2013-2014

中国及海外会展概览®

Directory of China & Overseas Exhibitions and Meetings

中国及海外会展概览编委会编辑
Edited By Editorial Board of
Directory of China & Overseas Exhibitions and Meetings

经济日报出版社

图书在版编目（CIP）数据

中国及海外会展概览：2013～2014/中国及海外会展概览编
-北京：经济日报出版社，2013.2
ISBN 978-7-80257-402-1

Ⅰ.①中… Ⅱ.①中… Ⅲ.①展览会—介绍—世界—2013～2014
Ⅳ.①G245

中国版本图书馆CIP数据核字（2013）第027538号

Diretory of China & Overseas Exhibitions and Meetings
2013-2014
Editoral Board of DCOEM

书名：中国及海外会展概览2013-2014

主　　编：张玉敏
责任编辑：陈嫔嫔 李进
封面设计：王　伟

出版发行：经济日报出版社
社　　址：北京市宣武区右安门内大街65号
邮政编码：100054
经　　销：全国新华书店
印　　刷：北京富泰印刷有限责任公司

开　　本：889×1194mm　1/16
字　　数：1000千字
印　　张：34
印　　次：2013年2月第一版 2013年2月第一次印刷

书　　号：ISBN 978-7-80257-402-1
定　　价：229.00元

特别感谢

给予本书大力支持的机构

With gratitude

to the many of organizations who have contributed to this Directory

亚洲国际博览馆	AsiaWorld-Expo
保昌展览搬运有限公司	BALtrans Exhibition & Removal Ltd
北京爱博西雅展览有限公司	Exposium-SIAL Exhibition Co Ltd
广东现代国际展览中心	Guangdong Modern International Exhibition Center
哈尔滨国际会展体育中心有限公司	Harbin International Conference Exhibmon & Sports Center Co Ltd
香港会议展览中心	Hong Kong Convention and Exhibition Centre
香港贸易发展局	Hong Kong Trade Development Council
澳门贸易投资促进局	Macao Trade and Investment Promotion Institute
沈阳国际展览中心	Shenyang International Exhibition Center
郑州国际会展中心	Zhengzhou International Convention & Exhibition Centre
全球国际货运有限公司	Schenker China Ltd
上海市国际展览有限公司	Shanghai International Exhibition Co Ltd
上海新国际博览中心有限公司	Shanghai New International Expo Center
显辉国际展览有限公司	Top Repute Co Ltd
澳门威尼斯人®度假村酒店会展及活动中心	The Venetian ® Macao - Resort - Hotel
亚洲博闻	UBM Asia
浙江中国小商品城集团股份有限公司	Zhejiang China Commodities City Group Co Ltd

前言

尽管欧洲经济出现了问题，亚洲展商在该地会展业的发展势头却丝毫不减。尤其在巴塞罗那举办的欧洲奖励旅游展览会上，中国展览商的影响力一年比一年强劲。

显而易见，亚洲不断参展的一个重要原因来源与国际特邀买家群体的青睐。欧洲奖励旅游展览会2011年的审计数据表明：3961个特邀买家中，32%的买家与亚洲展商建立了商业合作，还有51%的买家称愿意在未来与亚洲展商合作。这些资料均高于以往任何时期。

这些全球展会有助于公司产生直接收益，同时帮助其增强其品牌形象，发布新产品，进行市场调研，建立潜在客户数据库，保持与现有客户的联系，因而对支持全球商务至关重要。

例如，来自中国的展览商透露了展会管理如何发挥其最重要的职能——创造收益。这些展会必须能够吸引那些成为优秀行业领先者的买家。

2011年的研究进一步证实，专业会议组织者的发展有力地推动了会展行业的进步，与此同时，未来的中国展览商将广泛体验到参加会展所获得的经济利益。

在举办各种类型的会议和展会方面，中国以及亚洲其他地区作为入境市场，具有巨大的发展潜力。而欧洲成为亚洲寻求和赢得会展行业发展的风水宝地也便不足为奇了。

数据可以说明一切：去年欧洲奖励旅游展览会举办前，有64950对展览商与特邀买家进行了预约；3961个国际特邀买家中，66%的买家的购买预算超过了50万美元。

面临着严峻的经济形势，与任何其它媒体相比，无论是欧洲还是全球的展览商，都更努力地增加其营销份额。毫无疑问，随着欧洲奖励旅游展览会走过其第25个年头，展览商非常清晰地认识到，超过100个来自亚洲的目标市场、公司和服务营办商正准备于今年11月齐聚巴塞罗那。

Preface

Despite grim economic news from Europe,Asia continues to be strongly represented at exhibitions there-most notably at events such as EIBTM in Barcelona.

One of the key reasons for this ongoing participation is clearly the business being placed by the international hosted-buyer community.Statistics from the recordbreaking EIBTM2011 showed that 32 per cent of the 3961 hosted buyers placed business with Asian exhibitors,and another 51 per cent said they intended to place business.

Global events such as these are vital for supporting business globally as they enable companies to generate direct sales,while also enhancing brand image,launching new products,researching the market,building prospect databases and maintaining relationships with customers.

Exhibitors from China,for instance,have told how events management is one of their most important profitgenerating functions.Shows have to be effective in attracting buyers that turn into quality business leads.

Research conducted in 2011 confirmed that economic benefits from meetings will be felt throughout China in future as the growth in professional conference organisers helps push the conventions sector.

China and Asia offer huge potential for growth in the international inbound market for all types of meetings and events,so it is no surprise that Europe is a valuable place for them to seek and win that business.At EIBTM last year,for example,64950 scheduled appointments took place between exhibitors and hosted buyers,while 66 per cent of the 3961 international hosted buyers had budgets of over US$500000.

When times are tough, exhibitions work harder for a marketing budget than any other media. Little wonder then, that with EIBTM marking its 25th anniversary,more than 100 destinations,companies and service operators from Asia are preparing to descend on Barcelona in November.

目 录

会展概览

主编
张玉敏

编审
王亚东

编辑主任
黄继红

撰稿
方燕菁
吴超

高级客户主任
孙惠兰

编辑
李萌
钱小娟

编辑助理
马津

封面设计
王伟

电话：
010-6340 0061
010-8312 4138
010-8316 7137
传真：
010-8312 7130

读者服务和订购信息：
dcoem@live.cn
dcoem@qq.com
编辑部：
dcoem@qq.com
广告部：
expoinfo@dcoem.com

weibo.com/u/2402537562

博览世界网
www.dcoem.com

AsiaWorld-Expo

Contents

DCOEM

Editor-in-Chief
ZHANG Sarah

Editing Director
WANG Yadong

Senior Editors
HUANG Jihong

Contributors
FONG Gloria
WU Chao

Senior Account Manager
SUN Linda

Editor
LI Meng
QIAN Xiaojuan

Editorial Assistant
MA Jin

Art Director
WANG Wei

Telephone
86-10-6340 0061
86-10-8312 4138
Fax
86-10-8312 7130

Reader Service
dcoem@qq.com
Listing
dcoem@live.cn
Editorial Office
dcoem@qq.com
Advertising Office
expoinfo@qq.com

weibo.com/u/2402537562

www.dcoem.com

如何使用本书 | How to Use this Directory

全书国内会展信息有三大分类索引，便于查阅，具体方式如下：

分类一——按城市分类

这是国内会展信息的最主要章节，所有会展的基本信息按照先省区、后城市的汉语拼音顺序排列，城市中的信息再按照举办时间顺序排列。每条会展信息均有一个编号。编号的设置为便于您到后面的时间和行业分类中对应查询。

分类二——按行业分类

会展信息按行业分成78个分类。每个行业中，会展信息按照举办的时间顺序排列。通过编号，您可以在分类一中查到该展会的基本介绍。

分类三——按时间分类

展会在此按举办的时间顺序排列，通过每条信息的唯一编号，您可以在分类一中查到展会的基本介绍。

■ 重要提示

书中所列的展览和会议信息在编辑出版时，我们已经尽了最大努力核准无误，但个别展会的举办时间或地点等可能因故调整。因此，在决定参加、参观、出席展会之前，请您务必与主办和承办机构联系，获得确认。

★Exhibitions and Fairs in Mainland China

Register 1
Exhibitions and Fairs by City
This is the main chapter and contains basic exhibition and fairinformation in Mainland China. It is organized alphabetically byprovinces, alphabetically by city within each province, and chronologically within each city. To each exhibition there is a crossreference number which permits quick reference from register 2 and 3.

Register 2
Exhibitions and Fairs by Industry
This chapter lists exhibitions according 78 classifications. The exhibitions within the each branch are listed chronologically. A crossreference number is provided for quick access to more detailed information in register 1.

Register 3
Exhibitions and Fairs in Chronological Order
Exhibitions are listed in chronological order. A cross - reference number is provided for quick access to more detailed information in register 1.

★How to make phone call to China

1. Country code for China is 86.
2.Taking the phone number of 010-6340 0061 in the book as an example, 010 is the city code of Beijing. If you call from outside China, here is how you should dial: 86 10 6340 0061.
3. Area Code of HongKong is 852.

■ Warning

We have made best efforts to ensure the accuracy of the listed information at the time of editing. However, before making decision to participate an exhibition or conference, please always contact with the organizer for the very latest confirmation.

沈阳国际展览中心

SHEN YANG INTERNATIONAL EXHIBITION CENTER

国际化的设施、专业的管理、完善的服务

沈阳 将建设成为中国北方会展中心城市

Internationalized facilities, professional management, perfect services

Shenyang is going to be the center exhibition city of the northern China.

沈阳国际展览中心坐落于苏家屯区会展路9号，距市区12公里，距桃仙国际机场13公里。总用地面积95.9万平方米，计划分两期建设。一期建筑总面积16.6万平方米，室内展览面积10.56万平方米，室外展览面积20万平方米，综合服务区面积4万平方米。展馆按照国际专业化水准进行设计和建设，每个展厅既可独立办展，又能通过内部连廊彼此连通，使展区浑然一体。

展馆由8个单层、无柱、大跨度独立展厅组成，每厅面积1.32万平方米，可设625个国际标准展位。展馆由东西两侧各4个展厅组成，中间由双层连廊衔接，总体可容纳5000个国际标准展位，东、南、西、北面均设有观众登录厅，可举行各类礼仪活动。展馆北广场可举行开幕式、庆典及大型公益活动。

展馆设有1间1000人会议厅（内部可灵活分割），1间600人新闻发布厅，4间200人会议厅，6间50人会议室，3间贵宾会议室，2间洽谈室，可承接各种会议、会见、签约等活动。

展馆设有四星级宾馆、大型美食广场、集装箱场地、展品存放仓库、7500辆大型停车场等综合配套服务设施。

沈阳国际展览中心自开馆以来，接待了“汽博会”、“制博会”、“国家能源展”、“医博会”、“藏獒展”、“全国汽配展”、“全国制药机械展”“台湾名品展”、“中国美食节”、“广告节”、“全国糖酒会”等国家级、国际性大型展览项目，得到了社会各界一致认可。

Shenyang International Exhibition Centre (SYIEC) is located on No.9 Huizhan road, Sujiatun district. SYIEC is only 12km away from the unban district and 13km from Tiaoxian International Airport. The overall planning area of SYIEC is 959,000m^2, which is constructed in two phases. The first one covers 166,000m^2, including 105,600m^2 indoor exhibition area and 200,000m^2 outdoor exhibition area. The comprehensive servicing area occupies 40,000m^2. It is designed to meet international standard. Each hall can hold mini-exhibitions individually and can be connected by corridors into a comprehensive exhibition hall.

It is made up of 8 separated, single-level, column-free and spacious halls. Each hall occupies 13,200 square meters and it can accommodate 625 international standard booths. They are connected by corridors with 4 landing on east, north, west and south. We can supply 5,000 international standard booths. The north square can hold opening ceremony, celebration and public welfare activities.

One meeting room can accommodate 1000 people (can be subdivided as required), one conference room can accommodate 600 people, four meeting rooms accommodate 200 people, and six meeting rooms can accommodate 50 people, three VIP meeting rooms and two business rooms, which can provide activities such as meeting, interview and signing contracts.

SYIEC servicing zone includes supporting facilities such as one four-star hotel, a grand food hall, a container yard, a warehouse for displays and a large parking area for 7,500 vehicles.

Since its opening, SYIEC has held a number of national and international exhibitions, i.e., Auto Trade Fair, Equipment Manufacturing Exposition, National energy exhibition, CMEF, Exhibition of Chinese Tibetan mastiff, National Auto Parts Trade Fair, National Pharmaceutical Machinery Exposition, Food Festival, International Advertising Festival, China International Advertising Festival, Sugar and Alcoholic Commodities Fair, which were widely recognized and praised.

沈阳国际展览中心 Shenyang International Exhibition Center
地址：辽宁省沈阳市苏家屯区会展路9号 Add:No.9 Huizhan Road, Sujiatun District, Shenyang
电话TEL：024-89566744/55 传真FAX：024-89566778
E-mail：marketing@shenyang-expo.com
Web：www.shenyang-expo.com

2012中国专业贸易展80强排名

China Top 80 Trade Shows

排名 Rank	展会名称 Exhibition	展出面积 Exhibition Area(m^2)	参展商 Exhibitors	贸易观众 Trade Visiters	承办 Organizer	日期 Date	地点 Venue
1	第18届中国国际家具展览会 Furniture China	750,000	3,000	71,980	上海博华国际展览有限公司 Shanghai UBM Sinoexpo Intl Exh Co Ltd	9/11-15	上海新国际博览中心 Shanghai New Intl Expo Ctr
2	中国广州国际家具博览会(春季两期)(办公环境展/民用展) China Intl Furniture Fair	620,000	3,000	153,503	中国对外贸易广州展览公司 China Foreign Trade Guangzhou Exh General Corp	3/18-21 3/27-30	中国进出口商品交易会展馆 China Import & Export Fair Complex
3	第14届中国(广州)国际建筑装饰博览会 China (Guangzhou) Intl Bldg Decoration Fair	320,000	2,400	120,000	中国对外贸易广州展览公司/广州博亚展览发展有限公司 China Foreign Trade Guangzhou Exh General Corp	7/8-11	中国进出口商品交易会展馆 China Import & Export Fair Complex
4	第26届国际名家具(东莞)展览会 Intl Famous Furniture Fair (Guangdong)	270,000	1,000	117,820	东莞名家具俱乐部 Dongguan Famous Furniture Assn	3/16-20	广东现代国际展览中心 Guangdong Mordern Intl Exhibition Ctr
5	2012北京国际汽车展览会 Beijing Intl Automotive Exhibition	230,000	2,000	800,000 (观众总数)	中国国际贸易促进委员会汽车行业分会/中国汽车工业国际合作总公司/中国国际展览中心集团公司/中国汽车工程学会 CCPIT AUTO/ CNAICO/ CIEC/ SAE-China	4/25-5/2	中国国际展览中心（新馆）/中国国际展览中心（静安庄） China Intl Exh Ctr (New Venue)/ China Intl Exh Ctr (Jing'anzhuang)
6	第17届广州国际照明展览会 Guangzhou Intl Lighting Exhibition	210,000	2,931	100,465	广州光亚法兰克福展览有限公司 Messe Frankfurt Co Ltd	6/9-12	中国进出口商品交易会展馆 China Import & Export Fair Complex
7	第26届中国国际塑料橡胶工业展览会 The 26th Intl Exh on Plastics and Rubber Industries	210,000	2,700	100,000	雅式展览服务有限公司 Adsale Exh Services Ltd.	4/18-21	上海新国际博览中心 Shanghai New Intl Expo Ctr
8	第20届中国国际建筑装饰展览会 20th Expo Build China	200,000	2,200	100,000	上海博华国际展览有限公司 UBM SINOEXPO	4/9-12	上海新国际博览中心 Shanghai New Intl Expo Ctr
9	第19届中国(北京)国际建筑装饰及材料博览会 China Intl Bldg Decoration & Bldg Materials Expo	200,000	2,000	180,000	北京中装华港建筑科技展览有限公司 China B & D Exhibition Co Ltd	3/5-8	中国国际展览中心（新/老馆） China Intl Exh Ctr (New Venue/ Old Venue)
10	中国广州国际家具博览会(秋季) China Intl Furniture Fair (Guangzhou) Autumn	200,000	973	38,472	中国对外贸易广州展览总公司 China Foreign Trade Guangzhou Exh General Corp	9/7-10	中国进出口商品交易会展馆 China Import & Export Fair Complex
11	第10届中国(广州)国际汽车展览会 China (Guangzhou) Intl Automobile Fair	200,000	622	500,000	中国对外贸易广州展览总公司 China Foreign Trade Guangzhou Exh General Corp	11/23-12/2	中国进出口商品交易会展馆 China Import & Export Fair Complex
12	中国汽车用品暨改装汽车展览会 China Intl Expo for Auto Electronics, Accessories, Tuning & Car Products	200,000	6,000	180,000	北京雅森国际展览有限公司 YASN Intl Exhibit Ltd	2/14-17	中国国际展览中心（新馆） China Intl Exh Ctr (New Venue)

→
广东现代国际展览中心
Guangdong Modern International Exhibition Center
东莞国际会展中心
Dongguan International Convention and Exhibition Center

ufi Member 全球展览业协会 The Global Association of the Exhibition

中国展览馆协会 China Association for Exhibition Center

HKECIA 香港会议展览业协会 Hong Kong Exhibition & Convention Industry Association

DGCEIA 东莞市会议展览业协会 Dongguan Convention & Exhibition Industry Association

品牌展会 | BRAND EXHIBITION

1. 国际名家具（东莞）展览会 International Famous Furniture Fair (Dongguan)
2. 广东外商投资企业产品（内销）博览会 GuangDong Foreign-Invested Enterprises Commodities Fair
3. 中国东莞国际电脑资讯产品博览会 International Computer Communication &Consumer Electronic Products Exposition
4. 中国国际影视动漫版权保护和贸易博览会 China International Animation Copyright Fair
5. 国际模具展及金属加工展，国际橡塑胶、包装、压铸和铸造展 China Dongguan International Mould and Metalworking Exhibition, China Dongguan International Plastics Packing Rubber Die-casting & Foundry Exhibition
6. 国际鞋展 · 鞋机展 China Shoes · China Shoetecs
7. 中国（东莞）国际纺织制衣工业技术展览会 China (Dongguan) Int'l Textile & Clothing Industry Fair
8. 励华瓦楞展 · 彩盒展 Reed-huayin Sino-Corrugated & Folding Carton
9. 中国（广东）国际印刷技术展览会 China (Guangdong) Inte'l Print Technology Exhibition
10. 亚太地区压铸工业展览会 Asia-Pacific Die-casting Industry Exhibition
11. 广东国际汽车展示交易会 Guangdong International Auto Exhibition & Trade Fair

华南工业展览之都

MANUFACTURING PARTNER, SOURCING PLATFORM

公司一体化管理东莞两大专业会展场馆；
广东现代国际展览中心，室内展览面积10万平方米；
东莞国际会展中心，室内展览面积3万平方米；
已导入ISO9001:2000国际化标准管理体系，提供一站式A+服务。

Company manages integratively two big exhibition hall;
One is Guangdong Modern International Exhibition Center,covering a indoor exhibition space of one hundred thousand square meters;
Another is Dongguan International Convention and Exhibition Center with indoor exhibition space of thirty thousand square meters;
Company takes in ISO9000 quality management system and provides "One-stop A+" service to its customers.

广东现代会展管理有限公司
GD Modern Convention & Exhibition Management Co.,Ltd.

地址：东莞市厚街家具大道广东现代国际展览中心
Add/ Furniture Road, Houjie, Dongguan, Guangdong.P.R.China **P.C./** 523952
Tel/ 86-769-85981888, 85981868 **Fax/** 86-769-85981788
http://www.gdeexpo.com **E-mail/** gde@china.com

2012中国专业贸易展80强排名
China Top 80 Trade Shows

排名 Rank	展会名称 Exhibition	展出面积 Exhibition Area(m^2)	参展商 Exhibitors	贸易观众 Trade Visiters	承办 Organizer	日期 Date	地点 Venue
13	第9届中国(长春)国际汽车博览会 9th China Changchun Intl Auto Expo	190,000	136	650,000	中国贸促会长春分会 CCPIT Changchun Sub-Council	7/13-22	长春国际会展中心 Changchun Intl Conference & Exh Ctr
14	第18届中国义乌国际小商品博览会 China Yiwu Intl Commodities Fair	180,000	3,050	179,764	浙江省商务厅/ 义乌市人民政府 Department of Commerce of Zhejiang Province/ Yiwu Municipal People's Government	10/21-25	义乌国际博览中心（新馆） Yiwu Intl Expo Ctr (New Venue)
15	上海国际广告印刷包装纸业展览会 APPPEXPO	180,000	1,695	125,277	上海现代国际展览有限公司 Shanghai Modern Intl Exh Co Ltd	7/11-14	上海新国际博览中心 Shanghai New Intl Expo Ctr
16	第27届深圳国际家具展 Shenzhen Intl Furniture Exh	160,000	860	133,801	深圳市家具行业协会/ 深圳市德赛展览有限公司 Shenzhen Furniture Trade Assn/ Shenzhen Desy Exhibition Co,. Ltd	9/19-21	深圳会展中心 Shenzhen Convention & Exh Ctr
17	中国国际家用纺织品及辅料展览会 China Intl Trade Fair for Home Textiles and Accessories	138,000	1,330		中国贸促会纺织行业分会 CCPIT Textile Industry Sub-Council	8/28-30	上海新国际博览中心 Shanghai New Intl Expo Ctr
18	全国糖酒商品交易会(春季) China Natl Suger & Alcoholic Commodities Fair-Spring	130,000	2,300	40,000	中国糖业酒类集团公司 Off. Of China Natl Suger & Alcoholic Commodities Fair	3/23-26	成都世纪城新国际会展中心 Century City-New Intl Exh & Convention Ctr
19	九月香港珠宝首饰展览会 September Hong Kong Jewelry & Gem Fair	130,000	2,300	40,000	亚洲博闻 UBM Asia	9/19-23 9/21-25	亚洲国际博览馆/ 香港会议展览中心 AsiaWorld-Expo/ Hong Kong Convention & Exh Ctr
20	中国广州国际木工机械、家具配料展览会 Interzum guangzhou	130,000	1,058	56,582	科隆展览有限公司；中国对外贸易广州展览总公司 Koelnmesse Co Ltd; China Foreign Trade Guangzhou Exhibition Corp	3/27-30	中国进出口商品交易会展馆 Chinese Imp & Exp Fair Complex
21	第15届成都国际汽车展览会 15th Chengdu Motor Show	130,000	420	550,000	成都世纪城新国际会展中心；汉诺威米兰展览（上海）有限公司 Century City-New Intl Exh & Convention Ctr; Hannover Milano Fairs Shanghai Ltd.	9/1-9	成都世纪城新国际会展中心 Century City-New Intl Exh & Convention Ctr
22	第14届中国国际地面材料及铺装技术展览会 Domotexasia/China Floor	127,000	1,058	39,856	上海万耀企龙展览有限公司 VNU Exhibitions Asia	3/27-29	上海新国际博览中心 Shanghai New Intl Expo Ctr
23	中国国际医疗器械博览会(秋季) CMEF Autumn (Intl Medical Equipment Fair)	120,000	2,600	82,360	国药励展展览有限公司 Reed Sinopharm Exh Co Ltd	4/17-20	深圳会展中心 Shenzhen Convention & Exh Ctr
24	第12届世界制药原料中国展 CPhI China 2012	120,000	2,229	40,928	上海博华国际展览有限公司 UBM SINOEXPO	6/26-28	上海新国际博览中心 Shanghai New Intl Expo Ctr

TOP REPUTE CO. LTD. 显辉国际展览有限公司

Unit 2802, Shun Tak Centre, West Tower, Nos.168-200 Connaught Road Central, Hong Kong
香港干诺道中168-200号信德中心西座2802室
Tel: (852) 2851 8603 Fax: (852) 2851 8637
E-mail: topreput@top-repute.com Website: http://www.toprepute.com.hk

2013-2014 展会介绍 SHOW CALENDAR

中国 - 广州 CHINA - GUANGZHOU

Exhibition	2013	2014
SHOES & LEATHER – GUANGZHOU INTERNATIONAL EXHIBITION ON SHOES & LEATHER INDUSTRY – GUANGZHOU – 广州国际鞋类、皮革及工业设备展览会 – 暨 Incorporate with	29-31/5	28-30/5
GILE – GUANGZHOU INTERNATIONAL LEATHER EXHIBITION 广州国际皮革展览会	29-31/5	28-30/5
GITTME – GUANGZHOU INT'L TANNING TECHNOLOGY & MACHINERY EXHIBITION 广州国际皮革工业技术及生产设备展览会	29-31/5	28-30/5
IFLE – GUANGZHOU INTERNATIONAL FOOTWEAR & LEATHER PRODUCTS EXHIBITION – GUANGZHOU 广州国际鞋类、皮革制成品展览会	29-31/5	28-30/5

越南 - 胡志明市 VIETNAM - HO CHI MINH CITY

Exhibition	2013	2014
SHOES & LEATHER – VIETNAM INTERNATIONAL EXHIBITION ON SHOES & LEATHER INDUSTRY – VIETNAM 越南国际鞋类、皮革及工业设备展览会 – 暨 Incorporating	11-13/7	16-18/7
IFLE – VIETNAM INTERNATIONAL FOOTWEAR & LEATHER PRODUCTS EXHIBITION – VIETNAM 越南国际鞋类、皮革制成品展览会	11-13/7	16-18/7
GARMENT & FABRIC – VIETNAM VIETNAM INTERNATIONAL EXHIBITION ON GARMENT MANUFACTURING EQUIPMENT & FABRIC 越南国际制衣机械设备、面料展览会	11-13/7	16-18/7
VICB VIETNAM INTERNATIONAL CONSTRUCTION & BUILDING EXHIBITION – 越南国际建筑展览会 – 暨 Incorporating	18-20/7	2-4/7
RAHV – VIETNAM INTERNATIONAL EXHIBITION ON REFRIGERATION, AIR – CONDITIONING, HEATING & VENTILATION SYSTEM 越南国际制冷、空调、供暖、通风系统展览会	18-20/7	2-4/7
SECURITY & FIRE – VIETNAM VIETNAM INTERNATIONAL SECURITY SYSTEM & FIRE PROTECTION EQUIPMENT &TECHNOLOGY EXHIBITION 越南国际安防、技防、消防设备和技术展览会	18-20/7	2-4/7
LIGHTING VIETNAM VIETNAM INTERNATIONAL LIGHTING EQUIPMENT & TECHNOLOGY EXHIBITION 越南国际照明器材及技术展览会	18-20/7	2-4/7
IIME VIETNAM INTERNATIONAL INDUSTRIAL MACHINERY EXHIBITION – 越南国际工业机械展览会 – 暨 Incorporating	18-20/7	2-4/7
VIETNAM PLASTICS FAIR 越南国际塑胶机械及技术展览会	18-20/7	2-4/7
METALTECH 越南国际金属加工机械及技术展览会	18-20/7	2-4/7
PRINT & PACK 越南国际印刷包装机械及技术展览会	18-20/7	2-4/7
FOOD PACK 越南国际食品包装机械及技术展览会	18-20/7	2-4/7
AUTOMATION 越南国际自动化工业展览会	18-20/7	2-4/7

分行 BRANCH		电话 TELEPHONE	传真 FAX	电邮 E-MAIL
广州	GUANGZHOU	(86-20) 8363 1061	(86-20) 8363 1063	toprepute@toprepute.com.cn
上海	SHANGHAI	(86-21) 6279 1306 / 1291	(86-21) 6247 8552	topresha@sh163.net
越南	VIETNAM	(84-8) 3823 8828	(84-8) 3824 6351	info@toprepute.vn

2012中国专业贸易展80强排名
China Top 80 Trade Shows

排名 Rank	展会名称 Exhibition	展出面积 Exhibition Area(m^2)	参展商 Exhibitors	贸易观众 Trade Visiters	承办 Organizer	日期 Date	地点 Venue
36	中国（深圳）国际玩具及礼品展览会 China (Shenzhen) Intl Toys & Gifts Fair	110,000	3,300	410,000	励展华博展览(深圳)有限公司 Reed Huabo Exhibition (Shenzhen) Co	10/22-25	深圳会展中心 Shenzhen Convention & Exh Ctr
37	中国(深圳)国际礼品、工艺品、钟表及家庭用品展览会 China (Shenzhen) Intl Gifts, Handicraft, Watches & Houseware Fair	110,000	3,300	130,000	励展华博展览(深圳)有限公司 Reed Huabo Exhibition (Shenzhen) Co	4/25-28	深圳会展中心 Shenzhen Convention & Exh Ctr
38	上海国际酒店用品博览会 Hotelex	110,000	3,000	100,000	上海博华国际展览有限公司 UBM Sinoexpo	4/9-12	上海新国际博览中心 Shanghai New Intl Expo Ctr
39	中国国际医疗器械博览会(秋季) CMEF Autumn (Intl Medical Equipment Fair)	110,000	2,441	58,854	国药励展展览有限公司 Reed Sinopharm Exh Co Ltd	10/18-21	成都世纪城新国际会展中心 Century City-New Intl Exh & Convention Ctr
40	中国杨凌农业高新科技成果博览会 China Yangling Agricultural Hi-Tech Fair	110,000	1,700	155,000	陕西省人民政府 Shaanxi Provincial Government	11/20-24	杨凌农业科技展览中心 Yangling Agri Sci & Tech Exh Ctr
41	第21届中国国际专业音响·灯光·乐器及技术展览会 21th China Intl Exh on Pro Audio, Light, Music & Technology	110,000	1,200	200,000	中国演艺设备技术协会 China Entertainment Technology Assn	5/24-27	中国国际展览中心（新馆） China Intl Exh Ctr (New Venue)
42	中国国际自行车展览会 China Intl Bicyble Fair	110,000	1,200	120,000	上海协升展览有限公司 Shanghai Intl Exhibition Corp	4/26-29	上海新国际博览中心 Shanghai New Intl Expo Ctr
43	中国国际体育用品博览会(夏) China Sport Show (Spring)	110,000	1,100	70,000	国家体育总局体育器材装备中心 Sports Equipment Administrative Ctr of China General Administration of Sport	6/20-22	中国国际展览中心（新馆） China Intl Exh Ctr (New Venue)
44	第20届中国国际服装服饰博览会 20th China Intl Clothing & Accessories Fair	110,000	1,000	110,000	北京时尚博展国际展览有限公司/ 中国国际贸易中心股份有限公司 Beijing Fashion-EXPO Co Ltd/ China World Trade Center Co Ltd	3/26-29	中国国际展览中心（新馆） China Intl Exh Ctr (New Venue)
45	第11届中国国际门业展览会 China Intl Door Industry Exh	110,000	1,000	94,238	北京中装伟佳展览策划有限公司 Beijing WSJ United Strategy for Exh Co Ltd	2/21-24	中国国际展览中心（新馆） China Intl Exh Ctr (New Venue)
46	成都国际家具工业展览会 Intl Furniture Fair Chengdu	110,000	600	80,000	中国贸促会成都分会 CCPIT Chengdu Sub-Council	7/3-6	成都世纪城新国际会展中心 Century City-New Intl Exh & Convention Ctr

2012中国专业贸易展80强排名
China Top 80 Trade Shows

排名 Rank	展会名称 Exhibition	展出面积 Exhibition Area(m^2)	参展商 Exhibitors	贸易观众 Trade Visiters	承办 Organizer	日期 Date	地点 Venue
47	北京埃森国际焊接与切割展览会 Beijing Essen Welding & Cutting Fari	106,800	936	45,491	中国机械工程学会/ 中国机械工程学会焊接分会 Chinese Mechanical Engineering Society(CMES)/ Welding Institution of CMES	6/4-7	中国国际展览中心（新馆） China Intl Exh Ctr (New Venue)
48	中国(广州)国际广告标识展 Sign China	100,000	1,600	70,000	广州闻信展览服务有限公司 UBM Trust Co Ltd	2/20-23	中国进出口商品交易会展馆 Chinese Imp & Exp Fair Complex
49	上海国际机床展 Shanghai Intl Machine Tool Fair	100,000	1,200	98,900	上海东博展览有限公司 Eastpo Intl Expo Co Ltd	7/3-6	上海新国际博览中心 Shanghai New Intl Expo Ctr
50	中国国际焙烤展览会 China Intl Trade Fair For Bakery & Confectionery	100,000	1,000	150,000	中国焙烤食品糖制品工业协会 China Assn of Bakery & Confectionery	5/10-12	上海新国际博览中心 Shanghai New Intl Expo Ctr
51	中国国际日用品消费品博览会 China Intl Consumer Goods Fair	100,000	1,000	110,000	宁波市对外贸易服务中心有限公司 Ningbo Foreign Trade Service Center Co Ltd	6/8-11	宁波国际会展中心 Ningbo Intl Conference & Exh Ctr
52	广东国际汽车展示交易会 Guangdong Intl Auto Exh & Trade Fair	100,000	800	211,000	东莞中汽会展有限公司 China Natl Automobile Con & Exh Dongguan Co Ltd	9/29-10/4	广东现代国际展览中心 Gangdong Modern Intl Exh Ctr
53	第23届国际制冷、空调、供暖、通风及食品冷冻加工展览会 China Refrigeraion	90,000	900	30,000	北京贸促会/ 中国制冷协会 CCPIT Beijing	4/11-13	中国国际展览中心（新馆） China Intl Exh Ctr (New Venue)
54	香港国际珠宝展 Hong Kong Intl Jewellery Show	88,617	3,100	2,675	香港贸易发展局 Hong Kong Trade Development Council	2/16-20	香港会议展览中心 Hong Kong Convention & Exh Ctr
55	香港贸发局香港礼品及赠品展 HKTDC Hong Kong Gifts & Premium Fair	88,035	4,400	46,000	香港贸易发展局 Hong Kong Trade Development Council	4/27-30	香港会议展览中心 Hong Kong Convention & Exh Ctr
56	中国(上海)国际乐器展览会 MUSIC CHINA	86,000	1,606	60,172	上海国际展览中心有限公司/ 法兰克福展览（香港）有限公司 Intex Shanghai Co Ltd/ Messe Frankfurt (HK) Ltd	10/10-14	上海新国际博览中心 Shanghai New Intl Expo Ctr
57	2012北京国际汽车维修检测诊断设备及汽车养护展览会 Auto Maintech	85,000	1,106	53,205	北京联通国际展览有限公司 Beijing Traders-Links Intl Exh Co Ltd	2/27-3/1	中国国际展览中心（新馆） China Intl Exh Ctr (New Venue)

2012中国专业贸易展80强排名
China Top 80 Trade Shows

排名 Rank	展会名称 Exhibition	展出面积 Exhibition Area(m^2)	参展商 Exhibitors	贸易观众 Trade Visiters	承办 Organizer	日期 Date	地点 Venue
58	第57届中国国际汽车服务业及汽车文化博览会暨全国汽车保修检测诊断设备（春季）展览会	85,000	1,100	55,000	北京通联国际展览有限公司 Beijing Traders-Link International Exhibition Co., Ltd.	2/27-3/1	中国国际展览中心（新馆） China Intl Exh Ctr (New Venue)
59	中国国际皮革展/中国国际箱包、裘革服装及服饰展/中国国际鞋类展 Moda Shanghai/All China Leather Exh/China Intl Footwear Fair	80,500	1,100	14,095	亚太区皮革展有限公司 Asia Pacific Leather Fair Ltd	9/4-6	上海新国际博览中心 Shanghai New Intl Expo Ctr
60	第79届中国电子展 China Electronics Fair	80,000	2,000	57,050	中国电子器材总公司 Creative Convention & Exh Co Ltd	4/10-12	深圳会展中心 Shenzhen Convention & Exh Ctr
61	第12届中国(深圳)国际品牌服装服饰交易会 12th China (Shenzhen) Intl Brand Clothing & Accessories Fair	80,000	1,000	110,000	深圳市服装行业协会 Shenzhen Garment Industry Assn	7/4-6	深圳会展中心 Shenzhen Convention & Exh Ctr
62	第21届中国(上海)国际婚纱摄影器材展览会暨国际儿童摄影、主题摄影、相册相框展览会（春季） China Wedding Expo	80,000	670	112,000	上海国际展览服务有限公司 Shanghai Intl Exh Service Co Ltd	2/15-18	上海新国际博览中心 Shanghai New Intl Expo Ctr
63	第12届中国北方国际自行车电动车展览会 The 12th China North Int'l Bicyole & E-Bike Exh	80,000	560	200,000	天津市华轮展览有限公司 Introduction to Tianjin Hualun Exh Co., Ltd.	3/23-25	梅江会展中心 Meijiang Convention Center
64	香港贸发局香港秋季电子产品展 HKTDC Hong Kong Electronics Fair (Autumn)	77,391	2,852		香港贸易发展局 Hong Kong Trade Development Council	10/13-16	香港会议展览中心 Hong Kong Convention & Exh Ctr
65	第22届中国(上海)国际婚纱摄影器材展览会暨国际儿童摄影、主题摄影、相册相框展览会（秋季） China Wedding Expo	76,000	600	130,000	上海国际展览服务有限公司 Shanghai Intl Exh Service Co Ltd	3/23-25	上海新国际博览中心 Shanghai New Intl Expo Ctr
66	中国国际食品添加剂及配料展览会 Food Ingredients China	71,600	1,179	32,791	中国食品添加剂和配料协会/中国贸促会轻工行业分会 China Food Additives & Ingredients Association; CCPIT Sub-council of Light Industry	3/28-30	上海世博展览馆 Shanghai World Expo Exhibition & Convention Center
67	全国药品交易会（秋季） Pharmchina-Autumn	70,000	2,000	100,000	国药励展展览有限责任公司 Reed Sinopharm Exh Co Ltd	12/4-6	中国进出口商品交易会展馆 China Import & Export Fair Complex
68	中国国际汽车零部件博览会 China Intl Auto Parts Expo	70,000	1,483	51,830	中国通用技术集团 Genertec International AE Co Ltd	10/26-28	中国国际展览中心 China Intl Exhibition Ctr

2012中国专业贸易展80强排名
China Top 80 Trade Shows

排名 Rank	展会名称 Exhibition	展出面积 Exhibition Area(m^2)	参展商 Exhibitors	贸易观众 Trade Visiters	承办 Organizer	日期 Date	地点 Venue
69	香港贸发局香港国际秋季灯饰展 HKTDC Hong Kong Intl Lighting Fair (Autumn)	68,533	2,300	33,319	香港贸易发展局 Hong Kong Trade Development Council	10/27-30	香港会议展览中心 Hong Kong Convention & Exh Ctr
70	中国义乌文化产品交易博览会 China Yiwu Cultural Products Trade Fair	68,000	1,372	92,395	义乌中国小商品城展览有限公司 Yiwu China Commodities City Exh Co Ltd	4/29-5/2	义乌国际博览中心 Yiwu Intl Expo Ctr
71	全国药品交易会（春季） Pharmchina-Spring	65,000	2,000	100,000	国药励展展览有限责任公司 Reed Sinopharm Exh Co Ltd	4/25-27	合肥滨湖国际会展中心
72	香港贸发局香港春季电子产品展 HKTDC Hong Kong Electronics Fair (Spring)	60,000	2,459	92,395	香港贸易发展局 Hong Kong Trade Development Council	4/13-16	香港会议展览中心 Hong Kong Convention & Exh Ctr
73	香港贸发局香港家庭用品展 HKTDC Hong Kong Houseware Fair	58,610	2,016	26,769	香港贸易发展局 Hong Kong Trade Development Council	4/20-23	香港会议展览中心 Hong Kong Convention & Exh Ctr
74	中国国际旅游交易会 China Intl Trade Mart	57,500	104	100,000	国家旅游局 Natl Tourism Administration	11/15-19	上海新国际博览中心 Shanghai New Intl Expo Ctr
75	亚太区美容展 COSMOPROF ASIA	57,400	1,633	45,100	亚洲博闻 UBM Asia	11/14-16	香港会议展览中心 Hong Kong Convention & Exh Ctr
76	香港贸发局香港玩具展 HKTDC Hong Kong Toys & Games Fair	57,269	1,900	33,000	香港贸易发展局 Hong Kong Trade Development Council	1/9-12	香港会议展览中心 Hong Kong Convention & Exh Ctr
77	香港珠宝首饰展览会 Hong Kong Jewelry & Gem Fair	56,000	1,500	22,452	亚洲博闻 UBM Asia	6/21-24	香港会议展览中心 Hong Kong Convention & Exh Ctr
78	第17届中国宁波国际住宅产品博览会 17th China Intl Exh on Housing Industry Product	55,000	1,000		宁波市城之新展览有限公司 Ningbo Chengzhixin Exhibition Co Ltd	11/2-5	宁波国际会议展览中心 Ningbo Intl Conference & Exh Ctr
79	中国电子展览会暨亚洲电子展 China Electronics Fair	50,000	1,300	52,023	中国电子器材总公司 Creative Convention & Exh Co Ltd	11/9-11	上海新国际博览中心 Shanghai New Intl Expo Ctr
80	中国义乌国际森林产品博览会 China Yiwu Intl Forest Products Fair	50,000	1,200	112,600	义乌市人民政府 Yiwu Municipal Government	11/1-4	义乌国际博览中心 Yiwu Intl Expo Ctr

东莞：华南工业展览之都

——东莞展览差异化定位浮出水面

东莞位于世界著名的制造业中心，丰厚的产业资源、一小时经济圈区位优势、全球化的发展格局和现代市场经济的飞速发展催生了东莞的会展经济。经过多年的培育和发展，东莞展览业不断成熟和壮大，差异化特征凸现，“华南工业展览之都”雏形逐渐浮出水面。

广东现代国际展览中心位处穗港走廊中断，雄踞珠三角中心，以珠三角产业集群为依托，正朝着“国际化，集约化，专业化，基地化”的华南最具竞争力的制造业展览基地目标努力奋斗。

完善的配套设施

广东现代国际展览中心共有6个大型展馆，可提供12万平方米的室内展览面积及9万平方米的室外展览面积，展馆经权威国际专家指导设计，展馆最高处有38.4米，最低也有12米，屋顶采用索网结构，保证了跨度90米，宽度260米的无柱大空间，展区自由分隔，展出面积可从5000平方米至5万平方米任意组合。展馆可设6450个国际标准摊位。独特的自身硬件优势，无论平面展位、还是空中布

《亚洲会
Martin Do
庆祝酒会
李玉霞女
惊喜，宣布
佳会议展
中心”。
理狄嘉麟先
理公司执行
贸易发展局

《亚洲
游》杂志（
昨晚（11月2
将于2013年
查结果中，
(简称“会展
膺“亚洲最
佳会议展览

《亚洲会
游》杂志是亚
威刊物，读者包
览活动的主办机
人士，自2001年
读者调查，期间
获推选为“亚洲
展览中心亚洲
展览中心”。

《亚洲会议展
游》杂志编辑Mart
在11月29日于会展

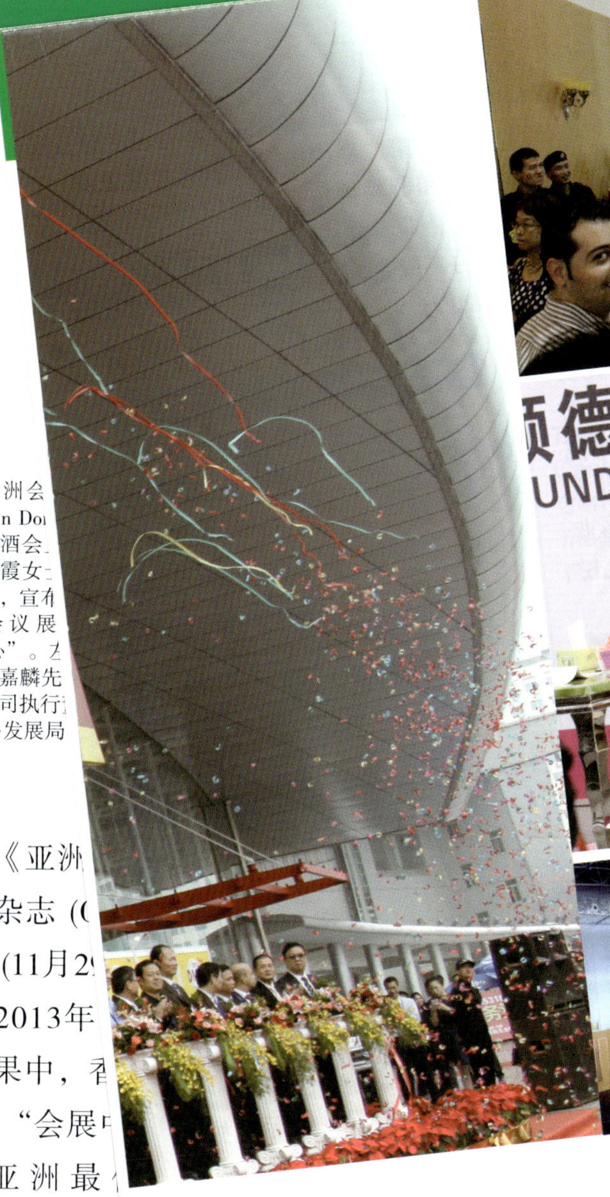

局均可充分满足客户不同规模的任何需求。

展馆配备先进的通讯网络系统，水电系统，安保系统，空调以及向导系统。面积为2700平方米的序厅，内设有展览公司现场办公室、商务中心、新闻中心、小件寄存室等服务区；馆内有大小11个功能会议厅，最大的一个可以容纳2000多人。

高效的交通网络

广东现代国际展览中心位于珠三角城市群中心点的东莞厚街，交通极为便利，以展馆为圆心，一小时车程可达广州、深圳、珠海、香港、澳门、中山、佛山、惠州等重要城市。临近广州、深圳、珠海、香港、澳门五大国际机场，每周国际航班达1600班以上，是上海的5倍，北京的7倍。深圳盐田港、东莞虎门港等多个国际港口可为海内外展商提供便利的运输服务。

连接广州深圳香港的广深港高铁已经在2011年8月完工通车，虎门站距展馆仅二公里。2012年2月，广深港高铁与武广高铁相连，虎门到武汉仅5小时。2012年底，广州到北京线路已经通车，仅需7小时59分车程。

在建的东莞地铁二号线，连通广深铁路，起点站广州，经东莞市中心、广东现代国际展览中心至深圳机场，全线预计于2013-2014年贯通，展览中心站设于展览中心前广场。

连通广州、东莞、深圳的穗莞深城际轨道预计也将于2011年年底建成通车，该项目东起广州，经东莞到达深圳机场。

结合高效的交通网络，东莞的国际贸易水平也大幅提升，配合中国-东盟自由贸易区的全面启动，吸引了大批东南亚的企业到莞进行贸易活动。

酒店及配套服务

东莞城市基础设施条件齐备，酒店业、餐饮业、娱乐业、均十分发达，从展览中心出发，10分钟车程内可达5家五星级酒店，三星级以上酒店十几家，镇内范围内足以解决一万

中食展：不断超越 高速扩张

2013年5月7日，第十四届中国国际食品和饮料展览会（SIAL China 2013）将在上海新国际博览中心举办。中食展由法国高美爱博展览集团和（中国）商业发展中心共同主办，于2000年首次创办，发展迅速，2012年首次超越日本国际食品与饮料展（FOODEX JAPAN），成为亚太地区最为令人瞩目的国际食品展！

数据显示，2012年中食展连续第二年递增25%，面积达73200平米，参展企业数量为1907家。专业观众比2011年增加22.4%，达40722名。2013年中食展将保持高增长的态势，展览面积、展商数量和观众数量均将增长15%左右，达到85000平米，2200家展商及46000名观众的总体规模。

据2012年年底统计，其中海外销售已完成八成。国内虽从2012年11月份才正式开始销售，热销仅仅两个月，就完成销售任务近七成。无论是海外销售，还是国内销售，均比去年同期销售进度加速。

海外方面，欧美国家经济低迷，但中国进口食品市场高速扩张，前景看好，吸引了60多个国家和地区的海外食品企业报名参展。不仅老展商积极报名，还吸引了捷克、罗马尼亚、哥伦比亚、比利时、瑞士、越南等新国家参展。香港贸发局代表香港地区首次参展，其所预定展台已不能满足参展企业的面积需求。

2013年的荣誉国为西亚翘楚的土耳其。土耳其是中食展的老参展国，历届参展效果甚佳，今年更将以1000平方米的规模，全面展示橄榄油、调味品、糖果、蜜饯、面食等多种特色产品。

国内招商一如既往，获得地方政府和协会的积极响应。山东、浙江、上海、宁波、乌鲁木齐、长春等省市的政府部门正积极筹备参展，以期推出当地的优质出口食品。此外，农业部对外经济合作中心将携陕西、山东、河南、山西、河北、辽宁、甘肃等七大苹果产区的优质苹果亮相果蔬专区，同时还展出中国优质鲜蔬和脱水冷冻蔬菜。中国水产流通与加工协会将率领大连獐子岛、上海水产集团等名企参展，并将推出水产品烹饪演示。中国乳制品工业协会将推出乳制品及婴幼儿食品专区，携海内外知名乳品及婴幼儿食品企业参展。由中国食品和包装机械工业协会与高美爱博展览集团共同主办的第十三届中国上海国际包装和食品加工技术展及由中国罐头工业协会主办的第六届上海国际罐藏食品及原辅材机械设备博览会亦将同期同地举办，报名情况也很踊跃，参展面积将进一步扩大。

值得注意的是，国内的海外食品代理商报名十分踊跃，所展示的产品线快速增容，展台面积扩大，装修档次提高，不乏大型海外食品代理公司。如大昌华嘉商业公司专为酒店业提供多系列产品，已在国内25个主要城市设立了营业处。铸池（上海）贸易公司2009年在上海成立，现已代理进口食品品牌40余种。中国的进口食品来自欧美、韩国、日本、东南亚等140多个国家和港澳台地区，得到广大市民的喜爱。专家预测，占到中国三分之二人口、约8亿多的年轻消费群，在未来十年将成为进口食品的消费主体。美国食品工业协会预测，到2018年，中国将成为全球最大的进口食品消费国，中国大陆进口食品市场规模将高达4800亿人民币，未来十年是中国进口食品的高速发展期。

2012年中食展的酒世界专馆集中了中外349家葡萄酒、烈性酒和酒精饮料的企业，面积达12000平方米，有8000名专业观众，获得许多海外参展国的表扬和支持。今年已经或正在报名的国家有法国、德国、意大利、希腊、匈牙利、南非、澳大利亚、美国以及一些南美国家。估计今年海内外酒类企业的参展规模将超过往年。为了营造更好的贸易洽谈氛围，根据海外参展商的要求，2013年酒专馆将设置专门的胸卡，对酒展馆观众组织专门的观众登记。据悉，主办方已于一月初同时开通了“中食展”和“酒世界专馆”的网上观众预登记。

名片

联系人：侯旭 徐亚骞
爱博西雅（北京）展览有限公司
电话：010-6588 6236，6588 9389,6588 9379
传真：010- 6588 6233
Email: xyz@sialchina.cn
中文官网：www.sialchina.cn

推荐参加下列机构主办的展览和会议

Recommend You the Exhibitions and Conferences Organized by Following Organizers

中国哈尔滨经济贸易洽谈会办公室	Administration Office of China Harbin Fair for Trade and Economic Cooperation
北京中装华港建筑科技展览有限公司	China B&D Exhibition co ltd
中国演艺设备技术协会	China Entertainment Technology Association
中国铸造协会	China Foundry Association
中国对外贸易广州展览总公司	China Foreign Trade Guangzhou Exhibition Corporation
中国昆明进出口商品交易会	China Import & Export Fair, Kunming
中国机械工程学会及焊接分会	Chinese Mechanical Engineering Society;Welding instution of CMES
中国贸促会轻工行业分会	CCPIT Sub-Council of Light Industry
中国国际贸易中心股份有限公司	China World Trade Center Co Ltd
北京爱博西雅展览有限公司	Exposium-SIAL Exhibition Co Ltd
广东省玩具协会	Guangdong Toy Association
香港贸易发展局	Hong Kong Trade Development Council
晋江市展务有限公司	Jinjiang Exhibition Affairs Co Ltd, Fujian
澳门贸易投资促进局	Macao Trade and Investment Promotion Institute
科隆展览中国有限公司	Koelnmesse Co Ltd China
励展博览集团	Reed Exhibitions
上海市国际展览有限公司	Shanghai International Exhibition Co Ltd
上海里扬展览服务有限公司	Shanghai Neon Exhibition Service Ltd
显辉国际展览有限公司	Top Repute Co Ltd
亚洲博闻	UBM Asia
宁波雅卓展览服务有限公司	Younage Exhibition Co Ltd
浙江中国小商品城集团股份有限公司	Zhejiang China Commodities City Group Co Ltd

国内展览会议 城市索引

Exhibitions and Fairs in Mainland China Index of Cities

北京 Beijing

2013/02/23-25
☎ 010-5820 3101, 5820 3102
🖷 010-5820 3100
✉ info_b@chinafish.cn
📱 1571797005
www.chinafish.cn
10

第二十三届中国国际钓鱼用品贸易展览会
地点：中国国际展览中心新馆，北京
内容：中国国际钓鱼用品贸易展览会（China Fish）中国唯一经商务部批准的国际性渔具展览会，经过22年的发展，已与美国ICAST、欧洲EFTTEX并称世界三大渔展。自1991年创办至今已连续成功举办了二十三届。主要展览渔具等周边产品，展会设有最佳新产品奖，受到国内外参展商和贸易商的青睐！
始办年份：1991
周期：每年一届
市场范围：国际性
性质：面向贸易观众
入场券价格：2013年2月8日前预注册免费
参展费用：标准展位9,200元/9m^2，光地8,500元/9m^2
上届规模：展览面积26,700m^2(国外展商面积1,500m^2)，参展商480家（国外展商41家，来自88个国家）
主办：北京澳钦润江展览有限公司；中国国际贸易中心股份有限公司
地址：北京市朝阳区建国路93号万达广场5号楼9层(100022)
联系人：杨女士，李小姐

China Fish 2013
23rd China Intl Fishing Tackle Trade Exhibition
Venue: China Intl Exhibition Center New Venue, Beijing
Profile: As the only exhibition authorized by MOFCOM with 22 years history, CHINAFISH is one of the top three fishing tackle exhibitions in the world, such as American ICAST and European EFTTEX. Since 1991, CHINAFISH has been hold 23th successfully, which shows products related fishing tackle. Best Product Showcase is established which is welcomed by exhibitors and buyers!
Established Year: 1991
Frequency: Annual
Market Area: International
Nature: Trade Only
Cost to Attend: Pre-register free
Participated Fee: Standard Booth RMB 9,200/9m^2, Raw Space RMB 8,500/9m^2
Statistics '12: Exhibition Area 26,700m^2 (foreigners 1,500m^2), Exhibitors 480 (foreigners 41, came from 88 countries)
Organizer: Beijing Admire Exhibition Co Ltd; China World Trade Center Co Ltd
Address: 9/F, Building 5, Wanda Plaza, No.93 Jianguo Road, Chaoyang District, Beijing
Contact: Alice

2013/03/01-04
☎ 010-5797 0888
🖷 010-5797 0999
✉ yuanyuhan@yasn.com.cn
📱 1979846251
www.yasn.net
20

第16届中国国际汽车用品展览会
地点：中国国际展览中心新馆，北京
内容：展出面积25万平米、14个馆精确分馆分区、汇集全球6000余家源头展商，专业观众将突破22万人，展品涵盖汽车电子、美容养护、太阳膜、汽车座垫、汽车脚垫、汽车内外饰、座套、把套、精品、环保用品、户外用品、轮胎/轮毂/油品等全行业产品类别。
始办年份：2005
周期：每年一届
市场范围：国际性
性质：面向公众
入场券价格：50元
上届规模 '12：展览面积250,000m^2，参展商6,103家（国外展商913家），贸易观众221,864人
主办：北京雅森国际展览有限公司
地址：北京市西城区裕民路18号北环中心A座505室(100029)
联系人：袁玉涵

16th China Intl Expo for Auto Electronics, Accessories, Tuning & Car Care Products
Venue: China Intl Exhibition Center New Venue, Beijing
Profile: The floor space will reach to 250,000m^2 with 14 exhibition halls, more than 6000 high-quality exhibitor and 220 thousand professional visitors will participate CIAACE 2013. The exhibits include: Auto Electronics, Car Care Products, Auto Solar Film, Auto Seat Cushion and cover, Auto Foot Mat, Auto Interior & Exterior Products, wheel hub, outdoor products
Established Year: 2005
Frequency: Annual
Market Area: International
Nature: Open to Public
Cost to Attend: RMB 50
Statistics '12: Exhibition Area 250,000m^2, Exhibitors 6,103 (foreigners 913), Trade Visitors 221,864
Organizer: YASN International Exhibition Co Ltd
Address: Suite 505, Tower A, North Ring Center, 18 Yumin Rd., Xicheng Dist., Beijing 100029, China

2013/03/07-10
☎ 010-8460 0901, 8460 0903
🖷 010-8460 0910
www.build-decor.com
25

第20届中国北京国际建筑装饰及材料博览会
地点：中国国际展览中心（新/老馆）同时举办
主办：北京中装华港建筑科技展览有限公司
地址：北京市朝阳区北三环东路6号中国国际展览中心一号馆四层388室

20th China Il Building Decorations & Building Materials Exposition
Venue: China Intl Exhibition Center (New Venue and Old Venue), Beijing
Organizer: China B & D Exhibition Co Ltd
Address: Rm.388, 4F, Hall 1, CIEC, No.6 East Beisanhuan Road, Beijing, China

2013/03/14-17
☎ 010-5933 9102
🖷 010-5933 9199
✉ raymond.zhang@reedhuaqun.com
📱 52109350
www.giftsbeijing.com
30

第27届中国北京国际礼品、赠品及家庭用品展览会
地点：中国国际展览中心，北京
内容：工艺品：陶瓷、水晶类、琉璃、金属类工艺品 赠品、促销品：广告促销品、福利、节庆促销品 品牌电子产品 纪念收藏品及钱币、邮票 有机食品 高档商务礼品：皮具、箱包、文化用品 家居用品：家具、家装用品、软装饰品、厨卫用品系列、家纺类产品 玩具及婴孕童用品：儿童及成人益智玩具、婴孕童日用品 旅游及户外用品：户外用品、健身及运动器械 媒体、协会、贸易服务及其它
始办年份：1999
周期：每年两届
性质：面向公众面和贸易观众
入场券价格：免费
参展费用：标准展位8,200元，光地7,800元/展位
上届规模：展览面积30,000m^2(国外展商面积2,000m^2)，参展商2,500家（国外展商100家，来自30个国家），参观人数60,000人（贸易观众35,000人）
主办：北京励展华群展览有限公司
地址：北京市朝阳区新源南路1-3号平安国际金融中心A座15层(100027)
联系人：张一萌，李晓瑞

27th China Beijing Intl Gifts, Premium & Houseware Exhibition
Venue: China Intl Exhibition Center, Beijing
Profile: Arts & Crafts, Electronic Appliances, Ceramics, Glassware, Collectables, Stationery, Household Goods, Pots, Hardware, Promotions, Packaging, Promotions, Gifts & Premium Products, Houseware, Home Textiles, Bags & Cases, Electronic Appliances, Kitchenware, Home Textiles, Bags, Sports & Leisure Products
Established Year: 1999
Frequency: Bi-annual
Nature: Open to Public
Cost to Attend: Free
Participated Fee: Standard Booth RMB 8,200, Raw Space RMB 7,800/booth
Statistics '12: Exhibition Area 30,000m^2 (foreigners 2,000m^2), Exhibitors 2,500 (foreigners 100, came from 30 countries), Visitors 60,000 (Trade Visitors 35,000)
Organizer: Reed Huaqun Exhibitions
Address: 15th Floor, Tower A, Ping An International Finance Center
Contact: Raymond, Xiaorui

2013/03/15-19
☎ 010-5245 8820
🖷 010-8954 3241
✉ houzhenhua618@163.com
40

2013北京园林展–第三届国际园林景观与美好人居展览会
地点：全国农业展览馆，北京
内容：成果展区(名人、名企、名项目)；设计(园林规划、景观、建筑、花园、别墅、居家园艺)及施工；花园与庭院设施、家具及用品系列；庭园用品及景观雕塑装饰品系列；仿真景观、户外园艺家具、休闲产品、户外健身器材和娱乐设施；园林防腐木及防腐木结构、塑木、木屋、木雕、摆饰和用品，园林石景、雕塑、观赏石；户外铺装、绿色建材、生态环保装饰材料；建筑钢结构、膜结构、遮阳、阳光房、暖棚；绿化苗木、花卉、造型盆景、草坪及屋顶绿化和施工技术；园艺工具机械
主办：中国林产工业协会；中国城市园林绿化局
承办：北京海墅展览策划有限公司
地址：北京市朝阳区八里庄西里1号远洋国际中心C座901室(100025)
联系人：赵飞，侯琳

Beijing Garden Show
Venue: National Agriculture Exhibition Center, Beijing
Organizer: Beijing Haishu Exhibition Co Ltd

2013/03/16-17
☎ 4000-365-520
🖷 010-8273 4029
50

中国（国际）婚博会
地点：国家会议中心，北京
主办：中国（国际）婚博会组委会
地址：北京市海淀区学清路8号科技财富中心B1506

Beijing Bridal Expo
Venue: China National Convention Center, Beijing
Organizer: Organizing Committee

2013/03/22-24
☎ 010-5933 9489
🖷 010-5933 9494
✉ asiagolfshow@reedguanghe.com
www.chinagolfshow.com
60

2013年第12届中国高尔夫球博览会（北京）
地点：国家会议中心，北京
内容：高尔夫个人用品消费区：球杆、球具及配件：球杆、杆身、握把、球、球Tee、球包、球杆套、球具制造设备、球具设计及加工技术、球杆试打设备、球杆测试设备 、训练辅助设备、挥杆分析器；服装服饰、鞋帽手套；时尚消费品：眼镜、手镯、高礼品、护肤用品、奖杯。球场设备设施及配套用品展区：各种高尔夫球车及配件；草坪机械：球场所需机械、设备、技术，包括剪草、打孔、清扫等机械及配件；灌溉设备：喷灌、排水设备和零配件；生物农药及化肥：草种、农药、化肥；球场设计建造，球场、练习场设备及用品：练习场设备，打击垫、给球机、收球设备、洗球机、分隔栏、球袋架、围网。高尔夫服务展区：球场投资开发咨询和管理公司；高尔夫赛事组织机构；高尔夫媒体；高尔夫教育培训机构（高尔夫教育、培训学院）；高尔夫球生活服务展区
主办：中国高尔夫球协会；北京励展光合展览有限公司

China Golf Show / PGA Merchandise Show-China
Venue: China National Convention Center, Beijing
Profile: Onsite activities and areas for golf course executives, industry professionals and golf enthusiasts include an indoor equipment testing center, fashion show, new product center and innovation area.
Organizer: Reed Guanghe Exhibitions

2013/03/26-29
☎ 010-6505 0546, 010-6505 4123
🖷 010-6505 3260
✉ zengqi@cwtc.com
guoxiaomeng@cwtc.com
chicintl@chiconline.com.cn
179461717
1607147516
www.chiconline.com.cn
weibo.com/u/1466173071
70

第21届中国国际服装服饰博览会
地点：中国国际展览中心新馆，北京
内容：中国国际服装服饰博览会(CHIC)由中国服装协会、中国国际贸易中心股份有限公司和中国贸促会纺织行业分会共同主办。创办于1993年，每年一届在北京举办。二十年来，CHIC伴随着中国服装产业的发展而不断壮大，已成长为亚洲地区最具规模与影响力的服装专业展会。
始办年份：1993
周期：每年一届
市场范围：国际性
性质：面向公众
入场券价格：20元
参展费用：海外展区：光地 1,980元/m^2，标准展位28,000元/12m^2，42,000元/18m^2；男装/都市休闲、休闲装、女装、皮革、皮草/羽绒：光地1880元/m^2，不设标展；童装/婴幼用品、时尚饰品：光地1,380元/m^2，标准展位25,100元/12m^2，37,600元/18m^2；"CHIC纯粹设计"主题展37,600元/18m^2
上届规模：展览面积110,000m^2(国外展商面积27,000m^2)，参展商1,000家（国外展商450家，来自21个国家），参观人数110,000人
主办：中国服装协会 中国国际贸易中心股份有限公司 中国贸促会纺织行业分会 北京时尚博展国际展览有限公司 中国国际贸易中心股份有限公司
地址：北京市建国门外大街1号国贸展厅二层展览部(100004)
联系人：曾琦先生，郭晓萌女士
msn：jjzeng72@hotmail.com
msn：guoxiaomeng7@live.cn

CHIC2013
2013 China Intl Clothing & Accessories Fair
Venue: China Intl Exhibition Center New Venue, Beijing
Profile: Established in 1993, China International Clothing & Accessories Fair (CHIC) has been held successfully for 20 years. With an exhibition area over 110,000 square meters, the past session witnessed over 110,000 professional visitors and more than 1000 brands from dozens of countries and regions in the world. CHIC has presently been the largest and one of the most important fashion fairs in Asia.
Established Year: 1993
Frequency: Annual
Market Area: International
Nature: Open to Public
Cost to Attend: RMB 20:-
Participated Fee: Raw Space RMB 1,980/m^2, Standard Booth RMB 28,000/12m^2, RMB 42,000/18m^2
Statistics '12: Exhibition Area 110,000m^2(foreigners 27,000m^2), Exhibitors 1,000 (foreigners 450, came from 21 countries), Visitors 110,000
Organizer: China National Garment Association; China World Trade Center Co Ltd; The Sub-council of Textile Industry; CCPIT Beijing Fashion-EXPO Co Ltd
Address: Exhibition Division, China World Trade Center Co Ltd, 2/F, Exhibition Hall, No. 1 Jianwai Ave., Beijing, China
Contact: Mr Jordan Zeng, Ms Cathy Guo

2013/03/27-29
☎ 010-8522 9505, 85229148, 8522 9504
🖷 010-8522 9300
✉ lzw@ccpittex.com
www.yarnexpo.com.cn
80

2013中国国际纺织纱线(春夏)展览会
地点：全国农业展览馆，北京
内容：天然纤维和纱线：棉、毛、丝、麻和其他，人造纤维和纱线：再生、合成纤维纱线，特种纤维和纱线，弹力纱线、花式纱线，计算机相关服务，研究检测服务，媒体及专业刊物
主办：中国贸促会纺织行业分会，法兰克福展览（香港）有限公司，中国棉纺织行业协会，中国毛纺织行业协会，中国化学纤维工业协会，中国麻纺行业协会，中国纺织信息中心
地址：北京东长安街12号546室 100742
联系人：李玉珏，林泽文，林英华

China International Trade Fair for Fibers and Yarns
Venue: National Agricultural Exhibition Center, Beijing
Organizer: The Sub-Council of Textile Industry, CCPIT; Messe Frankfurt (HK) Ltd
Address: Room 546, 12 East Chang An Street, Beijing 100742, China

2013/03/28-30
☎ 010-6505 8534, 6505 4124
🖷 010-65053260
✉ duyiming@cwtc.com
wanmingyue@cwtc.com
www.chinamed.net.cn
90

2013第二十五届国际医疗仪器设备展览会
地点：国家会议中心，北京
内容：医用X射线设备、防护设备及附属设备和部件与防护设备、装；医用超声仪器；医用冷疗、低温、冷藏设备及器具、医用磁共振；手术室、急救室、诊疗设备及器具；医用核素设备；医用电子仪器设备；临床检验分析仪器、物理治疗设备及中医器械；医用光学器具、仪器及内窥设备；手术器械；消毒和灭菌设备及

China Med
The Intl Medical Instruments and Equipment Exhibition
Venue: China National Convention Center, Beijing
Profile: CHINA MED is one of the most influential exhibitions in Chinese medical instruments and equipment industry. As the first UFI-approved international medical instruments and equipment exhibition in China, China Med is aiming to become the prevailing exhibition

器具；医用软件及信息处理系统；医用高频仪器设备；体外循环及血液自理设备、医用诊察器械；医用高能射线设备、病房护理设备及器具；植入材料和人工器官、口腔科设备及器具；应急救援；军队卫生设备
主办：中国人民解放军总后勤部卫生部；惠通兴业国际展览（北京）有限公司；中国国际贸易中心股份有限公司；杜塞尔多夫展览(中国)有限公司
承办：惠通兴业国际展览（北京）有限公司
联系人：刘芬

in China's medical instrument and equipment industry, a showcase of world-leading products and technologies, and a platform for the advanced academic theories and practice under the tenet of high-end event and academic authorization.
Established Year: 1989
Frequency: Annual
Organizer: Health Department of General Logistics Department, Chinese People's Liberation Army; China World Trade Center Co Ltd; Hui Tong Xing Ye Intl Exhibition (Beijing) Co Ltd; Messe Düsseldorf (Shanghai) Co Ltd
Contact: China World Trade Center Co Ltd

2013/04/07-09
☎ 010-8575 5043, 13161009232
🖷 010-5141 3308
✉ 1282429590@qq.com
www.mdexpo.com.cn
100

2013第十四届中国国际家庭医疗保健器械展览会
地点：中国国际展览中心，北京
内容：特别设置：医疗保健器械直销和体验营销展区、大型健康管理机构展区；家用治疗仪；家用检测器械；家用保健按摩器械；家用医疗康复器具；家用健康产品；家庭护理器具
参展费用：海外企业区豪华展位3,500美元/9m^2，12,800元/9m^2，标准展位10,800/9m^2
主办：中国医疗保健国际交流促进会
承办：北京世博威国际展览有限公司
联系人：周扬

14th China Intl Home Medical Health Care Recovery Products & Instrument (Beijing) Expo
Venue: China Intl Exhibition Center, Beijing
Participated Fee: USD 3,500/9m^2
Organizer: Beijing Shibowei International Exposition Co Ltd

2013/04/07-09
☎ 010-8575 4970, 13691567172
🖷 010-5141 3308
✉ jianbohui888@163.com
110

2013第十四届北京国际营养健康产业博览会
地点：中国国际展览中心，北京
内容：营养健康产品、保健产品、保健饮品、美容瘦身、无糖食品、食疗药膳产品、保健品包装:医药保健生产设备、包装设备、喷码设备、医药包装材料等
主办：中国保健营养理事会；中国医疗保健国际交流促进会；中国老年营养与食品专业委员会
承办：北京世博威国际展览有限公司
地址：北京市朝阳区朝阳路69号（财满街）1-4-904室
联系人：田振
msn：tianzhen868@hotmail.com

14th Beijing Nutrition and Health Industry Expo
Venue: China Intl Exhibition Center, Beijing
Organizer: Beijing Shibowei International Exposition Co Ltd

2013/04/07-09
☎ 010-8441 4052, 6478 7494
🖷 010-5804 3750
✉ fengfeng99@vip.163.com
www.cifie-expo.com
120

2013第十一届中国国际食品包装与加工设备展览会
地点：中国国际展览中心，北京
内容：食品加工机械、制药机械类加工机械设备。食品包装机械、包装材料及制品、食品生产技术、辅助机械设备及配件、食品管理和服务系统、食品信息化管理技术、食品零售业设施用品
主办：中国食品工业协会；国际食品加工包装协会；北京京贸国际展览有限公司
承办：北京京贸国际展览有限公司；京茂展览服务（上海）有限公司；中国食品工业协会市场发展部
地址：北京市望京西路48号金隅国际G座2705(100102)

11th China Beijing Intl Food Processing and Packaging Exhibition
Venue: China Intl Exhibition Center, Beijing
Profile: Food machinery, packaging machinery and processing industry
Organizer: Beijing Jingmao Intl Exhibition Co Ltd

2013/04/07-09
☎ 010-6478 7419, 13161911098
🖷 010-5804 3750
✉ expochina6695@163.com
www.icecream-expo.com
130

2013第九届中国国际冰淇淋乳制品展览会
2013中国国际冰淇淋乳制品新产品及原辅料设备采购交易会
地点：中国国际展览中心，北京
内容：冰淇淋冷饮制造生产设备；冰淇淋新工艺成品展示、配套包装、印刷、加工生产设备；香精香料添加剂及配料；商业冰淇淋机、原料、配料；仓储运输设备及其他与其相关的食品设备、器具、工具
主办：中国食品工业协会；北京京贸国际展览有限公司；北京京贸国际展览有限公司，京茂展览服务（上海）有限公司
地址：北京市望京西路48号金隅国际G座2705(100102)

9th Ice Cream Expo
Venue: China Intl Exhibition Center, Beijing
Organizer: Beijing Jingmao Intl Exhibition Co Ltd

2013/04/07-09
☎ 010-6478 7342
🖷 010-5804 3750
✉ fengfeng99@vip.163.com
www.baking-expo.com
140

2013第十届中国国际烘焙展览会
地点：中国国际展览中心，北京
内容：烘焙食品品牌、连锁店、代加工知名企业，食品、糕点（月饼）、面包、蛋糕、饼干、餐饮用原辅材料、装饰品及食品代加工（OEM）；焙烤设备及器具、包装等
主办：中国食品工业协会；中国烘焙食品协会；北京京贸国际展览有限公司
承办：北京京贸国际展览有限公司
地址：北京市望京西路48号金隅国际G座2705(100102)

10th China Intl Bakery Exhibition
Venue: China Intl Exhibition Center, Beijing
Organizer: Beijing Jingmao Intl Exhibition Co Ltd

2013/04/08-10
☎ 010-8460 0666
🖷 010-8460 0669
✉ cihe-hvac@163.com
QQ 386011611
www.ishc-cihe.com
150

2013中国国际供热通风空调、卫生洁具及城建设备与技术展览会
地点：中国国际展览中心新馆，北京
内容：锅炉、壁挂炉产品和技术；采暖散热器及配套产品和技术；地暖、电采暖产品和技术；空调及通风工程产品和技术；可再生能源、太阳能工程和太阳热能利用；热计量、热交换及配套件产品和技术；暖通自控系统产品和技术 ；泵、阀、管件及水处理设备 ；其它城建设备和技术
始办年份：2000
周期：每年一届
市场范围：国际性
性质：面向公众

China Intl Trade Fair for Sanitation, Heating, Ventilation & Air-conditioning
Venue: China Intl Exhibition Center New Venue, Beijing
Established Year: 2000
Frequency: Annual
Market Area: International
Nature: Open to Public
Cost to Attend: Free
Participated Fee: Standard Booth RMB 1,200/m^2, Raw Space RMB 1,100/m^2 (min 36m^2)
Statistics '12: Exhibition Area 70,000m^2 (foreigners 20,000m^2),

入场券价格：免费
参展费用：标准展位1,200元/m²，光地1,100元/m²（36m²起）
上届规模：展览面积70,000m²(国外展商面积20,000m²)，参展商900家（国外展商200家），参观人数30,000人（贸易观众15,000人）
主办：中国国际展览中心集团公司；北京中装泰格尔展览有限公司；法兰克福展览（上海）有限公司
地址：北京市朝阳区北三环东路6号中国国际展览中心一号馆四层380室(100028)
联系人：高倩

Exhibitors 900 (foreigners 200), Visitors 30,000 (Trade Visitors 15,000)
Organizer: CIEC
Contact: Gao Qian

2013/04/14-16
☎ 010-5620 9404, 13520554363
🖷 010-5228 3411
✉ yjj8511@163.com
QQ 771782572
www.fcechina.com
160

2013北京进口食品展
中国（北京）国际进口食品博览会
地点：全国农业展览馆，北京
内容：食品及饮料区、酒专区、水产品区、添加剂及配料区、包装及加工设备区
参展费用：标准展位9m²：国内企业12,800元，国外企业3,800美元；光地36m²起：国内企业1,280元/m²，国外企业380美元/m²
主办：北星国际展览（北京）有限公司
地址：北京市海淀区安宁庄西三条宜品上层大厦6单元407
联系人：闫俊杰

China Intl Import Food Exposition
Venue: National Agricultural Exhibition Center, Beijing
Participated Fee: Standard Booth 9m² USD 3,800, Raw Space (min 36m²) USD 380/m²
Organizer: Bei Xing Exhibition (Beijing) Co Ltd

2013/04/18-20
☎ 010-5822 0435, 5822 0408, 13552089378
🖷 010-5885 0839
✉ taopg@163.com
QQ 542315105
170

2013第二十二届中国北京国际美容化妆品博览会（春季）
地点：中国国际展览中心，北京
内容：美容产品，中医药养生及保健，SPA水疗及沐浴，包装及包装材料，医学整形美容及美容连锁加盟，美发产品
主办：北京世博联展览服务有限公司；北京市美发美容行业协会
地址：北京市朝阳区三元桥曙光西里甲1号第三置业B座1006室
联系人：江涛

22nd Chinese Intl Beauty & Cosmetic Expo in Beijing 2013
Venue: China Intl Exhibition Center, Beijing
Profile: Beauty products: skin care, perfume, body care, make-up, SPA, nail care, tattoo, fragrance and health care; Hairdressing products: hair wash, care, color and perm products, hair products, hair-nourishing & growth products, accessories for hair; Appliance products; Plastic-surgery; Materials
Organizer: Beijing Shibolian Exhibition Service Co Ltd; Beijing Hairdressing & Beauty Association
Address: Room 1006, Tower B, No.3 Zhiye Building, A- 1, Shuguang Xili, Sanyuanqiao, Beijing, China

---

2013/04/26-28
☎ 010-6878 4990，6878 4991
🖷 010-6878 4978
✉ 8006@_ccfa.org.cn
邮箱hyq@ccfa.org.cn
QQ 41556877
748644636
www.chinafranchiseexpo.com
180

2013第15届国际特许加盟展览会
地点：国家会议中心，北京
内容：零售业：超市、便利店、专卖店：食品、营养品、茶叶、药品、服装、图书、音像、礼品饰品、家居用品、化妆品其他 餐饮业：中式正餐、中式快餐、火锅、西式快餐、咖啡店、休闲饮品 服务业：教育培训、洗衣洗染、连锁酒店、家居装修、汽车维修、房屋中介、美容美体、健身保健、速递物流、图文图像、家政保洁、其它服务、供应商、设备、IT服务、咨询机构、地产企业
主办：中国连锁经营协会
地址：北京市西城区阜外大街22号外经贸大厦811-815(100037)
联系人：雷续红，郝永强

China Franchise Expo 2013
Venue: China National Convention Center, Beijing
Profile: Food retail, restaurants, fast foods, cafes, bars, pubs; hotels, motels; clothing, personal equipment; home & garden furnishings, fittings, maintenance, other property services
Organizer: China Chain Store & Franchise Association; CCPIT Beijing Sub-Council

---

2013/04/26-28
☎ 010-6878 4990，6878 4991
🖷 010-6878 4978
✉ 8006@_ccfa.org.cn
hyq@ccfa.org.cn
QQ 41556877
748644636
www.chinafranchiseexpo.com
190

2013中国创业投资展
地点：国家会议中心，北京
周期：每年一届
市场范围：全国性
性质：面向公众和贸易观众
入场券价格：免费
参展费用：标准展位9,900元/9m²，光地900元/m²
上届规模：展览面积8,000m²(国外展商面积1,000m²)，参展商120家（国外展商5家，来自3个国家），参观人数10,000人
主办：中国连锁经营协会
地址：北京市西城区阜外大街22号外经贸大厦811-815(100037)
联系人：雷续红，郝永强

China Intl Franchise Exhibition 2013
Venue: China National Convention Center, Beijing
Frequency: Annual
Market Area: National
Nature: Open to Public
Cost to Attend: Free
Participated Fee: Standard Booth RMB 9,900/9m², Raw Space RMB 900/m²
Statistics '12: Exhibition Area 8,000m²(foreigners 1,000m²), Exhibitors 120 (foreigners 5, came from 3 countries), Visitors 10,000
Organizer: China Chain Store & Franchise Association
Address: Room811, 8th Floor, Foreign Economic & Trade Plaza, No.22 Fuchengmenwai Str., Xicheng DIST., Beijing, China
Contact: Vivian Lei, Evan Hao

2013/04/30-05/03
☎ 010-6554 7002，6554 7003
🖷 010-6554 5213
✉ yvonne_ye@artbeijing.net
weibo.com/1747134133/profile
www.artbeijing.net
200

2013艺术北京博览会
地点：全国农业展览馆，北京
内容：艺术北京2013的展览主体依然是来自世界各地的百余家画廊和艺术机构，但在规模和面貌上都有全新的突破。并且，收藏家和广大艺术爱好者可以在欣赏前卫当代艺术的同时，感受经典传统艺术的精髓。
始办年份：2006
周期：每年一届
市场范围：国际性
性质：面向公众和贸易观众
入场券价格：50元
参展费用：2,000元/m²
主办：北京艾特菲尔文化有限公司
地址：北京市朝阳区望京阜通东大街6号方恒国际A座1808(100102)
联系人：范欣，叶枏

Art Beijing 2013
Venue: National Agricultural Exhibition Center, Beijing
Profile: Art Beijing 2012 will bring together domestic and international galleries and art institutions of the highest artistic standards on a larger scale than ever before. At this singular event, collectors and art lovers will experience both the essence of classical art and the cutting-edge avant-garde of today.
Established Year: 2006
Frequency: Annual
Market Area: International
Nature: Open to Public
Cost to Attend: RMB 50
Participated Fee: RMB 2,000/m²
Organizer: Beijing ArtFair Culture Co Ltd
Address: 1808, Fangheng International Center A, No., 6 Futong East Street, Wangjing, Chaoyang District, Beijing
Contact: Fan Xin, Yvonne Ye

2013/05/13-15
010-8776 6773，400-689-7986
010-8776 6773
bjgg@vip.163.com
252907551
www.beijingite.com
210

第15届北京国际玩具及幼教用品展览会
地点：全国农业展览馆新馆，北京
内容：文教用品：幼儿园图书、儿童出版物、书包、文具、绘画用品用具、橡皮泥、动画音像制品、植物标本，手工课程、游戏课程、科学实验课程、幼儿读物、左右脑开发教材等；教玩具类：各种积木、拼图、桌面玩具、益智玩具；幼儿园配套设备：安全地垫、地板、安全管理软件、新型白（黑）板、乐器、床具、课桌椅，户外滑梯、淘气堡、游艺机、儿童城堡、童车、电瓶车、摇摆车、儿童乐园、充气游乐设备、儿童游戏架、秋千、荡椅、转盘、蹦床、跷跷板、组合游乐玩具；幼儿园日用品
始办年份：1998
周期：每年一届
市场范围：国际性
性质：面向贸易观众
入场券价格：20元
参展费用：A区：标准展位8,800元/9m^2光地900元/m^2（36m^2起）角位加收500元；B区：标准展位7,800元/9m^2，光地800元/m^2（36m^2起）角位加收500元
上届规模：展览面积18,000m^2(国外展商面积23m^2)，参展商353家（国外展商5家），参观人数29,000人（贸易观众19,000人）
主办：中国国际贸易中心股份有限公司；北京南北展览有限公司
地址：北京市朝阳区百子湾路16号后现代城5A902(100124)
联系人：郭斌，许伟

15th Beijing Intl Toys & Preschool Tools Exhibition
Venue: National Agriculture Exhibition Center, Beijing
Profile: Educational Toys, Educational Articles, Kindergarten Supplies & Auxiliary Equipment, Animation Recreation Facilities
Established Year: 1998
Frequency: Annual
Market Area: International
Nature: Trade Only
Cost to Attend: RMB 20:-
Participated Fee: Standard Booth RMB 8,800/9m^2, Raw Space RMB 900/m^2 (min 36m^2), Corner Booth add RMB 500
Statistics '12: Exhibition Area 18,000m^2 (foreigners 23m^2), Exhibitors 353 (foreigners 5), Visitors 29,000 (Trade Visitors 19,000)
Organizer: China World Trade Center Co Ltd; Beijing Nanbei Exhibition Co Ltd
Address: Room 902, Block 5A, Post-Modern City, No. 16, Baiziwan Road, Chaoyang District, Beijing, China
Contact: Guo Bin

2013/05/14-18
010-5190 2394
010-5190 2393
chenqian@chinaprint.com.cn
www.chinaprint.com.cn
220

第八届北京国际印刷技术展览会
地点：中国国际展览中心新馆，北京
内容：印前、印刷、印后及纸加工设备、纸张和承印物、油墨和耗材、配套和基础设施、服务和软件业、其他
周期：四年一届
市场范围：国际性
性质：面向公众
入场券价格：10元
上届规模：展览面积110,000m^2(国外展商面积40,000m^2)，参展商1,284家（国外展商316家，来自25个国家），参观人数160,000人
主办：中国印刷及设备器材工业协会；中国国际展览中心集团公司；北京中印协华港国际展览有限公司
地址：北京市东城区光明路11号天玉大厦902室(100061)
联系人：陈芊，王金鸣

8th Beijing Intl Printing Technology Exhibition
Venue: China Intl Exhibition Center New Venue, Beijing
Profile: Prepress and Premedia, Print, Postpress and Paper Converting, Paper and substrates, Inks and Consumables, Components and Infrastructure, Services and Software, Others
Frequency: Every 4 years
Market Area: International
Nature: Open to Public
Cost to Attend: RMB 10:-
Statistics '09: Exhibition Area 110,000m^2(foreigners 40,000m^2), Exhibitors 1,284 (foreigners 316, came from 25 countries), Visitors 160,000
Organizer: Printing and Printing Equipment Industries Association of China; China Intl Exhibition Center Group Corp.; China Print Show Company Limited
Address: Room 902, Tianyu Building, 11 Guangming Road, Dongcheng District, Beijing, China
Contact: Mr Michael Chen, Mr Jason Wang

2013/05/15-17
010-6292 8860
010-6295 7691
www.cisile.com.cn
230

第十一届中国国际科学仪器及实验室装备展览会
CISILE2013
地点：中国国际展览中心，北京
内容：分析测试仪器，光学仪器及设备，电子光学仪器，实验室仪器与设备，生化仪器、生命科学及微生物检测仪器，材料力学性能试验设备、无损检测仪器，计量仪器，电工测量仪表，化学试剂和标准物质，行业专用仪器
主办：中国仪器仪表行业协会
承办：北京朗普展览有限公司
地址：北京市海淀区强佑清河新城甲1号楼919室(100085)

11th China Intl Scientific Instrument and Laboratory Equipment Exhibition
Venue: China Intl Exhibition Center, Beijing
Organizer: China Instrument Manufacturer' s Association

2013/05/21-24
010-6859 4811, 6859 4994, 6859 4910
010-6859 4995
info@ccpitmsc.org
www.chinamachine.org.cn
240

第一届国际矿业及冶金工业博览会暨产业交流大会
地点：全国农业展览馆，北京
周期：两年一届
主办：中国贸促会机械行业分会
地址：北京市西城区三里河路46号(100823)

1st Intl Exhibition and Congress for the Mining and Metallurgy Industry
Venue: National Agricultural Exhibition Center, Beijing
Profile: Machinery, equipment, products and services
Frequency: Biennial
Organizer: CCPIT Machinery Sub-Council
Address: 46 Sanlihe Road, Beijing 100823

2013/05/28-06/01
010-6590 7766
010-6590 6139
info@koelnmesse.cn
1007411920
www.urbantecchina.cn
250

2013京交会"中国国际城市智能化技术与服务大会"
地点：国家会议中心，北京
主办：科隆展览国际有限公司
地址：北京东三环北路8号亮马河大厦2座1018室(100004)

UrbanTec China Conference at CIFTIS 2013
Venue: China National Convention Center, Beijing
Organizer: KOELNMESSE
Address: Unit 1018, Landmark Tower II, No. 8 Dongsanhuan North Rd, Beijing 100004, China

2013/05/31-06/03
010-6715 6227, 6719 3152
010-6719 2832
cuikankan@sportshow.com.cn
www.sportshow.com.cn
260

中国国际体育用品博览会
地点：中国国际展览中心新馆，北京
内容：2013体博会继续使用北京新国展的全部8个展厅，展会整体规模达到11万平米，预计参展企业将超过1000家。2013体博会将继续按照不同类别体育用品及参展企业的行业特点，分为六大主题展区，分别是健身按摩康复设施展区、场馆设施及营造展区、网羽运动展区、户外休闲及轮滑，运动自行车展区、运动服饰及球类运动展区、海外展区。**始办年份**：1993
周期：每年一届
市场范围：国际性

2013 China Sport Show
Venue: China Intl Exhibition Center New Venue, Beijing
Established Year: 1993
Frequency: Annual
Market Area: International
Nature: Open to Public
Cost to Attend: RMB 10:-
Statistics '12: Exhibition Area 110,000m^2 (foreigners 5,000m^2), Exhibitors 1,100 (foreigners 40, came from 87 countries), Visitors 100,000 (Trade Visitors 70,000)

性质：面向公众和贸易观众
入场券价格：10元
上届规模 '12：展览面积110,000m²(国外展商面积5,000m²)，参展商1,100家（国外展商40家，来自87个国家），参观人数100,000人（贸易观众70,000人）
主办：国家体育总局；中国体育用品业联合会
承办：国家体育总局体育器材装备中心；华兴体育用品发展中心
地址：北京市东城区体育馆路3号(100763)
联系人：崔衎衎，王珏

Organizer: Sports Equipment Administrative Center of China Common Administration of Sport; China Glory Sporting Goods Promotion Company

2013/06/06-08
☎ 010-5763 5202, 13121717549
🖷 010-5299 8072
✉ twzlzhangqi@163.com
www.chinatruck.net.cn
270

2013中国（北京）国际卡车及零部件展览会
地点：中国国际展览中心，北京
内容：卡车、专用车展区：卡车：重型卡车、中型卡车、轻型卡车、微型卡车、牵引车、牵引半挂车；专用车：厢式汽车、罐式汽车、专用自卸车、起重举升汽车、仓栅式汽车、冷冻车、特种结构汽车；商用客车展区；新能源车展区；工程车展区；零部件展区，汽车用品及维修检测设备等
主办：中国物流行业协会；北京拓威国际展览有限公司
地址：北京市通州区杨庄南里长城国际D11-907室(101121)
联系人：张奇

China (Beijing) Intl Truck Exhibition 2013
Venue: China Intl Exhibition Center, Beijing
Organizer: Beijing Tuo Wei Exhibition Co Ltd

2013/06/07-10
☎ 010-8402 9994，6403 3098 转ext 203/205
🖷 010-84010152
✉ palmexpo@163.com
www.palmexpo.com
280

第二十二届中国国际专业音响、灯光、乐器及技术展览会
地点：中国国际展览中心新馆，北京
内容：1）专业音响器材：话筒、调音系统、扬声器、周边器材、录音系统等；2）专业舞台灯光器材：电脑灯、舞台灯、调光系统、LED视频、电光源产品等；3）舞台机械：升降台、车台、吊杆、防火幕、隔声幕等；4）乐器：键盘乐器、管乐器、弦乐器、打击乐器、电声乐器、电脑作曲器材等；5）专业用摄、录像设备：摄像机、录像机、三维动画系统、监视器等；6)音视频系统集成；7）专业类出版刊物：书籍、期刊、报纸、光碟等；8）其他：剧场座椅、剧场隔音材料、卡拉OK点歌器材等。
始办年份：1989
周期：每年一届
市场范围：国际性
性质：面向公众和贸易观众
入场券价格：免费
上届规模 '12：展览面积110,000m² (国外展商面积20,000m²)，参展商1,200家（国外展商180家，来自20个国家），参观人数200,000人（贸易观众30,000人）
主办：中国演艺设备技术协会；中华人民共和国文化部；中华人民共和国科学技术部；中国照明学会；中国民族管弦乐学会。
地址：北京市东城区安定门东大街28号雍和大厦东楼C座10层(100007)
联系人：（1）灯光音响部经理：赵清华；（2）乐器部经理：付淑娟

The 22nd China International Exhibition on Pro Audio, Light, Music & Technology
Venue: China Intl Exhibition Center New Venue, Beijing
Profile: 1) Professional Sound equipment: Microphone, Tuning system, Peripheral Component Equipment, Sound Recording System, etc: 2) Professional Stage & Light Equipment: Computer Lamp, Stage Lamp, Light control system, LED, Electric Light Source product, etc; 3) Stage machinery: Carrying LT, Turn-table, Boom, Safe Curtain, Sound Insulated Curtain, etc; 4) Musical Instrument: Keyboard instrument, Wind Instrument, Stringed Instrument, Percussion Instrument, Electro-acoustical Instrument, Computer Music composition equipment, etc; 5) Professional video camera & video equipment: Camera, Videotape Recorder, 3D Animation Systems, Monitor , etc; 6) Audio and video System Integration；7) Professional publications: Publication(Book), Periodical, Newspaper, Disc, etc; 8) Others: Theater Chair, Acoustic Celotex Material of Theater, KTV/VOD Equipment, etc.
Established Year: 1989
Frequency: Annual
Market Area: International
Nature: Open to Public
Cost to Attend: Free
Statistics '12: Exhibition Area 110,000m² (foreigners 20,000m²), Exhibitors 1,200 (foreigners 180, came from 20 countries), Visitors 200,000 (Trade Visitors 30,000)
Organizer: China Entertainment Technology Association; The Ministry of Culture, China; The Ministry of Science & Technology, China；China Illuminating Engineering Society
Address: 10 Fl., C, East Building, YongHe Plaza, No. 28, An Ding Men Dong Da Jie, Dong Cheng District, Beijing, China
Contact: Zhao Qinghua, Fu Shujuan

2013/06/26-28
☎ 021-5045 6700，5045 6700
🖷 021-5045 9355，5045 9355
✉ david.zhang@hmf-china.com
www.industrial-automation-beijing.com
290

北京国际工业智能及自动化展览会
地点：北京展览馆，北京
内容：面向工厂自动化全面解决方案、电气工程、机械工程、工业IT与制造业信息化、微系统技术的中国北方工业盛会
周期：每年一届
市场范围：国际性
性质：面向贸易观众
主办：中国机械工程协会；德国汉诺威展览公司；汉诺威米兰展览（上海）有限公司
联络：诺威米兰展览（上海）有限公司
地址：上海市浦东新区银霄路393号百安居浦东商务大厦301室汉(201204)
联系人：张曦

Industrial Automation Beijing
Venue: Beijing Exhibition Centre, Beijing
Profile: International Exhibition for Modern Factory / Process Automation Technology & Equipment
Frequency: Annual
Market Area: International
Nature: Trade Only
Organizer: Chinese Mechanical Engineering Society; Deutsche Messe AG; Hannover Milano Fairs Shanghai Ltd
Address: Hannover Milano Fairs Shanghai Ltd, Rm. 301, B&Q Pudong Office Tower, 393 Yinxiao Rd, Pudong, Shanghai
Contact: David Zhang

2013/06/28-30
☎ 010-6868 3796, 13621382017
🖷 010-6863 1368
✉ 511835548@qq.com
www.aiacte.com
300

2013亚洲国际智能制造装备产业展览会
地点：中国国际展览中心，北京
内容：高档数控机床与基础制造装备；精密和智能仪器仪表与试验设备；基础零部件、元器件及通用部件设备；智能专用装备；航天航空设备制造、机床制造和材料生产企业，复合材料制造装备、自动辅带/辅丝设备、构件加工机床、超声加工/高压水切割设备等。
主办：中国机械工业国际合作咨询服务中心；中国设备管理协会；北京华贸联展览有限责任公司
地址：北京市石景山区时代花园东街8号院3号楼1001室(100043)
联系人：胡金洲

Asia Intellect 2013
Asia Intl Intellect Equipment Manufacturer Industry Exhibition
Venue: China Intl Exhibition Center, Beijing
Profile:
Organizer: China Association of Plant Engineering; Beijing Sino-Trade Union Exhibition Co Ltd
Address: Room 1001, Building NO.3, Times-Garden, East Street NO.8, Shijingshan District, Beijing, 100043, China

2013/06/28-30
☎ 010-5753 2076
🖷 010-6863 1368
www.ciptc.org
310

2013第九届中国（北京）国际动力传动与控制技术展览会
地点：中国国际展览中心，北京
内容：流体动力系统及元件，液力元件，气动元件，密封技术；空气压缩机；机械传动元件；电传动；动力设备及发电机组；发电机组、移动电站；其他备用电源、发电机控制系统、仪器仪表及其相关零配件等。
周期：每年一届
主办：中国机械工业国际合作咨询服务中心；中国设备管理协会；北京华贸联展览有限责任公司
地址：北京石景山区时代花园东街8号院3号楼1001室(100043)

9th China (Beijing) Intl Power Transmission & Control Technology Exhibition 2013
Venue: China Intl Exhibition Center, Beijing
Frequency: Annual
Organizer: Beijing Sino-Trade Union Exhibition Co Ltd
Address: Room 1001, Building NO.3, Times-Garden, East Street NO.8, Shijingshan District, Beijing, 100043, China

2013/07/03-05
☎ 010-6590 7766转ext 736
🖷 010-6590 6139
✉ h.chen@koelnmesse.cn
www.windpowerasia.com
320

中国国际风能设备展览会
（原亚洲风能大会暨国际风能设备展览会）
地点：国家会议中心，北京
内容：风力发电机、配套设备及技术、相关服务与咨询
始办年份：2003
周期：每年一届
市场范围：国际性
性质：面向贸易观众
主办：科隆国际展览有限公司；中国贸促会北京市分会（CCPIT）北京国际展览中心（BIEC）
联络：科隆科隆展览中国有限公司
地址：北京市东三环北路8号亮马河大厦2座1018室(100004)
联系人：陈晗

Wind Power China
(Formerly Wind Power Asia)
Venue: China National Convention Center, Beijing
Profile: Wind Turbines, Accessory Equipment & Technologies, Service & Consulting
Established Year: 2003
Frequency: Annual
Market Area: International
Nature: Trade Only
Organizer: Koelnmesse; CCPIT; BIEC
Address: Koelnmesse, Unit 1018, Landmark Tower II, No8 Dongsanhuan North Rd. Beijing
Contact: Helen Chen

2013/07/03-05
☎ 010-6590 7766转ext 736
🖷 010-6590 6139
✉ h.chen@koelnmesse.cn
www.cleanenergyexpochina.com,
www.cleanenergyexpochina.cn
330

中国国际清洁能源博览会
地点：国家会议中心，北京
内容：光伏产业装备、光伏产品及配套控制设备、光伏发电工程及系统、太阳能光电应用产品、太阳能热利用产品、太阳能工程、生物质能发电、生物质能燃料、生物质燃烧技术、沼气技术、林业生物质能源植物培育等。
始办年份：2009
周期：每年一届
市场范围：国际性
性质：面向贸易观众
入场券价格：专业观众免费
主办：科隆展览国际有限公司
地址：北京东三环北路8号亮马河大厦2座1018室(100004)
联系人：陈晗

Clean Energy Expo China
Venue: China National Convention Center, Beijing
Profile: PV equipment and Accessories; Solar Cells and Other Technologies; Solar Electric Power Systems; Solar Thermal Products; PV Project and System Integrators; Biomass Power Generation Technology and Equipment; Liquid Bio-fuel and Solid Bio-fuel Technology; Biomass Gasification Technology; Methane Gas Technology and Equipment; Biomass Burning Technology; Biomass Briquette Technology; Biomass Energy Forestry Cultivation; Technologies and Applications of Hydroelectric Power & Geothermal Energy
Established Year: 2009
Frequency: Annual
Market Area: International
Nature: Trade Only
Cost to Attend: Free to Trade and Professional Visitors
Organizer: KOELNMESSE
Address: Unit 1018, Landmark Tower II, No. 8 Dongsanhuan North Rd, Beijing 100004, China
Contact: Helen Chen

2013/07/03-05
☎ 010-6590 7766
🖷 010-6590 6139
✉ info@koelnmesse.cn
www.emobilitychina.com
340

2013中国国际电动汽车充电设施及储能设备展览会
地点：国家会议中心，北京
主办：科隆展览国际有限公司
地址：北京东三环北路8号亮马河大厦2座1018室(100004)

eMobility China
Venue: China National Convention Center, Beijing
Organizer: KOELNMESSE
Address: Unit 1018, Landmark Tower II, No. 8 Dongsanhuan North Rd, Beijing 100004, China

2013/07/03-05
☎ 010-6590 7766
🖷 010-6590 6139
✉ info@koelnmesse.cn
www.emobilitychina.com
350

中国国际智能电网技术和设备展览会
地点：国家会议中心，北京
主办：科隆展览国际有限公司
地址：北京东三环北路8号亮马河大厦2座1018室(100004)

GridTec China 2013
Venue: China National Convention Center, Beijing
Organizer: KOELNMESSE
Address: Unit 1018, Landmark Tower II, No. 8 Dongsanhuan North Rd, Beijing 100004, China

2013/07/03-05
☎ 010-6590 7766转ext 736
🖷 010-6590 6139
✉ h.chen@koelnmesse.cn
www.gridtecchina.com
360

第五届中国国际生物质能展览暨技术研讨会
地点：国家会议中心，北京
周期：每年一届
市场范围：国际性
性质：面向贸易观众
主办：科隆国际展览有限公司
地址：北京市东三环北路8号亮马河大厦2座1018室(100004)
联系人：陈晗

Bio-Energy China
Venue: China National Convention Center, Beijing
Frequency: Annual
Market Area: International
Nature: Trade Only
Organizer: Koelnmesse; CCPIT
Address: Koelnmesse; Unit 1018, Landmark Tower II, No8 Dongsanhuan North Rd. Beijing
Contact: Helen Chen

2013/08/14-17
☎ 010-5933 9102
🖷 010-5933 9199
✉ raymond.zhang@reedhuaqun.com
☎ 52109350
www.giftsbeijing.com
370

第28届中国北京国际礼品、赠品及家庭用品展览会
地点：中国国际展览中心，北京
内容：工艺品：陶瓷、水晶类、琉璃、金属类工艺品 赠品、促销品：广告促销品、福利、节庆促销品 品牌电子产品 纪念收藏品及钱币、邮票 有机食品 高档商务礼品：皮具、箱包、文化用品 家居用品：家具、家装用品、软装饰品、厨卫用品系列、家纺类产品 玩具及婴孕童用品：儿童及成人益智玩具、婴孕童日用品

28th China Beijing Intl Gifts, Premium & Houseware Exhibition
Venue: China Intl Exhibition Center, Beijing
Profile: Arts & Crafts, Electronic Appliances, Ceramics, Glassware, Collectables, Stationery, Household Goods, Pots, Hardware, Promotions, Packaging, Promotions, Gifts & Premium Products, Houseware, Home Textiles, Bags & Cases, Electronic Appliances, Kitchenware, Home Textiles, Bags, Sports & Leisure Products

旅游及户外用品：户外用品、健身及运动器械 媒体、协会、贸易服务及其它
始办年份：1999
周期：每年两届
市场范围：国际性
性质：面向公众面和贸易观众
入场券价格：免费
参展费用：标准展位8,200元，光地7,800元/展位
上届规模：展览面积30,000m^2(国外展商面积2,000m^2)，参展商2,500家（国外展商100家，来自10个国家），参观人数60,000人（贸易观众55,000人）
主办：北京励展华群展览有限公司
地址：北京市朝阳区新源南路1-3号平安国际金融中心A座15层(100027)
联系人：张一萌，李晓瑞

Established Year: 1999
Frequency: Bi-annual
Market Area: International
Nature: Open to Public
Cost to Attend: Free
Participated Fee: Standard Booth RMB 8,200/booth, Raw Space RMB 7,800/booth
Statistics '12: Exhibition Area 30,000m^2 (foreigners 2,000m^2), Exhibitors 2,500 (foreigners 100, came from 10 countries), Visitors 60,000 (Trade Visitors 55,000)
Organizer: Reed Huaqun Exhibitions
Address: 15th Floor, Tower A, Ping An International Finance Center, Chaoyang Dist, Beijing 100027
Contact: Raymond, Xiaorui

2013/08/21-24
☎ 010-5205 5116, 5205 5295
🖷 010-5205 5156
✉ liran@birtv.com
✉ qulina@birtv.com
4067994
www.birtv.com
weibo.com/birtv
380

第二十二届北京国际广播电影电视设备展览会
地点：中国国际展览中心，北京
内容：国内历史最悠久、最具规模、最具权威的专业广播电影电视设备展览会
始办年份：1987
周期：每年一届
市场范围：国际性
性质：面向公众和贸易观众
入场券价格：专业观众免费
参展费用：标准展位3,150元/m^2，光地2,750元/m^2
主办：国家广播电影电视总局
承办：中国广播电视国际经济技术合作总公司
地址：北京市朝阳区广渠东路1号(100124)
联系人：李然，瞿丽娜
msn：eliran@163.com

Beijing Intl Radio, TV & Film Equipment Exhibition 2013 (BIRTV2013)
Venue: China Intl Exhibition Center, Beijing
Profile: The biggest and most-authoritative exhibition of professional Radio, TV & Film equipment in China
Established Year: 1987
Frequency: Annual
Market Area: International
Nature: Open to Public
Cost to Attend: Free to Trade and Professional Visitors
Participated Fee: Standard Booth RMB 3,150/m^2, Raw Space RMB 2,750/m^2
Sponsor: State Administration of Radio, Film and Television (SARFT)
Organizer China Radio & TV Co. for Intl Techno-Economic Cooperation
Address: No. 1, Guangqu East Road, Chaoyang District, Beijing 100124, China
Contact: Li Ran, Qu Lina
msn: eliran@163.com

2013/08/27-30
☎ 010-8280 0621, 8280 0630, 8280 0773, 8280 0975
🖷 010-8280 0857, 8280 0731
✉ zjl@cis.org.cn
lsh@cis.org.cn
zj@cis.org.cn
www.miconex.com.cn
390

第24届中国国际测量控制与仪器仪表展览会
地点：中国国际展览中心，北京
内容：多国仪器仪表展览会一直以厂商参与广泛、观众数量众多著称，因此也是采购人员、终端用户、研发工程师及技术经理不容错过的行业盛会。作为国内测量控制、仪器仪表及自动化行业的风向标，它已经成为全行业洞察企业动向以及整体市场波动的窗口。同时，多国仪器仪表展览会依靠中国仪器仪表学会的业内权威地位和丰富资源，在展会同期举办多场次学术会议、技术交流会、新品发布会和技术论坛。
始办年份：1973
周期：每年一届
市场范围：国际性
性质：面向贸易观众
入场券价格：免费
参展费用： 8号国际馆 24,000元/9m^2, 光地2,400元/m^2 (18m^2起)，1号馆1层 18,000元/9m^2, 1,800元/m^2 (18m^2起)，1号馆2层12,000元/9m^2, 光地1,200元/m^2 (18m^2起)
主办：中国仪器仪表学会；北京大陆恒科贸发展有限责任公司

MICONEX2013
24th Intl Conference and Fair Measurement Instrumentation and Automation
Venue: China Intl Exhibition Center, Beijing
Established Year: 1973
Frequency: Annual
Market Area: International
Nature: Trade Only
Cost to Attend: Free
Participated Fee: Standard Booth RMB 24,000/9m^2, Raw Space RMB 2,400/m^2 (min 18m^2)
Organizer: China Instrument & Control Society
Co-Organizer: BCH Tech & Trade Expo Ltd

2013/09/02-04
☎ 021-6488 0165
🖷 021-6412 6798
✉ zhanya2012@yahoo.com.cn
www.chinajyexpo.com/beijing
400

2013中国（北京）临床检验设备及用品展览会
地点：中国国际展览中心，北京
参展费用：标准展位：国内企业12,800元/9m^2，合资企业25,800元/9m^2，境外企业4,800美元/9m^2；豪华标准展位：国内企业15,800元/9m^2，合资企业28,800元/9m^2，境外企业5,280美元/9m^2；光地(36m^2起)：国内企业1,300元/m^2，合资企业2,600元/m^2，境外企业480元/m^2
主办：北京医学会；上海展亚展览服务有限公司
联系人：金成

China (Beijing) Clinical Examination Equipment and Products Exhibition 2013
Venue: China Intl Exhibition Center, Beijing
Participated Fee: Standard Booth USD 4,800/9m^2, Premium Booth USD 5,280/9m^2, Raw Space USD 480/m^2
Sponsor: Beijing Medical Association
Organizer: Shanghai Zhanya Exhibition Service Co Ltd

2013/09/02-04
☎ 021-6488 0957, 13062800785
🖷 021-6412 6798
✉ wujunexpo@yahoo.cn
www.cmedexpo.com
410

2013第十三届中国（北京）医疗器械展览会
地点：中国国际展览中心，北京
内容：医疗器械，诊断治疗设备，病房护理设备及器具，辅助设备，口腔医疗器械设备，医院远程医疗系统、医院医疗信息系统、医院办公自动化系统，医用敷料，眼科医疗设备、骨科医疗设备、临床检验设备及诊断试剂；手术室、急救室、诊疗室设备及器具
主办：北京医学会 (中华医学会北京分会)
承办：上海展亚展览服务有限公司
地址：上海市碧泉路36弄1号金霄大厦2304室
联系人：吴俊

The13th China (Beijing) Medical Devices Exhibition 2013
Venue: China Intl Exhibition Center, Beijing
Sponsor: Beijing Medical Association
Organizer: Shanghai Zhanya Exhibition Service Co Ltd

2013/09/05-07
☎ 4000 828 021-3428 0006
🖷 021-3428 0006
www.ch-solar.com
420

第13届中国光伏大会
地点：中国国际展览中心新馆，北京
内容：光伏生产设备、光伏电池、光伏相关零部件、光伏原材料、光伏应用产品、光伏工程及系统、光伏发电系统承包商、分布式光伏发电成套产品等
主办：中国可再生能源学会
承办：中国可再生能源学会光伏专业委员会；上海诺盖斯展览策划有限公司
地址：上海市徐汇区银都路298号九润商务大厦212室
联系人：董新利

13th China Photovoltaic Conference and Intl Photovoltaic Exhibition
Venue: China Intl Exhibition Center New Venue, Beijing
Sponsor: China Renewable Energy Society
Organizer: Shanghai New Grace Exhibition Planning

2013/09/05-07
☎ 021-6048 9706, 15026647473
🖷 021-5428 7017
✉ lead014@126.co
🐧 2403652767
www.csgptd.com
430

2013中国国际智能电网建设及输配电博览会
地点：中国国际展览中心新馆，北京
内容：智能电网及电力自动化技术设备：智能电网调度系统、智能配网自动化装置、电力系统自动化、变电站综合自动化、电网安全与控制、一体化测控、调度自动化集成系统、调度综合数据平台系统、电网网络安全、配网自动化系统、智能巡系统、安全稳定控制系统解决方案、电能监控系统及微机型继电保护、广域动态监测系统、电网稳定在线监控系统、配电网智能无功补偿装置、控制软件、变送器、自动化主站、远程测控终端（RTU）、调度模拟块、信息通信交换、以太网交换机、传输接入技术与设备、数据通信与网络技术**主办：**商务部中国国际经济合作学会，中国智能电网产业联盟
承办：上海励德展览展示服务有限公司
地址：上海市徐汇区银都路298号九润商务大厦210室(200231)
联系人：王晓阳

2013 China Intl Smart Grid and Electric Power Technology Exhibition
Venue: China Intl Exhibition Center New Venue, Beijing
Organizer: Shanghai Leader Exhibition Co Ltd

2013/09/10-13
☎ 010-6335 6966
🖷 010-6335 6960
✉ jiangxl@hardware-fair.com
www.hardware-fair.com
440

第二十四届中国国际五金博览会
地点：中国国际展览中心新馆，北京
内容：中国历史最久，底蕴最深，影响中国五金三代人的展会。参展产品涉及电动工具、手动工具、机械设备、焊接设备、机电产品等
始办年份：1952
周期：每年两届
市场范围：国际性
性质：面向贸易观众
上届规模：展览面积117,062m^2(国外展商面积22,245m^2)，参展商2,100家（国外展商441家，来自12个国家），贸易观众30,192人
主办：中国五金交电化工商业协会；北京金益友联展览有限公司
地址：北京市丰台区莱户营东街58号财富西环名苑9层901(100054)
联系人：姜晓莉

24th China Intl Hardware Fair
Venue: China Intl Exhibition Center New Venue, Beijing
Established Year: 1952
Frequency: Bi-annual
Market Area: International
Nature: Trade Only
Statistics '12: Exhibition Area 117,062m^2 (foreigners 22,245m^2), Exhibitors 2,100 (foreigners 441, came from 12 countries), Trade Visitors 30,192
Organizer: China Natl Hardware, Electric and Chemical Products Commercial Association; Beijing Jinyi Youlian Exhibition Co Ltd
Address: 9th Floor, Fortune West Plaza, 58 Caihuying, Fengtai District, Beijing, China
Contact: Jiang Xiaoli

2013/09/19-20
☎ 852-2827 6211
🖷 852-3749 7342
✉ info-hk@ubm.com
www.ubmasia.com
450

海洋工程中国峰会（北京）
地点：待定
主办：亚洲博闻有限公司
地址：香港湾仔港湾道26号华润大厦17楼

Offshore Engineering China (Beijing)
Venue: To be announced
Organizer: UBM Asia Ltd
Address: 17/F, China Resources Building, 26 Harbour Road, Wan Chai, Hong Kong

2013/09/13-15
☎ 010-5711 0218, 5713 0388
🖷 010-5281 8142, 5713 0388
🐧 1425530326
www.apechina.com
460

2013第七届中国国际汽车零部件博览会
地点：中国国际展览中心，北京
主办：通用国际广告展览有限公司

CIAPE
China Intl Auto Parts Expo
Venue: China Intl Exhibition Center, Beijing
Profile: Auto parts, equipment, new-energy, tuning cars, services and accessories
Organizer: China Intl Auto Parts Expo

2013/10/16-18
☎ 010-6863 9549，13681062477
🖷 010-8868 0811
✉ gjzhgxw@163.com
🐧 1394939314
www.bciffe.com
470

2013第十届中国（北京）国际热处理工业炉展览会
地点：中国国际展览中心，北京
内容：热处理领域：热处理炉、热处理生产线；过程控制仪器仪表、机电一体化控制技术、智能信息化管理技术；热处理质量控制、产品检测仪器；热处理及辅助设备、热处理工艺材料；加热元件、筑炉材料、耐火材料、耐热绝热保温材料；热处理工艺气氛、工业气体及其制备系统、气氛发生器；热处理设备配套元器件;表面处理和表面改性技术及设备；热处理相关的安全、节能、环保技术与设备等。工业炉领域：先进高效节能的工业炉窑、新型燃烧装置及燃烧技术；电热合金和加热元件、炉用材料、炉用机械及配套装置；炉用设备及技术；炉用余热回收及环保装置、换热器、冷却；炉用仪表及自动控制系统
始办年份：2003
周期：每年一届
市场范围：国际性
性质：面向公众和贸易观众
入场券价格：免费
参展费用：展位9,800元/9m^2，12,800元/12m^2，光地1,000元/m^2
上届规模：展览面积23,000m^2(国外展商面积3,000m^2)，参展商483家（国外展商120家，来自15个国家），参观人数35,000人（贸易观众30,000人）
主办：北京机械工程学会；北京机械工程学会热处理分会；北京机械工程学会工业炉分会；中国有色金属学会；中国设备管理协

10th China (Beijing) Intl Heat Treatment & Industrial Furnace Expo 2013
Venue: China Intl Exhibition Center, Beijing
Profile: Heat treatment fields: heat treatment furnaces, heat treatment production line; surface treatment and surface modify technology and equipments; heating and cooling new technology and new equipments; heat treatment auxiliary material and equipment; quality control of heat process, testing instruments and meters, automatic technology; electromechanical integration technology, technique software and computer control technology; heat treatment arts and crafts materials and auxiliary material, quenching media, penetrating agent, coating, etc.; new-type incendiary devices and technology; heat treatment energy-saving equipments and technology, surplus heat recovery processing, and relative environmental protection equipments and technology; induction heating equipment; furnace building materials, refractory materials, heating elements, heat-resistant insulation and thermal insulation materials, matched components. Industrial furnace fields
Established Year: 2003
Frequency: Annual
Market Area: International
Nature: Open to Public
Cost to Attend: Free

会；北京金属学会；北京铸锻行业协会；北京海闻展览有限公司
地址：北京市石景山区石景山路乙18号院万达广场C座1709(100040)
联系人：高雪玮

Participated Fee: RMB 9,800/9m², RMB 12,800/12m², Raw Space RMB 1,000/m²
Statistics '12: Exhibition Area 23,000m² (foreigners 3,000m²), Exhibitors 483 (foreigners 120, came from 15 countries), Visitors 35,000 (Trade Visitors 30,000)
Organizer: Beijing Hiven Exhibition Co Ltd
Address: C1709 Wan Da Plaza, B18 Shijiangshan Road, Beijing 100040, China
Contact: Gao Xue Wei

2013/10/16-18
☎ 010-8460 0329
📠 010-84600325 8460 0755
✉ lishu@ciec.com.cn
www.ilope-expo.com

2013第十八届中国国际光电产业博览会
地点：中国国际展览中心，北京
内容：激光材料、激光器及激光应用；红外材料、技术化及应用；光电显示及照明；光学元件、仪器、材料
参展费用：标准展位A区9,800元，B区8,800元，境外企业3,500美元；光地（36平方米起）A区980元/m²，B区880元/m²，境外企业350美元/m²，角位加收10%
主办：中国工业和信息化部；中国贸促会
承办：中国光学光协子行业协会；中国国际展览中心集团公司

Optoelectronics Industry Exposition (Beijing)
18th Intl Lasers, Optoelectronics and Photonics Exhibition (ILOPE2013)
Venue: China Intl Exhibition Center, Beijing
Profile: One of the most important and must-attend optoelectronic events in China. It helps you to find out how to get the best media exposure for your ILOPE investment and pay special attention to all the free publicity opportunities. Lasers, Infrared Sensors and Accessories/Opto-electric Display Material and Equipment/Optical Communications Equipment/Component, Devices and Sub-Systems
Established Year: 1991
Organizer: CIEC Exhibition Co Ltd

490
2013/10/16-18
☎ 010-6860 4260
📠 010-8868 0811
✉ zhanlan188@126.com
www.bcime.com

2013年第十届 中国（北京）国际冶金工业博览会
地点：中国国际展览中心，北京
内容：冶金（钢铁及有色金属）技术及设备；产品、制成品及辅助用品、钢铁产品、有色金属产品、金属制品、金属结构产品及各种应用材料、五金制品、 炭素材料及制品、各种铁合金产品等；辅助材料；冶金检测及自动化；用于冶金、热加工、机械加工、物料输送、动力传动、冶金轴承、减速机、切断、称重、润滑、液压、除尘、表面处理、起重、电气、工业窑炉、燃烧器、金属圆锯机、倒角机、磨削、抛光设备、冶金锯片、切割、机械设备及各种应用材料；耐火材料；冶金工业环境保护技术和设备以及设计与咨询
始办年份：2003
入场券价格：免费
参展费用：展位类型 展位规格 国内企业 合资企业 外资企业 展位/展期（3×3）m²
国内企业9,800元/9m²，12,800元/12m²，光地1,000元/m²；合资企业13,800元/9m²，16,800元/12m²，光地1,380元/m²；外资企业3,000美元/9m²，3,800元/12m²，光地 300美元/m²；光地36m²起。
上届规模：展览面积30,000m²(国外展商面积10,000m²)，参展商500家（国外展商100家），参观人数20,000人
主办：北京金属学会；中国有色金属学会；北京机械工程学会；中国设备管理协会
承办：北京海闻展览有限公司
地址：北京市石景山区石景山路乙18号院万达广场C座1709(100040)
联系人：刘春丽

10th China (Beijing) Intl Metallurgy Industry Exhibition 2013
Venue: China Intl Exhibition Center, Beijing
Established Year: 2003
Cost to Attend: Free
Participated Fee: USD 3,000/9m², USD 3,800/12m², Raw Space USD 300/m²
Statistics '12: Exhibition Area 30,000m² (foreigners 10,000m²), Exhibitors 500 (foreigners 100), Visitors 20,000
Organizer: Beijing Hiven Exhibition Co Ltd
Address: C1709 Wan Da Plaza, B18 Shijiangshan Road, Beijing 100040, China

500
2013/10/16-18
☎ 010-6863 9549，13681062477
📠 010-8868 0811
✉ gjzhgxw@163.com
www.bciffe.com

2013第十届中国（北京）国际铸造工业展览会
地点：中国国际展览中心，北京
内容：铸钢、铸铁、有色合金铸件；汽车、机床、船舶、工程机械、轨道交通、重型机机械、矿山机械、纺织机械、印刷机械、通用机械；输变电、电子通讯、石油化工、建筑五金、管道泵阀、市政工程、城市艺术类等铸件；铸造机械和设备、测量技术、表面处理技术、熔炉、焊接技术、环保技术、铸造模具；各类铸造原辅材料
始办年份：2003
市场范围：国际性
入场券价格：免费
参展费用：9,800元/9m², 12,800元/12m², 光地1,000元/m²
上届规模 '12：展览面积23,000m²(国外展商面积3,000m²)，参展商483家（国外展商120家，来自15个国家），参观人数35,000人（贸易观众30,000人）
主办：北京铸锻行业协会；北京机械工程学会铸造分会；北京机械工程学会；北京海闻展览有限公司
地址：北京市石景山区石景山路乙18号院万达广场C座1709(100040)
联系人：高雪玮

10th China (Beijing) Intl Foundry Industry Expo 2013
Venue: China Intl Exhibition Center, Beijing
Profile: Cast steel, cast iron, non-ferrous alloy cast parts(precision casting, pressure casting, lost foam casting, rotary casting, low-pressure casting; Automobile, machine tools, shipping, engineering plant, track traffic, heavy machinery, mining machine, textile machinery, printing machinery, general machinery; casting parts for power transmission and transformation, electrommunication, petroleum chemical industry; Foundry machinery and equipment, foundry equipment, casting mold, delivery technology, measuring technique, surface treatment, melting furnace, welding, environmental technology, casting molds; Casting raw and auxiliary material
Established Year: 2003
Market Area: International
Cost to Attend: Free
Participated Fee: RMB 9,800/9m², RMB 12,800/12m², Raw Space RMB 1,000/m²
Statistics '12: Exhibition Area 23,000m²(foreigners 3,000m²), Exhibitors 483 (foreigners 120, came from 15 countries), Visitors 35,000 (Trade Visitors 30,000)
Organizer: Beijing Hiven Exhibition Co Ltd
Address: C1709 Wan Da Plaza, B18 Shijiangshan Road, Beijing 100040, China
Contact: Gao Xue Wei

510
2013/10/17-18
☎ 852-2827 6211
📠 852-3749 7342
✉ info-hk@ubm.com
www.ubmasia.com

中国仿制药峰会（北京）
地点：待定
主办：亚洲博闻有限公司
地址：香港湾仔港湾道26号华润大厦17楼

NextGen China (Beijing)
Venue: To be announced
Organizer: UBM Asia Ltd
Address: 17/F, China Resources Building, 26 Harbour Road, Wan Chai, Hong Kong

2013/10/18-21
☎ 010-6859 4939, 6859 4882, 6859 5016
📠 010-68594995
✉ info@ccpitmsc.org
www.chinamachine.org.cn
520

第十二届北京国际工程机械展览与技术交流会
地点：北京九华国际会展中心，北京
周期：两年一届
主办：中国贸促会机械行业分会
地址：北京市西城区三里河路46号(100823)

Beijing Intl Construction Machinery Exhibition & Seminar
Venue: Jiuhua Intl Exhibition Center, Beijing
Frequency: Biennial
Organizer: CCPIT Machinery Sub-Council
Address: 46 Sanlihe Road, Xicheng Dist, Beijing 100823

2013/10/23-25
☎ 010-8808 2070, 13683554888
📠 010-8808 2034
✉ sunny.99@163.com
530

2013第十二届中国国际住宅产业博览会（节能环保低碳性大展）
地点：国家会议中心，北京
主办：住房和城乡建设部住宅产业化促进中心；中国房地产业协会；中国建筑文化中心；北京市住房和城乡建设委员会
承办：北京中建文博展览有限公司
地址：北京市海淀区三里河路13号中国建筑文化中心大厦四层、七层(100037)
联系人：陈星

12th China Intl Exhibition on Housing Industry
Venue: China National Convention Center, Beijing
Organizer: Center for Housing Industrialization
Address: 4/Fl., 13 Sanlihe Road, Haidian Dist., Beijing 100037

2013/11/13-15
☎ 010-5933 9102
📠 010-5933 9199
✉ raymond.zhang@reedhuaqun.com
52109350
www.giftsbeijing.com
540

北京国际礼品、赠品及家用精品年底展览会
地点：中国国际展览中心，北京
内容：工艺品：陶瓷、水晶类、琉璃、金属类工艺品 赠品、促销品：广告促销品、福利、节庆促销品 品牌电子产品 纪念收藏品及钱币、邮票 有机食品 高档商务礼品：皮具、箱包、文化用品 家居用品：家具、家装用品、软装饰品、厨卫用品系列、家纺类产品 玩具及婴孕童用品：儿童及成人益智玩具、婴孕童日用品 旅游及户外用品：户外用品、健身及运动器械 媒体、协会、贸易服务及其它
始办年份：1999
周期：每年一届
市场范围：国际性
性质：面向公众和贸易观众
入场券价格：免费
参展费用：标准展位8,200元，光地7,800元/展位
上届规模 '12：展览面积30,000m²(国外展商面积2,000m²)，参展商2,500家（国外展商100家，来自10个国家），参观人数60,000人（贸易观众55,000人）
主办：北京励展华群展览有限公司
地址：北京市朝阳区新源南路1-3号平安国际金融中心A座15层(100027)
联系人：张一萌，李晓瑞

Intl Gifts, Premium & Houseware Purchase Exhibition
Venue: China Intl Exhibition Center, Beijing
Profile: Arts & Crafts, Electronic Appliances, Ceramics, Glassware, Collectables, Stationery, Household Goods, Pots, Hardware, Promotions, Packaging, Promotions, Gifts & Premium Products, Houseware, Home Textiles, Bags & Cases, Electronic Appliances, Kitchenware, Home Textiles, Bags, Sports & Leisure Products
Established Year: 1999
Frequency: Annual
Market Area: International
Nature: Open to Public
Cost to Attend: Free
Participated Fee: Standard Booth RMB 8,200, Raw Space RMB 7,800/booth
Statistics '12: Exhibition Area 30,000m² (foreigners 2,000m²), Exhibitors 2,500 (foreigners 100, came from 10 countries), Visitors 60,000 (Trade Visitors 55,000)
Organizer: Reed Huaqun Exhibitions
Address: 15th Floor, Tower A, Ping An International Finance Center, South Xinyuan Road, Beijing 100027
Contact: Raymond, Xiaorui

重庆 Chongqing

2013/04/25-27
☎ 023-8632 5240
📠 023-6291 8806
✉ 408334091@qq.com
www.ccwpe.com
550

2013第十四届中国–中西部国际光电产业博览会
地点：重庆国际会议展览中心，重庆
内容：光学元件、仪器、材料展区：光学零件、光学镜片、镜头；分析仪器、测量仪器、工业仪器、设备、显微镜等光学应用；光学玻璃、薄膜材料、抛光粉等原料，清洁、洁净设备及工程。红外材料、技术、应用展区；激光材料、激光器、激光应用展区；光通信展区；光电显示、照明展区：LED 显示屏、OLED显示、显示器件； 液晶显示产品、液晶面板、其他LCD 显示产品；等离子技术、背投显示技术、VFD 、SED、LCOS、CDT ；各种发光二极管、LED 模块、LED 照明灯、其它LED照明产品 其他展区：触摸屏，平板显示与大屏幕，粘胶带，膜切、光学膜及高性能膜
承办：重庆九天亿地会展有限公司（原重庆九天展览策划有限公司）
地址：重庆市南岸区南坪西路27号福天大厦B座24-2室(400060)
联系人：杨茂盛

14th Midwest China (Chongqing) Photoelectricity, Laser & LED Industry Intl Exhibition
Venue: Chongqing Intl Convention & Exhibition Center, Chongqing
Profile: photoelectricity; improvement of laser technology; promoting expedite development of Midwest industry
Organizer: Chongqing Jiutian Exhibition Planning Co Ltd
Address: Room 24-2, Tower B of Futian House, No. 27 of West Road, Nanping, Chongqing 400060

2013/11/14-18
☎ 010-8260 6899
📠 010-8260 6883
✉ ciccyhuang@cnaico.com.cn
www.cnaico.com.cn
www.autochina.com.cn
560

2013第三届中国（重庆）汽车博览会
地点：重庆
主办：中国汽车工业国际合作总公司
地址：北京市海淀区中关村丹棱街3号A座

3rd China (Chongqing) Automobile Expo
Venue: Chongqing
Organizer: China Natl Automotive Industry Intl Corp
Address: Tower A, 3 Danling Street, Haidian District, Beijing, China
3rd China (Chongqing) Automobile Expo
Venue: Chongqing
Organizer: China Natl Automotive Industry Intl Corp
Address: Tower A, 3 Danling Street, Haidian District, Beijing, China

上海 Shanghai

2013/03/01-05
☎ 021-6353 9977
📠 021-3303 0072
www.ecf.gov.cn
570

中国华东进出口商品交易会
地点：上海新国际博览中心，上海
内容：设以下展区：服装、家用纺织品、日用消费品、装饰礼品
主办：上海外经贸商务展览有限公司

East China Fair
Venue: Shanghai New Intl Expo Center, Shanghai
Profile: Fashion, garments, home textiles, consumer goods, art deco gifts
Organizer: Shanghai International Trade Promotion Co Ltd

2013/03/04-06
☎ 021-5445 1965
🖷 021-5445 1968
✉ ctfegh@126.com
www.chpe.com.cn
580

2013第八届中国（上海）国际袜业采购交易会
地点：上海世博展览馆，上海
内容：长袜类，短袜类，袜机，袜业用原料
始办年份：2006
周期：每年一届
市场范围：国际性
性质：面向贸易观众
主办：中国同源有限公司，上海内衣行业协会
承办：上海歌华展览服务有限公司
地址：上海市田州路99号新安大楼1206-1208室(200233)
联系人：王刚

China (Shanghai) International Hosiery Purchasing Expo
Venue: Shanghai World Expo Exhibition & Convention Center, Shanghai
Established Year: 2006
Frequency: Annual
Market Area: International
Nature: Trade Only
Organizer: Shanghai Gehua Exhibition Planning Co Ltd
Address: Rm.1206-1208, Xin' an Building, No. 99 Tianzhou Rd, Shanghai 200233

2013/03/05-07
☎ 010-8522 9506, 8522 9504, 8522 9446, 8522 9546
🖷 010-8522 9300
✉ intertextile_home@ccpittex.com
www.intertextile-home.com.cn
590

中国国际家用纺织品及辅料（春夏）博览会
地点：上海世博展览馆，上海
内容：各类家用纺织品及辅料，计算机辅助设计与制造，相关出版物及网络
主办：中国纺织工业联合会
承办：中国贸促会纺织行业分会；中国家用纺织品行业协会；法兰克福展览（香港）有限公司
联系人：朱勤，林英华，何磊，罗洁，王小雷

intertextile Shanghai home textiles
China Intl Trade Fair for Textiles and Accessories
Venue: Shanghai World Expo Exhibition & Convention Center, Shanghai
Sponsor: China National Textile & Apparel Council
Organizer: China Home Textile Association; The Sub-Council of Textile Industry, CCPIT; Messe Frankfurt (HK) Ltd

2013/03/09-10
☎ 021-6432 7262, 6432 6970
🖷 021-6432 5551
www.chinawedding.com.cn
600

中国（国际）婚博会
地点：上海世博展览馆，上海
主办：中国（国际）婚博会组委会
地址：上海市徐汇区漕宝路82号光大会展中心E座1701-1702(200235)

China Wedding Expo
Venue: Shanghai World Expo Exhibition & Convention Center, Shanghai
Organizer: Organizing Committee

2013/03/11-13
☎ 021-5169 8082
🖷 021-5437 6242
cs.shjzexpo.com.cn
610

2013第二届上海国际人造板工业展览会
地点：上海世博展览馆，上海
内容：板材类；人造板机械类；木业化工展区；木制品展区；原木类
主办：上海木材行业协会
承办：上海京正展览服务有限公司
地址：上海市锦梅路1500弄6号14层C室(201104)
联系人：许微

Shanghai Intl Wood-Based Panels Industry Exhibition 2013
Venue: Shanghai World Expo Exhibition & Convention Center, Shanghai
Organizer: Shanghai Jingzheng Exhibition Service Co Ltd

2013/03/11-13
☎ 021-5169 8082
🖷 021-5437 6242
cs.shjzexpo.com.cn
620

2013（建筑.家具）贴面装饰板材及生产设备展览会
地点：上海世博中心，上海
内容：建筑装饰板，家具装饰板，橱壁柜装饰板，木门装饰板，辅料及设备
主办：上海木材行业协会；上海京正展览服务有限公司
地址：上海市 锦梅路1500弄6号14层C室(201104)
联系人：许微

2013 Veneer Decorative Plates Exhibition
Venue: Shanghai World Expo Exhibition & Convention Center, Shanghai
Organizer: Shanghai Jingzheng Exhibition Service Co Ltd

2013/03/12-14
☎ 010-6853 5399, 6853 5419
🖷 010-6853 5408
✉ shfairs-info@yahoo.cn
www.ckcf.cn
630

第95届中国针棉织品交易会
中国内衣服饰展览会
中国家纺家居展览会
地点：上海新国际博览中心，上海
内容：针织服饰：针织服装、家居服、内衣、文胸、男士内衣、袜品、运动休闲服、孕婴童服装；家纺家居用品：床上用品、毛类产品、夏凉产品、家居布艺、床品面料；丝绸类产品：丝绸家纺、丝绸服饰、丝绸面料
始办年份：1960
周期：每年一届
市场范围：全国性
性质：面向贸易观众
主办：中国纺织品商业协会
地址：北京市西城区三里河东路5号中商大厦12层(100045)

China Intl Trade Fair for Mode Underwear and Home Textile
Venue: Shanghai New Intl Expo Center, Shanghai
Profile: Underwear, loungewear, lingerie, pants, hosiery, casual clothes, knitted fabrics and accessories; Beddings, towel products, summer products, art cloth, home textiles fabrics and accessories; silk products
Frequency: Annual
Market Area: International
Nature: Trade Only
Organizer: China Textile Commerce Association
Address: No.5 Sanlihe East Road, Xicheng District, Beijing, China

2013/03/12-15
☎ 852-2827 6211
🖷 852-3749 7342
✉ info-hk@ubm.com
www.ubmasia.com
640

国际散杂货展览会暨研讨会-中国上海
地点：上海国际展览中心，上海
主办：亚洲博闻有限公司
地址：香港湾仔港湾道26号华润大厦17楼

Breakbulk China
Venue: INTEX Shanghai, Shanghai
Profile: provide breakbulk shippers the opportunity to learn about breakbulk cargo issues and meet with specialized cargo carriers, ports, terminals, freight forwarders, heavy equipment transportation companies and packers.
Organizer: UBM Asia Ltd
Address: 17/F, China Resources Building, 26 Harbour Road, Wan Chai, Hong Kong

2013/03/12-14
☎ 021-6277 5353转ext 610/ 609
🖷 021-6227 0002
✉ info@premiumfabric.com.cn
www.fashionshanghai.com
650

第十九届上海国际服装纺织品贸易博览会
地点：上海新国际博览中心，上海
内容：OEM-贴牌服装，Collection-正装/时装面料，Easy-运动/休闲面料，Compliment-辅料
主办：上海纺织技术服务展览中心
地址：上海市长寿路285号恒达广场25楼
联系人：田恩岗

Shanghai International Clothing & Textile Expo
Venue: Shanghai New Intl Expo Center, Shanghai
Profile: Silk, Silky aspects, Wool, Cotton, Knitted, Prints, Denim, Linen, Yarns, Fibers, Functional Fabrics, Fabrics Eco Friendly. Interlining, Embroidery/ Lace, zipper, button, ribbon, label. OEM/ODM clothing such as Ladies wear, Menswear, Children and Infants, wear, Sport and Casual Wear
Frequency: Annual
Organizer：Shanghai Textile Technology Service & Exhibition Center

2013/03/12-14
☎ 010-6335 6966
🖷 010-6335 6960
✉ jiangxl@hardware-fair.com
www.hardware-fair.com
660

第二十三届中国国际五金博览会
地点：上海新国际博览中心，上海
内容：中国国际五金博览会始于1952年，是中国历史最久，底蕴最深，影响中国五金三代人的展会。是亚洲规划最大、专业化程度最高、影响最广的国际性展会。参展产品涉及电动工具、手动工具、机械设备、焊接设备、机电产品等
周期：每年两届
市场范围：国际性
性质：面向贸易观众
入场券价格：免费
上届规模：展览面积117,062m^2(国外展商面积22,245m^2)，参展商2,100家（国外展商441家，来自12个国家），贸易观众30,192人
主办：中国五金交电化工商业协会；北京金益友联展览有限公司
地址：北京市丰台区菜户营东街58号财富西环名苑9层901(100054)
联系人：姜晓莉

23rd China Intl Hardware Fair
Venue: Shanghai New Intl Expo Center, Shanghai
Frequency: Bi-annual
Market Area: International
Nature: Trade Only
Cost to Attend: Free
Statistics '12: Exhibition Area 117,062m^2(foreigners 22,245m^2), Exhibitors 2,100 (foreigners 441, came from 12 countries), Trade Visitors 30,192
Organizer: China National Hardware, Electric and Chemical Products Commercial Association; Beijing Jinyi Youlian Exhibition Co Ltd
Address: 9th Floor, Fortune West Plaza, 58 Caihuying, Fengtai District, Beijing, China
Contact: Jiang Xiaoli

2013/03/12-14
☎ 010-6853 5420
🖷 010-6853 5408
✉ husheng@cttu.org
85797551
www.ckcf.cn
670

中国针棉织品交易会
地点：上海新国际博览中心，上海
内容：内衣、家居服、袜子、家纺（床上用品、毛巾、夏凉产品等）、相关面辅料
周期：每年一届
市场范围：全国性
性质：面向公众
入场券价格：免费
上届规模：展览面积50,000m^2，参展商360家，参观人数43,193人
主办：中国纺织品商业协会；中纺流通（北京）商务咨询有限公司
地址：北京市西城区三里河东路5号中商大厦12层(100045)
联系人：胡晟，金鑫
msn：kax1986612@hotmail.com

China Intl Trade Fair for Mode Underwear and Home Textiles
Venue: Shanghai New Intl Expo Center, Shanghai
Frequency: Annual
Market Area: National
Nature: Open to Public
Cost to Attend: Free
Statistics '12: Exhibition Area 50,000m^2, Exhibitors 360, Visitors 43,193
Organizer: China Textile Commerce Association; TexCoo Business Service Co Ltd
Address: NO.5 Sanlihe East Road, Xicheng District Beijing, China
Contact: Hu Sheng, Jin Xin

2013/03/13-15
☎ 021-6528 2319, 13816900991
🖷 021-6528 2319
✉ merry@aiexpo.com.cn
www.asiasolar.cc
680

第八届亚洲国际太阳能光伏工业展览会
地点：上海世博展览馆，上海
内容：太阳能电池组件，原材料，太阳能光电产品，太阳能光伏工程，太阳能光热发电系统，光热发电配套设备
主办：上海艾展展览服务有限公司
联系人：周洁

AsiaSolar Photovoltaic Industry Exhibition
Venue: Shanghai World Expo Exhibition & Convention Center, Shanghai
Profile: Solar Cell & Module, Manufacturing Equipment, Raw Materials, Related Components, Solar PV Products, Solar PV Engineering Services, Concentrating Solar Power System, Related equipment for Concentrating Solar Power
Organizer: Shanghai AiExpo Exhibition Services Co Ltd

2013/03/14-15
☎ 852-2827 6211
021-6517 3930
🖷 852-3749 7342
✉ info-hk@ubm.com
www.ubmasia.com
www.biomed-innovation.com
690

中国生物材料峰会
生物医用材料创新与发展中国峰会2013
地点：上海世纪皇冠假日酒店，上海
主办：亚洲博闻有限公司
地址：香港湾仔港湾道26号华润大厦17楼

Bio-Materials China
BioMed Innovation China 2013
Venue: Crown Plaza Century Park, Shanghai
Profile: Innovating the next generation, from concept to market.
Organizer: UBM Asia Ltd
Address: 17/F, China Resources Building, 26 Harbour Road, Wan Chai, Hong Kong

2013/03/18-21
☎ 400-630-8600
🖷 010-67156913
✉ awe@cheaa.com
www.appliance-expo.com
700

中国家电博览会-上海2013
地点：上海新国际博览中心，上海
主办：中国家用电器协会
承办：北京盛世协联会展服务有限公司
联系人：张丽娟

Appliance World Expo
Venue: Shanghai New Intl Expo Center, Shanghai
Sponsor: China Household Electrical Appliances Association
Organizer: Beijing ShengShiXieLian Expo Service Co Ltd

2013/03/19-21
☎ 021-5490 0077
🖷 021-5490 4537
✉ cpcashow@ying-zhan.com
www.cpcashow.com
710

第22届中国国际电子电路展览会
地点：上海世博展览馆，上海
内容：印制电路板制造，印制电路板设备，印制电路板原物料及化学品，电子组装设备，电子组装原物料，电子制造服务/合约制造，水处理技术及设备，洁净室技术及设备，学术研究机构，协会、咨询顾问，媒体
周期：每年一届
市场范围：国际性
性质：面向贸易观众
主办：上海颖展展览服务有限公司
地址：上海市漕溪北路41号汇嘉大厦23楼D座(200030)

CPCA SHOW 2013
22nd China Intl Electronic Circuits Exhibition
Venue: Shanghai World Expo Exhibition & Convention Center, Shanghai
Profile: PCB Manufacturing, PCB Equipment, PCB Raw Materials and Chemicals, Electronic Assembly Equipment, Electronic Assembly Materials, Electronic Manufacturing Services/ Contract Manufacturing, Water Treatment Technology / Equipment, Cleanrooms Technology/ Equipment, Research Institutes, Associations, Information & Consulting, News Media
Frequency: Annual
Market Area: International
Nature: Trade Only
Organizer: Shanghai Yingzhan Exhibition Service Co Ltd
Address: Unit D, 23/F, Hui-Jia Building, No. 41, Cao Xi Road (N) Shanghai 200030, China

2013/03/22-24
☎ 021-6432 9258
🖷 021-5171 4528
✉ 1724305609@qq.com
1724305609
www.meirongexpo.com
720

第18届上海美容美发化妆品博览会
地点：上海光大会展中心，上海
内容：美容护肤品、化妆品、美容仪器、中医美容、美容保健品、美体及瘦身、美发、彩妆香水、美甲纹绣、原料、生产设备及包装等
主办：上海秀博展览有限公司
地址：上海市漕宝路82号光大会展中心E座1905室(200235)
联系人：王小姐

Shanghai Beauty, Hairdressing & Cosmetics Expo
Venue: Shanghai Everbright Convention & Exhibition Center, Shanghai
Organizer: Shanghai Xiubo Exhibition Co Ltd
Address: Rm. 802, Seat D, Everbright Convention & Exhibition Center, 80 Caobao Road, Shanghai, 200235, China

2013/03/22-24
021-6432 9266, 13601838918
021-5171 4528
583017948
www.expo-ad.com
730

2013第14届上海国际广告四新展览会
地点：上海光大会展中心，上海
内容：广告制作设备；广告材料、物料；展览展示系统及广告标识；多媒体及触摸技术与设备
主办：中国同源有限公司
承办：上海秀博展览有限公司
地址：上海市漕宝路82号E座1905室(200235)
联系人：王中杰

14th Shanghai Intl Advertising Four New Exhibition
Venue: Shanghai Everbright Convention & Exhibition Center, Shanghai
Organizer: Shanghai Xiubo Exhibition Co Ltd
Address: Rm. 802, Seat D, Everbright Convention & Exhibition Center, 80 Caobao Road, Shanghai, 200235, China

2013/03/26-28
010-5979 5833, 6839 6330
010-5907 1335, 6839 6422
ccpitsli@yahoo.com.cn
www.fi-c.com
740

中国国际食品添加剂及配料展览会
地点：上海世博展览馆，上海
内容：食品添加剂、食品配料、食品加工助剂、相关设备技术及书籍、杂志
周期：每年一届
市场范围：国际性
性质：面向贸易观众
入场券价格：免费
上届规模 '12：展览面积71,600m²(国外展商面积20,000m²)，参展商1,179家（国外展商289家，来自30个国家），贸易观众32,791人
主办：中国食品添加剂和配料协会；中国贸促会轻工业分会
地址：北京市朝阳门外大街甲6号万通中心3座1402
联系人：张越宸
地址：北京市阜外大街22号(100020)，中国贸促会轻工行业分会
联系人：张昕

Food Ingredients China
Venue: Shanghai World Expo Exhibition & Convention Center, Shanghai
Profile: Food Ingredients, Food Additives, Food Supplements, Equipments and Instruments, Books and Magazines
Frequency: Annual
Market Area: International
Nature: Trade Only
Cost to Attend: Free
Statistics '12: Exhibition Area 71,600m²(foreigners 20,000m²), Exhibitors 1,179 (foreigners 289, came from 30 countries), Trade Visitors 32,791
Organizer: China Food Additives & Ingredients Association; CCPIT sub-council of Light Industry
Contact: Zhang Yuechen, Zhang Xin

2013/03/28-29
852-2827 6211, 021-6157 3930
852-3749 7342
info-hk@ubm.com
www.ubmasia.com
www.nextgen-china.com
750

中国仿制药峰会
地点：上海世纪皇冠假日酒店，上海
内容：在创新和竞争的循环下把握仿制药的商机
主办：亚洲博闻有限公司
地址：香港湾仔港湾道26号华润大厦17楼

NextGen China (Shanghai)
Venue: Crown Plaza Century Park Shanghai, Shanghai
Profile: Seizing the business opportunity of generic drugs in the cycle of innovation & competition
Organizer: UBM Asia Ltd
Address: 17/F, China Resources Building, 26 Harbour Road, Wan Chai, Hong Kong

2013/03/30-04/01
852-2827 6211
852-3749 7342
info-hk@ubm.com
www.ubmasia.com
www.pharma-manufacturing-china.com
760

中国药品生产与质量管理峰会
地点：上海
主办：亚洲博闻有限公司
地址：香港湾仔港湾道26号华润大厦17楼

Pharma Manufacturing China
Venue: Shanghai
Organizer: UBM Asia Ltd
Address: 17/F, China Resources Building, 26 Harbour Road, Wan Chai, Hong Kong

2013/04/01-03
852-2827 6211
021-6437 1178转ext 571
852-3749 7342
info-hk@ubm.com
helen.fan@ubmsinoexpo.com
http://finefood.hotelex.cn
770

上海国际葡萄酒与烈酒展览会
地点：上海新国际博览中心，上海
主办：亚洲博闻有限公司
地址：香港湾仔港湾道26号华润大厦17楼
承办：上海博华国际展览有限公司
地址：上海襄阳南路218号现代大厦八楼（200031）

Winexpo
Venue: Shanghai New Intl Expo Center, Shanghai
Organizer: UBM Asia Ltd
Address: 17/F, China Resources Building, 26 Harbour Road, Wan Chai, Hong Kong
Contact: Shanghai UBM Sinoexpo Intl Exhibition Co Ltd
Address: 8/F, Xian Dai Mansion, Xiang Yang Road(s), Shanghai 200031

2013/04/01-03
852-2827 6211
021-6437 1178转ext 173
852-3749 7342
info-hk@ubm.com
lily.jin@ubmsinoexpo.com
www.hotelex.cn
780

上海咖啡与茶用品展
地点：上海新国际博览中心，上海
主办：亚洲博闻有限公司
地址：香港湾仔港湾道26号华润大厦17楼
主办：上海博华国际展览有限公司
地址：上海襄阳南路218号现代大厦八楼（200031）

Expo Coffee&Tea
Venue: Shanghai New Intl Expo Center, Shanghai
Organizer: UBM Asia Ltd
Address: 17/F, China Resources Building, 26 Harbour Road, Wan Chai, Hong Kong
Contact: Shanghai UBM Sinoexpo Intl Exhibition Co Ltd
Address: 8/F, Xian Dai Mansion, Xiang Yang Road(s), Shanghai 200031

2013/04/01-03
852-2827 6211
021-6437 1178
852-3749 7342
info-hk@ubm.com
james.qiu@ubmsinoexpo.com
www.expolight.cn
790

中国(上海)国际建筑照明展览会暨中国（上海）LED展览会
地点：上海新国际博览中心，上海
主办：亚洲博闻有限公司
地址：香港湾仔港湾道26号华润大厦17楼
主办：上海博华国际展览有限公司
地址：上海襄阳南路218号现代大厦八楼（200031）

Expo Light
Venue: Shanghai New Intl Expo Center, Shanghai
Organizer: UBM Asia Ltd
Address: 17/F, China Resources Building, 26 Harbour Road, Wan Chai, Hong Kong
Contact: Shanghai UBM Sinoexpo Intl Exhibition Co Ltd
Address: 8/F, Xian Dai Mansion, Xiang Yang Road(s), Shanghai 200031

800
2013/04/01-03
☎ 852-2827 6211
021-6474 6138
🖷 852-3749 7342
✉ info-hk@ubm.com
annie.shi@ubmsinoexpo.com
www.ubmchina.com
www.expobuild.com

W3国际精品设计展
地点：上海新国际博览中心，上海
主办：亚洲博闻有限公司
地址：香港湾仔港湾道26号华润大厦17楼
主办：上海博华国际展览有限公司
地址：上海襄阳南路218号现代大厦八楼（200031）

Expo Deco
Venue: Shanghai New Intl Expo Center, Shanghai
Organizer: UBM Asia Ltd
Address: 17/F, China Resources Building, 26 Harbour Road, Wan Chai, Hong Kong
Contact: Shanghai UBM Sinoexpo Intl Exhibition Co Ltd
Address: 8/F, Xian Dai Mansion, Xiang Yang Road(s), Shanghai 200031

810
2013/04/01-03
☎ 852-2827 6211
021-6437 1178转ext 117
🖷 852-3749 7342
✉ info-hk@ubm.com
annie.shi@ubmsinoexpo.com
www.expobuild.com

中国国际建筑装饰展览会
地点：上海新国际博览中心，上海
主办：亚洲博闻有限公司
地址：香港湾仔港湾道26号华润大厦17楼
主办：上海博华国际展览有限公司
地址：上海襄阳南路218号现代大厦八楼（200031）

Expo Build China
Venue: Shanghai New Intl Expo Center, Shanghai
Organizer: UBM Asia Ltd
Address: 17/F, China Resources Building, 26 Harbour Road, Wan Chai, Hong Kong
Contact: Shanghai UBM Sinoexpo Intl Exhibition Co Ltd
Address: 8/F, Xian Dai Mansion, Xiang Yang Road(s), Shanghai 200031

820
2013/04/01-03
☎ 852-2827 6211
021-6437 1178
🖷 852-3749 7342
✉ info-hk@ubm.com
Bill.wu@ubmsinoexpo.com
www.ecobuildchina.com

ecobuild
世界节能环保与生态建筑中国展

世界节能环保与生态建筑中国展
地点：上海新国际博览中心，上海
主办：亚洲博闻有限公司
地址：香港湾仔港湾道26号华润大厦17楼
主办：上海博华国际展览有限公司
地址：上海襄阳南路218号现代大厦八楼（200031）

Ecobuild China
Venue: Shanghai New Intl Expo Center, Shanghai
Organizer: UBM Asia Ltd
Address: 17/F, China Resources Building, 26 Harbour Road, Wan Chai, Hong Kong
Contact: Shanghai UBM Sinoexpo Intl Exhibition Co Ltd
Address: 8/F, Xian Dai Mansion, Xiang Yang Road(s), Shanghai 200031

830
2013/04/01-03
☎ 852-2827 6211
021-6437 1178
🖷 852-3749 7342
✉ info-hk@ubm.com
www.ubmasia.com

HDE
上海酒店设计与工程展览会
Shanghai Hospitality Design & Engineering Expo

上海酒店设计与工程展览会
地点：上海新国际博览中心，上海
主办：亚洲博闻有限公司
地址：香港湾仔港湾道26号华润大厦17楼
主办：上海博华国际展览有限公司
地址：上海襄阳南路218号现代大厦八楼（200031）

Shanghai Hospitality Design & Engineering Expo
Venue: Shanghai New Intl Expo Center, Shanghai
Organizer: UBM Asia Ltd
Address: 17/F, China Resources Building, 26 Harbour Road, Wan Chai, Hong Kong
Contact: Shanghai UBM Sinoexpo Intl Exhibition Co Ltd
Address: 8/F, Xian Dai Mansion, Xiang Yang Road(s), Shanghai 200031

840
2013/04/01-09
☎ 852-2827 6211
021-6437 1178
🖷 852-3749 7342
✉ info-hk@ubm.com
Jack.liu@UBMSinoexpo.com
www.chinacleanexpo.com

CCE
China Clean Expo 2013

中国清洁博览会
地点：上海新国际博览中心，上海
周期：每年一届
主办：亚洲博闻有限公司
地址：香港湾仔港湾道26号华润大厦17楼
主办：上海博华国际展览有限公司
地址：上海襄阳南路218号现代大厦八楼（200031）

China Clean Expo
Venue: Shanghai New Intl Expo Center, Shanghai
Frequency: Annual
Organizer: UBM Asia Ltd
Address: 17/F, China Resources Building, 26 Harbour Road, Wan Chai, Hong Kong
Contact: Shanghai UBM Sinoexpo Intl Exhibition Co Ltd
Address: 8/F, Xian Dai Mansion, Xiang Yang Road(s), Shanghai 200031

850
2013/04/01-03
☎ 852-2827 6211
021-6437 1178
🖷 852-3749 7342
✉ hotelfurniure@ubmsinoexpo.com
www.hotelex-fur.com

Hotel Furniture

中国国际酒店家具展
地点：上海新国际博览中心，上海
周期：每年一届
市场范围：国际性
性质：面向贸易观众
主办：亚洲博闻有限公司
地址：香港湾仔港湾道26号华润大厦17楼
主办：上海博华国际展览有限公司
地址：上海襄阳南路218号现代大厦八楼（200031）

Hotel Furniture China
Venue: Shanghai New Intl Expo Center, Shanghai
Frequency: Annual
Market Area: International
Nature: Trade Only
Organizer: UBM Asia Ltd
Address: 17/F, China Resources Building, 26 Harbour Road, Wan Chai, Hong Kong
Contact: Shanghai UBM Sinoexpo Intl Exhibition Co Ltd
Address: 8/F, Xian Dai Mansion, Xiang Yang Road(s), Shanghai 200031

2013/04/01-03
☎ 852-2827 6211
021-6437 1178
📠 852-3749 7342
✉ info-hk@ubm.com
hotelex@ubm.com
www.hotelex.cn
860

上海国际酒店用品博览会
地点：上海新国际博览中心，上海
内容：酒店、餐饮、酒吧一站式的采购平台，提供建材、清洁、照明整体的解决方案。同时举办的展览有：餐饮设备及供应展、烘焙展、桌面用品展、咖啡与茶用品展、食品及饮料展、康体健身与休闲娱乐展、布草及纺织品展、酒店家具展、客房电器及用品展、酒店智能产品及安全防卫设备展
周期：每年一届
市场范围：国际性
性质：面向贸易观众
主办：亚洲博闻有限公司
地址：香港湾仔港湾道26号华润大厦17楼
主办：上海博华国际展览有限公司
地址：上海襄阳南路218号现代大厦八楼（200031）

Hotelex Shanghai
Venue: Shanghai New Intl Expo Center, Shanghai
Profile: Hotelex will stand at a new historical point and continue to focus on the low-carbon development of the hotel industry and the development direction of global hotel industry.
Frequency: Annual
Market Area: International
Nature: Trade Only
Organizer: UBM Asia Ltd
Address: 17/F, China Resources Building, 26 Harbour Road, Wan Chai, Hong Kong
Contact: Shanghai UBM Sinoexpo Intl Exhibition Co Ltd
Address: 8/F, Xian Dai Mansion, Xiang Yang Road(s), Shanghai 200031

2013/04/01-03
☎ 852-2827 6211
021-6437 1178转ext 571
📠 852-3749 7342
✉ info-hk@ubm.com
helen.fan@ubmsinoexpo.com
www.expofinefood.com
870

上海高端食品与饮料展
地点：上海新国际博览中心，上海
内容：美食、美酒、饮料、冰激凌、烘焙
主办：亚洲博闻有限公司
地址：香港湾仔港湾道26号华润大厦17楼
主办：上海博华国际展览有限公司
地址：上海襄阳南路218号现代大厦八楼（200031）

Expo Finefood
Venue: Shanghai New Intl Expo Center, Shanghai
Profile: Fine food, wines, drinks, ice cream, baked food
Organizer: UBM Asia Ltd
Address: 17/F, China Resources Building, 26 Harbour Road, Wan Chai, Hong Kong
Contact: Shanghai UBM Sinoexpo Intl Exhibition Co Ltd
Address: 8/F, Xian Dai Mansion, Xiang Yang Road(s), Shanghai 200031

2013/04/01-03
☎ 852-2827 6211
021-6437 1178转ext 171
📠 852-3749 7342
✉ info-hk@ubm.com
exposhop@ubmsinoexpo.com
www.exposhop.com.cn
880

上海国际商场设计、装饰与用品博览会
地点：上海新国际博览中心，上海
内容：针对各类大中型商场，百货店，小型商店，商铺等综合商贸零售产业及实体提供一站式采购平台的大型展会，是目前在中国独一无二的汇集商场商铺的各类解决方案和应用的专业活动，其展品范围包括标识和标牌、货架和展示柜、IT和安防、自动售货机，商场设计与装饰、家具与建材、照明与清洁等。
周期：每年一届
市场范围：国际性
性质：面向贸易观众
主办：亚洲博闻有限公司
地址：香港湾仔港湾道26号华润大厦17楼
主办：上海博华国际展览有限公司
地址：上海襄阳南路218号现代大厦八楼（200031）

Expo Shop
Venue: Shanghai New Intl Expo Center, Shanghai
Profile: One-stop purchasing stage, especially for shopping malls, department stores, small stores, and shops. It is the only exhibition involves solutions and applications for shops in China. The exhibition including sign and label, shelves and display cabinet, IT and security, vending machine, shop design and decoration, furniture and building material, lighting and cleaning.
Frequency: Annual
Market Area: International
Nature: Trade Only
Organizer: UBM Asia Ltd
Address: 17/F, China Resources Building, 26 Harbour Road, Wan Chai, Hong Kong
Contact: Shanghai UBM Sinoexpo Intl Exhibition Co Ltd
Address: 8/F, Xian Dai Mansion, Xiang Yang Road(s), Shanghai 200031

2013/04/01-03
☎ 852-2827 6211
021-6115 4999
📠 852-3749 7342
✉ info-hk@ubm.com
ceramics@ubmsinoexpo.com
www.ceramics-china.cn
890

中国国际建筑陶瓷及卫浴科技精品展览会
地点：上海新国际博览中心，上海
内容：建筑陶瓷、精品卫浴、马赛克、墙体地面材料、石材、陶板、涂料釉料。
主办：亚洲博闻有限公司
地址：香港湾仔港湾道26号华润大厦17楼
主办：上海博华国际展览有限公司
地址：上海襄阳南路218号现代大厦八楼（200031）

Ceramics, Tile & Sanitary Ware China
Venue: Shanghai New Intl Expo Center, Shanghai
Organizer: UBM Asia Ltd
Address: 17/F, China Resources Building, 26 Harbour Road, Wan Chai, Hong Kong
Contact: Shanghai UBM Sinoexpo Intl Exhibition Co Ltd
Address: 8/F, Xian Dai Mansion, Xiang Yang Road(s), Shanghai 200031

2013/04/08-10
☎ 010-5856 5888
📠 010-5856 6000
✉ wangping@biec.com.cn
www.cr-expo.com
900

第二十四届国际制冷、空调、供暖、通风及食品冷冻加工展览会
地点：上海新国际博览中心，上海
内容：制冷、空调、供暖、通风及食品冷冻加工
始办年份：1987
周期：每年一届
市场范围：国际性
入场券价格：免费
参展费用：1,300元/m^2
上届规模 '12：展览面积40,231m^2(国外展商面积8,288m^2)，参展

24th Intl Exhibition for Refrigeration, Air-conditioning, Heating and Ventilation, Frozen Food Processing, Packaging and Storage
Venue: Shanghai New Intl Expo Center, Shanghai
Profile: Refrigeration, Air-conditioning, Heating and Ventilation, Frozen Food Processing, Packaging and Storage
Established Year: 1987
Frequency: Annual
Market Area: International
Cost to Attend: Free

商1,109家（国外展商229家，来自31个国家），贸易观众45,758人
主办：中国贸促会北京市分会北京国际展览中心
地址：北京市西城区月坛北街26号恒华国际大厦A座6层601室(100045)
联系人：彭璐，王平

Participated Fee: RMB 1,300/m^2
Statistics '12: Exhibition Area 40,231m^2(foreigners 8,288m^2), Exhibitors 1,109 (foreigners 229, came from 31 countries), Trade Visitors 45,758
Organizer: CCPIT Beijing Sub-council Beijing Intl Exhibition Centre
Address: Suite 601, Floor 6, Henghua Intl Mansion, 26, Yuetanbeijie, Xicheng District, Beijing 100045, China
Contact: Peng Lu, Wang Ping

2013/04/08-10
☎ 021-5197 8782, 5197 8781, 5197 8780
🖷 021-5101 0898
✉ cwee@dr-expo.com.cn
www.cwee.com.cn
910

2013第七届中国（上海）国际风能展览会暨研讨会
地点：上海新国际博览中心，上海
内容：风力发电机组、海上风电设备及技术、服务与咨询、风电场
主办：中国农业机械工业协会风能设备分会（风力机械分会）；中国可再生能源学会风能专业委员会；中国电机工程学会可再生能源发电专业委员会（原风力与潮汐专委会）；世界风能协会（World Wind Energy Association）；ISPC（上海跨国采购中心）
承办：上海德瑞展览策划有限公司
地址：上海浦东金豫路100号1号楼926室(201206)

7th China (Shanghai) Intl Wind Energy Exhibition and Conference
Venue: Shanghai New Intl Expo Center, Shanghai
Organizer: MPZhongmao Deray (Shanghai) Intl Pte Ltd
Address: Room 926, Building1, 100 Jin Yu Road, Pudong, Shanghai 201206

2013/04/08-10
☎ 021-5197 8782, 5197 8781, 5197 8780
🖷 021-5101 0898
✉ cwee@mpzhongmao-dr.com
www.powerchinashow.com
920

2013上海第十二届中国国际动力设备发电机组展览会
地点：上海新国际博览中心，上海
内容：发动机，发电机组，配套设备、零部件、油品，通用动力设备，生产工艺、设备
参展费用：国内标摊1,300元/m^2，国外标摊360美元/m^2；国内特装360元/m^2，国外特装320美元/m^2，特装36m^2
主办：中国内燃机工业协会；上海跨国采购中心
承办：上海德瑞展览策划有限公司
地址：上海浦东金豫路100号1号楼926室(201206)

12th China (Shanghai) Intl Power and Generating Sets Exhibition
Venue: Shanghai New Intl Expo Center, Shanghai
Participated Fee: Standard Booth USD 360/m^2, Raw Space USD 320/m^2 (min 36m^2)
Organizer: MPZhongmao Deray (Shanghai) Intl Pte Ltd
Address: Room 926, Building1, 100 Jin Yu Road, Pudong, Shanghai 201206

2013/04/08-11
☎ 021-2231 7108, 2231 7101
🖷 021-2231 7183
✉ Alex.wang@reedexpo.com.cn mailto:Alex.wang@reedexpo.com.cn
www.sino-corrugated.com
925

2013中国国际瓦楞展
地点：上海新国际博览中心，上海
主办：励展博览集团(上海分公司)
地址：上海市闸北区裕通路100号洲际中心42楼
联系人：王文杰

SinoCorrugated 2013
Venue: Shanghai New Intl Expo Center, Shanghai
Organizer: Reed Exhibitions
Contact: Reed Exhibitions Shanghai Branch
Address: 42F, Intercontinental Center, 100 Yutong Road, Zhabei District, Shanghai 200070, China

---

2013/04/10-12
☎ 021-6413 7426, 6413 3729, 15821476635
🖷 021-6091 9309
✉ xumengxuan2013@163.com
📱 1935446758
www.rhbzexpo.com
930

2013国际日化包装机械设备展览会
同期举办
第十四届国际表面活性剂和洗涤剂展览会
地点：上海光大会展中心，上海
内容：日化原料、日化包装、日化机械设备、OEM、ODM等供应链产品
主办：中国日用化学工业研究院
承办：中国日用化学工业信息中心；上海怡涵展览服务有限公司
联系人：徐梦萱

Daily Chemical Packaging Machinery Exhibition
Surfactants and Detergents Exhibition
Venue: Shanghai Everbright Convention & Exhibition Center, Shanghai
Organizer: Shanghai Yihan Exhibition Co Ltd

2013/04/10-12
☎ 021-6460 5459
🖷 021-6119 8626
✉ shszexpo@yahoo.com.cn
www.luxuryexpo.org
940

2013上海国际高端生活方式（奢侈品）展览会
地点：上海世博展览馆，上海
内容：顶级跑车、房车、越野车、礼宾车、摩托车、私人飞机、豪华游艇等；顶级豪华别墅、地产、移民留学、私人豪华旅游、顶级酒店、度假村、私人金融及银行服务；顶级珠宝、香水、名表、名笔、化妆品、定制服装鞋帽、奢侈包装；顶级艺术品、古玩；顶级白酒、红酒、雪茄；顶级会所、高尔夫球会、游艇俱乐部
参展费用：标准展位(9m^2)：国内企业22,800元，国外企业4,000美元；光地（36m^{2}起）：国内企业2,000元/m^2, 国外企业400美元/m^2
主办：中国奢侈品贸易委员会
承办：上海顺展展览服务有限公司
地址：上海市莘建路228弄闵富大厦1号楼2104室(201100)

2013 Shanghai Intl High-end Lifestyle Exhibition
Venue: Shanghai World Expo Exhibition & Convention Center, Shanghai
Participated Fee: Standard Booth USD 4,000/9m^2, Raw Space USD 400/m^2
Organizer: Shanghai Shunzhan Exhibition Service Co Ltd
Address: Room 2104, Building 1, Minfu Mansion, Lane 228, Xinjian Road, Shanghai

---

2013/04/11-14
☎ 852-2827 6211
021-6437 1178
🖷 852-3749 7342
✉ info-hk@ubm.com
els@ubmsinoexpo.com
www.expolifestyle.com
950

ELS
Expo Life Style
for luxury and excellence

中国（上海）尚品生活展
地点：上海世博展览馆，上海
主办：亚洲博闻有限公司
地址：香港湾仔港湾道26号华润大厦17楼
承办：上海博华国际展览有限公司

Expo Life Style for Luxury and Excellence
Venue: Shanghai World Expo Exhibition & Convention Center, Shanghai
Organizer: UBM Asia Ltd
Address: 17/F, China Resources Building, 26 Harbour Road, Wan Chai, Hong Kong
Contact: Shanghai UBM Sinoexpo International Exhibition Co Ltd

2013/04/11-14
☎ 852-2827 6211
021-6437 1178
℻ 852-3749 7342
✉ info-hk@ubm.com
helena.gao@ubmsinoexpo.com
www.boatshowchina.cn
960

中国（上海）国际游艇展
地点：上海世博展览馆，上海
内容：船艇及豪华游艇：动力艇及帆船、豪华及超豪华游艇、橡皮艇、充气艇、游览船；码头、休闲活动及服务：房产公司、码头开发商、港口和船坞设备、码头设备、出版发行公司、信息顾问服务公司、行业标准机构、船艇设计公司；复合材料及设备：动力装置、推进系统、配套设备、硬件、便携式设备、通讯导航设备、发动机/驱动器、救生装置；水上运动：独木舟和皮筏、潜水、帆船运动、帆板、水橇设备、潜水装置、航行及帆船驾驶课程，便携式健康运动设备；观光：旅游局、旅馆及观光地、水岸别墅、租赁公司；生活方式：时尚、奢侈品、高级内部装饰及家具公司
周期：每年一届
主办：亚洲博闻有限公司
地址：香港湾仔港湾道26号华润大厦17楼
承办：上海博华国际展览有限公司
地址：上海市襄阳南路218号现代大厦8楼（200031）

China (Shanghai) International Boat Show
Venue: Shanghai World Expo Exhibition & Convention Center, Shanghai
Frequency: Annual
Organizer: UBM Asia Ltd
Address: 17/F, China Resources Building, 26 Harbour Road, Wan Chai, Hong Kong
Contact: Shanghai UBM Sinoexpo International Exhibition Co Ltd
Address: 8F Xian Dai Mansion, 218 Xiang Yang Road (S), Shanghai 200030, China

2013/04/11-14
☎ 852-2827 6211
021-6437 1178
℻ 852-3749 7342
021-6437 4988
✉ info-hk@ubm.com
king.wang@ubmsinoexpo.com
www.expoleisure.com
970

中国（上海）休闲产业展
地点：上海新国际博览中心，上海
主办：亚洲博闻有限公司
地址：香港湾仔港湾道26号华润大厦17楼
承办：上海博华国际展览有限公司
地址：上海市襄阳南路218号现代大厦8楼（200031）

Expo Leisure
Venue: Shanghai New Intl Expo Center, Shanghai
Organizer: UBM Asia Ltd
Address: 17/F, China Resources Building, 26 Harbour Road, Wan Chai, Hong Kong
Contact: Shanghai UBM Sinoexpo International Exhibition Co Ltd
Address: 8F Xian Dai Mansion, 218 Xiang Yang Road (S), Shanghai 200030, China

2013/04/12-14
☎ 021-2281 7535
℻ 021-5836 1665
✉ xiyaohua@ciec.com.cn
www.adc-expo.com
980

第十届中国国际成人保健及生殖健康展览会
地点：上海国际展览中心，上海
主办：中国国际展览中心集团公司
承办：北京中展海外展览有限公司；上海市生殖健康产业
地址：上海市浦东新区浦东南路1085号1311室(200120)

China Adult-Care Expo
Venue: INTEX Shanghai, Shanghai
Organizer: CIEC Overseas Exhibition Co Ltd

2013/04/17-19
☎ 021-2325 5318, 13918072400
℻ 021-2325 5111
✉ jenny@shanghaimart.com.cn
www.apparelchina.org
990

2013（春季）上海纺织服装展览会
地点：上海世贸商城，上海
内容：服装、面料、辅料
始办年份：1999
周期：每年一届
市场范围：全国性
性质：面向公众和贸易观众
入场券价格：免费
主办：上海世界贸易商城有限公司
地址：上海市延安西路2299号(200336)

Shanghai Textile & Apparel Trade Fair (Spring) 2013
Venue: Shanghai Mart, Shanghai
Established Year: 1999
Frequency: Annual
Market Area: National
Nature: Open to Public
Cost to Attend: Free
Organizer: Shanghai Mart

2013/04/17-20
☎ 021-6295 8367, 6295 6677
℻ 021-6278 0038
✉ intexcl@sh163.net
QQ 2546527197
www.hortiflorexpo.com
1000

第15届中国国际花卉园艺展览会
地点：上海世博展览馆，上海
内容：涉及鲜花、盆花、观叶植物、苗木、草坪、种籽（球）、种苗、仿真植物、生物技术、花盆、园林机械、温室设备、灌溉系统、花园家具、彩色地坪、屋顶绿化、城市景观以及各种园艺、花卉、园林的配套产品等
周期：每年一届
市场范围：国际性
入场券价格：免费
上届规模2012：展览面积8,500m²(国外展商面积2,000m²)，参展商405家（国外展商79家，来自24个国家），贸易观众16,586人
主办：中国花卉协会；上海国际展览中心有限公司；长城国际展览有限责任公司
地址：上海市娄山关路55号8楼(200336)
联系人：崔琳，郑轶多
msn：chui730new@hotmail.com

15th Hortiflorexpo IPM Shanghai
Venue: Shanghai World Expo Exhibition & Convention Center, Shanghai
Frequency: Annual
Market Area: International
Cost to Attend: Free
Statistics'12: Exhibition Area 8,500m²(foreigners 2,000m²), Exhibitors 405 (foreigners 79, came from 24 countries), Trade Visitors 16,586
Organizer: China Flower Association; Intex Shanghai Co Ltd; China Great Wall Intl Exhibition Co Ltd
Address: 8F, 55 Loushanguan Rd., Shanghai 200336, China
Contact: Catherine Cui, David Zheng

2013/04/17-19
☎ 010-6853 5315, 6853 5401
℻ 010-010-6853 5015
✉ ciosh@ciosh.com
www.ciosh.com
1010

2013第86届中国劳动保护用品交易会
地点：上海光大会展中心，上海
内容：个体防护用品，职业服装及材料，安全生产监测仪表，安全生产设备，安全生产科技咨询培训、劳动防护技术交流讲座、行业媒体、评估认证机构等
主办：中国纺织品商业协会
承办：中纺流通（北京）商务咨询有限公司
地址：北京市西城区三里河东路5号中商大厦12层（100045）

86th China Occupational Safety & Health Goods Expo
Venue: Shanghai Everbright Convention & Exhibition Center, Shanghai
Profile: Personal Protective Equipment, Uniforms and Protective Wear & Material, Monitoring Instrument, Safety of Workplace Installation, Environment Security, Industrial Cleaning Products.
Organizer: China Textile Commerce Association; TexCoo Business Service Co Ltd
Address: No.5 Sanlihe East Road, Xicheng District, Beijing 100045

2013/04/17-19
☎ 021-6279 2828
🖷 021-6386 6972
✉ wwn@siec-ccpit.com
www.chinainterdye.com
1020

第十三届中国国际染料工业暨有机颜料、纺织化学品展览会
地点：上海世博展览馆，上海
内容：各类染料、中间体、有机颜料和纺织化学品、各类助剂和整理助剂、各种纺织用化学制品、配套生产、分析检测和监控设备以及印染设备和三废处理设备，印花材料，印花相关设备等
始办年份：2001
周期：每年一届
市场范围：国际性
性质：面向贸易观众
主办：中国染料工业协会；中国印染行业协会；中国贸促会上海市分会；中国国际商会上海商会；上海国际展览服务有限公司
地址：上海市延安中路841号8楼(200040)
联系人：王薇娜女士

CHINA INTERDYE 2013
Venue: Shanghai World Expo Exhibition & Convention Center, Shanghai
Profile: Dyestuff, intermediates, organic pigments, textile chemicals, various auxiliaries and finishing agents, various chemicals for textiles, and equipment for related production, analysis, inspection, testing, and monitoring, as well as dyeing and printing equipment and the equipment for the treatment of "three wastes" , Printing materials, printing-related equipment, etc.
Established Year: 2001
Frequency: Annual
Market Area: International
Nature: Trade Only
Organizer: China Dyestuff Industry Association; China Dyeing and Printing Association; CCPIT Shanghai Sub-Council; Shanghai Chamber of Commerce of China Chamber of International Commerce; Shanghai International Exhibition Service Co Ltd
Address: Shanghai International Exhibition Service Co Ltd, 8/F, No.841 Yan An Zhong Road, Shanghai, 200040, China
Contact: Ms Weina Wang

2013/04/21-29
☎ 021-6279 2828
🖷 021-6545 5124
✉ lyg@siec-ccpit.com
www.autoshanghai.org
1030

第十五届上海国际汽车工业展览会
地点：上海新国际博览中心，上海
内容：各类轿车、商务车、客车、卡车、特种车、汽车设计及新概念产品、各类汽车零部件、汽车音响、轮胎、汽车检测维修设备、汽车用品等
始办年份：1985
周期：两年一届
市场范围：国际性
性质：面向公众和贸易观众
主办：中国汽车工业协会；中国贸促会上海市分会；中国贸促会汽车行业分会；上海市国际展览有限公司；德国慕尼黑国际博览集团/IMAG国际交易会及展览会有限公司
地址：上海市延安中路841号8楼上海市国际展览有限公司(200040)
联系人：陆洋先生

AUTO SHANGHAI 2013
Venue: Shanghai New Intl Expo Center, Shanghai
Profile: All kinds of concept cars, saloon cars, sports car, passenger cars, commercial vehicles, parts and fittings of autos, acoustics of autos, inspection and maintenance equipments of auto, auto article
Established Year: 1985
Frequency: Biennial
Market Area: International
Nature: Open to Public
Organizer: China Association of Automobile Manufacturers; CCPIT Shanghai Sub-Council; CCPIT, Automotive Sub-Council; Shanghai International Exhibition Co Ltd; MMG-Messe Muenchen International / IMAG-International Messe-und Ausstellungsdienst GmbH
Address: Shanghai International Exhibition Co Ltd, 8/F, No.841 Yan An Zhong Road, Shanghai 200040, China
Contact: Mr Lu Yang

2013/04/22-24
☎ 021-6247 3101
🖷 021-6247 2950
✉ info@printechexpo.com
www.printechexpo.com
1040

Printech2013票据标签打印展览会
地点：上海展览中心，上海
内容：打印机（热敏、针式机、热转印、喷墨、激光；打印机（票据、标签、证卡、条码）；条码扫描器、POS机；标签、不干胶、热敏纸、打印纸、复印纸、收银纸、票据纸及相关印刷设备；打印机复印机耗材、零部件；标签印制技术及设备、自动识别与防伪技术
主办：上海市计算机行业协会；上海文化用品行业协会；上海广会文化传媒有限公司；Grand Expo Inc. (USA)
地址：上海市镇宁路200号欣安大厦东楼24B(200040)

Printech Digital Printing & Label Expo
Venue: Shanghai Exhibition Center, Shanghai
Organizer: Shanghai Grand Culture Media Co Ltd
Address: 24B, East Wing, Xin'an Building, 200 Zhenning Rd., Shanghai 200040, China

2013/04/22-24
☎ 021-6289 5385
🖷 021-6247 2950
✉ info@ReChinaexpo.com.cn
www.ReChinaexpo.com.cn
1050

第十一届亚洲打印耗材展览会
地点：上海展览中心，上海
内容：墨盒、硒鼓、色带、碳粉、墨水及连续供墨系统；兼容、再生、循环使用的打印机和复印机通用耗材；芯片、感光鼓、各类辊、膜、空盒等配件和原材料；打印耗材的制造、翻新、灌装、测试等设备和工具；相纸、票据纸、彩喷纸、热敏纸等办公打印用纸；打印设备与耗材的技术、信息、包装等服务类产品
主办：Recharger Magazine (USA)；中国计算机行业协会耗材专委会；ReChina Expo Inc. (USA)；上海广会会展有限公司
地址：上海市镇宁路200号欣安大厦东楼24B(200040)
联系人：顾小姐，朱小姐

ReChina Asia Expo
Venue: Shanghai Exhibition Center, Shanghai
Profile: Ink cartridges, toner cartridges, ribbons, toner, ink and CISS; Compatible, remanufactured and renewable consumables for printers and copiers; Chips, OPC drums, various rollers, sleeves, empties; Manufacturing, remanufacturing, filling, testing equipment & tools for printer consumables; paper
Organizer: Shanghai Grand Expo Co Ltd
Address: 24B East Wing Xin'an Building, 200 Zhenning Road, Shanghai 200040 China

2013/04/22-24
☎ 010-6211 5995
🖷 010-6211 7993
✉ show@interweighing.com
cwia@weighment.com
www.weighment.com
www.interweighing.com
1060

2013中国国际衡器展览会
地点：上海光大会展中心，上海
主办：中国衡器协会
地址：北京市北三环西路43号青云当代大厦12B10室(100086)

InterWEIGHING
China Intl Weighing Instrument Exhibition
Venue: Shanghai Everbright Convention & Exhibition Center, Shanghai
Profile: All kinds of scales, balance, weighing system, indicator, load cell, testing instrument and device, electronic component and materials used in weighing instrument.
Organizer: China Weighing Instrument Association

2013/04/26-28
☎ 021-3127 9896, 3119 4620
🖷 86-021-31275478
✉ haiyan.wang@hnzmedia.com
www.biochina.org.cn
1070

中国（上海）国际生物质能和沼气大会暨展览会
地点：上海世博展览馆，上海
内容：生物质能发电设备；生物汽油转化设备和技术；生物柴油转化设备和技术；生物质气化,生物质气利用设备和技术；生物质固体颗粒燃料设备和技术；沼气技术与产品应用；转化,贮存,输送,利用设备；沼气行业新技术和设备；能源工程；合同能源管理
主办：中国可再生能源学会生物质能专业委员会；鸿与智工业媒体集团

China (Shanghai) Intl Bioenergy and Biogas Conference and Exhibition
Venue: Shanghai World Expo Exhibition & Convention Center, Shanghai
Organizer: HNZ Industry Media Group

2013/05/07-09
☎ 010-6588 6235，6588 9379
🖷 010-6588 6233
✉ xyz@sialchina.cn
www.sialchina.cn

1080

SIAL 2013 The Asian Food Marketplace China

中国国际食品和饮料展览会

地点：上海新国际博览中心，上海
内容：打造亚洲食品第一展-法国SIAL国际食品和饮料展览会创建于1964年，每两年一届，迄今已有40多年的历史，现已成为全球食品和饮料行业最大的展览贸易盛会。自2000年SIAL展移植中国以来，已成功举办了十三届，已成为中国规模最大、层次最高、效益最好的国际食品展。并成为亚洲最大的国际食品展。中食展SIAL China, 推动食品贸易的加速器 卓有成效的食品贸易盛会 每年，SIAL China 展会引领亚洲乃至全球买家来到上海，共同搭建中国食品行业最有影响力的商贸平台。专业贸易商涵盖了从食品进出口商、经销商、批发与零售商、超市与综合卖场，到酒店、餐饮业等食品与饮料采购的各个领域。 高质量的观众为参展商带来了众多的商机以及合作交流的机遇。 SIAL China 2012展会迎来了40,722位专业观众，其中14.5%（5,905位）来自中国大陆以外。中国最具国际化的食品与饮料贸易盛会 73,200平方米展出面积（相比2011年增长25%）。来自海内外69个国家和地区的1,907家展商（相比2011年增长25%）亮相SIAL China 2012。众多海外展商的加盟，一方面反映了食品贸易全球化的大趋势，同时SIAL China 再次体现了其高度国际性。SIAL China国内参展商来自24个省市自治区。农业部对外经济合作中心、中国乳制品工业协会、中国水产流通与加工协会以及山东、浙江、上海、福州、宁波、甘肃一如既往组织自己的龙头企业集体参展。中国罐头工业协会也再度组织罐头企业集体亮相本展。 众多丰富活动，提升展会价值 中食展为企业接触专业买家提供了多种渠道，通过丰富多彩的展期活动，给参展企业带来高附加值的参展效果。中国国际葡萄酒及烈性酒Best Buy评酒会，从参赛酒的外观、嗅觉、口感，并且从性价比的角度进行评选，只对参展商开放，由专业酒类销售人员、品酒师、调酒师、专栏作家、媒体记者等专业人士组成品鉴组，推选出不同类别的奖项 葡萄酒创新论坛，对葡萄产地，不同的葡萄品种以及著名的葡萄酒品牌进行介绍。产地展示区：对全球主要葡萄产地的地理位置以及参加本届展会的主要葡萄酒产地进行宣传和介绍。根据展会参展国，介绍全球产地。葡萄品种专区：着重介绍源自欧洲的主要品种的葡萄，同时请观众对不同葡萄品种酿制的葡萄酒进行品尝。名牌葡萄酒推介：根据创新、商业业绩和价值创造三项标准，筛选了一些著名品牌且致力于开拓葡萄酒与烈酒市场的展商在这里进行展示，对观众介绍他们的各种创新产品。每个品牌对自己产品的不同特点以及成功的历史进行了详细的介绍，并邀请与会观众品尝他们的美酒佳酿。食品趋势与创新大奖，中国市场的最新资讯平台！专设食品发展大趋势及创新产品展示区，经专家挑选符合世界食品发展趋势和创新的参展产品，在展示区集中展示并颁发了奖项。SIAL美食厨房，与国际厨师协会Escoffier 合作。欣赏国际厨师协会ESCOFFIER主厨们带来的原汁原味的西餐厨艺表演，发现美食烹饪的创意。亚洲青年希望厨师大赛- 埃斯科菲厨师协会中国区组织。- 来自亚洲中国大陆、中国香港、中国澳门、新加坡、韩国、泰国、越南和菲律宾的8名青年厨师进行紧张的角逐。厨师团队赛 - 4个从大中华区五星级酒店中甄选的厨师团队，角逐第一届最佳厨师团队奖。- 澳门团队则获得了第一届最佳厨师团队奖。举办"21Food国际买家见面会"。邀请了来自美国、泰国、中国香港、智利、澳大利亚、巴基斯坦、埃及、菲律宾、德国、丹麦、俄罗斯、印度、卡塔尔、摩洛哥、荷兰、韩国等多个国家和地区的买家前来参会，举办现场一对一贸易洽谈。采购产品涵盖了农产品、罐头食品、海鲜成品、咖啡茶饮、休闲小吃、食品添加剂、调味品配料、食品机械各领域。
始办年份：2000
周期：每年一届
市场范围：国际性
性质：面向贸易观众
入场券价格：专业观众免费
上届规模：展览面积73,200m^2，参展商1,907家（国外展商69家），贸易观众40,722人）
主办：法国高美爱博展览集团；北京爱博西雅展览有限公司
地址：北京市朝外大街22号泛利大厦1605室 （100020）(100020)
联系人：候旭，徐亚骞

Sial china 2013

Venue: Shanghai New Intl Expo Center, Shanghai
Established Year: 2000
Frequency: Annual
Market Area: International
Nature: Trade Only
Cost to Attend: Free to Trade and Professional Visitors
Statistics '12: Exhibition Area 73,200m^2, Exhibitors 1,907 (foreigners 69), Trade Visitors 40,722
Organizer: COMEXPOSIUMExposium-Sial Exhibition Co Ltd
Address: Suite 1605, Prime Tower, No.22 Chaoyangmenwai Dajie, Beijing 100020, China
Contact: Hou Xu，Henry Xu

2013/05/07-09
☎ 010-6338 1401/ 1402 / 1403
🖷 010-63381405
✉ ccmf-china@163.com
www.ccmfchina.cn

1090

2013第六届上海国际罐藏食品及原辅材料、机械设备博览会

地点：上海新国际博览中心，上海
内容：罐藏食品生产企业；机械设备配套企业；包装配套；行业经销商、代理商；
上届规模2012：展览面积73,200m^2，参展商1,907家（国外展商家，来自69个国家），参观人数40,722人
主办：中国罐头工业协会；北京中罐国联展览有限责任公司
地址：北京宣武区广安门外大街168号朗琴国际中座1215室（100055）

6th Shanghai Intl Canned Food and Materials Facility Exhibition

Venue: Shanghai New Intl Expo Center, Shanghai
Statistics '12: Exhibition Area 73,200m^2, Exhibitors 1,907 came from 69 countries, Visitors 40,722
Organizer: China Canned Food Industry Association

2013/05/16-19
☎ 021-6475 2979, 3414 0164（直线）
🖷 021-6475 2907
✉ hexiangdm@163.com
t.sina.com.cn/dongmaoexpo
www.tea-shexpo.com

1100

2013第十届中国（上海）国际茶业博览会

地点：上海国际展览中心，上海
内容：各类名茶；再加工茶；茶具产品；茶叶包装；泡茶用水；加工机械；茶叶技术；茶工艺品；茶延伸品
主办：上海东贸展览服务有限公司
地址：上海市徐汇区沪闵路9116号A座1006室
联系人：何湘

China Tea Expo, Shanghai 2013

Venue: INTEX Shanghai, Shanghai
Organizer: Shanghai Dongmao Exhibition Service Co Ltd

2013/05/16-18
☎ 021-6295 2907
📠 021-6278 0038
✉ intexljs@sh163.net
www.china-aid.com
1110

第八届中国国际养老及康复医疗博览会
地点：上海世博展览馆，上海
内容：我国养老及康复医疗领域规模最大、国际化程度最高的盛会。展览涉及老年人和残障人士康复医疗及护理服务、宜居建筑、健康养生、生活护理、养老服务等技术及管理成果，并涵盖老年人旅游、文化、教育、生活领域的服务产品展示。
始办年份：2000
周期：每年一届
市场范围：国际性
性质：面向公众
上届规模2012：展览面积17,000m^2(国外展商面积9,000m^2)，参展商348家（国外展商220家，来自16个国家），参观人数34,780人（贸易观众21,536人）
主办：上海市民政局；上海市老龄工作委员会办公室；上海市国际贸易促进委员会；上海国际展览中心有限公司
地址：上海市娄山关路55号新虹桥大厦8楼801-804室(200336)
联系人：李菊盛，朱筱曼

8th China Intl Exhibition of Senior Care Rehabilitation Medicine and Healthcare
Venue: Shanghai World Expo Exhibition & Convention Center, Shanghai
Profile: The leading show for senior care and rehabilitation medicine industry in China. It covers the products and services and related institutions, in rehabilitation and medicine, age-friendly buildings, health care products, nursing care and the other service relating to old persons travel, culture, education, and living.
Established Year: 2000
Frequency: Annual
Market Area: International
Nature: Open to Public
Statistics '12: Exhibition Area 17,000m^2(foreigners 9,000m^2), Exhibitors 348 (foreigners 220, came from 16 countries), Visitors 34,780 (Trade Visitors 21,536)
Organizer: Shanghai Civil Affairs Bureau; Shanghai Municipal Committee on Ageing; CCPIT Shanghai Sub-council; INTEX Shanghai Co Ltd
Address: Room 801-804, Floor 8, New Town Mansion, 55 Lou Shan Guan Rd. Shanghai
Contact: Ms Lillian Lee, Ms Xiaoman Zhu

2013/05/16-18
☎ 021-3455 5169
📠 021-3327 5389
✉ 13564593938@163.com
QQ 1102706719
1120

2013中国（上海）竹制品展/春季竹礼品展
地点：上海世博展览馆，上海
内容：竹日用品：竹砧板、竹筷、竹茶具、竹餐具、竹凉席、竹窗帘、竹架、竹垫、竹餐垫、竹盒、竹篮、竹签、牙签、茶道用具等；竹工艺品：竹礼品、竹工艺品、竹雕艺术品、竹装饰品、竹乐器、根工艺、竹筒、竹扇、竹包装、竹木制品、编织工艺、藤草制品等；竹纤维产品：服饰、家纺、床上用品、保健枕、卫浴用品等；竹质化学制品：竹叶黄酮、竹炭、竹醋液等；竹笋食品：保鲜笋、笋干、罐头笋、竹饮料等；
主办：中国日用商品行业协会，上海雅辉展览有限公司
地址：上海漕溪路251弄望族城5号楼20F室(200235)
联系人：杨佳婵

China (Shanghai) Bamboo Product Exhibition
Venue: Shanghai World Expo Exhibition & Convention Center, Shanghai
Organizer: Shanghai Yahui Exhibition Service Co Ltd

2013/05/17-19
☎ 010-5957 4252, 15210314956
📠 010-5885 0889
✉ suchao_vip@163.com
QQ 593450087
www.hifair.cn
1130

2013第十届中国国际营养健康产业（上海）博览会
地点：上海光大会展中心，上海
内容：营养健康产品，保健产品，保健饮品，保健用品，美容瘦身，无糖食品，食疗药膳产品，保健品包装
主办：中国对外贸易经济合作企业协会
承办：北京海名汇博会展有限公司
地址：北京朝阳区广渠路21号金海国际5号楼2单元1801室(100124)
联系人：苏超

China (Shanghai) Intl Nutrition and Health Industry Expo 2013
Venue: Shanghai Everbright Convention & Exhibition Center, Shanghai
Organizer: Beijing Haiming Huibo Exhibition Co Ltd
Address: Room 1712, Building B, Golden Sea Commerce Rich Center, 21 Guangqu Road, Chaoyang District, Beijing 100124, China

^^8928
2013/05/20-22
☎ 021-5308 2200, 5308 3300
📠 021-5308 2151
✉ sxl@chinabeautyexpo.com
www.cbebaiwen.com
1140

2013第十二届上海国际日化原料包装机械设备展览会
中国美容博览会
地点：上海新国际博览中心，上海
内容：日化原料、日化包装、日化机械设备、OEM/ODM
主办：上海百文会展有限公司，中国贸促会轻工分会
地址：上海市西藏中路728号23F(200001)

Shanghai Intl COSMETECH Exhibition
China Beauty Expo
Venue: Shanghai New Intl Expo Center, Shanghai
Organizer: Shanghai Baiwen Exhibition Co Ltd

2013/05/22-24
☎ 021-3468 9029, 18721881895
📠 021-5601 3923
✉ dongsexpo@126.com
www.allconfs.org
1150

2013上海国际工业计算机及嵌入式系统展览会暨
2013 MCU技术创新与嵌入式应用大会
2013人机界面技术创新与应用大会
地点：上海光大会展中心，上海
内容：工业计算机及板卡工业计算机嵌入式主板数据采集板通信板I/O接口其他各种功能板卡；嵌入式技术MCU/DSP/FPGA/单片机总线控制器/接口IC模拟芯片/AD/DA电源管理/功率器件嵌入式存储/工业存储传感器/光电元件操作系统、中间件及应用软件嵌入式开发工具；工业电源、嵌入式电源 其他 人机界面、工业显示
主办：中国自动化协会；全国工业自动化标准化委员会
承办：东世展览服务（上海）有限公司
地址：上海市罗芬路989弄3号201室(201908)
联系人：高健

Shanghai IPC & Embedded Expo 2013
Venue: Shanghai Everbright Convention & Exhibition Center, Shanghai
Organizer: Shanghai Dongs Expo Co Ltd

2013/05/24-26
☎ 021-5216 4993, 5216 4994
📠 021-5218 9400
✉ jay.xu@neon-expo.com
QQ 2558425391
www.kidsedu.cn
1160

第八届上海幼儿教育暨用品展
地点：上海世贸商城，上海
内容：国内唯一针对0-7岁以幼儿教育为主题的展会，自2006年举办以来为上千家企业成功拓展了销售渠道，成就了上万个家庭新主张。展会同期举办第八届全国幼儿园园长大会、连锁加盟规划 与研讨会、超级宝宝才艺大赛等9场会议，12场活动来丰富展会内容，以促进供需双方的贸易交流。展品范围：教育类、教具类、玩具类、书籍类、幼教用品类、幼儿园设施类、儿童家具类、服务机构类等
始办年份：2006
周期：每年一届
市场范围：国际性

The 8th Kids Education Expo 2013Shanghai
Venue: Shanghai Mart, Shanghai
Established Year: 2006
Frequency: Annual
Market Area: International
Nature: Open to Public
Cost to Attend: RMB 30
Participated Fee: Standard Booth RMB 8,800/7,800/6,800/9m^2, Raw Space RMB 880/780/680/m^2
Statistics '12: Exhibition Area 6,300m^2(foreigners 1,020m^2), Exhibitors 128 (foreigners 20, came from 7 countries), Visitors 31,082 (Trade Visitors 13,902)

性质：面向公众和贸易观众
入场券价格：30元
参展费用：标准展位8800元/7800元/6800元/9m^2，光地880元/780元/680元/m^2
上届规模：展览面积6,300m^2(国外展商面积1,020m^2)，参展商128家（国外展商20家，来自7个国家），参观人数31,082人（贸易观众13,902人）
主办：上海里扬展览服务有限公司
地址：上海市长宁区北翟路1158号鑫达大厦1号楼409室(200335)
联系人：徐先生，陆小姐

Organizer: SHANGHAI NEON EXHIBITION SERVICE LTD
Address: Room409, 4F, Xinda Plaza Building 2, No. 1158 Xiehe Road, Shanghai 200335, China

---

1170
2013/05/26-28
☎ 021-5566 0901
🖷 021-5566 0902
www.baichengcs.com

2013第101届中国上海国际鞋业皮具展CIFL暨GDS精品展
地点：上海展览中心，上海
内容：中高端革履、手袋、皮革制品及时尚配饰
预计规模：展览面积26,000m^2
主办：中国百货商业协会
承办：上海百承商务服务有限公司
地址：地址：上海市徐汇区中山西路1878弄 凯托大厦1号601室

101st Shanghai Intl Footwear & Leather Goods Exhibition & GDS Select
Venue: Shanghai Exhibition Center, Shanghai
Expectation: Gross Area 26,000m^2
Organizer: Shanghai Baicheng Commerce Service Co Ltd

1180
2013/05/29-31
☎ 021-6328 8899
🖷 021-6374 9188
✉ sphinxwang@gmail.com
www.biotech-china.com

中国国际生物技术和仪器设备博览会
同期举办：
2013中国（上海）科学仪器实验室装备及化学试剂展览会
2013中国（上海）诊断试剂和设备展览会
地点：上海世博展览馆，上海
内容：生物技术；分析仪器、实验室设备；医疗设备；试剂及耗材
承办：上海现代国际展览有限公司
地址：上海市盛泽路8号18楼(200002)
联系人：胡东

BIOTECH CHINA 2013
Intl Trade Fair & Congress for Biotechnology
Venue: Shanghai World Expo Exhibition & Convention Center, Shanghai
Organizer: Shanghai Modern International Exhibition Co Ltd
Address: 18F, No. 8 Shengze Road Shanghai, 200002, China

1190
2013/05/30-31
☎ 852-2827 6211
021-61573930, 6157 3919
🖷 852-3749 7342
021-6157 7299
✉ info-hk@ubm.com
conferencechina@ubm.com
www.ubmasia.com
www.sstconference.com

可持续船舶技术中国峰会
地点：上海
主办：亚洲博闻有限公司
地址：香港湾仔港湾道26号华润大厦17楼
地址:上海市南京西路388号仙乐斯广场9楼(200003)

3rd Sustainable Ship Technology Conference China
Venue: Shanghai
Organizer: UBM Asia Ltd
Address: 17/F, China Resources Building, 26 Harbour Road, Wan Chai, Hong Kong
Address: 9F, Ciros Plaza, No.388 West Nanjing Road, Shanghai 200003

1200
2013/06/04-06
☎ 021-6484 1883
🖷 021-6484 3366
✉ kuozhansales@163.com
www.mobileexpo.cn

2013第十五届上海国际手机产业展览会暨研讨会
地点：上海新国际博览中心，上海
内容：移动终端、相关配件及产品:半导体器件及IC电路，显示部件，包装附属品
主办：中国手机协会；中国触控协会
承办：上海扩展展览服务有限公司
地址：上海市徐汇区漕溪路251弄望族城5号楼602室(200235)
联系人：胡靖

CME2013
China Intl Mobile Phone Industry Exhibition & Seminar
Venue: Shanghai New Intl Expo Center, Shanghai
Organizer: Shanghai Kuozhan Exhibition Service Co Ltd

1210
2013/06/04-05
☎ 021-6279 2828
🖷 021-6545 5124
✉ zlei@siec-ccpit.com
www.iotconference.com

第四届中国国际物联网大会暨展览会
地点：上海世博展览馆，上海
内容：物联网相关应用领域：智能交通、车联网、移动支付、智能家居、智能医疗、智能电网、环境与安全检测、云计算及信息安全、工业及自动化控制、公共安全、智慧城市等
周期：每年一届
市场范围：国际性
性质：面向贸易观众
主办：中国贸促会上海市分会；上海市国际展览有限公司；美国克劳斯公司
地址：上海市延安中路841号8楼上海市国际展览有限公司(200040)
联系人：朱磊女士

IOT China Conference & Exhibition 2013
Venue: Shanghai World Expo Exhibition & Convention Center, Shanghai
Profile: Intelligent traffic, Telematics, _Mobile-payment, Intelligent home-wares, Intelligent healthcare, Smart power grid, environment & security surveillance, Cloud computing, information security, Industrial and automation control, Public security, Smart city
Frequency: Annual
Market Area: International
Nature: Trade Only
Organizer: CCPIT Shanghai Sub-Council; Shanghai Intl Exhibition Co Ltd; E.J.KRAUSE & ASSOCIATES, INC.
Address: Shanghai Intl Exhibition Co Ltd, 8/F, No.841 Yan An Zhong Road, Shanghai, 200040, China
Contact: Ms Julia Zhu

1220
2013/06/05-07
☎ 021-6488 0957, 13062800785
🖷 021-6412 6798
✉ wujunexpo@yahoo.cn
www.cmedexpo.com

2013第十二届中国（上海）国际医疗器械展览会
地点：上海世博展览馆，上海
内容：医疗器械；诊断治疗设备；病房护理设备及器具；辅助设备；口腔医疗器械设备；医用敷料；医用磁共振设备；手术室、急救室、诊疗室设备及器具；医疗软件及信息处理
主办：中国医促会；中国医疗保健国际交流促进会
承办：上海展亚展览服务有限公司
地址：上海市闵行区碧泉路36弄1号金霄大厦2304室
联系人：吴俊

China (Shanghai) Intl Medical Expo
Venue: Shanghai World Expo Exhibition & Convention Center, Shanghai
Organizer: Shanghai Zhanya Exhibition Service Co Ltd
Address: Unit 2304, Building Jinxiao, No 1, Lane 36, Biquan Road, Shanghai, China

2013/06/05-07
☎ 021-5417 5989, 15821242351
🖷 021-6412 6798
✉ 15821242351@139.com
www.chinaljexpo.com
1230

2013中国（上海）医疗美容及整形设备展览会
地点：上海世博展览馆，上海
内容：医疗整形美容机构、医疗整形手术器械及设备、耗材，激光美容仪器；医疗美容院校、医疗美容中心；功能性化妆、中草药美容产品；丰乳产品，减肥食品，SPA人身彩绘、纹身、美甲产品
上届规模：展览面积7,600m²，参展商373家，参观人数31,235人
主办：中国医促会，中国医疗保健国际交流促进会
承办：上海展亚展览服务有限公司
地址：上海市碧泉路36弄1号金霄大厦2304室
联系人：林翔

China (Shanghai) Medical Beauty and Plastic Surgery Equipment Exhibition 2013
Venue: Shanghai World Expo Exhibition & Convention Center, Shanghai
Statistics: Exhibition Area 7,600m², Exhibitors 373, Visitors 31,235
Organizer: Shanghai Zhanya Exhibition Service Co Ltd

2013/06/05-07
☎ 021-2553 3783, 15102178114
🖷 021-5156 1778
✉ info@shyhzl.com.cn
1519920954@qq.com
www.chybzl.com
1240

2013中国（上海）国际产业用纺织品及非织造布展览会
同期举办：
2013上海玻璃纤维及新型复合材料展览会
地点：上海世贸商城，上海
内容：非织造材料及相关深加工产品；纤维原料及化学助剂；产业用布；非织造材料及深加工技术与设备；非织造布；生产设备、深加工设计
主办：上海纺织品商业行业协会；上海雅辉展览有限公司
地址：上海市漕溪路251号5号楼20F(200235)
联系人：宋霞

2013 China (Shanghai) Trade Fair for Technical Textiles and Nonwovens
Venue: Shanghai Mart, Shanghai
Organizer: Shanghai Yahui Exhibition Service Co Ltd

2013/06/10-13
☎ 021-6279 2828
🖷 021-6545 5124
✉ yxf@siec-ccpit.com
www.shanghaitex.cn
1250

SHANGHAITEX 上海国际纺织工业展

第十六届上海国际纺织工业展览会
地点：上海新国际博览中心，上海
内容：织及织袜机械、印花、染整机械、纺纱、产业用布及非织造布机械、织造机械等不同的设备和技术
始办年份：1984
周期：两年一届
市场范围：国际性
性质：面向贸易观众
主办：上海纺织控股（集团）公司；中国贸促会上海市分会；中国国际商会上海商会；上海市国际展览有限公司；上海纺织技术服务展览中心；雅式展览服务有限公司
地址：上海市延安中路841号8楼上海市国际展览有限公司(200040)
联系人：姚秀芳女士

SHANGHAITEX 2013
Venue: Shanghai New Intl Expo Center, Shanghai
Profile: Knitting machine and hosiery machine; printing machine and dyeing and finishing machine; spinning machine, industry-used cloth machine and non-weaving machine; weaving machine and spare parts
Established Year: 1984
Frequency: Biennial
Market Area: International
Nature: Trade Only
Organizer: Shanghai Textile Holding (Group) Corporation; CCPIT Shanghai Sub-Council; Shanghai Chamber of Commerce of China Chamber of International Commerce; Shanghai International Exhibition Co Ltd; Shanghai Textile Technology Service Exhibition Center; Adsale Exhibition Services Ltd
Address: Shanghai International Exhibition Co Ltd, 8/F, No.841 Yan An Zhong Road, Shanghai, 200040, China
Contact: Ms Yao Xiufang

2013/06/18-21
☎ 010-6397 2404, 6398 3928
🖷 010-6398 0554
✉ yuany@cmes.org
xiangx@cmes.org
582468193
www.beijing-essen-welding.com
www.埃森焊接展.com
1270

BEIJING ESSEN WELDING & CUTTING
DVS GERMAN WELDING SOCIETY CMES
北京·埃森焊接与切割展览会

第十八届北京-埃森焊接与切割展览会
地点：上海新国际博览中心，上海
内容：焊接、切割、钎焊及粘接；消耗材料与其制备和原材料；检测设备及其耗材；焊前准备与焊后处理设备与技术；焊工安全和环境保护
始办年份：1987
周期：每年一届
市场范围：国际性
性质：面向公众和贸易观众
入场券价格：免费
参展费用：标准展位6,900-16,200元/展位，光地6,200-14,400元/展位
上届规模 '12：展览面积106,800m²(国外展商面积11,151m²)，参展商936家（国外展商202家，来自26个国家），参观人数45,491人（贸易观众22,436人）
主办：中国机械工程学会；中国机械工程学会焊接分会；中国焊接协会；中国焊接协会焊接设备分会；德国焊接学会；德国埃森展览公司；
承办：北京埃森焊接与切割展览会组委会
地址：北京市海淀区莲花小区2-5-1607_(100036)
联系人：袁艺，相茜

The 18th Beijing Essen Welding & Cutting Fair
Venue: Shanghai New Intl Expo Center, Shanghai
Profile: Welding, Cutting, Brazing and Adhesive bonding; Consumable Materials and their Manufacturing Equipment and Raw Materials; Inspection Equipment and Related Consumables; Pre- and Post-welding Treatment Equipment and Technology; Safety and Health for Welder & Environment Protection
Established Year: 1987
Frequency: Annual
Market Area: International
Nature: Open to Public
Cost to Attend: Free
Participated Fee: Standard Booth RMB 6,900-16,200/booth, Raw Space RMB 6,200-14,400/booth
Statistics '12: Exhibition Area 106,800m² (foreigners 11,151m²), Exhibitors 936 (foreigners 202, came from 26 countries), Visitors 45,491 (Trade Visitors 22,436)
Organizer: Chinese Mechanical Engineering Society (CMES); Welding Institution of CMES; China Welding Association (CWA); Welding Equipment Committee of CWA; German Welding Society (DVS) Messe Essen GmbH; The Organizing Committee of Beijing Essen Welding & Cutting Fair
Address: 2-5-1607 Lianhuaxiaoqu, Haidian District, Beijing 100036, China
Contact: Yuan Yi, Xiang Xi

2013/06/18-21
☎ 021-6279 2828
🖷 021-6545 5124
✉ slp@siec-ccpit.com
www.dmcexpo.com
1280

DMC 2013

2013中国国际模具、制造应用设备及相关工业展览会
地点：上海新国际博览中心，上海
内容：加工中心，数控铣床、磨床、镗床、车床、钻床等精密加工各类金切机床；各类电加工机床，激光加工设备，雕刻机；三坐标测量机及其它测量设备等；模具及模具制品，模具标准件；压铸机、冲床、各类压力机床等成形设备；塑料机械及橡胶机械；模具CAD / CAM / CAE等计算机集成制造技术；CAPP, PDM, ERP等模具生产管理技术；模具材料、冶金制品；工具、刃具，以及与模具相关的其它产品；各类模具生产用的辅料、辅助设备、包括抛光、研磨、装配夹具等
始办年份：1980
周期：两年一届
市场范围：国际性

DMC 2013
- China International Exhibition on Die & Mould, Metal Processing and Forming Industry
Venue: Shanghai New Intl Expo Center, Shanghai
Profile: Machining centre, CNC milling machining, jig grinding machines, boring machines, drilling machines, etc.; EDM machines, laser processing; coordinate measuring systems die & mould, standard die & mould components; various kinds of presses, punch, die casting machines, etc.; injection moulding machines, extruders, blow; moulding machines, injection & compression moulds, hotrunner system; die & mould CAD/CAE/CAM, computer integrated manufacturing technology, etc.; CAPP, PDM, ERP, etc.; cutting tools, spare parts and components, etc.; die & mould materials; die spotter

性质：面向贸易观众
主办：中国模具工业协会；上海市国际展览有限公司
地址：上海市延安中路841号8楼(200040)
联系人：盛来平先生

system, polishing system, NC tooling system, jig & fixture, engraving machines, etc.; auxilliary equipment for die & mould making; lubricant, remover, rust remover, etc.; heating & cooling units for die & mould
Established Year: 1980
Frequency: Biennial
Market Area: International
Nature: Trade Only
Organizer: China Die & Mould Industry Association; Shanghai International Exhibition Co Ltd
Address: Shanghai International Exhibition Co Ltd, 8/F, No.841 Yan An Zhong Road, Shanghai, 200040, China
Contact: Mr Sheng Laiping

2013/06/19-21
☎ 021-6279 2828
📠 021-6545 5124
✉ fjy@siec-ccpit.com
www.offshorewindchina.com
1290

2013上海国际海上风电及风电产业链大会暨展览会
地点：上海新国际博览中心，上海
内容：风电设备、风电配套服务、风电场开发、风电项目工程施工、储能设备等
周期：每年一届
市场范围：国际性
性质：面向贸易观众
主办：中国资源综合利用协会可再生能源专业委员会；中国可再生能源学会产业工业委员会；上海市国际展览有限公司
地址：上海市延安中路841号8楼上海市国际展览有限公司(200040)
联系人：费嘉奕女士

Offshore Wind China 2013
Venue: Shanghai New Intl Expo Center, Shanghai
Profile: equipment, services, wind farm development, construction and installation, energy storage equipment
Frequency: Annual
Market Area: International
Nature: Trade Only
Organizer: Chinese Renewable Energy Industries Association; Shanghai International Exhibition Co Ltd
Address: Shanghai International Exhibition Co Ltd, 8/F, No.841 Yan An Zhong Road, Shanghai, 200040, China
Contact: Ms Fei Jiayi

2013/06/20-22
☎ 010-5191 9091, 5191 9092
📠 010-5191 9089
✉ whyp@ccagm.org.cn
www.csfair.org.cn
1300

2013年107届中国文化用品商品交易会
地点：上海新国际博览中心，上海
内容：学生用品、文教用品、现代-办公及教学仪器设备、办公用品、电脑及IT数码产品、纸与纸制品、文房四宝、印刷与包装用品、照像器材、测量测绘用品、体育与健身器材、休闲娱乐用品、文具礼品与赠品、旅游用品、美术绘画用品、书写工具及生产设备、配件、办公耗材、办公家具、办公室用品、办公日杂品等
主办：中国百货商业协会
承办：中百文华展览（北京）有限公司
地址：北京市海淀区北蜂窝路21号(100038)

The 107th China Stationery Fair
Venue: Shanghai New Intl Expo Center, Shanghai
Organizer: China Commerce Association for General Merchandise

2013/06/24-25
☎ 852-2827 6211
021-6157 3930, 6157 3919
📠 852-3749 7342
✉ info-hk@ubm.com
conferencechina@ubm.com
www.ubmasia.com
www.cphichina-conference.com
1310

CPhI医药中国峰会
地点：上海
周期：每年一届
主办：亚洲博闻有限公司
地址：香港湾仔港湾道26号华润大厦17楼

CPhI On-site Modular Conferences
Venue: Shanghai
Frequency: Annual
Organizer: UBM Asia Ltd
Address: 17/F, China Resources Building, 26 Harbour Road, Wan Chai, Hong Kong

2013/06/25-27
☎ 852-2827 6211
021-6437 1178
📠 852-3749 7342
021-6437 0982
✉ info-hk@ubm.com
iris.feng@ubmsinoexpo.com
www.p-mec.cn
1320

医药包装材料精品中国展
2013世界制药机械、包装设备与材料中国展
地点：上海新国际博览中心，上海
周期：每年一届
主办：亚洲博闻有限公司
地址：香港湾仔港湾道26号华润大厦17楼
主办：上海博华国际展览有限公司
地址：上海市襄阳南路218号现代大厦8楼（200031）

InnoPack China
Venue: Shanghai New Intl Expo Center, Shanghai
Frequency: Annual
Organizer: UBM Asia Ltd
Address: 17/F, China Resources Building, 26 Harbour Road, Wan Chai, Hong Kong

2013/06/25-27
☎ 852-2827 6211 021-6437 1178
📠 852-3749 7342 021-6437 0982
✉ info-hk@ubm.com
chris.mao@ubmsinoexpo.com
www.cphi-china.cn
www.cphi-china.com
1330

世界制药原料中国展
地点：上海新国际博览中心，上海
始办年份：2010
市场范围：国际性
性质：面向贸易观众
主办：亚洲博闻有限公司
地址：香港湾仔港湾道26号华润大厦17楼
主办：上海博华国际展览有限公司
地址：上海市襄阳南路218号现代大厦8楼（200031）

CPhI China
Venue: Shanghai New Intl Expo Center, Shanghai
Frequency: Annual
Market Area: International
Nature: Trade Only
Organizer: UBM Asia Ltd
Address: 17/F, China Resources Building, 26 Harbour Road, Wan Chai, Hong Kong

2013/06/25-27
☎ 852-2827 6211
021-6437 1178
🖷 852-3749 7342
021-6437 0982
✉ info-hk@ubm.com
chris.mao@ubmsinoexpo.com
www.cphi-china.cn
www.cphi-china.com
1340

icse bringing outsourcing to CPhI China

世界合同定制服务中国展
地点：上海新国际博览中心，上海
内容：合同研发外包：合成定制、药物化学、分子药代动力学研究、制剂处方前及处方开发、临床前试验、临床试验、生物制药服务、计算机辅助的药物设计、工艺放大生产、生物检测、高效力药物开发、数据管理、新药申请等。 合同生产外包：工艺开发/优化、配方开发/优化、临床试验用药、化学或生物的原料药生产、中间体制造、制剂生产以及包装等。 咨询与服务：临床试验管理、咨询、资金和金融服务、一般商业顾问、法律服务、物流分析、法规咨询、训练；分析与检测、医疗器械定制服务等。
始办年份：2005
周期：每年一届
主办：亚洲博闻有限公司
地址：香港湾仔港湾道26号华润大厦17楼
主办：上海博华国际展览有限公司
地址：上海市襄阳南路218号现代大厦8楼（200031）

ICSE China
Venue: Shanghai New Intl Expo Center, Shanghai
Profile: Contract Research, Contract Manufacturing
Established Year: 2005
Organizer: UBM Asia Ltd
Address: 17/F, China Resources Building, 26 Harbour Road, Wan Chai, Hong Kong

2013/06/25-27
☎ 852-2827 6211
021-6437 1178
🖷 852-3749 7342
021-6437 0982
✉ info-hk@ubm.com
jessica.lin@ubmsinoexpo.com
www.fia-china.com
1350

亚洲食品配料、健康原料、天然原料中国展
第15届亚洲食品配料中国展
第15届健康原料、天然原料中国展
亚洲食品加工与包装、食品安全服务中国展
地点：上海新国际博览中心，上海
周期：每年一届
主办：亚洲博闻有限公司
地址：香港湾仔港湾道26号华润大厦17楼
主办：上海博华国际展览有限公司
地址：上海市襄阳南路218号现代大厦8楼

Food Ingredients (Fi) Asia-China
Health Ingredients (Hi)
Natural Ingredients (Ni) China
Venue: Shanghai New Intl Expo Center, Shanghai
Frequency: Annual
Organizer: UBM Asia Ltd
Address: 17/F, China Resources Building, 26 Harbour Road, Wan Chai, Hong Kong

2013/06/25-27
☎ 852-2827 6211 021-6437 1178
🖷 852-3749 7342
✉ info-hk@ubm.com
Farley.Wang@ubmsinoexpo.com
www.npcexpo.com
1360

npc

天然及营养保健品中国展
地点：上海新国际博览中心，上海
主办：亚洲博闻有限公司
地址：香港湾仔港湾道26号华润大厦17楼
主办：上海博华国际展览有限公司
地址：上海市襄阳南路218号现代大厦8楼

Natural & Nutraceutical Products China
Venue: Shanghai New Intl Expo Center, Shanghai
Organizer: UBM Asia Ltd
Address: 17/F, China Resources Building, 26 Harbour Road, Wan Chai, Hong Kong
Contact: Shanghai UBM Sinoexpo International Exhibition Co Ltd

2013/06/25-27
☎ 852-2827 6211
021-6437 1178
🖷 852-3749 7342
021-6437 0982
✉ info-hk@ubm.com
iris.feng@ubmsinoexpo.com
www.p-mec.cn
1370

P-MEC PHARMACEUTICAL MACHINERY & EQUIPMENT CONVENTION CHINA

世界制药机械、包装设备与材料中国展
世界生化、分析仪器与实验室装备中国展
地点：上海新国际博览中心，上海
内容：生化仪器、分析仪器、实验室成套设备、行业专用仪器设备等产品
周期：每年一届
市场范围：国际性
性质：面向贸易观众
主办：亚洲博闻有限公司
地址：香港湾仔港湾道26号华润大厦17楼
主办：上海博华国际展览有限公司
地址：上海市襄阳南路218号现代大厦8楼

P-MEC China
Pharmaceutical Machinery & Equipment Convention China
Venue: Shanghai New Intl Expo Center, Shanghai
Frequency: Annual
Market Area: International
Nature: Trade Only
Organizer: UBM Asia Ltd
Address: 17/F, China Resources Building, 26 Harbour Road, Wan Chai, Hong Kong

2013/06/26-28
☎ 852-2827 6211
021-6157 7223
🖷 852-3749 7342
✉ info-hk@ubm.com
hubert.guan@ubm.com
www.concreteshowchina.com
1380

CONCRETE SHOW CHINA | SHANGHAI

中国国际混凝土产业展览会
地点：上海世博展览馆，上海
主办：亚洲博闻有限公司
地址：香港湾仔港湾道26号华润大厦17楼
联络：博闻中国

Concrete Show China 2013
Venue: Shanghai World Expo Exhibition & Convention Center, Shanghai
Organizer: UBM Asia Ltd
Address: 17/F, China Resources Building, 26 Harbour Road, Wan Chai, Hong Kong
Contact: UBM China

2013/06/26-28
☎ 021-6136 8987, 6136 8997
🖷 021-6136 8986
✉ cict@cictexpo.com
www.cictexpo.com
1390

2013中国（上海）国际切削刀具暨工具展览会
地点：上海光大会展中心，上海
内容：表面刀具各类系列产品；孔加工刀具各类系列产品；螺纹加工工具各类系列产品；齿轮加工刀具各类系列产品；切断刀具各类系列产品；测量、夹具、计算机软件等
主办：中国机械工业金属切削刀具技术协会；灵硕集团控股有限公司
承办：上海灵硕会展服务有限公司；上海傲展会展服务有限公司
地址：上海市陆家浜路1332号南开大厦1410
联系人：白少东

China Intl Cuttings Tools Exhibition
Venue: Shanghai Everbright Convention & Exhibition Center, Shanghai
Organizer: Shanghai LingShuo Exhibition Service Co Ltd

2013/07/02-05
☎ 021-5239 6999
🖷 021-5101 0002
✉ eastpo@eastpo.net
www.eastpo.net
1400

第15届上海国际机床展
地点：上海新国际博览中心，上海
内容：金切机床、金属成形机床、制造单元/系统及自动化设备、机床零部件及辅助设备、工夹具、检测和测量、特种加工机床及专业设备、相关制造技术设备
主办：上海东博展览有限公司；中国社会经济调查研究中心
承办：上海东博文化发展有限公司

15th Shanghai Intl Machine Tool Fair
Venue: Shanghai New Intl Expo Center, Shanghai
Organizer: Eastpo Exhibition Co Ltd

2013/07/04-07
☎ 021-6279 2828
🖷 021-6386 6972
✉ interphoto@siec-ccpit.com
www.interphoto.com.cn
1410

第十五届中国（上海）国际摄影器材和数码影像展览会
地点：上海世博展览馆，上海
内容：影像输入、相机零件及附件、摄影器材及耗材、影像存储、影像处理、影像输出、数码影像等设备、产品、技术及服务等
始办年份：1998
周期：每年一届
市场范围：国际性
性质：面向公众和贸易观众
主办：中国贸促会上海市分会；中国国际商会上海商会；中国信息产业商会数字影像产业分会；上海市摄影家协会；上海市国际展览有限公司
地址：上海市延安中路841号8楼上海市国际展览有限公司(200040)
联系人：张莉娜女士

PHOTO & IMAGING SHANGHAI 2013
Venue: Shanghai World Expo Exhibition & Convention Center, Shanghai
Profile: Equipment for image input, camera parts & accessories, photographic equipment and consumables, image storing, image editing, image processing, image output, digital imaging and related products, technologies and services
Established Year: 1998
Frequency: Annual
Market Area: International
Nature: Open to Public
Organizer: CCPIT Shanghai Sub-Council; Shanghai Chamber of Commerce of China Chamber of International Commerce; China Information Industry Trade Association Digital Image Committee; Shanghai Photographers' Association,; Shanghai International Exhibition Co Ltd
Address: Shanghai International Exhibition Co Ltd, 8/F, No.841 Yan An Zhong Road, Shanghai 200040, China
Contact: Ms Lina Zhang

2013/07/10-13
☎ 021-6328 8899
🖷 86-021-6374 9188
✉ mie@chinamie.com
www.apppexpo.com
www.chinamie.com
1420

第二十一届上海国际印刷包装纸业展览会
地点：上海新国际博览中心，上海
内容：印前、CTP、数字快速印刷；彩色印刷、胶印、轮转印刷；标签、柔凹印、丝网、特种印刷、功能性印刷包装；印后、包装印刷机械设备及印刷包装产品
主办：上海现代国际展览有限公司
地址：上海市黄浦区盛泽路8号18楼

Shanghai Intl AD, Print, Pack, Paper Expo
Venue: Shanghai New Intl Expo Center, Shanghai
Frequency: Annual
Organizer: Shanghai Modern Intl Exhibition Co Ltd
Address: 18F No.8 ShengZe Road. Shanghai 200002

2013/07/10-13
☎ 021-6328 8899
🖷 86-021-6374 9188
✉ mie@chinamie.com
www.apppexpo.com
www.chinamie.com
1430

2013第二十一届上海国际广告技术设备展览会
地点：上海新国际博览中心，上海
内容：数字喷墨印刷；打印机及耗材；数字标牌广告机；标识、标牌设备及标识；展览展示、POP及商用设施；新媒体技术设备；LED
周期：每年一届
市场范围：国际性
主办：上海现代国际展览有限公司；上海广告设备器材供应商协会；上海市广告协会
地址：上海市黄浦区盛泽路8号18楼

Shanghai Intl AD & Sign Technology Equipment Exhibition
Venue: Shanghai New Intl Expo Center, Shanghai
Frequency: Annual
Market Area: International
Organizer: Shanghai Modern Intl Exhibition Co Ltd
Address: 18F No.8 ShengZe Road. Shanghai 200002

2013/07/17-19
☎ 852-2827 6211
0571-8839 3239
🖷 852-3749 7342
0571-8838 8829
✉ info-hk@ubm.com
www.cbmexpo.com
1440

CBME孕婴童展
CBME童装展

CBME孕婴童展、CBME童装展
地点：上海新国际博览中心，上海
内容：母婴用品，车床、汽座及家具，玩具、教育及纪念品，孕婴童食品、保健品，童装、婴装、童鞋及配饰，孕装、内衣及配饰
始办年份：2001
预计规模：总面积103,500m^2，4,800个展位，参展商1,200家，1,900品牌，观众90,000人次，预计来自全球80个国家及地区
主办：亚洲博闻有限公司
地址：香港湾仔港湾道26号华润大厦17楼

Shanghai International Children-Baby-Maternity Industry Expo
Venue: Shanghai New Intl Expo Center, Shanghai
Established Year: 2001
Expectation: Gross Area 103,500m^2, Booths 4,800, Exhibitors 1,200, Brands 1,900, Visitors 90,000 come from 80 countries and regions
Organizer: UBM Asia Ltd
Address: 17/F, China Resources Building, 26 Harbour Road, Wan Chai, Hong Kong

2013/07/18-19
☎ 852-2827 6211
021-6157 3930, 6157 3919
🖷 852-3749 7342
021-61577299
✉ info-hk@ubm.com
conferencechina@ubm.com
www.ubmasia.com
1450

植入介入医疗器械中国峰会（上海）
地点：上海
主办：亚洲博闻有限公司
地址：香港湾仔港湾道26号华润大厦17楼

Implantable Medical Device Conference (Shanghai)
Venue: Shanghai
Organizer: UBM Asia Ltd
Address: 17/F, China Resources Building, 26 Harbour Road, Wan Chai, Hong Kong

2013/08/01-03
☎ 010-5933 9102
🖷 010-5933 9199
✉ raymond.zhang@reedhuaqun.com
52109350
www.giftsbeijing.com
1460

2013年上海国际家庭用品、促销品及工艺品创意设计展览会
地点：上海世博展览馆，上海
内容：工艺品：陶瓷、水晶类、琉璃、金属类工艺品 赠品、促销品：广告促销品、福利、节庆促销品 品牌电子产品 纪念收藏品及钱币、邮票 有机食品 高档商务礼品：皮具、箱包、文化用品 家居用品：家具、家装用品、软装饰品、厨卫用品系列、家纺类产品 玩具及婴孕童用品：儿童及成人益智玩具、婴孕童日用品 旅游及户外用品：户外用品、健身及运动器械 媒体、协会、贸易服务及其它
周期：每年一届

Shanghai Intl Houseware, Premium, Arts & Crafts Creative Design Exhibition 2013
Venue: Shanghai World Expo Exhibition & Convention Center, Shanghai
Profile: Arts & Crafts, Electronic Appliances, Ceramics, Glassware, Collectables, Stationery, Household Goods, Pots, Hardware, Promotions, Packaging, Promotions, Gifts & Premium Products, Houseware, Home Textiles, Bags & Cases, Electronic Appliances, Kitchenware, Home Textiles, Bags, Sports & Leisure Products
Frequency: Annual
Market Area: International

市场范围：国际性
性质：面向公众和贸易观众
入场券价格：免费
参展费用：标准展位8,200元，光地7,800元/展位
上届规模：展览面积17,000m^2 (国外展商面积1,000m^2)，参展商800家（国外展商30家，来自10个国家），参观人数23,000人（贸易观众20,000人）
主办：北京励展华群展览有限公司
地址：北京市朝阳区新源南路1-3号平安国际金融中心A座15层(100027)
联系人：张一萌，李晓瑞

Nature: Open to Public
Cost to Attend: Free
Participated Fee: Standard Booth RMB 8,200, Raw Space RMB 7,800/booth
Statistics '12: Exhibition Area 17,000m^2 (foreigners 1,000m^2), Exhibitors 800 (foreigners 30, came from 10 countries), Visitors 23,000 (Trade Visitors 20,000)
Organizer: Reed Huaqun Exhibitions
Address: 15th Floor, Tower A, Ping An International Finance Center, 1-3 South Xinyuan Road, Beijing 100027
Contact: Raymond, Xiaorui

2013/08/01-03
☎ 010-5933 9341
🖷 010-5933 9390
www.zbfair.com.cn
1470

2013第107届中国日用百货商品交易会
暨中国现代家庭用品博览会
地点：上海新国际博览中心，上海
内容：五金制品：家用五金、餐具、厨具、炊具；陶瓷、玻璃、竹木制品：陶瓷制品、玻璃、工艺礼品、竹木制品；塑料制品：家用塑料制品、收纳箱；家居用品：清洁用具、浴室用品、休闲用品、家用衡器、家用纺织品、烟具、雨具、一次性用品；不锈钢制品：杯壶、家用小电器
主办：励展华百展览（北京）有限公司
地址：北京市朝阳区新源南路1-3号平安国际金融中心A座15层01-03, 05室(100027)
联系人：廖静

107th China Daily-use Articles Trade Fair
China Modern Home Expo
Venue: Shanghai New Intl Expo Center, Shanghai
Organizer: Reed Huabai Exhibitions

2013/08/15-18
☎ 010-8455 6616, 6617
🖷 010-8207 4505
✉ qinghua.wei@reedsinopharm.com
www.chinadentalshow.com
1480

中华口腔医学会第15次全国口腔医学学术会议
（2013年会）
2013（上海）国际口腔设备器材博览会
地点：上海光大会展中心，上海
主办：中华口腔医学会，国药励展展览有限责任公司
地址：北京市朝阳区新源南路1-3号平安国际金融中心B座15层

15th CSA Annual Meeting
2013 China Dental Show
Venue: Shanghai Everbright Convention & Exhibition Center, Shanghai
Organizer: Reed Sinopharm Exhibitions Co Ltd
Address: 15th Floor, Tower B, Ping An International Finance Center, No.1-3, Xinyuan South Road, Chaoyang District, Beijing 100027

2013/08/15-17
☎ 021-6384 2404, 6384 1462
🖷 021-6384 2439
邮箱sbmia@126.com
expo.sbmia.org.cn
1490

第九届中国(上海)国际门窗幕墙及建筑遮阳展览会
第九届中国(上海)国际建筑节能及新型建材展览会
第九届中国（上海）国际室内供暖系统及新能源设备展览会
第15届上海国际别墅配套设施博览会
地点：上海新国际博览中心，上海
上届规模：参观人数55,480人
主办：上海现代国际展览有限公司；上海市建筑材料行业协会
地址：上海市卢湾区普安路128号1601-1602室上海市建筑材料行业协会(200021)

9th Shanghai Intl Energy-saving & Advanced Building Materials Exhibition
Venue: Shanghai New Intl Expo Center, Shanghai
Organizer: Shanghai Building Materials Industry Association; Shanghai Modern Intl Exhibition Co Ltd

---

2013/08/20-23
☎ 852-2827 6211
021-6157 7215
🖷 852-3749 7342
✉ info-hk@ubm.com
vicky.sang@ubm.com
www.careshow.com.cn
1500

国际养老产业(上海)展览会暨峰会
地点：上海世博展览馆，上海
主办：亚洲博闻有限公司
地址：香港湾仔港湾道26号华润大厦17楼

Care Show China
Venue: Shanghai World Expo Exhibition & Convention Center, Shanghai
Organizer: UBM Asia Ltd
Address: 17/F, China Resources Building, 26 Harbour Road, Wan Chai, Hong Kong

---

2013/08/20-22
☎ 020-8989 9051, 8989 9051
🖷 020-8989 9050, 8989 9050
✉ cnibf@zhenweiexpo.com
731160817
744306173
www.cnibf.net
1510

第五届中国（上海）国际电池产品及技术展览会
地点：上海新国际博览中心，上海
内容：新型电池；新型动力、储能电池；新型电池生产设备、测试仪器、充电器；新型电池材料及零配件；各系列电池环保设备、回收处理技术；新能源汽车；新能源产业基地成果展示
周期：每年一届
市场范围：国际性
性质：面向贸易观众
入场券价格：免费
参展费用：标准展位8,800元/9m^2，光地880元/m^2
上届规模 '12：展览面积20,000m^2 (国外展商面积5,000m^2)，参展商400家（国外展商39家，来自36个国家），贸易观众12,270人
主办：中国电子学会；广东省电源行业协会；广州振威国际展览有限公司
地址：广东省广州市琶洲大道东1号保利国际广场南塔5楼501-504(510308)
联系人：王东杰，何海锋
msn：hohiphone@homail.com

5th China (Shanghai) Intl Battery Industry Fair
Venue: Shanghai New Intl Expo Center, Shanghai
Profile: New type batteries; New type power, stored energy battery; Battery production equipments, testers, chargers; Battery material and accessories; Battery environmental protection equipments, recovery processing technologies; New energy vehicles; Achievement demonstration of new energy
Frequency: Annual
Market Area: International
Nature: Trade Only
Cost to Attend: Free
Participated Fee: Standard Booth RMB 8,800/9m^2, Raw Space RMB 880/m^2
Statistics '12: Exhibition Area 20,000m^2 (foreigners 5,000m^2), Exhibitors 400 (foreigners 39, came from 36 countries), Trade Visitors 12,270
Organizer: Chinese Institute of Electronics; Guangdong Power Supply Association; Guangzhou Zhenwei International Exhibition Co Ltd
Address: Unit 501-504,South Tower, Poly Intl Plaza, 1 Pazhou Road, Haizhu District, Guangzhou, Guangdong
Contact: Dongjie Wang, Felix Ho
msn: hohiphone@homail.com

2013/08/20-22
☎ 020-8989 9051, 8989 9051
🖷 020-8989 9050, 8989 9050
✉ ctef@zhenweiexpo.com
www.ctef.net
1520

中国（上海）国际化工技术装备展览会
地点：上海新国际博览中心，上海
内容：化工单元设备、化工非标专用设备、流体及流程工业设备、密封件及执行器、环保及防护设备、石油石化、日化及化学工程设备、仪器仪表等产品及技术。
周期：每年一届
市场范围：国际性
性质：面向贸易观众
入场券价格：专业观众免费
参展费用：标准展位：国内企业13,000元，国外企业30.000元；光地(36m²起，特装管理费30元/m²)：国内企业1,300元/m²，国外企业3,200元/m²
上届规模 '12：展览面积30,000m²（国外展商面积9,000m²），参展商350家（国外展商50家，来自33个国家），贸易观众25,600人
主办：中国化工机械动力技术协会；广东省石油和化学工业协会；广东省化工学会；广州振威国际展览有限公司
地址：广东省广州市琶洲大道东1号保利国际广场南塔5楼501-504(510308)
联系人：盛莉，许栋林

5th China (Shanghai) Intl Chemical Technology & Equipment Fair
Venue: Shanghai New Intl Expo Center, Shanghai
Profile: Chemical unit equipment, Chemical non-standard equipment, Fluid and process of industrial equipment, Seals and actuator, Environmental protection and protective equipment, Petroleum and petrochemical equipment, Chemical equipment, Chemical engineering equipment and Instruments and apparatuses
Frequency: Annual
Market Area: International
Nature: Trade Only
Cost to Attend: Free to Trade and Professional Visitors
Participated Fee: Standard Booth USD 30,000, Raw Space RMB 3,200/m² (min 36m², management fee RMB 30/m²)
Statistics '12: Exhibition Area 30,000m² (foreigners 9,000m²), Exhibitors 350 (foreigners 50, came from 33 countries), Trade Visitors 25,600)
Organizer: China Chemical Industrial Mechanism Power Technology Association; Guangdong Petroleum and Chemical Industry Association; Chemical industry and Engineering Society of Guangdong; Guangzhou Zhenwei International Exhibition Co Ltd
Address: Unit 501-504,South Tower, Poly Intl Plaza, 1 Pazhou Road, Haizhu District, Guangzhou, Guangdong
Contact: Sheng Li，Xu Donglin

2013/08/27-30
☎ 010-8522 9506, 8522 9504, 8522 9446
🖷 010-8522 9300
✉ intertextile_home@ccpittex.com
www.intertextile-home.com.cn
1530

中国国际家用纺织品及辅料（秋冬）博览会
地点：上海新国际博览中心，上海
内容：各类家用纺织品及辅料，计算机辅助设计与制造，相关出版物及网络
主办：中国纺织工业联合会
承办：中国贸促会纺织行业分会；中国家用纺织品行业协会；法兰克福展览（香港）有限公司
联系人：朱勤，林英华，何磊，罗洁，王小雷

intertextile Shanghai home textiles
China Intl Trade Fair for Textiles and Accessories
Venue: Shanghai New Intl Expo Center, Shanghai
Sponsor: China National Textile & Apparel Council
Organizer: China Home Textile Association; The Sub-Council of Textile Industry, CCPIT; Messe Frankfurt (HK) Ltd

---

2013/09/02-03
☎ 852-2827 6211
021-6157 7214, 021-6157 7249
🖷 852-3749 7342
✉ info-hk@ubm.com
crystal.yang@ubm.com
carol.yin@ubm.com
www.tfmchina.com
1540

营销和广告创新技术展示会暨研讨会
地点：上海世贸商城，上海
内容：中国最具规模的整合营销、广告技术和电子商务盛典
主办：亚洲博闻有限公司
地址：香港湾仔港湾道26号华润大厦17楼

TFM&A China
Technology for Marketing & Advertising
Venue: Shanghai Mart, Shanghai
Organizer: UBM Asia Ltd
Address: 17/F, China Resources Building, 26 Harbour Road, Wan Chai, Hong Kong

---

2013/09/02-03
☎ 852-2827 6211
021-6157 7214, 021-6157 7249
🖷 852-3749 7342
✉ info-hk@ubm.com
crystal.yang@ubm.com
www.ece-china.com
1550

中国电子商务服务及产品展示会
地点：上海世贸商城，上海
市场范围：国际性
性质：面向贸易观众
上届规模：展览面积6,000m²
主办：亚洲博闻有限公司
地址：香港湾仔港湾道26号华润大厦17楼

eCommerce Expo China
Venue: Shanghai Mart, Shanghai, Shanghai
Market Area: International
Nature: Trade Only
Statistics '12: Exhibition Area 6,000m²
Organizer: UBM Asia Ltd
Address: 17/F, China Resources Building, 26 Harbour Road, Wan Chai, Hong Kong

---

2013/09/02-03
☎ 852-2827 6211
021-6157 7203
🖷 852-3749 7342
✉ info-hk@ubm.com
judith.fang@ubm.com
www.ubmasia.com
1560

中国国际呼叫中心管理大会
地点：上海世贸商城，上海
主办：亚洲博闻有限公司
地址：香港湾仔港湾道26号华润大厦17楼

ACCE China
Venue: ShanghaiMart, Shanghai
Organizer: UBM Asia Ltd
Address: 17/F, China Resources Building, 26 Harbour Road, Wan Chai, Hong Kong

---

2013/09/02-03
☎ 852-2827 6211
021-6157 7203
🖷 852-3749 7342
✉ info-hk@ubm.com
judith.fang@ubm.com
ww.ubmasia.com
1570

中国呼叫中心技术设备及解决方案博览会
地点：上海世贸商城，上海
主办：亚洲博闻有限公司
地址：香港湾仔港湾道26号华润大厦17楼

Call Center Expo China
Venue: ShanghaiMart, Shanghai
Organizer: UBM Asia Ltd
Address: 17/F, China Resources Building, 26 Harbour Road, Wan Chai, Hong Kong

2013/09/03-06
☎ 010-6603 9351, 6603 9043
🖷 010-6606 7681
✉ applas@applas.com
www.applas.com
1580

第十三届亚太国际塑料橡胶工业展览会
地点：上海新国际博览中心，上海
内容：注射成型机、中空成型机、辅助机械、吹膜机、挤出机、流延设备、编织机、塑料印刷设备、塑料包装设备、混炼设备、压延设备、仪器设备、检测设备、后加工设备、模具、零配件、机械手、橡胶机械、氟塑料及氟硅材料、塑料回收设备、塑料橡胶原辅材料及半成品
始办年份：1997
周期：两年一届
市场范围：国际性
性质：面向贸易观众
入场券价格：免费
参展费用：标准展位1,200元/m^2，光地1,100元/m^2
上届规模 '11：展览面积45,000m2，参展商826家，参观人数42,433人（贸易观众36,492人）
主办：中国轻工业联合会；中国石油和化学工业联合会；中国机电产品进出口商会；中国联合装备集团公司；中国轻工机械协会
承办：北京中轻合力国际展览有限公司
地址：北京市西城区西黄城根南街33号(100032)
联系人：李晓晔，张晓晨

13th Asian-pacific Intl Plastics & Rubber Industry Exhibition
Venue: Shanghai New Intl Expo Center, Shanghai
Profile: Injection moulding machine, Blow moulding machine, Auxiliary machine, Blown film extruder, Extruder, Cast film machine, Weave machine, Plastics printing machine, Plastics packaging machine, Mixer, Calendar, Instrument, Test equipment, Post processing equipment, Die, Components, Robot, Rubber machine, Fluoride plastics and fluorine & silicon, Plastics recycling equipment, Plastics and rubber raw/auxiliary materials, Final/semi-finished products
Established Year: 1997
Frequency: Biennial
Market Area: International
Nature: Trade Only
Cost to Attend: Free
Participated Fee: Standard Booth RMB 1,200/m^2, Raw Space RMB 1,100/m^2
Statistics '11: Exhibition Area 45,000m2, Exhibitors 826, Visitors 42,433 (Trade Visitors 36,492)
Organizer: China National Light Industry Council; China Petroleum and Chemical Industry Federation; China Chamber of Commerce for Import & Export of Machinery & Electronic Products; China National United Equipment Group Corp; China Light Industry Machinery Association; Beijing Zhongqing Heli International Exhibition Co Ltd
Address: No.33 Xihuangchenggen South Street, Xicheng District, Beijing 100032, China
Contact: Li Xiaoye, Zhang Xiaochen

2013/09/04-06
☎ 852-2827 6211
020-8666 0158
🖷 852-3749 7342
020-8667 2235
✉ info-hk@ubm.com
info-china@ubm.com
www.ciffchina.com
1590

中国国际鞋类展
地点：上海新国际博览中心，上海
内容：鞋类，手袋及皮具，皮衣，时尚配饰，行李箱包，业内相关服务
周期：每年一届
市场范围：国际性
性质：面向贸易观众
主办：亚太区皮革展有限公司；中国皮革协会
承办：亚洲博闻有限公司
地址：香港湾仔港湾道26号华润大厦17楼
国内联络：博闻(广州)中国有限公司
联系人：陈小姐

China International Footwear Fair
Venue: Shanghai New Intl Expo Center, Shanghai
Frequency: Annual
Market Area: International
Nature: Trade Only
Organizer: UBM Asia Ltd
Address: 17/F, China Resources Building, 26 Harbour Road, Wan Chai, Hong Kong

2013/09/04-06
☎ 852-2827 6211
020-8666 0158
🖷 852-3749 7342
020-8667 2235
✉ info-hk@ubm.com
info-china@ubm.com
www.ciffchina.com
www.aclechina.com
1600

中国国际箱包、裘革服装及服饰展
地点：上海新国际博览中心，上海
内容：鞋类,手袋及皮具，皮衣，时尚配饰，行李箱包，业内相关服务
周期：每年一届
市场范围：国际性
性质：面向贸易观众
主办：亚太区皮革展有限公司；中国皮革协会
承办：亚洲博闻有限公司
地址：香港湾仔港湾道26号华润大厦17楼
国内联络：博闻(广州)中国有限公司
联系人：陈小姐

Moda Shanghai
Venue: Shanghai New Intl Expo Center, Shanghai
Frequency: Annual
Market Area: International
Nature: Trade Only
Organizer: UBM Asia Ltd
Address: 17/F, China Resources Building, 26 Harbour Road, Wan Chai, Hong Kong

2013/09/04-06
☎ 852-2827 6211
020-8666 0158
🖷 852-3749 7342
020-8667 2235
✉ info-hk@ubm.com
info-china@ubm.com
www.aclechina.com
1610

中国国际皮革展
地点：上海新国际博览中心，上海
内容：生皮及原皮，半制成革及制成革。稀有皮革，人造革，合成/天然物料，化工原料及染料，配件及配饰，部件及工具，制革机器，生产技术（如：电脑辅助设计及生产系统）
周期：每年一届
市场范围：国际性
性质：面向贸易观众
主办：亚太区皮革展有限公司；中国皮革协会
承办：亚洲博闻有限公司
地址：香港湾仔港湾道26号华润大厦17楼
国内联络：博闻(广州)中国有限公司
联系人：陈小姐

All China Leather Exhibition
Venue: Shanghai New Intl Expo Center, Shanghai
Frequency: Annual
Market Area: International
Nature: Trade Only
Organizer: UBM Asia Ltd
Address: 17/F, China Resources Building, 26 Harbour Road, Wan Chai, Hong Kong

2013/09/04-06
☎ 010-6524 2231转ext 608, 010-6442 1448
✉ fany@icif.cn
www.icif.cn
1620

2013（第十二届）中国国际化工展览会
地点：上海世博展览馆，上海
主办：全国化工国际展览交流中心

ICIF CHINA
12th China Intl Chemical Industry Fair
Venue: Shanghai World Expo Exhibition & Convention Center, Shanghai
Organizer: China Intl Exhibition Center of Chemical Industry; CCPIT Sub-council of Chemical Industry

2013/09/11-14
☎ 852-2827 6211
021-6437 1178
🖷 852-3749 7342
021-6115 4988
✉ info-hk@ubm.com
william.yuan@ubmsinoexpo.com
www.fmcchina.com.cn
http://expo.fmcchina.com.cn
1630

中国国际家具配件及材料精品展览会
第十九届中国国际家具生产设备及原辅材料展览会

地点：上海世博展览馆，上海
内容：家具生产材料与配件，家具配件，原木、木材，弹簧、气弹簧，家具生产材料，板材，填充物(海绵、乳胶等) 家具半成品与部件，木皮、贴皮，驱动马达，家具五金，锁，脚轮；家具装饰材料，家用纺织品面料，家具装饰五金；纸藤、纸布，办公家具布料，家具装饰材料，家具商标牌，无纺布、非织造布，装饰纸、装潢薄膜，家具艺术玻璃，皮革 封边，家具保护垫，织带、松紧带，贴面、装饰板材，家具化工产品，粘合剂，树脂，干燥剂，分离剂，油漆、涂料，磨具、磨料，清洁剂、清洗剂，家具制造检测、设计与工程服务，检测认证，软件设计，工程服务
周期：每年一届
主办：亚洲博闻有限公司
地址：香港湾仔港湾道26号华润大厦17楼
联络：上海博华国际展览有限公司

FMC Premium
Furniture Manufacturing & Supply China 2013

Venue: Shanghai World Expo Exhibition & Convention Center, Shanghai
Profile: Woodworking machinery and tools, furniture raw materials, furniture coating and chemicals, furniture hardware and fitting, furniture panels & surface deco
Expectation: Exhibition Area 71,000m^2, Exhibitors 850, Visitors 35,000
Frequency: Annual
Organizer: UBM Asia Ltd
Address: 17/F, China Resources Building, 26 Harbour Road, Wan Chai, Hong Kong
Contact: Shanghai UBM Sinoexpo International Exhibition Co Ltd

2013/09/11-15
☎ 852-2827 6211
021-+8437 1178
🖷 852-3749 7342
021-6437 0982
✉ info-hk@ubm.com
officefurniture@ubmsinoexpo.com
www.furniture-china.cn/office
1640

第十九届中国国际办公家具展览会

地点：上海新国际博览中心，上海
内容：办公家具：办公椅，会议椅/会客椅，办公沙发，办公桌，会议桌，电脑桌，文件柜，档案柜，储藏柜，保险柜，屏风，高隔断，系统办公家具，个人工作站，其他办公家具 商用家具：公共座椅，公共交通用家具，机场家具，影剧院/礼堂家具，运动场馆家具，医院家具，学校家具，图书馆家具，实验室家具，定制及其他商用家具
周期：每年一届
主办：亚洲博闻有限公司
地址：香港湾仔港湾道26号华润大厦17楼
联络：上海博华国际展览有限公司

Office Furniture China

Venue: Shanghai New Intl Expo Center, Shanghai
Profile: Office Furniture: Office Chair, Meeting Room Chair, Office Sofa, Office Desk, Meeting Room Table, Computer Desk, Filing Cabinet, Storage, Safe Cabinet, Screen, Partition, System Furniture, Workstation, Other Office Furniture Commercial Furniture: Public Seating, Public Transportation Furniture, Airport Furniture, Theatre / Auditoria Furniture, Sports Furniture, Hospital Furniture, School Furniture, Library Furniture, Laboratory Furniture, Contract or Other Commercial Furniture
Frequency: Annual
Organizer: UBM Asia Ltd
Address: 17/F, China Resources Building, 26 Harbour Road, Wan Chai, Hong Kong
Contact: Shanghai UBM Sinoexpo International Exhibition Co Ltd
Address: 6 F. Xian Dai Mansion, 218 Xiang Yang Road (S), Shanghai, 200031

2013/09/11-15
☎ 852-2827 6211
021-6437 1178
🖷 852-3749 7342
021-6437 0982
✉ info-hk@ubm.com
nancy.huang@ubmsinoexpo.com
www.furniture-china.cn/furnishing
1650

中国国际家居饰品展览会

地点：上海新国际博览中心，上海
主办：亚洲博闻有限公司
地址：香港湾仔港湾道26号华润大厦17楼
联络：上海博华国际展览有限公司
地址：上海市襄阳南路218号现代大厦六楼（200031）

Home Furnishing China

Venue: Shanghai New Intl Expo Center, Shanghai
Profile: Furnishing, Decorative Painting, Fabrics / Beddings, Decorative Lighting, Decorative Carpet, Spa Appliances
Frequency: Annual
Organizer: UBM Asia Ltd
Address: 17/F, China Resources Building, 26 Harbour Road, Wan Chai, Hong Kong
Contact: Shanghai UBM Sinoexpo International Exhibition Co Ltd
Address: 6 F. Xian Dai Mansion, 218 Xiang Yang Road (S), Shanghai, 200031

2013/09/11-15
☎ 852-2827 6211
021-6437 1178
🖷 852-3749 7342
021-6437 1178
✉ info-hk@ubm.com
jacqueline.ji@ubmsinoexpo.com
dod.furniture-china.cn
1660

Design of Designers
中国国际设计师作品展示交易会

地点：上海新国际博览中心，上海
主办：亚洲博闻有限公司
地址：香港湾仔港湾道26号华润大厦17楼
联络：上海博华国际展览有限公司
地址：上海市襄阳南路218号现代大厦六楼（200031）

Design of Designers
- China Intl Design Trading Expo

Venue: Shanghai New Intl Expo Center, Shanghai
Organizer: UBM Asia Ltd
Address: 17/F, China Resources Building, 26 Harbour Road, Wan Chai, Hong Kong
Contact: Shanghai UBM Sinoexpo International Exhibition Co Ltd
Address: 6 F. Xian Dai Mansion, 218 Xiang Yang Road (S), Shanghai, 200031

2013/09/11-15
☎ 852-2827 6211
021-6437 1178
🖷 852-3749 7342
021-6437 0982
eric.xia@ubmsinoexpo.com
www.furniture-china.cn/kitchen
1670

中国国际橱柜展览会
地点： 上海新国际博览中心，上海
主办： 亚洲博闻有限公司
地址： 香港湾仔港湾道26号华润大厦17楼
联络： 上海博华国际展览有限公司
地址： 上海市襄阳南路218号现代大厦六楼（200031）

Kitchen & Cabinet China
Venue: Shanghai New Intl Expo Center, Shanghai
Organizer: UBM Asia Ltd
Address: 17/F, China Resources Building, 26 Harbour Road, Wan Chai, Hong Kong
Contact: Shanghai UBM Sinoexpo International Exhibition Co Ltd
Address: 6 F. Xian Dai Mansion, 218 Xiang Yang Road (S), Shanghai, 200031

2013/09/14-16
☎ 010-6878 4990, 6878 4991
🖷 010-6878 4978
✉ 8006@ccfa.org.cn
hyq@ccfa.org.cn
QQ 41556877
748644636
www.chinafranchiseexpo.com
1680

2013国际特许加盟（上海）展览会
地点： 上海国际展览中心，上海
内容： 作为中国南方地区规模最大、档次最高的特许加盟展览会，已经成功举办九届，累计展出千余个特许加盟品牌，参观观众二十余万人次。历经九载，展会已经成为特许加盟品牌开拓中国南方市场必不可少的推广平台，同时也成为了海外特许品牌进入中国的不二之选，更是投资人寻找加盟项目的最佳良机。
始办年份： 2004
周期： 每年一届
市场范围： 国际性
性质： 面向公众和贸易观众
入场券价格： 50元
参展费用： 一层：标准展位12,600元/9m^2，光地1,200元/m^2；二层：标准展位10,800元/9m^2，光地1,000元/m^2
上届规模 '12：展览面积8,000m^2 (国外展商面积1,000m^2)，参展商170家（国外展商50家，来自8个国家），参观人数10,000人
主办： 中国连锁经营协会
地址： 北京市西城区阜外大街22号外经贸大厦811-815 (100037)
联系人： 雷续红，郝永强

Shanghai International Franchise Exhibition 2013
Venue: INTEX Shanghai, Shanghai
Profile: China Franchise Expo is recognized as the largest and most diversified franchise exhibition in Asia. As one of series Exhibitions, the forthcoming China Franchise Expo Shanghai Session - Shanghai International Franchise Exhibition (SIFE) will celebrate its 8th Anniversary, and will coupled with the Beijing exhibition to satisfy the customers around the world. Every year, the exhibition showcases a range of franchise companies across a variety of sectors and thousands of investors, entrepreneurs and business owners have visited the exhibition to seek the business, to gain the market intelligence.
Established Year: 2004
Frequency: Annual
Market Area: International
Nature: Open to Public
Cost to Attend: RMB 50:-
Participated Fee: 1st Fl, Standard Booth RMB 12,600/9m^2, Raw Space RMB 1,200/m^2; 2nd Fl, Standard Booth RMB 10,800/9m^2, Raw Space RMB 1,000/m^2
Statistics '12: Exhibition Area 8,000m^2 (foreigners 1,000m^2), Exhibitors 170 (foreigners 50, came from 8 countries), Visitors 10,000
Organizer: China Chain Store & Franchise Association
Address: Room 811, 8th Floor, Foreign Economic & Trade Plaza, No. 22 Fuchengmenwai Str., Xicheng Dist., Beijing, China
Contact: Vivian Lei, Evan Hao

2013/09/15-17
☎ 852-2827 6211
🖷 852-3749 7342
✉ info-hk@ubm.com
www.ubmasia.com
1690

Cloud Connect China
地点： 上海国际会议中心，上海
主办： 亚洲博闻有限公司
地址： 香港湾仔港湾道26号华润大厦17楼

Cloud Connect China
Venue: Shanghai International Convention Centre, Shanghai
Organizer: UBM Asia Ltd
Address: 17/F, China Resources Building, 26 Harbour Road, Wan Chai, Hong Kong

2013/09/25-27
☎ 021-6160 8555转260, 256
🖷 021-5876 9332
✉ interior@china.messefrankfurt.com
www.il-china.com
1700

2013中国（上海）国际时尚家居用品展览会
同期举办：
Paperworld-China中国国际文具及办公用品展览会
地点： 上海新国际博览中心，上海
内容： 厨房用品、桌面用品、厨房工具、家电；礼品杂货：手工艺品、文具、花艺、熏香蜡烛、珠宝首饰、时尚创意品、设计师作品；家居家具装饰，布艺，户外园艺
性质： 面向贸易观众
参展费用： 光地（30m^{2}起）：A区优越展区1,600元/m^2，B区普通展区1,200元/m^2；标准展位（9m^{2}起）：A区优越展区1,900元/m^2，B区普通展区1,400元/m^2
主办： 法兰克福展览（上海）有限公司
地址： 上海浦东新区银城中路488号太平金融大厦15层1503室(200120)
联系人： 陈征小姐、李婷小姐、王润泽先生

interiorlifestyle China
China Intl Trade Fair for Household Products and Accessories
Venue: Shanghai New Intl Expo Center, Shanghai
Nature: Trade Only
Participated Fee: Raw Space (min 30m^2) RMB 1,200-1,600/m^2, Standard Booth (min 9m^2) RMB 1,400-1,900元/m^2
Organizer: Messe Frankfurt (Shanghai) Co Ltd
Address: Room 1503, 15/F, Taiping Finance Tower, 488 Middle Yincheng Road, Pudong New Area, Shanghai 200120

2013/09/25-28
☎ 010-6521 1282, 8774 7364
🖷 010-6513 5820, 8776 6609
✉ cisma@cisma.com.cn
www.cisma.com.cn
1710

2013中国国际缝制设备展览会
地点： 上海新国际博览中心，上海
内容： 中国国际缝制设备展览会CISMA是全球最大的缝制设备展览会，展品包括了缝前、缝制、缝后各类机器以及CAD/CAM设计系统以及面辅料和零件
周期： 两年一届
市场范围： 国际性
性质： 面向公众和贸易观众
入场券价格： 免费

China Intl Sewing Machinery & Accessories Show 2013
Venue: Shanghai New Intl Expo Center, Shanghai
Profile: The world largest sew equipment exhibition. It covers the products of pre-sewing, sewing & stitching, after- sewing, CAD/CAM and accessories.
Frequency: Biennial
Market Area: International
Nature: Open to Public
Cost to Attend: Free

上届规模 '11：展览面积103,500m^2，参展商1,182家（国外展商180家，来自18个国家），参观人数32,130人
主办：中国缝制机械协会
地址：北京市朝阳区百子湾路16号百子园5C-706(100022)
联系人：牟迎华, 张乐

Statistics '11: Exhibition Area 103,500m^2, Exhibitors 1,182 (foreigners 180, came from 18 countries), Visitors 32,130
Organizer: China Sewing Machinery Association
Address: 5C-706, Baiziyuan, No.16, Baiziwan Road, Chaoyang District, Beijing, China
Contact: Mu Yinghua, Zhang Le

2013/09/25-26
☎ 852-2827 6211
010-5765 2822
🖷 852-3749 7342
✉ info-hk@ubm.com
alston.tian@ubm.com
www.medtecchina.com
1720

上海国际医疗设备设计与技术展览会
地点：上海世博展览馆，上海
主办：亚洲博闻有限公司
地址：香港湾仔港湾道26号华润大厦17楼

MEDTEC China
Venue: Shanghai World Expo Exhibition & Convention Center, Shanghai
Profile: China's Only Dedicated Trade Show for Medical Device Design and Manufacturing
Organizer: UBM Asia Ltd
Address: 17/F, China Resources Building, 26 Harbour Road, Wan Chai, Hong Kong

2013/10/10-12
☎ 021-3782 1152, 6775 7823
🖷 021-3782 1409, 6451 6467
✉ sifse2009@163.com
Kim.yang@gehuaexpo.com
www.sifse.com
1730

2013第八届上海国际渔业博览会
暨第八届上海国际水产养殖展览会
地点：上海新国际博览中心，上海
主办：上海水产行业协会；上海歌华展览策划有限公司
地址：上海市泶亭南路129号秀森大厦1101室(201615)

8th Shanghai Intl Fisheries & Seafood Exposition
Venue: Shanghai New Intl Expo Center, Shanghai
Organizer: Shanghai Gehua Exhibition Service Co Ltd.
Address: Suite 1403, Shengli Building, No. 9120, Humin Road, Shanghai 200235, China

2013/10/15-17
☎ 010-6603 8881, 6590 7766
🖷 010-6603 3964, 6590 6139
✉ huanan@tjpa-china.org
g.pan@koelnmesse.cn
www.china-kids-expo.com
1740

中国婴童展
同期举办：
第十二届中国国际玩具及模型展览会
地点：上海新国际博览中心，上海
内容：旨在帮助海内外童车、儿童安全座椅、童床及婴童家具、童装童鞋、洗护用品等婴童用品厂家与品牌商开拓内销与外贸市场，促进全球营销网络布局完善，提升品牌知名度和影响力。2013年中国婴童展与全球规模第三、内地最大的第12届中国国际玩具、幼教用品及设备展览会、中国玩具展品牌授权馆共同举行
始办年份：2002
周期：每年一届
市场范围：国际性
性质：面向贸易观众
入场券价格：专业观众免费
参展费用：标准展位1,150元/m^2（12m^2起），光地950元/m^2（角位加收15%，36m^2起）
上届规模 '12：展览面积83,000m^2，参展商1,014家（来自110个国家），参观人数65,780人
主办：中国玩具和婴童用品协会；科隆展览（中国）有限公司
联络：中国玩具和婴童用品协会
地址：北京市复兴门内大街101号百盛写字楼9008室（100031）
联系人：华楠
联络：科隆展览（中国）有限公司
地址：北京市东三环北路8号亮马河大厦2座1018室（100004）
联系人：潘容

China Kids Expo
China International Baby Carriers & Baby Articles fair
Venue: Shanghai New Intl Expo Center, Shanghai
Profile: a leading international trade event in mainland china showcasing a big range of infant and baby products include baby strollers, car seats, infant wear, feeding products, bicycles, children's furniture and beddings etc. Unique from others, the fair offers international buyers the opportunity to meet the greatest number of export-ready Chinese manufacturers, especially for baby strollers and child car seats. Co-hosted by China Toy & Juvenile Products Association and Koelnmesse, China Kids Expo is held in every October in Shanghai concurrently with China Toy Expo, the biggest international toy fair in mainland China, and Brand Licensing Hall
Established Year: 2002
Frequency: Annual
Market Area: International
Nature: Trade Only
Cost to Attend: Free to Trade and Professional Visitors
Participated Fee: Standard Booth RMB 1,500/m^2 (min 12m^2), Raw Space RMB 950/m^2, min 36m^2, corner unit add 15%
Statistics '12: Exhibition Area 83,000m^2, Exhibitors 1,014 came from 110 countries, Visitors 65,780
Organizer: China Toy & Juvenile Products Association; Koelnmesse Co Ltd
Address: Koelnmesse Co Ltd, Unit 1018 Landmark Tower II, No.8 Dongsanhuan N. Rd., Beijing 100004 China

2013/10/15-17
☎ 010-6603 8881
🖷 010-6603 3964
✉ jinxiaohui@tjpa-china.org
www.china-toy-expo.com
1750

第12届中国国际玩具、幼教用品及设备展览会
地点：上海新国际博览中心，上海
始办年份：2002
周期：每年一届
市场范围：国际性
性质：面向贸易观众
入场券价格：专业观众免费
参展费用：标准展位1,150元/m^2（12m^2起），光地950元/m^2（角位加收15%，36m^2起）
上届规模 '12：展览面积83,000m^2，参展商1,014家（国外展商家，来自110个国家），参观人数65,780人
主办：中国玩具和婴童用品协会
地址：北京市复兴门内大街101号百盛写字楼9008室中国玩具和婴童用品协会(100031)
联系人：金晓辉

12th Intl Trade Fair for Toys & Preschool Educational Resources
Venue: Shanghai New Intl Expo Center, Shanghai
Established Year: 2002
Frequency: Annual
Market Area: International
Nature: Trade Only
Cost to Attend: Free to Trade and Professional Visitors
Participated Fee: Standard Booth RMB 1,500/m^2 (min 12m^2), Raw Space RMB 950/m^2, min 36m^2, corner unit add 15%
Statistics '12: Exhibition Area 83,000m^2, Exhibitors 1,014 came from 110 countries, Visitors 65,780
Organizer: China Toy & Juvenile Products Association
Address: No. 101 Fu Xing Men Nei Street Beijing 100031, China
Contact: Xiao Hui King

2013/10/20-22
☎ 010-8575 4970
🖷 010-5141 3308
✉ jianbohui888@163.com
QQ 421267652
www.bjjianbohui.com
1760

2013第十五届上海国际营养健康产业博览会
地点：上海国际展览中心，上海
内容：营养健康产品，保健产品，保健饮品，美容瘦身，无糖食品，食疗药膳产品，保健品包装
主办：中国保健营养理事会；中国医疗保健国际交流促进会；中国老年营养与食品专业委员会
承办：北京世博威国际展览有限公司
地址：北京市朝阳区朝阳路69号（财满街）1-4-904室
联系人：田振
msn：tianzhen868@hotmail.com

2013 China (Shanghai) Intl Nutrition and Health Industry Expo 2013
Venue: INTEX Shanghai, Shanghai
Organizer: Beijing Shibowei Intl Exhibition Co Ltd

2013/10/21-23
☎ 010-8522 9024, 8522 9098, 8522 9436
🖷 010-8522 9059
✉ chinaknitting@ccpittex.com
www.chinaknitting.com.cn
1770

中国国际针织博览会
地点：上海新国际博览中心，上海
内容：内衣、文胸、毛衫、针织休闲装/运动装/T恤、塑身/健身服、泳装/沙滩装、家居服/睡衣、袜类、针织面料、针织辅料、针织机械
主办：中国纺织工业联合会
承办：中国针织工业协会；中国贸促会纺织行业分会
联系人：车立超，陈博，金俊

China Intl Knitting Trade Fair
Venue: Shanghai New Intl Expo Center, Shanghai
Organizer: The Sub-Council of Textile Industry, CCPIT TEX.

2013/10/21-23
☎ 010-8522 9148, 8522 9504
🖷 010-8522 9300
✉ lzw@ccpittex.com
lyh@ccpittex.com
www.yarnexpo.com.cn
1780

中国国际纺织纱线（秋冬）展览会
地点：上海新国际博览中心，上海
内容：各类纺织纤维、纱线及CAD等
主办：中国纺织工业联合会
承办：中国贸促会纺织行业分会；法兰克福展览（香港）有限公司；中国棉纺织行业协会；中国毛纺织行业协会；中国化学纤维工业协会；中国麻纺行业协会；中国纺织信息中心

China Intl Trade Fair for Fibres and Yarns
Venue: Shanghai New Intl Expo Center, Shanghai
Organizer: The Sub-Council of Textile Industry, CCPIT TEX.

2013/10/21-24
☎ 010-8522 9440, 8522 9488, 8522 9463
🖷 010-8522 9296
✉ intertextile.sh@ccpittex.com
www.intertextile.com.cn
1790

中国国际纺织面料及辅料（秋冬）博览会
地点：上海新国际博览中心，上海
内容：各类纺织服装面料、辅料、计算机CAD/CAM系统，相关出版物及网络
主办：中国纺织工业联合会
承办：中国贸促会纺织行业分会；中国纺织信息中心；法兰克福展览（香港）有限公司
联系人：王壮飞，于欣，沈桢，马一丹

China Intl Trade Fair for Apparel Fabrics and Accessories
Venue: Shanghai New Intl Expo Center, Shanghai
Organizer: The Sub-Council of Textile Industry, CCPIT TEX

2013/10/23-25
☎ 852-2827 6211
🖷 852-3749 7342
✉ info-hk@ubm.com
www.since13.com
1800

中国国际非织造布研讨会及展览会
地点：上海世博展览馆，上海
主办：亚洲博闻有限公司
地址：香港湾仔港湾道26号华润大厦17楼

SINCE'13
- The 15th Intl Nonwovens Exhibition
Venue: Shanghai World Expo Exhibition & Convention Center, Shanghai
Organizer: UBM Asia Ltd
Address: 17/F, China Resources Building, 26 Harbour Road, Wan Chai, Hong Kong

2013/10/23-25
☎ 021-3251 6618, 3251 6628
🖷 021-3251 6698
✉ expo@vtexpo.com.cn
www.imwexpo.com
1810

第十二届电磁兼容暨微波技术展览会
地点：上海光大会展中心，上海
内容：用于通讯、电子、航空航天、军工、计算机、网络、无线电、仪器仪表、汽车、交通、医疗、船舶、电力等领域的电磁兼容设备、测试仪器、材料及元件等
周期：每年一届
市场范围：国际性
性质：面向公众和贸易观众
入场券价格：免费
主办：上海优创展览服务有限公司
地址：上海市曹杨路505号尚诚国际大厦505室(200063)
联系人：徐以敏

IME/China 2013
Intl Conference & Exhibition on Microwave and Antenna
Venue: Shanghai Everbright Convention & Exhibition Center, Shanghai
Frequency: Annual
Market Area: International
Nature: Open to Public
Cost to Attend: Free
Organizer: Viewtran Exhibition Service Co Ltd

2013/10/28-30
☎ 021-3641 1666, 6592 9965
🖷 021-6528 2319
✉ info@aiexpo.com.cn
www.sippe.org.cn
1820

第八届上海国际石油石化天然气技术装备展览会
同期举办：2013上海国际页岩气峰会
地点：上海新国际博览中心，上海
内容：石油石化技术装备展；石油天然气管道储运展；石油石化自动化及仪器仪表展
主办：中国石油学会；中国机电产品进出口商会；中国贸促会上海浦东分会
承办：上海艾展展览服务有限公司；上海艾能展览有限公司

8th Shanghai Intl Petroleum Petrochemical Natural Gas Technology Equipment Exhibition
Venue: Shanghai New Intl Expo Center, Shanghai
Organizer: Shanghai AiRui Exhibition Co Ltd; Shanghai AiExpo Exhibition Services Co Ltd
Address: Room 1309-1310.Building A, Fudan Software Park, No.15 Changyi Road, Shanghai 200441

2013/10/28-31
☎ 021-5045 6700, 5045 6700
🖷 021-5045 9355，5045 9355
✉ ally.huang@hmf-china.com
www.ptc-asia.com
1830

2013亚洲国际动力传动与控制技术展览会
地点：上海新国际博览中心，上海
内容：机械和电气传动、流体传动与控制、压缩空气技术、机械零部件、轴承、内燃机和燃气轮机的国际盛会
始办年份：1991
周期：每年一届
市场范围：国际性
性质：面向贸易观众
上届规模 '12：展览面积80,500m^2
主办：中国液压气动密封件工业协会；中国机械通用零部件工业协会；汉诺威米兰展览(上海)有限公司；德国汉诺威展览公司
地址：上海市浦东新区银霄路393号百安居浦东商务大厦301室汉诺威米兰展览（上海）有限公司(201204)
联系人：黄荔

PTC ASIA 2013
Venue: Shanghai New Intl Expo Center, Shanghai
Profile: International Exhibition for Electrical and Mechanical Power Transmission, Fluid Power Transmission, Compressed Air Technology, Machine Parts, Bearings, Internal Combustion Engines, and Gas Turbines
Established Year: 1991
Frequency: Annual
Market Area: International
Nature: Trade Only
Statistics '12: Exhibition Area 80,500m^2
Organizer: Deutsche Messe; Hannover Milano Fairs Shanghai Ltd; China Hydraulics Pneumatics & Sales Association; China General Machine Components Industry Association
Address: Rm. 301, B&Q Pudong Office Tower, 393 Yinxiao Rd, Pudong, Shanghai 201204 (Hannover Milano Fairs Shanghai Ltd)
Contact: Ally Huang

2013/10/28-31
☎ 021-5045 6700, 5045 6700
🖷 021-5045 9355, 5045 9355
✉ jelly.wang@hmf-china.com
www.ccmat-asia.com
1840

2013亚洲国际物流技术与运输系统展览会
地点：上海新国际博览中心，上海
内容：物料搬运、自动化技术、运输系统、物流和运输车辆的国际盛会
周期：每年一届
市场范围：国际性
性质：面向贸易观众
主办：中国物流与采购联合会；中国机械工程学会；德国汉诺威展览公司；汉诺威米兰展览（上海）有限公司
地址：上海市浦东新区银霄路393号百安居浦东商务大厦301室汉诺威米兰展览（上海）有限公司(201204)
联系人：汪萍

CeMAT 2013
Venue: Shanghai New Intl Expo Center, Shanghai
Profile: International Exhibition for Materials Handling, Automation Technology, Transport Systems, Logistics and Trucks
Frequency: Annual
Market Area: International
Nature: Trade Only
Organizer: Deutsche Messe; Hannover Milano Fairs Shanghai Ltd; China Federation of Logistics and Purchasing; Chinese Mechanical Engineering Society
Address: Rm. 301, B&Q Pudong Office Tower,393 Yinxiao Rd, Pudong, Shanghai 201204 (Hannover Milano Fairs Shanghai Ltd)
Contact: Jelly Wang

2013/10/29-11/01
☎ 010-8221 2866转ext 6002/6005
🖷 010-82212857
✉ chinapharm@ccpie.org
www.china-pharm.net
1850

第十八届中国国际医药（工业）展览会暨技术交流会
地点：上海新国际博览中心，上海
内容：制药机械展区，包装设备展区，药用辅料展区，生物工程及相关技术展区，分析检测展区，流体设备展区，洁净系统展区，行业相关服务
入场券价格：预登记免费
主办：中国医药国际交流中心；杜塞尔多夫展览(上海)有限公司

China-Pharm 2013
18th Intl Pharmaceutical Industry Exhibition
Venue: Shanghai New Intl Expo Center, Shanghai
Cost to Attend: Free for Pre-registered Visitors
Organizer: China Center for Pharmaceutical Intl Exchange

2013/10/30-11/01
☎ 852-2811 8897
🖷 852-2516 5024
✉ power@adsale.com.hk
www.epchinashow.com
1860

第九届上海国际电力设备及技术展览会
第八届上海国际电工装备展览会
地点：上海世博展览馆，上海
主办：中国电力企业联合会；雅式展览服务有限公司
承办：中国电力企业联合会国际合作部
地址：香港北角渣华道321号6楼雅式展览服务有限公司
联系人：冯佩珠，邓庆寿

9th Intl Exhibition on Electric Power Equipment and Technology
8th Intl Exhibition on Electrical Equipment
Venue: Shanghai World Expo Exhibition & Convention Center, Shanghai
Organizer: Adsale Exhibition Services Ltd

2013/11/05-09
☎ 021-2206 8393, 2206 8395, 2206 8888
🖷 021-6289 5703, 6279 0302
✉ calvin@shanghaiexpogroup.com
Markgao@shanghaiexpogroup.com
candyyao@shanghaiexpogroup.com
www.ciif-expo.com
1870

第15届中国国际工业博览会
地点：上海新国际博览中心，上海
主办：国家发展和改革委员会；商务部；工信部；科学技术部；教育部；中国科学院；中国工程院，中国贸促会；上海市人民政府
承办：上海东浩国际服务贸易（集团）有限公司；汉诺威展览(上海)有限公司
联系人：袁宏慧，高林，姚辰

China Intl Industry Fair
Venue: Shanghai New Intl Expo Center, Shanghai
Organizer: Shanghai Eastbest Intl (Group) Co Ltd

2013/11/08-11
☎ 852-2858 6179, 2516 1677
020-8666 0158
🖷 852-3749 7542
020-8867 7120
✉ salescjgf-hk@ubm.com
Info-china@ubm.com
www.jewellerynetasia.com
1880

上海国际黄金珠宝玉石展览会
地点：上海世博展览中心，上海
始办年份：2003
周期：每年一届
性质：面向公众和贸易观众
主办：亚洲博闻有限公司
地址：香港湾仔港湾道26号华润大厦17楼
国内联络：博闻(广州)展览有限公司
地址：广州市流花路中国大酒店商业大厦1159 - 1164室 (510015)

China International Gold, Jewellery & Gem Fair - Shanghai
Venue: Shanghai World Expo Exhibition & Convention Center, Shanghai
Established Year: 2003
Frequency: Annual
Nature: Open to Public
Organizer: UBM Asia Ltd
Address: 17/F, China Resources Building, 26 Harbour Road, Wan Chai, Hong Kong
Contact: UBM China (Guangzhou) Ltd （Mainland China）

2013/11/11-13
☎ 010-5166 2329转16/ 58/ 35
🖷 010-6813 2578, 6818 9519
✉ choisc@ceac.com.cn
www.icef.com.cn
1890

第82届中国电子展
同期举办：2013年亚洲电子展
地点：上海新国际博览中心，上海
内容：消费类电子：家庭娱乐，汽车电子产品，个人电脑与个人信息产品，网络计算产品 商业与工业用途：电子仪器，电子元器件，通讯设备
主办：中国电子器材总公司；香港贸易发展局；日本电子信息技术产业协会；韩国电子信息通信产业振兴会；台湾区电机电子工业同业公会
承办：中电会展与信息传播有限公司
地址：北京市复兴路49号
联系人：崔承哲、刘洪、关冰

82nd China Electronics Fair
Asia Electronics Exhibition in Shanghai (AEES 2013
2013 China LED Fair (Shanghai)
Venue: Shanghai New Intl Expo Center, Shanghai
Profile: A Gateway to Enter the World's Fastest Growing Electronics & ICT Markets
Established Year: 1964
Organizer: China Electronics Appliance Corp.

2013/11/12-14
☎ 010--6441 6187, 6441 4966
✉ fany@icif.cn
jiang@expo.cncic.gov.cn
www.waterchem.com.cn
1990

2013（第九届）中国国际水处理化学品、水溶性高分子技术及应用展览会
地点：上海世博展览馆，上海
主办：全国化工国际展览交流中心
地址：北京市和平街北口樱花东街5号（100029）

WATERCHEM+TECH
9th China Intl Exhibition on Water-Treatment Chemicals, Technologies and Applications
Venue: Shanghai World Expo Exhibition & Convention Center, Shanghai
Organizer: International Exhibition Center of China Chemical Industry

2013/11/12-14
☎ 010- 6445 2729, 6442 1448
✉ renfei111@126.com
www.chinasurfactant.com

2000

2013中国国际工业表面活性剂技术及应用展览会
地点：上海世博展览馆，上海
内容：表面活性剂，表面活性剂原料，工业清洗剂、皮革助剂、农药乳化剂及其他复配表面活性剂，表面活性剂工业用分析测试仪器及设备
主办：全国化工国际展览交流中心
地址：北京市和平街北口樱花东街5号（100029）

SURFACTANTCHEM+TECH
China Intl Exhibition on Industrial Surfactants, Technologies and Applications
Venue: Shanghai World Expo Exhibition & Convention Center, Shanghai
Organizer: International Exhibition Center of China Chemical Industry

2013/11/20-22
☎ 021-6279 2828
🖷 021-6545 5124
✉ yilei@siec-ccpit.com
www.sfchina.net
插入LOGO

2010

第二十六届中国国际表面处理展览会
地点：上海新国际博览中心，上海
内容：机械式精饰工艺、电镀及化学式处理、涂装及涂料产品、涂料原材料、仪器、设备及服务
始办年份：1983
周期：每年一届
市场范围：国际性
性质：面向贸易观众
主办：中贸推广国际有限公司；新展星展览（深圳）有限公司上海分公司；上海市国际展览有限公司
地址：上海市延安中路841号8楼上海市国际展览有限公司（200040）
联系人：益磊女士

SFCHINA 2013
Venue: Shanghai New Intl Expo Center, Shanghai
Profile: Mechanical finishing, chemical finishing & electroplating, coating applications and coating products, raw materials, machinery, services and others
Established Year: 1983
Frequency: Annual
Market Area: International
Nature: Trade Only
Organizer: Sinostar International Ltd; New Expostar (SZ) Co Ltd Shanghai Branch; Shanghai International Exhibition Co Ltd
Address: Shanghai International Exhibition Co Ltd , 8/F, No.841 Yan An Zhong Road, Shanghai 200040, China
Contact: Ms Carrie Yi

2013/11/20-22
☎ 021-6279 2828
🖷 021-6545 5124
✉ yilei@siec-ccpit.com
www.sfchina.net

2020

第十八届届中国国际涂料展览会
地点：上海新国际博览中心，上海
内容：机械式精饰工艺、电镀及化学式处理、涂装及涂料产品、涂料原材料、仪器、设备及服务
始办年份：1996
周期：每年一届
市场范围：国际性
性质：面向贸易观众
主办：中贸推广国际有限公司；新展星展览（深圳）有限公司上海分公司；上海市国际展览有限公司
地址：上海市延安中路841号8楼(200040)
联系人：益磊女士

CHINACOAT 2013
Venue: Shanghai New Intl Expo Center, Shanghai
Profile: Mechanical finishing, chemical finishing & electroplating, coating applications and coating products, raw materials, machinery, services and others
Established Year: 1996
Frequency: Annual
Market Area: International
Nature: Trade Only
Organizer: Sinostar International Ltd; New Expostar (SZ) Co Ltd Shanghai Branch; Shanghai International Exhibition Co Ltd
Address: Shanghai International Exhibition Co Ltd, 8/F, No.841 Yan An Zhong Road, Shanghai, 200040, China
Contact: Ms Carrie Yi

2013/11/20-22
☎ 021-5450 0848
🖷 021-5171 4505
✉ shmrhu@163.com
www.floor-expo.net

2030

2013第10届中国（上海）国际地坪工业展览会
地点：上海新国际博览中心，上海
内容：环氧地坪，砂浆地坪，混凝土地坪，耐磨地坪，弹性地材，防静电地坪，地坪机械，地坪清洁，地坪处理，表面处理技术，地坪保养等
始办年份：2004
周期：每年一届
市场范围：国际性
性质：面向贸易观众
入场券价格：免费
上届规模：展览面积12,000m^2
主办：中国建筑材料联合会地坪材料分会；上海展业展览有限公司
地址：上海市漕宝路400号明申商务Room 1808,(200233)
联系人：胡钰
msn：kennyhu@live.com

10th China (Shanghai) Intl Floor Industry Expo 2013
Venue: Shanghai New Intl Expo Center, Shanghai
Profile: Epoxy floor, mortar floor, concrete floor, resistance floor , elastic material, antistatic flooring, floor machinery, floor cleaning equipment, surface treatment technology , polyurethane, floor maintenance agent
Established Year: 2004
Frequency: Annual
Market Area: International
Nature: Trade Only
Cost to Attend: Free
Statistics '12: Exhibition Area 12,000m^2
Organizer: China Building Materials Industry Association Floor Branch; Shanghai Zhanye Exhibition Co Ltd
Address: Room 1808, Mingshen Business Square, No 400 Caobao Rd., Shanghai 200233, China
Contact: Kenny Hu
msn: kennyhu@live.com

2013/11/20-22
☎ 021-5450 0848
🖷 021-5171 4505
✉ shmrhu@163.com
www.baowenzhan.com.cn

2040

2013第11届中国（上海）国际保温材料与节能技术展览会
地点：上海新国际博览中心，上海
内容：岩棉，矿棉，玻璃棉，玻璃纤维，聚氨酯保温，酚醛保温，EPS，无机保温材料，岩棉生产线，气凝胶，保温砂浆，泡沫玻璃，保温装饰一体板，VIP真空绝热板等保温材料及设备
始办年份：2003
周期：每年一届
市场范围：国际性
性质：面向贸易观众
入场券价格：免费
上届规模：展览面积12,000m^2
主办：中国绝热节能材料协会；上海展业展览有限公司
地址：上海市漕宝路400号明申商务广场1808室(200233)
联系人：胡钰
msn：kennyhu@live.com

11th China (Shanghai) Insulating Materials and Energy-saving Technology Expo
Venue: Shanghai New Intl Expo Center, Shanghai
Profile: Rock wool, mineral wool, glass wool, fiberglass, Polyurethane insulation, phenolic foam insulation, inorganic insulating material, rock wool lines, aerogel, thermal insulation mortar, foam glass, insulation integration insulation board, VIP vacuum insulation panel
Established Year: 2003
Frequency: Annual
Market Area: International
Nature: Trade Only
Cost to Attend: Free
Statistics '12: Exhibition Area 12,000m^2
Organizer: China Insulation & Energy Efficiency Materials Association; Shanghai Zhanye Exhibition Co Ltd
Address: Room 1808, Mingshen Business Square, No 400 Caobao Rd., Shanghai 200233, China
Contact: Kenny Hu
msn: kennyhu@live.com

2013/11/20-22
☎ 021-5450 0848
🖷 021-5171 4505
✉ shmrhu@163.com
www.baowenzhan.com
2050

2013第9届中国（上海）国际干混砂浆技术及产品展览会
地点：上海新国际博览中心，上海
内容：干混砂浆，可再分散乳胶粉，纤维素醚，砂浆成品及辅材，砂浆生产及施工设备，砂浆添加剂及原料等
始办年份：2005
周期：每年一届
市场范围：国际性
性质：面向贸易观众
入场券价格：免费
上届规模：展览面积12,000m^2
主办：中国建筑业协会材料分会预拌砂浆推广委员会；上海展业展览有限公司
地址：上海市漕宝路400号明申商务广场1808室(200233)
联系人：胡钰
msn：kennyhu@live.com

9th China (Shanghai) Intl Dry Mix Mortar Technology and Product Expo 2013
Venue: Shanghai New Intl Expo Center, Shanghai
Profile: Dry mix mortar, re-dispersible latex powder, cellulose ether, mortar product and auxiliary, mortar production and construction equipment, mortar additives and raw materials
Established Year: 2005
Frequency: Annual
Market Area: International
Nature: Trade Only
Cost to Attend: Free
Statistics '12: Exhibition Area 12,000m^2
Organizer: Pre-mixed Mortar Promotion Association of China Construction Industry Association Materials Branch; Shanghai Zhanye Exhibition Co Ltd
Address: Room 1808, Mingshen Business Square, No 400 Caobao Rd., Shanghai 200233, China
Contact: Kenny Hu
msn: kennyhu@live.com

2013/11/26-28
☎ 010-6590 7766转ext 736
🖷 010-6590 6139
✉ h.chen@koelnmesse.cn
www.cihs.com.cn
www.hardwareshow-china.com
2060

2013 中国国际五金展
–科隆国际五金展 强力推动
地点：上海新国际博览中心，上海
内容：工具；建筑五金及DIY家装；锁具、安防产品及配件
始办年份：2001
周期：每年一届
市场范围：国际性
性质：面向贸易观众
主办：中国五金制品协会；德国科隆国际展览有限公司；全国工商联五金机电商会；中国贸促会轻工行业分会
承办：科隆国际展览有限公司；北京时瑞展览有限公司；上海大陆工具发展有限公司
地址：北京市朝阳区东三环北路8号亮马河大厦二座1018室，科隆国际展览有限公司(100004)
联系人：陈晗

China Intl Hardware Show
- Powered by PRACTICAL WORLD
Venue: Shanghai New Intl Expo Center, Shanghai
Profile: Tools; DIY and Building Hardware; Security, Locks and Fittings
Established Year: 2001
Frequency: Annual
Market Area: International
Nature: Trade Only
Organizer: China National Hardware Association; Koelnmesse; All-China Chamber of Commerce in Hardware, Mechanical and Electric Industry; Light Industry Sub-Council, CCPIT
Organizer: Koelnmesse; Beijing Triuni Exhibition Co Ltd; China Tool Development Co Ltd
Address: Koelnmesse, Unit 1018, Landmark Tower II, No. 8 Dongsanhuan North Rd, Beijing 100004, China
Contact: Helen Chen

2013/11/28-30
☎ 010-8810 2253，88102255
🖷 010-8810 2269
✉ liuding@chgie.com
邮箱wenhui@chgie.com
www.chinafvf.com
2070

2013中国国际果蔬、加工技术及物流展览会
地点：上海光大会展中心，上海
主办：中国出入境检验检疫协会；中国果品流通协会
承办：长城国际展览有限责任公司

China World Fruit & Vegetable Trade Fair 2013
Venue: Shanghai Everbright Convention & Exhibition Center, Shanghai
Sponsor: China Entry-Exit Inspection and Quarantine Association; China Fruit Marketing Association
Organizer: China Great Wall Intl Exhibition Co Ltd

2013/12/03-06
☎ 852-2827 6211
🖷 852-3749 7347
✉ marintec-hk@ubm.com
www.marintecchina.com
2080

中国国际海事技术学术会议和展览会
地点：上海新国际博览中心，上海
内容：船级社，计算机系统、网络和软件，咨询服务，疏浚设备，环境保护装备和设施，起重和升降设备，轮机工程和船用设备，补给和物流，海事出版，导航和通讯系统，离岸工程，滑油和润滑，油漆和涂料，港口和码头设备，港口和水路工程 港务局和码头作业公司，港口建设，港口设施，推进系统/ 泵和阀，冷冻系统 安全、救援和保护设备，船舶设计和建造，船舶工程，船舶营运和管理，船舶登记和检验，船坞和修船厂，电讯 贸易协会和出口委员会，仓库和配货系统
周期：两年一届
市场范围：国际性
性质：面向贸易观众
主办：亚洲博闻有限公司
地址：香港湾仔港湾道26号华润大厦17楼

Marintec China
Venue: Shanghai New Intl Expo Center, Shanghai
Frequency: Biennial
Market Area: International
Nature: Trade Only
Organizer: UBM Asia Ltd
Address: 17/F, China Resources Building, 26 Harbour Road, Wan Chai, Hong Kong

天津 Tianjin

2013/05/17-20
☎ 022-8370 1182, 8370 1162
🖷 022-8370 1009
✉ 2576788865@qq.com
www.tjlpz.com
2090

2013 第六届天津国际礼品、工艺品及家居用品博览会
地点：天津国际展览中心，天津
内容：礼品及赠品类、工艺品类、家居精品类、编织及藤铁工艺品类
主办：天津市工艺美术行业协会
地址：天津市南开区红旗南路中海御湖瀚苑3-1-3003室
联系人：万林

6th Tianjin Intl Gifts, Crafts & Household Goods Expo
Venue: Tianjin Intl Exhibition Center, Tianjin
Organizer: Tianjin Art & Crafts Association

2013/05/18-20
☎ 010-5114 9598, 13641075609
🖷 010-8954 3241
✉ yanhongkun321@163.com
2314642895
2100

2013第七届中国（天津）国际厨房、卫浴设施展览会
地点：天津梅江会展中心，天津
内容：厨房电器、厨房家电展区；厨房家具区；卫浴洁具及五金配件区；建筑陶瓷展区
参展费用：国内：光地900元/m^2（36m^{2}起），标准展位9,000元角位加10%；国际：光地210美元/m^2(36m^{2}起），标准展位2,100美元
主办：中国国际商会
承办：北京天威会展有限公司
地址：北京市通州区小潞邑152室(101125)
联系人：闫坤

Tianjin Kitchen and Sanitary Facilities Show
Venue: Meijiang Convention Center, Tianjin
Participated Fee: Raw Space USD 210/m^2 (min 36m^2, Standard Booth USD 2,100/booth
Organizer: Beijing Tianwei Exhibition Co Ltd

2013/05/18-20
☎ 010-5601 0887
🖷 010-5601 0887
✉ 1677362313@qq.com
2110

2013第七届中国（天津）国际太阳能及光伏展览会
地点：天津梅江会展中心，天津
内容：太阳能光照明系统；太阳能光伏材料及配件；太阳能光伏材料及配件；太阳能光伏系统；太阳能光伏材料及配件
市场范围：全国性
参展费用：国内：光地900元/m^2（36m^{2}起），标准展位9,000元角位加10%；国际：光地210美元/m^2(36m^{2}起），标准展位2,100美元
主办：中国国际商会
承办：汉维展览有限公司（汉维中国）
联系人：赵刚

Tianjin Solar and Photovoltaic Exhibition
Venue: Meijiang Convention Center, Tianjin
Market Area: National
Participated Fee: Raw Space USD 210/m^2 (min 36m^2, Standard Booth USD 2,100/booth
Organizer: Hanwei Exhibition Co Ltd

2013/05/30-06/02
☎ 022-2377 2599
🖷 022-2377 2518
✉ ddhaowei@gmail.com
www.jbhtj.com
2120

2013第二届天津国际营养健康产业博览会
2013天津国际茶业及茶艺博览会
地点：天津国际展览中心，天津
内容：高端营养保健品，高端酒水饮品，茶叶茶艺，高端食用油，有机和绿色产品，包装印刷设备
主办：中国营养协会
承办：天津诚尚优美广告有限公司
联系人：赵云

2nd Tianjin Intl Exposition of Nutrition and Health Industries 2013
Tianjin Intl Tea and Tea Art Expo
Venue: Tianjin Intl Exhibition Center, Tianjin
Profile: Health care products, healthy wine and beverage, tea and tea art, edible oil, organic and green food
Organizer: Tianjin Integrity and Grace Advertising Co Ltd

福建-晋江 Fujian-Jinjiang

2013/04/18-21
☎ 0595-8560 0609, 8566 4572
🖷 0595-8567 4572
✉ jif@cn-jif.com
www.cn-jif.com
2130

第十五届中国（晋江）国际鞋业博览会
地点：美旗城2号展馆，福建晋江
内容：作为亚洲最大的专业鞋业品牌展会之一，每届展会来自国（境）外10多个国家（地区）的展商占总展位数三分之一，与会专业买家遍布70多个国家（地区）和国内二十多个省（市）。
始办年份：1999
周期：每年一届
市场范围：国际性
性质：面向贸易观众
参展费用：标准展位5,000元，光地500元/m^2
主办：福建省人民政府；中国贸促会；中国轻工业联合会
承办：晋江市人民政府；晋江市制工业协会
地址：中国福建省晋江市青阳外经贸大厦3楼
联系人：李志达，丁燕燕

The 15th Jinjiang Footwear Intl Exposition, China
Venue: No.2 Exhibition Hall, Machi City, Jinjiang, Fujian
Profile: Footwear products (include sport shoes, casual shoes, canvas shoes, sandals& slippers working shoes and football shoes of various kinds),shoes materials & accessories, leathers (synthetic and imitation leather, PU , all kinds of leather), chemical raw materials, shoe-making & leather-making equipment, and relative researches, designs, information journals & books ,etc.
Established Year: 1999
Frequency: Annual
Market Area: International
Nature: Trade Only
Participated Fee: Standard Booth RMB 5,000/booth, Raw Space RMB 500/m^2
Organizer: Fujian Province Government; CCPIT; China National Light Industry Council
Address: 3F Foreign Economy & Trade Bldg., Qingyang, Jinjiang, Fujian

福建-厦门 Fujian-Xiamen

2013/04/12-15
☎ 0592-266 9867, 266 9866
🖷 0592-266 9868
✉ fuailan@chinafair.org.cn, ciipc18@chinafair.org.cn
www.straitsfair.org.cn
2140

第17届海峡两岸机械电子商品交易会
暨 厦门对台进出口商品交易会
地点：厦门会议展展中心，福建厦门
内容：机械设备，仪器仪表暨工控设备，模具、工具及材料，物流设备，节能照明产品等
主办：中国机电产品进出口商会；台湾区电机电子工业同业公会；厦门市人民政府
承办：厦门市对台贸易促进中心

17th China Xiamen Machinery and Electronics Exhibition (CXMEE)
Venue: Xiamen Intl Conference & Exhibition Center, Xiamen, Fujian
Organizer: Xiamen Promotion Center for Trade to Taiwan

2013/09/08-11
☎ 0592-266 9825, 266 9827
🖷 0592-266 9830
✉ cifit@chinafair.org.cn
www.chinafair.org.cn
2150

第十七届中国国际投资贸易洽谈会
地点：厦门国际会展中心，福建厦门
始办年份：1997
周期：每年一届
市场范围：国际性
性质：面向公众
主办：中华人民共和国商务部（MOFCOM）
承办：福建省人民政府；厦门市人民政府；商务部投资促进事务局
地址：福建厦门市湖滨北路108号振业大厦8-10层(361012)

The China International Fair for Investment and Trade
Venue: Xiamen International Conference & Exhibition Center, Xiamen, Fujian
Established Year: 1997
Frequency: Annual
Market Area: International
Nature: Open to Public
Organizer: MOFCOM
Address: 8-10/Fl., 108 North Hubin Road, Xiamen, Fujian 361012, China

甘肃-兰州 Gansu-Lanzhou

2013/04/27-02
☎ 010-8260 6899
🖷 010-8260 6883
www.cnaico.com.cn
www.autochina.com.cn
2160

2013年中国西部（兰州）国际汽车博览会　春季
地点：甘肃兰州
主办：中国汽车工业国际合作总公司
地址：北京市海淀区中关村丹棱街3号A座

2013 West China (Lanzhou) Automobile Expo -Spring
Venue: Lanzhou, Gansu
Organizer: China National Automotive Industry Intl Corp
Address: A, 3 Danling Street, Zhongguancun, Haidian Dist., Beijing, China

2013/08/22-27
☎ 010-8260 6899
🖷 010-8260 6883
✉ ciccyhuang@cnaico.com.cn
www.cnaico.com.cn,
www.autochina.com.cn
2170

2013年中国西部（兰州）国际汽车博览会　秋季
地点：甘肃兰州
预计规模：总面积40,000m^2
主办：中国汽车工业国际合作总公司
地址：北京市海淀区中关村丹棱街3号A座

2013 West China (Lanhou) Automobile Expo -Autumn
Venue: Lanzhou, Gansu
Expectation: Gross Area 40,000m^2
Organizer: China National Automotive Industry Intl Corp
Address: A, 3 Danling Street, Zhongguancun, Haidian Dist., Beijing, China

2013/03/16-20
☎ 0769-2242 3217, 13532778552
🖷 0769-2242 4631
✉ wumin0597@163.com
www.3f.net.cn
2180

第29届国际名家具（东莞）展览会
暨名家具机械、材料展览会
地点：广东现代国际展览中心，广东东莞
内容：木工机械：木材加工机械、家具生产机械、人造板生产机械、喷涂、涂装设备、雕刻机械、床垫机械、缝纫设备、软体机械、包装机械、刀具、机械配件、手动工具、磨具、测试仪器、木材运输及吊卸设备；原辅材料区：板材、木材、木皮、贴纸、地板、玻璃、石材、金属、皮革、布料、胶膜、海绵、塑胶、五金、橱柜五金、油漆、涂料、粘合剂、清洁剂、拉手、导轨、沙发脚、锁、连接固件
主办：东莞市人民政府
承办：东莞名家具俱乐部
地址：东莞市厚街镇商贸中心五楼
联系人：吴闽

IFM
29th Intl Famous Furniture Woodworking Machinery & Material Fair
Venue: GD Modern Intl Exhibition Center, Dongguan, Guangdong
Organizer: Dongguan Furniture Famous Club
Address: 5Fl. Trade Center, Houjie Town, Dongguan, Guangdong

2013/04/10-13
☎ 020-8761 2356, 8761 5755
🖷 020-8730 5903
✉ pc@paper-com.com.cn
www.dfmshow.com
2190

2013第十四届中国（东莞）国际鞋机鞋材工业技术展
地点：广东现代国际展览中心，广东东莞
内容：鞋类机械，鞋材及辅料，合成皮机械，皮革化工原料，袋类/箱包机械，注塑设备，电脑辅助设备
主办：通讯展览公司
地址：广州市环市东路477号海洋地质大厦四层M2室(510075)

14th China (Dongguan) Intl Footwear Machinery & Material Industry Fair
Venue: GD Modern Intl Exhibition Center, Dongguan, Guangdong
Organizer: Paper Communication Exhibition Service
Address: Rm. 15,5/F. Wha Shing Center , 11 Shing Ypi St. Kwun Tong , Kowloon , Hong Kong.

2013/04/30-05/02
☎ 0769-8598 1555
🖷 0769-2299 2793
www.gdautoshow.com
2200

第十三届广东国际汽车展示交易会
内容：汽车（含轿车、越野车、商用车及特种车）；汽车及其零部件；汽车生产制造设备、工艺装备；各种检测、测试、试验仪器和设备；计算机开发设计系统及应用技术；汽车工业生产的新工艺、新材料；汽车工业新能源技术与产品；汽车工业环保技术与产品；汽车用品、装饰件、美容品；汽车维修设备。
周期：每年一届
市场范围：国际性
主办：中国汽车工业国际合作总公司
承办：东莞中汽会展有限公司

13th Guangdong Intl Auto Exhibition & Trade fair
Venue: Dongguan, Guangdong
Frequency: Annual
Market Area: International
Organizer: China National Automotive Industry International Corp

2013/05/20-22
☎ 020-8359 9695
🖷 020-8358 9272
http://hk.allallinfo.com
2210

2013东莞国际纺织品印花工业技术展览会
地点：广东现代国际展览中心，广东东莞
主办：香港浩瀚资讯传媒集团有限公司

2013 China Intl Textile Printing Industrial Technology Exposition
Venue: GD Modern Intl Exhibition Center, Dongguan, Guangdong
Organizer: Hong Kong Allallinfo Media Group Ltd

2013/05/30-06/01
☎ 0769-2238 8565
🖷 0769-2238 8575
2220

2013华南国际汽车改装及赛车展览会
地点：广东现代国际展览中心，广东东莞
主办：东莞市龙亨展览有限公司

Southern China Intl Car Tuning and Racing Exhibition
Venue: GD Modern Intl Exhibition Center, Dongguan, Guangdong
Organizer: Dongguan South Dragon Expo Limited

2013/05/30 06/01
☎ 0769-2238 8565
🖷 0769-2238 8575
www.ssf-expo.net
2230

2013 东莞国际电镀工业、表面处理及涂料展
地点：广东现代国际展览中心，广东东莞
主办：东莞市龙亨展览有限公司

Southorn China Exhibition on Elcctro plating, Surfacc Finiching and Coatings
Venue: GD Modern Intl Exhibition Center, Dongguan, Guangdong
Organizer: Dongguan South Dragon Expo Limited

2013/06/04-07
☎ 0769-8326 2748
🖷 0769-8326 2758
✉ dgszma@126.com
www.dgzzexpo.com
2240

2013东莞振宗工业园区展览会
地点：广东现代国际展览中心，广东东莞
主办：东莞振宗展览有限公司

Dongguan Zhenzong Industry Park Exhibition
Venue: GD Modern Intl Exhibition Center, Dongguan, Guangdong
Organizer: Dongguan Zhenzong Exhibition Co Ltd

2013/06/19-22
☎ 0769-8598 1609, 8598 1610
🖷 0769-8590 9318
www.gdfecf.com
2250

2013中国加工贸易产品博览会
地点：广东现代国际展览中心，广东东莞
主办：组委会秘书处，广东现代会展管理有限公司营销中心

2013 China Processing Trade Products Fair
Venue: GD Modern Intl Exhibition Center, Dongguan, Guangdong
Organizer: GD Modern Intl Exhibition Management Co Ltd

2013/06/21-24
☎ 400 663 5811
🖷 0769-8899 8787
✉ wintickfair@163.com
www.tea-tickfair.com
2260

第7届东莞-春季茶博会
地点：常平会展中心，广东东莞
主办：迪亿会展（香港）有限公司

7th Dongguan-Spring Tea Expo
Venue: Changping Exhibition Center, Dongguan, Guangdong
Organizer: Tick Fair Company Limited

2013/07/17-19
☎ 852-2276 9000
🖷 852-2276 9846
2270

中国国际电线电缆及设备交易会
地点：广东现代国际展览中心，广东东莞
主办：UL安全检定国际有限公司

UL Wire & Cable Intl Fair 2013
Venue: GD Modern Intl Exhibition Center, Dongguan, Guangdong
Organizer: Underwriters Laboratories Inc

2013/08/21-23
☎ 021-2231 7000
🖷 021-2231 7181
www.sino-foldingcarton.com
2280

中国国际彩盒展
地点：广东现代国际展览中心，广东东莞
内容：专注于彩盒后道加工的展览会。展会聚焦彩盒领域前沿资讯、发布行业权威技术与市场发展动态、为彩盒生产企业提供最新生产加工解决方案。
周期：每年一届
主办：上海励欣展览有限公司

SinoFoldingCarton
Venue: GD Modern Intl Exhibition Center, Dongguan, Guangdong
Frequency: Annual
Organizer: Reed Exhibitions

2013/09/05-09
☎ 0769-8590 0111
🖷 0769-8558 5780
www.3f.net.cn
2290

第三十届国际名家具（东莞）展览会
地点：广东现代国际展览中心，广东东莞
主办：东莞名家具俱乐部

30th Intl Famous Furniture Fair (Dongguan)
Venue: GD Modern Intl Exhibition Center, Dongguan, Guangdong
Organizer: Dongguan Famous Furniture Club

2013/09/29-04
☎ 0769-8598 1555
🖷 0769-2299 2793
www.gdautoshow.com
2300

第十四届广东国际汽车展示交易会
地点：广东现代国际展览中心，广东东莞
内容：汽车（含轿车、越野车、商用车及特种车）；汽车及其零部件；汽车生产制造设备、工艺装备；各种检测、测试、试验仪器和设备；计算机开发设计系统及应用技术；汽车工业生产的新工艺、新材料；汽车工业新能源技术与产品；汽车工业环保技术与产品；汽车用品、装饰件、美容品；汽车维修设备。
市场范围：国际性
主办：中国汽车工业国际合作总公司
承办：东莞中汽会展有限公司

14th Guangdong Intl Auto Exhibition & Trade fair
Venue: GD Modern Intl Exhibition Center, Dongguan, Guangdong
Market Area: International
Organizer: China National Automotive Industry International Corp

2013/11/01-03
☎ 852-2811 8897, 0755-8232 6251
🖷 852-2516 5024, 0755-8232 6252
www.chinashoesexpo.com
2310

第十六届 中国东莞国际鞋展 -鞋机展-鞋材展
地点：广东现代国际展览中心，广东东莞
始办年份：2003
周期：每年一届
市场范围：国际性
性质：对公众和观众开放
主办：中国轻工工艺品进出口商会；中国贸促会广东省分会；雅式展览服务有限公司；杜塞尔多夫展览（上海）有限公司；广东现代会展管理有限公司及东莞市皮鞋业协会

Dongguan Shoes & China Shoetes
Venue: GD Modern Intl Exhibition Center, Dongguan, Guangdong
Established Year: 2003
Frequency: Annual
Market Area: International
Nature: Open to Public and Trade Visitors
Organizer: Adsales Exhibition Service Co Ltd

2013/11/06-08
☎ 010-5820 7013
🖷 010-5820 6476
2320

包装产业周
地点：广东现代国际展览中心，广东东莞
主办：美狮传媒集团

Packaging Industry Week
Venue: GD Modern Intl Exhibition Center, Dongguan, Guangdong
Organizer: M.Success Media Group

2013/11/13-16
☎ 020-8761 2356, 852-2950 1999
021-6304 5419
🖷 020-8730 5903, 852-2341 0379
021-6418 1136
www.dmpshow.com
2330

第十五届东莞国际橡塑胶、包装、压铸和铸造展
地点：广东现代国际展览中心，广东东莞
主办：广东讯展会议展览有限公司

15th China Dongguan Intl Plastics Packing Rubber Diecasting & Foundry Exhibition
Venue: GD Modern Intl Exhibition Center, Dongguan, Guangdong
Organizer: Paper Communication Exhibition Services

2013/11/13-16
☎ 020-8761 2356,852-2950 1999,
021-6304 5419
🖷 020-8730 5903, 852-2341 0379
021-6418 1136
www.dmpshow.com
2340

第十五届东莞国际模具展及金属加工展
地点：广东现代国际展览中心，广东东莞
主办：广东讯展会议展览有限公司，广东现代会展管理有限公司营销中心

15th China Dongguan Intl Mould and Metalworking Exhibition
Venue: GD Modern Intl Exhibition Center, Dongguan, Guangdong
Organizer: Paper Communication Exhibition Services

2013/12/21-2014/01/05
☎ 0769-8590 9009
🖷 0769-8583 0960, 8583 0970
2350

2013第十三届东莞嘉年华时尚生活用品购物节
地点：广东现代国际展览中心，广东东莞
主办：奥华国际展览有限公司

13th Dongguan Carnival
Venue: GD Modern Intl Exhibition Center, Dongguan, Guangdong
Organizer: Auwa Intl Exhibition Co Ltd

2013/12/28-31
☎ 852-8211 2668,0769-8383 5898
🖷 852-3405 8801
www.tea-tickfair.com
2360

广东（厚街）茶业博览会
地点：广东现代国际展览中心，广东东莞
主办：迪亿会展(香港)有限公司

Guangdong (Houjie) Tea Expo
Venue: GD Modern Intl Exhibition Center, Dongguan, Guangdong
Organizer: Tick Fair Company Limited

广东-广州 Guangdong-Guangzhou

2013/03/01-04
☎ 852-2827 6211
020-3810 6261,3810 6263
🖷 852-3749 7342
020-3810 6200
✉ info-hk@ubm.com
led-trust@ubm.com
www.ledchina-gz.com
2370

广州国际LED展
地点：中国进出口商品交易会展馆，广东广州
主办：亚洲博闻有限公司
地址：香港湾仔港湾道26号华润大厦17楼
联络：广州闻信展览服务有限公司
地址：广州市天河区林和东华庭路4号富力天河商务大厦1806-1807室（510610）

LED China
Venue: China Import & Export Fair Complex, Guangzhou, Guangdong
Organizer: UBM Asia Ltd
Address: 17/F, China Resources Building, 26 Harbour Road, Wan Chai, Hong Kong
Contact: UBM Trust Co Ltd
Address: Rm 1806-1807 Fu Li Tian He Business Mansion, No 4 Hua Ting Rd, Lin He Dong Rd, Guangzhou 510610, Guangdong, China

LED CHINA

2013/03/09-11
☎ 020-8625 9008, 8625 7099
🖷 020-8625 9533
✉ info@gdbeautyexpo.com
www.gdbeautyexpo.com
2380

广州国际美博会
地点：中国进出口商品交易会展馆，广东广州
内容：国际馆，专业美容馆，日化馆，养生馆，发品馆，美甲纹绣馆，包装器材馆
主办：广东省美容美发化妆品行业协会
地址：广东省广州市广园西路121号美博城A座写字楼五楼(510400)

Guangdong Intl Beauty Expo
Venue: China Import & Export Fair Complex, Guangzhou, Guangdong
Profile: Intl Brands, beauty salon, personal care, nature health, hair salon, nail and tattoo, packaging
Organizer: Guangdong Beauty & Cosmetic Association
Address: 5th Floor, Building A121 Guang Yuan Road (West) Guangzhou 510400, China

2013/03/18-21
☎ 010-8522 9446, 8522 9504
🖷 010-8522 9300
✉ intertextile_home@ccpittex.com
2390

中国（广州）国际家用纺织品及辅料博览会
地点：中国进出口商品交易会展馆，广东广州
内容：各类家用纺织品及辅料,计算机辅助设计与制造,相关出版物及网络
主办：中国纺织工业联合会，中国对外贸易中心（集团）
承办：中国家用纺织品行业协会；中国对外贸易广州展览总公司；中国贸促会纺织行业分会，法兰克福展览（香港）有限公司
联系人：何磊，林英华

China (Guangzhou) Intl Trade Fair for Home Textiles and Accessories-Autumn Edition
Venue: China Import & Export Fair Complex, Guangzhou, Guangdong
Organizer: The Sub-Council of Textile Industry CCPIT

2012/03/04-06
☎ 020-8912 8281, 8912 8291
🖷 020-8912 8222转ext 8406
✉ huangwj@fairwindow.com.cn
www.waterchina-gz.com
2400

第14届中国（广州）国际给排水、水处理技术与设备展览会暨2013中国（广州）国际泵、阀门、管道展览会
地点：中国进出口商品交易会展馆，广东广州
内容：供水系统，排水系统,建筑上下水系统;水工程施工设计与咨询，给排水绘图软件；纯净水、蒸馏水、矿泉水、高纯水等制水技术、设备及产品；节水技术与设备；水景工程与泳池系统；工业循环冷却水、锅炉补给水处理；膜分离技术与设备；水处理药剂、水处理技术、材料及通用设备；水过滤设备、消毒设备；泵类产品，阀类产品，各类管材、管道结头等。
始办年份：2000
周期：每年一届
市场范围：国际性
性质：面向贸易观众
入场券价格：业内观众凭名片登记
参展费用：标准展位：A区15,000元/9m^2，B区8,500元/9m^2，光地：A区1,300元/m^2，B区950元/m^2（36m^{2}起）
上届规模 '12：展览面积12,000m^2，参展商200家，参观人数15,000人
主办：中国对外贸易中心（集团）；中国水利企业协会脱盐分会；中国对外贸易广州展览总公司；青岛阿迪埃脱盐中心
地址：广州市新港东路980号广交会展馆C区16号馆A层(510035)
联系人：黄先生，陈小姐

Water, Wastewater & Water Treatment China 2013 and Pump, Valve & Pipe China 2013
Venue: China Import & Export Fair Complex, Guangzhou, Guangdong
Profile: Desalination Technology & Equipment Water Treatment Technology & Equipment End Products of Water Purification Technology &Equipment Fluid Automation and Automatic Control Equipment
Established Year: 2000
Frequency: Annual
Market Area: International
Nature: Trade Only
Participated Fee: Standard Booth: Area A RMB 15,000/9m^2, Area B RMB 8,500/9m^2, Raw Space: Area A RMB 1,300/m^2, Area B RMB 950/m^2 (min 36m^2)
Statistics '12: Exhibition Area 12,000m^2, Exhibitors 200, Visitors 15,000
Organizer: China Foreign Trade Center (Group); China Desalination Association; China Foreign Trade Guangzhou Exhibition General Corp; Qingdao Intl Desalination Center
Address: Floor A, Hall 16 Canton Fair Complex, No. 980 Xingang Dong Road, Guangzhou, Guangdong, China

2013/03/04-06
☎ 020-8912 8282
🖷 020-8912 8222转ext 8406
✉ zhangh@fairwindow.com.cn
www.siaf-china.com
2410

中国广州国际工业自动化技术及装备展览会
地点：中国进出口商品交易会展馆，广东广州
内容：传动、机械驱动系统及零部件、电子零部件及辅助设备、机电零部件及辅助设备、辅助设备、感应技术（传感器）、控制系统、工业用电脑装备、工业自动化软件、接口技术、低电压开关装置、人机界面装置、工业自动化技术交流、培训及咨询、组

SPS - Industrial Automation Fair Guangzhou
Venue: China Import & Export Fair Complex, Guangzhou, Guangdong
Profile: Drive Systems and Components, Electromechanical Components and Peripheral Equipment, Sensor Technology, Control Technology, IPCs, Industrial Software, Interface Technology, Low Voltage - Switching Devices, Human-Machine-Interface Devices, Industrial Communication,

装系统、材料处理装置、连动技术、集成化系统、分解设备、微系统技术、机器零部件、工业机器人
始办年份：1996
周期：每年一届
市场范围：国际性
性质：面向贸易观众
入场券价格：业内观众凭名片登记
参展费用：标准展台：A区12,000元/9m²，B区8,500元/9m²，光地：A区1,050元/m²，B区750元/m²（36m²起）
上届规模 '12：展览面积21,500m²，参展商354家，参观人数22,189人
主办：中国对外贸易中心（集团）；德国法兰克福展览有限公司；中国对外贸易广州展览总公司；广州光亚法兰克福展览有限公司；德国美赛高法兰克福展览有限公司；广州富洋展览有限公司
地址：广州市新港东路980号广交会展馆C区16号馆A层(510035)
联系人：张先生

Training and Consulting, Assembly Equipment, Materials Handling Devices, Integrated Systems, Dismantling Equipment, Micro Technology, Machine Components, Industrial Robot
Established Year: 1996
Frequency: Annual
Market Area: International
Nature: Trade Only
Participated Fee: Standard Booth: Area A RMB 15,000/9m², Area B RMB 8,500/9m², Raw Space: Area A RMB 1,300/m², Area B RMB 950/m² (min 36m²)
Statistics '12: Exhibition Area 21,500m², Exhibitors 354, Visitors 22,189
Organizer: China Foreign Trade Center (Group); Messe Frankfurt Exhibition GmbH; China Foreign Trade Guangzhou Exhibition General Corp; Guangzhou Guangya Messe Frankfurt Co Ltd; Mesago Messe Frankfurt GmbH; Guangzhou Overseas Trade Fairs Ltd
Address: Floor A, Hall 16 Canton Fair Complex, No.980 Xingang Dong Road, Guangzhou, Guangdong, China

---

2013/03/04-06
☎ 020-8912 8268, 8912 8283
🖷 020-8912 8222转ext 8406
✉ pfp@fairwindow.com.cn
www.PrintingSouthChina.com
www.SinoLabelChina.com
2420

第二十届华南国际印刷工业展览会
暨2013中国国际标签印刷技术展览会
地点：中国进出口商品交易会展馆，广东广州
内容：各种印刷设备、材料及资讯；
始办年份：1994
周期：每年一届
市场范围：国际性
性质：面向贸易观众
入场券价格：业内观众凭名片登记
参展费用：标准展位9,000元/9m²，光地880元/m²（36m²）
上届规模 '12：展览面积51,000m²（国外展商652家），贸易观众51,702人
主办：广东省新闻出版局；中国对外贸易中心（集团）；雅式展览服务有限公司；广东省出版集团有限公司；中国对外贸易广州展览总公司；北京雅展展览服务有限公司
地址：广州市新港东路980号广交会展馆C区16号馆A层(510035)
联系人：周小姐，刘小姐

20th South China Intl Exhibition on Printing Industry
China Intl Exhibition on Label Printing Technology 2013
Venue: China Import & Export Fair Complex, Guangzhou, Guangdong
Profile: Pre-press Equipment & Software, Digital Printing Equipment, Label, Flexor & Gravure Printing Equipment, Offset Printing Equipment & Machinery, Screen Printing, Package Printing, Binding Equipment, Printing Materials & Accessories
Established Year: 1994
Frequency: Annual
Market Area: International
Nature: Trade Only
Participated Fee: Standard Booth RMB 9,000/9m², Raw Space RMB 880/m² (min 36m²)
Statistics '12: Exhibition Area 51,000m², Exhibitors 652, Trade Visitors 51,702
Organizer: Administration of Press and Publication of Guangdong Pronvince; China Foreign Trade Center (Group); Adsale Exhibition Services Ltd; Guangdong Provincial Publishing Group; China Foreign Trade Guangzhou Exhibition General Corp; Beijing Adsale Exhibition Services Ltd
Address: Floor A, Hall 16 Canton Fair Complex, No. 980 Xingang Dong Road, Guangzhou, Guangdong, China

---

2013/03/07-09
☎ 020-8626 6696
🖷 020-8626 6690
✉ iris.han@hmf-china.com
www.gitf.com.cn
2430

2013广州国际旅游展览会
地点：中国进出口商品交易会展馆，广东广州
内容：亚太地区最重要的国际旅游展览年会之一
始办年份：1993
周期：每年一届
市场范围：国际性
性质：面向公众和贸易观众
上届规模：展览面积22,000m²
主办：汉诺威米兰展览（上海）有限公司
地址：广州市新港东路1000号保利世贸中心西塔1808室汉诺威米兰展览会（中国）有限公司广州代表处(510308)
联系人：韩霭文

Guangzhou Intl Travel Fair 2013
Venue: China Import & Export Fair Complex, Guangzhou, Guangdong
Profile: One of the Most Important International Annual Travel Fairs in Asia-Pacific Region
Established Year: 1993
Frequency: Annual
Market Area: International
Nature: Open to Public
Statistics '12: Exhibition Area 22,000m²
Organizer: Hannover Milano Fairs Shanghai Limited
Address: Hannover Milano Fairs China Ltd - Guangzhou, 1808 West Tower, Poly World Trade Center, 1000 Xingang East Road, Haizhu District, Guangzhou, Guangdong, China
Contact: Iris Han

2013/03/09-10
☎ 020-2808 7012, 2808 7035
🖷 020-2808 7070
2440

中国（国际）婚博会
地点：保利世贸博览馆，广东广州
主办：中国（国际）婚博会组委会
地址：广东省广州市海珠区新港东路琶洲中洲交易中心1203-1204（510335）

China (Intl) Wedding Expo
Venue: Poly World Trade Expo Center, Guangzhou, Guangdong

2013/03/09-12
☎ 020-8356 1590, 8354 6339, 8356 7322
✉ music@ste.cn
www.soundlight.cn
2450

2013第十届中国（广州）国际乐器展览会
地点：中国进出口商品交易会展馆，广东广州
内容：钢琴和键盘乐器弦乐器打击乐器电声乐器民族乐器管乐器手风琴口琴乐谱及书籍乐器配件音乐相关电脑硬件软件协会及媒体设备其他
主办：广东省科学技术厅广东省文化厅；中国轻工业乐器信息中心；广东省对外科技交流中心承办：广东国际科技贸易展览公司（广东科展）
联系人：马静、冯梅、崔华、银联晓、杨琳

ProSound + Light Guangzhou
Venue: China Import & Export Fair Complex, Guangzhou, Guangdong
Organizer: Guangdong International Science & Technology Exhibition Company (STE)

2013/03/13-15
☎ 010-8455 6622, 8455 6625
🖷 010-6237 3998
www.chinalabexpo.com
2460

广州国际分析测试及实验室设备展览会暨技术研讨会
地点：保利世贸展览馆，广东广州
内容：实验室产品：科学仪器，试剂/消耗品，玻璃制品，实验室家具
主办：国药励展展览有限责任公司；广东省对外科技交流中心；广东国际科技贸易展览公司
联系人：魏小姐，郭小姐

China Lab 2013
China Analytic & Laboratory Equipment Expo & Conference
Venue: Poly World Trade Expo Center, Guangzhou, Guangdong
Organizer: Reed Exhibitions; Sinopharm Group Co., Ltd.; Guangdong International Science & Technology Exhibition Company (STE)

2013/03/18-21
☎ 020-8912 8022, 8912 8016
🖷 020-8912 8222转ext 8115
✉ hhc@fairwindow.com.cn
www.fairwindow.com
2470

2013中国广州国际家居饰品、家纺布艺展览会
地点：中国进出口商品交易会展馆，广东广州
内容：家居饰品 地毯、地毯类 人造花卉类 画、镜及框类 树脂、塑料及金属工艺类 陶瓷、玻璃类 灯饰类 电话、时钟类 木、石（雕）刻类、小件家具、其它
主办：中国对外贸易中心（集团）
承办：中国对外贸易广州展览总公司
地址：广州市海珠区新港东路980号广交会展馆C区16号馆A层(510335)
联系人：余金玲 小姐，周文缨 小姐

Home Textile
Venue: China Import & Export Fair Complex, Guangzhou, Guangdong
Organizer: China Foreign Trade Guangzhou Exhibition General Corporation
Address: Floor A, Hall 16, Area C, Canton Fair Complex, No.980 Xingang Dong Road, Haizhu District, Guangzhou, Guangdong

2013/03/18-20
☎ 020-8908 9067, 8908 0321
🖷 020-8908 0322
✉ info@windoorexpo.com
www.windoorexpo.com
2480

2013年第十九届全国铝门窗幕墙行业年会暨铝门窗幕墙新产品博览会
地点：保利世贸博览馆，广东广州
内容：铝门窗幕墙系列；铝门窗幕墙相关系列产品；铝门窗幕墙各类生产、加工、安装设备； 建筑节能玻璃、光伏与建筑一体化；建筑遮阳系列；相关工业协会及技术
主办：中国建筑金属结构协会铝门窗幕墙委员会；广州市城博展览有限公司
联系人：谢荔晖

Aluminum Window, Door, Facade & Curtain Wall Expo 2013
Venue: Poly World Trade Expo Center, Guangzhou, Guangdong
Organizer: Guangzhou Citi Expositions Ltd

2013/03/18-21
☎ 020-8912 8021, 020-8912 8016
🖷 020-89128222
www.ciff-gz.com
2490

第三十一届中国（广州）国际家具博览会
地点：中国进出口商品交易会展馆，广东广州
内容：民用家具、办公家具、户外家具、家居饰品用品、家纺布艺、木工机械/五金配件
周期：每年两届
市场范围：国际性
性质：面向贸易观众
入场券价格：40元
上届规模 '12：展览面积680,000m^2，参展商3,454家来自130个国家，参观人数178,036人
主办：中国对外贸易中心(集团)中国对外贸易广州展览总公司
地址：广州市海珠区新港东路980广交会展馆C区A层(510335)

31st China Intl Furniture Fair (Guangzhou)
Venue: China Import & Export Fair Complex, Guangzhou, Guangdong
Profile: Home Furniture, Office Show, Outdoor, Homedecor & Housewares, Hometextile, Furniture Materials, Machinery
Frequency: Bi-annual
Market Area: International
Nature: Trade Only
Cost to Attend: RMB 40:-
Statistics '12: Exhibition Area 680,000m^2, Exhibitors 3,454 came from 130 countries, Visitors 178,036
Organizer: China Foreign Trade Guangzhou Exhibition General Corporation
Address: Floor A, Hall 16, Area C, Canton Fair Complex, No.980 Xingang Dong Road, Haizhu District, Guangzhou, Guangdong

2013/03/27-30
☎ 020-8755 2468
020-8755 2468转ext 12
🖷 020-8755 2970
020-8755 2970
✉ k.lee@koelnmesse.cn
www.interzum-guangzhou.cn
2500

中国广州国际木工机械、家具配料展览会
地点：中国进出口商品交易会展馆，广东广州
内容：木工机械、软体机械、家具工具及刀具、海绵塑料及PVC、家具皮革及面料、家具及厨具五金、化工原料、板材、木皮及粘面纸、其它
周期：每年一届
市场范围：国际性
性质：面向贸易观众
入场券价格：20元
参展费用：标准展位7,900元，光地790元/m^2
主办：中国对外贸易中心（集团）；科隆国际展览有限公司
联络：中国对外贸易广州展览总公司
地址：广州市海珠区新港东路980号广交会展馆C区A层(510014)
联络：科隆国际中国有限公司
地址：广州市天河区天河北路183号大都会广场3311室(510620)
联系人：李伟莉

interzum guangzhou
China Intl Woodworking Machinery & Furniture Raw Materials Fair (Guangzhou)
Venue: China Import & Export Fair Complex, Guangzhou, Guangdong
Profile: Woodworking Machinery, Mattress & Sewing Machinery, Tools & Cutter, Aerated Plastics & PVC, Furniture Leather & Fabrics, Furniture & Kitchen Hardware, Industrial Chemical, Wood, Panel & Paper Overlay, Others
Frequency: Annual
Market Area: International
Nature: Trade Only
Cost to Attend: RMB 20:-
Participated Fee: Standard Booth RMB 7,900/booth, Raw Space RMB 790/m^2
Organizer: China Foreign Trade Center (Group); Koelnmesse GmbH
Contact: China Foreign Trade Guangzhou Exhibition Corp.
Address: Floor A, Hall 16, Area C, Canton Fair Complex, No.980 Xingang Dong Road, Haizhu District, Guangzhou, Guangdong, China
Contact: Koelnmesse Co Ltd
Address: Room3311, Metro Plaza, No.183 Tianhe Road (North), TianHe District, Guangzhou
Contact: Karen Lee

2013/03/29-31
☎ 020-2831 4758/68/78
🖷 020-8257 9220
www.biometricchina.net
2510

2013中国（广州）国际生物识别技术展览会
地点：保利世贸博览馆，广东广州
主办：广东省对外经济合作企业协会；亚洲建筑技术联盟协会；广东省五金制品协会；香港鸿威国际展览集团
承办：广州市鸿威展览服务有限公司
地址：广州市天河区车陂路318号美景花苑202 203(510660)
联系人：020-2831 4758/68/78

China Guangzhou Intl Biometric Identification Technology Exhibition 2013
Venue: Poly World Trade Expo Center, Guangzhou, Guangdong
Organizer: Guangzhou Grandeur Exhibition Services Co., Ltd

2013/04/01-04
☎ 852-2827 6211
020 - 3810 6261、 3810 6263
🖷 020 - 3810 6200
852-3749 7342
✉ info-hk@ubm.com
led-trust@ubm.com
info-trust@ubm.com
www.ledchina-gz.com
2520

中国（广州）国际广告标识展
地点：中国进出口商品交易会展馆，广东广州
内容：户内外数码喷绘写真设备、UV平板打印机、数码纺织印花机、热转印机、数码影像技术输出设备、条幅机、冷裱机、热裱机、拼接机、覆膜机；喷墨写真墨水、油墨、喷绘布、写真布、蓬盖布、网格布、单透膜、冷裱膜、车身贴、即时贴、背胶、反光材料、相纸等数码打印耗材；激光雕刻机、激光切割机、激光打标机、广告雕刻机、刀具及相关配件；弯字机、刻字机、开槽机、抛光机、吸塑机；展览展示器材、便携式展具系

Sign China
Venue: China Import & Export Fair Complex, Guangzhou, Guangdong
Profile: Indoor & Outdoor Large Format Printer, Inkjet Printer, UV Flatbed Printer, Textile Printer, Thermal Transfer Equipment, Digital Image Output Equipment, Banner Machine, Laminating Machine, Splicing Machine, Screen Printing Equipment; Ink, Printing Ink, Flex, Tents, Mesh, One-way Vision Vinyl, Laminates, Automobile Decal/ Graphics, Adhesive Film, Sticker, Reflective Materials, Inkjet Printer

列、舞台桁架及其他POP产品；灯箱、3D立体产品、多媒体广告机及其他发光产品；标牌、标识产品、三面及多面翻；压克力板材、PVC发泡板、铝塑板、KT板等各类广告板材；广告礼品
始办年份：2005
周期：每年一届
市场范围：国际性
主办：亚洲博闻有限公司
地址：香港湾仔港湾道26号华润大厦17楼
承办：广州闻信展览服务有限公司
地址：广州市天河区林和东华庭路4号富力天河商务大厦1806-1807室（510610）

Paper; Engraving Machine, Laser Engraver, Laser Marking Machine, Engraver, Cutting Tools and Components; Bending Machine, Carving Machine, Slotting Machine, Polishing Machine, Plastic Vacuum Forming Machine; Exhibition and Display Equipment, Portable Display, Stage Display Shelf and other POP items; Lightbox, 3D Products, Multimedia Advertising Machine and other Illuminated Products; Signage, Specialty Sign, Multiple-face Display; Acrylic Panel, PVC Foam Board, Aluminum Composite Panel, KT Board; Promotional Gift, Design Book, Picture Bank and Software, Post Production Technology and Other Miscellaneous; Advertisement Media
Established Year: 2005
Frequency: Annual
Market Area: International
Organizer: UBM Asia Ltd
Address: 17/F, China Resources Building, 26 Harbour Road, Wan Chai, Hong Kong

2013/04/08-10
☎ 020-8358 7012, 8358 7037
🖷 020-8358 7016
✉ expo@ctoy.cn
babyfair@ctoy.cn
www.chinababyfair.com
2530

第4届广州国际婴童用品展
地点：保利世贸博览馆，广东广州
内容：婴儿推车、座椅、幼儿学步车、童车、婴儿纸尿片、婴儿电子用品、婴儿食品、保健品、婴儿玩具、奶瓶奶嘴、婴童床及用品、婴童服、鞋、帽、婴童护肤及沐浴品、婴童教育用品
始办年份：2010
周期：每年一届
市场范围：国际性
性质：面向贸易观众
入场券价格：免费
参展费用：标准展位7,000元/9m^2，光地730元/m^2
上届规模 '12：展览面积47,200m^2，参展商912家，参观人数33,910人（贸易观众5,183人）
主办：广东省玩具协会；广州力通展览服务有限公司
地址：广州市淘金北路正平南街1号金源楼2楼(510095)
联系人：郑小姐，王小姐

4th Guangzhou Intl Baby Product Fair
Venue: Poly World Trade Expo Center, Guangzhou, Guangdong
Profile: Baby Wear, Baby Food, Baby Shoes, Baby Bed/Cot, Baby Booster Seat, Bedding Item, Mother Care, Stroller & Gear, Skincare and Bath Product, Baby Toy and Activity, Feeding and Nursery, Medicine Spoon, Baby Toothbrush, Milk Powder Container
Established Year: 2010
Frequency: Annual
Market Area: International
Nature: Trade Only
Cost to Attend: Free
Participated Fee: Standard Booth RMB 7,000/9m^2, Raw Space RMB 730/m^2
Statistics '12: Exhibition Area 47,200m^2, Exhibitors 912, Visitors 33,910 (Trade Visitors 5,183)
Organizer: Guangdong Toy Association; Guangzhou Litong Exhibition Service Co Ltd
Address: 2F., No.1 Zhengping Street South, Taojin Road North, Guangzhou, Guangdong, China
Contact: Ms Zheng, Ms Wang

2013/04/08-10
☎ 020-8358 7012, 8358 7037
🖷 020-8358 7016
✉ expo@ctoy.cn
fair@ctoy.cn
www.chinatoyfair.com
2540

第25届广州国际玩具及模型展
地点：保利世贸博览馆，广东广州
内容：电子电动玩具、塑胶玩具、布毛绒玩具、娃娃玩具、充气玩具、木制、纸品玩具、学习机、游乐设施、童车、童床、玩具、模型配套产品、动漫形象授权、模型
始办年份：1989
周期：每年一届
市场范围：国际性
性质：面向贸易观众
入场券价格：免费
参展费用：标准展位7,000元/9m^2，光地730元/m^2
上届规模 '12：展览面积47,200m^2，参展商912家，参观人数33,910人
主办：广东省玩具协会；广州力通展览服务有限公司
地址：广州市淘金北路正平南街1号金源楼2楼（510095）
联系人：郑小姐，姚小姐

25th Guangzhou Intl Toy and Hobby Fair
Venue: Poly World Trade Expo Center, Guangzhou, Guangdong
Profile: Electronic and Electrical Toys, Amusement Play-sets, Plastic Toys, Baby Strollers, Ride-ons, Cribs, Plush and Cloth Toys, Toy and Model Supporting Products, Dolls, Animation and Comic Character Licensing, Inflatable Toys, Models, Wooden and Paper Toys, Learning Systems
Established Year: 1989
Frequency: Annual
Market Area: International
Nature: Trade Only
Cost to Attend: Free
Participated Fee: Standard Booth RMB 7,000/9m^2, Raw Space RMB 730/m^2
Statistics '12: Exhibition Area 47,200m^2, Exhibitors 912, Visitors 33,910
Organizer: Guangdong Toy Association; Guangzhou Litong Exhibition Service Co Ltd
Address: 2F., No. 1 Zhengping Street South, Taojin Road North, Guangzhou, Guangdong, China
Contact: Ms Zheng

2013/04/15-05/05
☎ 4000 888 999（境内）
852-2877 1318（香港）
86-20-28 888 999 (overseas)
www.cantonfair.org.cn
2550

第113届中国进出口商品交易会
地点：中国进出口商品交易会展馆，广东广州
内容：第一期4月15-19日展出：家用电器，电子消费品，电子电气产品，计算机及通讯产品，大型机械及设备，小型机械，五金，工具，自行车，摩托车，汽车配件，建筑及装饰材料，卫浴设施，照明产品，化工产品，车辆（室外），工程机械（室外），进口展区等展区。
第二期 4月23-27日展出：餐厨用具，日用陶瓷，工艺陶瓷，家居装饰品，玻璃工艺品，节日用品，玩具，礼品及赠品，钟表眼镜，家居用品，土特产品，个人护理用具，浴室用品，编织及藤铁工艺品，家具，园林产品，铁石制品（室外）等展区。
第三期5月01-05日展出：男女装，内衣，运动服及休闲服，童装，服装饰物与配件，裘革皮羽绒及制品，纺织原料面料，鞋，箱包，地毯及挂毯，家用纺织品，办公文具，食品，医药及保健品，医疗器械、耗材、敷料，体育及旅游休闲用品等展区
承办：中国对外贸易中心

Canton Fair
113th China Import and Export Fair
Venue: China Import & Export Fair Complex, Guangzhou, Guangdong
Profile: April 15-19, Phase 1, Electronics & Household Electrical Appliances, Lighting Equipment, Vehicles & Spare Parts, Machinery, Hardware & Tools, Building Materials, Chemical Products, International Pavilion
April 23-27, Phase 2, Consumer Goods, Gifts, Home Decorations
May 1-5, Phase 3, Textiles & Garments, Shoes, Office Supplies, Cases & Bags, and Recreation Products, Medicines, Medical Devices and Health Products, Food, International Pavilion
Organizer: Organizer: China Foreign Trade Centre

2013/05/09-11
☎ 010-658 1456，5979 2007
🖷 010-8721 3827
✉ nbaking@126.com
🐧 1073934767
www.baking-china.org
2560

2013第十七届中国烘焙展览会
地点：中国进出口商品交易会展馆，广东广州
内容：烘焙食品加工设备、工具、器具及包装设备；西餐厅、咖啡厅、酒吧配料及设备；饼房店铺陈列设备、厨房设施、冷冻、冷藏设备；烘焙业专用原辅材料；专用辅料；食品添加剂；烘焙行业包装设计生产及包装材料、辅料；巧克力制品、仿真模型、蜡烛、蛋糕装饰材料；烘焙书籍、教育培训机构及烘焙企业管理系统
始办年份：1997
周期：每年一届
市场范围：国际性
性质：面向贸易观众
入场券价格：免费
参展费用：标准展位6,200元/9m²，光地620元/m²；国际展商：标准展位2,500美元/9m²，光地250美元/m²
上届规模 '12：展览面积50,000m²(国外展商面积1,200m²)，参展商773家（国外展商46家，来自13个国家），参观人数60,000人（贸易观众30,000人）
主办：中华全国工商业联合会烘焙业公会；北京中连鼎和烘焙食品技术有限公司
地址：北京市朝阳区广渠路3号竞园38A（100124）
联系人：张伟，骆磊
msn：timzhang724@hotmail.com

17th China Bakery Exhibition
Venue: China Import & Export Fair Complex, Guangzhou, Guangdong
Profile: Baking food processing and packaging equipment, tools; Restaurant, cafe, bar ingredients and equipment; Equipment for Pastry shop display, galley, refrigeration; Baking raw and auxiliary materials; dairy products; Chocolate, nuts, fruit, canned stuffing; Food additives; Packaging design, production, and materials; Decorating materials; Baking books, education and training institutions and enterprise management system
Established Year: 1997
Frequency: Annual
Market Area: International
Nature: Trade Only
Cost to Attend: Free
Participated Fee: Standard Booth USD 2,500/9m², Raw Space USD 250/m²
Statistics '12: Exhibition Area 50,000m²(foreigners 1,200m²), Exhibitors 773 (foreigners 46, came from 13 countries), Visitors 60,000 (Trade Visitors 30,000)
Organizer: All-China Bakery Association (A.C.B.A); Beijing Zhonglian Dinghe Bakery Technology Co Ltd
Address: 38A Building, Jingyuan, No.3 Guangqu Road, Chaoyang District, Beijing, China
Contact: Tim Zhang, Luo Lei
msn: timzhang724@hotmail.com

2013/05/10-12
☎ 020-2910 5318, 2910 5328, 2210 2943
🖷 020-2910 5322
✉ watersports@grandeurhk.com
www.chinaboatshow.org
2570

2013中国国际游艇产业博览会
同期举办：2013中国国际水系运动休闲博览会
地点：中国进出口商品交易会展馆，广东广州
内容：休闲艇、旅游观光船艇；竞技艇、运动艇；公务艇；游艇设计；游艇配件；配套服务；高端生活方式；水上运动器材及用品
主办：中国国际贸易促进会广东省委员会；广东省游艇行业协会
承办：广州市鸿威展览服务有限公司
地址：广州市越秀区东风东路836号东峻广场四座2303-2305室

China Intl Boat Show
Venue: China Import & Export Fair Complex, Guangzhou, Guangdong
Organizer: Guangzhou Grandeur Exhibition Services Co., Ltd
Address: Room 2303-2305, the 4th Tower, Dong Jun Plaza, NO.836 of Dong Feng Dong Road, Yuexiu District, Guangzhou, China

2013/05/10-12
☎ 021-5153 8487, 15083469713
🖷 021-6085 3106
✉ shdqzl.2008@163.com
www.china-dqe.com.cn
2580

2013第九届中国（广州）国际食品饮料展
地点：保利世贸博览馆，广东广州
内容：酒及酒精饮料区；饮料展区；粮油与辅料展区：粮油产品、肉制品、辅料；休闲食品展区：蜜饯、坚果、炒货、方便食品、儿童食品、保健食品、冲剂品； 绿色有机食品及营养食品区：特色农产品、有国际和国内认证的绿色/有机食品、营养食品；机械与包装展区
上届规模 '12：展览面积21,000m²，参展商538家，贸易观众28,000人
主办：中国食品土畜进出口商会；上海东琦展览服务有限公司
地址：上海市永泰路1960弄54号502室(200123)
联系人：程磊

9th China Intl Foodstuff (Guangzhou) Exposition 2013
Venue: Poly World Trade Expo Center, Guangzhou, Guangdong
Statistics '12: Exhibition Area 21,000m², Exhibitors 538, Trade Visitors 28,000
Organizer: Shanghai Dongqi Exhibition Service Co Ltd

2013/05/29-31
☎ 852-2851 8603
🖷 852-2851 8637
✉ topreput@top-repute.com
www.shoesleather-guangzhou.com
2590

广州国际鞋类、皮革及工业设备展览会
地点：中国进出口商品交易会展馆，广东广州
内容：鞋类机械、制革机、皮具机、皮革、原皮料、鞋材、化工、配件/辅料
始办年份：1991
周期：每年一届
市场范围：国际性
参展费用：3,150美元/9m²
上届规模 '12：参展商965家，参观人数36,800人
主办：显辉国际展览有限公司；广州市显辉展览服务有限公司
地址：香港干诺道中168-200号信德中心西座2802室

SHOES & LEATHER – GUANGZHOU 2013
International Exhibition on Shoes & Leather Industry-Guangzhou (Machinery & Raw Material)
Venue: China Import & Export Fair Complex, Guangzhou, Guangdong
Profile: Tanning machinery, shoes machinery, raw materials, leather etc.
Established Year: 1991
Frequency: Annual
Market Area: International
Participated Fee: USD 3,150 / booth (9m²)
Statistics '12: Exhibitors 965, Visitors 36,800
Organizer: Top Repute Co. Ltd Top Repute Co. Ltd (Guangzhou)
Address: Unit 2802, Shun Tak Centre, West Tower, Nos.168-200 Connaught Road Central, Hong Kong
Contact: Mr Dennis Lam

2013/05/29-31
☎ 852-2851 8603
🖷 852-2851 8637
✉ topreput@top-repute.com
www.ifle-china.com
2600

广州国际鞋类、皮革制成品展览会
地点：中国进出口商品交易会展馆，广东广州
内容：所有鞋类、皮包和箱包、皮革衣服和产品、时尚皮制饰物配件、知名品牌产品
周期：每年一届
市场范围：国际性
参展费用：2,070美元 / 9m²
上届规模 '12：参展商105家，参观人数5,500人
主办：显辉国际展览有限公司；广州市显辉展览服务有限公司
地址：香港干诺道中168-200号信德中心西座2802室
联系人：刘小姐

IFLE – GUANGZHOU 2013
International Footwear & Leather Products Exhibition Guangzhou
Venue: China Import & Export Fair Complex, Guangzhou, Guangdong
Profile: All kinds of footwear, Bags & Suitcases, Leather Garments, Leather Product, Fashion Accessories & Brand Name Products
Frequency: Annual
Market Area: International
Participated Fee: USD 2,070/ booth (9m²)
Statistics '12: Exhibitors 105, Visitors 5,500
Organizer: Top Repute Co. Ltd Top Repute Co. Ltd (Guangzhou)
Address: Unit 2802, Shun Tak Centre, West Tower, Nos.168-200 Connaught Road Central, Hong Kong.
Contact: Ms. Mandy Lau

2013/06/04-06
☎ 020-6108 9481
🖷 020-6108 9459, 6108 9469
✉ hujun7038@163.com
gzyfzl@qq.com
QQ 1356312831
http://blog.sina.com.cn/hujun7039
www.gzyfzl.com
2610

2013第22届中国（广州）国际医药保健产业博览会
2013第22届全国药品保健品（广州）交易会
第2届中国（广东）药店多元化采购交易会
地点：中国进出口商品交易会展馆，广东广州
主办：中国医药保健国际贸易促进会；广东省保健食品行业协会；广东药店联盟；广州市艺帆展览服务有限公司
地址：广州市天河区燕岭路25-27号银燕大厦201室(510507)
联系人：胡军

22nd China (Guangzhou) Intl Medicine Health Care Industry Expo 2013
2nd China (Guangdong) Pharmacy Purchasing Diversification Fair 2013
Venue: China Import & Export Fair Complex, Guangzhou, Guangdong
Organizer: Guangzhou Yifan Exhibition Service Co Ltd

2013/06/04-06
☎ 020-6108 9492, 020-6137 1549
🖷 020-6108 9459, 6108 9469
✉ gzyfzL2002@163.com
www.gzspzh.com
2620

2013第13届广州国际食品展暨广州进口食品展览会
第14届中国（广州）国际营养品-健康食品及有机产品展览会
地点：中国进出口商品交易会展馆，广东广州
内容：食品、饮料区；营养品及健康食品展区；进口食品展区；食品添加剂及配料区；食品包装及加工设备区
主办：国农业产业经济发展协会；中国粮油学会油脂分会；广东省保健食品行业协会；广州进口食品质量管理协会；广州市艺帆展览服务有限公司
地址：广东广州市天河区燕岭路25-27号201室(510507)
联系人：黄东

13th China (Guangzhou) Intl Food Exhibition and Guangzhou Import Food Exhibition 2013
14th China (Guangzhou) Intl Nutrition & Healthy Food and Organic Products Exhibition
Venue: China Import & Export Fair Complex, Guangzhou, Guangdong
Organizer: Guangzhou Yi Fan Exhibition Service Co Ltd

2013/06/05-07
☎ 020-8922 0105, 8922 0050, 13725309198
🖷 020-8922 0585
✉ china_ch@163.com
info@fce.cn
www.fce.cn/ciame
2630

2013第11届中国（广州）国际汽车零部件展览会
同期举行：2013中国汽车零部件（全球）采供峰会
地点：保利世贸博览馆，广东广州
内容：汽车零部件、零配件，发动机系统、底盘系统、制动系统、行驶系统、转向系统、车身系统、传动系统、排气系统、散热冷却系统、燃油系统，紧固件、密封件、摩擦材料，电机、轴承、蓄电池、滤清器、散热器、仪器仪表、离合器、离合片、刹车片、弹簧、减震器、保险杠、安全气囊、座椅、玻璃、车镜、车用空调、车灯、轮胎、轮毂、链条、防滑链，汽车线束、插接器；车用纺织品，汽车油漆、润滑油、机油、添加剂，汽车电子电器通讯、安全防盗，改装部件，汽车模具，汽车零部件制造技术，清洗设备及包装，新产品，节能环保与新能源技术及产品
主办：中国对外贸易经济合作企业协会
承办：广州一流展览服务有限公司
联系人：上官小姐

11th China (Guangzhou) Intl Auto Parts Expo 2013
11th China (Guangzhou) Intl Automotive Manufacturing Technology & Materials Show 2013
Venue: Poly World Trade Expo Center, Guangzhou, Guangdong
Organizer: First-class Exhibitions Co Ltd

2013/07/08-11
☎ 020-8912 8186, 8912 8198, 8961 6333
🖷 020-8912 8222转ext 303, 8961 6222
✉ cbd@fairwindow.com.cn
boya333@188.com
QQ 1692005827
www.cbd-china.com
2640

第十五届中国（广州）国际建筑装饰博览会
地点：中国进出口商品交易会展馆，广东广州
内容：厨房、衣柜、门窗、地材、卫陶、建筑装饰五金、装饰玻璃/移门、天花吊顶、墙纸/布艺及辅料、楼梯、建筑工程照明、建筑涂料及化学建材、石材、集成家居等
周期：每年一届
市场范围：全国性
性质：面向贸易观众
入场券价格：20元
参展费用：光地1000元/m^2，标准展位10,000元/9m^2
上届规模 '12：展览面积320,000m^2，参展商2,599家，参观人数120,235人
主办：中国对外贸易中心（集团）；中国建筑装饰协会；中国对外贸易广州展览总公司；广州博亚展览发展有限公司
地址：广州市新港东路980号广交会展馆(510335)
联系人：廖小姐，刘小姐

15th China (Guangzhou) Intl Building Decoration Fair
Venue: China Import & Export Fair Complex, Guangzhou, Guangdong
Profile: Kitchen, Sanitary Aare and Building Ceramics, Wardrobe, Floor Covering, Window & Door, Decorative Hardware, Decorative Glass/Slide Door, Ceiling, Wallpaper & Fabric, Stairs, Decorative Lighting, Coating & Chemicals, Stone, Household
Frequency: Annual
Market Area: National
Nature: Trade Only
Cost to Attend: RMB 20:-
Participated Fee: Raw Space 1,000/m^2, Standard Booth RMB 10,000/9m^2
Statistics '12: Exhibition Area 320,000m^2, Exhibitors 2,599, Visitors 120,235
Organizer: China Foreign Trade Center (Group); China Building Decoration Association; China Foreign Trade Guangzhou Exhibition General Corp; Guangzhou Boya Exhibition Development Co Ltd
Address: No.980 Xingang Dong Road, Guangzhou, Guangdong, China

2013/08/09-12
☎ 020-8923 1183, 18026221905, 13710171993
🖷 020-8923 6983
✉ 1549495155@qq.com
www.gzgigf.com
www.yijiaexpo.com
2650

2013广州国际服装节暨广州时装周
地点：中国进出口商品交易会展馆，广东广州
内容：成衣区、童装区、牛仔系列专区、皮衣皮具区，男女服装饰品、面辅料、各类纺织制衣设备及技术。创新设计廊之"创意梦工场"、流行趋势发布专区
主办：广州市人民政府
承办：广州怡佳展览服务有限公司；广州服装行业协会；广州经贸会展服务中心
地址：广州市海珠区新港东路1068号中洲国际商务中心南塔C座909室（510335）
联系人：刘炳霞

Guangzhou Fashion Week
Venue: China Import & Export Fair Complex, Guangzhou, Guangdong
Organizer: Guangzhou Yijia Expo Co Ltd

2013/08/10-12
☎ 020-8923 1214, 8923 1183, 18026221900
🖷 020-8923 6983
QQ 844860767
www.gzicte.com
www.gzgigf.com
2660

2013广州国际缝制制衣设备展
广州国际服装面辅料展览会
地点：中国进出口商品交易会展馆，广东广州
内容：工业缝纫机及其零部件；刺绣设备、裁剪、激光切割设备；整烫、定型、洗涤机械；服装服饰生产控制系统与输送设备；服装服饰CAD/CAM计算机设计、打版及制造系统；纺织服装面料、辅料
主办：广州市人民政府
承办：广州服装行业协会；广州经贸会展服务中心；广州怡佳展览服务有限公司
地址：广州新港东路1068号中洲国际商务中心南塔C座910-911（510335）
联系人：梁磊

Guangzhou Intertextile Apparel Fabrics
Guangzhou Textile Equipment Fair
Venue: China Import & Export Fair Complex, Guangzhou, Guangdong
Organizer: Guangzhou Yijia Expo Co Ltd

2013/08/16-18
☎ 020-3409 5949, 3409 5945, 13798083901
🖷 020-3409 5856
✉ 475782272@qq.com
www.gzyfzl.cpooo.com
2670

2013华南国际老年用品及康复保健器械展览会
同期举办：
医院装备展览会/家庭医疗器械展览会
地点：中国进出口商品交易会展馆，广东广州
内容：特殊医疗器械；特殊助行器械；生活辅助；家具和配件；文化通讯；日常护理用品；休闲娱乐
参展费用：标准展位9m²国内企业7800元，境外企业1,800美元，光地36m²起，国内企业780元/m²，境外企业180美元/m²
主办：中国老龄产业协会老年用品专业委员会；香港巴斯特国际会展集团公司；广东省医疗器械行业协会；广州市医疗器械行业协会
承办：广州益发展览有限公司
地址：广州市新港东路238号世港国际公寓B栋403（510405）
联系人：王梅斌

South China Intl Gerontic Products & Health Care Recovery Instrument Exhibition 2013
Venue: China Import & Export Fair Complex, Guangzhou, Guangdong
Participated Fee: Standard Booth USD 1,800/booth, Raw Space USD 180/m² (min 36m²)
Organizer: Guangzhou Yifa Exhibition Co Ltd

2013/09/02-04
☎ 010-67167461
🖷 010-67161520
✉ cspia@126.com
www.cspia.org
2680

第30届中国国际网印及数字技术展览会
地点：保利世贸博览馆，广东广州
内容：服装及织物印刷、移印、热转印、薄膜开关印刷、电子线路板及电子工业印刷、陶瓷和玻璃印刷、瓶具和容器印刷、广告及大幅面印刷、数字印刷等。
始办年份：1998
周期：每年一届
主办：中国印刷及设备器材工业协会_中国丝网印刷行业协会
地址：北京市东城区左安门内大街4号(100061)

China Screen Print 2013
Venue: Poly World Trade Expo Center, Guangzhou, Guangdong
Established Year: 1998
Frequency: Annual
Organizer: China Screen Printing Industry Association
Address: No. 4 Zuoanmennei Street, Dongcheng District, Beijing 100061, China

2013/09/07-10
☎ 020-8912 8021, 020-8912 8016
🖷 020-89128222
QQ 508487054
www.ciff-gz.com
2690

第三十二届中国（广州）国际家具博览会
地点：中国进出口商品交易会展馆，广东广州
周期：每年两届
市场范围：国际性
性质：面向贸易观众
入场券价格：40元
上届规模：展览面积200,000m²，参展商937家（国外展商130家），参观人数38,472人
主办：中国对外贸易中心(集团)；中国对外贸易广州展览总公司
地址：广州市海珠区新港东路980广交会展馆C区A层(510335_)

32nd China Intl Furniture Fair (Guangzhou)
Venue: China Import & Export Fair Complex, Guangzhou, Guangdong
Frequency: Annual
Market Area: International
Nature: Trade Only
Cost to Attend: RMB 40:-
Statistics '12: Exhibition Area 200,000m², Exhibitors 937 (foreigners 130), Visitors 38,472
Organizer: China Foreign Trade Guangzhou Exhibition General Corporation
Address: Floor A, Hall 16, Area C, Canton Fair Complex, No.980 Xingang Dong Road, Haizhu District, Guangzhou, Guangdong

2013/09/07-09
☎ 020-8989 9051
🖷 020-8989 9050
✉ hci@zhenweiexpo.com
www.hciexpo.com
2695

中国（广州）国际保健产业博览会
地点：中国进出口商品交易会展馆，广东广州
内容：展品涉及保健产业各范畴，包括：营养及保健食品展区、保健用品展区、医疗保健器械展区、睡眠用品展区，以及老年产业用品及设施展区。
周期：每年一届
市场范围：国际性
性质：面向公众和贸易观众
入场券价格：免费
参展费用：标准展位9m²，国内企业：A级展位9,000元；B级展位8,500元；国外企业25,000元；光地(36m²起,另加20元/m²特装管理费)：国内企业900元/m²，国外企业2,500元/m²
预计规模：展出面积50,000m²，参展商1,000，参观人数50,000人
主办：中国营养协会；中国睡眠研究会；中国医疗保健国际交流促进会；广东省保健食品行业协会；广州振威国际展览有限公司
地址：广州市海珠区琶洲大道东1号保利国际广场南塔501-504(510308)
联系人：刘育葵，马玉柱

China (Guangzhou) Intl Health Care Industry Exposition
Venue: China Import & Export Fair Complex, Guangzhou, Guangdong
Profile: All the products relating to the health care industry, for a better exhibition effects, HCI will divide 5 areas: Health-care Food Area, Health-care Supplies Area, Health-care and Medical Treatment Equipments Area, Sleeping Supplies Area, Elderly Industry Supplies and Facilities Area.
Frequency: Annual
Market Area: International
Nature: Open to Public
Cost to Attend: Free
Participated Fee: Standard Booth 9m² RMB 25,000, Raw Space (min 36m², management fee RMB 20/m²) RMB 2,500/m²
Expectation: Gross Area 50,000m², Exhibitors 1,000, Visitors 50,000
Organizer: China Nutrition Society; Chinese Sleep Research Society; CPAMM; Guangdong Health Care Industry Association; Guangzhou Zhenwei Intl Exhibition Co Ltd
Address: Unit 501-504, South Tower, Poly Plaza, No.1 Pazhou Road, Haizhu District, Guangzhou, 510308, China
Contact: Liu Yu Kui, Ma Yu Zhu

2013/09/24-26
☎ 020-8257 8826
🖷 020-8257 8756
✉ asiametal@china.messefrankfurt.com
www.amw-china.com
2698

广州国际金属加工工业展
地点：保利世贸博览馆，广东广州
内容：金属加工制造，金属成型机床，其他机床；精密工具、切削工具、气动和机械手工工具；金属材料，金属板材，金属制品；自动化与运动控制部件；其他制造技术设备
参展费用：光地（36m²起）1,100元/m²；标准展位（18m²起）24,000元/18m²
主办：广州光亚法兰克福展览有限公司
地址：广州市天河区林和西路161号中泰国际广场A2001室(510620)
联系人：刘蒋

asia metal
Guangzhou Intl Metalworking Industry Exhibition
Venue: Poly World Trade Expo Center, Guangzhou, Guangdong
Participated Fee: Raw Space (min 36m²) RMB 1,100/m², Standard Booth (min 18m²) RMB 24,000/18m²
Organizer: Guangzhou Guangya Messe Frankfurt Co Ltd

2013/12/12-15
☎ 020-8730 0161
🖷 020-8778 2615
www.fx306.com
www.gdfoxing.com
2700

第二十届广州酒店用品展览会
地点：中国进出口商品交易会展馆，广东广州
内容：陶瓷制品，酒店配套家具，酒店餐具系列，餐饮系列，酒店大堂系列，酒店客房用品，酒店服饰，饭店管理信息系统，清洁设备及用品，健身器材、康体设备。
主办：广东佛兴展览服务有限公司
地址：广州市番禺区大新商务广场515室

Guangzhou Hotel Show
Venue: China Import & Export Fair Complex, Guangzhou, Guangdong
Organizer: Guangzhou Foxing Exhibition Service Co Ltd

广东-深圳 Guangdong-Shenzhen

2013/02/26-01
☎ 852-2585 6179, 2516 1677
020-8666 0158
🖷 852-3749 7542
020-3749 7542
✉ salescjgf-hk@ubm.com
info-china@ubm.com
www.jewellerynetasia.com
2710

深圳国际黄金珠宝玉石展览会
地点：深圳会展中心，广东深圳
主办：亚洲博闻有限公司
地址：香港湾仔港湾道26号华润大厦17楼
内地联络：博闻（广州）展览有限公司
地址：广东广州市流花路中国大酒店商业大厦1159-1164室(510015)

China Intl Gold, Jewellery & Gem Fair-Shenzhen
Venue: Shenzhen Convention & Exhibition Centre, Shenzhen, Guangdong
Organizer: UBM Asia Ltd
Address: 17/F, China Resources Building, 26 Harbour Road, Wan Chai, Hong Kong

2013/04/10-12
☎ 010-5166 2329,
🖷 010-6818 9519
✉ cefinfo@ceac.com.cn
www.icef.com.cn
2720

第一届中国电子信息博览会
暨2013中国（深圳）消费电子展
地点：深圳会展中心，广东深圳
主办：深圳市人民政府；中国电子信息产业集团有限公司；中国电子视像行业协会；中国电子信息产业商会
承办：中电会展与信息传播有限公司；深圳会展中心管理有限责任公司
地址：北京市复兴路49号(100036)

China Information Technology Expo
81st China Electronic Fair
Venue: Shenzhen Convention & Exhibition Centre, Shenzhen, Guangdong
Organizer: China Electronics Appliance Corporation
Address: 49 Fuxing Road, Beijing 100036, China

2013/04/17-20
☎ 010-8455 6610
🖷 010-8202 2922
www.cmef.com.cn
2730

第69届中国国际医疗器械（春季）博览会
第16届中国国际医疗器械设计与制造技术（春季）展览会
地点：深圳会展中心，广东深圳
内容：涵盖了包括医用影像、体外诊断、电子、光学、急救、康复护理以及医疗信息技术、外包服务等上万种产品，直接并全面服务于医疗器械行业从源头到终端整条医疗产业链
主办：国药励展展览有限责任公司
地址：北京市朝阳区新源南路1-3号平安国际金融中心B座15层(100027)

69th China Intl Medical Equipment Fair-Spring
16th Intl Component Manufacturing & Design Show-Spring
Venue: Shenzhen Convention & Exhibition Centre, Shenzhen, Guangdong
Organizer: Reed Sinopharm Exhibitions Co Ltd

2013/06/08-13
☎ 010-8260 6899
🖷 010-8260 6883
✉ ciccyhuang@cnaico.com.cn
www.cnaico.com.cn
www.autochina.com.cn
2740

第十七届深圳-香港-澳门国际汽车博览会
地点：广东深圳
主办：中国汽车工业国际合作总公司
地址：北京市海淀区中关村丹棱街3号A座

17th Shenzhen-Hong Kong-Macao Intl Automobile Expo
Venue: Shenzhen, Guangdong
Organizer: China National Automotive Industry Intl Corp
Address: A, 3 Danling Street, Zhongguancun, Haidian Dist., Beijing, China

2013/07/08-10
☎ 0755-8347 2856转ext 803
🖷 0755-8347 2509
✉ chixingwen@gmail.com
www.szic.cn
2750

2013第十三届中国（深圳）国际品牌服装服饰交易会
深圳制衣设备展览会
地点：深圳会展中心，广东深圳
内容：品牌女装、男装、孕/婴/童服装、内衣、晚礼服、饰品、面料、辅料、皮具、皮草、制衣机械设备、服装软件、时尚信息、出版物等
参展费用：光地10,000～15,000元/9m^2（36m^{2}起），标准展位11,000元/9m^2
主办：深圳市服装行业协会
承办：环宇时尚展览（深圳）有限公司
地址：深圳市福田区车公庙泰然工业区中国有色大厦11楼 1113室
联系人：迟兴文

13th China Intl Fashion Brand Fair – Shenzhen
Shenzhen Textile Equipment Fair
Venue: Shenzhen Convention & Exhibition Centre, Shenzhen, Guangdong
Participated Fee: Raw Space RMB 10,000-15,000/9m^2 (min 36m^2), Standard Booth RMB 11,000/9m^2
Organizer: Shenzhen Garments Industry Association
Address: 11/F, China Youse Building Tairan Industrial Garden, Futian District, Shenzhen, Guangdong, China 518040

2013/07/11-13
☎ 010-8522 9702, 8522 9596, 8522 9062
🖷 010-8522 9296
2760

深圳国际纺织面料及辅料博览会
地点：深圳会展中心，广东深圳
内容：各类服装面料、辅料、计算机CAD/CAM系统，相关出版物及网络
主办：中国纺织工业联合会
承办：中国贸促会纺织行业分会；法兰克福展览（香港）有限公司；深圳市服装行业协会
联系人：吴知真，宋文，王壮飞

2013 Shenzhen Intl Trade Fair for Apparel Fabrics and Accessories
Venue: Shenzhen Convention & Exhibition Centre, Shenzhen, Guangdong
Organizer: The Sub-Council of Textile Industry CCPIT

2013/07/18-20
☎ 0755-8350 2448, 8350 2452
🖷 0755-8350 2435
✉ luis_wang@163.com
www.e66666.com
www.e66666.net
2770

2013第二十一届多人行国际电子、激光、线缆线束展览会
地点：深圳会展中心，广东深圳
内容：各类触摸屏，各类触摸屏软件，触摸屏材料和设备：玻璃基板、ITO导电玻璃、油墨、导电银浆、ITO薄膜 、薄膜开关、双面胶类、PET保护膜、OCA光学胶、柔性线路板、丝网印刷制版材料设备、LCD精密玻璃切割设备、丝印机、网版、UV机、烤箱、清洁、ESD保护清洁室、净化室耗材、ESD保护设备/设施、净化设备等
主办：深圳市多人行展览有限公司
地址：深圳市福田区新洲路天健名苑A座25A
联系人：王先生

21st DEX Intl Electronic, Laser, Harness Products Exhibition 2013
Venue: Shenzhen Convention & Exhibition Centre, Shenzhen, Guangdong
Organizer: Shenzhen Dowell Exhibition Co Ltd

2013/07/18-20
☎ 0755-8350 2448, 8350 2449
🖷 0755-8350 2435
✉ 1773060138@qq.com
www.drxzl.com
www.ad555.com
2780

2013多人行国际胶粘带、保护膜、光学膜及模切展览会
地点：深圳会展中心，广东深圳
内容：胶粘带，薄膜类，光学膜类，泡棉类，金属箔、橡胶、塑料、棉（布）、纸类、膜类、丝网类等可模切材料；原料及化工产品；设备及仪器，各种胶粘制品与光学膜制造加工过程相关设备。防护系统、分析、测量、测试仪器及相关控制系统、印刷设备。
主办：中国电子学会；广东省包装技术协会；广东省包装技术协会塑料包装委员会；深圳市光学光电子行业协会；深圳市多人行展览有限公司
地址：深圳市福田区新洲路天健名苑A座25A
联系人：丁小姐，但先生

2013 Dowell International Adhesive tape, Protective layer, Optical Film & Die-Cutting Exhibition
Venue: Shenzhen Convention & Exhibition Centre, Shenzhen, Guangdong
Organizer: Chinese Institute of Electronics (CIE); The Packaging Technology Association of Guangdong; Guangdong Packaging Technology Association of Plastic Packaging Committee; Shenzhen Optics and Optoelectronics Manufactures Association; Shenzhen Dowell Exhibition Co Ltd

2013/07/18-20
☎ 0755-8350 2448, 8350 2458
🖷 0755-8350 2435
✉ 1773060138@qq.com
www.drxzl.com
www.e66666.net
2790

2013多人行国际智能手机组装、触摸屏展览会
地点：深圳会展中心，广东深圳
内容：智能手机，手机元器件，手机配件，手机材料，手机设备。触摸屏，触摸屏软件，触摸屏材料和设备。丝网印刷 丝网印刷设备、丝网印刷材料、网版、UV机、烤箱、配件、油墨等。
主办：中国电子学会；深圳市光学光电子行业协会；深圳市多人行展览有限公司
地址：深圳市福田区新洲路天健名苑A座25A
联系人：雷小姐

2013 Dowell Intl Smartphone Assembly & Touch Screen Exhibition
Venue: Shenzhen Convention & Exhibition Centre, Shenzhen, Guangdong
Organizer: Chinese Institute of Electronics (CIE), Shenzhen Optics and Optoelectronics Manufactures Association, Shenzhen Dowell Exhibition Co Ltd

2013/07/18-20
☎ 0755-8350 2448, 8350 2458
🖷 0755-8350 2435
✉ 1773060138@qq.com
www.drxzl.com
www.e66666.cn
2800

2013多人行国际连接器、线束及设备展览会
地点：深圳会展中心，广东深圳
内容：连接器、接插件、配线器材、线束、电子线材、线束设备
主办：深圳市光学光电子行业协会；深圳市多人行展览有限公司
地址：深圳市福田区新洲路天健名苑A座25A
联系人：陈小姐、张小姐

2013 Dowell Intl Connector, Harness and Equipment Exhibition
Venue: Shenzhen Convention & Exhibition Centre, Shenzhen, Guangdong
Organizer: Chinese Institute of Electronics (CIE); Shenzhen Optics and Optoelectronics Manufactures Association; Shenzhen Dowell Exhibition Co Ltd

2013/07/18-20
☎ 0755-8350 2448, 8350 2458
🖷 0755-8350 2435
✉ 1773060138@qq.com
www.drxzl.com
www.e66666.net
2810

2013多人行国际移动电源展览会
地点：深圳会展中心，广东深圳
内容：各类移动电源，移动电源配件及材料、移动电源加工设备、检测设备。
主办：中国电子学会，深圳市光学光电子行业协会，深圳市多人行展览有限公司
地址：深圳市福田区新洲路天健名苑A座25A
联系人：刘小姐

2013 Dowell International Mobile Power Supply Exhibition
Venue: Shenzhen Convention & Exhibition Centre, Shenzhen, Guangdong
Organizer: Chinese Institute of Electronics (CIE); Shenzhen Optics and Optoelectronics Manufactures Association; Shenzhen Dowell Exhibition Co Ltd

2013/07/18-20
☎ 0755-8350 2448, 8350 2458
🖷 0755-8350 2435
www.drxzl.com
www.e66666.cn
2820

2013第21届中国国际电子设备、电子元器件及光电显示展览会
地点：深圳会展中心，广东深圳
内容：电子组装、代工设备 (OEM, ODM, EMS) ；电子元器件、电子组件；平板显示及配套产品、光电产品；激光产品；特设展区：阻容、开关展区；工业机器人、传动设备展区；点胶设备展区；清洗、净化、防静电展区。
主办：中国电子学会，深圳市光学光电子行业协会，深圳市多人行展览有限公司
地址：深圳市福田区新洲路天健名苑A座25A
联系人：刘小姐、何小姐、刘先生、李小姐

21st China Intl Electronic Equipment, Electronic Components and Optoelectronic Display Exhibition
Venue: Shenzhen Convention & Exhibition Centre, Shenzhen, Guangdong
Organizer: Chinese Institute of Electronics (CIE); Shenzhen Optics and Optoelectronics Manufactures Association; Shenzhen Dowell Exhibition Co Ltd

2013/07/18-20
☎ 0755-8350 2448, 8350 2458
🖷 0755-8350 2435
✉ 1773060138@qq.com
www.e66666.com
www.m669.com
2830

2013多人行国际激光展览会
地点：深圳会展中心，广东深圳
主办：中国电子学会，深圳市光学光电子行业协会，深圳市多人行展览有限公司
地址：深圳市福田区新洲路天健名苑A座25A
联系人：唐先生、陈小姐

2013 Dowell Intl Laser Exhibition
Venue: Shenzhen Convention & Exhibition Center, Shenzhen, Guangdong
Organizer: Chinese Institute of Electronics (CIE); Shenzhen Optics and Optoelectronics Manufactures Association; Shenzhen Dowell Exhibition Co Ltd

2013/10/26-27
☎ 0755-8366 3896
🖷 0755-8366 3926
✉ jade_li@idg.com.cn
www.androidworld.net.cn
2840

第二届安卓全球开发者大会
地点：深圳福田香格里拉酒店，广东深圳
内容：汇聚开发者、应用平台、设备制造商、运营商、渠道商、投资机构等商业人士的盛会，是一个主要针对基于Android平台的商业模式探讨、技术交流、移动应用推广的大会，也是一次很好的探索和寻求共同发展、合作共赢的契机。
周期：每年一届
市场范围：国际性
性质：面向公众和贸易观众
主办：IDG美国国际数据集团
承办：IDG爱奇会展有限公司
地址：深圳市福田中心区益田路4068号卓越时代广场2901A室(518048)
联系人：李小姐

2013 Android World Global Developers Conference
Venue: Futian Shangri-La, Shenzhen, Guangdong
Profile: The largest domestic meeting in scale for businessmen concerning developer, application platform, equipment manufacturer, operation, channel operation and investment institute, a great meeting for discussion, technical exchange, mobile application and promotion for commercial mode based on Android platform, and a good chance to search for joint development and win-win.
Frequency: Annual
Market Area: International
Nature: Open to Public
Organizer: International Data Group; IDG World Expo China Co Ltd
Address: Room 2901A, Excellence Times Square Building, Yitian Road, Futian District, Shenzhen, Guangdong
Contact: Ms Li

2013/11/25-27
☎ 13818317905
🖷 021-6484 3355
✉ 762263668@qq.com
2850

2013第十六届深圳国际手机产业展览会暨研讨会
地点：深圳会展中心，广东深圳
内容：移动终端，相关配件及产品，显示部件，包装附属品
周期：每年两届
参展费用：标准展位：国内企业15,800元/9m^2，角位16,800元/9m^2，境外企业4,800美元/9m^2；光地(36m2起)国内企业1,500元/m^2, 境外企业480美元/m^2
主办：中国手机协会；中国触控协会
承办：上海扩展展览服务有限公司
地址：上海市徐汇区漕溪路251弄望族城5号楼602室
联系人：胡靖

CME2013
Venue: Shenzhen Convention and Exhibition Center, Shenzhen, Guangdong
Frequency: Bi-annual
Participated Fee: Standard Booth USD 4,800/9m^2, Raw Space USD 480/m^2
Organizer: Shanghai Kuozhan Exhibition Co Ltd

广东-顺德 Guangdong-Shunde

2013/10/17-20
☎ 020-8755 2468 转ext 19
🖷 020-8755 2970
✉ g.liu@koelnmesse.cn
www.shundeexpo.cn,
www.shundeexpo.com
2860

中国顺德国际家用电器博览会
地点：顺德汇展中心，广东顺德
内容：不要错过这个了解家电行业最新潮流、最新技术以及开拓海内外销售渠道的最佳电器贸易平台。展品范围包括：黑色家电、白色家电、小家电、厨房家电、水家电，卫浴家电、家电配件以及家电相关服务与刊物等。
始办年份：2001
周期：每年一届
市场范围：国际性
主办：科隆展览有限公司；中国机电产品进出口商会；中国贸促会广东省分会；顺德区人民政府
承办：科隆展览有限公司
地址：广州市天河区天河北路183号大都会广场3311室（510620）
联系人：刘桂宜女士

China Shunde Intl Exposition for Household Electrical Appliances
Venue: Shunde Exhibition Center, Shunde, Guangdong
Profile: Don't miss this golden opportunity to keep up to date on the latest industry trends and developments network and do business with the local and international players in the household appliance industry. Exhibit profile includes: Black home appliances, white home appliances, small home appliances, kitchen and bathroom home appliances, water appliances, accessories and components, services and publications
Established Year: 2001
Frequency: Annual
Market Area: International
Sponsor: Koelnmesse Co Ltd; China Chamber of Commerce for Import and Export of Machinery and Electronic Products (CCCME); CCPIT Guangdong Sub-council (CCPIT GD); The People's Government of Shunde
Organizer: Koelnmesse Co Ltd
Address: Rm3311 Metro Plaza, No. 183 Tianhebei Road, Tianhe District, Guangzhou, Guangdong 510620 China
Contact: Ms Grace Liu

广西-南宁 Guangxi-Nanning

2013/06/20-23
☎ 010-8260 6899
🖷 010-8260 6883
www.cnaico.com.cn
www.autochina.com.cn
2870

2013第二届广西汽车文化节
地点：广西南宁
主办：中国汽车工业国际合作总公司
地址：北京市海淀区中关村丹棱街3号A座

2nd Guangxi Automobile Culture Festival
Venue: Nanning, Guangxi
Organizer: China National Automotive Industry Intl Corp
Address: A, 3 Danling Street, Zhongguancun, Haidian Dist., Beijing, China

2013/09/20-24
☎ 0771-581 3169，581 3135，581 3211
🖷 0771-581 3355
✉ liaison@caexpo.org
www.caexpo.org
weibo.com/dongmengbolanhui
2880

中国-东盟博览会
地点：南宁国际会展中心，广西南宁
内容：商品贸易专题，包括中国商品（工程机械及运输车辆、电力与新能源设备、新能源、食品加工与包装机械、建筑材料、电子电器、珠宝首饰、农产品、轻工产品等）、东盟商品（品牌展品、食品农产品、家具家居、工艺品及珠宝饰品、日用消费品、服务业产品等）、中国港澳台商品；投资合作专题，包括国际经济合作展（国际工程承包、劳务合作、资源开发、园区招商、信息通信、基础设施建设等）；先进技术专题，包括农业先进技术展和高新技术展；服务贸易专题，包括金融、教育、旅游；魅力

China-ASEAN Expo
Venue: Nanning Intl Convention & Exhibition Center, Nanning, Guangxi
Profile: Pavilion of Commodity Trade, Chinese Commodity Section（Engineering Machinery & Vehicles, Electric Power & New Energy Equipment, Food Processing & Packaging Machinery, Building Material, Electronics & Electrical Appliances, Jewelry, Agricultural）; ASEAN Commodity Section（Galleria of ASEAN Brands, Agro-based Products & Foodstuffs, Furniture & Furnishings Handicrafts & Jewelry, Consumer Goods, Services）Investment Cooperation;

之城专题；系列高规格国际会议论坛。
始办年份：2004
周期：每年一届
市场范围：国际性
性质：面向贸易观众
入场券价格：凭专业观众证件
参展费用：主会场(南宁国际会展中心) 标准展位：10,000元/9m²，室内光地1,000元/m²，室外光地75美元/m²，500元/m²；分会场：标准展位5,000元/9m²，室内光地500元/m²
上届规模 '12：4,600国际标准展位，参展商2,280家
主办：中国商务部和东盟10国经贸主管部门及东盟秘书处
承办：广西壮族自治区人民政府
地址：广西南宁市竹溪大道98号(530021)

Advanced Technology; Trade in Services; Cities of Charm
Established Year: 2004
Frequency: Annual
Market Area: International
Nature: Trade Only
Participated Fee: Main Venue: Standard Booth RMB 10,000/9m², Raw Space RMB 1,000/m², Outdoor USD 75/m²; Branch Venue: Standard Booth RMB 5,000/9m², Raw Space RMB 500/m²
Statistics '12: Total 4,600 booths, Exhibitors 2,280
Sponsor: The Ministries of Commerce/Trade & Industry of China and the 10 ASEAN countries as well as the Organizer ASEAN Secretariat
Address: No.98, Zhuxi Avenue, Nanning, Guangxi, China

2013/10/28-30
☎ 010-8455 6534, 13701064964
℻ 010-6235 8733
✉ xuetao.wu@reed-sinopharm.com
www.reed-sinopharm.com
2890

第四届中国兽医大会
地点：南宁国际会展中心，广西南宁
内容：兽用疫苗、生物制品、诊断试剂；(进入政府采购名录企业优先) - 兽医诊疗器械、兽医用材料、检验仪器、兽医用书籍及培训机构；畜禽、水产化学药品、原料药、添加剂、用品；宠物药品、宠物诊疗器械、诊断试剂、宠物食品、宠物用品
主办：中国兽医协会，中国动物疫病预防控制中心
承办：国药励展展览有限责任公司
地址：北京市朝阳区新源南路1-3号平安国际金融中心B座15层(100027)
联系人：吴学涛

4th Chinese Veterinary Conference
Venue: Nanning Intl Convention & Exhibition Center, Nanning, Guangxi
Organizer: Reed Sinopharm Exhibitions Co Ltd
Address:

2013/12/05-09
☎ 010-8260 6899
℻ 010-8260 6883
www.cnaico.com.cn
www.autochina.com.cn
2900

2013第六届中国—东盟（南宁）国际汽车展览会
地点：广西南宁
主办：中国汽车工业国际合作总公司
地址：北京市海淀区中关村丹棱街3号A座

6th China-ASEAN (Nanning) Intl Auto Exhibition
Venue: Nanning, Guangxi
Organizer: China National Automotive Industry Intl Corp
Address: A, 3 Danling Street, Zhongguancun, Haidian Dist., Beijing, China

贵州-贵阳 Guizhou-Guiyang

2013/04/11-15
☎ 010-8260 6899
℻ 010-8260 6883
www.cnaico.com.cn
www.autochina.com.cn
2910

2013第三届贵阳国际汽车展览会
地点：贵州贵阳
主办：中国汽车工业国际合作总公司
地址：北京市海淀区中关村丹棱街3号A座

3rd Guiyang Intl Automobile Exhibition
Venue: Guiyang, Guizhou
Organizer: China National Automotive Industry Intl Corp
Address: A, 3 Danling Street, Zhongguancun, Haidian Dist., Beijing, China

---

2013/05/16-18
☎ 0851-689 4453
℻ 0851-685 2878
✉ yaogan888@126.com
www.gzblh.com
2920

2013第8届中国(贵州)国际装备制造业博览会暨中国贵阳国际工业博览会
地点：贵阳国际会展中心，贵州贵阳
内容：投资环境及两化融合展区：航空航天、优势装备制造业科技创新成果，工业城市及工业园区、科研机构和大中专院校，军民两用技术，新型工业化示范基地，大中型企业、投融资机构、重点招商项目、现代服务、工业艺术设计。工业装备专题展区：数控机床、工模具及其附件；工业控制自动化及仪器仪表；五金工具、焊接与切割设备；锻造、冲压、锻压、工业炉及表面处理；流体机械及动力传动；工业与环卫清洁设备；节能环保、电力电工及电气自动化；LED及光电技术；铁路、城市轨道交通技术装备；农业机械、印刷包装及广告设备；结构钢材及加工设备
主办：贵州省人民政府
承办：贵阳市人民政府；贵州省经济和信息化委员会
地址：贵州省贵阳市中华北路181号省经信委干部培训中心5楼(550004)

8th China (Guizhou) Intl Equipment Manufacturing Exposition & China –Guiyang Intl Industry Expo
Venue: Guiyang Convention & Exhibition Center, Guiyang, Guizhou
Organizer: Guizhou Kebo Exhibition & Ad Co Ltd

2013/09/09-13
☎ 0851-528 3203, 0851-528 4027
邮箱exhibition@9expo.cn
www.9expo.cn
2930

2013第三届中国（贵州）国际酒类博览会
地点：贵阳国际会展中心，贵州贵阳
主办：贵州省政府

China (Guizhou) Intl Alcoholic Beverage Expo
Venue: Guiyang Convention & Exhibition Center, Guiyang Guizhou
Organizer: Department of Commerce of Guizhou Province

2013/10/31-03
☎ 010-8260 6899
℻ 010-8260 6883
www.cnaico.com.cn
www.autochina.com.cn
2940

第三届贵阳汽车文化节
地点：贵州贵阳
主办：中国汽车工业国际合作总公司
地址: 北京市海淀区中关村丹棱街3号A座

3rd Guiyang Automobile Culture Festival
Venue: Guiyang, Guizhou
Organizer: China National Automotive Industry Intl Corp
Address: A, 3 Danling Street, Zhongguancun, Haidian Dist., Beijing, China

河北-邯郸 Hebei-Handan

2013/04/28-02
☎ 010-8260 6899
🖷 010-8260 6883
www.cnaico.com.cn
www.autochina.com.cn
2950

中国（邯郸）国际汽车文化节
地点：河北邯郸
主办：中国汽车工业国际合作总公司
地址：北京市海淀区中关村丹棱街3号A座

China (Handan) Intl Automobile Culture Festival
Venue: Handan, Hebei
Organizer: China National Automotive Industry Intl Corp
Address: A, 3 Danling Street, Zhongguancun, Haidian Dist., Beijing, China

河北-唐山 Hebei-Tangshan

2013/05 -
☎ 010-8260 6899
🖷 010-8260 6883
✉ ciccyhuang@cnaico.com.cn
www.cnaico.com.cn
www.autochina.com.cn
2960

2013第十届中国（唐山）国际汽车博览会
地点：河北唐山
主办：中国汽车工业国际合作总公司
地址：北京市海淀区中关村丹棱街3号A座

10th China (Tangshan) Intl Automobile Expo
Venue: Tangshan, Hebei
Organizer: China National Automotive Industry Intl Corp
Address: A, 3 Danling Street, Zhongguancun, Haidian Dist., Beijing, China

黑龙江-哈尔滨 Heilongjiang-Harbin

2013/04/23-25
☎ 0451-8238 8901/02/04/05转8058
🖷 0451-8238 8903
✉ 2656083704@qq.com
2970

2013哈尔滨水处理展会
地点：哈尔滨国际会展体育中心，黑龙江哈尔滨
内容：给排水技术设备、污水处理设备、膜及膜分离技术设备、水消毒与软化除盐、水处理药剂与材料、饮水设备、仪器仪表与自控系统、容器：水箱、贮罐、贮桶、罐体、塑料容器、节水和废水资源化应用技术与设备
主办：中国贸促会哈尔滨市分会；哈尔滨市城乡建设委员会；哈尔滨市环境保护局；哈尔滨市水务局
承办：哈尔滨中信伟业展览有限公司
地址：哈尔滨市黄河路99号黄河绿园小区黄河大厦805室(150090)
联系人：杨洋

Harbin Water Treatment Exhibition
Venue: Harbin Intl Conference Exhibition and Sport Center, Harbin, Heilongjiang
Organizer: Harbin Zhongxin Weiye Exhibition Co Ltd

2013/04/23-25
☎ 0451-8238 8901
🖷 0451-8238 8903
✉ gu15146840836@163.com
2980

2013第11届中国哈尔滨国际门窗幕墙及加工设备展览会
地点：哈尔滨国际会展体育中心，黑龙江哈尔滨
内容：门系列，建筑门窗系列，玻璃、幕墙系列，五金系列，胶粘剂系列，设备与型材系列
主办：中国贸促会哈尔滨市分会；哈尔滨市城乡建设委员会；哈尔滨市住房保障和房产管理局
承办：哈尔滨中信伟业展览有限公司
地址：哈尔滨市南岗区黄河路99号黄河绿园小区黄河大厦805室(150090)

11th China (Harbin) Intl Door and Window Exhibition
Venue: Harbin Intl Conference Exhibition and Sport Center, Harbin, Heilongjiang
Organizer: Harbin Zhongxin Weiye Exhibition Co Ltd

2013/06/15-19
☎ 0451-8234 0100
🖷 0451-8234 0226, 8234 5874
✉ chn@ichtf.com
eng@ichtf.com
kor@ichtf.com
jpn@ichtf.com
www.ichtf.com
2990

HTF

第二十四届中国哈尔滨国际经济贸易洽谈会
地点：哈尔滨国际会展体育中心，黑龙江哈尔滨
内容：中国哈尔滨国际经济贸易洽谈会（以下简称哈洽会）是经中国政府批准举办的国家级、国际性大型经贸展览会，由中华人民共和国商务部、国家发展和改革委员会、中国贸促会、黑龙江省人民政府、浙江省人民政府和哈尔滨市人民政府共同主办，协办单位有俄罗斯联邦经济发展部、俄罗斯联邦地区发展部、日本国际贸易促进协会等10多个境外的政府部门与贸易促进机构共同协办。自1990年创办以来，累计有80多个国家和地区的近190多万中外客商参会参展，总成交额逾千亿美元。哈洽会将为中外客商打造一个投资洽谈，贸易对接和传播友谊的国际平台，成为中外客商开拓国际市场的风向标。
始办年份：1990
市场范围：国际性
性质：面向公众和贸易观众
入场券价格：50元
参展费用：1．室内国际标准展位：A、B、C厅展位 8,000元/9m^2，E厅展位 6,600 元/7.5m^2（3m×2.5m），展览设施包括三面展墙、一张洽谈桌、二把椅子、地毯、两只射灯、一个220V／3A（限500W以内）电源插座、纸篓、中英俄文企业楣板；特装展位：A、B、C厅光地 780元/m^2（36m^{2}起，按9m^{2}递增），E厅光地750元/m^2（30m^{2}起，按7.5m^{2}递增）；机电展区光地 500 元/m^2, 36m^{2}起，按9m^{2}递增；机电展区（展览篷房）标准展位:5,200元/9m^2，展览设施包括三面展墙、一张洽谈桌、三把椅子、两只

The 24th China Harbin International Economic and Trade Fair
Venue: Harbin Intl Conference Exhibition and Sport Center, Harbin, Heilongjiang
Profile: China Harbin International Economic and Trade Fair (Harbin Trade Fair) is a large-scale national level international fair approved by the Chinese government. The fair is sponsored by the Ministry of Commerce of the People's Republic of China, National Development and Reform Commission, CCPIT, the People's Government of Heilongjiang Province, the People's Government of Zhejiang Province, the People's Government of Harbin Municipality and co-sponsored by governmental departments and trade promotional institutions from over 10 countries including Ministry of Economic Development of the Russian Federation, Ministry of Regional Development of the Russian Federation, the Association of the Promotion of International Trade of Japan. Since its first session in 1990, 1.9 million exhibitors and visitors from more than 80 countries and regions attended the fair with over USD 100 billion contract volumes concluded. Harbin Trade Fair has become an international platform to develop trade negotiation, investment and cooperation for exhibitors and visitors from home and abroad, and the wind vane to explore overseas market.
Established Year: 1990
Market Area: International
Nature: Open to Public
Cost to Attend: RMB 50:-

射灯、一个220V／3A（限500W以内）电源插座、中英俄文企业楣板。展品装卸免费，设备演示连接电源用电缆自备，电费另付；机电展区（室外广场）展期200元/m²50m²起
上届规模 '12：展览面积86,000m²(国外展商面积10,000m²)，参展商2,200家家（国外展商220家家，来自21个国家），参观人数32万人（贸易观众12万人）
主办：中华人民共和国商务部；中华人民共和国国家发展和改革委员会；中国贸促会；黑龙江省人民政府；浙江省人民政府；哈尔滨市人民政府
承办：中国哈尔滨经济贸易洽谈会办公室
地址：中国哈尔滨市南岗区美顺街35号(150090)
联系人：张玉虹，袁笛

Participated Fee: Hall A、B、C RMB 8,000/9m², Hall E RMB 6,600 /7.5m² （3x2.5m）; Raw Space: Hall A、B、C RMB 780/m² (min 36m²), Hall E RMB 750元/m² (min 30m²), Outdoor Raw Space RMB 200/m² (min 50m²)
Statistics '12: Exhibition Area 86,000m² (foreigners 10,000m²), Exhibitors 2,200 (foreigners 220 came from 21 countries), Visitors 320,000 (Trade Visitors 120,000)
Organizer: Ministry of Commerce of the People' s Republic of China; National Development and Reform Commission, CCPIT; The People' s Government of Heilongjiang Province; The Peoples Government of Zhejiang Province; The People' s Government of Harbin Municipality
Contact: The Administration Office of China Harbin Economic and Trade Fair
Address: No.35 Meishun St., Nangang Dist., Harbin, Heilongjiang, China
Contact: Zhang Yuhong, Yuan Di

2013/09/05-08
☎ 010-6590 7766
🖷 010-6590 6139
✉ info@koelnmesse.cn
www.harbin-agri-expo.cn
3000

哈尔滨世界农业博览会
地点：哈尔滨国际会展体育中心，黑龙江哈尔滨
主办：科隆展览国际有限公司
地址：北京东三环北路8号亮马河大厦2座1018室(100004)

Agriculture & Food Expo Harbin
Venue: Harbin Intl Conference Exhibition and Sport Center, Harbin, Heilongjiang
Organizer: KOELNMESSE
Address: Unit 1018, Landmark Tower II, No. 8 Dongsanhuan North Rd, Beijing 100004, China

河南-洛阳 Henan-Luoyang

2013/04 -
☎ 010-8260 6899
🖷 010-8260 6883
✉ ciccyhuang@cnaico.com.cn
www.cnaico.com.cn
www.autochina.com.cn
3010

2013年中国洛阳国际汽车展览会
地点：河南洛阳
内容：2013年4月和10月
主办：中国汽车工业国际合作总公司
地址：北京市海淀区中关村丹棱街3号A座

China (Luoyang) Intl Automobile Exhibition
Venue: Luoyang, Henan
Organizer: China National Automotive Industry Intl Corp
Address: A, 3 Danling Street, Zhongguancun, Haidian Dist., Beijing, China

河南-郑州 Henan-Zhengzhou

2013/01 -
☎ 0371-6808 9866
www.zzicec.com
3020

中原珠宝风尚大典–中国（郑州）珠宝首饰博览会
地点：郑州国际会展中心，河南郑州

China (Zhengzhou) Jewellery Expo
Venue: Zhengzhou Intl Convention & Exhibition Center, Zhengzhou, Henan

2013/01-
☎ 0371-6808 9866
www.zzicec.com
3030

年货采购会
地点：郑州国际会展中心，河南郑州

New Year Shopping Festival
Venue: Zhengzhou Intl Convention & Exhibition Center, Zhengzhou, Henan

2013/03 -
☎ 0371-6808 9866
www.zzicec.com
3040

2013年春季第22届郑州中原广告展
地点：郑州国际会展中心，河南郑州

2013 Spring Zhengzhou Central Plain Advertisement Exhibition
Venue: Zhengzhou Intl Convention & Exhibition Center, Zhengzhou, Henan

2013/03 -
☎ 0371-6808 9866
www.zzicec.com
3050

第23届中原医疗器械（2013年春季）展览会
第23届中原口腔设备及材料（2013年春季）展览会
地点：郑州国际会展中心，河南郑州

2013 Spring Central Plain Intl Medical Apparatus and Instruments Exhibition
Venue: Zhengzhou Intl Convention & Exhibition Center, Zhengzhou, Henan

2013/03/12-14
☎ 0371-6675 9160
🖷 0371-6675 9136/7/8
✉ 1498843754@qq.com
www.dhbhz.com
3060

2013年第13届中国中部橱柜衣柜及配套材料博览会
地点：中原国际博览中心，河南郑州
内容：定制家居、橱柜、移门、配套材料展区
主办：大河报社，中原国际博览中心
地址：河南省郑州市郑汴路106号中原国际博览中心办公楼306室
联系人：常晓静

Central China Cabinet, Wardrobe and Supporting Materials Fair
Venue: Central China Intl Exhibition Center, Zhengzhou, Henan
Organizer: Dahe Newspaper; Central China Intl Exhibition Center

2013/04-
☎ 0371-6808 9866
www.zzicec.com
3070

2013春季中原住交会
地点：郑州国际会展中心，河南郑州

2013 Central China Real Estate Fair (Spring)
Venue: Zhengzhou Intl Convention & Exhibition Center, Zhengzhou, Henan

2013/04/-
☎ 0371-6808 9866
www.zzicec.com
3080

2013中国中部（郑州）国际装备制造业博览会
（暨第十五届中原国际装备制造业博览会）
地点：郑州国际会展中心，河南郑州

2013 Central China Intl Equipment Manufacturing Industry Expo
Venue: Zhengzhou Intl Convention & Exhibition Center, Zhengzhou, Henan

2013/04 -
☎ 0371-6808 9866
www.zzicec.com
3090

2013第十一届中国（郑州）社会公共安全产品博览会
地点：郑州国际会展中心，河南郑州

2013 China (Zhengzhou) Security Science Product Exhibition
Venue: Zhengzhou Intl Convention & Exhibition Center, Zhengzhou, Henan

2013/04 -
☎ 0371-6808 9866
www.zzicec.com
3100

2013大河新生活方式展（汽车展）
地点：郑州国际会展中心，河南郑州

A new way of life, 2013 Spring Dahe- Auto Show
Venue: Zhengzhou Intl Convention & Exhibition Center, Zhengzhou, Henan

2013/04/-
☎ 0371-6808 9866
www.zzicec.com
3110

全国宠物展
地点：郑州国际会展中心，河南郑州

National Pet Show
Venue: Zhengzhou Intl Convention & Exhibition Center, Zhengzhou, Henan

2013/04/-
☎ 010-6859 6265, 6852 7326
🖷 010-6852 7326, 6853 0069
www.camf.com.cn
3120

全国春季农机展
中国农业机械展览会
地点：郑州国际会展中心，河南郑州
主办：中国农业机械流通协会；中国农业机械化协会

CAMF
China Intl Agricultural Machinery Exhibition 2013
Venue: Zhengzhou Intl Convention & Exhibition Center, Zhengzhou, Henan
Organizer: China Agricultural Machinery Distribution Association; China Association of Agricultural Machinery Manufacturers

2013/05 -
☎ 0371-6808 9866
www.zzicec.com
3130

中部博览会
地点：郑州国际会展中心，河南郑州

Central China Expo
Venue: Zhengzhou Intl Convention & Exhibition Center, Zhengzhou, Henan

2013/05 -
☎ 0371-6808 9866
www.zzicec.com
3140

第三届中国郑州国际家具展
地点：郑州国际会展中心，河南郑州

The Third Zhengzhou International Furniture Fair
Venue: Zhengzhou Intl Convention & Exhibition Center, Zhengzhou, Henan

2013/05-
☎ 0371-6808 9866
www.zzicec.com
3150

欧亚国际酒店用品展
地点：郑州国际会展中心，河南郑州

(Zhengzhou) Intl Hotel Supplies Show
Venue: Zhengzhou Intl Convention & Exhibition Center, Zhengzhou, Henan

2013/05 -
☎ 0371-6808 9866
www.zzicec.com
3160

2013第九届中国食品包装及加工设备（郑州）展览会
地点：郑州国际会展中心，河南郑州
主办：郑州国际会展中心营销部

2013 China (Zhengzhou) Food Packaging and Processing Equipment Show
Venue: Zhengzhou Intl Convention & Exhibition Center, Zhengzhou, Henan

2013/05 -
☎ 0371-6808 9866
www.zzicec.com
3170

瑞城郑州全国糖酒食品交易会
地点：郑州国际会展中心，河南郑州

Ruicheng Zhengzhou Sugar and Wine Trade Fair
Venue: Zhengzhou Intl Convention & Exhibition Center, Zhengzhou, Henan

2013/05 -
☎ 0371-6808 9866
www.zzicec.com
3180

中国肉类工业（郑州）展览会
地点：郑州国际会展中心，河南郑州

China (Zhengzhou) Meat Industry Show
Venue: Zhengzhou Intl Convention & Exhibition Center, Zhengzhou, Henan

2013/05/27-29
☎ 0371-6097 0172
🖷 0371-6097 0173
www.lcexpo.cn
3190

2013中国（郑州）国际纺织面料、辅料及纱线展览会
2013第十届中国（郑州）国际缝纫设备展览会
地点：郑州国际会展中心，河南郑州
内容：面料、纤维、辅料；刺绣、花边、衬里
主办：河南省服装行业协会
承办：河南省商务厅；郑州大路展览有限公司

China (Zhengzhou) Intl Textile Fabrics, Accessories & Yarn Exhibition
2013 China (Zhengzhou) Sewing Equipments and Textile Show
Venue: Zhengzhou Intl Convention & Exhibition Center, Zhengzhou, Henan
Organizer: Zhengzhou Dalu Exhibition Co Ltd

2013/06 -
☎ 0371-6808 9866
www.zzicec.com
3200

2013年第五届中国郑州烘焙展览会
2013年第五届中国郑州食品保鲜及冷冻、冷藏技术展览会
地点：郑州国际会展中心，河南郑州

Zhengzhou Baking Technology Expo
Food Refrigeration Technology Show
Venue: Zhengzhou Intl Convention & Exhibition Center, Zhengzhou, Henan

2013/06 -
☎ 0371-6808 9866
www.zzicec.com
3210

2013年第三届中国（郑州）国际微型汽车配件博览会
2013年中国国际轿车配件（郑州）博览会
2013年中国润滑油及汽保设备展览会
地点：郑州国际会展中心，河南郑州

2013 China (Zhengzhou) Intl Mini-car Accessories Expo and Lubricants, Tires, Auto Maintenance Equipment Exhibition
Venue: Zhengzhou Intl Convention & Exhibition Center, Zhengzhou, Henan

2013/06 -
☎ 0371-6808 9866
www.zzicec.com
3220

2013河南省夏季种子信息交流暨产品展览会
地点：郑州国际会展中心，河南郑州

Henan Summer Seed Information Products Show
Venue: Zhengzhou Intl Convention & Exhibition Center, Zhengzhou, Henan

2013/06 -
☎ 0371-6808 9866
www.zzicec.com
3230

中原国际汽车博览会暨中原国际汽车文化旅游节
地点：郑州国际会展中心，河南郑州

Cars & Automotive Culture and Tourism Festival
Venue: Zhengzhou Intl Convention & Exhibition Center, Zhengzhou, Henan

2013/06 -
☎ 0371-6808 9866
www.zzicec.com
3240

2013年（海名）中国郑州珠宝首饰玉石展览会
2013年中国郑州奢侈品收藏品古典家具展览会
地点：郑州国际会展中心，河南郑州

2013 China (Haiming) Jewelry Show
Venue: Zhengzhou Intl Convention & Exhibition Center, Zhengzhou, Henan

2013/06/01-03
☎ 0371-5563 2776, 15937108871
🖷 0371-5569 0333
✉ 1404359262@qq.com
www.ciaaff.org
3250

2013年全国微型汽车配件展览会
地点：郑州国际会展中心，河南郑州
内容：轿车微车零部件；汽车改装及用品；汽车配件、汽车材料、通用部件节能、汽车用品、环保、新能源技术及产品
主办：中华全国工商业联合会汽车摩托车配件用品业商会；郑州市人民政府
承办：郑州东信展览有限公司；北京东信国际会展有限公司
地址：郑州市郑东新区商务内环路金成阳光世纪20号楼707室
联系人：王艳

2013 China (Zhengzhou) Intl Car & Mini Auto Parts Expo
Venue: Zhengzhou Intl Convention & Exhibition Center, Zhengzhou, Henan
Organizer: Dongxin Exhibition Group

2013/07 -
☎ 0371-6576 0078,6339 6977, 65760168
www.zzicec.com
3260

2013中国国际汽车后市场博览会暨
中国汽车用品（郑州）交易会
地点：郑州国际会展中心，河南郑州

China (Zhengzhou) Automobile Product Fair
Venue: Zhengzhou Intl Convention & Exhibition Center, Zhengzhou, Henan
Organizer: Hongda Exhibition

2013/08 -
☎ 0371-6808 9866
www.zzicec.com
3270

2013年（海名）中国郑州珠宝首饰玉石展览会
2013年中国郑州奢侈品收藏品古典家具展览会
地点：郑州国际会展中心，河南郑州

2013 China (Haiming) Jewelry Show
Venue: Zhengzhou Intl Convention & Exhibition Center, Zhengzhou, Henan

2013/08 -
☎ 0371-6808 9866
www.zzicec.com
3280

2013第十二届瑞城郑州全国糖酒食品交易会
2013第三届瑞城郑州国际葡萄酒及烈酒展览会
2013第三届瑞城郑州面业暨精品粮油交易会
地点：郑州国际会展中心，河南郑州

2013 Ruicheng-Zhengzhou Sugar and Wine Trade Fair
Zhengzhou Intl Wine Fair
Reicheng Flour, Food and Oil Fair
Venue: Zhengzhou Intl Convention & Exhibition Center, Zhengzhou, Henan

2013/08/23-25
☎ 0371-6369 6191
🖷 0371-6392 3100
✉ zzhmhz@126.com
www.zzhaiming.com
3290

2013第九届中国（郑州）国际机床及工模具展览会
2013年第八届中国郑州工业装备博览会
地点：郑州国际会展中心，河南郑州
主办：中国机械工程学会；河南省工业经济联合会；中国国际贸易促进联合会
承办：郑州海名汇博会展策划有限公司
地址：郑州市经七路37号和众商务中心502室
联系人：刘慧芳

2013 China Machine Tool, Expo
Venue: Zhengzhou Intl Convention & Exhibition Center, Zhengzhou, Henan
Organizer: Zhengzhou Haiming Huibo Exhibition Planning Co Ltd

2013/09 -
☎ 0371-6808 9866
www.zzicec.com
3300

第24届中原医疗器械（2013年秋季）展览会
地点：郑州国际会展中心，河南郑州

2013 Autumn Central Plain International Medical Instruments Exhibition
Venue: Zhengzhou Intl Convention & Exhibition Center, Zhengzhou, Henan

2013/09 -
☎ 0371-6808 9866
www.zzicec.com
3310

2013全国郑州商品交易会
地点：郑州国际会展中心，河南郑州

Zhengzhou National Commodity Fair
Venue: Zhengzhou Intl Convention & Exhibition Center, Zhengzhou, Henan

2013/09 -
☎ 0371-6808 9866
www.zicec.com
3320

第4届中国国际时尚发制品及美发用品展览会
地点：郑州国际会展中心，河南郑州

4th China Intl Fashion Hair Products and Hair Care Products Exhibition
Venue: Zhengzhou Intl Convention & Exhibition Center, Zhengzhou, Henan

2013/09/-
☎ 0371-6808 9866
www.zicec.com
3330

2013河南省家禽交易会
地点：郑州国际会展中心，河南郑州

2013 Henan Poultry Exhibition
Venue: Zhengzhou Intl Convention & Exhibition Center, Zhengzhou, Henan

2013/09 -
☎ 0371-6808 9866
www.zicec.com
3340

2013年中国郑州建筑节能及新型建材博览会
2013年中国郑州照明LED展览会
地点：郑州国际会展中心，河南郑州

2013 China (Zhengzhou) LED Lighting Exhibition
Venue: Zhengzhou Intl Convention & Exhibition Center, Zhengzhou, Henan

2013/10 -
☎ 0371-6808 9866
www.zicec.com
3350

2013河南省秋季种子信息交流暨产品展览会
2013河南省植保信息交流暨农药械交流会
地点：郑州国际会展中心，河南郑州

Henan Autumn Seed Information Products Show
Venue: Zhengzhou Intl Convention & Exhibition Center, Zhengzhou, Henan

2013/10/31-11/04
☎ 010-8260 6899
🖷 010-8260 6883
✉ ciccyhuang@cnaico.com.cn
www.cnaico.com.cn
www.autochina.com.cn
3360

2013年第六届郑州国际汽车展览会
地点：郑州国际会展中心，河南郑州
主办：中国汽车工业国际合作总公司
地址：北京市海淀区中关村丹棱街3号A座

6th Zhengzhou Intl Automobile Exhibition 2013
Venue: Zhengzhou Intl Convention & Exhibition Center, Zhengzhou, Henan
Organizer: China National Automotive Industry Intl Corp
Address: A, 3 Danling Street, Zhongguancun, Haidian Dist., Beijing, China

2013/11-
☎ 0371-6808 9866
www.zicec.com
3370

磨料磨具展览会
地点：郑州国际会展中心，河南郑州
主办：郑州国际会展中心营销部

Abrasives Exhibition
Venue: Zhengzhou Intl Convention & Exhibition Center, Zhengzhou, Henan

2013/11 -
☎ 0371-6808 9866
www.zicec.com
3380

秋季时尚（郑州）购物节
地点：郑州国际会展中心，河南郑州

Autumn Fashion Shopping Festival (Zhengzhou)
Venue: Zhengzhou Intl Convention & Exhibition Center, Zhengzhou, Henan

湖北-武汉 Hubei-Wuhan

2013/04/25-27
☎ 010-8455 6677
🖷 010-6203 3210
www.pharmchina.com.cn
3390

第69届全国药品交易会
地点：武汉国际博览中心，湖北武汉
内容：PHARMCHINA涵盖了医药制剂领域的所有产品，包括：化学药、中成药、生物制药、OTC药品、健康产品、医药相关技术与服务等，是洞悉医药领域变化和最新发展趋势的绝佳平台
主办：国药励展展览有限责任公司

PHARMCHINA
Venue: Wuhan Intl Expo Center, Wuhan, Hubei
Organizer: Reed Sinopharm Exhibitions Co Ltd

2013/04/25-27
☎ 010-8455 6677
🖷 010-6203 3210
www.apichina.com.cn
3400

第70届中国国际医药原料药、中间体、包装、设备交易会
地点：武汉国际博览中心，湖北武汉
主办：国药励展展览有限责任公司
地址：北京市朝阳区新源南路1-3号平安国际金融中心B座15层(100027)

APi China
Venue: Wuhan Intl Expo Center, Wuhan, Hubei
Profile: exhibition for the pharmaceutical manufacturing sector covering the complete spectrum of products from raw material, fine chemical, intermediate, ingredients, processing machinery and packaging machinery
Organizer: Reed Sinopharm Exhibitions Co Ltd

2013/05/18-20
☎ 010-5867 7700转ext 885
🖷 010-5867 7809
✉ liudan@caaa.cn
www.bio-energy-expo.com
3410

第四届（2013）中国国际生物质能源展
地点：武汉国际博览中心，湖北武汉
内容：沼气工程、技术、设备；能源工程；能源传输；有机肥处理与加工；检测、测量和系统控制；清洁能源机制CDM项目；金融、咨询、服务等
周期：每年一届
主办：中国畜牧业协会；德国农业协会
联系人：刘丹

Bio-Energy-Expo 2013
Trade Exhibition for Biogas-Technology and Management
4th Intl Bio-Energy Conference
Venue: Wuhan Intl Expo Center, Wuhan, Hubei
Frequency: Annual
Organizer: China Animal Agricultural Association (CAAA); DLG International GmbH

2013/05/23-28
☎ 010-8260 6899
🖷 010-8260 6883
✉ ciccyhuang@cnaico.com.cn
www.cnaico.com.cn
www.autochina.com.cn
3420

2013年第十一届华中国际汽车展览会
地点：湖北武汉
主办：中国汽车工业国际合作总公司
地址：北京市海淀区中关村丹棱街3号A座

11th Central China Automobile Exhibition
Venue: Wuhan, Hubei
Organizer: China National Automotive Industry Intl Corp
Address: A, 3 Danling Street, Zhongguancun, Haidian Dist., Beijing, China

2013/10/18-23
☎ 021-5045 6700，5045 6700
🖷 021-5045 9355，5045 9355
✉ karl.wang@hmf-china.com
www.wh-motorshow.com
3430

武汉国际汽车展览会
地点：武汉国际博览中心，湖北武汉
内容：中国中部地区最具规模的国际汽车展览会
始办年份：1995
周期：每年一届
市场范围：国际性
性质：面向公众和贸易观众
主办：成都世纪城新国际会展中心有限公司；汉诺威米兰展览（上海）有限公司；湖北省机械行业联合会；中国贸促会武汉市分会
地址：上海市浦东新区银霄路393号百安居浦东商务大厦301室汉诺威米兰展览（上海）有限公司(201204)
联系人：王飞

Wuhan Motor Show 2013
Venue: Wuhan Intl Expo Center, Wuhan, Hubei
Profile: Intel Exhibition for Automobile and Accessories
Established Year: 1995
Frequency: Annual
Market Area: International
Nature: Open to Public
Organizer: CCPIT Automotive Industry Committee; Chengdu Century City Convention & Exhibition Center; Hannover Milano Fairs Shanghai Ltd; Hubei Machinery Industry Federation; CCPIT Wuhan Sub-Council
Address: Hannover Milano Fairs Shanghai Ltd, Rm. 301, B&Q Pudong Office Tower, 393 Yinxiao Rd, Pudong, Shanghai
Contact: Karl Wang

2013/10/30-11/02
☎ 021-5045 6700，5045 6700
🖷 021-5045 9355，5045 9355
✉ austin.wang@hmf-china.com
http://ccvs.hmf-china.com
3440

2013中国国际商用车展览会
地点：武汉国际博览中心，湖北武汉
内容：国内权威商用车行业盛会
周期：两年一届
市场范围：国际性
性质：面向贸易观众
上届规模：展览面积60,000m^2
主办：湖北省人民政府；武汉市人民政府湖北省经济和信息化委员会；汉阳专用汽车研究所；汉诺威米兰展览（上海）有限公司；湖北省汽车行业协会；武汉新城国际博览中心；武汉经济技术开发区管委会；北京三达经济技术合作开发中心
地址：上海市浦东新区银霄路393号百安居浦东商务大厦301室汉诺威米兰展览（上海）有限公司(201204)
联系人：汪村彦

China Commercial Vehicles Show 2013
Venue: Wuhan Intl Expo Center, Wuhan, Hubei
Profile: Leading Trade Fair for Commercial Vehicles and Accessories in China
Frequency: Biennial
Market Area: International
Nature: Trade Only
Statistics '11: Exhibition Area 60,000m^2
Organizer: Hubei Provincial People's Government; Wuhan Municipal People's Government; Hubei Economy and Information Technology Commission; Hanyang Special Purpose Vehicle Institute; Hannover Milano Fairs Shanghai Ltd; Hubei Auto Industry Association; Wuhan New City Intl Expo Center Co Ltd; Administrative Commission of Wuhan Economic & Technological Development Zone; Beijing Sanda Economic and Technological Center
Address: Hannover Milano Fairs Shanghai Ltd, Rm. 301, B&Q Pudong Office Tower, 393 Yinxiao Rd, Pudong, Shanghai, China
Contact: Austin Wang

2013/11/29-12/02
☎ 010-8260 6899
🖷 010-8260 6883
✉ ciccyhuang@cnaico.com.cn
www.cnaico.com.cn
www.autochina.com.cn
3450

2013楚天汽车文化节
地点：湖北武汉
主办：中国汽车工业国际合作总公司
地址：北京市海淀区中关村丹棱街3号A座

Hubei Automobile Culture Festival
Venue: Wuhan, Hubei
Organizer: China National Automotive Industry Intl Corp
Address: A, 3 Danling Street, Zhongguancun, Haidian Dist., Beijing, China

湖北-株洲 Hubei-Zhuzhou

2013/11 -
☎ 010-8260 6899
🖷 010-8260 6883
www.cnaico.com.cn
www.autochina.com.cn
3460

中国（株洲）国际汽车及新能源汽车展示交易会
地点：湖南株州
主办：中国汽车工业国际合作总公司
地址：北京市海淀区中关村丹棱街3号A座

China (Zhuzhou) Intl Automobile and New Energy Car Exhibition
Venue: Zhuzhou, Hunan
Organizer: China National Automotive Industry Intl Corp
Address: A, 3 Danling Street, Zhongguancun, Haidian Dist., Beijing, China

内蒙古-包头 Inner Mongolia-Baotou

2013/08/30-09/01
☎ 400 676 3090
🖷 400 676 3090转ext 8
✉ 804402058@qq.com
804402058
www.nmgexpo.com/food
3470

第九届内蒙古国际食品博览会
地点：包头国际会展中心，内蒙古包头
内容：加工机械及包装材料展区，酒类及软饮料展区，茶类展区，餐饮调味品展区，绿色食品、有机食品、农副土特产展区，冷冻包装食品展区
主办：内蒙古自治区食品安全委员会
承办：内蒙古艾克思博会展有限公司
地址：内蒙古呼和浩特市新华东街长安金座B座1906室(010000)
联系人：郑峰

9th Inner Mongolia Food Expo
Venue: Baotou, Inner Mongolia
Organizer: Inner Mongolia Aikesi Conference and Exhibition Co Ltd

2013/09 -
☎ 010-8260 6899
🖷 010-8260 6883
✉ ciccyhuang@cnaico.com.cn
www.cnaico.com.cn
www.autochina.com.cn
3480

第三届中国包头国际汽车展览会
地点：内蒙古包头
主办：中国汽车工业国际合作总公司
地址：北京市海淀区中关村丹棱街3号A座

3rd China (Inner Mongolia) Intl Automobile Exhibition
Venue: Baotou, Inner Mongolia
Organizer: China National Automotive Industry Intl Corp
Address: A, 3 Danling Street, Zhongguancun, Haidian Dist., Beijing, China

内蒙古-呼和浩特 Inner Mongolia-Hohhot

2013/04/12-14
☎ 400 676 3090
🖷 400 676 3090转ext 8
✉ 804402058@qq.com
804402058
www.nmgexpo.com/food
3490

第八届内蒙古国际食品博览会
地点：呼和浩特国际会展中心，内蒙古呼和浩特
主办：内蒙古自治区食品安全委员会
地址：内蒙古呼和浩特市新华东街长安金座B座1906室(010000)
联系人：郑峰

8th Inner Mongolia Intl Food Expo
Venue: Hohhot, Inner Mongolia
Organizer: Inner Mongolia Aikesi Conference and Exhibition Co Ltd

2013/07/19-23
☎ 010-8260 6899
🖷 010-8260 6883
✉ ciccyhuang@cnaico.com.cn
www.cnaico.com.cn
www.autochina.com.cn
3500

2013年第五届呼和浩特国际汽车展览会
地点：内蒙古呼和浩特
预计规模：总面积50,000m^2
主办：中国汽车工业国际合作总公司
地址：北京市海淀区中关村丹棱街3号A座
联系人：姜东，黄燕，卞祖新，何朗

5th Hohhot Intl Automobile Exhibition 2013
Venue: Hohhot, Inner Mongolia
Expectation: Gross Area 50,000m^2
Organizer: China National Automotive Industry Intl Corp
Address: A, 3 Danling Street, Zhongguancun, Haidian Dist., Beijing, China

2013/09 -
☎ 010-8260 6899
🖷 010-8260 6883
✉ ciccyhuang@cnaico.com.cn
www.cnaico.com.cn
www.autochina.com.cn
3510

呼和浩特汽车文化节
地点：内蒙古呼和浩特
主办：中国汽车工业国际合作总公司
地址：北京市海淀区中关村丹棱街3号A座

Hohhot Automobile Culture Festival
Venue: Hohhot, Inner Mongolia
Organizer: China National Automotive Industry Intl Corp
Address: A, 3 Danling Street, Zhongguancun, Haidian Dist., Beijing, China

内蒙古-鄂尔多斯 Inner Mongolia-Ordos

2013/05/30-03
☎ 010-8260 6899
🖷 010-8260 6883
✉ ciccyhuang@cnaico.com.cn
www.cnaico.com.cn
www.autochina.com.cn
3520

2013第四届鄂尔多斯国际汽车展览会
地点：内蒙古鄂尔多斯
预计规模：总面积40,000m²
主办：中国汽车工业国际合作总公司
地址：北京市海淀区中关村丹棱街3号A座

4th Ordos Intl Automobile Exhibition
Venue: Ordos, Inner Mongolia
Expectation: Gross Area 40,000m²
Organizer: China National Automotive Industry Intl Corp
Address: A, 3 Danling Street, Zhongguancun, Haidian Dist., Beijing, China

江苏-常州 Jiangsu-Changzhou

2013/04/29-05/01
电话：13961278026
13584369405
www.0519net.com
3530

第五届中国常州汽车博览会
地点：常州国际会展中心，江苏常州
周期：每年两届
市场范围：地区性
性质：面向公众和贸易观众
上届规模：展览面积30,000m²，贸易观众100,000人
主办：江苏上游传媒公司

China (Changzhou) Automobile Expo
Venue: Changzhou Intl Exhibition Center, Changzhou, Jiangsu
Frequency: Bi-annual
Market Area: Regional
Nature: Open to Public
Statistics '12: Exhibition Area 30,000m², Trade Visitors 100,000
Organizer: Jiangsu Ahead Media Co

2013/06/30-07/02
☎ 0519-89851052
🖷 0519-89851052
✉ expocz@126.com
3540

第六届中国常州电动车展览会
地点：常州国际会展中心，江苏常州
周期：每年一届
市场范围：全国性
性质：面向贸易观众
上届规模：展览面积25,000m²，贸易观众10,000人
主办：青岛金奥广告策划有限公司

6th China (Changzhou) Electric Cars Exhibition
Venue: Changzhou Intl Exhibition Center, Changzhou, Jiangsu
Frequency: Annual
Market Area: National
Nature: Trade Only
Statistics '12: Exhibition Area 25,000m², Exhibitors , Trade Visitors 10,000)
Organizer: Qingdao Jinao AD Co Ltd

2013/08/04-04
☎ 0519-89851052
🖷 0519-89851052
✉ expocz@126.com
3550

2013年中国（常州）汽车配件交易会
地点：常州国际会展中心，江苏常州
周期：每年一届
市场范围：全国性
性质：面向贸易观众
上届规模：展览面积10,000m²，贸易观众10,000人
主办：北京慧聪国际资讯有限公司；慧聪商情广告（北京）有限公司

2013 China (Changzhou) Auto Parts Fair
Venue: Changzhou Intl Exhibition Center, Changzhou, Jiangsu
Frequency: Annual
Market Area: National
Nature: Trade Only
Statistics '12: Exhibition Area 10,000m², Trade Visitors 10,000
Organizer: HC Group

江苏-连云港 Jiangsu-Lianyungang

2013/06/10-13
☎ 010-8260 6899
🖷 010-8260 6883
✉ ciccyhuang@cnaico.com.cn
www.cnaico.com.cn
www.autochina.com.cn
3560

第五届连云港-大陆桥汽车贸易博览会
地点：江苏连云港
主办：中国汽车工业国际合作总公司
地址：北京市海淀区中关村丹棱街3号A座

5th Lianyungang-Continental Bridge Automobile Trade Fair
Venue: Lianyungang, Jiangsu
Organizer: China National Automotive Industry Intl Corp
Address: A, 3 Danling Street, Zhongguancun, Haidian Dist., Beijing, China

江苏-南京 Jiangsu-Nanjing

2013/04/28-05/02
☎ 010-8260 6899
🖷 010-8260 6883
✉ ciccyhuang@cnaico.com.cn
www.cnaico.com.cn
www.autochina.com.cn
3570

2013年第六届中国（南京）国际汽车博览会
地点：江苏南京
主办：中国汽车工业国际合作总公司
地址：北京市海淀区中关村丹棱街3号A座

6th China (Nanjing) Intl Automobile Expo
Venue: Nanjing, Jiangsu
Organizer: China National Automotive Industry Intl Corp
Address: A, 3 Danling Street, Zhongguancun, Haidian Dist., Beijing, China

2013/05/09-11
☎ 025-8555 2818, 8555 0655
🖷 025-8555 0655
✉ shbj88@188.com
www.chinabojin.net
3580

2013年第十五届中国国际（江苏）医博会
暨华东地区医院管理高级论坛
地点：南京国际展览中心，江苏南京
主办：南京市卫生局；南京市食品药品监督管理局
承办：南京博贸展览有限公司
联系人：张祥杰

15th China (Jiangsu) Intl Medical Expo
East China Hospital Management Forum
Venue: Nanjing Intl Exhibition Center, Nanjing, Jiangsu
Organizer: Nanjing BoMao Exhibition Co Ltd

2013/05/19-21
☎ 010-6562 3308, 6562 3306, 6562 3355
📠 010-8571 2120
✉ hospitalbuild@iirchina.com
www.hospitalbuildchina.cn
3590

2013中国国际医院建设、装备及管理展览会暨第14届全国医院建设大会
地点：南京博览中心，江苏南京
内容：医院建设策划设计；环境与医疗空间设计及绿色建材；医用洁具系统；绿色能源及环保节能；医用中央空调及通风系统，水净化、直饮水及污水处理系统；医疗垃圾与废弃物处理系统；医疗支持系统及专业工程；实验室装备；数字化医院及计算机网络系统
主办：卫生部医院管理研究所；英富曼会展（北京）有限公司
承办：《中国医院建筑与装备》杂志社；北京经卫联合医药信息研究所
联系人：任小姐

Hospital Build & Infrastructure Exhibition & Congress China 2013
14th China Hospital Construction Forum
Venue: Nanjing Intl Expo Center, Nanjing, Jiangsu
Organizer: NIHA informa exhibitions; Beijing Jingwei United Institute of Medical Information

2013/05/25-27
☎ 0531-8582 7333, 1333513316
📠 0531-8639 1116
www.ghjbh.com
3600

2013营养健康产业（南京）博览会
地点：南京规划建设展览馆，江苏南京
内容：营养健康产品；膳食补充剂类；有机产品类；药妆/功能性化妆品类；保健产品类；；功能性纺织品类；无糖食品；医药保健产品生产/包装类
主办：中国医药保健品协会；中国营养健康产业学会；中国医保产业国际交流协会；济南歌华展览服务有限公司
联系人：李伟

China (Nanjing) Nutrition and Health Industry Exposition 2013
Venue: Nanjing, Jiangsu
Organizer: Jinan Gehua Exhibition Co Ltd

2013/05/30-06/01
☎ 025-5231 5808
📠 025-5231 5918
www.njzfexpo.com
3610

2013第十二届南京国际纺织品面料、辅料博览会
地点：南京国际展览中心，江苏南京
周期：每年一届
主办：中国贸促会南京市分会；南京中纺展览有限公司

12th Nanjing Intl Textiles Fabrics Accessories Exhibition 2013
Venue: Nanjing Intl Exhibition Center, Nanjing, Jiangsu
Frequency: Annual
Organizer: CCPIT Nanjing Sub-Council; Nanjing Zhongfang Exhibition Co Ltd

2013/10/14-16
☎ 021-5081 9232, 5081 2190, 5081 1358
📠 021-5081 3069
✉ ambchina@messe-stuttgart.com.cn
http://messe-stuttgart.com.cn
3620

2013 中国（南京）国际金属加工展览会
地点：南京国际博览中心，江苏南京
内容：机床、刀具、机床零部件、模具制造等金属加工 各个领域的创新产品和技术
周期：每年一届
主办：江苏省经济和信息化委员会；德国斯图加特展览公司
承办：江苏省机械行业协会；南京机电行业协会；斯图加特展览（南京）有限公司
联系人：曹莉芳，周晖，张蕊倩

AMB China
China Metal Working & Forming Exhibition
Venue: Nanjing Intl Expo Center, Nanjing, Jiangsu
Frequency: Annual
Organizer: Jiangsu Economic & Information Technology Commission; Landesmesse Stuttgart GmbH

2013/11/04-06
☎ 025-6856 9817, 6856 7479, 6856 9815
📠 025-6856 9810
✉ info@expo800.com
www.expo800.com
3630

2013中国（国际）精密制造及技术展
地点：南京国际博览中心，江苏南京
主办：中国机械通用零部件工业协会；中国精密制造分会（筹）；南京投资促进委员会
承办：江苏网展科技有限公司
地址：江苏省南京市珠江路600号谷阳世纪大厦1806室

China (Intl) Precision Machine Technology Expo
Venue: Nanjing Intl Expo Center, Nanjing, Jiangsu
Organizer: Jiangsu Wangzhan Tech Co Ltd

江苏-苏州 Jiangsu-Suzhou

2013/05/08-10
☎ 021-6304 5419
📠 021-6418 1136
✉ cnshow-xunzhan@yahoo.cn
3640

2013第九届苏州电路板展览会
苏州电子线路板展览会
同期举办：
苏州电子组装展览会
苏州表面贴装展览会
地点：苏州国际博览中心，江苏苏州
内容：电路板本业：各类面板、多层板、软板等电路板制造、设计、代工。电路板设备：包含干制程/湿制程相关设备、电路板用检测设备。电路板用原物料与化学品。周边相关设备、零组件。电子组装设备、材料（SMT）
周期：每年一届
上届规模 '12：展览面积18,000m^2，参展商305家，参观人数20,115人
主办：海峡经济科技合作中心
承办：展昭国际企业股份有限公司；上海讯展会议展览有限公司
联系人：王资红（先生）

Suzhou Assembly Show
Suzhou SMT Show
Venue: Suzhou Intl Expo Center, Suzhou, Jiangsu
Frequency: Annual
Statistics '12: Exhibition Area 18,000m^2, Exhibitors 305, Visitors 20,115
Organizer: Shanghai Xunzhan Convention & Exhibition Ltd.

2013/09/18-22
☎ 010-8260 6899
📠 010-8260 6883
✉ ciccyhuang@cnaico.com.cn
www.cnaico.com.cn
www.autochina.com.cn
3650

2013第十届中国（苏州）国际汽车工业博览会
地点：江苏苏州
主办：中国汽车工业国际合作总公司
地址：北京市海淀区中关村丹棱街3号A座

10th China (Suzhou) Intl Automobile Industry Expo
Venue: Suzhou, Jiangsu
Organizer: China National Automotive Industry Intl Corp
Address: A, 3 Danling Street, Zhongguancun, Haidian Dist., Beijing, China

江苏-泰州 Jiangsu-Taizhou

2013/04 -
☎ 010-8260 6899
🖷 010-8260 6883
✉ ciccyhuang@cnaico.com.cn
www.cnaico.com.cn
www.autochina.com.cn
3660

泰州国际汽车展览会
地点：江苏泰州
主办：中国汽车工业国际合作总公司
地址：北京市海淀区中关村丹棱街3号A座

Taizhou Intl Automobile Exhibition
Venue: Taizhou, Jiangsu
Organizer: China National Automotive Industry Intl Corp
Address: A, 3 Danling Street, Zhongguancun, Haidian Dist., Beijing, China

江苏-盐城 Jiangsu-Yancheng

2013/09/18-22
☎ 010-8260 6899
🖷 010-8260 6883
✉ ciccyhuang@cnaico.com.cn
www.cnaico.com.cn
www.autochina.com.cn
3670

东部沿海（盐城）国际汽车博览会
地点：江苏盐城
主办：中国汽车工业国际合作总公司
地址：北京市海淀区中关村丹棱街3号A座

East Coast (Yancheng) Intl Automobile Expo
Venue: Yancheng, Jiangsu
Organizer: China National Automotive Industry Intl Corp
Address: A, 3 Danling Street, Zhongguancun, Haidian Dist., Beijing, China

江西-南昌 Jiangxi-Nanchang

2013/10/18-21
☎ 010-8260 6899
🖷 010-8260 6883
✉ ciccyhuang@cnaico.com.cn
www.cnaico.com.cn
www.autochina.com.cn
3680

2013年第八届南昌国际汽车展览会
地点：江西南昌
主办：中国汽车工业国际合作总公司
地址：北京市海淀区中关村丹棱街3号A座

8th Nanchang Intl Automobile Exhibition
Venue: Nanchang, Jiangxi
Organizer: China National Automotive Industry Intl Corp
Address: A, 3 Danling Street, Zhongguancun, Haidian Dist., Beijing, China

辽宁-大连 Liaoning-Dalian

2013/04/11-14
☎ 0411-8253 8642, 13352212336
🖷 0411-8253 8678
✉ my12336@126.com
1504987187
www.sinoexhibition.com/jz
3690

2013年大连建材展
第十八届中国国际建筑装饰材料展览会
地点：大连星海会展中心/大连世界博览广场，辽宁大连
内容：门窗，幕墙，五金及设备，工程公司；洁具，陶瓷，石材，水泥制品；铺地材料，铺装技术及设备；橱柜及厨房电器，配套用品；油漆，涂料，防水材料，橡塑制品；采暖，空调，通风，燃气技术及太阳能产品；照明灯饰，LED显示器，美化工程及园林设施；大型工艺品，室内装饰用品及居室用品；管材，管件，阀门；智能小区，监控系统，楼宇对讲设备；建筑五金，电动工具展区
始办年份：1995
周期：每年一届
市场范围：国际性
性质：面向公众和贸易观众
入场券价格：免费
参展费用：5,500元/展位
主办：大连北方国际展览股份有限公司
地址：大连市中山区同兴街25号世界贸易大厦25F(116001)
联系人：王常虹

CHINA BUILD 18th
18th China Intl Construction & Decoration Materials Exhibition
Venue: Dalian World Expo Center, Dalian, Liaoning
Established Year: 1995
Frequency: Annual
Market Area: International
Nature: Open to Public
Cost to Attend: Free
Participated Fee: RMB 5,500/booth
Organizer: Dalian Northern Intl Exhibition Ltd

2013/05/15-17
☎ 0411-8253 2845
🖷 0411-8264 4331
✉ zhanghongling.8@126.com
www.industry-expo.com
3700

2013大连国际物流技术及包装工业展览会
第11届大连国际塑料橡胶工业展览会
第14届大连国际机床、工具暨模具展览会
地点：大连世界博览广场，辽宁大连
内容：仓储设备，物料搬运设备，起重设备，输送设备及物流的完整系统，物流配送车辆，物流服务
参展费用：标准展位6,000元/9m^2，光地600元/m^2（36m^{2}起）
主办：辽宁省人民政府；大连市人民政府
承办：中国贸促会大连市分会；中国国际商会大连商会；大连国际商会展览公司
地址：大连市中山区解放街9号万达大厦1004室(116001)
联系人：张洪玲

Dalian Intl Logistics Technology and Packaging Industry Exhibition
Dalian Intl Plastic and Rubber Industry Exhibition
14th Dalian Intl Machine Tool and Mold Exhibition
Venue: Dalian World Expo Center, Dalian, Liaoning
Participated Fee: Standard Booth RMB 6,000/booth, Raw Space RMB 600/m^2 (min 36m^2)
Organizer: CCPIT Dalian Sub-Council

2013/11/05-07
☎ 010-5919 4405
🖷 010-6591 8986
✉ joy@agri.gov.cn
jeff@agri.gov.cn
www.cafte.gov.cn
3710

第十八届中国国际渔业博览会
地点：大连世界博览广场，辽宁大连
内容：水产品加工及贸易、渔业机械设备、海洋捕捞、养殖饲料及病害防治、质量控制、相关服务及媒体
始办年份：1996
周期：每年一届
市场范围：国际性
性质：面向贸易观众
入场券价格：国内观众100元
上届规模 '12：展览面积48,000m^2(国外展商面积19,000m^2)，参展商930家（国外展商400家，来自44个国家），贸易观众20,000人
主办：中国贸促会农业行业委员会
地址：北京市朝阳区麦子店街20号楼8层(100125)
联系人：张晓颖，潘久

18th China Fisheries & Seafood Expo
Venue: Dalian World Expo Center, Dalian, Liaoning
Profile: Seafood products, seafood processing equipment, aquaculture products and supplies, fishing equipment, associated services
Established Year: 1996
Frequency: Annual
Market Area: International
Nature: Trade Only
Statistics '12: Exhibition Area 48,000m^2(foreigners 19,000m^2), Exhibitors 930 (foreigners 400, came from 44 countries), Trade Visitors 20,000
Organizer: CCPIT-Agriculture Industry Committee
Address: 8th Floor, 20 Building, Maizidian Street, Chaoyang District, Beijing 100125, China
Contact: Joy Zhang, Jeff Pan

辽宁-锦州 Liaoning-Jinzhou

2013/05/07-10
☎ 010-8260 6899
🖷 010-8260 6883
✉ ciccyhuang@cnaico.com.cn
www.cnaico.com.cn
www.autochina.com.cn
3720

2013年中国锦州国际汽车展览会
地点：辽宁锦州
主办：中国汽车工业国际合作总公司
地址：北京市海淀区中关村丹棱街3号A座

China (Jinzhou) Intl Automobile Exhibition
Venue: Jinzhou, Liaoning
Organizer: China National Automotive Industry Intl Corp
Address: A, 3 Danling Street, Zhongguancun, Haidian Dist., Beijing, China

辽宁-盘锦 Liaoning-Panjin

2013/04/27-30
☎ 010-8260 6899
🖷 010-8260 6883
www.cnaico.com.cn
www.autochina.com.cn
3730

2013年中国（盘锦）国际汽车展览会
地点：辽宁盘锦
主办：中国汽车工业国际合作总公司
地址：北京市海淀区中关村丹棱街3号A座

China (Panjin) Intl Automobile Exhibition
Venue: Panjin, Liaoning
Organizer: China National Automotive Industry Intl Corp
Address: A, 3 Danling Street, Zhongguancun, Haidian Dist., Beijing, China

辽宁-沈阳 Liaoning-Shenyang

2013/03/15-18
☎ 024-2389 2399, 2388 5066
🖷 024-2389 2399, 2388 5066
QQ 1718168458
3740

2013辽宁第十八届国际广告/标识/数码影像/LED光电照明暨灯饰展
地点：辽宁工业展览馆，辽宁沈阳
内容：广告写真、喷绘，雕刻、热转印设备及耗材，标识标牌、灯箱、展示器材、三面翻、POP设备及材料，广告摄影技术设备、感光材料、办公打印设备及耗材，广告礼品、书籍，LED、显示屏、LED广告标识、LED元件及器材，舞台灯光、电影电视灯光、调光控制设备控光器件，室内外灯饰、光电照明设备材料及组件、城市亮化产品等
始办年份：1995
周期：每年一届
市场范围：全国性
性质：面向公众和贸易观众
入场券价格：免费
参展费用：5,000元/展位，光地500元/m^2
上届规模 '12：展览面积15,000m^2，参展商400家，参观人数40,000人
主办：辽宁省服务业委员会；辽宁省展览业协会；辽宁省展览贸易集团；辽宁工业展览馆；沈阳市世博会展服务中心；辽宁艾菲传媒有限公司
地址：辽宁沈阳市和平区龙泉路15号东印商务228室(110004)
联系人：朱樱

2013 Liaoning 18th Intl Adverting/Signal/Digital Images/LED Lighting Exhibition
Venue: Liaoning Industrial Exhibition Hall, Shenyang, Liaoning
Profile: Advertisement Photos, Printing, Carving, Heating Trans print and consumption, Signal labels, Lighting box, exhibiting equipment, Three-side turning, POP equipment and material, Advertisement film technology and equipment, sensitization materials, Office Printing equipment and consumption, Advertisement gift, LED Display; Lighting for stage, film and TV, indoor and outdoor lighting
Established Year: 1995
Frequency: Annual
Market Area: National
Nature: Open to Public
Cost to Attend: Free
Participated Fee: RMB 5,000/booth, Raw Space RMB 500/m^2
Statistics '12: Exhibition Area 15,000m^2, Exhibitors 400, Visitors 40,000
Organizer: Liaoning Industry of Service Council; Liaoning Association of Exhibition; Liaoning Exhibition Trade Group; Liaoning Industry Exhibition Hall; Shenyang Shibo Exhibition Service Center; Liaoning Effect Media Company
Address: Rm 228, 15 Longquan Road, Heping Dist., Shenyang, Liaoning 110004, China
Contact: Zhu Ying

2013/04/10-13
☎ 024-2392 1795
🖷 024-2392 2432
✉ bfexpo@126.com
QQ 506079733
www.bfexpo.com.cn
3750

2013第十四届东北国际机床与金属加工展览会
地点：沈阳国际展览中心，辽宁沈阳
内容：机床类，模具类，相关制造技术与设备
上届规模：参观人数48,200人
主办：沈阳市人民政府；中国贸易促进委员会辽宁省分会
承办：沈阳市工装模具行业协会；沈阳市装备制造业行业协会；北方工商业展览服务有限责任公司
地址：沈阳市三好街93号金源大厦5F(110004)

14th Northeast Intl Machine Tool and Metalworking Exhibition 2013
Venue: Shenyang International Exhibition Center, Shenyang, Liaoning
Statistics '12: Visitors 48,200
Organizer: Northern Industrial & Commercial Exhibition Co Ltd
Address: 5 Fl., 93 Sanhao Street, Shenyang, Liaoning 110004, China

2013/06/27-02
☎ 010-8260 6899
🖷 010-8260 6883
✉ ciccyhuang@cnaico.com.cn
www.cnaico.com.cn
www.autochina.com.cn
3760

2013年第十二届中国沈阳汽车工业博览会
地点：辽宁沈阳
主办：中国汽车工业国际合作总公司
地址：北京市海淀区中关村丹棱街3号A座

12th China (Shenyang) Automobile Industry Expo
Venue: Shenyang, Liaoning
Organizer: China National Automotive Industry Intl Corp
Address: A, 3 Danling Street, Zhongguancun, Haidian Dist., Beijing, China

2013/09/13-17
☎ 024-2391 1801
🖷 024-2325 0180
www.cnzbh.com
3770

第十二届中国国际装备制造业博览会–机床模具展
地点：沈阳国际展览中心，辽宁沈阳
内容：金属切削机床、金属成形机床、特种加工机床及专用设备、检验和测量设备、数控系统、数显装置和机床电器、机床零部件及辅助设备、磨料磨具、刀具、工夹具及相关产品
周期：每年一届
主办：中国贸促会；辽宁省人民政府
承办：沈阳市人民政府；沈阳金之诺会展有限公司
地址：辽宁省沈阳市和平区和平北大街94号星光大厦二楼

12th China Intl Equipment Manufacturing Exposition -Machine Tools & Mould Exhibition
Venue: Shenyang Intl Exhibition Center, Shenyang, Liaoning
Frequency: Annual
Organizer: Jinnoc Intl Exhibition Co Ltd

陕西-西安 Shaanxi-Xi' an

2013/03/14-17
☎ 029-8815 3802, 15389409298
🖷 029-8831 4333
✉ liluoluo.joyful@163.com
www.cwieme.com
3780

2013年第十六届中国西部国际装备制造业博览会
西部国际五金机电工具贸易展览会
地点：陕西西安
内容：热处理技术；表面处理；；热处理质量控制；机电一体化技术、工艺软件及微机控制技术；热处理工艺材料及辅助材料、淬火介质、渗剂、涂料等；新型燃烧装置及技术；热处理节能设备与技术，余温回收处理以及相关环保设备与技术；感应加热设备；筑炉材料、耐火材料、加热元件、耐热绝热保温材料及与热处理设备相关的配套元器件。工业炉窑技术及设备；铸造、锻造技术及设备；铸造原材料；热处理炉。耐火材料领域；电炉、工业炉配件产品；切割装备及辅件
周期：每年一届
市场范围：全国性
主办：中国贸易促进委员会，中国机械工业联合会，陕西省振兴装备制造业领导小组，西安市人民政府，成都市人民政府
承办：西安曲江三之联会展有限公司#
地址：西安市科技路37号海星城市广场B座24层
联系人：张玉华

China West Intl Equipment Manufacturing Exposition
Venue: Xi' an Qujiang Intl Conference & Exhibition Center, Xi' an, Shaanxi
Profile: Machine Tool and Mold Exhibition Reverse Procurement, D Printer and Technology; Industrial Automation and Control Technology, Instrumentation, Measuring And Testing; Welding and Cutting Equipment; Fluid Machinery and Power Transmission; Plastics and Rubber Machinery, Printing and Packaging Technology.
Frequency: Annual
Market Area: National
Organizer: Xi'an Joint Exhibition Co Ltd

2013/05/16-18
☎ 029-8535 9326, 15191581180
🖷 029-8522 9308
huazhan2008@huazhan.com.cn
www.xajdzh.com
www.xahz.wanye68.com
3790

第十四届西安国际酒店设备及用品展览会
同期举办：
第六届西安国际酒店家具展览会
第六届西安国际烘焙、咖啡、茶展览会
第六届西安国际食品、葡萄酒、饮料及酒店餐饮服务展览会
地点：西安曲江国际会展中心，陕西西安
内容：餐饮厨房设备用品区，清洁设备用品区，洗涤设备用品区，酒店家具区，桌面用品区，客房、大堂用品区，纺织布艺制服区，烘焙、咖啡设备用品区，茶展区，食品乳制品区，酒类饮料及餐饮服务区，康体娱乐智能区
主办：陕西省旅游局；陕西省旅游协会；陕西旅游饭店协会；陕西省烹饪餐饮行业协会；陕西省饭店协会
承办：陕西省旅游服务公司；西安华展展览有限公司；西安曲江千秋展览策划有限公司
地址：西安市雁展路6号曲江会展国际B座1102室(710061)
联系人：高建伟

14th Xi'an Intl Hospitality Equipment & Supplies Fair
Venue: Xi' an Qujiang Intl Conference & Exhibition Center, Xi'an, Shaanxi
Frequency: Annual
Organizer: Xian Huazhan Exhibition Co Ltd
Address: Room B1102, 6 Yanzhan Road, Xi' an, Shaanxi 710061, China

2013/05/23-25
☎ 0411-3960 7302, 13390515632
🖷 0411-8457 5260
✉ bithuiyi@163.com
3800

2013第四届神经科技大会
地点：曲江国际会议中心，陕西西安
主办：中国医药生物技术协会；国家外国专家局国外人才信息交流中心
承办：百奥泰国际会议（大连）有限公司
联系人：郗蕊

BIT's 4th Annual World Congress of Neuro Talk 2013
Venue: Xi'an Qujiang Intl Conference Center, Xi'an, Shaanxi
Organizer: BIT Congress Inc

山东-广饶 Shandong-Guangrao

2013/05/15-17
☎ 010-5225 9949
🖷 010-5225 9863
✉ yangliu1818@163.com
QQ 1264704231
www.zonro.cn
3810

2013第十届中国国际轮胎资源循环利用展览会
地点：山东广饶国际会展中心，山东广饶
内容：旨在从轮胎橡胶产业链的角度出发，充分借助十广饶轮胎展这个在业界已享有较高声誉和规模的政府支持的橡胶轮胎、汽车配件产业基地举办的专业展览会的优势，集橡胶行业客户资源共享，参观观众资源共享，政府优质的服务工作共享的优厚的条件。服务企业，引领市场，促进发展，创造商机

10th China Intl Tire Cyclic Utilization Expo 2013
Venue: Guangrao Convention Center, Guangrao, Shandong
Established Year: 2002
Frequency: Annual
Market Area: International
Nature: Open to Public
Cost to Attend: Free

始办年份：2002
周期：每年一届
市场范围：国际性
性质：面向公众和贸易观众
入场券价格：免费
参展费用：光地500元/m²(36m²起)
主办：中国物流与采购联合会；中国轮胎翻修与循环利用协会
承办：中融商汇（北京）国际会展有限公司
地址：北京市丰台区南三环刘家窑芳群公寓C座1204室(100078)
联系人：杨柳，田盈

Participated Fee: Raw Space RMB 500/m² (min 36m²)
Organizer: China Tyre Retreading, Repairing & Recycling Association; Zhongrong Shanghui (Beijing) Intl Exhibition Co Ltd

山东-济南 Shandong-Jinan

2013/03/10-12
☎ 0531-8238 6077, 13370507991
🖷 0531-8238 5199转808
✉ shibo6666@126.com
www.sdddc.net
www.weilaiqiche.com
3820

2013第7届山东国际自行车电动车及零部件展览会
地点：济南国际会展中心，山东济南
内容：高档自行车、运动自行车、休闲自行车、折叠自行车、儿童车、滑板车等；轻型电动两轮车、电动摩托车、电动三轮车、摩托车、燃油助力车等；低速电动四轮车、电动公交车、电动旅游观光车、太阳能电动车、电动客车、电动清洁车等新能源汽车；各种电源、电机、控制器、轮胎等零部件，电池修复仪等配套辅助产品；机械加工、流水线、检测仪器；行业协会、检测中心及行业媒体
主办：山东省自行车电动车行业协会；山东省经济和信息化委员会；济南市人民政府,山东省轻工业协会；山东省国际经济贸易联合会；山东省电动车产业化办公室
承办：济南世博展览策划有限公司；中国贸促会济南市分会
地址：济南市花园路189-1号336室
联系人：张先生

Shandong Intl Electric-Bicycle and Spare Parts Exhibition
Venue: Jinan Intl Convention & Exhibition Center, Jinan, Shandong
Organizer: CCPIT Jinan Sub-Council; Jinan Shibo Exhibition Planning Co Ltd

2013/03/03-05
☎ 0531-8121 9080, 8651 2556, 8887 9849
🖷 0531-8887 9893
www.chinaieme.com/gongyezhidong
3830

2013第12届中国（山东）国际工业自动化应用技术展览会
地点：济南国际会展中心，山东济南
内容：工业控制与自动化展区、工厂自动化设备展区、仪器仪表展区、无损检测展区
主办：山东省人民政府，中国机械工业联合会

12th China (Shandong) Intl Industrial Automation Applied Technology Exhibition
Venue: Jinan Intl Convention & Exhibition Center, Jinan, Shandong
Organizer: Shandong Zhenghua Exhibitions

2013/03/31-04/02
☎ 0531-8796 1189, 8718 2646, 13465313231
🖷 0531-8718 2646
✉ wm87961189@163.com
QQ 284686960
www.shhzexpo.com
3840

2013中国（济南）国际LED光电产业博览会
地点：济南国际会展中心，山东济南
内容：照明及灯饰产品， LED光电城市亮化，LED元件及器材，配套产品
参展费用：标准展位3,600元/9m²，光地400元/m²（光地36m²起）
主办：山东省照明电器协会；山东照明学会
承办：上海汇展商贸有限公司
地址：山东省济南市槐村街25号3F(250022)
联系人：吴明

China (Jinan) Intl LED Expo
Venue: Jinan Intl Convention & Exhibition Center, Jinan, Shandong
Participated Fee: Standard Booth RMB 3,600/booth, Raw Space RMB 400/m² (min 36m²)
Organizer: Shanghai Huizhan Trade Co Ltd

2013/04/18-20
☎ 0531-8312 5466
🖷 0531-8816 0483
✉ xinzhan86@163.com
www.sdntzh.com
3850

2013第16届中国济南供热采暖、热泵空调产品与技术展览会
第四届山东电采暖节能应用研讨会
地点：济南国际会展中心，山东济南
内容：采暖类、锅炉类、集中供热设备、空调：商用及家用中央空调系统、环保空调、冷暖空调机组、新风系统等
主办：济南市人民政府；山东建筑大学；中国国际贸易促进联合会；山东省土木建筑学会；中国建筑装饰协会；山东省经济和信息化委员会
承办：济南信展展览有限公司（山东省建设科技协会理事单位）
地址：济南市华龙路28号智能园五层(250100)

16th China Jinan Heating, Heat Pump Air Conditioning Products and Technology Exhibition
Venue: Jinan Intl Convention & Exhibition Center, Jinan, Shandong
Organizer: Jinan Xinzhan Exhibition Co Ltd

2013/05/06-08
☎ 010-6320 5144, 6320 3094
🖷 010-6320 3494
✉ jixieexpo@126.com
www.cihmexpo.cn
3860

2013中国国际水利机械及施工装备展览会
地点：济南国际会展中心，山东济南
内容：水利专用机械，通用施工机械
参展费用：A区展位：光地680元/m²，标准展台6,800元/展位；B区展位：光地580元/m²，标准展台5,800元/展位
主办：中国水利学会；水利部综合事业局；济南市政府；山东省水利厅（待定）；湖南省水利厅

China Intl Hydraulic Machinery and Construction Equipment Exhibition
Venue: Jinan Intl Convention & Exhibition Center, Jinan, Shandong
Participated Fee: Area A, Raw Space RMB 680/m², Standard Booth RMB 6,800/booth; Area B, Raw Space RMB 580/m², Standard Booth RMB 5,800/booth
Organizer: Chinese Hydraulic Engineering Society

2013/05/24-26
☎ 0531-8235 0000
🖷 0531-88927900
www.zmqgsp.com
3870

2013第七届全国食品博览会暨糖酒商品交易会
地点：济南国际会展中心，山东济南
内容：酒水展区，饮料展区，食品展区，乳制品展区，调味品展区，肉制品展区，食品包装及加工机械专区
主办：山东省食品工业办公室；中国贸促会山东省委员会

7th National Food Expo and Sugar and Alcoholic Commodities Fair
Venue: Jinan Intl Convention & Exhibition Center, Jinan, Shandong
Organizer: Shandong Food Industry Association; Jinan Zhongmao Exhibition Co Ltd

山东-青岛 Shandong-Qingdao

3880
2013/03/07-09
☎ 0532-5555 2901, 13615320907
🖷 0532-5555 2903
✉ jndaiming@126.com
www.foundry-china.cn

2013第十一届青岛国际铸造、热处理及工业炉展览会
地点：青岛国际会展中心，山东青岛
内容：铸品，锻造件，压铸设备，压铸模具，铸造技术，热处理，工业炉领域，耐火材料领域，产品质量控制、检测用仪器、仪表
主办：中国金属学会；青岛市人民政府
承办：青岛金诺会展有限公司
地址：青岛市福州南路87号福林大厦902室（266071）
联系人：戴明

Qingdao Intl Casting, Heat Treatment and Furnace Exhibition
Venue: Qingdao Intl Convention & Exhibition Center, Qingdao, Shandong
Organizer: Qingdao Jinnoc Exhibition Co Ltd
Address: Room 902, 87 South Fuzhou Road, Qingdao 266071, Shandong

3890
2013/04/04-07
☎ 010-8260 6899
🖷 010-8260 6883
✉ ciccyhuang@cnaico.com.cn
www.cnaico.com.cn
www.autochina.com.cn

青岛春季汽车文化节
地点：山东青岛
主办：中国汽车工业国际合作总公司
地址：北京市海淀区中关村丹棱街3号A座

Qingdao Spring Automobile Culture Festival
Venue: Qingdao, Shandong
Organizer: China National Automotive Industry Intl Corp
Address: A, 3 Danling Street, Zhongguancun, Haidian Dist., Beijing, China

3900
2013/04/06-08
☎ 0532-8079 1062, 15154425657
🖷 0532-8079 1027
http://chinabwe.qdcese.com

2013中国（青岛）国际建筑给排水展览会
第七届中国（青岛）建筑节能和可再生能源建筑应用博览会
地点：青岛国际会展中心，山东青岛
内容：建筑供水系统；建筑中水系统；消防给水系统；建筑内部排水系统；建筑热水系统；建筑饮水系统；管道类；泵阀类；配套产品类；配件类
主办：中国建筑材料联合会；青岛市人民政府
承办：青岛市城乡建设委员会；青岛市建筑节能协会；青岛海宸国际会展有限公司
地址：青岛 苗岭路9号（青岛国际会展中心）5-8F
联系人：李占胜

China (Qingdao) Intl Building Water Technology Energy Fair
Venue: Qingdao Intl Convention & Exhibition Center, Qingdao, Shandong
Organizer: Qingdao Haichen International Expo Co Ltd
Address: 5-8F, 9 Miaoling Road, Qingdao, Shandong 266061, China

3910
2013/04/06-08
☎ 0532-8395 1056
🖷 0532-8395 1197
www.expotuliao.com

第三届中国（青岛）国际建筑装饰涂料及化学建材展览会
地点：青岛国际会展中心，山东青岛
内容：涂料产品：建筑外围涂料，家居装饰涂料，特种涂料，胶粘剂与涂料原材料，化工原料；木器漆；涂料相关工具、设备；行业相关技术和服务、研发
主办：中国建筑材料联合会；青岛市人民政府
承办：青岛市城乡建设委员会；青岛市建筑节能协会；青岛海宸国际会展有限公司
地址：中国青岛苗岭路9号（青岛国际会展中心）5-8F(266061)

Qingdao Architectural Coatings and Chemical Building Materials
Venue: Qingdao Intl Convention & Exhibition Center, Qingdao, Shandong
Organizer: Qingdao Haichen International Expo Co Ltd
Address: 5-8F, Miaoling Road, Qingdao, Shandong 266061, China

3920
2013/04/06-08
☎ 0532-8383 1786
🖷 0532-8384 1887
www.qdcese.cn

第六届中国（青岛）国际太阳能与建筑一体化应用产品技术展览会
地点：青岛国际会展中心，山东青岛
内容：太阳能热利用，太阳能光伏、光电，太阳能配件，太阳能其他产品，可与建筑完美结合的新能源技术
主办：中国建筑材料联合会；青岛市人民政府；海展集团
承办：青岛市城乡建设委员会；青岛市建筑节能协会；青岛海宸国际会展有限公司
地址：中国青岛国际会展中心5-8F（苗岭路9号）(266061)
联系人：刘娜

Qingdao Intl Solar Energy Fair
Venue: Qingdao Intl Convention & Exhibition Center, Qingdao, Shandong
Organizer: Qingdao Haichen International Expo Co Ltd
Address: 5-8F, Miaoling Road, Qingdao, Shandong 266061, China

3930
2013/04/06-08
☎ 0532-8079 1078, 15092298301
🖷 0532-8395 1197
www.qdmbjsj.com

第二届中国（青岛）国际新型建筑模板、脚手架及施工技术展览会
地点：青岛国际会展中心，山东青岛
内容：新型建筑模板相关产品和技术；脚手架相关产品和技术；高空施工技术平台；固定式液压升降台；高空作业车、高空取料机、防护产品
主办：中国建筑材料联合会；青岛市人民政府
承办：青岛市城乡建设委员会；青岛市建筑节能协会；青岛海宸国际会展有限公司
地址：山东青岛苗岭路9号（青岛国际会展中心）5-8F(266061)
联系人：闫红

Qingdao Intl Building Cyclostyle & Scaffold Fair
Venue: Qingdao Intl Convention & Exhibition Center, Qingdao, Shandong
Organizer: Qingdao Haichen International Expo Co Ltd
Address: 5-8F, Miaoling Road, Qingdao, Shandong 266061, China

3940
2013/04/06-08
☎ 0532-8395 1056
🖷 0532-8395 1197
www.qdcese.com

第七届中国（青岛）国际外墙保温及新型墙体产品技术展览会
地点：青岛国际会展中心，山东青岛
内容：新型外墙装饰板材，建筑保温系统，新型墙体材料，保温、隔热材料，屋面保温系统，干混砂浆产品，添加剂及技术设备
主办：中国建筑材料联合会；青岛市人民政府；
承办：青岛市城乡建设委员会；青岛市建筑节能协会；青岛海宸国际会展有限公司
地址：青岛苗岭路9号（青岛国际会展中心）5-8F(266061)

Qingdao Building External Wall insulation and New Wall Materials Exhibition
Venue: Qingdao Intl Convention & Exhibition Center, Qingdao, Shandong
Organizer: Qingdao Haichen International Expo Co Ltd
Address: 5-8F, Miaoling Road, Qingdao, Shandong

3950
2013/04/06-08
☎ 0532-8395 1056
🖷 0532-8395 1197
www.qdcese.com

第七届中国（青岛）国际干混砂浆、地坪产品及技术设备展览会
地点：青岛国际会展中心，山东青岛
内容：建筑砂浆产品；砂浆添加剂；物流与施工设备；生产与检测设备；砂浆原料；地坪材料；地坪产品；地坪机械；其他：各类地坪的应用技术、施工
主办：中国建筑材料联合会；青岛市人民政府
承办：青岛市城乡建设委员会；青岛市建筑节能协会；青岛海宸国际会展有限公司
地址：青岛苗岭路9号（青岛国际会展中心）5-8F(266061)

7th China (Qingdao) Dry-mixed mortar, Floor Exhibition
Venue: Qingdao Intl Convention & Exhibition Center, Qingdao, Shandong
Organizer: Qingdao Haichen International Expo Co Ltd
Address: 5-8F, Miaoling Road, Qingdao, Shandong

3960
2013/04/06-08
☎ 0532-8380 3552, 18678617975
🖷 0532-8395 1086
www.qdlszm.com

第三届中国（青岛）国际绿色照明产品及技术应用展览会
地点：青岛国际会展中心，山东青岛
内容：LED照明；室内照明；户外照明；LED光源；照明配套产品
主办：中国建筑材料联合会；青岛市人民政府
承办：青岛市城乡建设委员会；青岛市建筑节能协会；青岛海宸国际会展有限公司
地址：中国青岛国际会展中心5-8F（苗岭路9号）(266061)
联系人：张福宽

Qingdao Intl Green Lighting Fair
Venue: Qingdao Intl Convention & Exhibition Center, Qingdao, Shandong
Organizer: Qingdao Haichen International Expo Co Ltd
Address: 5-8F, Miaoling Road, Qingdao, Shandong

3970
2013/04/09-11
☎ 0532-5555 2996, 13589340811
🖷 0532-5555 2903
✉ wfei622@126.com
www.rubbere.com

2013第十届中国国际橡胶技术（青岛）展览会
地点：青岛国际会展中心，山东青岛
内容：橡胶机械设备；橡胶原材料；橡胶助剂；非轮胎橡胶制品；其它专区
主办：山东省橡胶行业协会；国家轮胎工艺与控制工程技术研究中心；中国石油石油化工研究院
承办：青岛金诺国际会展有限公司
地址：青岛市福州南路87号福林大厦902室
联系人：王飞

10th China Intl Rubber Technology (Qingdao) Fair
Venue: Qingdao Intl Convention & Exhibition Center, Qingdao, Shandong
Organizer: Qingdao Jinnoc Exhibition Co Ltd
Address: Room 902, 87 South Fuzhou Road, Qingdao 266071, Shandong

3980
2013/04/27-29
☎ 0532-5555 2901, 5555 2902
🖷 0532-5555 2903
www.china-spjx.com.cn

2013第十届中国(青岛)国际肉类工业展览会
第十届中国国际食品加工与包装设备（青岛）展览会
第五届中国国际食品保鲜及冷冻、冷藏技术设备展览会
地点：青岛国际会展中心，山东青岛
内容：肉食及成品；原料和相关；加工与设备；低温物流设备与技术；包装物流
主办：中国食品工业协会，青岛市人民政府，青岛金诺会展有限公司

10th China Intl Food Processing & Packaging Equipment (Qingdao) Exhibition
10th China (Qingdao) Intl Meat Industry Exhibition
5th China Intl Technology Equipment Fair of Food Fresh Keeping, Freezing
Venue: Qingdao Intl Convention & Exhibition Center, Qingdao, Shandong
Organizer: Qingdao Jinnoc Exhibition Co Ltd
Address: 902, Fulin Building, 87 South Fuzhou Road, Qingdao, Shandong 266071, China
Contact: Nina Ren

3990
2013/06/07-09
☎ 0532-8501 2515
🖷 0532-8501 2915
✉ qd-fair@163.com
QQ 1007079648
www.qdlanbo.com

2013第四届中国（青岛）国际卡车、商用车及零部件展览会
地点：青岛国际会展中心，山东青岛
内容：卡车及专用车；工程车；商用车；零部件
参展费用：豪华标准展位（18m²起）13,800元/9m²；标准展位8,800元/9m²，角位9,800元/9m²；光地（36m²起）880元/m²，室外光地680元/m²
主办：中国国际机械工业协会；中国国际贸易发展联合会；青岛蓝博会展有限公司
地址：青岛市南区山东路48号 华宇大厦206室

China (Qingdao) Intl Commercial Vehicle Exhibition
Venue: Qingdao Intl Convention & Exhibition Center, Qingdao, Shandong
Participated Fee: Premium Booth (min 18m²), RMB 13,800/9m²; Standard Booth RMB 8,800/9m², Corner Booth RMB 9,800/9m²; Indoor Raw Space (min 36m²) RMB 880/m², Outdoor Raw Space RMB 680/m²
Organizer: Qingdao Lanbo Conference & Exhibition Co Ltd
Address: Room 206, Huayu Building, Shandong Road, Nan Dist., Qingdao, Shandong, China

4000
2013/06/28-30
☎ 0532-8501 1486
🖷 0532-8501 2624
www.tex532.com

2013第15届中国（青岛）国际面料、辅料及纱线展览会
地点：青岛国际会展中心，山东青岛
内容：功能/运动装面料，休闲装面料，泳装面料，时尚女装面料，正装面料，辅料，家纺面料，纱线，其他
主办：青岛市人民政府；中国贸促会山东省委员；中国国际商会山东商会
承办：青岛海名国际会展有限公司
地址：青岛市山东路52号华嘉大厦4楼(266071)

15th China (Qingdao) Intl Fabric, Yarn and Accessories Exhibition
Venue: Qingdao Intl Convention & Exhibition Center, Qingdao, Shandong
Organizer: Qingdao Haiming Exhibition Co Ltd

4010
2013/07/16-19
☎ 0532-8079 1060, 15020044991
🖷 0532-8395 1062
www.stoneqd.cn

第七届中国（青岛）国际石材工业及机械设备展览会
地点：青岛国际会展中心，山东青岛
内容：石材类，板材类，人造石类，墓碑类，艺术石，石材机械及加工设备，养护材料及设备
主办：青岛市人民政府；山东省石材行业协会；海展集团
承办：青岛海宸国际会展有限公司
地址：山东青岛苗岭路9号（青岛国际会展中心）5-8F(266061)
联系人：公正

China (Qingdao) Intl Stone Products & Machinery Exhibition
Venue: Qingdao Intl Convention & Exhibition Center, Qingdao, Shandong
Organizer: Qingdao Haichen International Expo Co Ltd
Address: 5-8F, Miaoling Road, Qingdao, Shandong 266061, China

4020
2013/07/17-19
☎ 0532-8380 3552, 18678617975
🖷 0532-8395 1086
www.floorqd.cn

第七届中国（青岛）国际地板及整木家装展览会
地点：青岛国际会展中心，山东青岛
内容：地板展区，竹地板展区，地板配件展区，整木家装
主办：中国建筑材料联合会；青岛市城乡建设委员会；海展集团
承办：青岛海宸国际会展有限公司
地址：青岛苗岭路9号（青岛国际会展中心）5-8F(266061)
联系人：张宽

Qingdao Floor and Entire Wooden Decoration Exhibition
Venue: Qingdao Intl Convention & Exhibition Center, Qingdao, Shandong
Organizer: Qingdao Haichen International Expo Co Ltd
Address: 5-8F, Miaoling Road, Qingdao, Shandong 266061, China

2013/07/17-19
☎ 0532-8395 1161, 15866885895
🖷 0532-8384 1887
www.qdcainuan.com
4030

第四届中国（青岛）国际供热采暖系统产品及技术应用展览会
地点：青岛国际会展中心，山东青岛
内容：地暖、电采暖产品和技术；发泡水泥、模块地暖等供热采暖产品和技术；供暖系统自动化与配套设备；空调制冷通风及热泵节能技术设备
主办：住房和城乡建设部建筑节能中心；青岛市城乡建设委员会；海展集团
承办：青岛市建筑节能协会；青岛市供热协会；青岛海宸国际会展有限公司
地址：山东青岛苗岭路9号（青岛国际会展中心）5-8F(266061)
联系人：孟翔

Qingdao Intl Heating System Product & Technology Utilization Fair
Venue: Qingdao Intl Convention & Exhibition Center, Qingdao, Shandong
Organizer: Qingdao Haichen International Expo Co Ltd
Address: 5-8F, Miaoling Road, Qingdao, Shandong

2013/07/17-19
☎ 0532-8395 1081, 8395 1190
🖷 0532-8384 1887
www.wooddoorqd.cn
4040

第九届中国（青岛）国际木门展览会
地点：青岛国际会展中心，山东青岛
内容：实木及各类门、窗，门窗辅助材料；木工机械及生产加工设备、烤漆设备；门业涂料、油漆化工产品；门控门禁技术及门窗五金配件
主办：中国木材与木制品流通协会木门窗专业委员会；海展集团
承办：青岛海宸国际会展有限公司
地址：山东青岛苗岭路9号（青岛国际会展中心）5-8F(266061)

9th Qingdao Intl Wooden Door Exhibition
Venue: Qingdao Intl Convention & Exhibition Center, Qingdao, Shandong
Organizer: Qingdao Haichen International Expo Co Ltd
Address: 5-8F, Miaoling Road, Qingdao, Shandong 266061, China

2013/07/17-19
☎ 0532-8395 1073, 13553007412
🖷 0532-8395 1197
www.qdmsmw.com
4050

第二届中国（青岛）国际木屋、木结构及配套设施展览会
地点：青岛国际会展中心，山东青岛
内容：木结构建筑，木屋、木结构材料，木塑景观型材，木屋、木结构设备
主办：中国建筑材料联合会；山东省经济和信息化委员会；青岛市人民政府；**承办：**山东省建筑材料工业协会，青岛市城乡建设委员会，青岛海宸国际会展有限公司
地址：青岛苗岭路9号（青岛国际会展中心）5-8F(266061)
联系人：于娟

Qingdao Intl Wood House Exhibition
Venue: Qingdao Intl Convention & Exhibition Center, Qingdao, Shandong
Organizer: Qingdao Haichen International Expo Co Ltd
Address: 5-8F, Miaoling Road, Qingdao, Shandong 266061, China

2013/07/17-19
☎ 0532-8395 1012
🖷 0532-8395 1189
www.qdcwjt.com
4060

第二届中国（青岛）橱柜衣柜展览会
地点：青岛国际会展中心，山东青岛
内容：整体橱柜、集成厨房，整体衣柜、整体书柜、衣帽间等，橱柜、衣柜饰面材料；整体家装
主办：中国建筑材料联合会；青岛市城乡建设委员会；海展集团
承办：青岛海宸国际会展有限公司
地址：青岛苗岭路9号（青岛国际会展中心）5-8F(266061)

China (Qingdao) Intl Cabinet and Wardrobe Exhibition
Venue: Qingdao Intl Convention & Exhibition Center, Qingdao, Shandong
Organizer: Qingdao Haichen International Expo Co Ltd
Address: 5-8F, Miaoling Road, Qingdao, Shandong 266061, China

2013/08/09-11
☎ 0532-8501 7066
🖷 0532-8583 3615
4070

2013第十二届青岛国际电子电路板展览会
2013青岛国际胶粘带、保护膜及光学膜展
胶粘剂及密封剂展
地点：青岛国际会展中心，山东青岛
内容：电路板本业，电路板设备，电路板用原物料与化学品，周边相关设备、零组件，电子成品组装代工服务、洁净室技术及服务、净水技术及设备。
周期：每年一届
主办：中国电子学会元件分会；中国国际贸易促进联合会；广东省电子商会；亚洲经贸发展促进中心
承办：青岛德尔展览有限公司

12th Qingdao Electronic Circuit Board Fair
Venue: Qingdao Intl Convention & Exhibition Center, Qingdao, Shandong
Frequency: Annual
Organizer: Qingdao Deer Exhibition Co Ltd

2013/08/15-17
☎ 0532-5555 2919, 13589340811
🖷 0532-5555 2903
✉ sujiao85785101@163.com
www.china-sujiao.com
4080

第15届中国青岛国际塑料橡胶工业展览会
2013青岛国际塑料原料及改性技术展览会
地点：青岛国际会展中心，山东青岛
内容： 注射成型生产技术设备、机械手臂（取出机）、中央供料及辅机设备/模具及模具零组件制造设备。挤出生产技术及设备；塑胶机械、橡胶/轮胎机械及配套产品、测试及控制仪器、表面处理、打光设备、后处理设备；中空成型生产技术及设备；相关配套设备及各类零件；原材料、添加剂；塑料及橡胶原物料、添加剂、色母粒等成品及半成品。软包装加工、制膜、印刷、复合等机械设备**主办：**中国贸促会机械行业分会；中国国际商会机械行业商会；青岛市人民政府；青岛金诺国际会展有限公司
地址：青岛市福州南路87号福林大厦902室
联系人：王飞

15th China (Qingdao) Intl Plastics & Rubber Industry Exhibition
China Qingdao Intl Exhibition of Plastic Raw Materials and Modified Technology
Venue: Qingdao Intl Convention & Exhibition Center, Qingdao, Shandong
Organizer: Qingdao Jinnoc Exhibition Co Ltd
Address: Room 902, 807 South Fuzhou Road, Qingdao 266071, Shandong

2013/08/15-17
☎ 0532-5555 2901, 5555 2902
🖷 0532-5555 2903
✉ service@china-jinnuo.com
www.china-ptce.com
4090

2013第15届中国青岛国际动力传动与控制技术展览会
地点：青岛国际展会中心，山东青岛
内容：流体动力传动，机械传动、零部件及制造设备，轴承，直线运动系统，电气传动，压缩气体技术，内燃机及小型燃汽轮机
主办：中国贸促会机械行业分会；山东省自动化学会
承办：青岛金诺会展有限公司
地址：山东省青岛市福州南路87号福林大厦902室

15th China Intl Power Transmission & Control Technology (Qingdao) Exhibition
Venue: Qingdao Intl Convention & Exhibition Center, Qingdao, Shandong
Organizer: Qingdao Jinnoc Exhibition Co Ltd
Address: 902, Fulin Building, 87 South Fuzhou Road, Qingdao, Shandong 266071, China

2013/08/15-17
☎ 0532-5555 2901, 5555 2902
🖷 0532-5555 2903
✉ service@china-jinnuo.com
www.zd-yiqi.com
4100

2013第15届中国青岛国际仪器仪表及测试测量技术展览会
第15届中国青岛国际工业自动化及控制技术展览会
地点：青岛国际会展中心，山东青岛
内容：工业自动化及控制技术，工业自动化（生产及过程自动化），电气传动，机器人技术，工业自动化信息技术及软件，微系统技术，仪器仪表及测试测量技术，自动化仪器仪表，科学仪器，电子与电工测量仪器，元器件及附件

15th China Qingdao Industrial Automation and Control Technology Exhibition
15th China Qingdao Intl Instruments and Test and Measurement Technology Exhibition
Venue: Qingdao Intl Convention & Exhibition Center, Qingdao, Shandong
Organizer: Qingdao Jinnoc Exhibition Co Ltd

主办：中国贸促会机械行业分会；中国计算机用户协会智能控制分会；山东省自动化学会；青岛市人民政府
承办：青岛金诺会展有限公司
地址：山东省青岛市福州南路87号福林大厦902室

Address: 902, Fulin Building, 87 South Fuzhou Road, Qingdao, Shandong 266071, China

2013/10/23-25
☎ 010-6876 7728
🖷 010-6876 7765
✉ wangc@autoid-china.com.cn
www.aimchina.org.cn
4110

第二十届国际自动识别及物联网技术展览会
地点：青岛国际会展中心，山东青岛
内容：条码技术及产品，射频识别技术及产品，生物特征识别技术及产品，物联网相关技术产品，其它自动识别技术及上下游关联产品，自动识别与信息化相关技术集成应用解决方案及产品，自动识别技术在零售、工业制造、医疗卫生、食品安全、安防、防伪等行业应用的解决方案。
主办：中国物品编码中心；中国自动识别技术协会
承办：北京源智天成科技有限公司
地址：北京市海淀区阜成路16号航天科技大厦附楼401室
联系人：王灿

SCAN CHINA 2013
20th Intl Exhibition of Automatic Identification Technology
Venue: Qingdao Intl Convention & Exhibition Center, Qingdao, Shandong
Organizer: Automatic Identification Manufacture Association of China

山东-烟台 Shandong-Yantai

2013/04/11-14
☎ 010-8260 6899
🖷 010-8260 6883
✉ ciccyhuang@cnaico.com.cn
www.cnaico.com.cn
www.autochina.com.cn
4120

2013年烟台春季汽车展销会
地点：山东烟台
主办：中国汽车工业国际合作总公司
地址：北京市海淀区中关村丹棱街3号A座

2013 Yantai Spring Automobile Show and Sale
Venue: Yantai, Shandong
Organizer: China National Automotive Industry Intl Corp
Address: A, 3 Danling Street, Zhongguancun, Haidian Dist., Beijing, China

2013/07/05-07
☎ 0535-628 0001, 628 0002
🖷 0535-628 0003
✉ mail@wine-china.org
4130

第七届烟台国际葡萄酒博览会
地点：烟台国际博览中心，山东烟台
内容：品牌葡萄酒，果酒及原酒（红葡萄酒、白葡萄酒、桃红葡萄酒、香槟、雪莉酒、朗姆酒、冰酒、白兰地、威士忌等），礼品酒及工艺品，葡萄酒相关产品，酒庄、酒窖，酒吧，中西美食，葡萄酒俱乐部，葡萄酒文化旅游，葡萄酒文化艺术，葡萄酒书刊网站
始办年份：2007
周期：每年一届
市场范围：国际性
性质：面向公众和贸易观众
参展费用：国内展商5,000元/展位，角位加收500元/个，光地450元/m^2(36m^2起)；海外展商1,200美元/展位，角位加收100美元/展位，光地100美元/m^2(36m^2起)
上届规模 '12：展览面积18,000m^2(国外展商面积3,000m^2)，参展商530家（国外展商76家，来自19个国家），参观人数50,000人（贸易观众5,000人）
主办：国际葡萄及葡萄酒组织（OIV）；中国酒类流通协会；烟台市人民政府；山东省商务厅
承办：高美艾博（上海）有限公司
地址：山东省烟台市莱山区新苑路5号合普生物主楼五层(264003)
联系人：王丹萍女士，王晓燕女士

7th Yantai Intl Wine Exposition
Venue: Yantai Intl Expo Center, Yantai, Shandong
Profile: Grape wines, fruit wines, proto-wines, related wine products, chateaus and wine clubs, wine culture tourism, wine culture arts, gift wines and works of art, wine magazines and websites, etc
Established Year: 2007
Frequency: Annual
Market Area: International
Nature: Open to Public
Participated Fee: USD 1,200/booth, Corner Booth add USD 100/booth, Raw Space USD 100/m^2(min 36m^2)
Statistics '12: Exhibition Area 18,000m^2 (foreigners 3,000m^2), Exhibitors 530 (foreigners 76, came from 19 countries), Visitors 50,000 (Trade Visitors 5,000)
Organizer: Yantai City
Address: 5/F, Hepu Biology Main Building, No. 5 Xinyuan Road, Laishan District, Yantai 264003, Shandong, China

2013/09/05-09
☎ 010-8260 6899
🖷 010-8260 6883
✉ ciccyhuang@cnaico.com.cn
www.cnaico.com.cn
www.autochina.com.cn
4140

2013第九届烟台国际汽车工业展览会
地点：山东烟台
主办：中国汽车工业国际合作总公司
地址：北京市海淀区中关村丹棱街3号A座

9th Yantai Intl Automobile Industry Exhibition 2013
Venue: Yantai, Shandong
Organizer: China National Automotive Industry Intl Corp
Address: A, 3 Danling Street, Zhongguancun, Haidian Dist., Beijing, China

2013/09/26-28
☎ 0535-660 5511, 661 1833
🖷 0535-6280 003
✉ yantai310@yahoo.com
20584045
www.fruitveg-expo.cn
4150

第十四届国际果蔬、食品博览会
地点：烟台国际博览中心，山东烟台
内容：优质干果、鲜果及制成品，脱水蔬菜、冷冻蔬菜及各类蔬菜加工产品等；乳制品、肉制品、豆制品、调味品、罐头食品、速冻食品、面食点心等；果汁（肉）饮料、功能饮料、保健饮料、茶叶、保健酒等；化肥、有机肥、农药、塑料薄膜及其它农用生产资料等；果蔬种苗、花卉等；果蔬栽培、采收、保鲜储藏技术与设备，自动化控制与温室工程，无公害生产技术与设备，加工技术与设备，包装材料与设备，园艺工具，灌溉设备，食品、饮料生产加工机械，渔业机械；农机汽车工程机械；水产品
始办年份：1999
周期：每年两届
市场范围：国际性
性质：面向公众
主办：联合国亚洲及太平洋经济社会委员会；联合国亚太农业工程与机械中心；联合国亚太技术转让中心
承办：山东省烟台市人民政府；山东省商务厅；山东省科学技术厅；山东省农业厅；山东省林业局、山东省供销合作社联合社；山东省农业机械管理局
地址：山东省烟台市莱山区新苑路5号合普生物主楼5层(264003)
联系人：王晓燕

11th Intl Fruit/Vegetable/Food Exposition
Venue: Yantai Intl Expo Center, Yantai, Shandong
Profile: High-quality fresh, dried and processed fruits, dehydrated vegetables, frozen vegetables and other processed vegetables from northern China; dairy products, meat products, bean products, seasonings, canned food, quick-frozen food, health-care food, cookies, chocolates; beverage, fruit juice drinks, functional drinks, health-care drinks, tea, alcoholic drinks; fertilizers, organic fertilizers, pesticides, storage equipments, automatic control and green-house engineering, treatment technology and equipments, processing technology and equipments
Established Year: 1999
Frequency: Bi-annual
Market Area: International
Nature: Open to Public
Organizer: United Nations Economic and Social Commission for Asia; Pacific (ESCAP); United Nations Asian and Pacific Center for Agricultural Engineering and Machinery (APCAEM-ESCAP), Asian and Pacific Center for Transfer of Technology (APCTT-ESCAP)
Address: 5th Floor, 5 Xinyuan Road, Laishan District, Yantai, Shandong Province, China

山西-大同 Shanxi-Datong

2013/08/23-28
☎ 010-8260 6899
🖷 010-8260 6883
✉ ciccyhuang@cnaico.com.cn
www.cnaico.com.cn
www.autochina.com.cn
4160

中国（大同）国际汽车文化节
地点： 山西大同
主办： 中国汽车工业国际合作总公司
地址： 北京市海淀区中关村丹棱街3号A座

China (Datong) Intl Automobile Culture Festival
Venue: Datong, Shanxi
Organizer: China National Automotive Industry Intl Corp
Address: A, 3 Danling Street, Zhongguancun, Haidian Dist., Beijing, China

四川-成都 Sichuan-Chengdu

2013/03/02-03
☎ 028-8538 0226,8538 2006
🖷 028-8535 2015，8538 2015
✉ 695149355@qq.com
695149355
4170

成都婚庆博览会
地点： 成都世纪城新国际会展中心，四川成都
内容： 涉及婚纱摄影，婚纱礼服，婚庆公司，婚宴酒楼，珠宝首饰，婚礼用品，蜜月旅游等行业。不仅齐聚来自全球千余家婚庆品牌，新人可一站式轻松采购结婚所需，更聚焦了世界前沿婚庆品牌新品发布潮流看点。
周期： 每年两届
市场范围： 地区性
性质： 面向公众和贸易观众
入场券价格： 20元
参展费用： 标准展位4,800元/9m²，光地550元/m²
上届规模： 展览面积5,328m²，参展商70家，参观人数21,952人
主办： 成都市博览局；成都市民政局；成都市商务局
承办： 成都国际商务会展服务中心；591结婚网；成都世纪城新国际会展中心
地址： 四川省成都市世纪城路198号世纪城国际会议中心8楼(610041)
联系人： 杨会兰，张倍

Chengdu Wedding Fair
Venue: New Intl Convention & Expo Center Chengdu Century City, Chengdu, Sichuan
Profile: Various sectors ranged from wedding photography, wedding dress, wedding planning, wedding catering, jewellery, to honey-moon travels. It does not only gather thousands of global wedding brands for newly married couples to choose but also attract top brands to release their new products.
Frequency: Bi-annual
Market Area: Regional
Nature: Open to Public
Cost to Attend: RMB 20:-
Participated Fee: Standard Booth RMB 4,800/9m², Raw Space RMB 550/m²
Statistics '12: Exhibition Area 5,328m², Exhibitors 70, Visitors 21,952
Organizer: Chengdu Expo Bureau; Chengdu Civil Affairs Bureau; Chengdu Municipal Bureau of Commerce
Organizer: Chengdu Intl Business Conference and Exhibition Service Center; 591 wed.com; Chengdu Century City New Intl Exhibition and Convention Center
Address: 8th Floor, Century City International Conference Center, No. 198, Century City Road, Chengdu, Sichuan 610041, China
Contact: Tracy Yang, Jessica Zhang

2013/03/28-31
☎ 010-8836 3768, 6831 7248, 6831 6827
🖷 info@qgtjh.com
www.qgtjh.com
4180

2013年春季成都全国糖酒会
地点： 成都世纪城新国际会展中心，四川成都
内容： 各种酒类、食品、饮料、调味品、食品添加剂、食品包装、食品机械的生产或销售
始办年份： 1955
周期： 每年两届
主办： 中国糖业酒类集团公司；成都市人民政府
承办： 中糖新世纪国际会展（北京）有限公司；成都市博览局

China Food & Drinks Fair
Venue: New Intl Convention & Expo Center Chengdu Century City, Chengdu, Sichuan
Established Year: 1955
Frequency: Bi-annual
Organizer: China National Sugar and Alcohol Group Corp

2013/04/02-04
☎ 028-8608 0319
🖷 028-8608 0309
✉ 1971397976@qq.com
www.cdmee.cn
4190

2013第12届西部成都医疗器械展览会
第十期医院领导干部管理培训班
第七届检验医学学术会
四川省康复学术年会
地点： 成都世纪城新国际会展中心，四川成都
内容： 影像设备，心脑电监护设备，检验生化及实验室设备与试剂，辅助设备，其他设备
主办： 四川省医院协会；四川省农村卫生协会；四川省输血协会；四川省康复学会
承办： 成都市天一展览服务有限公司
联系人： 张静

12th West China (Chengdu) Medical Equipment Exhibition
Venue: New Intl Convention & Expo Center Chengdu Century City, Chengdu, Sichuan
Organizer: Chengdu Tanya Exhibition Service Co Ltd

2013/04/10-12
☎ 028-6810 1913, 13709088591
🖷 028-6810 1918
✉ cdcd@vip.sohu.com
4200

2013中国四川国际天然气汽车、加气站设备展览会
地点： 成都世纪城新国际会展中心，四川成都
内容： 天然气汽车整车展区：天然气专用车，零部件展区，零部件及专用装备，电池及其它蓄能装置，燃料转换系统，控制元器件，加气设施类展区，加气站设备，深冷设备展区；其他设备及技术展区，燃料
参展费用： 标准展位8,200元，美元2500，光地（36m²起）900元/m²，250美元/m²
主办： 四川省清洁汽车产业协会
承办： 成都环达中油展览有限公司
地址： 成都市二环路南四段10号岷江大楼505
联系人： 韩东

China (Sichuan) Natural?Gas?Vehicle and Gas Station Equipment Exhibition
Venue: New Intl Convention & Expo Center Chengdu Century City, Chengdu, Sichuan
Participated Fee: Standard Booth USD 2,500/booth, Raw Space (min 36m²) USD 250/m²
Organizer: Chengdu Huada Zhongyou Exhibition Co Ltd

2013/04/18-20
☎ 028-8624 7166
🖷 028-8624 1828
✉ 444189398@qq.com
4210

2013年建材行业大型展览会
地点：成都世纪城新国际会展中心，四川成都
内容：创意设计，建筑装饰企业，室内装饰材料：厨房用品及配套设施，卫浴陶瓷，室内装饰门窗、楼梯及木制品，地铺材料，软装配饰，建筑装饰五金，涂料，整体家居，石材，天花吊顶材料，室内新型材料，室内供暖系统、热泵及通风设备，玻璃制品
参展费用：标准展位：境内企业6,500元，境外企业1,800美元，角位加收20%。光地（$36m^2$起）境内企业650元/m^2，境外企业180美元/m^2
主办：四川省住房和城乡建设厅；成都陈设艺术行业协会；成都市建筑装饰协会
联系人：刘凤贤

Building Material Industry Exhibition
Venue: New Intl Convention & Expo Center Chengdu Century City, Chengdu, Sichuan
Participated Fee: Standard Booth USD 1,800, Corner Booth add 20%, Raw Space ($36m^2$) USD 180/m^2
Organizer: Chengdu Building Decoration Association

2013/04/18-20
☎ 028-8692 2808
🖷 028-6647 6338
4220

2013中国成都创意设计展暨建筑装饰博览会
地点：成都世纪城新国际会展中心，四川成都
内容：创意设计：建筑装饰设计机构、建筑装饰设计师、陈设艺术设计师、住宅工业化部品产品设计师
主办：四川省住房和城乡建设厅；成都陈设艺术行业协会；成都市建筑装饰协会
地址：成都市东马道街19号
联系人：林先生

2013 China Chengdu Creative Design Exhibitions and Architecture Decoration Fair
Venue: New Intl Convention & Expo Center Chengdu Century City, Chengdu, Sichuan
Organizer: Chengdu Building Decoration Association

2013/04/18-20
☎ 028-8624 2818, 18280328306
🖷 028-8624 1828
✉ 137315520@qq.com
4230

2013中国成都厨房用品及配套设施展览会
地点：成都世纪城新国际会展中心，四川成都
内容：厨房电器及设备：烟机、灶具、电磁炉、微波炉、烤炉、电烤箱、电饼铛、面包机、洗碗机、榨汁机、咖啡机（壶）、电水壶、直饮机、电饭煲、电冰箱、冷藏柜、电暖器，厨具洗刷设备、抽排风设备、水处理设备、垃圾处理设备等。
主办：四川省住房和城乡建设厅；成都市建筑装饰协会；成都陈设艺术行业协会
地址：成都市青羊区东胜街1号青羊物业大厦618室
联系人：杨翔宇

China (Chengdu) Kitchen Supplies and Ancillary Facilities Exhibition
Venue: New Intl Convention & Expo Center Chengdu Century City, Chengdu, Sichuan
Organizer: Chengdu Building Decoration Association

2013/06/20-22
☎ 010-5166 2329转16/ 58/ 35
🖷 010-6813 2578, 6818 9519
✉ guanbing@ceac.com.cn
www.icef.com.cn
4240

2013年中国(成都)电子展
地点：成都世纪城新国际会展中心，四川成都
主办：中国电子器材总公司
承办：中电会展与信息传播有限公司
地址：北京市复兴路49号702（100036）

China Electronics Fair West Show 2013
Venue: New Intl Convention & Expo Center Chengdu Century City, Chengdu, Sichuan
Organizer: China Electronics Appliance Corp

2013/07/03-06
☎ 028-8627 9311
🖷 028-8628 0491
✉ 1393127834@qq.com
www.iffcd.com
4250

2013第十四届成都国际家具工业展览会
地点：成都世纪城新国际会展中心，四川成都
内容：家具馆：民用家具、办公家具、宾馆家具、厨房家具等；综合馆：家居饰品、布艺、皮革等；机械馆：木工机械、刀具、配件料等；辅料馆：家具原辅料、五金配件、五金工具，家具五金，五金制品，装饰材料
主办：成都市人民政府；四川省商务厅
承办：中国贸促会成都市分会，四川省家具进出口商会
地址：成都市东马道街19号
联系人：林先生

Intl Furniture Fair Chengdu
Venue: New Intl Convention & Expo Center Chengdu Century City, Chengdu, Sichuan
Organizer: CCPIT Chengdu Sub-Council

2013/07/18-20
☎ 028-8692 5628
🖷 028-6647 6338
✉ zznk@yeah.net
QQ 7547808
4260

2013第十七届中国西部（成都）五金机电商品展览会
地点：成都世纪城新国际会展中心，四川成都
内容：五金工具，机械设备，机电产品，五金制品类，其他产品
参展费用：标准展位（3x3m）：特别展区5,500元，普通展区5,000元，光地（$36m^2$起）550元/m^2
主办：中国贸易促进委员会；中国机械工业联合会；成都市人民政府；
承办：西安三联科技会展有限公司

17th China West Intl Equipment Manufacturing Exposition
Venue: New Intl Convention & Expo Center Chengdu Century City, Chengdu, Sichuan
Participated Fee: Standard Booth RMB 5,000/$9m^2$, Raw Space (min $36m^2$) RMB 550/m^2
Organizer: Xi'an Joint Exhibition Co., Ltd

2013/07/19-21
☎ 029-8815 3802, 15389409298
🖷 029-8831 4333
✉ liluoluo.joyful@163.com
www.cwieme.com
4270

2013第十七届中国西部国际装备制造业博览会
地点：成都世纪城新国际会展中心，四川成都
内容：热处理技术，工业炉窑技术及设备，铸造、锻造技术及设备；铸造装备；模具；检测设备；耐火材料领域；电炉、工业炉配件产品；焊接及切割技术；切割装备及辅件；热处理产业科研机构、大专院校
主办：中国贸易促进委员会；中国机械工业联合会；陕西省振兴装备制造业领导小组；西安市人民政府，成都市人民政府
承办：西安曲江三之联会展有限公司
地址：西安市科技路37号海星城市广场B座24层
联系人：张玉华

17th China West Intl Equipment Manufacturing Exposition
Venue: New Intl Convention & Expo Center Chengdu Century City, Chengdu, Sichuan
Organizer: Xi'an Joint Exhibition Co., Ltd

2013/08/31-09/08
☎ 021-5045 6700, 5045 6700
🖷 021-5045 9355, 5045 9355
✉ karl.wang@hmf-china.com
www.cd-motorshow.com
4280

第十六届成都国际汽车展览会
地点：成都世纪城新国际会展中心，四川成都
内容：西部地区顶级的专业汽车展览会
周期：每年一届
市场范围：国际性
性质：面向公众和贸易观众
上届规模：展览面积130,000m^2

Chengdu Motor Show 2013
Venue: New Intl Convention & Expo Center Chengdu Century City, Chengdu, Sichuan
Profile: Intl Exhibition for Automobile and Accessories
Frequency: Annual
Market Area: International
Nature: Open to Public

主办：成都市人民政府；成都世纪城新国际会展中心；汉诺威米兰展览（上海）有限公司_
地址：上海市浦东新区银霄路393号百安居浦东商务大厦301室汉诺威米兰展览（上海）有限公司(201204)
联系人：王飞

Statistics '12: Exhibition Area 130,000m²
Organizer: Chengdu Municipal Government; New Intl Convention & Exposition Center Chengdu Century City; Hannover Milano Fairs Shanghai Ltd
Address: Hannover Milano Fairs Shanghai Ltd, Rm. 301, B&Q Pudong Office Tower,393 Yinxiao Rd, Pudong, Shanghai 201204, China
Contact: Karl Wang

2013/09/18-21
☎ 028-8514 4168, 6557 3957, 023-8630 8303
🖷 028-8514 4168, 6557 3958, 023-8630 8323
✉ cdcwmte@cwmte.cn
www.cwmte.com.cn
4290

2013第14届立嘉国际机床展览会-成都展会
地点：成都世纪城新国际会展中心，四川成都
内容：金属切削机床类、锻压机床类、工夹量具类、数控与自动化类、模具及材料类、计算机应用技术、工业货柜、工具柜、仓储、物流设备、其他机械加工新技术新设备。
主办：成都立嘉会议展览有限公司
地址：成都市高新区世纪城路920号6栋2单元28层2号
联系人：孙俊良

Jiali Intl Machinery Exhibition - Chengdu
Venue: New Intl Convention & Expo Center Chengdu Century City, Chengdu, Sichuan
Organizer: Chengdu Jiali Conference and Exhibition Co Ltd

2013/11/14-16
☎ 010-6878 4996，6878 4998
🖷 010-6878 4978
✉ yw@ccfa.org.cn
50161389
www.chinaretailexpo.com
4300

第十五届中国连锁店展览会
地点：成都世纪城新国际会展中心，四川成都
内容：目前国内规模最大、最具权威性的零售品牌、零售技术、设备专业展览，也是跨国快消品企业参与度最高的零售业展会。历经十四届的成功举办，已发展成为目前国内零售领域内规模最大、影响力最高的展会活动之一。展商包括连锁百强企业、商用设施设备、技术供应商、商品供应商。展览会设有零售信息技术、商用设施设备、特色商品和农产品等主题展区。
始办年份：1999
周期：每年一届
市场范围：全国性
性质：面向贸易观众
入场券价格：免费
参展费用：标准展位8,000元/9m²，光地展位800元/m²
上届规模：展览面积43,000m²（国外展商面积8,600m²），参展商283家（国外展商60家，来自6个国家），贸易观众19,000人
主办：中国连锁经营协会
地址：北京市西城区阜外大街22号外经贸大厦811-815（100037）
联系人：杨雯，沈静

China Shop - China Retail Trade Fair
Venue: New Intl Convention & Expo Center Chengdu Century City, Chengdu, Sichuan
Profile: The most influential and forward-looking event in China, Focus and support from thousands of retailers and suppliers for 14 years. This is the best place to show the latest, safety and delicate food and produce technology from both China and abroad, and to open Chinese retailing gate, to meet your Chinese buyers, agents and partners. A valuable opportunity to save your procurement cost to 40%-60% compared to overseas markets. This is the integrative event including different theme pavilions, leadership Summit, match-making activities, seminars and high-level dialogues.
Established Year: 1999
Frequency: Annual
Market Area: National
Nature: Trade Only
Cost to Attend: Free
Participated Fee: Standard Booth RMB 8,000/9m², Raw Space RMB 800/m²
Statistics '12: Exhibition Area 43,000m² (foreigners 8,600m²), Exhibitors 283 (foreigners 60, came from 6 countries), Trade Visitors 19,000
Organizer: China Chain Store & Franchise Association
Address: Room811, 8th Floor, Foreign Economic & Trade Plaza, No 22 Fuchengmenwai Str., Xicheng Dist., Beijing 100037, China
Contact: Sharon Yang, Shen Jingo

新疆-乌鲁木齐 Xinjiang-Urumqi

^^8958
2013/04/10-12
☎ 0991-610 8088, 13579965359
🖷 0991-610 8099
✉ ranwei139@sina.com
www.ceaeexpo.com
4310

2013年亚欧能源产业博览会
地点：新疆国际会展中心，新疆乌鲁木齐
内容：大型能源企业成果形象展示，煤电、煤化工与煤炭装备展区，石油石化与天然气技术展区，发电与输电能源展区，新能源展区，新能源与可再生能源、风能风电、太阳能光伏产业展区，大型设备展区
主办：乌鲁木齐市人民政府；新疆维吾尔自治区商务厅
承办：乌鲁木齐市商务（粮食）局；新疆华和国际商务咨询有限公司；新疆雷诺展览有限公司
地址：新疆乌鲁木齐市阿勒泰路83号皓翔金山大厦401(830054)
联系人：冉伟

EuroAsia Energy Industry Expo 2013
Venue: Xinjiang Intl Convention & Exhibition Center, Urumqi, Xinjiang
Organizer: Xinjiang R-space Expo Co Ltd

云南-昆明 Yunnan-Kunming

2013/06/06-10
☎ 0871-226 9387, 18987140763
🖷 0871-716 7954
✉ kmfair@kmfair.org
1223235543
www.kmfair.org
4320

首届中国-南亚博览会
原南亚商品展
地点：昆明国际会展中心，云南昆明
内容：展会设置机电、生物资源、家居建材等商品专业展馆和境外来展馆、南亚馆等专题展馆
参展费用：标准展位5,000元/9m²
主办：国家商务部、重庆、四川、云南、贵州、广西、西藏、成都（省、自治区、市）人民政府
承办：云南省人民政府
地址：昆明市春城路289号(650011)
联系人：苟帅

First South Asia Expo
Venue: Kunming Intl Convention & Exhibition Center, Kunming, Yunnan
Participated Fee: Standard Booth RMB 5,000/9m²
Organizer: The People's Government of Yunnan Province
Address: 289 Chunchen Road, Kunming 650011, Yunnan, China

2013/06/06-10
☎ 0871-226 9387, 18987140763
🖷 0871-716 7954
✉ kmfair@kmfair.org
1223235543
www.kmfair.org
4330

第二十一届昆交会
– 第二十一届中国昆明进出口商品交易会
地点：昆明国际会展中心，云南昆明
内容：包括商品、技术进出口、国内外招商引资及经济技术合作项目洽谈等，设有机电、生物资源、家居建材等商品专业馆和投资促进、境外来展等专题展馆。
始办年份：1993
周期：每年一届
市场范围：国际性
性质：面向公众和贸易观众
主办：国家商务部，云南省人民政府
承办：云南省人民政府
地址：昆明市春城路289号(650011)
联系人：荀帅

The 21th Kunming Fair
- The 21th China Import & Export Fair, Kunming
Venue: Kunming Intl Convention & Exhibition Center, Kunming, Yunnan
Profile: Kunming Fair covers import and export trade and technology, investment promotion, and economic and technological cooperation. There are pavilions for all sectors from Machinery & Electronics; Biological Resources; Household Building Materials. There are also theme pavilions, including International Pavilion and Investment
Established Year: 1993
Frequency: Annual
Market Area: International
Nature: Open to Public
Organizer: The People’s Government of Yunnan Province
Address: 289 Chunchen Road, Kunming 650011, Yunnan, China

浙江-杭州 Zhejiang-Hangzhou

2013/03/21-24
☎ 010-5129 8656转ext 131
🖷 010-6478 7582
✉ liuxuezhu@talent-expo.com
www.OutdoorHangZhou.com
4340

第6届中国（杭州）国际花园户外家具及休闲用品展
地点：杭州和平国际会展中心，浙江杭州
内容：户外家具系列，户外运动系列
参展费用：标准展位：国内展商8,800元/9m²，海外展商1,250欧元/9m²；光地(36m²起)：820元/m²，海外展商120欧元/m²
主办：中国轻工工艺品进出口商会；杭州市人民政府；浙江省商务厅
承办：杭州市对外贸易经济合作局；北京泰莱特展览有限责任公司
地址：(100038)
联系人：刘雪竹

Outdoor Lifestyle Hangzhou 2013
Venue: Hangzhou Peace Intl Exhibition and Conference Center, Hangzhou, Zhejiang
Participated Fee: Standard Booth EUR 1,250/9m², Raw Space (min 36m²) EUR 120/m²
Organizer: Beijing Talent-Expo Co Ltd

2013/04 -
☎ 010-8260 6899
🖷 010-8260 6883
✉ ciccyhuang@cnaico.com.cn
www.cnaico.com.cn
www.autochina.com.cn
4350

第七届杭州春季汽车展销会
地点：浙江杭州
内容：2013年4月或5月
主办：中国汽车工业国际合作总公司
地址：北京市海淀区中关村丹棱街3号A座

7th Hangzhou Spring Automobile Show and Sale
Venue: Hangzhou, Zhejiang
Organizer: China National Automotive Industry Intl Corp
Address: A, 3 Danling Street, Zhongguancun, Haidian Dist., Beijing, China

2013/10 -
☎ 010-8260 6899
🖷 010-8260 6883
✉ ciccyhuang@cnaico.com.cn
www.cnaico.com.cn
www.autochina.com.cn
4360

2013年第十四届中国杭州国际汽车工业展览会
地点：浙江杭州
主办：中国汽车工业国际合作总公司
地址：北京市海淀区中关村丹棱街3号A座

14th China (Hangzhou) Auto Industry Exhibition
Venue: Hangzhou, Zhejiang
Organizer: China National Automotive Industry Intl Corp
Address: A, 3 Danling Street, Zhongguancun, Haidian Dist., Beijing, China

2013/10/26-28
☎ 852-2827 6211
020-8666 0158
🖷 852-3749 7342
020-8667 7120
✉ info-hk@ubm.com
info-china@ubm.com
http://exhibitions.jewellerynetasia.com/hzj
4370

Treasures Hangzhou

珠光魅影–杭州
地点：上海金茂君悦大酒店，浙江杭州
主办：亚洲博闻有限公司
地址：香港湾仔港湾道26号华润大厦17楼
国内联络：博闻(广州)展览有限公司
地址：广州市流花路中国大酒店商业大厦1159-1164室 (510015)

Treasures Hangzhou
Venue: Hyatt Regency, Hangzhou, Zhejiang
Organizer: UBM Asia Ltd
Address: 17/F, China Resources Building, 26 Harbour Road, Wan Chai, Hong Kong

浙江-宁波 Zhejiang-Ningbo

2013/03/14-17
☎ 0574-8784 9308, 2771 6625
🖷 0574-8784 9306
✉ younage@younage.com
www.chinamaching.cn
4380

ChinaMach2013 中国国际机械工业展览会

2013中国国际机械工业展览会
地点：宁波国际贸易展览中心，浙江宁波
内容：金属加工机床、金属成形机床、电加工和线切割机床、工控自动化、工业机器人、数控系统、数显装置、机床附件、工量具、粉末冶金生产装备、焊接切割设备、硬质合金、特种金属功能材料、高端金属结构材料、模具及材料配件、物料搬运设备。
始办年份：2000
周期：每年一届
市场范围：国际性
性质：面向公众和贸易观众
参展费用：标准展位6,800元/个，光地680元/平方米

2013China International Machinery Industry Exhibition
Venue: Ningbo Intex Center, Ningbo, Zhejiang
Profile: Metal cutting machine tool, Metal forming machine tool, EDM and wire cutting machine, FMC/FMS & automatic devices, CNC system, Machine tool components and accessories, Tooling, fixture and related products, Plastic and rubber machinery and equipment Packing and printing equipment, Welding and cutting equipment, Automation and industrial control, Instrument and apparatus.
Established Year: 2000
Frequency: Annual
Market Area: International

上届规模：展览面积25,020m^2(国外展商面积31m^2)，参展商315家（国外展商346家，来自12个国家），参观人数12,800人（贸易观众5,647人）
主办：宁波市人民政府；中国机械设备工程股份有限公司；宁波雅卓展览服务有限公司；西麦克国际展览公司
地址：宁波市江东区百丈东路650号7楼（315040）
联系人：施国平，薛层

Nature: Open to Public
Participated Fee: Standard Booth RMB 6,800/Booth, Raw Space RMB 680/m^2
Statistics '12: Exhibition Area 25,020m^2 (foreigners 31m^2), Exhibitors 315 (foreigners 346, came from 12 countries), Visitors 12,800 (Trade Visitors 5,647)
Organizer: Younage Exhibition Co Ltd; CMEC International Exhibition Company
Address: 7/Fl, 650 East Baizhang Road, Jiangdong District, Ningbo, Zhejiang 315040, China

---

2013/03/29-31
☎ 0574-8725 4009
🖷 0574-8725 4017
✉ Stationeryfair@163.com
expo.21wenju.com
QQ 934667450
4390

第10届中国国际文具礼品博览会
地点：宁波国际会展中心，浙江宁波
内容：文具及办公用品，办公设备及电脑周边产品、耗材，办公家具：办公桌椅、保险箱、文件柜，文具、礼品生产加工设备、零部件，礼品、赠品、工艺品、家庭用品
主办：中国贸促会；宁波市人民政府
承办：中国贸促会宁波分会；宁海县人民政府；宁波高新区文讯科技有限公司；宁海县商务局；宁波中博国际展览有限公司
地址：宁波市江东区会展路181号办公二区7C05

10th China Intl Stationery & Gifts Exposition
Venue: Ningbo Intex Center, Ningbo, Zhejiang
Profile: stationery & office supplies; writing instrument; paper and paper products; office equipment, exhaustible materials of computer; crafts; artist products stationery & gift producing and processing machines, parts; gifts, presents; arts
Established Year: 2004
Frequency: Annual
Market Area: International
Organizer: CCPIT Ningbo Sub-Council; Ninghai Municipal People' s Government
Address: Room 7C05 Office Building 11, No.181 Huizhan Road, Jiangdong, Ningbo, Zhejiang

---

2013/03/29-31
☎ 0574-8721 6329, 15258282728
🖷 0574-8725 4017
✉ 15258282728@163.com
QQ 1049185526
4400

2013宁波国际时尚礼品及家庭用品展览会
地点：宁波国际会议展览中心，浙江宁波
内容：礼品、工艺品、赠品、纪念品；家居用品、家纺、家庭装饰品；运动及旅游用品、休闲用品；文具及文化用品；皮具、箱包；家用小电器
主办：宁波高新区文讯科技有限公司
地址：宁波江东会展路 181 号办公二区 7C04(315040)
联系人：邹小姐

Ningbo Gift and Housewear Exhibition
Venue: Ningbo Intex Center, Ningbo, Zhejiang
Organizer: Ningbo Wenxun Tech Co Ltd

2013/05/23-25
☎ 0574-8778 4337, 5668 5188
🖷 0574-8777 3480
✉ nbdongbo@163.com
www.intertextile.net
www.nb-tex.com
4410

2013第十一届宁波国际纺织面料、辅料及纱线博览会
地点：宁波国际会展中心，浙江宁波
内容：纺织面料；服装辅料；家用纺织品；纺织原料；纱线；辅助设备；纺织服装媒体
主办：宁波市服装协会；宁波江东东博展览有限公司
地址：宁波市世纪大道689号新天地商务大厦12幢6楼(315040)
联系人：张小姐

11th Ningbo Intl Textile Fabrics, Accessories & Yarns Exhibition 2013
Venue: Ningbo Intl Conference & Exhibition Center, Ningbo, Zhejiang
Organizer: Ningbo Jiangdong Dongbo?Exhibition?Co Ltd
Address: 6Fl., 12 New World Commercial Building, 689 Century Ave., Ningbo, Zhejiang 315040, China

---

2013/06/19-21
☎ 0574-8784 9308, 2771 6625
🖷 0574-8784 9308, 2771 6625
✉ younage@younage.com
www.china-mts.cn
4420

2013宁波国际海事会议和展览会
地点：宁波国际贸易展览中心，浙江宁波
内容：船舶工程、航运与海事服务、港口建设与营运、海事安全、海洋科技与装备、物流技术设备。
周期：每年一届
市场范围：国际性
性质：面向公众和贸易观众
参展费用：标准展位：国内单位9,000元/9m^2，海外单位2,800美元/9m^2；光地：国内单位850元/m^2，海外单位260美元/m^2
上届规模：展览面积11,000m^2 (国外展商面积27m^2)，参展商132家来自11个国家，参观人数3,551人（贸易观众1,600人）
主办：浙江省船舶行业协会；宁波市经济和信息化委员会；宁波市江东区人民政府；
承办：宁波雅卓展览服务有限公司；美国克劳斯国际展览公司；宁波市船舶工业行业协会
地址：宁波市江东区百丈东路650号7楼（315040）
联系人：施国平，薛层

China Maritime Tech Security Expo 2013
Venue: Ningbo Intex Center, Ningbo, Zhejiang
Frequency: Annual
Market Area: International
Nature: Open to Public
Participated Fee: USD 2,800/9m^2, Raw Space USD 260/m^2
Statistics '12: Exhibition Area 11,000m^2 (foreigners 27m^2), Exhibitors 132 came from 11 countries, Visitors 3,551 (Trade Visitors 1,600)
Organizer: Zhejiang Association of Shipbuilding; Ningbo Economic and Information Technology Commission; The People' s Government of Ningbo Jiangdong District; Younage Exhibition Co Ltd; E.J. Krause & Associates Inc; Ningbo Association of Shipbuilding Industry
Address: 7/Fl, 650 East Baizhang Road, Jiangdong District, Ningbo, Zhejiang 315040, China

---

2013/11/29-12/01
☎ 0574-8784 9308, 2771 6625
🖷 0574-8784 9306
✉ younage@younage.com
www.home-lifes.com
4430

2013中国宁波家居与时尚生活产品展览会
地点：宁波国际贸易展览中心，浙江宁波
内容：家居用品、智能家居、时尚生活用品及服务
市场范围：国际性
性质：面向公众和贸易观众
参展费用：国内单位7,500元/9m^2，海外单位2,000美元/9m^2，光地：国内单位680元/m^2，海外单位180美元/m^2
主办：宁波市工商业联合会；宁波市工业设计联合会；雅卓展览服务有限公司；美国克劳斯国际展览有限公司；
承办：宁波雅卓展览服务有限公司；美国克劳斯国际展览公司
地址：宁波市江东区百丈东路650号7楼（315040）
联系人：施国平，薛层

2013 Ningbo International Home & Lifestyle Products Exhibition
Venue: Ningbo Intex Center, Ningbo, Zhejiang
Market Area: International
Nature: Open to Public
Participated Fee: USD 2,000/9m^2, Raw Space USD 180/m^2
Organizer: Younage Exhibition Co Ltd; E.J. Krause & Associates, Inc
Address: 7/Fl, 650 East Baizhang Road, Jiangdong District, Ningbo, Zhejiang 315040, China

浙江-台州 Zhejiang-Taizhou

2013/09/25-28
☎ 0576-8253 1122, 8253 1100
www.china-pec.com
4440

2013塑胶会
－第十三届中国塑料交易会
地点：台州市国际会展中心，浙江台州
内容：机械类、机床工具、原料类
周期：每年一届
主办：路桥区政府；台州经济和信息化委员会；台州商务局
联络：组委会
地址：浙江省台州市路桥区腾达路1号台州市国际会展中心

China PET '13
12th China Plastics Exhibition & Conference
Venue: Taizhou Intl Convention & Exhibition Center, Taizhou, Zhejiang
Profile: Plastic products and parts, moulds and equipment, machines, raw material and auxiliary
Frequency: Annual
Contact: The Organizing Committee

浙江-温岭 Zhejiang-Wenling

2013/05-
☎ 010-8260 6899
📠 010-8260 6883
✉ ciccyhuang@cnaico.com.cn
www.cnaico.com.cn
www.autochina.com.cn
4450

2013温岭汽车展览会
地点：浙江温岭
内容：2013年5月或6月
主办：中国汽车工业国际合作总公司
地址：北京市海淀区中关村丹棱街3号A座

Wenling Auto Exhibition 2013
Venue: Wenling, Zhejiang
Organizer: China National Automotive Industry Intl Corp
Address: A, 3 Danling Street, Zhongguancun, Haidian Dist., Beijing, China

浙江-温州 Zhejiang-Wenzhou

2013/03/15-17
☎ 0577-8890 2222, 8895 8601
📠 0577-8890 1788
http://ce.donnor.com
4460

2013中国（温州）国际机床、工模具及塑胶工业展览会
地点：温州国际会展中心，浙江温州
内容：金切机床、金属成型机床、特种加工机床与专用设备类；制造单元/系统、自动化设备、工夹具与检测仪器类；机电产品与通用机械类；模具类；塑胶机械与原材料类等。
始办年份：2003
周期：每年一届
市场范围：地区性
性质：面向贸易观众
参展费用：国际区6,800元/9m^{2}展位,国内A区6,800元/9m^{2}展位，国内B区6,300元/9m^2；光地（36m^2）：国际区700元/m^2，国内A区700元/m^2，国内B区650元/m^2
上届规模：展览面积35,000m^2，参展商420家
主办：浙江德纳展览有限公司
地址：浙江省温州市龙湾区上江路198号新世纪商务大厦B-1403（325011）
联系人：石宪伟, 林晓东

2013 China (Wenzhou) Intl Machine Tool & Plastics Industry Equipment Exhibition
Venue: Wenzhou Intl Convention & Exhibition Center, Wenzhou, Zhejiang
Established Year: 2003
Frequency: Annual
Market Area: Regional
Nature: Trade Only
Participated Fee: RMB 6,800/9m^2, Raw Space RMB 700/m^2 (min 36m^2)
Statistics '12: Exhibition Area 35,000m^2, Exhibitors 420
Organizer: Donnor Exhibition Co Ltd
Address: B-1403, New Century Business Building, No.198 Shangjiang Rd, Wenzhou , Zhejiang 325011, China

2013/03/15-17
☎ 0577-8890 2222, 8890 5008
📠 0577-8890 1788
✉ machine@donnor.com
📱 1501542550
http://me.donnor.com
4470

2013中国（温州）国际工业博览会
地点：温州国际会展中心，浙江温州
内容：机械设备、自动化设备与电气系统、焊接切割技术与五金设备、五金机电与周边设备。
周期：每年一届
市场范围：地区性
性质：面向贸易观众
参展费用：标准展位5,800元/9m^2，光地（36m^{2}起）600元/m^2
主办：浙江德纳展览有限公司
地址：浙江省温州市龙湾区上江路198号新世纪商务大厦B-1403（325011）
联系人：徐建英，林晓东

2013 China (Wenzhou) Intl Industry Equipment
Venue: Wenzhou Intl Convention & Exhibition Center, Wenzhou, Zhejiang
Frequency: Annual
Market Area: Regional
Nature: Trade Only
Participated Fee: Standard Booth RMB 5,800/9m^2, Raw Space (min 36m^2) RMB 600/m^2
Organizer: Donnor Exhibition Co Ltd
Address: B-1403, New Century Business Building, 198 Shangjiang Rd., Wenzhou, Zhejiang 325011, China

2013/04/11-14
☎ 0577-8890 2222, 8890 5186
📠 0577-8890 1788
✉ vicky@donnor.net
📱 1205985714
4480

2013第十一届中国（温州）国际汽车展览会
地点：温州国际会展中心，浙江温州
始办年份：2003
周期：每年一届
市场范围：地区性
性质：面向公众和贸易观众
入场券价格：35元
参展费用：室内光地500元/m^2（200m^{2}起），室外光地200元/m^2（100m^{2}起），标准展位5,000元/9m^2
上届规模：展览面积42,000m^2，参观人数80,000人
主办：温州市汽车流通行业协会；浙江德纳展览有限公司
地址：浙江省温州市龙湾区上江路198号新世纪商务大厦B-1403（325011）
联系人：苏苗守，陈赛君
msn：victoria19840616@hotmail.com

11th Wenzhou Intl Auto Expo
Venue: Wenzhou Intl Convention & Exhibition Center, Wenzhou, Zhejiang
Established Year: 2003
Frequency: Annual
Market Area: Regional
Nature: Open to Public
Cost to Attend: RMB 35:-
Participated Fee: Raw Space RMB 500/m^2 (min 200m^2), Outdoor Raw Space RMB 200/m^2 (min 100m^2) , Standard Booth RMB 5,000/9m^2
Statistics '12: Exhibition Area 42,000m^2, Visitors 80,000
Organizer: Donnor Exhibition Co Ltd
Address: B-1403, New Century Business Building, 198 Shangjiang Rd., Wenzhou, Zhejiang 325011, China
Contact: Su Miaoshou, Vicky

2013/07/10-12
☎ 0577-8890 2222, 8890 5168
🖷 0577-8890 1788
✉ optics@donnor.com
1205985714
www.opticsfair.cn

4490

2013第十一届中国（温州）国际眼镜业展览会
地点：温州国际会展中心，浙江温州
内容：太阳镜与运动眼镜、老视镜、镜片及毛胚、眼镜架、眼镜包装、原辅材料及配件 专用工具、制造设备、验光配镜仪器及设备、隐形眼镜及护理产品、零售及店铺 设计、陈列设备及技术、眼镜连锁品牌
始办年份：2003
周期：每年一届
市场范围：国际性
性质：面向公众和贸易观众
入场券价格：免费
参展费用：国内企业标准展位5,800元/9m^2，光地600元/m^2；海外企业标准展位2,000美元/展位9m^2，光地200美元/m^2
上届规模：参展商400家，参观人数10,799人
主办：温州市人民政府；浙江省眼镜行业协会；温州市眼镜商会；温州德纳展览有限公司
地址：浙江省温州市龙湾区上江路198号新世纪商务大厦B-1403（325011）
联系人：苏苗守，陈赛君

11th Wenzhou Intl Optics Fair, China
Venue: Wenzhou Intl Convention & Exhibition Center, Wenzhou, Zhejiang
Profile: Sunglasses and sports spectacles, presbyopic glasses, lens & optical blanks, frames, packaging, raw and auxiliary materials, spare parts, tools, manufacturing equipments, optometry instruments, contact lens & care products, retail and shop design, display equipment and technology, chain glasses enterprises, etc.
Established Year: 2003
Frequency: Annual
Market Area: International
Nature: Open to Public
Cost to Attend: Free
Participated Fee: Standard Booth USD 2,000/9m^2, Raw Space USD 200/m^2
Statistics '12: Exhibitors 400, Visitors 10,799
Organizer: Wenzhou Municipal People's Government; Zhejiang Optometric & Optical Association; Wenzhou Glasses Chamber of Commerce; Wenzhou Donnor Exhibition Co Ltd
Address: B-1403, New Century Business Building, 198 Shangjiang Rd., Wenzhou, Zhejiang 325011, China
Contact: Su Miaoshou, Vicky

2013/08/29-31
☎ 0577-8890 2222, 8890 5881
🖷 0577-8890 1788
✉ sewing@donnor.com
1954851663
www.wzsew.com

4500

2013中国（温州）国际缝制设备展览会
地点：温州国际会展中心，浙江温州
内容：缝纫刺绣设备、缝合封包设备、预缩粘合设备、激光雕切设备、熨烫整理设备、（缝制设备）设计系统、其他设备、辅料、信息服务
周期：每年一届
市场范围：地区性
性质：面向贸易观众
参展费用：标准展位7,800元/9m^2，9,800元/12m^2，光地（36m^{2}起）800元/m^2
主办：浙江德纳展览有限公司
地址：浙江省温州市龙湾区上江路198号新世纪商务大厦B-1403（325011）
联系人：林良材，林晓东

2013 China (Wenzhou) Intl Sewing Equipment Fair
Venue: Wenzhou Intl Convention & Exhibition Center, Wenzhou, Zhejiang
Frequency: Annual
Market Area: Regional
Nature: Trade Only
Participated Fee: Standard Booth RMB 7,800/9m^2, RMB 9,800/12m^2, Raw Space (min 36m^2) RMB 800/m^2
Organizer: Donnor Exhibition Co Ltd
Address: B-1403, New Century Business Building, 198 Shangjiang Rd., Wenzhou, Zhejiang 325011, China

浙江-义乌 Zhejiang-Yiwu

2013/04/20-22
☎ 0579-8541 5491，8541 5012
🖷 0579-8541 5077
✉ louj@chinafairs.org
imported.yiwufair.com

4510

义乌进口商品展
地点：义乌国际博览中心，浙江义乌
内容：继2012年成功举办首届义乌进口商品展后，第二届义乌进口商品展将于2013年4月20日在义乌国际博览中心隆重举行。首届义乌进口商品展暨第七届义乌消费品交易会共设国际标准展位800余个，参展企业近500家。其中进口商品展设展位400余个，共有来自全球80多个国家和地区的展品同台展示，为企业开拓中国内销市场搭建了一个绝佳的商贸平台。
周期：每年一届
市场范围：地区性
性质：面向公众和贸易观众
主办：中华人民共和国商务部外贸发展事务局；义乌市人民政府；
承办：浙江中国小商品城集团股份有限公司
地址：浙江省义乌市宗泽东路59号国际博览中心(322000)
联系人：张远兰，楼剑

Yiwu Imported Commodities Fair
Venue: Yiwu Intl Expo Center, Yiwu, Zhejiang
Profile: Following with the success of the 1st Yiwu Imported Commodities Fair, the 2nd Yiwu Imported Commodities Fair will be held in Yiwu International Expo Center in 20th April 2013. The 1st Yiwu Imported Commodities Fair and the 7th Yiwu Sourcing Fair: Consumer Goods totally set up 800 international standard booths, almost 500 enterprises participated. While Imported Commodities Fair set up over 400 standard booths, with over 80 nations and regions exhibiting their characteristic products. The fair established an excellent platform to exploit China's domestic market for all cooperation.
Frequency: Annual
Market Area: Regional
Nature: Open to Public
Organizer: Zhejiang China Commodities City Group Company Limited

2013/04/20-22
☎ 0579-8541 5222, 8541 5003
🖷 0579-8541 5005, 8541 5444
www.hardwareexpo.cn

4520

第10届中国国际五金电器博览会
地点：义乌国际博览中心，浙江义乌
内容：五金工具、日用五金、建筑五金、电子电器、机械机电
始办年份：2004
周期：每年一届
市场范围：全国性
性质：面向贸易观众
入场券价格：30元
参展费用：6,000元/展位
上届规模：展览面积30,000m^2，参展商897家，贸易观众11,386人
主办：中国五金交电化工商业协会；义乌市人民政府；浙江中国小商品城集团股份有限公司；义乌市五金家电行业协会
地址：浙江省义乌市宗泽东路59号综合楼3楼(322000)
联系人：朱旭杉，唐薛红

The10th China Intl Hardware & Electrical Appliances Trade Fair
Venue: Yiwu Intl Expo Centre, Yiwu, Zhejiang
Profile: Hardware & Tools Daily Hardware category Building Hardware Electrical products Mechanical Equipment
Established Year: 2004
Frequency: Annual
Market Area: National
Nature: Trade Only
Cost to Attend: RMB 30:-
Participated Fee: RMB 6,000/booth
Statistics '12: Exhibition Area 30,000m^2, Exhibitors 897, Trade Visitors 11,386
Organizer: China National Hardware Electric and Chemical Products Commercial Association; Yiwu Municipal People's Government; Zhejiang China Commodities City Group Co Ltd; Yiwu Hardware & Electrical Appliances Trade Association

2013/04/20-22
☎ 0579-8541 5333
🖷 0579-8541 5005
✉ 462155971@qq.com
4530

2013中国义乌消费品交易会–家居家具展
地点：义乌国际博览中心，浙江义乌
内容：家庭用品：塑料制品、竹木纸制日用品、清洁卫生用品、妇婴用品、宠物用品、洗化用品、医药保健及个人护理用品、日杂用品、酒店用品、家用电器、家用厨具、生活用品、清洁用品、厨房用品、浴室用品、雨具等；家居家纺：家居家具、箱包皮具、皮带、地毯、家用纺织品、床上用品、布艺、辅料配件等；工艺家装：工艺品、圣诞用品、礼品赠品、礼品包装、树脂工艺、传统工艺、旅游工艺品、家居装饰、画框相框、仿真工艺、编制工艺品、水晶玻璃、陶瓷工艺品、金属工艺品、饰品配件、汽车装饰用品、玩具、园艺及户外用品、休闲用品等；服装鞋帽
参展费用：标准展位5,800元 /9m^2，角位加收800元，光地550元/m^2（18m^{2}起），角位800元
主办：中华人民共和国商务部外贸发展事务局；义乌市人民政府
承办：浙江中国小商品城集团股份有限公司；浙江省绗缝工艺协会；浙江远大国际会展有限公司
地址：义乌国际博览中心综合楼3楼（322000）
联系人：吴秦安

China (Yiwu) Housewear and Furniture Exhibition
Venue: Yiwu Intl Expo Centre, Yiwu, Zhejiang
Participated Fee: Standard Booth RMB 5,800/9m^2, Corner Booth add USB 800, Raw Space RMB 550/m^2 (min 18m^2), Corner Booth add RMB 800
Organizer: Zhejiang China Commodities City Group Company Limited

2013/04/20-22
☎ 0579-8540 8040
🖷 0579-8509 6977
✉ zjyw201005@163.com
www.guojiqinxi.com
4540

中国（义乌）时尚发制品与美发用品展览会
同期举办：第二届国际进口商品展
地点：义乌国际博览中心，浙江义乌
内容：假发类：男女装假发、工艺发条、教习发、化纤发条、接发、发环、发块、发把、发帘、手织发、化学纤维、天然纺织原料等其他假发类原材料。美发用品及器材类：美发、护发、染发、生发产品；发剪、发梳、电吹风、电夹板、美发工具设备；整发器、洗护发用品、染发剂、药水。发饰品类：发夹、头饰、头花、发簪、发珠、发带、发环。包装及设备类：各类相关包装制品；相关配套产品及生产用机器设备等。进口展区：高档发制品、原材料、饰品、假发护理品及美发用品。万圣节节日用品、节日服饰及配件、派对道具、派对服饰、节日面具
主办：中华人民共和国商务部外贸发展事务局；义乌市人民政府
承办：浙江中国小商品城集团股份有限公司；杭州创杰展览服务有限公司
地址：义乌时代广场A座30-31楼3001-3101室
联系人：陈真

China (Yiwu) Hair Products and Hairdressing Supplies Exhibition 2013
Venue: Yiwu Intl Expo Centre, Yiwu, Zhejiang
Organizer: Zhejiang China Commodities City Group Company Limited

2013/04/27-30
☎ 0579-8541 5444, 8541 5999
🖷 0579-8541 5386, 8541 5477
✉ 573721403@qq.com
573721403
www.ssofair.com
4550

第8届中国义乌文化产品交易博览会
地点：义乌国际博览中心，浙江义乌
内容：中国义乌文化产品交易博览会创办于2006年，2008年被评为"中国最具影响力的文化品牌展会"，2010年升格为由国家文化部、浙江省人民政府主办，浙江省文化厅和义乌人民政府承办的文体行业唯一外贸主导型国家级展会。参展范围有：印刷包装、文体用品、圣诞文化用品、十字绣框画工艺品、佛教文化用品、景德镇陶瓷、文化创意产品、书画古玩、工艺美术
始办年份：2006
周期：每年一届
市场范围：国际性
性质：面向公众和贸易观众
入场券价格：30元
参展费用：4,800元/展位，光地500元/m^2
上届规模：展览面积68,000m^2（国外展商面积620m^2），参展商1,372家（国外展商25家，来自8个国家），参观人数92,000人（贸易观众5,700人）
主办：中华人民共和国文化部；浙江省人民政府 ；浙江省文化厅；浙江省文化产业促进会；义乌市人民政府
联络：义乌中国小商品城展览有限公司
地址：浙江省义乌市宗泽东路59号 (322000)
联系人：陈静美，叶旻昊

The 8th China Yiwu Cultural Products Trade Fair
Venue: Yiwu Intl Expo Center, Yiwu, Zhejiang
Profile: Firstly held in 2006, China Yiwu Cultural Products Trade Fair was chosen as "the most influential brand fair of cultural industry in China" in 2008. In 2010, it becomes the only national-level foreign trade-oriented fair of stationery & sports industry. It is hosted by the Ministry of Cultural of the PRC and the People's Government of Zhejiang Province and is organized by the Department of Culture of Zhejiang Province and Yiwu Municipal people's government. It contains exhibition items as printing & packing, stationery & sports products, Christmas cultural, articles, cross-stitch, frame pictures and crafts, Buddhist cultural products, Jingdezhen's ceramics, cultural and creative products, antique & painting, crafts & arts
Established Year: 2006
Frequency: Annual
Market Area: International
Nature: Open to Public
Cost to Attend: RMB 30:-
Participated Fee: RMB 4,800/booth, Raw Space RMB 500/m^2
Statistics '12: Exhibition Area 68,000m^2 (foreigners 620m^2), Exhibitors 1,372 (foreigners 25 came from 8 countries), Visitors 92,000 (Trade Visitors 5,700)
Organizer: Ministry of Cultural of the PRC; The People's Government of Zhejiang Province; Department of Culture of Zhejiang Province; Zhejiang Association for Promoting Culture Industry; Yiwu Municipal People's Government
Address: Yiwu China Commodities City Exhibition Co Ltd, 59 Zongze Dong Road, Yiwu, Zhejiang 322000, China
Contact: Chen Jingmei, Ye Minhao

2013/05/09-12
☎ 010-8260 6899
🖷 010-8260 6883
✉ ciccyhuang@cnaico.com.cn
www.cnaico.com.cn
www.autochina.com.cn
4560

2013年第八届义乌汽车展览会
地点：浙江义乌
主办：中国汽车工业国际合作总公司
地址：北京市海淀区中关村丹棱街3号A座

8th Yiwu Automobile Exhibition 2013
Venue: Yiwu, Zhejiang
Organizer: China National Automotive Industry Intl Corp
Address: A, 3 Danling Street, Zhongguancun, Haidian Dist., Beijing, China

2013/05/24-27
☎ 0579-8541 5002, 8518 8851
🖷 0579-8541 5412
✉ Service@chinafairs.org
www.tourismfair.cn
4570

中国国际旅游商品博览会
地点：义乌国际博览中心，浙江义乌
内容：简称"旅博会"是由国家旅游局、浙江省人民政府主办，已连续举办4届，每年5月24日～27日在浙江义乌举行。分设旅游装备品、户外休闲用品、酒店用品、旅游纪念品、旅游商品创意研发、进口商品等行业。
始办年份：2009
主办：国家旅游局；浙江省人民政府；中国旅游协会；浙江省旅游局；义乌市人民政府
联络：义乌中国小商品城展览有限公司
联系人：胡松团，丁小康

China Intl Tourism Commodities Fair
Venue: Yiwu Intl Expo Center, Yiwu, Zhejiang
Established Year: 1995
Contact: Zhejiang China Commodities City Group Company Limited

2013/10/21-25
☎ 0579-8541 5800, 8541 5888
✉ Service@chinafairs.org
www.chinafairs.org
4580

中国义乌国际小商品博览会
地点：义乌国际博览中心，浙江义乌
内容：简称"义博会"创办于1995年，是经国务院批准的日用消费品类国际性展会，由商务部、浙江省人民政府等联合主办，已连续举办17届，每年10月21日～25日在浙江义乌举行。分设五金、电子电器、工艺品、文化办公用品、体育及休闲用品、箱包及皮具、日用品、饰品及饰品配件、针纺织品、玩具及儿童用品等10个行业，另设电子商务及贸易服务、进口商品、来料加工、浙江省山海协作等4个专区
始办年份：1995
主办：中华人民共和国商务部；浙江省人民政府；中国贸促会；中国轻工业联合会；中国商业联合会；浙江省商务厅；义乌市人民政府
联络：义乌中国小商品城展览有限公司
联系人：虞东民，贾文俊

China Yiwu Intl Commodities Fair
Venue: Yiwu Intl Expo Center, Yiwu, Zhejiang
Profile: Stationery & Office Products, Sports & Recreational Articles, Toys & Children' s Products, Household Textiles, Knitwear Garment & Accessories, Crafts, Daily Necessities, Jewelry & Accessories, Cosmetics & Cleaning Products, Leather& Cases & Bags, Hardware, Electronic & Electrical Appliances, Crystal & Glassware, E-commerce & Trade Services, Foreign goods
Established Year: 1995
Sponsor: Ministry of Commerce of the People' s Republic of China; The People' s Government of Zhejiang Province; China Council for the Promotion of International Trade; China National Light Industry Council; China General Chamber of Commerce
Organizer: Department of Commerce of Zhejiang Province; Yiwu Municipal People' s Government
Contact: Zhejiang China Commodities City Group Company Limited

2013/11/01-04
☎ 0579-8541 5001,8541 5125
🖷 0579-8541 5244
www.forestryfair.com
4590

第6届中国义乌国际森林产博览会
地点：义乌国际博览中心，浙江义乌
内容：家具、木结构木建材、木竹工艺品、木竹日用品、森林食品、花卉园艺、森林旅游、林业装备等八大行业。
始办年份：2008
周期：每年一届
市场范围：国际性
性质：面向公众和贸易观众
入场券价格：30元
参展费用：3,800元/展位，光地400元/m^2
上届规模：展览面积64,000m^2（国外展商面积6,111m^2），参展商1,418家（国外展商35家，来自36个国家），参观人数606,000人（贸易观众9,243人）
主办：国家林业局；浙江省人民政府中国林业产业联合会；浙江省林业厅；义乌市人民政府；浙江省人民政府台湾事务办公室
地址：浙江省义乌市宗泽东路59号综合楼三楼展览（322000）
联系人：孙甜，吴晗妃

6th China Yiwu Intl Forest Products Fair
Venue: Yiwu Intl Expo Center, Yiwu, Zhejiang
Profile: Bamboo & wood household supplies, Bamboo & wood handicrafts, Bamboo & wood articles for daily use, Forest leisure products, Forest food products, Flower and gardening products, Forestry machinery
Established Year: 2008
Frequency: Annual
Market Area: International
Nature: Open to Public
Cost to Attend: RMB 30:-
Participated Fee: RMB 3,800/booth, Raw Space RMB 400/m^2
Statistics '12: Exhibition Area 64,000m^2 (foreigners 6,111m^2), Exhibitors 1,418 (foreigners 35, came from 36 countries), Visitors 606,000 (Trade Visitors 9,243)
Organizer: The State Forestry Administration (SFA); The People' s Government of Zhejiang Province; China National Forestry Industry Association; The Forestry Department of Zhejiang Province; Yiwu Municipal People' s Government; The Office of Taiwan Affairs of People' s Government of Zhejiang Province

浙江-永康 Zhejiang-Yongkang

2013/03/29-31
☎ 0579-8711 1210
🖷 0579-8711 7336
✉ dsl314@163.com
📱 13968890383
http://weibo.com/u/2492128384
www.donnor.com
4600

2013第六届永康国际机械装备及工模具展览会
地点：永康国际会展中心，浙江永康
内容：机床及工模具类，塑胶工业机械及原料类，五金技术、焊接与切割类，涂装及表面处理类，木工机械及原料类：实木加工机械设备，板式加工机械设备，辅助加工机械设备，雕刻机及辅助设备、原材料
始办年份：2008
周期：每年一届
市场范围：国际性
入场券价格：免费
主办：永康市人民政府
承办：浙江德纳展览有限公司
地址：浙江省永康市九铃东路3090号邮政大楼1206室(321300)
联系人：王轩

6th Yongkang Intl Equipment and Machine Tools Exhibition
Venue: Yongkang Intl Convention & Exhibition Center, Yongkang, Zhejiang
Established Year: 2008
Frequency: Annual
Market Area: International
Cost to Attend: Free
Organizer: Zhejiang Donnor Exhibition Co Ltd

其他 Others

☎ 010-8455 6613, 8455 6618
✉ yuhui.wang@reedsinopharm.com
wei.wei@reedsinopharm.com
www.ceme365.com
4610

国际应急医学救援展览会
地点：待定
内容：救援管理行业的采购及学习平台，提供贸易及交流机会，产品展示的首要平台
主办：国药励展展览责任有限公司
地址：北京市朝阳区新源南路 1-3 号平安国际金融中心B 座15 层 (100027)

China Intl Emergency Medical Expo (CEME)
Venue: to be confirmed
Profile: A unique & dedicated event specifically focusing on natural healthcare products in China
Organizer: Reed Sinopharm Exhibitions

2013 -
☎ 00852-2827 6211
🖷 00852-3749 7342
✉ info-hk@ubm.com
awards.icmichina.cn
4620

CCCS™
客户联络中心标准委员会

中国最佳呼叫中心及最佳管理人系列评选奖项
地点：待定
主办：亚洲博闻有限公司
地址：香港湾仔港湾道26号华润大厦17楼

CCCS Best Call Center Awards
Venue: to be confirmed
Organizer: UBM Asia Ltd
Address: 17/F, China Resources Building, 26 Harbour Road, Wan Chai, Hong Kong

2013 -
☎ 00852-2827 6211
🖷 00852-3749 7342
✉ info-hk@ubm.com
www.gdcchina.com
4630

游戏开发者大会–中国
地点：待定
主办：亚洲博闻有限公司
地址：香港湾仔港湾道26号华润大厦17楼

Game Developers Conference, China
Venue: to be confirmed
Organizer: UBM Asia Ltd
Address: 17/F, China Resources Building, 26 Harbour Road, Wan Chai, Hong Kong

2013/10 -
☎ 0771-261 5620
🖷 0771-263 0917
4640

2013中国国际社会公共安全产品博览会
2013年SSC第六届中外安防产品采购洽谈会
地点：待定
主办：越中会展商务有限公司

Public Safety and Security Expo
Venue: to be confirmed
Organizer: Vietnam-China Conference Business Co Ltd

国内展览会议
行业索引

Exhibitions and Conferences in Mainland China
Index of Industry/ Profession – Classification

1、综合博览会
General Fair

年货采购会
New Year Shopping Festival
2013/01
河南郑州Henan-Zhengzhou 3030

中国华东进出口商品交易会
East China Fair
2013/03/01-05
上海Shanghai 570

2013春季中原住交会
2013 Central China Real Estate Fair(Spring)
2013/04
河南郑州Henan-Zhengzhou 3070

第113届中国进出口商品交易会
Canton Fair
113th China Import and Export Fair
2013/04/15-05
广东广州Guangdong-Guangzhou 2550

义乌进口商品展
Yiwu Imported Commodities Fair
2013/04/20-22
浙江义乌Zhejiang-Yiwu 4510

中部博览会
Central China Expo
2013/05
河南郑州Henan-Zhengzhou 3130

第二十一届昆交会
(第二十一届中国昆明进出口商品交易会)
The 21th Kunming Fair
(The 21th China Import & Export Fair, Kunming)
2013/06/06-10
云南昆明Yunnan-Kunming 4330

第一届中国-南亚博览会
First South Asia Expo
2013/06/06-10
云南昆明Yunnan-Kunming 4320

第二十四届中国哈尔滨国际经济贸易洽谈会
The 24th China Harbin Intl Economic and Trade Fair
2013/06/15-19
黑龙江哈尔滨Heilongjiang-Harbin 2990

2013全国郑州商品交易会
Zhengzhou National Commodity Fair
2013/09
河南郑州Henan-Zhengzhou 3310

中国—东盟博览会
China-ASEAN Expo
2013/09/20-24
广西南宁Guangxi-Nanning 2880

中国义乌国际小商品博览会
China Yiwu Intl Commodities Fair
2013/10/21-25
浙江义乌Zhejiang-Yiwu 4580

1、安全
Safety and Security

2013第十一届中国（郑州）社会公共安全产品博览会
China (Zhengzhou)Security Science Product Exhibition
2013/04
河南郑州Henan-Zhengzhou 3090

2013第86届中国劳动保护用品交易会
86th China Occupational Safety & Health Goods Expo
2013/04/17-19
上海Shanghai 1010

2013中国国际社会公共安全产品博览会
SSC第六届中外安防产品采购洽谈会
Public Safety and Security Expo
2013/10 4640

国际应急医学救援展览会
China Intl Emergency Medical Expo (CEME)
2013 4610

2、包装
Packaging

2013中国国际瓦楞展
SinoCorrugated 2013
2013/04/08-11
上海Shanghai 925

2013国际日化包装机械设备展览会
同期举办
第十四届国际表面活性剂和洗涤剂展览会
Daily Chemical Packaging Machinery Exhibition
Surfactants and Detergents Exhibition
2013/04/10-12
上海Shanghai 930

2013大连国际物流技术及包装工业展览会
Dalian Intl Logistics Technology and Packaging Industry Exhibition
Dalian Intl Plastic and Rubber Industry Exhibition
14th Dalian Intl Machine Tool and Mold Exhibition
2013/05/15-17
辽宁大连Liaoning-Dalian 3700

2013第十二届上海国际日化原料包装机械设备展览会
Shanghai Intl COSMETECH Exhibition
2013/05/20-22
上海Shanghai 1140

医药包装材料精品中国展
InnoPack China
2013/06/25-27
上海Shanghai 1320

第二十一届上海国际印刷包装纸业展览会
Shanghai Intl AD, Print, Pack, Paper Expo
2013/07/10-13
上海Shanghai 1420

中国国际彩盒展
SinoFoldingCarton
2013/08/21-23
广东东莞Guangdong-Dongguan 2280

包装产业周
Packaging Industry Week
2013/11/06-08
广东东莞Guangdong-Dongguan 2320

第十五届东莞国际橡塑胶、包装、压铸和铸造展
15th China Dongguan Intl Plastics Packing Rubber Diecasting & Foundry Exhibition
2013/11/13-16
广东东莞Guangdong-Dongguan 2330

3、材料
Materials

2013第11届中国（上海）国际保温材料与节能技术展览会
11th China (Shanghai) Insulating Materials and Energy-saving Technology Expo
2013/11/20-22
上海Shanghai 2040

4、宠物
Pets

全国宠物展
National Pet Show
2013/04
河南郑州Henan-Zhengzhou 3110

5、船艇、海事
Boats, Ship Building

中国(上海)国际游艇展
China (Shanghai) Intl Boat Show
2013/04/11-14
上海Shanghai 960

2013中国国际游艇产业博览会
同期举办：
2013中国国际水系运动休闲博览会
China Intl Boat Show
2013/05/10-12
广东广州Guangdong-Guangzhou 2570

可持续船舶技术中国峰会
Sustainable Ship Technology Conference
2013/05/30-31
上海Shanghai 1190

2013宁波国际海事会议和展览会_
China Maritime Tech Security Expo 2013
2013/06/19-21
浙江宁波Zhejiang-Ningbo 4420

海洋工程中国峰会（北京）
Offshore Engineering China (Beijing)
2013/09/19-20
北京Beijing 450

中国国际海事技术学术会议和展览会
Marintec China
2013/12/03-06
上海Shanghai 2080

7、灯光照明、灯饰
Lighting

广州国际LED展
LED China
2013/03/01-04
广东广州Guangdong-Guangzhou 2370

2013中国（济南）国际LED光电产业博览会
China (Jinan) Intl LED Expo
2013/03/31-04/02
山东济南Shandong-Jinan 3840

第三届中国（青岛）国际绿色照明产品及技术应用展览会
Qingdao Intl Green Lighting Fair
2013/04/06-08
山东青岛Shandong-Qingdao 3960

2013辽宁第十八届国际广告/标识/数码影像/LED光电照明暨灯饰展
2013 Liaoning 18th Intl Adverting/Signal/Digital Images/LED Lighting Exhibition
2013/03/15-18
辽宁沈阳Liaoning-Shenyang 3740

中国(上海)国际酒店与建筑照明展览会
Expo Light
2013/04/01-03
上海Shanghai 790

8、电池、电源 Battery &Power Supply

2013多人行国际移动电源展览会
Dowell Intl Mobile Power Supply Exhibition
2013/07/18-20
广东深圳Guangdong-Shenzhen 2810

第五届中国（上海）国际电池产品及技术展览会
5th China (Shanghai) Intl Battery Industry Fair
2013/08/20-22
上海Shanghai 1510

9、电力、电工 Electric Power, Electrical Engineering

中国国际智能电网技术和设备展览会
GridTec China 2013
2013/07/03-05
北京Beijing 350

2013中国国际智能电网建设及输配电博览会
China Intl Smart Grid and Electric Power Technology Exhibition
2013/09/05-07
北京Beijing 430

第九届上海国际电力设备及技术展览会
第八届上海国际电工装备展览会
9th Intl Exhibition on Electric Power Equipment and Technology
8th Intl Exhibition on Electrical Equipment
2013/10/30-11/01
上海Shanghai 1860

10、电子 Electronics

第22届中国国际电子电路展览会
CPCA SHOW 2013
22nd China Intl Electronic Circuits Exhibition
2013/03/19-21
上海Shanghai 710

第一届中国电子信息博览会暨
2013中国（深圳）消费电子展
China Information Technology Expo
81st China Electronic Fair
2013/04/10-12
广东深圳Guangdong-Shenzhen 2720

2013第十四届中国-中西部国际光电产业博览会
14th Midwest China (Chongqing) Photoelectricity, Laser & LED Industry Intl Exhibition
2013/04/25-27
重庆Chongqing 550

2013第九届苏州电路板展览会-
苏州电子线路板展览会
同期举办：苏州电子组装展览会
苏州表面贴装展览会
Suzhou Assembly Show
2013/05/08-10
江苏苏州Jiangsu-Suzhou 3640

2013年中国(成都)电子展
China Electronics Fair West Show 2013
2013/06/20-22
四川成都Sichuan-Chengdu 4240

2013多人行国际智能手机组装、触摸屏展览会
Dowell Intl Smartphone Assembly & Touch screen exhibition
2013/07/18-20
广东深圳Guangdong-Shenzhen 2790

2013多人行国际连接器、线束及设备展览会
Dowell Intl connector, harness and Equipment Exhibition
2013/07/18-20
广东深圳Guangdong-Shenzhen 2800

2013第21届中国国际电子设备、电子元器件及光电显示展览会
21th China Intl Electronic Equipment, Electronic Components and Optoelectronic Display Exhibition
2013/07/18-20
广东深圳Guangdong-Shenzhen 2820

2013多人行国际激光展览会
Dowell Intl Laser Exhibition
2013/07/18-20
广东深圳Guangdong-Shenzhen 2830

2013第二十一届多人行国际电子、激光、线缆线束展览会
21st DEX Intl Electronic, Laser, Harness Products Exhibition 2013
2013/07/18-20
广东深圳Guangdong-Shenzhen 2770

2013第十二届青岛国际电子电路板展览会
12th Qingdao Electronic Circuit Board Fair
2013/08/09-11
山东青岛Shandong-Qingdao 4070

2013第十八届中国国际光电产业博览会
Optoelectronics Industry Exposition (Beijing)
2013/10/16-18
北京Beijing 480

第十二届电磁兼容暨微波技术展览会
IME/China 2013
Intl Conference & Exhibition on Microwave and Antenna
2013/10/23-25
上海Shanghai 1810

第82届中国电子展 同期举办：2013年亚洲电子展
82nd China Electronics Fair
Asia Electronics Exhibition in Shanghai (AEES 2013)
China LED Fair (Shanghai)
2013/11/11-13
上海Shanghai 1890

广州国际LED展
LED China
2013/03/01-04
广东广州Guangdong-Guangzhou 2370

第17届海峡两岸机械电子商品交易会
暨厦门对台进出口商品交易会
17th China Xiamen Machinery and Electronics Exhibition (CXMEE)
2013/04/12-15
福建厦门Fujian-Xiamen 2140

2013东莞振宗工业园区展览会
Dongguan Zhenzong Industry Park Exhibition
2013/06/04-07
广东东莞Guangdong-Dongguan 2240

11、动漫、游戏 Comics and Games

游戏开发者大会-中国
Game Developers Conference, China
2013 4630

12、房地产 Real Estate

2013第十二届中国国际住宅产业博览会
（节能环保低碳性大展）
12th China Intl Exhibition on Housing Industry
2013/10/23-25
北京Beijing 530

13、纺织、服装、服饰及生产机械 Clothing, Textile and Related Machinery

2013第八届中国（上海）国际袜业采购交易会
China (Shanghai) Intl Hosiery Purchasing Expo
2013/03/04-06
上海Shanghai 580

2013第12届中国（上海）纺织品面辅料博览会
12th China（Shanghai）Textiles, Fabrics & Accessories Exhibition
2013/03/05-07
上海Shanghai 590

中国针棉织品交易会
China Intl Trade Fair for Mode Underwear and Home Textiles
2013/03/12-14
上海Shanghai 670

第十九届上海国际服装纺织品贸易博览会
Shanghai Intl Clothing & Textile Expo
2013/03/12-14
上海Shanghai 650

第95届中国针棉织品交易会
（中国内衣服饰展览会、中国家纺家居展览会）
China Intl Trade Fair for Mode Underwear and Home Textile
2013/03/12-14
上海Shanghai 630

中国（广州）国际家用纺织品及辅料博览会
China （Guangzhou） Intl Trade Fair for Home Textiles and Accessories-Autumn Edition
2013/03/18-21
广东广州Guangdong-Guangzhou 2390

第21届中国国际服装服饰博览会
（CHIC2013）
China Intl Clothing & Accessories Fair
2013/03/26-29
北京Beijing 70

2013中国国际纺织纱线(春夏)展览会
China Intl Trade Fair for Fibers and Yarns
2013/03/27-29
北京Beijing 80

2013 (春季)上海纺织服装展览会
Shanghai Textile & Apparel Trade Fair (Spring) 2013
2013/04/17 19
上海Shanghai 990

第十三届中国国际染料工业暨有机颜料、纺织化学品展览会
CHINA INTERDYE 2013
2013/04/17-19
上海Shanghai 1020

2013东莞国际纺织品印花工业技术展览会
China Intl Textile Printing Industrial Technology Exposition

2013/05/20-22
广东东莞Guangdong-Dongguan 2210

2013第十一届宁波国际纺织面料、辅料及纱线博览会
11th Ningbo Intl Textile Fabrics, Accessories & Yarns Exhibition 2013
2013/05/23-25
浙江宁波ZhejiangNingbo 4410

2013中国（郑州）国际纺织面料、辅料及纱线展览会
China (Zhengzhou) Intl Textile Fabrics, Accessories & Yarn Exhibition
2013 China (Zhengzhou) Sewing Equipments and Textile Show
2013/05/27-29
河南郑州Henan-Zhengzhou 3190

2013第十二届南京国际纺织品面料、辅料博览会
12th Nanjing Intl Textiles Fabrics Accessories Exhibition 2013
2013/05/30-06/01
江苏南京Jiangsu-Nanjing 3610

2013中国（上海）国际产业用纺织品及非织造布展览会
同期举办：2013上海玻璃纤维及新型复合材料展览会
China (Shanghai) Trade Fair for Technical Textiles and Nonwovens
2013/06/05-07
上海Shanghai 1240

第十六届上海国际纺织工业展览会
SHANGHAITEX 2013
2013/06/10-13
上海Shanghai 1250

2013第15届中国（青岛）国际面料、辅料及纱线展览会
15th China (Qingdao) Intl Fabric, Yarn and Accessories Exhibition
2013/06/28-30
山东青岛Shandong-Qingdao 4000

2013第十三届中国（深圳）国际品牌服装服饰交易会
13th China Intl Fashion Brand Fair – Shenzhen
Shenzhen Textile Equipment Fair
2013/07/08-10
广东深圳Guangdong-Shenzhen 2750

深圳国际纺织面料及辅料博览会
Shenzhen Intl Trade Fair for Apparel Fabrics and Accessories
2013/07/11-13
广东深圳Guangdong-Shenzhen 2760

CBME孕婴童展、CBME童装展
Shanghai Intl Children-Baby-Maternity Industry Expo
2013/07/17-19
上海Shanghai 1440

2013广州国际服装节暨广州时装周
Guangzhou Fashion Week
2013/08/09-12
广东广州Guangdong-Guangzhou 2650

2013广州国际缝制制衣设备展
广州国际服装面辅料展览会
Guangzhou Intertextile Apparel Fabrics
2013/08/10-12
广东广州Guangdong-Guangzhou 2660

中国国际家用纺织品及辅料（秋冬）博览会
intertextile Shanghai home textiles
China Intl Trade Fair for Textiles and Accessories
2013/08/27-30
上海Shanghai 1530

2013中国（温州）国际缝制设备展览会
China (Wenzhou) Intl Sewing Equipment Fair
2013/08/29-31
浙江温州Zhejiang-Wenzhou 4500

中国国际箱包、裘革服装及服饰展
Moda Shanghai
2013/09/04-06
上海Shanghai 1600

2013中国国际缝制设备展览会
China Intl Sewing Machinery & Accessories Show 2013
2013/09/25-28
上海Shanghai 1710

中国国际针织博览会
China Intl Knitting Trade Fair
2013/10/21-23
上海Shanghai 1770

中国国际纺织纱线（秋冬）展览会
China Intl Trade Fair for Fibres and Yarns
2013/10/21-23
上海Shanghai 1780

中国国际纺织面料及辅料（秋冬）博览会
China Intl Trade Fair for Apparel Fabrics and Accessories
2013/10/21-24
上海Shanghai 1790

中国国际非织造布研讨会及展览会
15th Intl Nonwovens Exhibition
2013/10/23-25
上海Shanghai 1800

14、高新技术 New Hi-Tech

2013京交会"中国国际城市智能化技术与服务大会"
UrbanTec China Conference at CIFTIS 2013
2013/05/28-06/01
北京Beijing 250

15、工程机械 Construction Machinery

中国国际混凝土产业展览会
Concrete Show China 2013
2013/06/26-28
上海Shanghai 1380

第十二届北京国际工程机械展览与技术交流会
Beijing Intl Construction Machinery Exhibition & Seminar
2013/10/18-21
北京Beijing 520

16、广播、电影、电源、舞台设备 Broadcasting, Film, Television & Stage Equipment

第二十二届中国国际专业音响、灯光、乐器及技术展览会
22nd China Intl Exhibition on Pro Audio,Light,Music & Technology
2013/06/07-10
北京Beijing 280

第二十二届北京国际广播电影电视设备展览会
(BIRTV2013)
Beijing Intl Radio, TV & Film Equipment Exhibition
2013/08/21-24
北京Beijing 380

17、广告、标识、媒介 Advertising, Signs and Media

2013年春季第22届郑州中原广告展
Spring Zhengzhou Central Plain Advertisment Exhibition
2013/03
河南郑州Henan-Zhengzhou 3040

2013辽宁第十八届国际广告/标识/数码影像/LED光电照明暨灯饰展
Liaoning 18th Intl Adverting/Signal/Digital Images/LED Lighting Exhibition
2013/03/15-18
辽宁沈阳Liaoning-Shenyang 3740

2013第14届上海国际广告四新展览会
14th Shanghai Intl Advertising Four New Exhibition
2013/03/22-24
上海Shanghai 730

中国（广州）国际广告标识展
Sign China
2013/04/01-04
广东广州Guangzhou-Guangzhou 2520

2013第二十一届上海国际广告技术设备展览会
Shanghai Intl AD & Sign Technology Equipment Exhibition
2013/07/10-13
上海Shanghai 1430

营销和广告创新技术展示会暨研讨会
TFM&A China
2013/09/02-03
上海Shanghai 1540

18、化工 Chemical Industry

第十三届中国国际染料工业暨有机颜料、纺织化学品展览会
CHINA INTERDYE 2013
2013/04/17-19
上海Shanghai 1020

2013东莞国际纺织品印花工业技术展览会
2013 China Intl Textile Printing Industrial Technology Exposition
2013/05/20-22
广东东莞Guangdong-Dongguan 2210

2013第十二届上海国际日化原料包装机械设备展览会
Shanghai Intl COSMETECH Exhibition
2013/05/20-22
上海Shanghai 1140

2013多人行国际胶粘带、保护膜、光学膜及模切展览会
Dowell Intl Adhesive tape, protective layer, Optical film & Die-Cutting Exhibition
2013/07/18-20
广东深圳Guangdong-Shenzhen 2780

中国（上海）国际化工技术装备展览会
5th China (Shanghai) Intl Chemical Technology & Equipment Fair
2013/08/20-22
上海Shanghai 1520

2013（第十二届）中国国际化工展览会
ICIF CHINA
2013/09/04-06
上海Shanghai 1620

2013（第九届）中国国际工业表面活性剂技术及应用展览会
SURFACTANTCHEM+TECH
2013/11/12-14
上海Shanghai 2000

第二十六届中国国际表面处理展览会
SFCHINA 2013
2013/11/20-22
上海Shanghai 2010

第十八届届中国国际涂料展览会
CHINACOAT 2013
2013/11/20-22
上海Shanghai 2020

19、婚庆 Wedding Show

成都婚庆博览会
Chengdu Wedding Fair
2013/03/02-03
四川成都Sichuan-Chengdu 4170

中国（国际）婚博会
China Wedding Expo
2013/03/09-10
上海Shanghai 600

中国（国际）婚博会
China (Intl) Wedding Expo
2013/03/09-10
广东广州GuangdongGuangzhou 2440

中国（国际）婚博会
Beijing Bridal Expo
2013/03/16-17
北京Beijing 50

20、家具、木工机械 Furniture, Wood Working

2013年第13届中国中部橱柜衣柜及配套材料博览会
Central China Cabinet, Wardrobe and Supporting Materials Fair
2013/03/12-14
河南郑州Henan-Zhengzhou 3060

第29届国际名家具（东莞）展览会暨名家具机械、材料展览会
IFM 29th Intl Famous Furniture Woodworking Machinery & Material Fair
2013/03/16-20
广东东莞Guangdong-Dongguan 2180

第三十一届中国（广州）国际家具博览会
31st China Intl Furniture Fair (Guangzhou)
2013/03/18-21
广东广州Guangdong-Guangzhou 2490

第6届中国（杭州）国际花园户外家具及休闲用品展
Outdoor Lifestyle Hangzhou 2013
2013/03/21-24
浙江杭州Zhejiang-Hangzhou 4340

中国广州国际木工机械、家具配料展览会
interzum guangzhou
China Intl Woodworking Machinery & Furniture Raw Materials Fair (Guangzhou)
2013/03/27-30
广东广州Guangdong-Guangzhou 2500

上海国际酒店用品博览会暨中国国际酒店家具展
Hotel Furniture China
2013/04/01-03
上海Shanghai 850

第十四届西安国际酒店设备及用品展览会
同期举办：
第六届西安国际酒店家具展览会
第六届西安国际烘焙、咖啡、茶展览会
第六届西安国际食品、葡萄酒、饮料及酒店餐饮服务展览会
14th Xi'an Intl Hospitality Equipment & Supplies Fair
2013/05/16-18
陕西西安Shaanxi-Xi'an 3790

第三届中国郑州国际家具展
Third Zhengzhou Intl Furniture Fair
2013/05
河南郑州HenanZhengzhou 3140

2013第十四届成都国际家具工业展览会
Intl Furniture Fair Chengdu
2013/07/03-06
四川成都Sichuan-Chengdu 4250

第二届中国（青岛）橱柜衣柜展览会
China (Qingdao) Intl Cabinet and Wardrobe Exhibition
2013/07/17-19
山东青岛Shandong-Qingdao 4060

第七届中国（青岛）国际地板及整木家装展览会
Qingdao Floor and Entire Wooden Decoration Exhibition
2013/07/17-19
山东青岛Shandong-Qingdao 4020

第二届中国（青岛）国际木屋、木结构及配套设施展览会
Qingdao Intl Wood House Exhibition
2013/07/17-19
山东青岛Shandong-Qingdao 4050

第九届中国（青岛）国际木门展览会
9th Qingdao Intl Wooden Door Exhibition
2013/07/17-19
山东青岛Shandong-Qingdao 4040

第三十届国际名家具（东莞）展览会
30th Intl Famous Furniture Fair (Dongguan)
2013/09/05-09
广东东莞Guangdong-Dongguan 2290

第三十二届中国（广州）国际家具博览会
32nd China Intl Furniture Fair (Guangzhou)
2013/09/07-10
广东广州Guangdong-Guangzhou 2690

中国国际橱柜展览会
Kitchen & Cabinet China
2013/09/11-15
上海Shanghai 1670

第十九届中国国际办公家具展览会
Office Furniture China
2013/09/11-15
上海Shanghai 1640

中国国际家具配件及材料精品展览会
FMC Premium
2013/09/11-14
上海Shanghai 1630

第6届中国义乌国际森林产博览会
6th China Yiwu Intl Forest Products Fair
2013/11/01-04
浙江义乌Zhejiang-Yiwu 4590

21、建筑、建材、建筑装饰材料及机械 Building, Construction, Decoration, Materials and Machinery

第二十届中国北京国际建筑装饰及材料博览会
20th China Intl Building Decorations & Building Materials Exposition
2013/03/7-10
北京Beijing 25

2013(建筑.家具)贴面装饰板材及生产设备展览会
Veneer Decorative Plates Exhibition
2013/03/11-13
上海Shanghai 620

2013第二届上海国际人造板工业展览会
Shanghai Intl Wood-Based Panels Industry Exhibition 2013
2013/03/11-13
上海Shanghai 610

2013年第十九届全国铝门窗幕墙行业年会暨铝门窗幕墙新产品博览会
Aluminum Window, Door, Facade & Curtain Wall Expo 2013
2013/03/18-20
广东广州Guangdong-Guangzhou 2480

中国国际建筑陶瓷及卫浴科技精品展览会
Ceramics, Tile & Sanitary Ware China
2013/04/01-03
上海Shanghai 890

上海国际商场设计、装饰与用品博览会
Expo Shop
2013/04/01-03
上海Shanghai 8880

中国国际建筑装饰展览会
Expo Build China
2013/04/01-03
上海Shanghai 810

第二届中国（青岛）国际新型建筑模板、脚手架及施工技术展览会
Qingdao Intl Building Cyclostyle & Scaffold Fair
2013/04/06-08
山东青岛Shandong-Qingdao 3930

第六届中国（青岛）国际太阳能与建筑一体化应用产品技术展览会
Qingdao Intl Solar Energy Fair
2013/04/06-08
山东青岛Shandong-Qingdao 3920

第三届中国（青岛）国际建筑装饰涂料及化学建材展览会
Qingdao Architectural coatings and Chemical Building Materials
2013/04/06-08
山东青岛Shandong-Qingdao 3910

第七届中国（青岛）国际外墙保温及新型墙体产品技术展览会
Qingdao Building External Wall insulation and New Wall Materials Exhibition
2013/04/06-08
山东青岛Shandong-Qingdao 3940

第七届中国（青岛）国际干混砂浆、地坪产品及技术设备展览会
7th China (Qingdao) Dry-mixed mortar, Floor Exhibition
2013/04/06-08
山东青岛Shandong-Qingdao 3950

2013中国（青岛）国际建筑给排水展览会
第七届中国（青岛）建筑节能和可再生能源建筑应用博览会
China (Qingdao) Intl Building Water Technology Energy Fair
2013/04/06-08
山东青岛Shandong-Qingdao 3900

2013年大连建材展
第十八届中国国际建筑装饰材料展览会
CHINA BUILD 18th
18th China Intl Construction & Decoration Materials Exhibition
2013/04/11-14
辽宁大连Liaoning-Dalian 3690

2013年建材行业大型展览会
Building Material Industry Exhibition
2013/04/18-20
四川成都Sichuan-Chengdu 4210

2013中国（成都）厨房用品及配套设施展览会
China (Chengdu) Kitchen Supplies and Ancillary Facilities Exhibition
2013/04/18-20
四川成都Sichuan-Chengdu 4230

2013中国成都创意设计展暨建筑装饰博览会
China Chengdu Creative Design Exhibitions and Architecture Decoration Fair
2013/04/18-20
四川成都Sichuan-Chengdu 4220

2013第11届中国哈尔滨国际门窗幕墙及加工设备展览会
11th China (Harbin) Intl Door and Window Exhibition
2013/04/23-25
黑龙江哈尔滨Heilongjiang-Harbin 2980

2013第七届中国（天津）国际厨房、卫浴设施展览会
Tianjin Kitchen and Sanitary Facilities Show
2013/05/18-20
天津Tianjin 2100

2013中国国际医院建设、装备及管理展览会暨第14届全国医院建设大会
Hospital Build & Infrastructure Exhibition & Congress China 2013
14th China Hospital Construction Forum
2013/05/19-21
江苏南京Jiangsu-Nanjing 3590

第十五届中国（广州）国际建筑装饰博览会
15th China (Guangzhou) Intl Building Decoration Fair
2013/07/08-11
广东广州Guangdong-Guangzhou 2640

第七届中国（青岛）国际石材工业及机械设备展览会
China (Qingdao) Intl Stone Products & Machinery Exhibition
2013/07/16-19
山东青岛Shandong-Qingdao 4010

第九届中国（青岛）国际木门展览会
9th Qingdao Intl Wooden Door Exhibition
2013/07/17-19
山东青岛Shandong-Qingdao 4040

第九届中国(上海)国际门窗幕墙及建筑遮阳展览会/第九届中国(上海)国际建筑节能及新型建材展览会
9th Shanghai Intl Energy-saving & Advanced Building Materials Exhibition
2013/08/15-17
上海Shanghai 1490

2013年中国郑州建筑节能及新型建材博览会/ 中国郑州照明LED展览会
China (Zhengzhou) LED Lighting Exhibition
2013/09
河南郑州Henan-Zhengzhou 3340

中国国际家具配件及材料精品展览会
FMC Premium
2013/09/11-14
上海Shanghai 1630

2013第10届中国（上海）国际地坪工业展览会
10th China (Shanghai) Intl Floor Industry Expo 2013
2013/11/20-22
上海Shanghai 2030

2013第9届中国（上海）国际干混砂浆技术及产品展览会
9th China (Shanghai) Intl Dry Mix Mortar Technology and Product Expo
2013/11/20-22
上海Shanghai 2050

22、交通、运输、物流 Transportation and Logistics

国际散杂货展览会暨研讨会-中国上海
Breakbulk China
2013/03/12-15
上海Shanghai 640

2013大连国际物流技术及包装工业展览会
Dalian Intl Logistics Technology and Packaging Industry Exhibition
Dalian Intl Plastic and Rubber Industry Exhibition
14th Dalian Intl Machine Tool and Mold Exhibition
2013/05/15-17
辽宁大连Liaoning-Dalian 3700

第二十届国际自动识别及物联网技术展览会
SCAN CHINA 2013
2013/10/23-25
山东青岛Shandong-Qingdao 4110

2013亚洲国际物流技术与运输系统展览会
CeMAT 2013
2013/10/28-31
上海Shanghai 1840

2013中国国际果蔬、加工技术及物流展览会
China World Fruit & Vegetable Trade Fair 2013
2013/11/28-30
北京Beijing 2070

23、教育 Education

第八届上海幼儿教育暨用品展
The 8th Kids Education Expo 2013Shanghai
2013/05/24-26
上海Shanghai 1160

第12届中国国际玩具、幼教用品及设备展览会
12thIntl Trade Fair for Toys & Preschool Educational Resources
2013/10/15-17
上海Shanghai 1750

24、金属加工、冶金、铸造技术设备 Metalworking, Metallurgy & Foundry

2013第十一届青岛国际铸造、热处理及工业炉展览会
Qingdao Intl Casting, Heat Treatment and Furnace Exhibition
2013/03/07-09
山东青岛Shandong-Qingdao 3880

2013第十四届东北国际机床与金属加工展览会
14th Northeast Intl Machine Tool and Metalworking Exhibition
2013/04/10-13
辽宁沈阳Liaoning-Shenyang 3750

2013第8届中国（贵州）国际装备制造业博览会暨中国贵阳国际工业博览会
8th China (Guizhou) Intl Equipment Manufacturing Exposition & China - Guiyang Intl Industry Expo
2013/05/16-18
贵州贵阳Guizhou-Guiyang 2920

第一届国际矿业及冶金工业博览会暨产业交流大会
1st Intl Exhibition and Congress for the Mining and Metallurgy Industry
2013/05/21-24
北京Beijing 240

广州国际金属加工工业展
asia metal
Guangzhou Intl Metalworking Industry Exhibition
2013/09/24-26
广东广州Guangdong-Guangzhou 2698

2013 中国（南京）国际金属加工展览会
AMB China
China Metal Working & Forming Exhibition
2013/10/14-16
江苏南京Jiangsu-Nanjing 3620

2013第十届中国（北京）国际热处理工业炉展览会
10th China (Beijing) Intl Heat Treatment & Industrial Furnace Expo
2013/10/16-18
北京Beijing 470

2013年第十届 中国（北京）国际冶金工业博览会
10th China (Beijing) Intl Metallurgy Industry Exhibition
2013/10/16-18
北京Beijing 490

2013第十届中国（北京）国际铸造工业展览会
10th China (Beijing) Intl Foundry Industry Expo 2013
2013/10/16-18
北京Beijing 500

第十五届东莞国际橡塑胶、包装、压铸和铸造展
15th China Dongguan Intl Plastics Packing Rubber Diecasting & Foundry Exhibition
2013/11/13-16
广东东莞Guangdong-Dongguan 2330

25、酒店业 Hospitality

中国(上海)国际酒店与建筑照明展览会
Expo Light
2013/04/01-03
上海Shanghai 790

上海酒店设计与工程展览会
Shanghai Hospitality Design & Engineering Expo
2013/04/01-03
上海Shanghai 830

上海国际酒店用品博览会
Hotelex Shanghai
2013/04/01-03
上海Shanghai 860

上海国际酒店用品博览会暨中国国际酒店家具展
Hotel Furniture China
2013/04/01-03
上海Shanghai 850

中国清洁博览会
China Clean Expo
2013/04/01-09
上海Shanghai 840

欧亚国际酒店用品展
(Zhengzhou) Intl Hotel Supplies Show
2013/05
河南郑州Henan-Zhengzhou 3150

第十四届西安国际酒店设备及用品展览会
同期举办：
第六届西安国际酒店家具展览会
第六届西安国际烘焙、咖啡、茶展览会
第六届西安国际食品、葡萄酒、饮料及酒店餐饮服务展览会

14th Xi'an Intl Hospitality Equipment & Supplies Fair
2013/05/16-18
陕西西安Shaanxi-Xi'an 3790

广州12月酒店用品展览会
Guangzhou Hotel Show
2013/12/12-15
广东广州Guangdong-Guangzhou 2700

26、机械、制造、工业装备、自动化 Machinery, Machine Tools and Technology & Automation

2013第12届中国（山东）国际工业自动化应用技术展览会
12th China (Shandong) Intl Industrial Automation Applied Technology Exhibition
2013/03/03-05
山东济南Shandong-Jinan 3830

中国广州国际工业自动化技术及装备展览会
SPS - Industrial Automation Fair Guangzhou
2013/03/04-06
广东广州Guangdong-Guangzhou 2410

2013中国国际机械工业展览会
China Intl Machinery Industry Exhibition
2013/03/14-17
浙江宁波Zhejiang-Ningbo 4380

2013年第十六届中国西部国际装备制造业博览会/西部国际五金机电工具贸易展览会
China West Intl Equipment Manufacturing Exposition
2013/03/14-17 3780

2013中国（温州）国际机床、工模具及塑胶工业展览会
China (Wenzhou) Intl Machine Tool & Plastics Industry Equipment
2013/03/15-17
浙江温州Zhejiang-Wenzhou 4460

2013中国（温州）国际工业博览会
China (Wenzhou) Intl Industry Equipment
2013/03/15-17
浙江温州Zhejiang-Wenzhou 4470

2013第六届永康国际机械装备及工模具展览会
6th Yongkang Intl Equipment and Machine Tools Exhibition
2013/03/29-31
浙江永康Zhejiang-Yongkang 4600

2013中国中部（郑州）国际装备制造业博览会暨第十五届中原国际装备制造业博览会
Central China Intl Equipment Manufacturing Industry Expo
2013/04
河南郑州Henan-Zhengzhou 3080

2013上海第十二届中国国际动力设备发电机组展览会
12th China (Shanghai) Intl Power and Generating Sets Exhibition
2013/04/08-10
上海Shanghai 920

2013第十届中国国际橡胶技术（青岛）展览会
10th China Intl Rubber Technology (Qingdao) Fair
2013/04/09-11
山东青岛Shandong-Qingdao 3970

2013第十四届东北国际机床与金属加工展览会
14th Northeast Intl Machine Tool and Metalworking Exhibition
2013/04/10-13
辽宁沈阳Liaoning-Shenyang 3750

第17届海峡两岸机械电子商品交易会暨厦门对台进出口商品交易会
17th China Xiamen Machinery and Electronics Exhibition (CXMEE)
2013/04/12-15
福建厦门Fujian-Xiamen 2140

2013中国国际水利机械及施工装备展览会
China Intl Hydraulic Machinery and Construction Equipment Exhibition
2013/05/06-08
山东济南Shandong-Jinan 3860

2013第六届上海国际罐藏食品机械设备博览会
6th shanghai Intl Canned Food and Materials Facility Exhibition
2013/05/07-09
上海Shanghai 1090

2013第8届中国（贵州）国际装备制造业博览会暨中国贵阳国际工业博览会
8th China (Guizhou) Intl Equipment Manufacturing Exposition & China-Guiyang Intl Industry Expo
2013/05/16-18
贵州贵阳Guizhou-Guiyang 2920

2013东莞振宗工业园区展览会
Dongguan Zhenzong Industry Park Exhibition
2013/06/04-07
广东东莞Guangdong-Dongguan 2240

第十八届北京-埃森焊接与切割展览会
The 18th Beijing Essen Welding & Cutting Fair
2013/06/18-21
上海Shanghai 1270

2013中国国际模具、制造应用设备及相关工业展览会
DMC 2013 (China Intl Exhibition on Die & Mould, Metal Processing and Forming Industry)
2013/06/18-21
上海Shanghai 1280

2013中国加工贸易产品博览会
China Processing Trade Products Fair
2013/06/19-22
广东东莞Guangdong-Dongguan 2250

北京国际工业智能及自动化展览会
Industrial Automation Beijing
2013/06/26-28
北京Beijing 290

2013中国(上海)国际切削刀具暨工具展览会
China Intl Cuttings Tools Exhibition
2013/06/26-28
上海Shanghai 1390

2013年第十二届中国沈阳汽车工业博览会
12th China (Shenyang) Automobile Industry Expo
2013/06/27-02
辽宁沈阳Liaoning-Shenyang 3760

2013亚洲国际智能制造装备产业展览会
Asia Intl Intellect Equipment Manufacturer Industry Exhibition
2013/06/28-30
北京Beijing 300

2013第九届中国（北京）国际动力传动与控制技术展览会
9th China (Beijing) Intl Power Transmission & Control Technology Exhibition
2013/06/28-30
北京Beijing 310

第15届上海国际机床展
15th Shanghai Intl Machine Tool Fair
2013/07/02-05
上海Shanghai 1400

2013第十七届中国西部国际装备制造业博览会
17th China West Intl Equipment Manufacturing Exposition
2013/07/19-21
四川成都Sichuan-Chengdu 4270

2013第15届中国青岛国际动力传动与控制技术展览会
15th China Intl Power Transmission & Control Technology (Qingdao) Exhibition
2013/08/15-17
山东青岛Shandong-Qingdao 4090

2013第九届中国（郑州）国际机床及工模具展览会
2013 China Machine Tool Expo
2013/08/23-25
河南郑州Henan-Zhengzhou 3290

第十一届中国国际装备制造业博览会-机床模具展
12th China Intl Equipment Manufacturing Exposition -Machine Tools & Mould Exhibition
2013/09/13-17
辽宁沈阳Liaoning-Shenyang 3770

2013第14届立嘉国际机床展览会-成都展会
Jiali Intl Machinery Exhibition - Chengdu
2013/09/18-21
四川成都Sichuan-Chengdu 4290

2013亚洲国际动力传动与控制技术展览会
PTC ASIA 2013
2013/10/28-31
上海Shanghai 1830

2013中国（国际）精密制造及技术展
China (Intl) Precision Machine Technology Expo
2013/11/04-06
江苏南京Jiangsu-Nanjing 3630

第15届中国国际工业博览会
China Intl Industry Fair
2013/11/05-09
上海Shanghai 1870

第二十六届中国国际表面处理展览会
SFCHINA 2013
2013/11/20-22
上海Shanghai 2010

磨料磨具展览会
Abrasives Exhibition
2013/11
河南郑州Henan-Zhengzhou 3370

27、矿业 Mining

第一届国际矿业及冶金工业博览会暨产业交流大会
1st Intl Exhibition and Congress for the Mining and Metallurgy Industry
2013/05/21-24
北京Beijing 240

28、空调、制冷、供暖、通风 Air-conditioning, Heating, Refrigeration, Ventilation

第二十四届国际制冷、空调、供暖、通风及食品冷冻加工展览会
24th Intl Exhibition for Refrigeration, Air-conditioning, Heating and Ventilation, Frozen Food Processing, Packaging and Storage
2013/04/08-10
上海Shanghai 900

2013中国国际供热通风空调、卫生洁具及城建设备与技术展览会

China Intl Trade Fair for Sanitation, Heating, Ventilation & Air-conditioning
2013/04/08-10
北京Beijing 150

2013第16届中国济南供热采暖、热泵空调产品与技术展览会/第四届山东电采暖节能应用研讨会
16th China Jinan Heating, Heat Pump Air Conditioning Products and Technology Exhibition
2013/04/18-20
山东济南Shandong-Jinan 3850

第四届中国（青岛）国际供热采暖系统产品及技术应用展览会
Qingdao Intl Heating System Product & Technology Utilization Fair
2013/07/17-19
山东青岛Shandong-Qingdao 4030

29、零售业、营销 Retail

上海国际商场设计、装饰与用品博览会
Expo Shop
2013/04/01-03
上海Shanghai 8880

2013国际特许加盟（上海）展览会
Shanghai Intl Franchise Exhibition 2013
2013/09/14-16
上海Shanghai 1680

第十五届中国连锁店展览会
China Shop
(China Retail Trade Fair)
2013/11/14-16
四川成都Sichuan-Chengdu 4300

30、礼品 Gifts

第27届中国北京国际礼品、赠品及家庭用品展览会
27th China Beijing Intl Gifts, Premium & Houseware Exhibtion
2013/03/14-17
北京Beijing 30

2013宁波国际时尚礼品及家庭用品展览会
Ningbo Gift and Housewear Exhibition
2013/03/29-31
浙江宁波Zhejiang-Ningbo 4400

第10届中国国际文具礼品博览会
10th China Intl Stationery & Gifts Exposition
2013/03/29-31
浙江宁波Zhejiang-Ningbo 4390

2013中国最大的竹制品展/春季竹礼品展
China (Shanghai) Bamboo Product Exhibition
2013/05/16-18
上海Shanghai 1120

2013 第六届天津国际礼品、工艺品及家居用品博览会
6th Tianjin Intl Gifts, Crafts & Household Goods Expo
2013/05/17-20
天津Tianjin 2090

2013年上海国际家庭用品、促销品及工艺品创意设计展览会
Shanghai Intl Houseware, Premuium, Arts & Crafts Creative Design Exhibition 2013
2013/08/01-03
上海Shanghai 1460

第28届中国北京国际礼品、赠品及家庭用品展览会
28th China Beijing Intl Gifts, Premium & Houseware Exhibtion
2013/08/14-17
北京Beijing 370

北京国际礼品、赠品及家用精品年底展览会
Intl Gifts, Premium & Houseware Purchase Exhibiton
2013/11/13-15
北京Beijing 540

31、旅游 Tourism

2013广州国际旅游展览会
Guangzhou Intl Travel Fair
2013/03/07-09
广东广州Guangdong-Guangzhou 2430

中国国际旅游商品博览会
China Intl Tourism Commodities Fair
2013/05/24-27
浙江义乌Zhejiang-Yiwu 4570

32、美容美发、化妆品、个人护理、水疗、整形 Cosmetics,Hairdressing, Personal Care, Spa, Plastic Surgery

广州国际美博会
Guangdong Intl Beauty Expo
2013/03/09-11
广东广州Guangdong-Guangzhou 2380

第18届上海美容美发化妆品博览会
Shanghai Beauty, Hairdressing & Cosmetics Expo
2013/03/22-24
上海Shanghai 720

2013第二十二届中国北京国际美容化妆品博览会(春季)
22nd Chinese Intl Beauty & Cosmetic Expo in Beijing
2013/04/18-20
北京Beijing 170

中国(义乌)时尚发制品与美发用品展览会
同期举办：
第二届国际进口商品展
China (Yiwu) Hair Products and Hairdressing Supplies Exhibition 2013
2013/04/20-22
浙江义乌Zhejiang-Yiwu 4540

2013中国（上海）医疗美容及整形设备展览会
China (Shanghai) Medical Beauty and Plastic Surgery Equipment Exhibition
2013/06/05-07
上海Shanghai 1230

第4届中国国际时尚发制品及美发用品展览会
4th China Intl Fashion Hair Products and Hair Care Products Exhibition
2013/09
河南郑州Henan-Zhengzhou 3320

33、农业、林业、渔业、畜牧业 Agriculture, Forestry, Fishery &Animal Husbandry

2013北京园林展-第三届国际园林景观与美好人居展览会
Beijing Garden Show
2013/03/15-19
北京Beijing 40

全国春季农机展
CAMF
2013/04
河南郑州Henan-Zhengzhou 3120

第15届中国国际花卉园艺展览会
15th Hortiflorexpo IPM Shanghai
2013/04/17-20
上海Shanghai 1000

2013河南省夏季种子信息交流暨产品展览会
Henan Summer Seed Information Products Show
2013/06
河南郑州Henan-Zhengzhou 3220

2013河南省家禽交易会
Henan Poultry Exhibition
2013/09
河南郑州Henan-Zhengzhou 3330

哈尔滨世界农业博览会
Agriculture & Food Expo Harbin
2013/09/05-08
黑龙江哈尔滨Heilongjiang-Harbin 3000

2013河南省秋季种子信息交流暨产品展览会/河南省植保信息交流暨农药械交流会
Henan Autumn Seed Information Products Show
2013/10
河南郑州Henan-Zhengzhou 3350

2013第八届上海国际渔业博览会
8th Shanghai Intl Fisheries & Seafood Exposition
2013/10/10-12
上海Shanghai 1730

第四届中国兽医大会
4th Chinese Veterinary Conference
2013/10/28-30
广西南宁Guangxi-Nanning 2890

第6届中国义乌国际森林产博览会
6th China Yiwu Intl Forest Products Fair
2013/11/01-04
浙江义乌Zhejiang-Yiwu 4590

第十八届中国国际渔业博览会
18th China Fisheries & Seafood Expo
2013/11/05-07
辽宁大连Liaoning-Dalian 3710

2013中国国际果蔬、加工技术及物流展览会
China World Fruit & Vegetable Trade Fair
2013/11/28-30
北京Beijing 2070

34、汽车、摩托车、电动车 Automobiles, Motorcycles and Electric Cars

第16届中国国际汽车用品展览会
16th China Intl Expo For Auto Electronics, Accessories, Tuning & Car Care Products
2013/03/01-04
北京Beijing 20

第七届杭州春季汽车展销会
7th Hangzhou Spring Automobile Show and Sale
2013/04
浙江杭州Zhejiang-Hangzhou 4350

泰州国际汽车展览会
Taizhou Intl Automobile Exhibition
2013/04
江苏泰州Jiangsu-Taizhou 3660

2013大河新生活方式展（汽车展）
A new way of life；2013 Spring Dahe- Auto Show
2013/04
河南郑州Henan-Zhengzhou 3100

2013年中国洛阳国际汽车展览会
China (Luoyang) Intl Automobile Exhibition
2013/04
河南洛阳Henan-Luoyang 3010

青岛春季汽车文化节
Qingdao Spring Automobile Culture Festival
2013/04/04-07
山东青岛Shandong-Qingdao 3890

2013中国四川国际天然气汽车、加气站设备展览会
China (Sichuan) Natural Gas Vehicle and Gas Station Equipment Exhibition
2013/04/10-12
四川成都Sichuan-Chengdu 4200

2013年烟台春季汽车展销会
Yantai Spring Automobile Show and Sale
2013/04/11-14
山东烟台Shandong-Yantai 4120

2013第三届贵阳国际汽车展览会
3rd Guiyang Intl Automobile Exhibition
2013/04/11-15
贵州贵阳Guizhou-Guiyang 2910

2013第十一届中国（温州）国际汽车展览会
11th Wenzhou Intl Auto Expo
2013/04/11-14
浙江温州Zhejiang-Wenzhou 4480

第十五届上海国际汽车工业展览会
AUTO SHANGHAI 2013
2013/04/21-29
上海Shanghai 1030

2013年中国（盘锦）国际汽车展览会
China (Panjin) Intl Automobile Exhibition
2013/04/27-30
辽宁盘锦Liaoning-Panjin 3730

2013年中国西部（兰州）国际汽车博览会•春季
2013 West China (Lanzhou) Automobile Expo -Spring
2013/04/27-02
甘肃兰州Gansu-Lanzhou 2160

中国（邯郸）国际汽车文化节
China (Handan) Intl Automobile Culture Festival
2013/04/28-02
河北邯郸Hebei-Handan 2950

2013年第六届中国（南京）国际汽车博览会
6th China (Nanjing) Intl Automobile Expo
2013/04/28-02
江苏南京Jiangsu-Nanjing 3570

第四届中国常州汽车博览会
China (Changzhou) Automobile Expo
2013/04/29-01
江苏常州Jiangsu-Changzhou 3530

第十三届广东国际汽车展示交易会
13th Guangdong Intl Auto Exhibition & Trade Fair
2013/04/30-02
广东东莞Guangdong-Dongguan 2200

2013第十届中国（唐山）国际汽车博览会
10th China (Tangshan) Intl Automobile Expo
2013/05
河北唐山Hebei-Tangshan 2960

2013温岭汽车展览会
Wenling Auto Exhibition
2013/05
浙江温岭Zhejiang-Wenling 4450

2013年中国锦州国际汽车展览会
China (Jinzhou) Intl Automobile Exhibition
2013/05/07-10
辽宁锦州Liaoning-Jinzhou 3720

2013年第八届义乌汽车展览会
8th Yiwu Automobile Exhibition 2013
2013/05/09-12
浙江义乌Zhejiang-Yiwu 4560

2013第十届中国国际轮胎资源循环利用展览会
10th China Intl Tire Cyclic Utilization Expo 2013
2013/05/15-17
山东广饶Shandong-Guangrao 3810

2013年第十一届华中国际汽车展览会
11th Central China Automobile Exhibition
2013/05/23-28
湖北武汉Hubei-Wuhan 3420

2013第四届鄂尔多斯国际汽车展览会
4th Ordos Intl Automobile Exhibition
2013/05/30-06/03
内蒙古鄂尔多斯Inner Mongolia-Ordos 3520

2013华南国际汽车改装及赛车展览会
Southern China Intl Car Tuning and Racing Exhibition
2013/05/30-06/01
广东东莞Guangdong-Dongguan 2220

2013年第三届中国（郑州）国际微型汽车配件博览会/中国国际轿车配件（郑州）博览会/中国润滑油及汽保设备展览会
China (Zhengzhou) Intl Mini-car Accessories Expo and Lubricants, Tires, Auto Maintenance Equipment Exhibition
2013/06
河南郑州Henan-Zhengzhou 3210

中原国际汽车博览会暨中原国际汽车文化旅游节
Cars & Automotive Culture and Tourism Festival
2013/06
河南郑州Henan-Zhengzhou 3230

2013年全国微型汽车配件展览会
China (Zhengzhou) Intl Car & Mini Auto Parts Expo
2013/06/01-03
河南郑州Henan-Zhengzhou 3250

2013第十一届中国(广州)国际汽车零部件展览会
同期举行：
中国汽车零部件(全球)采供峰会
11th China (Guangzhou) Intl Auto Parts Expo
2013/06/05-07
广东广州Guangdong-Guangzhou 2630

2013中国（北京）国际卡车及零部件展览会
China (Beijing) Intl Truck Exhibition 2013
2013/06/06-08
北京Beijing 270

2013第四届中国（青岛）国际卡车、商用车及零部件展览会
China (Qingdao) Intl Commercial Vehicle Exhibition
2013/06/07-09
山东青岛Shandong-Qingdao 3990

第十七届深圳-香港-澳门国际汽车博览会
17th Shenzhen-Hong Kong-Macao Intl Automobile Expo
2013/06/08-13
广东深圳Guangdong-Shenzhen 2740

第五届连云港-大陆桥汽车贸易博览会
5th Lianyungang-Continental Bridge Automobile Trade Fair
2013/06/10-13
江苏连云港Jiangsu-Lianyungang 3560

2013第二届广西汽车文化节
2nd Guangxi Automobile Culture Festival
2013/06/20-23
广西南宁Guangxi-Nanning 2870

第六届中国常州电动车展览会
6th China (Changzhou) Electric Cars Exhibition
2013/06/30-07/02
江苏常州Jiangsu-Changzhou 3540

2013中国国际汽车后市场博览会暨中国汽车用品（郑州）交易会
China (Zhengzhou) Automobile Product Fair
2013/07
河南郑州Henan-Zhengzhou 3260

2013中国国际电动汽车充电设施及储能设备展览会
eMobility China
2013/07/03-05
北京Beijing 340

2013年第五届呼和浩特国际汽车展览会
5th Hohhot Intl Automobile Exhibition
2013/07/19-23
内蒙古呼和浩特Inner Mongolia-Hohhot 3500

2013年中国（常州）汽车配件交易会
China (Changzhou) Auto Parts Fair
2013/08/04
江苏常州Jiangsu-Changzhou 3550

2013年中国西部（兰州）国际汽车博览会-秋季
West China (Lanhou) Automobile Expo-Autumn
2013/08/22-27
甘肃兰州Gansu-Lanzhou 2170

中国（大同）国际汽车文化节
China (Datong) Intl Automobile Culture Festival
2013/08/23-28
山西大同Shanxi-Datong 4160

第十六届成都国际汽车展览会
Chengdu Motor Show 2013
2013/08/31-09/08
四川成都Sichuan-Chengdu 4280

呼和浩特汽车文化节
Hohhot Automobile Culture Festival
2013/09
内蒙古呼和浩特Inner Mongolia-Hohhot 3510

第三届中国包头国际汽车展览会
3rd China (Inner Mongolia) Intl Automobile Exhibition
2013/09
内蒙古包头Inner Mongolia-Baotou 3480

2013第九届烟台国际汽车工业展览会
9th Yantai Intl Automobile Industry Exhibition 2013
2013/09/05-09
山东烟台Shandong-Yantai 4140

2013第七届中国国际汽车零部件博览会
CIAPE
2013/09/13-15
北京Beijing 460

2013第十届中国（苏州）国际汽车工业博览会
10th China (Suzhou) Intl Automobile Industry Expo
2013/09/18-22
江苏苏州Jiangsu-Suzhou 3650

东部沿海（盐城）国际汽车博览会
East Coast (Yancheng) Intl Automobile Expo
2013/09/18-22
江苏盐城Jiangsu-Yancheng 3670

第十四届广东国际汽车展示交易会
14th Guangdong Intl Auto Exhibition & Trade fair
2013/09/29-10/04
广东东莞Guangdong-Dongguan 2300

2013年第十四届中国杭州国际汽车工业展览会
14th China (Hangzhou) Auto Industry Exhibition
2013/10
浙江杭州Zhejiang-Hangzhou 4360

2013年第八届南昌国际汽车展览会
8th Nanchang Intl Automobile Exhibition
2013/10/18-21
广西南昌Guangxi-Nanchang 3680

武汉国际汽车展览会
Wuhan Motor Show
2013/10/18-23
湖北武汉Hubei-Wuhan 3430

2013中国国际商用车展览会
China Commercial Vehicles Show
2013/10/30-11/02
湖北武汉Hubei-Wuhan 3440

2013年第六届郑州国际汽车展览会
6th Zhengzhou Intl Automobile Exhibition 2013
2013/10/31-11/04
河南郑州Henan-Zhengzhou 3360

第三届贵阳汽车文化节
3rd Guiyang Automobile Culture Festival
2013/10/31-11/03
贵州贵阳Guizhou-Guiyang 2940

中国（株洲）国际汽车及新能源汽车展示交易会
China (Zhuzhou) Intl Automobile and New Energy Car Exhibition
2013/11
湖南株洲Hunan-Zhuzhou 3460

2013第三届中国（重庆）汽车博览会
3rd China (Chongqing) Automobile Expo
2013/11/14-18
重庆Chongqing 560

2013楚天汽车文化节
Hubei Automobile Culture Festival
2013/11/29-12/02
湖北武汉Hubei-Wuhan 3450

2013第六届中国-东盟（南宁）国际汽车展览会
6th China-ASEAN (Nanning) Intl Auto Exhibition
2013/12/05-09
广西南宁Guangxi-Nanning 2900

35、清洁 Cleaning

中国清洁博览会
China Clean Expo
2013/04/01-09
上海Shanghai 840

36、设计 Design

W3国际精品设计展
Expo Deco
2013/04/01-03
上海Shanghai 800

上海国际商场设计、装饰与用品博览会
Expo Shop
2013/04/01-03
上海Shanghai 8880

2013中国成都创意设计展暨建筑装饰博览会
China Chengdu Creative Design Exhibitions and Architecture Decoration Fair
2013/04/18-20
四川成都Sichuan-Chengdu 4220

Design of Designers
中国国际设计师作品展示交易会
China Intl Design Trading Expo
2013/09/11-15
上海Shanghai 1660

上海国际医疗设备设计与技术展览会
MEDTEC China
2013/09/25-26
上海Shanghai 1720

37、摄影、数码影像 Photography & Image

第十五届中国（上海）国际摄影器材和数码影像展览会
PHOTO & IMAGING SHANGHAI 2013
2013/07/04-07
上海Shanghai 1410

38、食品、饮料、茶、咖啡、酒及生产资料 Food, Beverage, Tea, Coffee, Spirit & Processing

中国国际食品添加剂及配料展览会
Food Ingredients China
2013/03/26-28
上海Shanghai 740

2013年春季成都全国糖酒会
China Food & Drinks Fair
2013/03/28-31
四川成都Sichuan-Chengdu 4180

上海咖啡与茶用品展
Expo Coffee&Tea
2013/04/01-03
上海Shanghai 780

上海国际葡萄酒与烈酒展览会
Winexpo
2013/04/01-03
上海Shanghai 770

上海高端食品与饮料展
Expo Finefood
2013/04/01-03
上海Shanghai 870

2013第九届中国国际冰淇淋乳制品展览会/中国国际冰淇淋乳制品新产品及原辅料设备采购交易会
9th Ice Cream Expo
2013/04/07-09
北京Beijing 130

2013第十届中国国际烘焙展览会
10th China Intl Bakery Exhibition
2013/04/07-09
北京Beijing 140

2013第十一届中国国际食品包装与加工设备展览会
11th China Beijing Intl Food Processing and Packaging Exhibition
2013/04/07-09
北京Beijing 120

第八届内蒙古国际食品博览会
8th Inner Mongolia Intl Food Expo
2013/04/12-14
内蒙古呼和浩特Inner Mongolia-Hohhot 3490

2013北京进口食品展-中国（北京）国际进口食品博览会
China Intl Import Food Exposition
2013/04/14-16
北京Beijing 160

2013第十届中国(青岛)国际肉类工业展览会
10th China (Qingdao) Intl Meat Industry Exhibition

5th China Intl Technology Equipment Fair of Food Fresh Keeping, Freezing
2013/04/27-29
山东青岛Shandong-Qingdao 3980

2013第九届中国食品包装及加工设备（郑州）展览会
2013 China (Zhengzhou) Food Packaging and Processing Equipment Show
2013/05
河南郑州Henan-Zhengzhou 3160

瑞城郑州全国糖酒食品交易会
Ruicheng Zhengzhou Sugar and Wine Trade Fair
2013/05
河南郑州Henan-Zhengzhou 3170

中国肉类工业（郑州）展览会
China (Zhengzhou) Meat Industry Show
2013/05
河南郑州Henan-Zhengzhou 3180

中国国际食品和饮料展览会
Sial china 2013
2013/05/07-09
上海Shanghai 1080

2013第十七届中国烘焙展览会
17th China Bakery Exhibition
2013/05/09-11
广东广州Guangdong-Guangzhou 2560

2013第九届中国（广州）国际食品饮料展
9th China Intl Foodstuff (Guangzhou) Exposition
2013/05/10-12
广东广州Guangdong-Guangzhou 2580

2013第十届中国(上海)国际茶业博览会
China Tea Expo, Shanghai 2013
2013/05/16-19
上海Shanghai 1100

2013第十届中国国际营养健康产业（上海）博览会
China (Shanghai) Intl Nutrition and Health Industry Expo 2013
2013/05/17-19
上海Shanghai 1130

2013第七届全国食品博览会暨糖酒商品交易会
7th National Food Expo and Sugar and Alcoholic Commodities Fair
2013/05/24-26
山东济南Shandong-Jinan 3870

2013营养健康产业（南京）博览会
China (Nanjing) Nutrition and Health Industry Exposition
2013/05/25-27
江苏南京Jiangsu-Nanjing 3600

2013第二届天津国际营养健康产业博览会
2nd Tianjin Intl Exposition of Nutrition and Health Industries
2013/05/30-06/02
天津Tianjin 2120

2013年第五届中国郑州烘焙展览会/第五届中国郑州食品保鲜及冷冻、冷藏技术展览会
Zhengzhou Baking Technology Expo/ Food Refrigeration Technology Show
2013/06
河南郑州Henan-Zhengzhou 3200

2013第13届广州国际食品展暨广州进口食品展览会
13th China(Guangzhou) Intl Food Exhibition And Guangzhou Import Food Exhibition
2013/06/04-06
广东广州Guangdong-Guangzhou 2620

亚洲食品配料、健康原料、天然原料中国展
Food Ingredients Asia-China
2013/06/25-27
上海Shanghai 1350

天然及营养保健品中国展
Nutraceutical Products China
2013/06/25-27
上海Shanghai 1360

第七届烟台国际葡萄酒博览会
7th Yantai Intl Wine Exposition
2013/07/05-07
山东烟台Shandong-Yantai 4130

2013第十二届瑞城郑州全国糖酒食品交易会/第三届瑞城郑州国际葡萄酒及烈酒展览会/第三届瑞城郑州面业暨精品粮油交易会
Ruicheng-Zhengzhou Sugar and Wine Trade Fair and Zhengzhou Intl Wine Fair
2013/08
河南郑州Henan-Zhengzhou 3280

第九届内蒙古国际食品博览会
9th Inner Mongolia Food Expo
2013/08/30-09/01
内蒙古包头Inner Mongolia- 3470

2013第三届中国（贵州）国际酒类博览会
China (Guizhou) Intl Alcoholic Beverage Expo
2013/09/09-13
贵州贵阳Guizhou-Guiyang 2930

第十四届国际果蔬、食品博览会
11th Intl Fruit/Vegetable/Food Exposition
2013/09/26-28
山东烟台Shagndong-Yantai 4150

2013第十五届上海国际营养健康产业博览会
China (Shanghai) Intl Nutrition and Health Industry Expo
2013/10/20-22
上海Shanghai 1760

秋季时尚（郑州）购物节
Autumn Fashion Shopping Festival (Zhengzhou)
2013/11
河南郑州Henan-Zhengzhou 3380

广东（厚街）茶业博览会
Guangdong (Houjie) Tea Expo
2013/12/28-31
广东东莞Guangdong-Dongguan 2360

39、实验室设备 Laboratory

广州国际分析测试及实验室设备展览会暨技术研讨会
China Lab 2013
China Analytic & Laboratory Equipment Expo & Conference
2013/03/13-15
广东广州Guangdong-Guangzhou 2460

CISILE2013
第十一届中国国际科学仪器及实验室装备展览会
11th China Intl Scientific Instrument and Laboratory Equipment Exhibition
2013/05/15-17
北京Beijing 230

中国国际生物技术和仪器设备博览会
同期举办：中国（上海）科学仪器、实验室装备及化学试剂展览会/中国（上海）诊断试剂和设备展览会
BIOTECH CHINA 2013
Intl Trade Fair & Congress for Biotechnology
2013/05/29-31
上海Shanghai 1180

40、石油、石化、天然气 Petroleum, Gas, Petrochemical

第八届上海国际石油石化天然气技术装备展览会/上海国际页岩气峰会
8th Shanghai Intl Petroleum Petrochemical Natural Gas Technology Equipment Exhibition
2013/10/28-30
上海Shanghai 1820

41、水、水处理 Water Treatment

第十四届中国（广州）国际给排水、水处理技术与设备展览会暨2013中国（广州）国际泵、阀门、管道展览会
Water, Wastewater & Water Treatment China and Pump, Valve & Pipe China
2013/03/04-06
广东广州Guangdong-Guangzhou 2400

2013哈尔滨水处理展会
Harbin Water Treatment Exhibition
2013/04/23-25
黑龙江哈尔滨Heilongjiang-Harbin 2970

2013（第九届）中国国际水处理化学品、水溶性高分子技术及应用展览会
WATERCHEM+TECH
2013/11/12-14
上海Shanghai 1990

42、塑料、橡胶 Plastics & Rubbers

2013第十届中国国际橡胶技术（青岛）展览会
10th China Intl Rubber Technology (Qingdao) Fair
2013/04/09-11
山东青岛Shandong-Qingdao 3970

2013第十届中国国际轮胎资源循环利用展览会
10th China Intl Tire Cyclic Utilization Expo
2013/05/15-17
山东广饶Shandong-Guangrao 3810

2013第15届中国青岛国际塑料橡胶工业展览会/青岛国际塑料原料及改性技术展览会
15th China (Qingdao) Intl Plastics & Rubber Industry Exhibition/ China Qingdao Intl Exhibition of Plastic Raw Materials and Modified Technology
2013/08/15-17
山东青岛Shandong-Qingdao 4080

第十三届亚太国际塑料橡胶工业展览会
13th Asian-pacific Intl Plastics & Rubber Industry Exhibition
2013/09/03-06
上海Shanghai 1580

塑交会
(2013第十三届中国塑料交易会)
China PET '13
-12th China Plastics Exhibition & Conference
2013/09/25-28
浙江台州Zhejiang-Taizhou 4440

第十五届东莞国际橡塑胶、包装、压铸和铸造展
15th China Dongguan Intl Plastics Packing Rubber Diecasting & Foundry Exhibition
2013/11/13-16
广东东莞Guangdong-Dongguan 2330

43、特许经营、连锁加盟 Franchising

2013第15届国际特许加盟展览会
China Franchise Expo 2013
2013/04/26-28
北京Beijing 180

2013国际特许加盟（上海）展览会
Shanghai Intl Franchise Exhibition 2013
2013/09/14-16
上海Shanghai 1680

第十五届中国连锁店展览会
China Retail Trade Fair (China Shop)
2013/11/14-16
四川成都Sichuan-Chengdu 4300

44、体育、休闲 Sports & Leisure

第二十三届中国国际钓鱼用品贸易展览会
China Fish 2013
(23rd China Intl Fishing Tackle Trade Exhibition)
2013/02/23-25
北京Beijing 10

2013年第12届中国高尔夫球博览会（北京）
China Golf Show / PGA Merchandise Show-China
2013/03/22-24
北京Beijing 60

中国(上海)国际游艇展
China (Shanghai) Intl Boat Show
2013/04/11-14
上海Shanghai 960

中国(上海)休闲产业展
Expo Leisure
2013/04/11-14
上海Shanghai 970

2013中国国际游艇产业博览会
同期举办：
中国国际水系运动休闲博览会
China Intl Boat Show
2013/05/10-12
广东广州Guangdong-Guangzhou 2570

中国国际体育用品博览会
China Sport Show
2013/05/31-06/03
北京Beijing 260

45、投资、创业 Investment

2013中国创业投资展
China Intl Franchise Exhibition
2013/04/26-28
北京Beijing 190

第十七届中国国际投资贸易洽谈会
The China Intl Fair for Investment and Trade
2013/09/08-11
福建厦门Fujian-Xiamen 2150

46、玩具、婴幼儿用品 Toys & Children's Products

第25届广州国际玩具及模型展
25th Guangzhou Intl Toy and Hobby Fair
2013/04/08-10
广东广州Guangdong-Guangzhou 2540

第4届广州国际婴童用品展
4th Guangzhou Intl Baby Product Fair
2013/04/08-10
广东广州Guangdong-Guangzhou 2530

第15届北京国际玩具及幼教用品展览会
15th Beijing Intl Toys & Preschool Tools Exhibition
2013/05/13-15
北京Beijing 210

第八届上海幼儿教育暨用品展
8th Kids Education Expo 2013 Shanghai
2013/05/24-26
上海Shanghai 1160

CBME孕婴童展、CBME童装展
Shanghai Intl Children-Baby-Maternity Industry Expo
2013/07/17-19
上海Shanghai 1440

第12届中国国际玩具、幼教用品及设备展览会
12thIntl Trade Fair for Toys & Preschool Educational Resources
2013/10/15-17
上海Shanghai 1750

中国婴童展
同期举办：
第十二届中国国际玩具及模型展览会
China Kids Expo
China Intl Baby Carriers & Baby Articles fair
2013/10/15-17
上海Shanghai 1740

47、文化产业 Culture Industry

第8届中国义乌文化产品交易博览会
8th China Yiwu Cultural Products Trade Fair
2013/04/27-30
浙江义乌Zhejiang-Yiwu 4550

2013年107届中国文化用品商品交易会
107th China Stationery Fair
2013/06/20-22
上海Shanghai 1300

48、文具、办公用品 Stationery &Office Supplies

第10届中国国际文具礼品博览会
10th China Intl Stationery & Gifts Exposition
2013/03/29-31
浙江宁波Zhejiang-Ningbo 4390

第十一届亚洲打印耗材展览会
ReChina Asia Expo
2013/04/22-24
上海Shanghai 1050

第8届中国义乌文化产品交易博览会
8th China Yiwu Cultural Products Trade Fair
2013/04/27-30
浙江义乌Zhejiang-Yiwu 4550

49、五金、工具 Hardware and Tools

第二十三届中国国际五金博览会
23rd China Intl Hardware Fair
2013/03/12-14
上海Shanghai 660

2013年第十六届中国西部国际装备制造业博览会/西部国际五金机电工具贸易展览会
China West Intl Equipment Manufacturing Exposition
2013/03/14-17 3780

第10届中国国际五金电器博览会
The10th China Intl Hardware & Electrical Appliances Trade Fair
2013/04/20-22
浙江义乌Zhejiang-Yiwu 4520

2013中国国际衡器展览会
InterWEIGHING
China Intl Weighing Instrument Exhibition
2013/04/22-24
上海Shanghai 1060

2013第十七届中国西部(成都)五金机电商品展览会
17th China West Intl Equipment Manufacturing Exposition
2013/07/18-20
四川成都Sichuan-Chengdu 4260

第二十四届中国国际五金博览会
24th China Intl Hardware Fair
2013/09/10-13
北京Beijing 440

磨料磨具展览会
Abrasives Exhibition
2013/11
河南郑州Henan-Zhengzhou 3370

第十五届东莞国际模具展及金属加工展
15th China Dongguan Intl Mould and Metalworking Exhibition
2013/11/13-16
广东东莞Guangdong-Dongguan 2340

2013 中国国际五金展
-《科隆国际五金展》强力推动
China Intl Hardware Show
- Powered by PRACTICAL WORLD
2013/11/26-28
上海Shanghai 2060

50、线、缆 Cable &Wire

中国国际电线电缆及设备交易会
UL Wire & Cable Intl Fair 2013
2013/07/17-19
广东东莞Guangdong-Dongguan 2270

2013多人行国际连接器、线束及设备展览会
Dowell Intl connector, harness and Equipment Exhibition
2013/07/18-20
广东深圳Guangdong-Shenzhen 2800

51、消费电子、家用电器 Consumer Electronics & Appliances

中国家电博览会-上海2013
Appliance World Expo
2013/03/18-21
上海Shanghai 700

游戏开发者大会-中国
Game Developers Conference, China
2013 4630

中国顺德国际家用电器博览会
China Shunde Intl Exposition for Household Electrical Appliances
2013/10/17-20
广东顺德Guangdong-Shunde 2860

52、消费品、家居用品 Consumer Goods

2013中国广州国际家居饰品、家纺布艺展览会
Home Textile
2013/03/18-21
广东广州Guangdong-Guangzhou 2470

第6届中国（杭州）国际花园户外家具及休闲用品展
Outdoor Lifestyle Hangzhou
2013/03/21-24
浙江杭州Zhejiang-Hangzhou 4340

2013上海国际高端生活方式（奢侈品）展览会
Shanghai Intl High-end Lifestyle Exhibition
2013/04/10-12
上海Shanghai 940

中国(上海)尚品生活展
Expo Life Style For Luxury and Excellence
2013/04/11-14
上海Shanghai 950

2013中国义乌消费品交易会-家居家具展
China (Yiwu) Housewear and Furniture Exhibition
2013/04/20-22
浙江义乌Zhejiang-Yiwu 4530

2013中国最大的竹制品展/春季竹礼品展
China (Shanghai) Bamboo Product Exhibition
2013/05/16-18
上海Shanghai 1120

2013 第六届天津国际礼品、工艺品及家居用品博览会
6th Tianjin Intl Gifts, Crafts & Household Goods Expo
2013/05/17-20
天津Tianjin 2090

2013第107届中国日用百货商品交易会暨中国现代家庭用品博览会
107th China Daily-use Articles Trade Fair & China Modern Home Expo
2013/08/01-03
上海Shanghai 1470

第28届中国北京国际礼品、赠品及家庭用品展览会
28th China Beijing Intl Gifts, Premium & Houseware Exhbition
2013/08/14-17
北京Beijing 370

中国国际家居饰品展览会
Home Furnishing China
2013/09/11-15
上海Shanghai 1650

2013中国（上海）国际时尚家居用品展览会
同期举办：
中国国际文具及办公用品展览会
interiorlifestyle China
China Intl Trade Fair for Household Products and Accessories
Paperworld-China
2013/09/25-27
上海Shanghai 1700

秋季时尚（郑州）购物节
Autumn Fashion Shopping Festival (Zhengzhou)
2013/11
河南郑州Henan-Zhengzhou 3380

北京国际礼品、赠品及家用精品年底展览会
Intl Gifts, Premium & Houseware Purchase Exhibiton
2013/11/13-15
北京Beijing 540

2013中国宁波家居与时尚生活产品展览会
Ningbo Intl Home& Lifestyle Products Exhibition
2013/11/29-12/01
浙江宁波Zhejiang-Ningbo 4430

2013第十三届东莞嘉年华时尚生活用品购物节
13th Dongguan Carnival
2013/12/21-2014/01/05
广东东莞Guangdong-Dongguan 2350

53、鞋、皮革 Shoes & Leather

2013第十四届中国(东莞)国际鞋机鞋材工业技术展
14th China (Dongguan) Intl Footwear Machinery & Material Industry Fair
2013/04/10-13
广东东莞Guangdong-Dongguan 2190

第十五届中国（晋江）国际鞋业博览会
The 15th Jinjiang Footwear Intl Exposition, China
2013/04/18-21
福建晋江Fujian-Jinjiang 2130

2013第101届中国上海国际鞋业皮具展CIFL暨GDS精品展
101st Shanghai Intl Footwear & Leather Goods Exhibition & GDS Select
2013/05/26-28
上海Shanghai 1170

广州国际鞋类、皮革及工业设备展览会
SHOES & LEATHER – GUANGZHOU 2013
Intl Exhibition on Shoes & Leather Industry - Guangzhou (Machinery & Raw Material)
2013/05/29-31
广东广州Guangdong-Guangzhou 2590

广州国际鞋类、皮革制成品展览会
IFLE – GUANGZHOU 2013
Intl Footwear & Leather Products Exhibition - Guangzhou
2013/05/29-31
广东广州Guangdong-Guangzhou 2600

中国国际皮革展
All China Leather Exhibition
2013/09/04-06
上海Shanghai 1610

中国国际箱包、裘革服装及服饰展
Moda Shanghai
2013/09/04-06
上海Shanghai 1600

中国国际鞋类展
China Intl Footwear Fair
2013/09/04-06
上海Shanghai 1590

第十六届中国东莞国际鞋展-鞋机展-鞋材展
Dongguan Shoes & China Shoetes
2013/11/01-03
广东东莞Guangdong-Dongguan 2310

54、新能源、节能 New Energy, Energy-Saving

第八届亚洲国际太阳能光伏工业展览会
AsiaSolar Photovoltaic Industry Exhibition
2013/03/13-15
上海Shanghai 680

世界节能环保与生态建筑中国展
Ecobuild China
2013/04/01-03
上海Shanghai 820

第六届中国（青岛）国际太阳能与建筑一体化应用产品技术展览会
Qingdao Intl Solar Energy Fair
2013/04/06-08
山东青岛Shandong-Qingdao 3920

2013第七届中国(上海)国际风能展览会暨研讨会
7th China (Shanghai) Intl Wind Energy Exhibition and Conference
2013/04/08-10
上海Shanghai 910

2013年亚欧能源产业博览会
EuroAsia Energy Industry Expo 2013
2013/04/10-12
新疆乌鲁木齐Xinjiang-Urumqi 4310

2013中国四川国际天然气汽车、加气站设备展览会
China (Sichuan) Natural Gas Vehicle and Gas Station Equipment Exhibition
2013/04/10-12
四川成都Sichuan-Chengdu 4200

中国（上海）国际生物质能和沼气大会暨展览会
China (Shanghai) Intl Bioenergy and Biogas Conference and Exhibition
2013/04/26-28
上海Shanghai 1070

2013第七届中国（天津）国际太阳能及光伏展览会
Tianjin Solar and Photovoltaic Exhibition
2013/05/18-20
天津Tianjin 2110

第四届（2013）中国国际生物质能源展
Bio-Energy-Expo 2013
Trade Exhibition for Biogas-Technology and Management
4th Intl Bio-Energy Conference
2013/05/18-20
湖北武汉Hubei-Wuhan 3410

2013上海国际海上风电及风电产业链大会暨展览会
Offshore Wind China 2013
2013/06/19-21
上海Shanghai 1290

中国国际清洁能源博览会
Clean Energy Expo China
2013/07/03-05
北京Beijing 330

中国国际风能设备展览会
（原亚洲风能大会暨国际风能设备展览会）
Wind Power China
(Formerly Wind Power Asia)
2013/07/03-05
北京Beijing 320

第五届中国国际生物质能展览暨技术研讨会
Bio-Energy China
2013/07/03-05
北京Beijing 360

第13届中国光伏大会
13th China Photovoltaic Conference and Intl Photovoltaic Exhibition
2013/09/05-07
北京Beijing 420

中国（株洲）国际汽车及新能源汽车展示交易会
China (Zhuzhou) Intl Automobile and New Energy Car Exhibition
2013/11
湖南株州Hunan-Zhuzhou 3460

2013第11届中国（上海）国际保温材料与节能技术展览会
11th China (Shanghai) Insulating Materials and Energy-saving Technology Expo
2013/11/20-22
上海Shanghai 2040

55、信息技术、通信技术 Information Technology & Communication Technology

中国最佳呼叫中心及最佳管理人系列评选奖项
CCCS Best Call Center Awards
2013 4620

第十一届亚洲打印耗材展览会
ReChina Asia Expo
2013/04/22-24
上海Shanghai 1050

2013上海国际工业计算机及嵌入式系统展览会暨2013MCU技术创新与嵌入式应用大会/人机界面技术创新与应用大会
Shanghai IPC & Embedded Expo 2013
2013/05/22-24
上海Shanghai 1150

第四届中国国际物联网大会暨展览会
IOT China Conference & Exhibition 2013
2013/06/04-05
上海Shanghai 1210

2013第十五届上海国际手机产业展览会暨研讨会
CME2013
2013/06/04-06
上海Shanghai 1200

2013亚洲国际智能制造装备产业展览会
Asia Intl Intellect Equipment Manufacturer Industry Exhibition
2013/06/28-30
北京Beijing 300

2013多人行国际智能手机组装、触摸屏展览会
Dowell Intl Smartphone Assembly & Touch Screen Exhibition
2013/07/18-20
广东深圳Guangdong-Shenzhen 2790

中国呼叫中心技术设备及解决方案博览会
Call Center Expo China
2013/09/02-03
上海Shanghai 1570

中国国际呼叫中心管理大会
ACCE China
2013/09/02-03
上海Shanghai 1560

中国电子商务服务及产品展示会
eCommerce Expo China
2013/09/02-03
上海Shanghai 81550

营销和广告创新技术展示会暨研讨会
TFM&A China
2013/09/02-03
上海Shanghai 1540

Cloud Connect China
2013/09/15-17
上海Shanghai 1690

第二十届国际自动识别及物联网技术展览会
SCAN CHINA 2013
2013/10/23-25
山东青岛Shandong-Qingdao 4110

第二届安卓全球开发者大会
Android World Global Developers Conference
2013/10/26-27
广东深圳Guangdong-Shenzhen 2840

2013第十六届深圳国际手机产业展览会暨研讨会
CME2013
2013/11/25-27
广东深圳Guangdong-Shenzhen 2850

56、养老产业 Elder Support Industry

2013华南国际老年用品及康复保健器械展览会
同期举办：
医院装备展览会/家庭医疗器械展览会
South China Intl Gerontic Products & Health Care Recovery Instrument Exhibition
2013/08/16-18
广东广州Guangdong-Guangzhou 2670

国际养老产业(上海)峰会
Care Show China
2013/08/20-23
上海Shanghai 1500

57、眼镜 Optics

2013第十一届中国（温州）国际眼镜业展览会
11th Wenzhou Intl Optics Fair, China
2013/07/10-12
浙江温州Zhejiang-Wenzhou 4490

58、印刷 Printing

第二十届华南国际印刷工业展览会暨2013中国国际标签印刷技术展览会
20th South China Intl Exhibition on Printing Industry/ China Intl Exhibition on Label Printing Technology
2013/03/04-06
广东广州Guangdong-Guangzhou 2420

Printech2013
票据标签打印展览会
Printech Digital Printing & Label Expo
2013/04/22-24
上海Shanghai 1040

第十一届亚洲打印耗材展览会
ReChina Asia Expo
2013/04/22-24
上海Shanghai 1050

第八届北京国际印刷技术展览会
8th Beijing Intl Printing Technology Exhibition
2013/05/14-18
北京Beijing 220

第二十一届上海国际印刷包装纸业展览会暨中国西部国际印刷包装产业博览会
Shanghai Intl AD, Print, Pack, Paper Expo
2013/07/10-13
上海Shanghai 1420

第30届中国国际网印及数字技术展览会
China Screen Print 2013
2013/09/02-04
广东广州Guangdong-Guangzhou 2680

59、应急救灾 Emergency Rescue

国际应急医学救援展览会
China Intl Emergency Medical Expo (CEME)
2013 4610

60、仪器仪表 Instrument

2013中国国际衡器展览会
InterWEIGHING
China Intl Weighing Instrument Exhibition
2013/04/22-24
上海Shanghai 1060

CISILE2013
第十一届中国国际科学仪器及实验室装备展览会
11th China Intl Scientific Instrument and Laboratory Equipment Exhibition
2013/05/15-17
北京Beijing 230

2013第15届中国青岛国际仪器仪表及测试测量技术展览会/第15届中国青岛国际工业自动化及控制技术展览会
15th China Qingdao Industrial Automation and Control Technology Exhibition/ 15th China Qingdao Intl Instruments and Test and Measurement Technology Exhibition
2013/08/15-17
山东青岛Shandong-Qingdao 4100

第24届中国国际测量控制与仪器仪表展览会
MICONEX2013
24th Intl Conference and Fair Measurement Instrumentation and Automation
2013/08/27-30
北京Beijing 390

61、艺术 Arts

2013艺术北京博览会
Art Beijing 2013
2013/04/30-05/03
北京Beijing 200

62、医药、医疗设备、生物、保健 Medical Equipment, Pharmaceuticals & Health Care

国际应急医学救援展览会
China Intl Emergency Medical Expo (CEME)
2013 4610

第23届中原医疗器械（2013年春季）展览会/第23届中原口腔设备及材料（2013年春季）展览会
Spring Central Plain Intl Medical Apparatus and Instruments Exhibition
2013/03
河南郑州Henan-Zhengzhou 3050

中国生物材料峰会，生物医用材料创新与发展中国峰会
Bio-Materials China，BioMed Innovation China 2013
2013/03/14-15
上海Shanghai 690

中国仿制药峰会
NextGen China (Shanghai)
2013/03/28-29
上海Shanghai 750

2013中国（广州）国际生物识别技术展览会
China Guangzhou Intl Biometric Identification Technology Exhibition
2013/03/29-31
广东广州Guangdong-Guangzhou 2510

中国药品生产与质量管理峰会
Pharma Manufacturing China
2013/03/30-04/01
上海Shanghai 760

2013第12届西部成都医疗器械展览会
12th West China (Chengdu) Medical Equipment Exhibition
2013/04/02-04
四川成都Sichuan-Chengdu 4190

2013第十四届北京国际营养健康产业博览会
14th Beijing Nutrition and Health Industry Expo
2013/04/07-09
北京Beijing 110

2013第十四届中国国际家庭医疗保健器械展览会
14th China Intl Home Medical Health Care Recovery Products & Instrument (Beijing) Expo
2013/04/07-09
北京Beijing 100

第70届中国国际医药原料药、中间体、包装、设备交易会
7th China (Shanghai) Intl Wind Energy Exhibition and Conference
2013/04/08-10
湖北武汉Hubei-Wuhan 3400

第十届中国国际成人保健及生殖健康展览会
China Adult-Care Expo
2013/04/12-14
上海Shanghai 980

第69届中国国际医疗器械（春季）博览会/第16届中国国际医疗器械设计与制造技术（春季）展览会
69th China Intl Medical Equipment Fair-Spring/ 16th Intl Component Manufacturing & Design Show-Spring
2013/04/17-20
广东深圳Guangdong-Shenzhen 2730

第69届全国药品交易会
PHARMCHINA
2013/04/25-27
湖北武汉Hubei-Wuhan 3390

2013年第十五届中国国际（江苏）医博会暨华东地区医院管理高级论坛
15th China (Jiangsu) Intl Medical Expo
East China Hospital Management Forum
2013/05/09-11
江苏南京Jiangsu-Nanjing 3580

第八届中国国际养老及康复医疗博览会
8th China Intl Exhibition of Senior Care Rehabilitation Medicine and Healthcare
2013/05/16-18
上海Shanghai 1110

2013第四届神经科技大会
BIT's 4th Annual World Congress of Neuro Talk 2013
2013/05/23-25
陕西西安Shaanxi-Xi'an 3800

2013营养健康产业（南京）博览会
China (Nanjing) Nutrition and Health Industry Exposition 2013
2013/05/25-27
江苏南京Jiangsu-Nanjing 3600

中国国际生物技术和仪器设备博览会
同期举办：2013中国（上海）科学仪器、实验室装备及化学试剂展览会/中国（上海）诊断试剂和设备展览会
BIOTECH CHINA 2013
Intl Trade Fair & Congress for Biotechnology
2013/05/29-31
上海Shanghai 1180

2013第二届天津国际营养健康产业博览会
2nd Tianjin Intl Exposition of Nutrition and Health Industries
2013/05/30-06/02
天津Tianjin 2120

2013第22届中国（广州）国际医药保健产业博览会/第22届全国药品保健品（广州）交易会
22nd China (Guangzhou) Intl Medicine Health Care Industry Expo
2013/06/04-06
广东广州Guangdong-Guangzhou 2610

2013第十二届中国（上海）国际医疗器械展览会
China (Shanghai) Intl Medical Expo
2013/06/05-07
上海Shanghai 1220

2013中国（上海）医疗美容及整形设备展览会
China (Shanghai) Medical Beauty and Plastic Surgery Equipment Exhibition
2013/06/05-07
上海Shanghai 1230

CPhI医药中国峰会
CPhI On-site Modular Conferences
2013/06/24-25
上海Shanghai 1310

天然及营养保健品中国展
Nutraceutical Products China
2013/06/25-27
上海Shanghai 1360

世界制药机械、包装设备与材料中国展 世界生化、分析仪器与实验室装备中国展
P-MEC China
2013/06/25-27
上海Shanghai 1370

世界合同定制服务中国展
ICSE China
2013/06/25-27
上海Shanghai 1340

世界制药原料中国展
CPhI China
2013/06/25-27
上海Shanghai 1330

植入介入医疗器械中国峰会（上海）
Implantable Medical Device Conference (Shanghai)
2013/07/18-19
上海Shanghai 1450

中华口腔医学会第15次全国口腔医学学术会议（2013年会）/2013(上海)国际口腔设备器材博览会
15th CSA Annual Meeting
2013 China Dental Show
2013/08/15-18
上海Shanghai 1480

2013华南国际老年用品及康复保健器械展览会
同期举办：医院装备展览会/家庭医疗器械展览会
South China Intl Gerontic Products & Health Care Recovery Instrument Exhibition
2013/08/16-18
广东广州Guangdong-Guangzhou 2670

第24届中原医疗器械（2013年秋季）展览会
2013 Autumn Central Plain Intl Medical Instruments Exhibition
2013/09
河南郑州Henan-Zhengzhou 3300

2013中国（北京）临床检验设备及用品展览会
China (Beijing) Clinical Examination Equipment and Products Exhibition
2013/09/02-04
北京Beijing 400

2013第十三届中国（北京）医疗器械展览会
13th China (Beijing) Medical Devices Exhibition
2013/09/02-04
北京Beijing 410

中国（广州）国际保健产业博览会
China (Guangzhou) Intl Health Care Industry Exposition
2013/09/07-09
广东广州Guangdong-Guangzhou 2695

上海国际医疗设备设计与技术展览会
MEDTEC China
2013/09/25-26
上海Shanghai 1720

中国仿制药峰会（北京）
NextGen China (Beijing)
2013/10/17-18
北京Beijing 510

2013第十五届上海国际营养健康产业博览会
China (Shanghai) Intl Nutrition and Health Industry Expo
2013/10/20-22
上海Shanghai 1760

第十八届中国国际医药（工业）展览会暨技术交流会
China-Pharm 2013
18th Intl Pharmaceutical Industry Exhibition
2013/10/29-11/01
上海Shanghai 1850

63、乐器 Musical Instrument

2013第十届中国（广州）国际乐器展览会
ProSound + Light Guangzhou
2013/03/09-12
广东广州Guangdong-Guangzhou 2450

第二十二届中国国际专业音响、灯光、乐器及技术展览会
The 22nd China Intl Exhibition on Pro Audio, Light, Music & Technology
2013/06/07-10
北京Beijing 280

64、纸业 Paper

2013中国国际瓦楞展
SinoCorrugated 2013
2013/04/08-11
上海Shanghai 925

第二十一届上海国际印刷包装纸业展览会暨2013年3月份中国西部国际印刷包装产业博览会
Shanghai Intl AD, Print, Pack, Paper Expo
2013/07/10-13
上海Shanghai 1420

65、珠宝 Jewelry

中原珠宝风尚大典-中国（郑州）珠宝首饰博览会
China (Zhengzhou) Jewellery Expo
2013/01
河南郑州Henan-Zhengzhou 3020

深圳国际黄金珠宝玉石展览会
China Intl Gold, Jewellery & Gem Fair-Shenzhen
2013/02/26-03/01
广东深圳Guangdong-Shenzhen 2710

2013年（海名）中国郑州珠宝首饰玉石展览会/中国郑州奢侈品收藏品古典家具展览会
China (Haiming) Jewelery Show
2013/06
河南郑州Henan-Zhengzhou 3240

2013年（海名）中国郑州珠宝首饰玉石展览会/ 中国郑州奢侈品收藏品古典家具展览会
2013 China (Haiming) Jewelery Show
2013/08
河南郑州Henan-Zhengzhou 3270

珠光魅影-杭州
Treasures Hangzhou
2013/10/26-28
浙江杭州Zhejiang-Hangzhou 4370

上海国际黄金珠宝玉石展览会
China Intl Gold, Jewellery & Gem Fair - Shanghai
2013/11/08-11
上海Shanghai 1880

66、自行车 Bikes

2013第7届山东国际自行车电动车及零部件展览会
Shandong Intl Electric-Bicycle and Spare Parts Exhibition
2013/03/05-07
山东济南Shandong-Jinan 3820

第六届中国常州电动车展览会
6th China (Changzhou) Electric Cars Exhibition
2013/06/30-07/02
江苏常州Jiangsu-Changzhou 3540

国内展览会议
日期索引
Exhibitions and Conferences in Chronological Order

2013

January 2013 一月

February 2013 二月

March 2013 三月

2013/03/12-15
国际散杂货展览会暨研讨会-中国上海
Breakbulk China
上海Shanghai 640

2013/03/13-15
第八届亚洲国际太阳能光伏工业展览会
AsiaSolar Photovoltaic Industry Exhibition
上海Shanghai 680

2013/03/13-15
广州国际分析测试及实验室设备展览会暨技术研讨会
China Lab 2013
China Analytic & Laboratory Equipment Expo & Conference
广东广州Guangdong-Guangzhou 2460

2013/03/14-17
第27届中国北京国际礼品、赠品及家庭用品展览会
27th China Beijing Intl Gifts, Premium & Houseware Exhibtion
北京Beijing 30

2013/03/14-15
中国生物材料峰会
生物医用材料创新与发展中国峰会
Bio-Materials China
BioMed Innovation China
上海Shanghai 690

2013/03/14-17
2013年第十六届中国西部国际装备制造业博览会/西部国际五金机电工具贸易展览会
China West Intl Equipment Manufacturing Exposition
- 3780

2013/03/14-17
2013中国国际机械工业展览会
China Intl Machinery Industry Exhibition
浙江宁波Zhejiang-Ningbo 4380

2013/03/15-18
辽宁第十八届国际广告/标识/数码影像/LED光电照明暨灯饰展
Liaoning 18th Intl Adverting/Signal/Digital Images/LED Lighting Exhibition
辽宁沈阳Liaoning-Shenyang 3740

2013/03/15-19
2013北京园林展-
第三届国际园林景观与美好人居展览会
Beijing Garden Show
北京Beijing 40

2013/03/15-17
中国（温州）国际机床、工模具及塑胶工业展览会
China (Wenzhou) Intl Machine Tool & Plastics Industry Equipment
浙江温州Zhejiang-Wenzhou 4460

2013/03/15-17
2013中国（温州）国际工业博览会
China (Wenzhou) Intl Industry Equipment
浙江温州Zhejiang-Wenzhou 4470

2013/03/16-17
中国（国际）婚博会
Beijing Bridal Expo
北京Beijing 50

2013/03/16-20
第29届国际名家具（东莞）展览会暨名家具机械、材料展览会
IFM 29th Intl Famous Furniture Woodworking Machinery & Material Fair
广东东莞Guangdong-Dongguan 2180

2013/03/18-21
第三十一届中国（广州）国际家具博览会
31st China Intl Furniture Fair (Guangzhou)
广东广州Guangdong-Guangzhou 2490

2013/03/18-21
中国家电博览会-上海2013
Appliance World Expo
上海Shanghai 700

2013/03/18-21
中国（广州）国际家用纺织品及辅料博览会
China (Guangzhou0 Intl Trade Fair for Home Textiles and Accessories-Autumn Edition
广东广州Guangdong-Guangzhou 2390

2013/03/18-21
2013中国广州国际家居饰品、家纺布艺展览会
Home Textile
广东广州Guangdong-Guangzhou 2470

2013/03/18-20
第十九届全国铝门窗幕墙行业年会暨铝门窗幕墙新产品博览会
Aluminum Window, Door, Facade & Curtain Wall Expo
广东广州Guangdong-Guangzhou 2480

2013/03/19-21
第22届中国国际电子电路展览会
CPCA SHOW 2013
22nd China Intl Electronic Circuits Exhibition
上海Shanghai 710

2013/03/21-24
第6届中国（杭州）国际花园户外家具及休闲用品展
Outdoor Lifestyle Hangzhou 2013
浙江杭州Zhejiang-Hangzhou 4340

2013/03/22-24
2013第14届上海国际广告四新展览会
14th Shanghai Intl Advertising Four New Exhibition
上海Shanghai 730

2013/03/22-24
第18届上海美容美发化妆品博览会
Shanghai Beauty, Hairdressing & Cosmetics Expo
上海Shanghai 720

2013/03/22-24
第12届中国高尔夫球博览会（北京）
China Golf Show
PGA Merchandise Show-China
北京Beijing 60

2013/03/26-28
中国国际食品添加剂及配料展览会
Food Ingredients China
上海Shanghai 740

2013/03/26-29
第21届中国国际服装服饰博览会
CHIC2013
-China Intl Clothing & Accessories Fair
北京Beijing 70

2013/03/27-30
中国广州国际木工机械、家具配料展览会
interzum guangzhou
-China Intl Woodworking Machinery & Furniture Raw Materials Fair (Guangzhou)
广东广州Guangdong-Guangzhou 2500

2013/03/27-29
2013中国国际纺织纱线(春夏)展览会
China Intl Trade Fair for Fibers and Yarns
北京Beijing 80

2013/03/28-29
中国仿制药峰会
NextGen China (Shanghai)
上海Shanghai 750

2013/03/28-31
2013年春季成都全国糖酒会
China Food & Drinks Fair
四川成都Sichuan-Chengdu 4180

2013/03/29-31
2013第六届永康国际机械装备及工模具展览会
6th Yongkang Intl Equipment and Machine Tools Exhibition
浙江永康Zhejiang-Yongkang 4600

2013/03/29-31
2013中国（广州）国际生物识别技术展览会
China Guangzhou Intl Biometric Identification Technology Exhibition
广东广州Guangdong-Guangzhou 2510

2013/03/29-31
第10届中国国际文具礼品博览会
10th China Intl Stationery & Gifts Exposition
浙江宁波Zhejiang-Ningbo 4390

2013/03/29-31
2013宁波国际时尚礼品及家庭用品展览会
Ningbo Gift and Housewear Exhibition
浙江宁波Zhejiang-Ningbo 4400

2013/03/30-04/01
中国药品生产与质量管理峰会
Pharma Manufacturing China
上海Shanghai 760

2013/03/31-04/02
2013中国（济南）国际LED光电产业博览会
China (Jinan) Intl LED Expo
山东济南Shandong-Jinan 3840

April 2013 四月

2013/04-
第七届杭州春季汽车展销会
7th Hangzhou Spring Automobile Show and Sale
浙江杭州Zhejiang-Hangzhou 4350

2013/04-
泰州国际汽车展览会
Taizhou Intl Automobile Exhibition
江苏泰州Jiangsu-Taizhou 3660

2013/04-
中国中部（郑州）国际装备制造业博览会
暨第十五届中原国际装备制造业博览会
Central China Intl Equipment Manufacturing Industry Expo
河南郑州Henan-Zhengzhou 3080

2013/04-
2013大河新生活方式展（汽车展）
A new way of life
2013 Spring Dahe- Auto Show
河南郑州Henan-Zhengzhou 3100

2013/04-
2013春季中原住交会
Central China Real Estate Fair(Spring)
河南郑州Henan-Zhengzhou 3070

2013/04-
2013第十一届中国（郑州）社会公共安全产品博览会
China (Zhengzhou) Security Science Product Exhibition
河南郑州Henan-Zhengzhou 3090

2013/04-
全国春季农机展
CAMF
河南郑州Henan-Zhengzhou 3120

2013/04-
全国宠物展
National Pet Show
河南郑州Henan-Zhengzhou 3110

2013/04-
2013年中国洛阳国际汽车展览会
China (Luoyang) Intl Automobile Exhibition
河南洛阳Henan-Luoyang 3010

2013/04/01-03
中国国际建筑陶瓷及卫浴科技精品展览会
Ceramics, Tile & Sanitary Ware China
上海Shanghai 890

2013/04/01-03
世界节能环保与生态建筑中国展
Ecobuild China
上海Shanghai 820

2013/04/01-03
中国国际建筑装饰展览会
Expo Build China
上海Shanghai 810

2013/04/01-03
W3国际精品设计展
Expo Deco
上海Shanghai 800

2013/04/01-03
中国(上海)国际酒店与建筑照明展览会
Expo Light
上海Shanghai 790

2013/04/01-03
上海咖啡与茶用品展
Expo Coffee&Tea
上海Shanghai 780

2013/04/01-03
上海国际葡萄酒与烈酒展览会
Winexpo
上海Shanghai 770

2013/04/01-03
上海酒店设计与工程展览会
Shanghai Hospitality Design & Engineering Expo
上海Shanghai 830

2013/04/01-03
上海国际商场设计、装饰与用品博览会
Expo Shop
上海Shanghai 8880

2013/04/01-03
上海高端食品与饮料展
Expo Finefood
上海Shanghai 870

2013/04/01-03
上海国际酒店用品博览会
Hotelex Shanghai
上海Shanghai 860

2013/04/01-03
上海国际酒店用品博览会暨中国国际酒店家具展
Hotel Furniture China
上海Shanghai 850

2013/04/01-04
中国（广州）国际广告标识展
Sign China
广东广州Guangzhou-Guangzhou 2520

2013/04/01-09
中国清洁博览会
China Clean Expo
上海Shanghai 840

2013/04/02-04
第12届西部成都医疗器械展览会
12th West China (Chengdu) Medical Equipment Exhibition
四川成都Sichuan-Chengdu 4190

2013/04/04-07
青岛春季汽车文化节
Qingdao Spring Automobile Culture Festival
山东青岛Shandong-Qingdao 3890

2013/04/06-08
第二届中国（青岛）国际新型建筑模板、脚手架及施工技术展览会
Qingdao Intl Building Cyclostyle & Scaffold Fair
山东青岛Shandong-Qingdao 3930

2013/04/06-08
第三届中国（青岛）国际建筑装饰涂料及化学建材展览会
Qingdao Architectural coatings and Chemical Building Materials
山东青岛Shandong-Qingdao 3910

2013/04/06-08
第七届中国（青岛）国际外墙保温及新型墙体产品技术展览会
Qingdao Building External Wall insulation and New Wall Materials Exhibition
山东青岛Shandong-Qingdao 3940

2013/04/06-08
第七届中国（青岛）国际干混砂浆、地坪产品及技术设备展览会
7th China (Qingdao) Dry-mixed mortar, Floor Exhibition
山东青岛Shandong-Qingdao 3950

2013/04/06-08
中国（青岛）国际建筑给排水展览会/第七届中国（青岛）建筑节能和可再生能源建筑应用博览会
China (Qingdao) Intl Building Water Technology Energy Fair
山东青岛Shandong-Qingdao 3900

2013/04/06-08
第三届中国（青岛）国际绿色照明产品及技术应用展览会
Qingdao Intl Green Lighting Fair
山东青岛Shandong-Qingdao 3960

2013/04/06-08
第六届中国（青岛）国际太阳能与建筑一体化应用产品技术展览会
Qingdao Intl Solar Energy Fair
山东青岛Shandong-Qingdao 3920

2013/04/07-09
第十四届北京国际营养健康产业博览会
14th Beijing Nutrition and Health Industry Expo
北京Beijing 110

2013/04/07-09
第十四届中国国际家庭医疗保健器械展览会
14th China Intl Home Medical Health Care Recovery Products & Instrument (Beijing) Expo
北京Beijing 100

2013/04/07-09
第九届中国国际冰淇淋乳制品展览会-中国国际冰淇淋乳制品新产品及原辅料设备采购交易会
9th Ice Cream Expo
北京Beijing 130

2013/04/07-09
第十届中国国际烘焙展览会
10th China Intl Bakery Exhibition
北京Beijing 140

2013/04/07-09
第十一届中国国际食品包装与加工设备展览会
11th China Beijing Intl Food Processing and Packaging Exhibition
北京Beijing 120

2013/04/08-10
第二十四届国际制冷、空调、供暖、通风及食品冷冻加工展览会
24th Intl Exhibition for Refrigeration, Air-conditioning, Heating and Ventilation, Frozen Food Processing, Packaging and Storage
上海Shanghai 900

2013/04/08-10
中国国际供热通风空调、卫生洁具及城建设备与技术展览会
China Intl Trade Fair for Sanitation, Heating, Ventilation & Air-conditioning
北京Beijing 150

2013/04/08-10
第25届广州国际玩具及模型展
25th Guangzhou Intl Toy and Hobby Fair
广东广州Guangdong-Guangzhou 2540

2013/04/08-10
第4届广州国际婴童用品展
4th Guangzhou Intl Baby Product Fair
广东广州Guangdong-Guangzhou 2530

2013/04/08-10
上海第十二届中国国际动力设备发电机组展览会
12th China (Shanghai) Intl Power and Generating Sets Exhibition
上海Shanghai 920

2013/04/08-10
第70届中国国际医药原料药、中间体、包装、设备交易会
7th China (Shanghai) Intl Wind Energy Exhibition and Conference
湖北武汉Hubei-Wuhan 3400

2013/04/08-10
第七届中国(上海)国际风能展览会暨研讨会
7th China (Shanghai) Intl Wind Energy Exhibition and Conference
上海Shanghai 910

2013/04/08-11
2013中国国际瓦楞展
SinoCorrugated 2013
上海Shanghai 925

2013/04/09-11
第十届中国国际橡胶技术（青岛）展览会
10th China Intl Rubber Technology (Qingdao) Fair
山东青岛Shandong-Qingdao 3970

2013/04/10-12
国际日化包装机械设备展览会
同期举办：
第十四届国际表面活性剂和洗涤剂展览会
Daily Chemical Packaging Machinery Exhibition
Surfactants and Detergents Exhibition
上海Shanghai 930

2013/04/10-13
第十四届东北国际机床与金属加工展览会
14th Northeast Intl Machine Tool and Metalworking Exhibition
辽宁沈阳Liaoning-Shenyang 3750

2013/04/10-13
第十四届中国(东莞)国际鞋机鞋材工业技术展
14th China (Dongguan) Intl Footwear Machinery & Material Industry Fair
广东东莞Guangdong-Dongguan 2190

2013/04/10-12
2013年亚欧能源产业博览会
EuroAsia Energy Industry Expo 2013
新疆乌鲁木齐Xinjiang-Urumqi 4310

2013/04/10-12
2013中国四川国际天然气汽车、加气站设备展览会
China (Sichuan) Natural Gas Vehicle and Gas Station Equipment Exhibition
四川成都Sichuan-Chengdu 4200

2013/04/10-12
第一届中国电子信息博览会暨2013中国（深圳）消费电子展

China Information Technology Expo
81st China Electronic Fair
广东深圳Guangdong-Shenzhen 2720

2013/04/10-12
上海国际高端生活方式（奢侈品）展览会
Shanghai Intl High-end Lifestyle Exhibition
上海Shanghai 940

2013/04/11-14
烟台春季汽车展销会
Yantai Spring Automobile Show and Sale
山东烟台Shandong-Yantai 4120

2013/04/11-14
中国(上海)休闲产业展
Expo Leisure
上海Shanghai 970

2013/04/11-14
中国(上海)尚品生活展
Expo Life Style For Luxury and Excellence
上海Shanghai 950

2013/04/11-14
第十一届中国（温州）国际汽车展览会
11th Wenzhou Intl Auto Expo
浙江温州Zhejiang-Wenzhou 4480

2013/04/11-14
2013年大连建材展/第十八届中国国际建筑装饰材料展览会
CHINA BUILD 18th
18th China Intl Construction & Decoration Materials Exhibition
辽宁大连Liaoning-Dalian 3690

2013/04/11-14
中国(上海)国际游艇展
China (Shanghai) Intl Boat Show
上海Shanghai 960

2013/04/11-15
第三届贵阳国际汽车展览会
3rd Guiyang Intl Automobile Exhibition
贵州贵阳Guizhou-Guiyang 2910

2013/04/12-14
第八届内蒙古国际食品博览会
8th Inner Mongolia Intl Food Expo
内蒙古呼和浩特Inner Mongolia-Hohhot 3490

2013/04/12-15
第17届海峡两岸机械电子商品交易会暨厦门对台进出口商品交易会
17th China Xiamen Machinery and Electronics Exhibition (CXMEE)
福建厦门Fujian-Xiamen 2140

2013/04/12-14
第十届中国国际成人保健及生殖健康展览会
China Adult-Care Expo
上海Shanghai 980

2013/04/14-16
北京进口食品展-中国（北京）国际进口食品博览会
China Intl Import Food Exposition
北京Beijing 160

2013/04/15-05
第113届中国进出口商品交易会
Canton Fair
113th China Import and Export Fair
广东广州Guangdong-Guangzhou 2550

2013/04/17-19
第十三届中国国际染料工业暨有机颜料、纺织化学品展览会
CHINA INTERDYE 2013
上海Shanghai 1020

2013/04/17-19
(春季)上海纺织服装展览会
Shanghai Textile & Apparel Trade Fair (Spring)
上海Shanghai 990

2013/04/17-19
第86届中国劳动保护用品交易会
86th China Occupational Safety & Health Goods Expo
上海Shanghai 1010

2013/04/17-20
第69届中国国际医疗器械（春季）博览会/第16届中国国际医疗器械设计与制造技术（春季）展览会
69th China Intl Medical Equipment Fair-Spring/16th Intl Component Manufacturing & Design Show-Spring
广东深圳Guangdong-Shenzhen 2730

2013/04/17-20
第15届中国国际花卉园艺展览会
15th Hortiflorexpo IPM Shanghai
上海Shanghai 1000

2013/04/18-21
第十五届中国（晋江）国际鞋业博览会
The 15th Jinjiang Footwear Intl Exposition, China
福建晋江Fujian-Jinjiang 2130

2013/04/18-20
第16届中国济南供热采暖、热泵空调产品与技术展览会/第四届山东电采暖节能应用研讨会
16th China Jinan Heating, Heat Pump Air Conditioning Products and Technology Exhibition
山东济南Shandong-Jinan 3850

2013/04/18-20
第二十二届中国北京国际美容化妆品博览会(春季)
22nd Chinese Intl Beauty & Cosmetic Expo in Beijing
北京Beijing 170

2013/04/18-20
建材行业大型展览会
Building Material Industry Exhibition
四川成都Sichuan-Chengdu 4210

2013/04/18-20
中国成都创意设计展暨建筑装饰博览会
China Chengdu Creative Design Exhibitions and Architecture Decoration Fair
四川成都Sichuan-Chengdu 4220

2013/04/18-20
中国（成都）厨房用品及配套设施展览会
China (Chengdu) Kitchen Supplies and Ancillary Facilities Exhibition
四川成都Sichuan-Chengdu 4230

2013/04/20-22
第10届中国国际五金电器博览会
10th China Intl Hardware & Electrical Appliances Trade Fair
浙江义乌Zhejiang-Yiwu 4520

2013/04/20-22
义乌进口商品展
Yiwu Imported Commodities Fair
浙江义乌Zhejiang-Yiwu 4510

2013/04/20-22
中国(义乌)时尚发制品与美发用品展览会
同期举办：第二届国际进口商品展
China (Yiwu) Hair Products and Hairdressing Supplies Exhibition
浙江义乌Zhejiang-Yiwu 4540

2013/04/20-22
中国义乌消费品交易会-家居家具展
China (Yiwu) Housewear and Furniture Exhibition
浙江义乌Zhejiang-Yiwu 4530

2013/04/21-29
第十五届上海国际汽车工业展览会
AUTO SHANGHAI 2013
上海Shanghai 1030

2013/04/22-24
中国国际衡器展览会
InterWEIGHING
China Intl Weighing Instrument Exhibition
上海Shanghai 1060

2013/04/22-24
Printech 2013
票据标签打印展览会
Printech Digital Printing & Label Expo
上海Shanghai 1040

2013/04/22-24
第十一届亚洲打印耗材展览会
ReChina Asia Expo
上海Shanghai 1050

2013/04/23-25
第11届中国哈尔滨国际门窗幕墙及加工设备展览会
11th China (Harbin) Intl Door and Window Exhibition
黑龙江哈尔滨Heilongjiang-Harbin 2980

2013/04/23-25
哈尔滨水处理展会
Harbin Water Treatment Exhibition
黑龙江哈尔滨Heilongjiang-Harbin 2970

2013/04/25-27
第69届全国药品交易会
PHARMCHINA
湖北武汉Hubei-Wuhan 3390

2013/04/25-27
第十四届中国-中西部国际光电产业博览会
14th Midwest China (Chongqing) Photoelectricity, Laser & LED Industry Intl Exhibition
重庆Chongqing 550

2013/04/26-28
中国创业投资展
China Intl Franchise Exhibition
北京Beijing 190

2013/04/26-28
第15届国际特许加盟展览会
China Franchise Expo 2013
北京Beijing 180

2013/04/26-28
中国（上海）国际生物质能和沼气大会暨展览会
China (Shanghai) Intl Bioenergy and Biogas Conference and Exhibition
上海Shanghai 1070

2013/04/27-30
中国（盘锦）国际汽车展览会
China (Panjin) Intl Automobile Exhibition
辽宁盘锦Liaoning-Panjin 3730

2013/04/27-29
第十届中国(青岛)国际肉类工业展览会
10th China (Qingdao) Intl Meat Industry Exhibition
山东青岛Shandong-Qingdao 3980

2013/04/27-30
第8届中国义乌文化产品交易博览会
8th China Yiwu Cultural Products Trade Fair
浙江义乌Zhejiang-Yiwu 4550

2013/04/27-05/02
中国西部（兰州）国际汽车博览会-春季
West China (Lanzhou) Automobile Expo -Spring
甘肃兰州Gansu-Lanzhou 2160

2013/04/28-05/02
中国（邯郸）国际汽车文化节
China (Handan) Intl Automobile Culture Festival
河北邯郸Hebei-Handan 2950

2013/04/28-05/02
第六届中国（南京）国际汽车博览会

6th China (Nanjing) Intl Automobile Expo
江苏南京Jiangsu-Nanjing 3570

2013/04/29-05/01
第四届中国常州汽车博览会
China (Changzhou) Automobile Expo
江苏常州Jiangsu-Changzhou 3530

2013/04/30-05/02
第十三届广东国际汽车展示交易会
13th Guangdong Intl Auto Exhibition & Trade fair
广东东莞Guangdong-Dongguan 2200

2013/04/30-05/03
2013艺术北京博览会
Art Beijing 2013
北京Beijing 200

May 2013 五月

2013/05-
第十届中国（唐山）国际汽车博览会
10th China (Tangshan) Intl Automobile Expo
河北唐山Hebei-Tangshan 2960

2013/05-
2013温岭汽车展览会
Wenling Auto Exhibition
浙江温岭Zhejiang-Wenling 4450

2013/05-
第九届中国食品包装及加工设备（郑州）展览会
China (Zhengzhou) Food Packaging and Processing Equipment Show
河南郑州Henan-Zhengzhou 3160

2013/05-
瑞城郑州全国糖酒食品交易会
Ruicheng Zhengzhou Sugar and Wine Trade Fair
河南郑州Henan-Zhengzhou 3170

2013/05
中国肉类工业（郑州）展览会
China (Zhengzhou) Meat Industry Show
河南郑州Henan-Zhengzhou 3180

2013/05-
欧亚国际酒店用品展
(Zhengzhou) Intl Hotel Supplies Show
河南郑州Henan-Zhengzhou 3150

2013/05-
第三届中国郑州国际家具展
The Third Zhengzhou Intl Furniture Fair
河南郑州Henan-Zhengzhou 3140

2013/05-
中部博览会
Central China Expo
河南郑州Henan-Zhengzhou 3130

2013/05/06-08
中国国际水利机械及施工装备展览会
China Intl Hydraulic Machinery and Construction Equipment Exhibition
山东济南Shandong-Jinan 3860

2013/05/07-09
中国国际食品和饮料展览会
Sial china 2013
上海Shanghai 1080

2013/05/07-09
2013第六届上海国际罐藏食品机械设备博览会
6th Shanghai Intl Canned Food and Materials Facility Exhibition
上海Shanghai 1090

2013/05/07-10
中国锦州国际汽车展览会
China (Jinzhou) Intl Automobile Exhibition
辽宁锦州Liaoning-Jinzhou 3720

2013/05/08-10
第九届苏州电路板展览会
-苏州电子线路板展览会
同期举办：
苏州电子组装展览会
苏州表面贴装展览会
Suzhou Assembly Show
江苏苏州Jiangsu-Suzhou 3640

2013/05/09-12
第八届义乌汽车展览会
8th Yiwu Automobile Exhibition
浙江义乌Zhejiang-Yiwu 4560

2013/05/09-11
第十七届中国烘焙展览会
17th China Bakery Exhibition
广东广州Guangdong-Guangzhou 2560

2013/05/09-11
第十五届中国国际（江苏）医博会暨华东地区医院管理高级论坛
15th China (Jiangsu) Intl Medical Expo
East China Hospital Management Forum
江苏南京Jiangsu-Nanjing 3580

2013/05/10-12
第九届中国（广州）国际食品饮料展
9th China Intl Foodstuff (Guangzhou) Exposition
广东广州Guangdong-Guangzhou 2580

2013/05/10-12
中国国际游艇产业博览会
同期举办：
中国国际水系运动休闲博览会
China Intl Boat Show
广东广州Guangdong-Guangzhou 2570

2013/05/13-15
第15届北京国际玩具及幼教用品展览会
15th Beijing Intl Toys & Preschool Tools Exhibition
北京Beijing 210

2013/05/14-18
第八届北京国际印刷技术展览会
8th Beijing Intl Printing Technology Exhibition
北京Beijing 220

2013/05/15-17
第十届中国国际轮胎资源循环利用展览会
10th China Intl Tire Cyclic Utilization Expo
山东广饶Shandong-Guangrao 3810

2013/05/15-17
大连国际物流技术及包装工业展览会
Dalian Intl Logistics Technology and Packaging Industry Exhibition/ Dalian Intl Plastic and Rubber Industry Exhibition
辽宁大连Liaoning-Dalian 3700

2013/05/15-17
CISILE2013
第十一届中国国际科学仪器及实验室装备展览会
11th China Intl Scientific Instrument and Laboratory Equipment Exhibition
北京Beijing 230

2013/05/16-18
第八届中国国际养老及康复医疗博览会
8th China Intl Exhibition of Senior Care Rehabilitation Medicine and Healthcare
上海Shanghai 1110

2013/05/16-18
第8届中国（贵州）国际装备制造业博览会暨中国贵阳国际工业博览会
8th China (Guizhou) Intl Equipment Manufacturing Exposition
& China-Guiyang Intl Industry Expo
贵州贵阳Guizhou-Guiyang 2920

2013/05/16-18
中国最大的竹制品展
春季竹礼品展
China (Shanghai) Bamboo Product Exhibition
上海Shanghai 1120

2013/05/16-19
第十届中国(上海)国际茶业博览会
China Tea Expo, Shanghai 2013
上海Shanghai 1100

2013/05/16-18
第十四届西安国际酒店设备及用品展览会
同期举办：
第六届西安国际酒店家具展览会/第六届西安国际烘焙、咖啡、茶展览会/第六届西安国际食品、葡萄酒、饮料及酒店餐饮服务展览会
14th Xi'an Intl Hospitality Equipment & Supplies Fair
陕西西安Shaanxi-Xi'an 3790

2013/05/17-19
第十届中国国际营养健康产业（上海）博览会
China (Shanghai) Intl Nutrition and Health Industry Expo
上海Shanghai 1130

2013/05/17-20
第六届天津国际礼品、工艺品及家居用品博览会
6th Tianjin Intl Gifts, Crafts & Household Goods Expo
天津Tianjin 2090

2013/05/18-20
第七届中国（天津）国际厨房、卫浴设施展览会
Tianjin Kitchen and Sanitary Facilities Show
天津Tianjin 2100

2013/05/18-20
第七届中国（天津）国际太阳能及光伏展览会
Tianjin Solar and Photovoltaic Exhibition
天津Tianjin 2110

2013/05/18-20
第四届（2013）中国国际生物质能源展
Bio-Energy-Expo 2013
Trade Exhibition for Biogas-Technology and Management/ 4th Intl Bio-Energy Conference
湖北武汉Hubei-Wuhan 3410

2013/05/19-21
中国国际医院建设、装备及管理展览会暨第14届全国医院建设大会
Hospital Build & Infrastructure Exhibition & Congress China/ 14th China Hospital Construction Forum
江苏南京Jiangsu-Nanjing 3590

2013/05/20-22
东莞国际纺织品印花工业技术展览会
China Intl Textile Printing Industrial Technology Exposition
广东东莞Guangdong-Dongguan 2210

2013/05/20-22
第十二届上海国际日化原料包装机械设备展览会
Shanghai Intl COSMETECH Exhibition
上海Shanghai 1140

2013/05/21-24
第一届国际矿业及冶金工业博览会暨产业交流大会
1st Intl Exhibition and Congress for the Mining and Metallurgy Industry
北京Beijing 240

2013/05/22-24
上海国际工业计算机及嵌入式系统展览会暨2013MCU技术创新与嵌入式应用大会/人机界面技术创新与应用大会

Shanghai IPC & Embedded Expo
上海Shanghai 1150

2013/05/23-25
2013第十一届宁波国际纺织面料、辅料及纱线博览会
11th Ningbo Intl Textile Fabrics, Accessories & Yarns Exhibition 2013
浙江宁波Zhejiang-Ningbo 4410

2013/05/23-25
2013第四届神经科技大会
BIT's 4th Annual World Congress of Neuro Talk 2013
陕西西安Shaanxi-Xi'an 3800

2013/05/23-28
第十一届华中国际汽车展览会
11th Central China Automobile Exhibition
湖北武汉Hubei-Wuhan 3420

2013/05/24-27
中国国际旅游商品博览会
China Intl Tourism Commodities Fair
浙江义乌Zhejiang-Yiwu 4570

2013/05/24-26
第八届上海幼儿教育暨用品展
8th Kids Education Expo 2013 Shanghai
上海Shanghai 1160

2013/05/24-26
第七届全国食品博览会暨糖酒商品交易会
7th National Food Expo and Sugar and Alcoholic Commodities Fair
山东济南Shandong-Jinan 3870

2013/05/25-27
营养健康产业（南京）博览会
China (Nanjing) Nutrition and Health Industry Exposition
江苏南京Jiangsu-Nanjing 3600

2013/05/26-28
第101届中国上海国际鞋业皮具展CIFL暨GDS精品展
101st Shanghai Intl Footwear & Leather Goods Exhibition & GDS Select
上海Shanghai 1170

2013/05/27-29
中国（郑州）国际纺织面料、辅料及纱线展览会
China (Zhengzhou) Intl Textile Fabrics, Accessories & Yarn Exhibition
河南郑州Henan-Zhengzhou 3190

2013/05/28-06/01
京交会
-中国国际城市智能化技术与服务大会
UrbanTec China Conference at CIFTIS 2013
北京Beijing 250

2013/05/29-31
广州国际鞋类、皮革及工业设备展览会
SHOES & LEATHER- GUANGZHOU 2013
-Intl Exhibition on Shoes & Leather Industry-Guangzhou (Machinery & Raw Material)
广东广州Guangdong-Guangzhou 2590

2013/05/29-31
广州国际鞋类、皮革制成品展览会
IFLE- GUANGZHOU 2013
Intl Footwear & Leather Products Exhibition-Guangzhou
广东广州Guangdong-Guangzhou 2600

2013/05/29-31
中国国际生物技术和仪器设备博览会
同期举办：
中国（上海）科学仪器、实验室装备及化学试剂展览会/中国（上海）诊断试剂和设备展览会
BIOTECH CHINA 2013
Intl Trade Fair & Congress for Biotechnology
上海Shanghai 1180

2013/05/30-31
可持续船舶技术中国峰会
Sustainable Ship Technology Conference
上海Shanghai 1190

2013/05/30-06/01
华南国际汽车改装及赛车展览会
Southern China Intl Car Tuning and Racing Exhibition
广东东莞Guangdong-Dongguan 2220

2013/05/30-06/01
第十二届南京国际纺织品面料、辅料博览会
12th Nanjing Intl Textiles Fabrics Accessories Exhibition
江苏南京Jiangsu-Nanjing 3610

2013/05/30-06/02
第二届天津国际营养健康产业博览会
2nd Tianjin Intl Exposition of Nutrition and Health Industries
天津Tianjin 2120

2013/05/30-06/03
第四届鄂尔多斯国际汽车展览会
4th Ordos Intl Automobile Exhibition
内蒙古鄂尔多斯Inner Mongolia-Ordos 3520

2013/05/31-06/03
中国国际体育用品博览会
2013 China Sport Show
北京Beijing 260

June 2013 六月

2013/06-
第五届中国郑州烘焙展览会/第五届中国郑州食品保鲜及冷冻、冷藏技术展览会
Zhengzhou Baking Technology Expo/ Food Refrigeration Technology Show
河南郑州Henan-Zhengzhou 3200

2013/06-
第三届中国（郑州）国际微型汽车配件博览会/ 中国国际轿车配件（郑州）博览会/ 中国润滑油及汽保设备展览会
China (Zhengzhou) Intl Mini-car Accessories Expo and Lubricants, Tires, Auto Maintenance Equipment Exhibition
河南郑州Henan-Zhengzhou 3210

2013/06-
河南省夏季种子信息交流暨产品展览会
Henan Summer Seed Information Products Show
河南郑州Henan-Zhengzhou 3220

2013/06-
中原国际汽车博览会暨中原国际汽车文化旅游节
Cars & Automotive Culture and Tourism Festival
河南郑州Henan-Zhengzhou 3230

2013/06-
（海名）中国郑州珠宝首饰玉石展览会/ 中国郑州奢侈品收藏品古典家具展览会
China (Haiming) Jewelery Show
河南郑州Henan-Zhengzhou 3240

2013/06/01-03
全国微型汽车配件展览会
China (Zhengzhou) Intl Car & Mini Auto Parts Expo
河南郑州Henan-Zhengzhou 3250

2013/06/04-05
第四届中国国际物联网大会暨展览会
IOT China Conference & Exhibition
上海Shanghai 1210

2013/06/04-07
东莞振宗工业园区展览会
Dongguan Zhenzong Industry Park Exhibition
广东东莞Guangdong-Dongguan 2240

2013/06/04-06
第22届中国（广州）国际医药保健产业博览会/ 第22届全国药品保健品（广州）交易会
22nd China (Guangzhou) Intl Medicine Health Care Industry Expo
广东广州Guangdong-Guangzhou 2610

2013/06/04-06
第十五届上海国际手机产业展览会暨研讨会
CME2013
上海Shanghai 1200

2013/06/04-06
第13届广州国际食品展暨广州进口食品展览会
13th China(Guangzhou) Intl Food Exhibition And Guangzhou Import Food Exhibition
广东广州Guangdong-Guangzhou 2620

2013/06/05-07
第十二届中国（上海）国际医疗器械展览会
China (Shanghai) Intl Medical Expo
上海Shanghai 1220

2013/06/05-07
中国（上海）国际产业用纺织品及非织造布展览会
同期举办：2013上海玻璃纤维及新型复合材料展览会
China (Shanghai) Trade Fair for Technical Textiles and Nonwovens
上海Shanghai 1240

2013/06/05-07
中国（上海）医疗美容及整形设备展览会
China (Shanghai) Medical Beauty and Plastic Surgery Equipment Exhibition
上海Shanghai 1230

2013/06/05-07
第十一届中国(广州)国际汽车零部件展览会同期举行：中国汽车零部件(全球)采供峰会
11th China (Guangzhou) Intl Auto Parts Expo
广东广州Guangdong-Guangzhou 2630

2013/06/06-08
中国（北京）国际卡车及零部件展览会
China (Beijing) Intl Truck Exhibition
北京Beijing 270

2013/06/06-10
第二十一届昆交会
-第二十一届中国昆明进出口商品交易会
The 21th Kunming Fair-
The 21th China Import & Export Fair, Kunming
云南昆明Yunnan-Kunming 4330

2013/06/06-10
第一届中国-南亚博览会
First South Asia Expo
云南昆明Yunnan-Kunming 4320

2013/06/07-10
第二十二届中国国际专业音响、灯光、乐器及技术展览会
The 22nd China Intl Exhibition on Pro Audio, Light, Music & Technology
北京Beijing 280

2013/06/07-09
第四届中国（青岛）国际卡车、商用车及零部件展览会
China (Qingdao) Intl Commercial Vehicle Exhibition
山东青岛Shandong-Qingdao 3990

2013/06/08-13
第十七届深圳-香港-澳门国际汽车博览会
17th Shenzhen-Hong Kong-Macao Intl Automobile Expo
广东深圳Guangdong-Shenzhen 2740

2013/06/10-13
第五届连云港-大陆桥汽车贸易博览会
5th Lianyungang-Continental Bridge Automobile Trade Fair
江苏连云港Jiangsu-Lianyungang 3560

2013/06/10-13
第十六届上海国际纺织工业展览会
SHANGHAITEX 2013
上海Shanghai 1250

2013/06/15-19
第二十四届中国哈尔滨国际经济贸易洽谈会
The 24th China Harbin Intl Economic and Trade Fair
黑龙江哈尔滨Heilongjiang-Harbin 2990

2013/06/18-21
第十八届北京-埃森焊接与切割展览会
The 18th Beijing Essen Welding & Cutting Fair
上海Shanghai 1270

2013/06/18-21
中国国际模具、制造应用设备及相关工业展览会
DMC 2013
(China Intl Exhibition on Die & Mould, Metal Processing and Forming Industry)
上海Shanghai 1280

2013/06/19-21
上海国际海上风电及风电产业链大会暨展览会
Offshore Wind China 2013
上海Shanghai 1290

2013/06/19-21
2013宁波国际海事会议和展览会_
China Maritime Tech Security Expo 2013
浙江宁波Zhejiang-Ningbo 4420

2013/06/19-22
中国加工贸易产品博览会
China Processing Trade Products Fair
广东东莞Guangdong-Dongguan 2250

2013/06/20-23
第二届广西汽车文化节
2nd Guangxi Automobile Culture Festival
广西南宁Guangxi-Nanning 2870

2013/06/20-22
中国(成都)电子展
China Electronics Fair West Show
四川成都Sichuan-Chengdu 4240

2013/06/20-22
107届中国文化用品商品交易会
107th China Stationery Fair
上海Shanghai 1300

2013/06/24-25
CPhI医药中国峰会
CPhI On-site Modular Conferences
上海Shanghai 1310

2013/06/25-27
亚洲食品配料、健康原料、天然原料中国展
Food Ingredients Asia-China
上海Shanghai 1350

2013/06/25-27
天然及营养保健品中国展
Nutraceutical Products China
上海Shanghai 1360

2013/06/25-27
医药包装材料精品中国展
InnoPack China
上海Shanghai 1320

2013/06/25-27
世界制药机械、包装设备与材料中国展
世界生化、分析仪器与实验室装备中国展
P-MEC China
上海Shanghai 1370

2013/06/25-27
世界合同定制服务中国展
ICSE China
上海Shanghai 1340

2013/06/25-27
世界制药原料中国展
CPhI China
上海Shanghai 1330

2013/06/26-28
北京国际工业智能及自动化展览会
Industrial Automation Beijing
北京Beijing 290

2013/06/26-28
中国国际混凝土产业展览会
Concrete Show China 2013
上海Shanghai 1380

2013/06/26-28
中国(上海)国际切削刀具暨工具展览会
China Intl Cuttings Tools Exhibition
上海Shanghai 1390

2013/06/27-07/02
第十二届中国沈阳汽车工业博览会
12th China (Shenyang) Automobile Industry Expo
辽宁沈阳Liaoning-Shenyang 3760

2013/06/28-30
亚洲国际智能制造装备产业展览会
Asia Intl Intellect Equipment Manufacturer Industry Exhibition
北京Beijing 300

2013/06/28-30
第九届中国（北京）国际动力传动与控制技术展览会
9th China (Beijing) Intl Power Transmission & Control Technology Exhibition
北京Beijing 310

2013/06/28-30
第15届中国（青岛）国际面料、辅料及纱线展览会
15th China (Qingdao) Intl Fabric, Yarn and Accessories Exhibition
山东青岛Shandong-Qingdao 4000

2013/06/30-07/02
第六届中国常州电动车展览会
6th China (Changzhou) Electric Cars Exhibition
江苏常州Jiangsu-Changzhou 3540

July 2013 七月

2013/07-
中国国际汽车后市场博览会暨中国汽车用品（郑州）交易会
China (Zhengzhou) Automobile Product Fair
河南郑州Henan-Zhengzhou 3260

2013/07/02-05
第15届上海国际机床展
15th Shanghai Intl Machine Tool Fair
上海Shanghai 1400

2013/07/03-05
中国国际电动汽车充电设施及储能设备展览会
eMobility China
北京Beijing 340

2013/07/03-05
中国国际智能电网技术和设备展览会
GridTec China 2013
北京Beijing 350

2013/07/03-05
中国国际清洁能源博览会
Clean Energy Expo China
北京Beijing 330

2013/07/03-05
中国国际风能设备展览会
原亚洲风能大会暨国际风能设备展览会
Wind Power China
Formerly Wind Power Asia
北京Beijing 320

2013/07/03-05
第五届中国国际生物质能展览暨技术研讨会
Bio-Energy China
北京Beijing 360

2013/07/03-06
第十四届成都国际家具工业展览会
Intl Furniture Fair Chengdu
四川成都Sichuan-Chengdu 4250

2013/07/04-07
第十五届中国（上海）国际摄影器材和数码影像展览会
PHOTO & IMAGING SHANGHAI 2013
上海Shanghai 1410

2013/07/05-07
第七届烟台国际葡萄酒博览会
7th Yantai Intl Wine Exposition
山东烟台Shandong-Yantai 4130

2013/07/08-11
第十五届中国（广州）国际建筑装饰博览会
15th China (Guangzhou) Intl Building Decoration Fair
广东广州Guangdong-Guangzhou 2640

2013/07/08-10
第十三届中国（深圳）国际品牌服装服饰交易会
13th China Intl Fashion Brand Fair-Shenzhen
Shenzhen Textile Equipment Fair
广东深圳Guangdong-Shenzhen 2750

2013/07/10-12
第十一届中国（温州）国际眼镜业展览会
11th Wenzhou Intl Optics Fair, China
浙江温州Zhejiang-Wenzhou 4490

2013/07/10-13
第二十一届上海国际广告技术设备展览会
Shanghai Intl AD & Sign Technology Equipment Exhibition
上海Shanghai 1430

2013/07/10-13
第二十一届上海国际印刷包装纸业展览会暨2013年3月份中国西部国际印刷包装产业博览会
Shanghai Intl AD, Print, Pack, Paper Expo
上海Shanghai 1420

2013/07/11-13
深圳国际纺织面料及辅料博览会
Shenzhen Intl Trade Fair for Apparel Fabrics and Accessories
广东深圳Guangdong-Shenzhen 2760

2013/07/16-19
第七届中国（青岛）国际石材工业及机械设备展览会
China (Qingdao) Intl Stone Products & Machinery Exhibition
山东青岛Shandong-Qingdao 4010

2013/07/17-19
第二届中国（青岛）橱柜衣柜展览会
China (Qingdao) Intl Cabinet and Wardrobe Exhibition
山东青岛Shandong-Qingdao 4060

2013/07/17-19
第七届中国（青岛）国际地板及整木家装展览会
Qingdao Floor and Entire Wooden Decoration Exhibition
山东青岛Shandong-Qingdao 4020

2013/07/17-19
第二届中国（青岛）国际木屋、木结构及配套设施展览会
Qingdao Intl Wood House Exhibition
山东青岛Shandong-Qingdao 4050

2013/07/17-19
中国国际电线电缆及设备交易会
UL Wire & Cable Intl Fair 2013
广东东莞Guangdong-Dongguan 2270

2013/07/17-19
第九届中国（青岛）国际木门展览会
9th Qingdao Intl Wooden Door Exhibition
山东青岛Shandong-Qingdao 4040

2013/07/17-19
第四届中国（青岛）国际供热采暖系统产品及技术应用展览会
Qingdao Intl Heating System Product & Technology Utilization Fair
山东青岛Shandong-Qingdao 4030

2013/07/17-19
CBME孕婴童展、CBME童装展
Shanghai Intl Children-Baby-Maternity Industry Expo
上海Shanghai 1440

2013/07/18-19
植入介入医疗器械中国峰会（上海）
Implantable Medical Device Conference (Shanghai)
上海Shanghai 1450

2013/07/18-20
第十七届中国西部(成都)五金机电商品展览会
17th China West Intl Equipment Manufacturing Exposition
四川成都Sichuan-Chengdu 4260

2013/07/18-20
多人行国际胶粘带、保护膜、光学膜及模切展览会
Dowell Intl Adhesive Tape, Protective Layer, Optical film & Die-Cutting Exhibition
广东深圳Guangdong-Shenzhen 2780

2013/07/18-20
多人行国际智能手机组装、触摸屏展览会
Dowell Intl Smartphone Assembly & Touch Screen Exhibition
广东深圳Guangdong-Shenzhen 2790

2013/07/18-20
多人行国际连接器、线束及设备展览会
Dowell Intl Connector, Harness and Equipment Exhibition
广东深圳Guangdong-Shenzhen 2800

2013/07/18-20
多人行国际移动电源展览会
Dowell Intl Mobile Power Supply Exhibition
广东深圳Guangdong-Shenzhen 2810

2013/07/18-20
第21届中国国际电子设备、电子元器件及光电显示展览会
21th China Intl Electronic Equipment, Electronic Components and Optoelectronic Display Exhibition
广东深圳Guangdong-Shenzhen 2820

2013/07/18-20
多人行国际激光展览会
Dowell Intl Laser Exhibition
广东深圳Guangdong-Shenzhen 2830

2013/07/18-20
第二十一届多人行国际电子、激光、线缆线束展览会
21st DEX Intl Electronic, Laser, Harness Products Exhibition
广东深圳Guangdong-Shenzhen 2770

2013/07/19-21
第十七届中国西部国际装备制造业博览会
17th China West Intl Equipment Manufacturing Exposition
四川成都Sichuan-Chengdu 4270

2013/07/19-23
第五届呼和浩特国际汽车展览会
5th Hohhot Intl Automobile Exhibition
内蒙古呼和浩特Inner Mongolia-Hohhot 3500

August 2013 八月

2013/08-
（海名）中国郑州珠宝首饰玉石展览会/中国郑州奢侈品收藏品古典家具展览会
China (Haiming) Jewelery Show
河南郑州Henan-Zhengzhou 3270

2013/08-
第十二届瑞城郑州全国糖酒食品交易会/第三届瑞城郑州国际葡萄酒及烈酒展览会/第三届瑞城郑州面业暨精品粮油交易会
Ruicheng-Zhengzhou Sugar and Wine Trade Fair and Zhengzhou Intl Wine Fair
河南郑州Henan-Zhengzhou 3280

2013/08/01-03
上海国际家庭用品、促销品及工艺品创意设计展览会
Shanghai Intl Houseware, Premuium, Arts & Crafts Creative Design Exhibition
上海Shanghai 1460

2013/08/01-03
第107届中国日用百货商品交易会暨中国现代家庭用品博览会
107th China Daily-use Articles Trade Fair & China Modern Home Expo
上海Shanghai 1470

2013/08/04-04
中国（常州）汽车配件交易会
China (Changzhou) Auto Parts Fair
江苏常州Jiangsu-Changzhou 3550

2013/08/09-11
第十二届青岛国际电子电路板展览会
12th Qingdao Electronic Circuit Board Fair
山东青岛Shandong-Qingdao 4070

2013/08/09-12
广州国际服装节暨广州时装周
Guangzhou Fashion Week
广东广州Guangdong-Guangzhou 2650

2013/08/10-12
广州国际缝制制衣设备展
广州国际服装面辅料展览会
Guangzhou Intertextile Apparel Fabrics
广东广州Guangdong-Guangzhou 2660

2013/08/14-17
第28届中国北京国际礼品、赠品及家庭用品展览会
28th China Beijing Intl Gifts, Premium & Houseware Exhibtion
北京Beijing 370

2013/08/15-17
第九届中国(上海)国际门窗幕墙及建筑遮阳展览会/第九届中国(上海)国际建筑节能及新型建材展览会
9th Shanghai Intl Energy-saving & Advanced Building Materials Exhibition
上海Shanghai 1490

2013/08/15-17
第15届中国青岛国际塑料橡胶工业展览会/青岛国际塑料原料及改性技术展览会
15th China (Qingdao) Intl Plastics & Rubber Industry Exhibition/ China Qingdao Intl Exhibition of Plastic Raw Materials and Modified Technology
山东青岛Shandong-Qingdao 4080

2013/08/15-17
第15届中国青岛国际动力传动与控制技术展览会
15th China Intl Power Transmission & Control Technology (Qingdao) Exhibition
山东青岛Shandong-Qingdao 4090

2013/08/15-17
第15届中国青岛国际仪器仪表及测试测量技术展览会/第15届中国青岛国际工业自动化及控制技术展览会
15th China Qingdao Industrial Automation and Control Technology Exhibition/ 15th China Qingdao Intl Instruments, Test and Measurement Technology Exhibition
山东青岛Shandong-Qingdao 4100

2013/08/15-18
中华口腔医学会第15次全国口腔医学学术会议（2013年会）/2013(上海)国际口腔设备器材博览会
15th CSA Annual Meeting
2013 China Dental Show
上海Shanghai 1480

2013/08/16-18
华南国际老年用品及康复保健器械展览会同期举办：医院装备展览会/家庭医疗器械展览会
South China Intl Gerontic Products & Health Care Recovery Instrument Exhibition 2013
广东广州Guangdong-Guangzhou 2670

2013/08/20-22
第五届中国（上海）国际电池产品及技术展览会
5th China (Shanghai) Intl Battery Industry Fair
上海Shanghai 1510

2013/08/20-22
中国（上海）国际化工技术装备展览会
5th China (Shanghai) Intl Chemical Technology & Equipment Fair
上海Shanghai 1520

2013/08/20-23
国际养老产业(上海)峰会
Care Show China
上海Shanghai 1500

2013/08/21-24
第二十二届北京国际广播电影电视设备展览会
BIRTV2013
Beijing Intl Radio, TV & Film Equipment Exhibition
北京Beijing 380

2013/08/21-23
中国国际彩盒展
SinoFoldingCarton
广东东莞Guangdong-Dongguan 2280

2013/08/22-27
中国西部（兰州）国际汽车博览会-秋季
West China (Lanhou) Automobile Expo -Autumn
甘肃兰州Gansu-Lanzhou 2170

2013/08/23-28
中国（大同）国际汽车文化节
China (Datong) Intl Automobile Culture Festival
山西大同Shanxi-Datong 4160

2013/08/23-25
第九届中国（郑州）国际机床及工模具展览会
China Machine Tool Expo
河南郑州Henan-Zhengzhou 3290

2013/08/27-30
第24届中国国际测量控制与仪器仪表展览会
MICONEX2013
24th Intl Conference and Fair Measurement Instrumentation and Automation
北京Beijing 390

2013/08/27-30
中国国际家用纺织品及辅料（秋冬）博览会
intertextile Shanghai home textiles
China Intl Trade Fair for Textiles and Accessories
上海Shanghai 1530

2013/08/29-31
中国（温州）国际缝制设备展览会
China (Wenzhou) Intl Sewing Equipment Fair
浙江温州Zhejiang-Wenzhou 4500

2013/08/30-09/01
第九届内蒙古国际食品博览会
9th Inner Mongolia Food Expo
内蒙古包头Inner Mongolia- 3470

2013/08/31-09/08
第十六届成都国际汽车展览会
Chengdu Motor Show 2013
四川成都Sichuan-Chengdu 4280

September 2013 九月

2013/09-
呼和浩特汽车文化节
Hohhot Automobile Culture Festival
内蒙古呼和浩特Inner Mongolia-Hohhot 3510

2013/09-
第24届中原医疗器械（2013年秋季）展览会
2013 Autumn Central Plain Intl Medical Instruments Exhibition
河南郑州Henan-Zhengzhou 3300

2013/09-
2013全国郑州商品交易会
Zhengzhou National Commodity Fair
河南郑州Henan-Zhengzhou 3310

2013/09-
第4届中国国际时尚发制品及美发用品展览会
4th China Intl Fashion Hair Products and Hair Care Products Exhibition
河南郑州Henan-Zhengzhou 3320

2013/09-
河南省家禽交易会
Henan Poultry Exhibition
河南郑州Henan-Zhengzhou 3330

2013/09-
中国郑州建筑节能及新型建材博览会/中国郑州照明LED展览会
China (Zhengzhou) LED Lighting Exhibition
河南郑州Henan-Zhengzhou 3340

2013/09-
第三届中国包头国际汽车展览会
3rd China (Inner Mongolia) Intl Automobile Exhibition
内蒙古包头Inner Mongolia-Baotou 3480

2013/09/02-04
第30届中国国际网印及数字技术展览会
China Screen Print 2013
广东广州Guangdong-Guangzhou 2680

2013/09/02-03
中国呼叫中心技术设备及解决方案博览会
Call Center Expo China
上海Shanghai 1570

2013/09/02-03
中国国际呼叫中心管理大会
ACCE China
上海Shanghai 1560

2013/09/02-03
中国电子商务服务及产品展示会
eCommerce Expo China
上海Shanghai 81550

2013/09/02-03
营销和广告创新技术展示会暨研讨会
TFM&A China
上海Shanghai 1540

2013/09/02-04
中国（北京）临床检验设备及用品展览会
China (Beijing) Clinical Examination Equipment and Products Exhibition
北京Beijing 400

2013/09/02-04
第十三届中国（北京）医疗器械展览会
13th China (Beijing) Medical Devices Exhibition
北京Beijing 410

2013/09/03-06
第十三届亚太国际塑料橡胶工业展览会
13th Asian-pacific Intl Plastics & Rubber Industry Exhibition
上海Shanghai 1580

2013/09/04-06
（第十二届）中国国际化工展览会
ICIF CHINA
上海Shanghai 1620

2013/09/04-06
中国国际皮革展
All China Leather Exhibition
上海Shanghai 1610

2013/09/04-06
中国国际箱包、裘革服装及服饰展
Moda Shanghai
上海Shanghai 1600

2013/09/04-06
中国国际鞋类展
China Intl Footwear Fair
上海Shanghai 1590

2013/09/05-08
哈尔滨世界农业博览会
Agriculture & Food Expo Harbin
黑龙江哈尔滨Heilongjiang-Harbin 3000

2013/09/05-09
第九届烟台国际汽车工业展览会
9th Yantai Intl Automobile Industry Exhibition
山东烟台Shandong-Yantai 4140

2013/09/05-09
第三十届国际名家具（东莞）展览会
30th Intl Famous Furniture Fair (Dongguan)
广东东莞Guangdong-Dongguan 2290

2013/09/05-07
中国国际智能电网建设及输配电博览会
China Intl Smart Grid and Electric Power Technology Exhibition
北京Beijing 430

2013/09/05-07
第13届中国光伏大会
13th China Photovoltaic Conference and Intl Photovoltaic Exhibition
北京Beijing 420

2013/09/07-10
第三十二届中国（广州）国际家具博览会
32nd China Intl Furniture Fair (Guangzhou)
广东广州Guangdong-Guangzhou 2690

2013/09/07-09
中国（广州）国际保健产业博览会
China (Guangzhou) Intl Health Care Industry Exposition
广东广州Guangdong-Guangzhou 2695

2013/09/08-11
第十七届中国国际投资贸易洽谈会
The China Intl Fair for Investment and Trade
福建厦门Fujian-Xiamen 2150

2013/09/09-13
第三届中国（贵州）国际酒类博览会
China (Guizhou) Intl Alcoholic Beverage Expo
贵州贵阳Guizhou-Guiyang 2930

2013/09/10-13
第二十四届中国国际五金博览会
24th China Intl Hardware Fair
北京Beijing 440

2013/09/11-15
中国国际设计师作品展示交易会
Design of Designers
China Intl Design Trading Expo
上海Shanghai 1660

2013/09/11-15
中国国际橱柜展览会
Kitchen & Cabinet China
上海Shanghai 1670

2013/09/11-14
中国国际家具配件及材料精品展览会
FMC Premium
上海Shanghai 1630

2013/09/11-15
第十九届中国国际办公家具展览会
Office Furniture China
上海Shanghai 1640

2013/09/11-15
中国国际家居饰品展览会
Home Furnishing China
上海Shanghai 1650

2013/09/13-15
2013第七届中国国际汽车零部件博览会
CIAPE
北京Beijing 460

2013/09/13-17
第十一届中国国际装备制造业博览会 机床模具展
12th China Intl Equipment Manufacturing Exposition -Machine Tools & Mould Exhibition
辽宁沈阳Liaoning-Shenyang 3770

2013/09/14-16
国际特许加盟（上海）展览会
Shanghai Intl Franchise Exhibition
上海Shanghai 1680

2013/09/15-17
Cloud Connect China
上海Shanghai 1690

2013/09/18-22
第十届中国（苏州）国际汽车工业博览会
10th China (Suzhou) Intl Automobile Industry Expo
江苏苏州Jiangsu-Suzhou 3650

2013/09/18-22
东部沿海（盐城）国际汽车博览会
East Coast (Yancheng) Intl Automobile Expo
江苏盐城Jiangsu-Yancheng 3670

2013/09/18-21
第14届立嘉国际机床展览会-成都展会
Jiali Intl Machinery Exhibition - Chengdu
四川成都Sichuan-Chengdu 4290

2013/09/19-20
海洋工程中国峰会（北京）
Offshore Engineering China (Beijing)
北京Beijing 450

2013/09/20-24
中国-东盟博览会
China-ASEAN Expo
广西南宁Guangxi-Nanning 2880

2013/09/24-26
广州国际金属加工工业展

asia metal
Guangzhou Intl Metalworking Industry Exhibition
广东广州Guangdong-Guangzhou 2698

2013/09/25-28
中国国际缝制设备展览会
China Intl Sewing Machinery & Accessories Show
上海Shanghai 1710

2013/09/25-28
塑交会
第十三届中国塑料交易会
China PET '13
12th China Plastics Exhibition & Conference
浙江台州Zhejiang-Taizhou 4440

2013/09/25-26
上海国际医疗设备设计与技术展览会
MEDTEC China
上海Shanghai 1720

2013/09/25-27
中国（上海）国际时尚家居用品展览会同期举办：
中国国际文具及办公用品展览会
interiorlifestyle China
China Intl Trade Fair for Household Products and Accessories
Paperworld-China
上海Shanghai 1700

2013/09/26-28
第十四届国际果蔬、食品博览会
11th Intl Fruit/Vegetable/Food Exposition
山东烟台Shagndong-Yantai 4150

2013/09/29-10/04
第十四届广东国际汽车展示交易会
14th Guangdong Intl Auto Exhibition & Trade fair
广东东莞Guangdong-Dongguan 2300

October 2013 十月

2013/10-
第十四届中国杭州国际汽车工业展览会
14th China (Hangzhou) Auto Industry Exhibition
浙江杭州Zhejiang-Hangzhou 4360

2013/10-
中国国际社会公共安全产品博览会/ SSC第六届中外安防产品采购洽谈会
Public Safety and Security Expo
\- 4640

2013/10-
河南省秋季种子信息交流暨产品展览会/河南省植保信息交流暨农药械交流会
Henan Autumn Seed Information Products Show
河南郑州Henan-Zhengzhou 3350

2013/10/10-12
第八届上海国际渔业博览会
8th Shanghai Intl Fisheries & Seafood Exposition
上海Shanghai 1730

2013/10/14-16
中国（南京）国际金属加工展览会
AMB China
China Metal Working & Forming Exhibition
江苏南京Jiangsu-Nanjing 3620

2013/10/15-17
第12届中国国际玩具、幼教用品及设备展览会
12th Intl Trade Fair for Toys & Preschool Educational Resources
上海Shanghai 1750

2013/10/15-17
中国婴童展同期举办第十二届中国国际玩具及模型展览会
China Kids Expo
China Intl Baby Carriers & Baby Articles fair
上海Shanghai 1740

2013/10/16-18
第十届中国（北京）国际热处理工业炉展览会
10th China (Beijing) Intl Heat Treatment & Industrial Furnace Expo
北京Beijing 470

2013/10/16-18
第十届 中国（北京）国际冶金工业博览会
10th China (Beijing) Intl Metallurgy Industry Exhibition
北京Beijing 490

2013/10/16-18
第十届中国（北京）国际铸造工业展览会
10th China (Beijing) Intl Foundry Industry Expo
北京Beijing 500

2013/10/16-18
第十八届中国国际光电产业博览会
Optoelectronics Industry Exposition (Beijing)
北京Beijing 480

2013/10/17-18
中国仿制药峰会（北京）
NextGen China (Beijing)
北京Beijing 510

2013/10/17-20
中国顺德国际家用电器博览会
China Shunde Intl Exposition for Household Electrical Appliances
广东顺德Guangdong-Shunde 2860

2013/10/18-21
第八届南昌国际汽车展览会
8th Nanchang Intl Automobile Exhibition
广西南昌Guangxi-Nanchang 3680

2013/10/18-23
武汉国际汽车展览会
Wuhan Motor Show 2013
湖北武汉Hubei-Wuhan 3430

2013/10/18-21
第十二届北京国际工程机械展览与技术交流会
Beijing Intl Construction Machinery Exhibition & Seminar
北京Beijing 520

2013/10/20-22
第十五届上海国际营养健康产业博览会
China (Shanghai) Intl Nutrition and Health Industry Expo
上海Shanghai 1760

2013/10/21-25
中国义乌国际小商品博览会
China Yiwu Intl Commodities Fair
浙江义乌Zhejiang-Yiwu 4580

2013/10/21-23
中国国际针织博览会
China Intl Knitting Trade Fair
上海Shanghai 1770

2013/10/21-23
中国国际纺织纱线（秋冬）展览会
China Intl Trade Fair for Fibres and Yarns
上海Shanghai 1780

2013/10/21-24
中国国际纺织面料及辅料（秋冬）博览会
China Intl Trade Fair for Apparel Fabrics and Accessories
上海Shanghai 1790

2013/10/23-25
中国国际非织造布研讨会及展览会
The 15th Intl Nonwovens Exhibition
上海Shanghai 1800

2013/10/23-25
第二十届国际自动识别及物联网技术展览会
SCAN CHINA 2013
山东青岛Shandong-Qingdao 4110

2013/10/23-25
第十二届中国国际住宅产业博览会
（节能环保低碳性大展）
12th China Intl Exhibition on Housing Industry
北京Beijing 530

2013/10/23-25
第十二届电磁兼容暨微波技术展览会
IME/China 2013
Intl Conference & Exhibition on Microwave and Antenna
上海Shanghai 1810

2013/10/26-27
第二届安卓全球开发者大会
2013 AndroidWorld Global Developers Conference
广东深圳Guangdong-Shenzhen 2840

2013/10/26-28
珠光魅影-杭州
Treasures Hangzhou
浙江杭州Zhejiang-Hangzhou 4370

2013/10/28-30
第八届上海国际石油石化天然气技术装备展览会同期举办上海国际页岩气峰会
8th Shanghai Intl Petroleum Petrochemical Natural Gas Technology Equipment Exhibition
上海Shanghai 1820

2013/10/28-30
第四届中国兽医大会
4th Chinese Veterinary Conference
广西南宁Guangxi-Nanning 2890

2013/10/28-31
亚洲国际物流技术与运输系统展览会
CeMAT 2013
上海Shanghai 1840

2013/10/28-31
亚洲国际动力传动与控制技术展览会
PTC ASIA 2013
上海Shanghai 1830

2013/10/29-11/01
第十八届中国国际医药（工业）展览会暨技术交流会
China-Pharm 2013
18th Intl Pharmaceutical Industry Exhibition
上海Shanghai 1850

2013/10/30-11/01
第九届上海国际电力设备及技术展览会/第八届上海国际电工装备展览会
9th Intl Exhibition on Electric Power Equipment and Technology/ 8th Intl Exhibition on Electrical Equipment
上海Shanghai 1860

2013/10/30-11/02
中国国际商用车展览会
China Commercial Vehicles Show
湖北武汉Hubei-Wuhan 3440

2013/10/31-11/03
第三届贵阳汽车文化节
3rd Guiyang Automobile Culture Festival
贵州贵阳Guizhou-Guiyang 2940

2013/10/31-11/04
第六届郑州国际汽车展览会
6th Zhengzhou Intl Automobile Exhibition
河南郑州Henan-Zhengzhou 3360

November 2013 十一月

2013/11-
中国（株州）国际汽车及新能源汽车展示交易会
China (Zhuzhou) Intl Automobile and New Energy Car Exhibition
湖南株州Hunan-Zhuzhou 3460

2013/11-
磨料磨具展览会
Abrasives Exhibition
河南郑州Henan-Zhengzhou 3370

2013/11-
秋季时尚（郑州）购物节
Autumn Fashion Shopping Festival (Zhengzhou)
河南郑州Henan-Zhengzhou 3380

2013/11/01-03
第十六届中国东莞国际鞋展-鞋机展-鞋材展
Dongguan Shoes & China Shoetes
广东东莞Guangdong-Dongguan 2310

2013/11/01-04
第6届中国义乌国际森林产博览会
6th China Yiwu Intl Forest Products Fair
浙江义乌Zhejiang-Yiwu 4590

2013/11/04-06
中国（国际）精密制造及技术展
China (Intl) Precision Machine Technology Expo
江苏南京Jiangsu-Nanjing 3630

2013/11/05-07
第十八届中国国际渔业博览会
18th China Fisheries & Seafood Expo
辽宁大连Liaoning-Dalian 3710

2013/11/05-09
第15届中国国际工业博览会
China Intl Industry Fair
上海Shanghai 1870

2013/11/06-08
包装产业周
Packaging Industry Week
广东东莞Guangdong-Dongguan 2320

2013/11/08-11
上海国际黄金珠宝玉石展览会
China Intl Gold, Jewellery & Gem Fair - Shanghai
上海Shanghai 1880

2013/11/11-13
第82届中国电子展
同期举办: 2013年亚洲电子展
82nd China Electronics Fair
Asia Electronics Exhibition in Shanghai (AEES 2013)/
2013 China LED Fair (Shanghai)
上海Shanghai 1890

2013/11/12-14
（第九届）中国国际水处理化学品、水溶性高分子技术及应用展览会
WATERCHEM+TECH
上海Shanghai 1990

2013/11/12-14
（第九届）中国国际工业表面活性剂技术及应用展览会
SURFACTANTCHEM+TECH
上海Shanghai 2000

2013/11/13-16
第十五届东莞国际模具展及金属加工展
15th China Dongguan Intl Mould and Metalworking Exhibition
广东东莞Guangdong-Dongguan 2340

2013/11/13-16
第十五届东莞国际橡塑胶、包装、压铸和铸造展
15th China Dongguan Intl Plastics Packing Rubber Diecasting & Foundry Exhibition
广东东莞Guangdong-Dongguan 2330

2013/11/13-15
北京国际礼品、赠品及家用精品年底展览会
Intl Gifts, Premium & Houseware Purchase Exhibiton
北京Beijing 540

2013/11/14-18
第三届中国（重庆）汽车博览会
3rd China (Chongqing) Automobile Expo
重庆Chongqing 560

2013/11/14-16
第十五届中国连锁店展览会
China Shop
-China Retail Trade Fair
四川成都Sichuan-Chengdu 4300

2013/11/20-22
第10届中国（上海）国际地坪工业展览会
10th China (Shanghai) Intl Floor Industry Expo
上海Shanghai 2030

2013/11/20-22
第9届中国（上海）国际干混砂浆技术及产品展览会
9th China (Shanghai) Intl Dry Mix Mortar Technology and Product Expo
上海Shanghai 2050

2013/11/20-22
第11届中国（上海）国际保温材料与节能技术展览会
11th China (Shanghai) Insulating Materials and Energy-saving Technology Expo
上海Shanghai 2040

2013/11/20-22
第二十六届中国国际表面处理展览会
SFCHINA 2013
上海Shanghai 2010

2013/11/20-22
第十八届届中国国际涂料展览会
CHINACOAT 2013
上海Shanghai 2020

2013/11/25-27
第十六届深圳国际手机产业展览会暨研讨会
CME2013
广东深圳Guangdong-Shenzhen 2850

2013/11/26-28
中国国际五金展
-《科隆国际五金展》强力推动
China Intl Hardware Show
- Powered by PRACTICAL WORLD
上海Shanghai 2060

2013/11/28-30
2013中国国际果蔬、加工技术及物流展览会
China World Fruit & Vegetable Trade Fair 2013
北京Beijing 2070

2013/11/29-12/01
2013中国宁波家居与时尚生活产品展览会
2013 Ningbo Intl Home& Lifestyle Products Exhibition
浙江宁波Zhejiang-Ningbo 4430

2013/11/29-12/02
2013楚天汽车文化节
Hubei Automobile Culture Festival
湖北武汉Hubei-Wuhan 3450

December 2013 十二月

2013/12/03-06
中国国际海事技术学术会议和展览会
Marintec China
上海Shanghai 2080

2013/12/05-09
第六届中国-东盟（南宁）国际汽车展览会
6th China-ASEAN (Nanning) Intl Auto Exhibition
广西南宁Guangxi-Nanning 2900

2013/12/12-15
广州12月酒店用品展览会
Guangzhou Hotel Show
广东广州Guangdong-Guangzhou 2700

2013/12/28-31
广东（厚街）茶业博览会
Guangdong (Houjie) Tea Expo
广东东莞Guangdong-Dongguan 2360

2013/12/21-2014/01/05
2013第十三届东莞嘉年华时尚生活用品购物节
13th Dongguan Carnival
广东东莞Guangdong-Dongguan 2350

中国香港展览会议

Exhibitions and Conferences in Hong Kong, China

日期 Date	展览会议 Event	地点 Venue	主办 Organizer
2013.1.7-8	亚洲授权业研讨会 Asian Licensing Conference	香港会议展览中心 Hong Kong Convention and Exhibition Centre	香港贸易发展局 Hong Kong Trade Development Council ☎ 852-1830 668 🖷 852-2824 0249 ✉ hktdc@hktdc.org www.hktdc.com/hklicensingshow 详细介绍见☆1 Detail see ☆1
2013.1.7-9	香港贸发局香港国际授权展 HKTDC Hong Kong International Licensing Show	香港会议展览中心 Hong Kong Convention and Exhibition Centre	香港贸易发展局 Hong Kong Trade Development Council ☎ 852-1830 668 🖷 852-2824 0249 ✉ hktdc@hktdc.org www.hktdc.com/hklicensingshow 详细介绍见☆2 Detail see ☆2
2013.1.7-10	香港贸发局香港玩具展 HKTDC Hong Kong Toys & Games Fair	香港会议展览中心 Hong Kong Convention and Exhibition Centre	香港贸易发展局 Hong Kong Trade Development Council ☎ 852-1830 668 🖷 852-2824 0249 ✉ exhibitions@hktdc.org www.hktdc.com/hktoyfair 详细介绍见☆3 Detail see ☆3
2013.1.7-10	香港贸发局香港婴儿用品展 HKTDC Hong Kong Baby Products Fair	香港会议展览中心 Hong Kong Convention and Exhibition Centre	香港贸易发展局 Hong Kong Trade Development Council ☎ 852-1830 668 🖷 852-2824 0249 ✉ exhibitions@hktdc.org www.hktdc.com/hkbabyfair 详细介绍见☆4 Detail see ☆4
2013.1.7-10	香港国际文具展 Hong Kong International Stationery Fair	香港会议展览中心 Hong Kong Convention and Exhibition Centre	香港贸易发展局 Hong Kong Trade Development Council ☎ 852-1830 668 🖷 852-2824 0249 ✉ exhibitions@hktdc.org www.hkstationeryfair.com 详细介绍见☆5 Detail see ☆5
2013.1.14-15	亚洲金融论坛 The Asian Financial Forum	香港会议展览中心 Hong Kong Convention and Exhibition Centre	香港贸易发展局 Hong Kong Trade Development Council ☎ 852-1830 668 🖷 852-2824 0249 ✉ aff@hktdc.org www.asianfinancialforum.com 详细介绍见☆6 Detail see ☆6

日期 Date	展览会议 Event	地点 Venue	主办 Organizer
2013.1.14-17	香港贸发局香港时装节秋冬系列 HKTDC Hong Kong Fashion Week for Fall/Winter	香港会议展览中心 Hong Kong Convention and Exhibition Centre	香港贸易发展局 Hong Kong Trade Development Council ☎ 852-1830 668 🖷 852-2824 0249 ✉ exhibitions@hktdc.org www.hktdc.com/hkfashionweekfw 详细介绍见☆7 Detail see☆7
2013.1.14-17	香港贸发局香港国际时尚荟萃 HKTDC World Boutique, Hong Kong	香港会议展览中心 Hong Kong Convention and Exhibition Centre	香港贸易发展局 Hong Kong Trade Development Council ☎ 852-1830 668 🖷 852-2824 0249 ✉ exhibitions@hktdc.org www.hktdc.com/worldboutiquehk 详细介绍见☆8 Detail see☆8
2013.1.26-27	英国教育展 Education UK Exhibition 2013, Hong Kong	香港会议展览中心 Hong Kong Convention and Exhibition Centre	英国文化协会 British Council ☎ 852-2913 5100 🖷 852-2913 5166 ✉ enquiries@britishcouncil.org.hk www.educationuk.org.hk
2013.1.31-2.3	香港贸发局教育及职业博览 HKTDC Education & Careers Expo	香港会议展览中心 Hong Kong Convention and Exhibition Centre	香港贸易发展局 Hong Kong Trade Development Council ☎ 852-1830 668 🖷 852-2824 0249 ✉ exhibitions@hktdc.org www.hktdc.com/hkeducationexpo 详细介绍见☆9 Detail see☆9
2013.1.31-2.5	香港宠物节 The 8th Hong Kong Pet Show	香港会议展览中心 Hong Kong Convention and Exhibition Centre	展汇博览有限公司 World Hong Kong Investment Limited ✉ marketing@petshow.com.hk www.petshow.com.hk
2013.2.1-2	乐活博览2013 Lohas Expo 2013	香港会议展览中心 Hong Kong Convention and Exhibition Centre	盈柏广告策划有限公司 Inspire Advertising & Marketing Limited ☎ 852-2786 0998 🖷 852-2786 0983 ✉ contact@lohasexpohk.com www.lohasexpohk.com
2013.2.2-3	2013喜迎春冠军猫展 Spring Championship Cat Show	香港会议展览中心 Hong Kong Convention and Exhibition Centre	展汇博览有限公司 World Hong Kong Investment Limited ✉ cmarketing@petshow.com.hk www.petshow.com.hk
2013.2.2-3	第183及184届全犬种冠军狗展 The 183rd & 184th All Breed Champion Dog Shows	香港会议展览中心 Hong Kong Convention and Exhibition Centre	展汇博览有限公司 World Hong Kong Investment Limited ✉ cmarketing@petshow.com.hk www.petshow.com.hk
2013.2.15-17	第70届情人节婚纱、婚宴及结婚服务博览 70th Valentine's Wedding Service & Banquet Expo	香港会议展览中心 Hong Kong Convention and Exhibition Centre	香港亚洲展览(集团)有限公司 Hongkong-Asia Exhibition (Holdings) Ltd ☎ 852-2591 9823 🖷 852-2573 3311 ✉ hkexhi@hka.com.hk www.iweddingclub.com

日期 Date	展览会议 Event	地点 Venue	主办 Organizer
2013.2.22-24	2013年“BB春季购物节”暨“儿童成长教育展” Baby Expo in Spring & Child Growth Education Expo	香港会议展览中心 Hong Kong Convention and Exhibition Centre	荷花集团 Eugene Group Limited ☎ 852-2811 4522 🖷 852-2565 0258 ✉ marketing@eugenegroup.com.hk www.iweddingclub.com
2013.2.25-27	Airline Retail Conference	亚洲国际博览馆 AsiaWorld-Expo	Airline Retail Conference ☎ +44-20 7749 2313 ✉ info@airlineretail.com www.airlineretail.com
2013.2.25-28	2013香港国际毛皮时装展览会 Hong Kong International Fur & Fashion Fair	香港会议展览中心 Hong Kong Convention and Exhibition Centre	香港毛皮业协会 Hong Kong Fur Federation ☎ 852-2367 4646 🖷 852-2739 0799 ✉ fur@hkff.org www.hkff.org
2013.2.25-27	Airline Retail Conference	亚洲国际博览馆 AsiaWorld-Expo	Airline Retail Conference ☎ (44) 20 7749 2313 ✉ info@airlineretail.com www.airlineretail.com 详细介绍见☆10 Detail see☆10
2013.3.4-7	三月亚洲时尚首饰及配饰展 Asia's Fashion Jewellery & Accessories Fair - March	亚洲国际博览馆 AsiaWorld-Expo	亚洲博闻有限公司 UBM Asia Limited ☎ 852-2585 6179, 2585 6127 🖷 852-3749 7542, 3749 7344 ✉ salesafj-hk@ubm.com www.asiafja.com 详细介绍见☆11 Detail see☆11
2013.3.5-9	香港贸发局香港国际珠宝展 HKTDC Hong Kong International Jewellery Show	香港会议展览中心 Hong Kong Convention and Exhibition Centre	香港贸易发展局 Hong Kong Trade Development Council ☎ 852-1830 668 🖷 852-2824 0249 ✉ exhibitions@hktdc.org www.hktdc.com/hkjewelleryshow 详细介绍见☆12 Detail see☆12
2013.3.11-14	亚太区国际教育协会年会暨展览 APAIE Conference & Exhibition 2013	亚洲国际博览馆 AsiaWorld-Expo	香港中文大学 The Chinese University of Hong Kong ☎ 852-3943 7597 🖷 852-2603 5402 ✉ apaie2013@cuhk.edu.hk www.apaie.org 详细介绍见☆13 Detail see☆13
2013.3.12-14	TOC集装箱供应链亚洲展 TOC Container Supply Chain Asia 2013	香港会议展览中心 Hong Kong Convention and Exhibition Centre	TOC Events Worldwide ☎ +44 -2070174391 ✉ sean.deane@toc-events.com www.tocevents-americas.com

日期 Date	展览会议 Event	地点 Venue	主办 Organizer
2013.3.13-15	香港国际春季成衣及时装材料展 Interstoff Asia Essential - Spring 2013	香港会议展览中心 Hong Kong Convention and Exhibition Centre	法兰克福展览（香港）有限公司 Messe Frankfurt HK Ltd ☎ 852-2802 7728 🖷 852-2598 8771 ✉ textile@hongkong.messefrankfurt.com www.messefrankfurt.com.hk
2013.3.15-17	C3日本动玩博览2013 C3 in Hong Kong 2013	香港会议展览中心 Hong Kong Convention and Exhibition Centre	SOTSU CO., LTD ☎ 852-2418 8881 🖷 852-2481 6594 ✉ info@c3hk.com.hk www.c3hk.com.hk
2013.3.15-17	香港婚宴暨世界名酒博览2013 Hong Kong Wedding Banquet & World Wine Expo	香港会议展览中心 Hong Kong Convention and Exhibition Centre	隽杰国际展览有限公司 Audace International Fairs Limited ☎ 852-2367 8385 🖷 852-2367 8488 ✉ info@expo.com.hk www.wedding.expo.com.hk
2013.3.15-17	香港婚纱暨海外婚礼博览2013 Hong Kong Wedding & Overseas Wedding Expo	香港会议展览中心 Hong Kong Convention and Exhibition Centre	隽杰国际展览有限公司 Audace International Fairs Limited ☎ 852-2367 8385 🖷 852-2367 8488 ✉ info@expo.com.hk www.wedding.expo.com.hk
2013.3.18-20	LINC Asia-Pacific 2013	亚洲国际博览馆 AsiaWorld-Expo, Hong Kong	CongO Congress Organisation and more GmbH ☎ +49-89 1295440 🖷 +49-89 13936704 ✉ info@cong-o.de www.lincasiapacific.com 详细介绍见☆14 Detail see☆14
2012.3.18-21	香港贸发局香港国际影视展 HKTDC Hong Kong Intl Film & TV Market (FILMART)	香港会议展览中心 Hong Kong Convention and Exhibition Centre	香港贸易发展局 Hong Kong Trade Development Council ☎ 852-1830 668 🖷 852-2824 0249 ✉ hktdc@hktdc.org www.hktdc.com/hkfilmart 详细介绍见☆15 Detail see☆15
2012.3.18-22	Mines and Money Hong Kong 2013	香港会议展览中心 Hong Kong Convention and Exhibition Centre	Beacon Events Ltd ☎ 852-2531 6130 🖷 852-2586 1999 ✉ lstemp@beaconevents.com pablo.martin@aspermontuk.com www.minesandmoney.com/hongkong
2012.3.19-21	亚洲商务航空展览会 Asian Business Aviation	香港机场商用航空中心 The Hong Kong Business Aviation Centre	励展博览集团 Reed Exhibitions ☎ 010-5933 9364 ✉ adeline.desages@reedexpo.com.cn www.asianaerospace.com 详细介绍见☆16 Detail see☆16

日期 Date	展览会议 Event	地点 Venue	主办 Organizer
2012.3.19-21	亚洲国际航空展览会暨论坛 Asian Aerospace 2013 Asian Aerospace International Expo and Congress	亚洲国际博览馆 AsiaWorld-Expo	励展博览集团 Reed Exhibitions Ltd ☎ 852-2965 1603 🖷 852-2824 0246 ✉ brian.thomas@reedexpo.com.hk www.asianaerospace.com 详细介绍见☆17 Detail see☆17
2012.3.19-21	亚洲航空物流技术展览会 Air Freight Asia	亚洲国际博览馆 AsiaWorld-Expo	励展博览集团 Reed Exhibitions Ltd ☎ 010-5933 9209 ✉ martin.du@reedexpo.com.cn www.airfreightasia.com 详细介绍见☆18 Detail see☆18
2013.3.21-23	USANA 亚太区年会2013 USANA Asia Pacific Convention 2013	亚洲国际博览馆 AsiaWorld-Expo	USANA Health Sciences ☎ 852-2162 1888 ✉ dist.serv@hk.usana.com 详细介绍见☆19 Detail see☆19
2013.3.25-27	时尚汇集(春季) Fashion Access - Spring Show	香港会议展览中心 Hong Kong Convention and Exhibition Centre	亚太区皮革展有限公司 （亚洲博闻有限公司及 SIC集团合办） APLF Limited ☎ 852-2827 6211 020-8666 0158 🖷 852-3479 7346 020-8667 2235 ✉ info@aplf.com www.aplf.com 详细介绍见☆20 Detail see ☆20
2013.3.25-27	2013年亚太区皮革展 – 原料及制造技术展 APLF-MM&T Asia Pacific Leather Fair 2013 - Materials, Manufacturing and Technology	香港会议展览中心 Hong Kong Convention and Exhibition Centre	亚太区皮革展有限公司 （亚洲博闻有限公司及 SIC集团合办） APLF Limited ☎ 852-2827 6211 020-8666 0158 🖷 852-3479 7346 020-8667 2235 ✉ sales@aplf.com Info-china@ubm.com www.mmt.aplf.com 详细介绍见☆21 Detail see☆21
2013.3.25-27	国际服装业高峰论坛 Prime Source Forum Hong Kong	香港会议展览中心 Hong Kong Convention and Exhibition Centre	亚洲博闻 ☎ 852-2827 6211 020-8666 0158 🖷 852-3479 7346 020-8667 2235 ✉ sales@aplf.com Info-china@ubm.com www.primesourceforum.com 详细介绍见☆22 Detail see☆22
2012.3.26-27	香港国际时尚内衣泳装展-原材料-品牌加工 Interfiliere hong kong - mode lingerie 2013	香港会议展览中心 Hong Kong Convention and Exhibition Centre	欧罗维特 Eurovet Asia Ltd ☎ 852-2815 0667 🖷 852-2815 0691 ✉ hongkong@eurovet.fr www.hongkong-mode-lingerie.com

日期 Date	展览会议 Event	地点 Venue	主办 Organizer
2012.3.27-28	亚洲智能卡工业展 Cartes in Asia 2013	亚洲国际博览馆 AsiaWorld-Expo	Comexposium ☎ +33-01 7677 1300 🖷 +33-01 5330 9514 ✉ isabelle.alfano@comexposium.com www.cartes-asia.com 详细介绍见☆23 Detail see☆23
2013.4.5-9	第11届香港国际武术节 11th Hong Kong Wushu Intl Championship	亚洲国际博览馆 AsiaWorld-Expo	香港国际武术节组委会 ☎ 852-6444 4699 🖷 852-3011 9565 ✉ hkwsj@hkwsj.com www.hkwsj.com
2013.4.6-9	香港贸发局香港国际春季灯饰展 HKTDC Hong Kong Intl Lighting Fair (Spring Edition)	香港会议展览中心 Hong Kong Convention and Exhibition Centre	香港贸易发展局 Hong Kong Trade Development Council ☎ 852-1830 668 🖷 852-2824 0249 ✉ exhibitions@hktdc.org www.hktdc.com/hklightingfairse 详细介绍见☆24 Detail see☆24
2013.4.12-15	环球资源电子产品及零件采购交易会 China Sourcing Fair - Electronics & Components Spring 2012	亚洲国际博览馆 AsiaWorld-Expo	环球资源 Global Sources Exhibitions ☎ 852-8199 7308 🖷 852-8199 7628 ✉ visit@chinasourcingfair.com www.chinasourcingfair.com 详细介绍见☆25 Detail see☆25
2013.4.12-15	环球资源安防产品采购交易会 China Sourcing Fair - Security Product Spring 2013	亚洲国际博览馆 AsiaWorld-Expo	环球资源 Global Sources Exhibitions ☎ 852-8199 7308 🖷 852-8199 7628 ✉ visit@chinasourcingfair.com www.chinasourcingfair.com 详细介绍见☆26 Detail see☆26
2013.4.12-15	环球资源韩国电子产品及零件采购交易会 Korea Sourcing Fair - Electronics & Components Spring 2012	亚洲国际博览馆 AsiaWorld-Expo	环球资源 Global Sources Exhibitions ☎ 852-8199 7308 🖷 852-8199 7628 ✉ visit@chinasourcingfair.com www.koreasourcingfair.com 详细介绍见☆27 Detail see☆27
2013.4.13-16	香港贸发局香港春季电子产品展 HKTDC Hong Kong Electronics Fair (Spring Edition)	香港会议展览中心 Hong Kong Convention and Exhibition Centre	香港贸易发展局 Hong Kong Trade Development Council ☎ 852-1830 668 🖷 852-2824 0249 ✉ exhibitions@hktdc.org www.hktdc.com/hkelectronicsfairse 详细介绍见☆28 Detail see☆28

日期 Date	展览会议 Event	地点 Venue	主办 Organizer
2013.4.13-16	香港贸发局国际资讯科技博览 HKTDC International ICT Expo	香港会议展览中心 Hong Kong Convention and Exhibition Centre	香港贸易发展局 Hong Kong Trade Development Council ☎ 852-1830 668 🖷 852-2824 0249 ✉ exhibitions@hktdc.org www.hktdc.com/ictexpo 详细介绍见☆29 Detail see☆29
2013.4.19-22	环球资源婴儿及儿童产品采购交易会 China Sourcing Fair - Baby & Children's Products	亚洲国际博览馆 AsiaWorld-Expo	环球资源 Global Sources Exhibitions ☎ 852-8199 7308 🖷 852-8199 7628 ✉ visit@chinasourcingfair.com www.chinasourcingfair.com 详细介绍见☆30 Detail see☆30
2013.4.19-22	环球资源圣诞及节日产品采购交易会 China Sourcing Fair - Christmas & Seasonal Products Spring 2013	亚洲国际博览馆 AsiaWorld-Expo	环球资源 Global Sources Exhibitions ☎ 852-8199 7308 🖷 852-8199 7628 ✉ visit@chinasourcingfair.com www.chinasourcingfair.com 详细介绍见☆31 Detail see☆31
2013.4.19-22	环球资源礼品及赠品采购交易会 China Sourcing Fair - Gifts & Premiums	亚洲国际博览馆 AsiaWorld-Expo	环球资源 Global Sources Exhibitions ☎ 852-8199 7308 🖷 852-8199 7628 ✉ visit@chinasourcingfair.com www.chinasourcingfair.com 详细介绍见☆32 Detail see☆32
2013.4.19-22	环球资源家居用品采购交易会 China Sourcing Fair - Home Products	亚洲国际博览馆 AsiaWorld-Expo	环球资源 Global Sources Exhibitions ☎ 852-8199 7308 🖷 852-8199 7628 ✉ visit@chinasourcingfair.com www.chinasourcingfair.com 详细介绍见☆33 Detail see☆33
2013.4.19-22	环球资源医疗及健康用品采购交易会 China Sourcing Fair - Medical & Health Products	亚洲国际博览馆 AsiaWorld-Expo	环球资源 Global Sources Exhibitions ☎ 852-8199 7308 🖷 852-8199 7628 ✉ visit@chinasourcingfair.com www.chinasourcingfair.com 详细介绍见☆34 Detail see☆34
2013.4.19-22	环球资源太阳能及节能产品采购交易会 China Sourcing Fair - Solar & Energy Saving Products Spring 2013	亚洲国际博览馆 AsiaWorld-Expo	环球资源 Global Sources Exhibitions ☎ 852-2814 5605 🖷 852-2580 7988 ✉ visit@chinasourcingfair.com www.chinasourcingfair.com 详细介绍见☆35 Detail see☆35

日期 Date	展览会议 Event	地点 Venue	主办 Organizer
2013.4.19-22	环球资源印度家居用品采购交易会 India Sourcing Fair - Home Products	亚洲国际博览馆 AsiaWorld-Expo	环球资源 Global Sources Exhibitions ☎ 852-8199 7308 🖷 852-8199 7628 ✉ visit@chinasourcingfair.com www.india-sourcingfair.com
2013.4.19-22	环球资源韩国礼品及赠品采购交易会 Korea Sourcing Fair - Gifts & Premiums	亚洲国际博览馆 AsiaWorld-Expo	环球资源 Global Sources Exhibitions ☎ 852-8199 7308 🖷 852-8199 7628 ✉ visit@chinasourcingfair.com www.koreasourcingfair.com 详细介绍见☆36 Detail see☆36
2013.4.19-22	香港贸发局香港家庭用品展 HKTDC Hong Kong Houseware Fair	香港会议展览中心 Hong Kong Convention and Exhibition Centre	香港贸易发展局 Hong Kong Trade Development Council ☎ 852-1830 668 🖷 852-2824 0249 ✉ exhibitions@hktdc.org www.hktdc.com/hkhousewarefair 详细介绍见☆37 Detail see☆37
2013.4.20-23	香港贸发局香港家用纺织品展 HKTDC Hong Kong Houseware Fair	香港会议展览中心 Hong Kong Convention and Exhibition Centre	香港贸易发展局 Hong Kong Trade Development Council ☎ 852-1830 668 🖷 852-2824 0249 ✉ exhibitions@hktdc.org www.hktdc.com/hkhousewarefair 详细介绍见☆38 Detail see☆38
2013.4.27-30	香港贸发局香港礼品及赠品展 HKTDC Hong Kong Gifts & Premium Fair	香港会议展览中心 Hong Kong Convention and Exhibition Centre	香港贸易发展局 Hong Kong Trade Development Council ☎ 852-1830 668 🖷 852-2824 0249 ✉ exhibitions@hktdc.org www.hktdc.com/hkgiftspremiumfair 详细介绍见☆39 Detail see☆39
2013.4.27-30	环球资源流行服饰配件采购交易会 China Sourcing Fair - Fashion Accessories	亚洲国际博览馆 AsiaWorld-Expo	环球资源 Global Sources Exhibitions ☎ 852-8199 7308 🖷 852-8199 7628 ✉ visit@chinasourcingfair.com www.chinasourcingfair.com 详细介绍见☆40 Detail see☆40
2013.4.27-30	环球资源服装及面料采购交易会 China Sourcing Fair - Garments & Textiles	亚洲国际博览馆 AsiaWorld-Expo	环球资源 Global Sources Exhibitions ☎ 852-8199 7308 🖷 852-8199 7628 ✉ visit@chinasourcingfair.com www.chinasourcingfair.com 详细介绍见☆41 Detail see☆41

日期 Date	展览会议 Event	地点 Venue	主办 Organizer
2013.4.27-30	环球资源内衣及泳衣采购交易会 China Sourcing Fair - Underwear & Swimwear	亚洲国际博览馆 AsiaWorld-Expo	环球资源 Global Sources Exhibitions ☎ 852-8199 7308 🖷 852-8199 7628 ✉ visit@chinasourcingfair.com www.chinasourcingfair.com 详细介绍见☆42 Detail see☆42
2013.4.27-30	环球资源印度服装及配饰采购交易会 India Sourcing Fair - Garments & Accessories	亚洲国际博览馆 AsiaWorld-Expo	环球资源 Global Sources Exhibitions ☎ 852-8199 7308 🖷 852-8199 7628 ✉ visit@chinasourcingfair.com www.indiasourcingfair.com 详细介绍见☆43 Detail see☆43
2013.4.27-30	香港国际印刷及包装展 Hong Kong Intl Printing & Packaging Fair	亚洲国际博览馆 AsiaWorld-Expo	香港贸易发展局 Hong Kong Trade Development Council ☎ 852-1830 668 🖷 852-2824 0249 ✉ exhibitions@hktdc.org www.hkprintpackfair.com 详细介绍见☆44 Detail see☆44
2013.5.7-9	第三届亚洲乘客体验会议 Future Travel Experience Asia 2013	亚洲国际博览馆 AsiaWorld-Expo	PPS Publications Limited ☎ 44 (0) 1293 783 851 🖷 44 (0) 1293 782 959 www.futuretravelexperience.com/fteasia 详细介绍见☆45 Detail see☆45
2013.5.7-10	第十五届国际食品及饮料、酒店、餐厅及餐饮设备、供应及服务展览会 HOFEX 2013 - The 15th International Exhibition of Food & Drink, Hotel, Restaurant & Food Service Equipment, Supplies & Services	香港会议展览中心 Hong Kong Convention & Exhibition Centre	香港展览服务有限公司 Hong Kong Exhibition Services Ltd ☎ 852-2804 1500 🖷 852-2528 3103 ✉ exhibit@hkesallworld.com www.hofex.com
2013.5.7-10	香港长者博览暨亚洲银发产品展2013 Hong Kong Senior Fair and Senior Expo Asia 2013	香港会议展览中心 Hong Kong Convention & Exhibition Centre	纵延展业有限公司 Vertical Expo Services Company Ltd ☎ 852-2528 0062 🖷 852-2528 0072 ✉ hksf@verticalexpo.com www.hkseniorfair.com
2013.5.14-16	香港贸发局香港国际医疗器材及用品展 HKTDC Hong Kong Intl Medical Devices and Supplies Fair	香港会议展览中心 Hong Kong Convention and Exhibition Centre	香港贸易发展局 Hong Kong Trade Development Council ☎ 852-1830 668 🖷 852-2824 0249 ✉ exhibitions@hktdc.org www.hktdc.com/hkmedicalfair 详细介绍见☆46 Detail see☆46
2013.5.16-18	亚洲殡仪及墓园博览暨会议 Asia Funeral and Cemetery Expo & Conference	香港会议展览中心 Hong Kong Convention and Exhibition Centre	纵延展业有限公司 Vertical Expo Services Company Limited ☎ 852-2528 0062 🖷 852-2528 0072 ✉ afe@verticalexpo.com www.verticalexpo.com

日期 Date	展览会议 Event	地点 Venue	主办 Organizer
2013.5.17-19	第12届The Parents' Journal儿童、婴儿国际品牌购物展 12th Parents' Journal Intl Children & Baby Brands Expo	香港会议展览中心 Hong Kong Convention and Exhibition Centre	百家宝集团有限公司 Peegaboo Corporation Limited ☎ 852-3741 1720 🖷 852-3741 1725 ✉ info@peegaboo.com
2013.5.23-26	香港国际艺术展 Hong Kong International Art Fair	香港会议展览中心 Hong Kong Convention and Exhibition Centre	Asian Art Fairs Ltd ☎ 852-3127 5529 🖷 852-3127 5524 ✉ hongkonginfo@artbasel.com www.hongkongartfair.com basel.artbasel.com
2013.5.25-27	国际古玩展 International Antiques Fair	香港会议展览中心 Hong Kong Convention and Exhibition Centre	翟氏投资有限公司 Chak's Investment Limited ☎ 852-2548 8702 🖷 852-2559 8568 ✉ chaks@netvigator.com info@chaksinvestment.com www.iaf.com.hk
2013.5.31-6.1	香港贸发局创业日 HKTDC Entrepreneur Day	香港会议展览中心 Hong Kong Convention and Exhibition Centre	香港贸易发展局 Hong Kong Trade Development Council ☎ 852-1830 668 🖷 852-2824 0249 ✉ entrepreneurday@hktdc.org www.hktdc.com/eday
2013.5.31-6.4	ISN World Congress of Nephrology 2013	香港会议展览中心 Hong Kong Convention and Exhibition Centre	International Society of Nephrology ☎ 852-2559 9973 🖷 852-2547 9528 ✉ info@wcn2013.org www.wcn2013.org
2013.6.1-2	第十四届香港国际教育展 The 14th Hong Kong International Education Expo	香港会议展览中心 Hong Kong Convention and Exhibition Centre	立新国际展览有限公司 Neway Intl Trade Fairs Limited ☎ 852-2561 5566 🖷 852-2811 9156 ✉ info@newayfairs.com www.newayfairs.com
2013.6.4-6	亚洲零售博览会 Retail Asia Expo 2013	香港会议展览中心 Hong Kong Convention and Exhibition Centre	Diversified Events Hong Kong LLC ☎ 852-3105 3970 🖷 852-3105 3974 ✉ info@retailasiaexpo.com www.retailasiaexpo.com
2013.6.7-9	第71届夏日婚纱、婚宴及结婚服务博览暨第14届香港婚嫁美容及化妆节2013 71th Summer Wedding Service & Banquet Expo incorporating 14th HK Beauty & Wedding Fiesta 2013	香港会议展览中心 Hong Kong Convention and Exhibition Centre	香港亚洲展览(集团)有限公司 Hongkong-Asia Exhibition (Holdings) Ltd ☎ 852-2591 9823 🖷 852-2573 3311 ✉ hkexhi@hka.com.hk www.iweddingclub.com
2013.6.8-9	SMART Investment and International Property Expo 2012	香港会议展览中心 Hong Kong Convention and Exhibition Centre	Corporate Consumer Communications Limited ☎ 852-2944 6430 🖷 852-2944 6424 ✉ info@3c-ltd.com www.smartexpos.com

日期 Date	展览会议 Event	地点 Venue	主办 Organizer
2013.6.8	青联招工日2013 HKUYA Job Fair 2013	香港会议展览中心 Hong Kong Convention and Exhibition Centre	香港青年联会有限公司 Hong Kong United Youth Association Limited ☎ 852-2598 9385 🖷 852-2598 9767 ✉ mail@hkyua.org.hk www.smartexpos.com
2013.6.13-16	第27届香港国际旅游展 27th Intl Travel Expo	香港会议展览中心 Hong Kong Convention and Exhibition Centre	汇众展览服务有限公司 TKS Exhibition Services Ltd ☎ 852-3155 0600 🖷 852-3520 1500 ✉ travel@tkshk.com www.itehk.com
2013.6.13-16	第8届商务会奖旅游展 The 8th M.I.C.E. Travel Expo	香港会议展览中心 Hong Kong Convention and Exhibition Centre	汇众展览服务有限公司 TKS Exhibition Services Ltd ☎ 852-3155 0600 🖷 852-3520 1500 ✉ travel@tkshk.com www.itehk.com
2013.6.14-16	健康生活博览2013 Health Expo 2013	香港会议展览中心 Hong Kong Convention and Exhibition Centre	新城财经台 Metro Finance ☎ 852-3698 8000 🖷 852-2123 9868 www.metroradio.com.hk
2013.6.14-16	香港家居博览2013暨香港室内设计师巡礼 In-Home Expo 2013	香港会议展览中心 Hong Kong Convention and Exhibition Centre	展汇博览有限公司 World HK Exhibition Limited ☎ 852-2756 3488 ✉ marketing@world-hk.com.hk www.metroradio.com.hk
2013.6.16-20	Vinexpo Asia-Pacific 2013	香港会议展览中心 Hong Kong Convention and Exhibition Centre	VINEXPO OVERSEAS SA ☎ +33 5 56 56 00 22 🖷 +33 5 56 56 00 00 ✉ info@vinexpo.com www.vinexpo.com
2013.6.20-23	六月亚洲时尚首饰及配饰展 Asia's Fashion Jewellery & Accessories Fair - June	香港会议展览中心 Hong Kong Convention and Exhibition Centre	亚洲博闻有限公司 UBM Asia Limited ☎ 852-2585 6179, 2516 1677 🖷 852-3749 7542 ✉ salesafj-hk@ubm.com www.asiafja.com 详细介绍见☆47 Detail see☆47
2012.6.20-23	六月香港珠宝首饰展览会 June Hong Kong Jewellery & Gem Fair	香港会议展览中心 Hong Kong Convention and Exhibition Centre	亚洲博闻有限公司 UBM Asia Limited ☎ 852-2516 1677, 2585 6179 🖷 852-3749 7319 ✉ salesjgf-hk@ubm.com www.jewellerynetasia.com 详细介绍见☆48 Detail see☆48

日期 Date	展览会议 Event	地点 Venue	主办 Organizer
2013.7.8-11	香港贸发局香港时装节春夏系列 HKTDC Hong Kong Fashion Week for Spring/Summer	香港会议展览中心 Hong Kong Convention and Exhibition Centre	香港贸易发展局 Hong Kong Trade Development Council ☎ 852-1830 668 🖷 852-2824 0249 ✉ exhibitions@hktdc.org www.hktdc.com/hkfashionweekss 详细介绍见☆49 Detail see☆49
2013.7.17-23	香港贸发局香港书展 HKTDC Hong Kong Book Fair	香港会议展览中心 Hong Kong Convention and Exhibition Centre	香港贸易发展局 Hong Kong Trade Development Council ☎ 852-1830 668 🖷 852-2824 0249 ✉ exhibitions@hktdc.org www.hkbookfair.com 详细介绍见☆50 Detail see☆50
2012.8.15-17	香港国际茶展 Hong Kong International Tea Fair	香港会议展览中心 Hong Kong Convention and Exhibition Centre	香港贸易发展局 Hong Kong Trade Development Council ☎ 852-1830 668 🖷 852-2824 0249 ✉ exhibitions@hktdc.org www.hktdc.com/hkteafair 详细介绍见☆51 Detail see☆51
2013.8.15-17	国际现代化中医药及健康产品展览会暨会议 Intl Conference & Exhibition of the Modernization of Chinese Medicine & Health Products	香港会议展览中心 Hong Kong Convention and Exhibition Centre	香港贸易发展局 Hong Kong Trade Development Council ☎ 852-1830 668 🖷 852-2824 0249 ✉ exhibitions@hktdc.org www.hktdc.com/icmcm 详细介绍见☆52 Detail see☆52
2013.8.15-19	香港贸发局美食博览 HKTDC Food Expo	香港会议展览中心 Hong Kong Convention and Exhibition Centre	香港贸易发展局 Hong Kong Trade Development Council ☎ 852-1830 668 🖷 852-2824 0249 ✉ exhibitions@hktdc.org www.hktdc.com/hkfoodexpo 详细介绍见☆53 Detail see☆53
2013.9.4-5	亚洲营养食品展 2013 Vitafoods Asia 2013	亚洲国际博览馆 AsiaWorld-Expo	IIR Exhibitions ☎ +44-207 017 7036 🖷 +44-207 017 7818 ✉ vitafoods@informa.com www.vitafoodsasia.com
2013.9.4-6	亚洲国际水果蔬菜展览会 ASIA FRUIT LOGISTICA 2013	亚洲国际博览馆 AsiaWorld-Expo	全球产品会展有限公司 Global Produce Events GmbH ☎ +49-30 3038 2178 🖷 +49-30 3038 7060 ✉ info@gp-events.com www.asiafruitlogistica.com 详细介绍见☆54 Detail see☆54

日期 Date	展览会议 Event	地点 Venue	主办 Organizer
2013.9.4-6	亚洲营养食品展 2013 ASIA FRUIT LOGISTICA 2013	亚洲国际博览馆 AsiaWorld-Expo	全球产品会展有限公司 Global Produce Events GmbH ☎ +49-30 3038 2178 📠 +49-30 3038 7060 ✉ info@gp-events.com www.asiafruitlogistica.com 详细介绍见☆55 Detail see☆55
2013.9.4-8	香港贸发局香港钟表展 HKTDC Hong Kong Watch & Clock Fair	香港会议展览中心 Hong Kong Convention & Exhibition Centre	香港贸易发展局 Hong Kong Trade Development Council ☎ 852-1830 668 📠 852-2824 0249 ✉ exhibitions@hktdc.org www.hktdc.com/hkwatchfair 详细介绍见☆56 Detail see☆56
2013.9.11-14	九月亚洲时尚首饰及配饰展 Asia's Fashion Jewellery & Accessories Fair - September	亚洲国际博览馆 AsiaWorld-Expo	亚洲博闻有限公司 UBM Asia Limited ☎ 852-2585 6179, 2516 1677 📠 852-3749 7542 ✉ salesjgf-hk@ubm.com www.asiafja.com 详细介绍见☆57 Detail see☆57
2013.9.11-15	九月香港珠宝首饰展览会 September Hong Kong Jewellery & Gem Fair	亚洲国际博览馆 AsiaWorld-Expo	亚洲博闻有限公司 UBM Asia Limited ☎ 852-2516 1677, 2585 6179 📠 852-3749 7319 ✉ salesjgf-hk@ubm.com exhibitions.jewellerynetasia.com 详细介绍见☆58 Detail see☆58
2013.9.13-17	九月香港珠宝首饰展览会 -珠宝首饰成品 September Hong Kong Jewellery & Gem Fair	香港会议展览中心 Hong Kong Convention and Exhibition Centre	亚洲博闻有限公司 UBM Asia Limited ☎ 852-2516 1677, 2585 6179 📠 852-3749 7319 ✉ salesjgf-hk@ubm.com exhibitions.jewellerynetasia.com 详细介绍见☆59 Detail see☆59
2013.9.25-27	时尚汇集 (九月展) Fashion Access - September	香港会议展览中心 Hong Kong Convention and Exhibition Centre	亚太区皮革展有限公司 Asia Pacific Leather Fair Ltd ☎ 852-2827 6211，020-8666 0158 📠 852-3749 7346，020-8667 2235 ✉ sales@aplf.com info-china@ubm.com www.fashionaccess.aplf.com 详细介绍见☆60 Detail see☆60
2013.9.25-27	国际羊绒交易会 – 国际性的专业羊绒商贸展览盛会 Cashmere World - The International Trade Fair for the Cashmere Industry	香港会议展览中心 Hong Kong Convention and Exhibition Centre	亚太区皮革展有限公司 Asia Pacific Leather Fair Ltd ☎ 852-2827 6211, 020-8666 0158 📠 852-3749 7346, 020-8667 2235 ✉ sales@aplf.com, info-china@ubm.com www.fashionaccess.aplf.com 详细介绍见☆61 Detail see☆61

日期 Date	展览会议 Event	地点 Venue	主办 Organizer
2013.10.12-15	环球资源电子产品及零件采购交易会 China Sourcing Fair – Electronics & Components	亚洲国际博览馆 AsiaWorld-Expo	环球资源 Global Sources ☎ 852-8199 7308 🖷 852-8199 7628 ✉ visit@chinasourcingfair.com www.chinasourcingfair.com 详细介绍见☆62 Detail see☆62
2013.10.12-15	环球资源韩国电子产品及零件采购交易会 Korea Sourcing Fair - Electronics & Components	亚洲国际博览馆 AsiaWorld-Expo	环球资源 Global Sources ☎ 852-8199 7308 🖷 852-8199 7628 ✉ visit@chinasourcingfair.com www.koreasourcingfair.com 详细介绍见☆63 Detail see☆63
2013.10.12-15	环球资源安防产品采购交易会 China Sourcing Fair - Security Products	亚洲国际博览馆 AsiaWorld-Expo	环球资源 Global Sources ☎ 852-8199 7308 🖷 852-8199 7628 ✉ visit@chinasourcingfair.com www.chinasourcingfair.com 详细介绍见☆64 Detail see☆64
2013.10.13-16	香港贸发局香港秋季电子产品展 HKTDC Hong Kong Electronics Fair (Autumn Edition)	香港会议展览中心 Hong Kong Convention and Exhibition Centre	香港贸易发展局 Hong Kong Trade Development Council ☎ 852-1830 668 🖷 852-2824 0249 ✉ exhibitions@hktdc.org www.hktdc.com/hkelectronicsfairae 详细介绍见☆65 Detail see☆65
2013.10.13-16	国际电子组件及生产技术展 electronicAsia	香港会议展览中心 Hong Kong Convention and Exhibition Centre	香港贸易发展局 慕尼黑国际博览亚洲有公司 Hong Kong Trade Development Council MMI Asia Pte Ltd ☎ 852-1830 668 🖷 852-2824 0249 ✉ exhibitions@hktdc.org www.electronicasia.com 详细介绍见☆66 Detail see☆66
2013.10.19-22	环球资源婴儿及儿童产品采购交易会 China Sourcing Fair - Baby & Children's Products	亚洲国际博览馆 AsiaWorld-Expo	环球资源 Global Sources ☎ 852-8199 7308 🖷 852-8199 7628 ✉ visit@chinasourcingfair.com www.chinasourcingfair.com 详细介绍见☆67 Detail see☆67
2013.10.19-22	环球资源圣诞及节日产品采购交易会 China Sourcing Fair - Christmas & Seasonal Products	亚洲国际博览馆 AsiaWorld-Expo	环球资源 Global Sources ☎ 852-8199 7308 🖷 852-8199 7628 ✉ visit@chinasourcingfair.com www.chinasourcingfair.com 详细介绍见☆68 Detail see☆68

日期 Date	展览会议 Event	地点 Venue	主办 Organizer
2013.10.19-22	环球资源礼品及赠品采购交易会 China Sourcing Fair - Gifts & Premiums	亚洲国际博览馆 AsiaWorld-Expo	环球资源 Global Sources ☎ 852-8199 7308 🖷 852-8199 7628 ✉ visit@chinasourcingfair.com www.chinasourcingfair.com 详细介绍见☆69 Detail see☆69
2013.10.19-22	环球资源家居用品采购交易会 China Sourcing Fair - Home Products	亚洲国际博览馆 AsiaWorld-Expo	环球资源 Global Sources ☎ 852-8199 7308 🖷 852-8199 7628 ✉ visit@chinasourcingfair.com www.chinasourcingfair.com 详细介绍见☆70 Detail see☆70
2013.10.19-22	环球资源医疗及健康用品采购交易会 China Sourcing Fair - Medical & Health Products	亚洲国际博览馆 AsiaWorld-Expo	环球资源 Global Sources ☎ 852-8199 7308 🖷 852-8199 7628 ✉ visit@chinasourcingfair.com www.chinasourcingfair.com 详细介绍见☆71 Detail see☆71
2013.10.19-22	环球资源韩国礼品及赠品采购交易会 Korea Sourcing Fair – Gifts & Premiums	亚洲国际博览馆 AsiaWorld-Expo	环球资源 Global Sources ☎ 852-8199 7308 🖷 852-8199 7628 ✉ visit@chinasourcingfair.com www.chinasourcingfair.com 详细介绍见☆72 Detail see☆72
2013.10.27-30	环球资源流行服饰配件采购交易会 China Sourcing Fair – Fashion Accessories	亚洲国际博览馆 AsiaWorld-Expo	环球资源 Global Sources ☎ 852-8199 7308 🖷 852-8199 7628 ✉ visit@chinasourcingfair.com www.chinasourcingfair.com 详细介绍见☆73 Detail see☆73
2013.10.27-30	环球资源服装及面料采购交易会 China Sourcing Fairs - Garments & Textiles	亚洲国际博览馆 AsiaWorld-Expo	环球资源 Global Sources ☎ 852-8199 7308 🖷 852-8199 7628 ✉ visit@chinasourcingfair.com www.chinasourcingfair.com 详细介绍见☆74 Detail see☆74
2013.10.27-30	环球资源内衣及泳衣采购交易会 China Sourcing Fair – Underwear & Swimwear	亚洲国际博览馆 AsiaWorld-Expo	环球资源 Global Sources ☎ 852-8199 7308 🖷 852-8199 7628 ✉ visit@chinasourcingfair.com www.chinasourcingfair.com 详细介绍见☆75 Detail see☆75

日期 Date	展览会议 Event	地点 Venue	主办 Organizer
2013.10.27-30	环球资源印度服装及配饰采购交易会 India Sourcing Fair - Garments & Accessories	亚洲国际博览馆 AsiaWorld-Expo	环球资源 Global Sources ☎ +852-8199 7308 🖷 +852-8199 7628 ✉ visit@chinasourcingfair.com www.india-sourcingfair.com 详细介绍见☆76 Detail see☆76
2013.10.28-30	香港贸发局香港国际建筑装饰材料及五金展 HKTDC Hong Kong Intl Building and Decoration Materials & Hardware Fair	亚洲国际博览馆 AsiaWorld-Expo	香港贸易发展局 Hong Kong Trade Development Council ☎ 852-1830 668 🖷 852-2824 0249 ✉ exhibitions@hktdc.org www.hktdc.com/hkbdh 详细介绍见☆77 Detail see☆77
2013.10.27-30	香港贸发局香港国际秋季灯饰展 HKTDC Hong Kong Intl Lighting Fair (Autumn Edition)	香港会议展览中心 Hong Kong Convention & Exhibition Centre	香港贸易发展局 Hong Kong Trade Development Council ☎ 852-1830 668 🖷 852-2824 0249 ✉ exhibitions@hktdc.org www.hktdc.com/hklightingfairae 详细介绍见☆78 Detail see☆78
2013.10.28-31	国际环保博览 Eco Expo Asia - Intl Trade Fair on Environmental Protection	亚洲国际博览馆 AsiaWorld-Expo	香港贸易发展局 Hong Kong Trade Development Council ☎ 852-1830 668 🖷 852-2824 0249 ✉ exhibitions@hktdc.org www.ecoexpoasia.com 详细介绍见☆79 Detail see☆79
2013.10.28-30	亚洲运动用品展 Sports Source Asia	亚洲国际博览馆 AsiaWorld-Expo	香港贸易发展局 Hong Kong Trade Development Council ☎ 852-1830 668 🖷 852-2824 0249 ✉ exhibitions@hktdc.org www.sportssource-asia.com 详细介绍见☆80 Detail see☆80
2013.11.6-8	香港贸发局香港眼镜展 HKTDC Hong Kong Optical Fair	香港会议展览中心 Hong Kong Convention & Exhibition Centre	香港贸易发展局 Hong Kong Trade Development Council ☎ 852-1830 668 🖷 852-2824 0249 ✉ exhibitions@hktdc.org www.hktdc.com/hkopticalfair 详细介绍见☆81 Detail see☆81
2013.11.7-9	香港贸发局香港国际美酒展 HKTDC Hong Kong Intl Wine & Spirits Fair	香港会议展览中心 Hong Kon g Convention & Exhibition Centre	香港贸易发展局 Hong Kong Trade Development Council ☎ 852-1830 668 🖷 852-2824 0249 ✉ exhibitions@hktdc.org www.hktdc.com/hkwinefair 详细介绍见☆82 Detail see☆82

日期 Date	展览会议 Event	地点 Venue	主办 Organizer
2013.11.07	亚洲物流及航运会议 Asian Logistics and Maritime Conference	香港会议展览中心 Hong Kong Convention & Exhibition Centre	香港贸易发展局 Hong Kong Trade Development Council ☎ 852-1830 668 🖷 852-2824 0249 ✉ alc@hktdc.org www.asianlogisticsconference.com 详细介绍见☆83 Detail see☆83
2013.11.13-15	亚太区美容展 Cosmoprof Asia	香港会议展览中心 Hong Kong Convention & Exhibition Centre	亚太区美容展有限公司 Cosmoprof Asia Ltd. ☎ 852-2827 6211, 020-8666 0158 🖷 852-3749 7345, 3749 7310, 020-8626 6186, 8667 7120 ✉ cosmasia-hk@ubm.com info-china@ubm.com www.cosmoprof-asia.com 详细介绍见☆84 Detail see☆84
2013.11.27-29	中国新能源汽车展览会 China NEW ENERGY VEHICLE Show	亚洲国际博览馆 AsiaWorld-Expo	EUROPEXPO ☎ +33(0)1 49 52 14 07 🖷 +33(0)1 49 52 14 48 ✉ nev-hk@europ-expo.com www.nev-hk.com 详细介绍见☆85 Detail see☆85
2013.11.13-15	环球电子娱乐博览 GEEE! (Global Electronic Entertainment Expo)	亚洲国际博览馆 AsiaWorld-Expo	MP International (Asia Pacific) Limited ☎ 852-2509 3430 🖷 852-2689 5229 ✉ info@mphk.com www.mphk.com
2013.12	香港贸发局国际中小企博览 HKTDC World SME Expo	香港会议展览中心 Hong Kong Convention & Exhibition Centre	香港贸易发展局 Hong Kong Trade Development Council ☎ 852-1830 668 🖷 852-2824 0249 ✉ hktdc@hktdc.org www.hktdc.com/worldsmeexpo 详细介绍见☆86 Detail see☆86
2013.12	香港贸发局设计及创新科技博览 HKTDC Inno Design Tech Expo	香港会议展览中心 Hong Kong Convention & Exhibition Centre	香港贸易发展局 Hong Kong Trade Development Council ☎ 852-1830 668 🖷 852-2824 0249 ✉ hktdc@hktdc.org www.hktdc.com/innodesigntechexpo 详细介绍见☆87 Detail scc☆87
2013.12	亚洲知识产权营商论坛 Business of IP Asia Forum	香港会议展览中心 Hong Kong Convention & Exhibition Centre	香港贸易发展局 Hong Kong Trade Development Council ☎ 852-1830 668 🖷 852-2824 0249 ✉ bipasia@hktdc.org www.bipasiaforum.com 详细介绍见☆88 Detail see☆88

日期 Date	展览会议 Event	地点 Venue	主办 Organizer
2013.12.10-12	自主生活医疗保健展 Independent Healthcare Living Conference and Expo	亚洲国际博览馆 AsiaWorld-Expo	MP International (Asia Pacific) Limited ☎ 852-2509 3430 🖷 852-2689 5229 ✉ info@mphk.com www.mphk.com
2014.6.3-5	Build4Asia, Asian Securitex 2014	香港会议展览中心 Hong Kong Convention and Exhibition Centre	香港展览服务有限公司 ☎ 852-2804 1500 🖷 852-2528 3103 ✉ exhibit@hkesallworld.com www.build4asia.com

☆1
2013/01/07-08
☎ 852-1830 668
🖷 852-2824 0249
✉ licensingshow@hktdc.org
www.hktdc.com/asianlicensingconference

Asian Licensing Conference

7 – 8 January 2013

亚洲授权业研讨会
地点：香港会议展览中心
内容：国际知名的授权业代表将于研讨会上分享他们丰富的授权业经验，剖析最新的市场动向并阐述他们对授权业发展的看法，讲者们亦会向有兴趣开展授权业务的人士讲解授权业入门的知识和成功要诀。
上届规模2012：参加者572人，来自22个国家及地区
主办：香港贸易发展局
地址：香港湾仔港湾道一号会展广场办公大楼38字楼

Asian Licensing Conference
Venue: Hong Kong Convention & Exhibition Centre
Profile: Top-notch international licensing executives will share their extensive experience in the licensing industry, latest market trends and their insights on future industry developments in a series of thematic sessions. They will also introduce fundamentals of licensing for those who are interested in starting a licensing business.
Statistics 2012: Participants 572, from 22 countries and regions
Organiser: Hong Kong Trade Development Council
Address: 38/F, Office Tower, Convention Plaza, 1 Harbour Road, Wan Chai, Hong Kong

☆2
2013/01/07-09
☎ 852-1830 668
🖷 852-2824 0249
✉ hktdc@hktdc.org
www.hktdc.com/hklicensingshow

HKTDC
Hong Kong International Licensing Show
香港國際授權展

香港贸发局香港国际授权展
地点：香港会议展览中心
内容：产品、设计等授权活动包括品牌或设计、卡通人物、动漫及数码娱乐、艺术设计、专上学府品牌、知名企业品牌、娱乐名人、生活时尚及服饰、运动品牌、设计及市场推广服务、法律及专业顾问服务
上届规模2012：展出面积4,202平方米，参展商173家
主办：香港贸易发展局
地址：香港湾仔港湾道一号会展广场办公大楼38字楼

HKTDC Hong Kong International Licensing Show
Venue: Hong Kong Convention & Exhibition Centre
Profile: Properties and brands for licensing, animation & digital entertainment, art & design, characters, collegiate, corporate brands, entertainment, fashion & lifestyle, sports, design & marketing services, legal & professional services
Statistics 2012: Gross Area 4,202m^2, Exhibitors 173
Organiser: Hong Kong Trade Development Council
Address: 38/F, Office Tower, Convention Plaza, 1 Harbour Road, Wan Chai, Hong Kong

2013/01/07-10
☎ 852-1830 668
🖷 852-2824 0249
✉ exhibitions@hktdc.org
www.hktdc.com/hktoyfair

HKTDC
Hong Kong Toys & Games Fair
香港玩具展

香港贸发局香港玩具展
地点：香港会议展览中心
内容：糖果玩具、益智玩具及游戏、电子及遥控玩具、节目及派对用品、玩具零件及配件、嗜好玩具、魔术用具、综合玩具产品、户外及运动用品、纸品及玩具包装、软身玩具及洋娃娃、检测及认证服务、商贸服务、模型、机械玩具及动作玩偶、电玩游戏
上届规模2012：展出面积57,030平方米，参展商1,820家
主办：香港贸易发展局
地址：香港湾仔博览道1号香港会议展览中心博览商场13号展览事务部

HKTDC Hong Kong Toys & Games Fair
Venue: Hong Kong Convention & Exhibition Centre
Profile: Candy toys, educational toys & games, electronic & remote control toys, festive & party items, toy parts & accessories, hobby goods, magic items, multiple toys products/general merchandise, outdoor & sporting items, paper products & toy packaging, soft toys & dolls, testing, inspection & certification services, trade services, vehicles, mechanical toys & action figures, video games
Statistics 2012: Gross Area 57,030 m^2, Exhibitors 1,820
Organiser: Hong Kong Trade Development Council
Address: Exhibitions Department, Unit 13, Expo Galleria, Hong Kong Convention and Exhibition Centre, 1 Expo Drive, Wan Chai, Hong Kong

☆4
2013/01/07-10
☎ 852-1830 668
🖷 852-2824 0249
✉ exhibitions@hktdc.org
www.hktdc.com/hkbabyfair

HKTDC
Hong Kong Baby Products Fair
香港嬰兒用品展

香港贸发局香港婴儿用品展
地点： 香港会议展览中心
内容： 婴儿寝具及家具、婴儿礼品及纪念品、婴儿护肤及沐浴产品、婴儿玩具、游戏及教学用品、婴儿衣服及鞋、育婴及孕妇用品、育婴电器产品、婴儿手推车及婴儿椅
上届规模 2012：展出面积11,696平方米，参展商370家
主办： 香港贸易发展局
地址： 香港湾仔博览道1号香港会议展览中心博览商场13号展览事务部

HKTDC Hong Kong Baby Products Fair
Venue: Hong Kong Convention & Exhibition Centre
Profile: Baby bedding items and furniture, baby gift sets and souvenirs, baby skincare and bath products, baby toys and activity, baby wear and footwear, feeding, nursery & maternity products, nursery electrical appliances, strollers and gear
Statistics 2012: Gross Area 11,696m^2, Exhibitors 370
Organiser: Hong Kong Trade Development Council
Address: Exhibitions Department, Unit 13, Expo Galleria, Hong Kong Convention and Exhibition Centre, 1 Expo Drive, Wan Chai, Hong Kong

☆5
2013/01/07-10
☎ 852-1830 668
🖷 852-2824 0249
✉ exhibitions@hktdc.org
www.hkstationeryfair.com

Hong Kong International Stationery Fair
香港國際文具展

香港国际文具展
地点： 香港会议展览中心
内容： 美术用品、儿童文具及学校用品、电脑周边设备及配件、办公室设备用消耗品、礼品文具、办公室设备、纸品及印刷品、书写设备
上届规模 2012：展出面积4,901平方米，参展商210家
主办： 香港贸易发展局，法兰克福展览(香港)有限公司
地址： 香港湾仔博览道1号香港会议展览中心博览商场13号展览事务部

Hong Kong International Stationery Fair
Venue: Hong Kong Convention & Exhibition Centre
Profile: Artist supplies, children' s stationery & school supplies, computer peripherals & related accessories, consumables for office equipment, gift stationery, office equipment, paper & printing products, writing equipment
Statistics 2012: Gross Area 4,901m^2, Exhibitors 210
Organisers: Hong Kong Trade Development Council, Messe Frankfurt (HK) Ltd
Address: Exhibitions Department, Unit 13, Expo Galleria, Hong Kong Convention and Exhibition Centre, 1 Expo Drive, Wan Chai, Hong Kong

☆6
2013/01/14-15
☎ 852-1830 668
🖷 852-2824 0249
✉ aff@hktdc.org
www.asianfinancialforum.com

AFF
亞洲金融論壇
ASIAN FINANCIAL FORUM
環球金融新思維
The Voice in Global Finance

亚洲金融论坛
地点： 香港会议展览中心
内容： 亚洲金融论坛是一个环球金融会议，每届论坛均集中讨论重要而且广受关注的经济议题。为期两天的论坛汇聚全球最具影响力的金融专家、政府及监管机构代表以及区内的商界翘楚，深入探讨亚洲面对的发展机遇及挑战。
上届规模2012：参加者2,016人，来自32个国家及地区
主办： 香港贸易发展局，香港特别行政区政府
地址： 香港湾仔港湾道一号会展广场办公大楼38字楼

The Asian Financial Forum
Venue: Hong Kong Convention & Exhibition Centre
Profile: A global financial conference, the Asian Financial Forum (AFF) brings together some of the world' s most influential leaders in business, finance and government to share their insights on the market developments and trends in the Asian region.
Statistics 2012: Participants 2,016, from 32 countries and regions
Organiser: Hong Kong Trade Development Council, the Government of the Hong Kong Special Administrative Region
Address: 38/F, Office Tower, Convention Plaza, 1 Harbour Road, Wan Chai, Hong Kong

☆7
2013/01/14-17
☎ 852-1830 668
🖷 852-2824 0249
✉ exhibitions@hktdc.org
www.hktdc.com/hkfashionweekfw

HKTDC
Hong Kong Fashion Week for Fall/Winter
香港時裝節秋冬系列

香港贸发局香港时装节秋冬系列
地点：香港会议展览中心
内容：女装、男装、婴儿服装、运动服装、内衣、泳衣、新娘礼服及晚礼服、手袋、鞋、流行饰物、布料及纱线、钮扣、唛头、验证、测试及认证服务、时装杂志、专业商贸服务
上届规模 2012：展出面积40,598平方米，参展商1,649家
主办：香港贸易发展局
地址：香港湾仔博览道1号香港会议展览中心博览商场13号展览事务部

HKTDC Hong Kong Fashion Week for Fall/Winter
Venue: Hong Kong Convention & Exhibition Centre
Profile: Ladies' wear, men's wear, babies and children's wear, sportswear, lingerie, swimwear, bridal & evening wear, handbags, shoes, costume jewellery, fabrics & yarns, buttons, labels, inspection, testing & certification, fashion magazines, trade services
Statistics 2012: Gross Area 40,598m^2, Exhibitors 1,649
Organiser: Hong Kong Trade Development Council
Address: Exhibitions Department, Unit 13, Expo Galleria, Hong Kong Convention and Exhibition Centre, 1 Expo Drive, Wan Chai, Hong Kong

☆8
2013/01/14-17
☎ 852-1830 668
🖷 852-2824 0249
✉ exhibitions@hktdc.org
www.hktdc.com/worldboutiquehk

HKTDC
World Boutique, Hong Kong
香港國際時尚薈萃

香港贸发局香港国际时尚荟萃
地点：香港会议展览中心
内容：名牌时装及设计师系列、时装饰品、家居时尚用品及赠品
上届规模 2012：展出面积 8,593平方米，参展商229家
主办：香港贸易发展局
地址：香港湾仔博览道1号香港会议展览中心博览商场13号展览事务部

HKTDC World Boutique, Hong Kong
Venue: Hong Kong Convention & Exhibition Centre
Profile: Fashion designers' collection, branded fashion products, home fashion & lifestyle products, small gifts
Statistics 2012: Gross Area 8,593m^2, Exhibitors 229
Organiser: Hong Kong Trade Development Council
Address: Exhibitions Department, Unit 13, Expo Galleria, Hong Kong Convention and Exhibition Centre, 1 Expo Drive, Wan Chai, Hong Kong

☆9
2013/01/31-02/03
☎ 852-1830 668
🖷 852-2824 0249
✉ exhibitions@hktdc.org
www.hktdc.com/hkeducationexpo

HKTDC
Education & Careers Expo
教育及職業博覽

香港贸发局教育及职业博览
地点：香港会议展览中心
内容：大专院校及理工、大学、专科及进修学校、职业训练机构、语文学校、外地教育机构、政府部门、半政府机构、专业学会、私人机构、出版商及书店、教学／学习辅助器材
上届规模 2012：展出面积8,187平方米，参展商720家
主办：香港贸易发展局
地址：香港湾仔博览道1号香港会议展览中心博览商场13号展览事务部

HKTDC Education & Careers Expo
Venue: Hong Kong Convention & Exhibition Centre
Profile: Colleges & polytechnics, universities, school for continue education, vocational training, language schools, outside Hong Kong educational institutions, government departments, semi-government organisations, professional associations, private enterprises, book publishers/book stores, learning aids/educational equipment
Statistics 2012: Gross Area 8,187m^2, Exhibitors 720
Organiser: Hong Kong Trade Development Council
Address: Exhibitions Department, Unit 13, Expo Galleria, Hong Kong Convention and Exhibition Centre, 1 Expo Drive, Wan Chai, Hong Kong

☆10
2013/02/25-02/27
☎ (44) 20 7749 2313
✉ info@airlineretail.com
www.airlineretail.com

asia-pacific hong kong
arc.2013
AIRLINE RETAIL CONFERENCE

Airline Retail Conference
地点： 亚洲国际博览馆
内容： 航空服务
主办： Airline Retail Conference

Airline Retail Conference
Venue: AsiaWorld-Expo
Profile: Conference on Airline service
Organiser: Airline Retail Conference

☆11
2013/03/04-07
参展 To exhibit
☎ 852-2585 6179
📠 852-3749 7542
✉ salesafj-hk@ubm.com
参展 To visit
☎ 852-2585 6127
📠 852-3749 7344
✉ visitafj-hk@ubm.com
www.asiafja.com

Asia's Fashion Jewellery & Accessories Fair
亞洲時尚首飾及配飾展
4 - 7 March 2013
二〇一三年三月四至七日

三月亚洲时尚首饰及配饰展
地点： 亚洲国际博览馆
内容： 时尚首饰: 非贵金属首饰、珠子首饰、珐琅及白蜡首饰、宝石首饰、半宝石首饰、合成宝石或仿宝石首饰、玻璃首饰、天然物料首饰、塑料首饰、纯银首饰及配饰。时尚配饰: 皮带及配饰、时尚手表、发饰、手袋、钱包、头饰及颈饰; 时尚首饰原料: 珠子、宝石—未经打磨及打磨宝石、半宝石、合成宝石或仿宝石、首饰配件及组件、天然物料；陈列及包装: 陈列物料、礼盒
周期： 每年三届（三月、六月、九月）
市场范围： 国际性
展览性质： 只对专业观众开放
上届规模 2012：展商总数327家（来自15国家），贸易观众4,207人(来自92个国家和地区)
主办： 亚洲博闻有限公司

Asia's Fashion Jewellery & Accessories Fair - March
Venue: AsiaWorld-Expo, Hong Kong
Profile: Fashion Jewellery, Fashion Jewellery Materials, Fashion accessories, Display and packaging
Frequency: Three times a year (March, June, September)
Market Area: International
Nature: Trade only
Statistics 2011: Exhibitors 327 came from 15 countries and regions, Trade Visitors 4,207 came from 92 countries and regions
Organizer: UBM Asia Limited

☆12
2013/03/05-09
☎ 852-1830 668
📠 852-2824 0249
✉ exhibitions@hktdc.org
www.hktdc.com/hkjewelleryshow

HKTDC
Hong Kong International Jewellery Show
香港國際珠寶展

香港贸发局香港国际珠宝展
地点： 香港会议展览中心
内容： 珠宝首饰、银首饰、制成首饰、古董首饰、翡翠首饰、钻石、贵重宝石、南洋珠及大溪地珍珠、淡水珠及养珠、半宝石、珠宝配件、宝石陈列及包装用品、工具及仪器、珠宝刊物及服务、贸易商会、品牌表及时钟、成表及时钟
上届规模2012： 展出面积93,872平方米，参展商3,118家
主办： 香港贸易发展局
地址： 香港湾仔博览道1号香港会议展览中心博览商场13号展览事务部

HKTDC Hong Kong International Jewellery Show
Venue: Hong Kong Convention & Exhibition Centre, Hong Kong
Profile: Fine jewellery, silver jewellery, finished jewellery, antique jewellery, jade jewellery, diamonds, precious stones, south sea pearls & Tahiti pearls, fresh water & cultured pearls, semi-precious stones, jewellery accessories, jewellery display & packaging material, jewellery tools & equipment, trade publications & services, trade associations, brand name watches & clocks, complete watches & clocks
Statistics 2012: Gross Area93,872m^2, Exhibitors 3,118
Organiser: Hong Kong Trade Development Council
Address: Exhibitions Department, Unit 13, Expo Galleria, Hong Kong Convention and Exhibition Centre, 1 Expo Drive, Wan Chai, Hong Kong

☆13
2013/03/11-14
☎ 852-3943 7597
🖷 852-2603 5402
✉ apaie2013@cuhk.edu.hk
www.apaie.org

The Chinese University of Hong Kong

亚太国际教育协会年会暨展览
地点：　亚洲国际博览馆
内容：　国际教育课程及服务
主办：　香港中文大学

Asia-Pacific Association for International Education 2013 Conference and Exhibition
Venue: AsiaWorld-Expo
Profile: Organization' s programmes and services
Organiser: The Chinese University of Hong Kong

☆14
2013/03/18-20
☎ (49) 89 1295440
🖷 (49) 89 13936704
✉ info@cong-o.de
www.lincasiapacific.com

LINC Asia-Pacific 2013
地点：　亚洲国际博览馆
内容：　医疗服务
主办：　Congress Organisation and More GmbH

LINC Asia-Pacific 2013
Venue: AsiaWorld-Expo
Profile: Conference on medical topics
Organiser: Congress Organisation and More GmbH

☆15
2013/03/18-21
☎ 852-1830 668
🖷 852-2824 0249
✉ hktdc@hkTDC.org
www.hktdc.com/hkfilmart

HKTDC
Hong Kong International Film & TV Market (FILMART)
香港國際影視展

香港贸发局香港国际影视展
地点：　香港会议展览中心
内容：　电影、电视节目、动画、数码娱乐、有关产品及服务
上届规模 2012：展出面积14,624平方米，参展商596家
主办：　香港贸易发展局
地址：　香港湾仔港湾道1号会展广场办公大楼38楼

HKTDC Hong Kong International Film & TV Market (FILMART)
Venue: Hong Kong Convention & Exhibition Centre
Profile: Movies, TV programmes, animation, digital entertainment, related products & services
Statistics 2012: Gross Area 14,624m^2, Exhibitors 596
Organiser: Hong Kong Trade Development Council
Address: 38/F, Office Tower, Convention Plaza, 1 Harbour Road, Wan Chai, Hong Kong

☆16
2013.3.19-21
☎ 010-5933 9364
✉ adeline.desages@reedexpo.com.cn
www.asianaerospace.com

ABA Asian Business Aviation

亚洲商务航空展览会
地点：　香港机场商用航空中心
内容：　带您通往全球最具活力的中国与亚洲商务航空市场。产品和服务包括飞机内部设计、飞机维护与运营、飞机制造、飞机市场销售、管理和相关服务、机身和飞机组件、机场和机场运营、私人飞机运营、固定基地运营、商务和金融服务、教育培训、电子、 航空电子设备和仪器、发动机和推进器、飞行计划和导航、地面运营、行业组织、飞机中产区

和服务、出版、安全、安保和应急准备、工具和测试设备、交通服务。
主办： 励展博览集团

Asian Business Aviation
Venue: The Hong Kong Business Aviation Centre
Profile: Products & Services, Aircraft interior, Aircraft maintenance and operations, Aircraft manufacturers, Aircraft market sales, Management and related services, Airframe and aircraft components, Airports and airport operations, Private jet operators, FBOs, Business and financial services, Education training, Electronics, Avionics and instrumentation, Engines and propellers, Flight planning and navigation, Ground operations, Industry organizations, In-flight products and services, Publications, Safety, security and emergency preparation, Tools and test equipment, Transportation services.
Organizer: Reed Exhibitions

☆17
2013.3.19-21
☎ 852-2965 1603
🖷 852-2824 0246
✉ brian.thomas@reedexpo.com.hk
www.asianaerospace.com

ASIAN AEROSPACE INTERNATIONAL EXPO AND CONGRESS 2013

亚洲国际航空展览会暨论坛
地点： 亚洲国际博览馆
内容： 亚洲国际航空展览会暨论坛是亚洲领先商用及民用航空业展会，是世界上最大的专著于商用和民用航空市场的单一主题展览会和论坛。亚洲国际航空展览会将整合行业资源突出体现世界航空业对亚洲行业发展的高度关注，为那些具有远景规划的商业航空企业及专业人士提供独一无二的“一站式采购”机会，从而继续助力航空企业发展重要的战略伙伴关系，拉近中国，亚洲与世界的距离。
产品及服务： 飞机包租、运输服务，航空货运公司，航空物流、供应链管理，空中交通管制系统，飞机经纪人、经销商和分销商，飞机、机身构造制造商，飞机室内设计及设备-设备与服务，飞机零件和附件，航空公司，机场、航站楼管理，机场系统/基础设施、服务，航空电子设备及雷达系统，餐饮设备、服务，化学品、油漆、涂料，民用飞机设计与工程，元件工程维修和检查，复合材料/航空材料，顾问、代理，引擎制造商、零部件，金融、银行、租赁、保险服务， 固定基地运营商、燃油供应商，航班规划和气象服务，飞行培训、学校与服务机构、研究院，政府部门、立法机构，机场航空管理局、运营商、行政管理部门，地面支持设备、运输，直升飞机，航载娱乐、通信系统，维护、修理和检修、工程，媒体、出版，医疗、救援，安全、逃生、急救，安全系统、服务-飞机/机场，软件系统、服务与应用，模拟、培训设备与服务，太空、卫星设备与服务，系统制造商，测试设备与服务，行业协会、其他工业组织。
周期： 两年一届
主办： 励展博览集团

Asian Aerospace 2013
Asian Aerospace International Expo and Congress
Venue: AsiaWorld-Expo
Profile: Asian Aerospace (Asian Aerospace International Expo and Congress) is the leading B2B commercial aerospace event embraces key sectors – MRO, manufacturing, business aviation, interiors and training.
Asian Aerospace 2013 will also feature the popular AA Congress, in conjunction with Airline Business - the must attend event for lively discussion and engaging debate on air transport trends and infrastructure.
Frequency: Biennial
Organizer: Reed Exhibitions Ltd

☆18
2013.3.19-21
☎ 010-5933 9209
✉ martin.du@reedexpo.com.cn
www.airfreightasia.com

AIR FREIGHT ASIA 2013

亚洲航空物流技术展览会
地点： 亚洲国际博览馆
内容： 汇聚全球物流精英，引领亚洲空运展会。亚洲航空物流技术展览会暨论坛将在2013年竭诚为所有参与者提供一个宝贵的机会与业界同仁直面交流。。香港是一处东方航空运输及供应链管理的物流企业与西方同行交流的理想之地。位于中国南大门，香港地理位置优越，是亚洲乃至世界各国进入中国巨大市场的跳板。
周期： 两年一届
主办： 励展博览集团

Air Freight Asia
Venue: AsiaWorld-Expo
Profile: The Air Freight Asia Conference and Exhibition is a biennial event for the global air freight

industry. In 2013, logistics in supply chain management will be new element at the event. Hong Kong is where Eastern air freight and logistics business involved in supply chain management engage with their Western counterparts. Strategically located in South China, Hong Kong is the gateway to the China market or industries from across the globe.

Frequency: Biennial
Organizer: Reed Exhibitions

☆19
2013.3.21-23
☎ 852- 2162 1888
✉ dist.serv@hk.usana.com
http://apconvention.usana.com

USANA 亚太区年会2013
地点： 亚洲国际博览馆
主办： USANA Health Sciences

USANA Asia Pacific Convention 2013
Venue: AsiaWorld-Expo
Organizer: USANA Health Sciences

☆20
2013.3.25-27
☎ 852-2827 6211
020-20 8666 0158
🖷 852-3749 7346
020-20 8667 2235
✉ info@aplf.com
www.aplf.com

时尚汇集（春季）
手袋、行李箱包、鞋类、皮衣、裘皮服装及时尚配饰展（FAS）
地点： 香港会议展览中心
内容： 各类鞋类、箱包、手袋、皮带、钱包、皮衣、时尚配饰、传播媒介及其他
周期： 每年两届
市场范围： 国际性
展览性质： 仅向贸易观众开放
上届规模 2012：展商总数588家来自25个国家及地区，买家12,901人
主办： 亚太区皮革展有限公司 （亚洲博闻有限公司及 SIC集团合办）

Fashion Access - Spring Show
Venue: Hong Kong Convention & Exhibition Center
Profile: Variety of footwear; luggage; leather products; garment and finished decoration accessories; press and others
Frequency: Biannual
Market Area: International
Nature: Trade only
Statistics 2012: Exhibitors 588 came from 25 countries and regions, Buyers 12,901
Organizer: APLF Limited

☆21
2013/03/25-27
☎ 852-2827 6211
020-8666 0158
🖷 852-3479 7346
020-8667 2235
✉ sales@aplf.com
Info-china@ubm.com
www.mmt.aplf.com

2013年亚太区皮革展　原料及制造技术展
地点： 香港会议展览中心
内容： 皮革；化工；机械；配件等皮革原料；生产技术/品质认证及检测 / 其他服务
周期： 每年一届

市场范围：　国际性
展览性质：　面向贸易观众
上届规模 2012：买家19,089 人来自91个国家及地区
主办：　亚太区皮革展有限公司 （亚洲博闻有限公司及 SIC集团合办）

APLF-MM&T
Asia Pacific Leather Fair 2013 - Materials, Manufacturing and Technology
Venue: Hong Kong Convention and Exhibition Centre
Profile: Raw Materials ; Synthetic /Textiles; Chemicals & Dyes; Tanning & Footwear Machinery; Components & Accessories; Technology, Testing Laboratories and Other Services
Frequency: Annual
Market Area: International
Nature: Trade only
Statistics 2012: Buyers 19,089 came from 91 countries & regions
Organizer: APLF Ltd.

☆22
2013/03/25-27
☎ 852-2827 6211
020-20 8666 0158
🖷 852-3749 7346
020-20 8667 2235
✉ sales@aplf.com
info-china@ubm.com
www.fashionaccess.aplf.com

PRIME SOURCE FORUM HONG KONG

国际时尚服装业高峰论坛
地点：　香港会议展览中心
内容：　论坛云集全球高级管理人员，彼此就制造商、供货商及零售商所面对的挑战及机遇作出研讨，以改善成衣/纺织的生产与销售。这项国际盛事能让与会代表结识同业及各位专家，并可跟同业及竞争者就共同关注的事项交换意见。
周期：　每年一届
始办年份：　2006
主办：　亚太区皮革展有限公司 （亚洲博闻有限公司及 SIC集团合办）

Prime Source Forum 2012
Venue: Hong Kong Convention & Exhibition Center
Frequency: Annual
Established Year: 2006
Organizer: APLF Ltd

☆23
2013/03/27-28
☎ 33- 01 7677 1300
🖷 33- 01 5330 9514
✉ isabelle.alfano@comexposium.com
www.cartes-asia.com

CARTES SECURE CONNEXIONS EVENT ASIA

亚洲智能卡工业展
地点：　亚洲国际博览馆
内容：　面向卡制造、支付、安全、身份识别及移动性解决方案
主办：　Comexposium

CARTES in Asia 2013
Venue: AsiaWorld-Expo
Profile: Card manufacturing, payment, security, identification and mobility solutions
Organiser: Comexposium

☆24
2013/04/06-09
☎ 852-1830 668
🖷 852-2824 0249
✉ exhibitions@hktdc.org
www.hktdc.com/hklightingfairse

HKTDC
Hong Kong International Lighting Fair (Spring Edition)
香港國際春季燈飾展

香港贸发局香港国际春季灯饰展
地点：　香港会议展览中心
内容：　商业照明、环保照明、装饰照明、LED照明、灯饰配件及零件、零售及照明、专业及户外照明、贸易服务及刊物
上届规模 2012：展出面积25,322平方米，参展商954家
主办：　香港贸易发展局
地址：　香港湾仔博览道1号香港会议展览中心博览商场13号展览事务部

HKTDC Hong Kong International Lighting Fair (Spring Edition)
Venue: Hong Kong Convention & Exhibition Centre, Hong Kong

Profile: Commercial lighting, decorative lighting, green lighting, LED lighting, lighting accessories, parts & components, retail lighting, design & technology, technical and outdoor lighting, trade service & publication
Statistics 2012: Gross Area 25,322m^2, Exhibitors 954
Organiser: Hong Kong Trade Development Council
Address: Exhibitions Department, Unit 13, Expo Galleria, Hong Kong Convention and Exhibition Centre, 1 Expo Drive, Wan Chai, Hong Kong

☆25
2013/04/12-15
☎ 852- 8199 7308
🖷 852-8199 7628
✉ visit@chinasourcingfair.com
www.chinasourcingfair.com

环球资源电子产品及零件采购交易会
地点： 亚洲国际博览馆
内容： 电脑周边产、品 电脑终端机、网络产品、个人数码电子产品、消费类电子产品及配件、电子零件、连接件、电源设备、车载电子产品、全球定位系统、通信产品、智能手机、家庭影音娱乐设备、电子产品专用包、苹果产品周边配件、平板电脑及配件
主办： 环球资源

China Sourcing Fair – Electronics & Components
Venue: AsiaWorld-Expo
Profile: Computer Peripherals , iProducts Accessories, Consumer Electronics & Accessories, Personal Digital Electronics, In-Car Electronics, Telecom products, Electronic Components, Interconnects, Home Entertainment, Power Supplies, Smartphones, GPS, Tablets & accessories, Computer Terminals, Networking Products , Bags & cases
Organiser: Global Sources

☆26
2013/04/12-15
☎ 852- 8199 7308
🖷 852-8199 7628
✉ visit@chinasourcingfair.com
www.chinasourcingfair.com

环球资源安防产品采购交易会
地点： 亚洲国际博览馆
内容： CCTV及数码监视器、门禁系统及无线射频、 防盗报警器及传感器、家居安防及系统整合、安全及防火设备产品
主办： 环球资源

China Sourcing Fair – Security Products
Venue: AsiaWorld-Expo
Profile: CCTV & Digital Surveillance, Access Control & RFID, Home and system integration , Alarms, Fire and Safety products
Organiser: Global Sources

☆27
2013/04/12-15
☎ 852- 8199 7308
🖷 852-8199 7628
✉ visit@chinasourcingfair.com
www.chinasourcingfair.com

环球资源韩国电子产品及零件采购交易会
地点： 亚洲国际博览馆
内容： 消费类电子产品及配件、家庭影音娱乐设备、个人数码电子产品、通信及无线产品、移动电话及配件、车载电子产品、音响设备及配件、电脑终端机及周边产品、电子零件、安防产品、苹果产品周边配件、电子产品专用包、平板电脑及移动设备配件
主办： 环球资源

Korea Sourcing Fair – Electronics & Components
Venue: AsiaWorld-Expo
Profile: Telecom Products & Wireless, iProducts Accessories , Computer Peripherals , Consumer Electronics & Accessories, In-Car Electronics
Organiser: Global Sources

☆28
2013/04/13-16
☎ 852-1830 668
🖷 852-2824 0249
✉ exhibitions@hktdc.org
www.hktdc.com/hkelectronicsfairse

HKTDC

Hong Kong Electronics Fair (Spring Edition)
香港春季電子產品展

香港贸发局香港春季电子产品展
地点： 香港会议展览中心
内容： 视听产品、汽车零配件、健美产品、关键元件、数码影像产品、电子配件、电子游戏产品、电子制造服务、电子组件及生产技术、环保节能、高清显像、电子保健产品、家用电器、汽车电子及导航系统、办公室自动化及设备、个人电子产品、电子产品保护／储存设备、保安产品、智能手机及平板电脑配件、太阳能光伏技术、创新科技、电讯产品、检测和认证、商贸服务
上届规模 2012：展出面积65,923平方米，参展商2,511家
主办： 香港贸易发展局
地址： 香港湾仔博览道1号香港会议展览中心博览商场13号展览事务部

HKTDC Hong Kong Electronics Fair (Spring Edition)
Venue: Hong Kong Convention & Exhibition Centre
Profile: Audio & visual, auto parts & accessories, beauty and fitness, critical components, digital imaging, electronic accessories, electronic gaming, electronic manufacturing services (EMS), electronic parts, components and production technology, green and energy saving, HD (High Definition Display & Electronics), healthcare electronics, home appliances, in-vehicle electronics & navigation systems, office automation & equipment, personal electronics, protective & storage solutions for electronics, security products, smartphone & tablet accessories, solar photovoltaic technology, technology and innovation, telecommunication products, testing and certification & inspection, trade services
Statistics 2012: Gross Area 65,923m^2, Exhibitors 2,511
Organiser: Hong Kong Trade Development Council
Address: Exhibitions Department, Unit 13, Expo Galleria, Hong Kong Convention and Exhibition Centre, 1 Expo Drive, Wan Chai, Hong Kong

☆29
2013/04/13-16
☎ 852-1830 668
🖷 852- 2824 0249
✉ exhibitions@hktdc.org
www.hktdc.com/ictexpo

HKTDC

International ICT Expo
國際資訊科技博覽

香港贸发局国际资讯科技博览
地点： 香港会议展览中心
内容： 手机用程序及广告推广、云端运算及开放源码、数码生活及多媒体、电子物流及零售科技、企业解决方案及资讯科技外包服务、本土创意科技、智能电话及平板电脑、电讯、网络、及无线科技、商贸服务
上届规模 2012：展出面积8,597平方米，参展商590家
主办： 香港贸易发展局
地址： 香港湾仔博览道1号香港会议展览中心博览商场13号展览事务部

HKTDC International ICT Expo
Venue: Hong Kong Convention & Exhibition Centre, Hong Kong
Profile: Apps & mobile marketing, cloud computing & open source, digital living & multimedia, e-logistics & retail technologies, enterprise solutions & IT outsourcing, home-grown innovations, smartphone & tablet, telecom, networking & wireless technologies, trade services
Statistics 2012: Gross Area 8,597m^2, Exhibitors 590
Organiser: Hong Kong Trade Development Council
Address: Exhibitions Department, Unit 13, Expo Galleria, Hong Kong Convention and Exhibition Centre, 1 Expo Drive, Wan Chai, Hong Kong

☆30
2013/04/19-22
☎ 852-8199 7308
🖷 852- 8199 7628
✉ visit@chinasourcingfair.com
www.chinasourcingfair.com

global sources
Baby & Children's Products
China Sourcing Fair

环球资源婴儿及儿童产品采购交易会
地点： 亚洲国际博览馆
内容： 服装、床上用品、家具、安全产品、护理及沐浴产品、喂食产品、旅行产品、鞋类产品、流行服饰及配件、包袋、玩具、游戏及益智拼图、面具及服饰、户外游乐设施
主办： 环球资源

China Sourcing Fair – Baby & Children's Products
Venue: AsiaWorld-Expo
Profile: Toys, Baby & Children's Garment, Footwear, Baby Care Products, Bedding & Furniture
Statistics 2012: Gross Area 52,616m^2, Exhibitors 1,703
Organiser: Global Sources

☆31
2013/04/19-22
☎ 852- 8199 7308
🖷 852- 8199 7628
✉ visit@chinasourcingfair.com
www.chinasourcingfair.com

环球资源圣诞及节日产品采购交易会
地点：亚洲国际博览馆
内容：圣诞装饰、圣诞饰品、万圣节装饰、节日灯饰、派对装饰、复活节装饰、圣诞树、圣诞袜子、派对用品、情人节装饰
主办：环球资源

China Sourcing Fair – Christmas & Seasonal Products
Venue: AsiaWorld-Expo
Profile: Christmas & Seasonal, Party Products
Organiser: Global Sources

☆32
2013/04/19-22
☎ 852- 8199 7308
🖷 852- 8199 7628
✉ visit@chinasourcingfair.com
www.chinasourcingfair.com

环球资源礼品及赠品采购交易会
地点：亚洲国际博览馆
内容：运动及活动礼赠品、电子赠品、手表及时钟、文具及纸制品、礼盒、小饰品盒及珠宝盒、普通礼品、苹果产品促销配件
主办：环球资源

China Sourcing Fair – Gifts & Premiums
Venue: AsiaWorld-Expo
Profile: Stationery & Paper, Electronic premiums, Watches & clocks , General gifts, Promotional Bags , Gifts, trinkets and jewelry boxes , Flags, Banners & Accessories, Souvenir Items, Promotional iProduct Accessories, Brand zone
Organiser: Global Sources

☆33
2013/04/19-22
☎ 852- 8199 7308
🖷 852- 8199 7628
✉ visit@chinasourcingfair.com
www.chinasourcingfair.com

环球资源家居用品采购交易会
地点：亚洲国际博览馆
内容：厨具及餐桌用品、烘烤及烹饪用具、酒具及酒吧用具、玻璃及陶瓷制品、家居用品、宠物护理产品、浴室用品、家居装饰品、家用纺织品、家用电器、户外家具及装饰用品、运动及休闲用品、运动包袋及旅行产品、DIY及家居装饰产品
主办：环球资源

China Sourcing Fair – Home Products
Venue: AsiaWorld-Expo
Profile: Kitchenware & Tableware, Bakeware & cookware, Sports Bags & Travel Goods, Bathroom Products & Accessories, Household products , Home Decor , Glassware & Ceramic , Home Textiles, Home appliances, Outdoor furniture and decorations, Petcare Products, Wine and bar accessories, Sports & Leisure
Organiser: Global Sources

☆34
2013/04/19-22
☎ 852- 8199 7308
🖷 852- 8199 7628
✉ visit@chinasourcingfair.com
www.chinasourcingfair.com

环球资源医疗及健康用品采购交易会
地点：亚洲国际博览馆
内容：个人护理产品、健康及保健、家用医疗设备及供应、水疗设备及用品、美容化妆品

主办： 环球资源

China Sourcing Fair – Medical & Health Products
Venue: AsiaWorld-Expo
Profile: Medical & Health Products
Organiser: Global Sources

☆35
2013/04/19-22
☎ 852- 8199 7308
🖷 852- 8199 7628
✉ visit@chinasourcingfair.com
www.chinasourcingfair.com

global sources Solar & Energy Saving Products China Sourcing Fair

环球资源太阳能及节能产品采购交易会
地点： 亚洲国际博览馆
内容： 太阳能应用产品、LED家用照明
主办： 环球资源

China Sourcing Fair – Solar & Energy Saving Products
Venue: AsiaWorld-Expo
Profile: Energy Efficient Light and Accessories, Solar and Wind Power Products
Organiser: Global Sources

☆36
2013/04/19-22
☎ 852- 8199 7308
🖷 852- 8199 7628
✉ visit@chinasourcingfair.com
www.chinasourcingfair.com

global sources Gifts & Premiums Korea Sourcing Fair

环球资源韩国礼品及赠品采购交易会
地点： 亚洲国际博览馆
内容： 普通礼品、电子赠品、运动礼赠品、圣诞及节日礼品、旅行用品、礼品包装及配饰、纪念品、工艺品、保健及美容用品、家用电子产品、玻璃制品、家用器具、婴儿用品及护理品
主办： 环球资源

Korea Sourcing Fair – Gifts & Premiums
Venue: AsiaWorld-Expo
Profile: Korean Gifts & Premiums
Organiser: Global Sources

☆37
2013/04/20-23
☎ 852-1830 668
🖷 852- 2824 0249
✉ exhibitions@hktdc.org
www.hktdc.com/hkhousewarefair

HKTDC
Hong Kong Houseware Fair
香港家庭用品展

香港贸发局香港家庭用品展
地点： 香港会议展览中心
内容： 人造花饰、酒吧用具、浴室用具、美容及健身用品、蜡烛及香薰饰品、清洁用品、家具、园艺及户外用品、手工艺品、五金用具及自行装配产品、保健及个人护理产品、家居装饰品、厨具及厨房小器具、油画及艺术作品、宠物用品、长者用品、小型家庭电器、餐具、商贸服务
上届规模 2012：展出面积52,616平方米，参展商1,703家
主办： 香港贸易发展局
地址： 香港湾仔博览道1号香港会议展览中心博览商场13号展览事务部

HKTDC Hong Kong Houseware Fair
Venue: Hong Kong Convention & Exhibition Centre
Profile: Artificial flowers, bar accessories, bathroom accessories, beauty & fitness, candles & scent sensation, cleaning & supplies, furniture, gardening & outdoor accessories, handicrafts, hardware & DIY products, health & personal care items, home decorations, kitchenware and gadgets, paintings & objets d' Art, pet supplies, silver generation products, small electrical appliances, tableware, trade services
Statistics 2012: Gross Area 52,616m^2, Exhibitors 1,703
Organiser: Hong Kong Trade Development Council
Address: Exhibitions Department, Unit 13, Expo Galleria, Hong Kong Convention and Exhibition Centre, 1 Expo Drive, Wan Chai, Hong Kong

☆38
2013/04/20-23
☎ 852-1830 668
📠 852-2824 0249
✉ exhibitions@hktdc.org
www.hktdc.com/hkhometextilesfair

Hong Kong International Home Textiles and Furnishings Fair
香港國際家用紡織品展

香港贸发局香港国际家用纺织品展
地点： 香港会议展览中心
内容： 婴儿及寝室纺织品、浴室及厨房纺织品、地毡及铺地制品、装饰布艺及墙纸、窗户时尚及配件、设计及贸易服务
上届规模 2012：展出面积5,790平方米，参展商221家
主办： 香港贸易发展局
地址： 香港湾仔博览道1号香港会议展览中心博览商场13号展览事务部

HKTDC Hong Kong International Home Textiles and Furnishings Fair
Venue: Hong Kong Convention & Exhibition Centre
Profile: Baby & bedroom textiles, bathroom & kitchen textiles, carpet & floor coverings, upholstery & furnishing products, window' s fashion & accessories, design & trade services
Statistics 2012: Gross Area 5,790m^2, Exhibitors 221
Organiser: Hong Kong Trade Development Council
Address: Exhibitions Department, Unit 13, Expo Galleria, Hong Kong Convention and Exhibition Centre, 1 Expo Drive, Wan Chai, Hong Kong

☆39
2013/04/27-30
☎ 852-1830 668
📠 852-2824 0249
✉ exhibitions@hktdc.org
www.hktdc.com/hkgiftspremiumfair

Hong Kong Gifts & Premium Fair
香港禮品及贈品展

香港贸发局香港礼品及赠品展
地点： 香港会议展览中心
内容： 宣传赠品及赠品、公司礼品、时尚首饰及饰品、小型摆设及装饰品、综合礼品、绿色礼品、行李及旅游用品、包装产品、派对及节庆用品/新婚贺礼及用品、个人及健康礼品、画框及相架、文具及纸品、科技礼品、检测及认证服务、玩具及体育用品、雨伞及户外用品、钟表、商贸服务
上届规模 2012：展出面积79,079平方米，参展商3,805家
主办： 香港贸易发展局
地址： 香港湾仔博览道1号香港会议展览中心博览商场13号展览事务部

HKTDC Hong Kong Gifts & Premium Fair
Venue: Hong Kong Convention & Exhibition Centre, Hong Kong
Profile: Advertising gifts & premium, corporate gifts, fashion jewellery & accessories, figurines & decorations, general gift items, green gifts, luggage & travel goods, packaging, party & festive items/wedding favours, personal & well-being gifts, pictures & photo frames, stationery & paper, tech gifts, testing, inspection & certification, toys & sporting goods, umbrella and outdoor goods, watches & clocks, trade services
Statistics 2012: Gross Area 79,079m^2, Exhibitors 3,805
Organiser: Hong Kong Trade Development Council
Address: Exhibitions Department, Unit 13, Expo Galleria, Hong Kong Convention and Exhibition Centre, 1 Expo Drive, Wan Chai, Hong Kong

☆40
2013/04/27-30
☎ 852- 8199 7308
📠 852- 8199 7628
✉ visit@chinasourcingfair.com
www.chinasourcingfair.com

global sources Fashion Accessories China Sourcing Fair

环球资源流行服饰配件采购交易会
地点： 亚洲国际博览馆
内容： 休闲及时尚手袋、晚装包、皮包、发饰及配件、 头饰品、时尚珠宝首饰、围巾及披肩、时尚腰带、 时尚鞋类、手套类产品、袜类产品、 伞类产品
主办： 环球资源

China Sourcing Fair – Fashion Accessories
Venue: AsiaWorld-Expo
Profile: Headwear, Scarves & Gloves, Casual & Fashion Bags , Fashion jewelry , Socks, Fashion Belts, Evening Bags, Fashion Footwear
Organiser: Global Sources

☆41
2013/04/27-30
☎ 852- 8199 7308
📠 852- 8199 7628
✉ visit@chinasourcingfair.com
www.chinasourcingfair.com

环球资源服装及面料采购交易会
地点：　亚洲国际博览馆
内容：　服装成衣、运动装/休闲装、儿童服饰、毛衣及针织衫、面料、花边及服装辅料
主办：　环球资源

China Sourcing Fairs - Garments & Textiles
Venue: AsiaWorld-Expo
Profile: Casual wear, Garments, Sweater & Knitwear , Fabrics, Lace and Trimmings , Children's wear
Organiser: Global Sources

☆42
2013/04/27-30
☎ 852- 8199 7308
📠 852- 8199 7628
✉ visit@chinasourcingfair.com
www.chinasourcingfair.com

环球资源内衣及泳衣采购交易会
地点：　亚洲国际博览馆
内容：　内衣、泳衣及沙滩装、睡衣
主办：　环球资源

China Sourcing Fair – Underwear & Swimwear
Venue: AsiaWorld-Expo
Profile: Underwear & sleepwear , Swimwear & Beachwear
Organiser: Global Sources

☆43
2013/04/27-30
☎ 852- 8199 7308
📠 852- 8199 7628
✉ visit@chinasourcingfair.com
www.chinasourcingfair.com

环球资源印度服装及配饰采购交易会
地点：　亚洲国际博览馆
内容：　休闲及时尚手袋、晚装包、皮包、发饰及配件、帽类产品、太阳镜、时尚珠宝首饰、针织品、领带、围巾及披肩、时尚腰带、休闲及时尚鞋类产品、手套类产品、袜类产品、伞类产品、男女服装、服装辅料
主办：　环球资源

India Sourcing Fair - Garments & Accessories
Venue: AsiaWorld-Expo
Profile: Indian Garments & Accessories
Organiser: Global Sources

☆44
2013/04/27-30
☎ 852-1830 668
📠 852-2824 0249
✉ exhibitions@hktdc.org
www.hkprintpackfair.com

香港国际印刷及包装展
地点：　亚洲国际博览馆
内容：　印刷服务、包装服务、食品及饮料包装方案、环保印刷及包装方案、印刷耗材及包装材料、印刷及包装设备、数码印刷设备、综合包装方案、综合印前及贸易服务
上届规模 2012：展出面积7,976平方米，参展商345家
主办：　香港贸易发展局，华港国际展览有限公司
地址：　香港湾仔博览道1号香港会议展览中心博览商场13号展览事务部

Hong Kong International Printing & Packaging Fair

Venue: AsiaWorld-Expo

Profile: Printing services, packaging services, food and beverage packaging solutions, green printing & packaging solutions, printing consumables & packaging materials, printing & packaging equipment, digital printing equipment, integrated packaging solution, integrated pre-press & trade service

Statistics 2012: Gross Area 7,976m^2, Exhibitors 345

Organiser: Hong Kong Trade Development Council, CIEC Exhibition Company (HK) Limited

Address: Exhibitions Department, Unit 13, Expo Galleria, Hong Kong Convention and Exhibition Centre, 1 Expo Drive, Wan Chai, Hong Kong

☆45
2013/05/8-9
☎ 44 (0) 1293 783 851
🖷 44 (0) 1293 782 959
www.futuretravelexperience.com/fteasia

FUTURE TRAVEL EXPERIENCE ASIA
CHECK-IN // BAGGAGE // SECURITY // IMMIGRATION // BOARDING // ARRIVALS

Future Travel Experience Asia 2013

地点： 亚洲国际博览馆

内容： 旅游服务

主办： PPS Publications Limited

地址： 香港湾仔博览道1号香港会议展览中心博览商场13号展览事务部

Future Travel Experience Asia 2013

Venue: AsiaWorld-Expo

Profile: Conference on travel experience

Organiser: PPS Publications Limited

Address: Exhibitions Department, Unit 13, Expo Galleria, Hong Kong Convention and Exhibition Centre, 1 Expo Drive, Wan Chai, Hong Kong

☆46
2013/05/14-16
☎ 852-1830 668
🖷 852-2824 0249
✉ exhibitions@hktdc.org
www.hktdc.com/hkmedicalfair

HKTDC

Hong Kong International Medical Devices and Supplies Fair
香港國際醫療器材及用品展

香港贸发局香港国际医疗器材及用品展

地点： 香港会议展览中心

内容： 意外及急救设备、建筑科技及医院家具、中医设备、通讯、系统及资讯科技、牙科设备及用品、诊断、电子医疗设备/医疗科技、化验室设备、医疗设备部件及物料、医疗用品及消耗用品、物理治疗/整形外科/复康技术及设备、医疗纺织品、商贸服务及刊物

上届规模2012： 展出面积4,172平方米，参展商168家

主办： 香港贸易发展局

地址： 香港湾仔博览道1号香港会议展览中心博览商场13号展览事务部

HKTDC Hong Kong International Medical Devices and Supplies Fair

Venue: Hong Kong Convention & Exhibition Centre

Profile: Accident and emergency equipment, building technology and hospital furniture, chinese medical devices, communication, systems and information technology, dental equipment and supplies, diagnostics, electromedical equipment/medical technology, laboratory equipment, medical components and materials, medical supplies and disposables, physiotherapy / orthopaedic/ rehabilitation technology, textiles, trade services and publications

Statistics 2012: Gross Area 4,172m^2, Exhibitors 168

Organiser: Hong Kong Trade Development Council

Address: Exhibitions Department, Unit 13, Expo Galleria, Hong Kong Convention and Exhibition Centre, 1 Expo Drive, Wan Chai, Hong Kong

☆47
2013.6.20-23
☎ 852-2585 6179, 2516 1677
🖷 852-3749 7542
✉ salesafj-hk@ubm.com
www.asiafja.com

Asia's Fashion Jewellery & Accessories Fair
亚洲時尚首飾及配飾展
20 - 23 June 2013
二〇一三年六月二十至二十三日

六月亚洲时尚首饰及配饰展

地点： 香港会议展览中心

内容： 时尚首饰: 非贵金属首饰、珠子首饰、珐琅及白蜡首饰、宝石首饰、半宝石首饰、合成宝石或仿宝石首饰、玻璃首饰、天然物料首饰、塑料首饰、纯银首饰及配饰 时尚配饰: 皮带及配饰、时尚手表、发饰、手袋、钱包、头饰及颈饰 时尚首饰原料: 珠子、宝石—未经打磨及打磨宝石、半宝石、合成宝石或仿宝石、首饰配件及组件、天然物料 陈列及包装: 陈

列物料、礼盒
周期：　每年三届
市场范围：　国际性
性质：　只对贸易观众开放
上届规模 2012：展商总数400家（来自21国家及地区），贸易买家6,188人（来自90个国家及地区）
主办：　亚洲博闻有限公司

Asia's Fashion Jewellery & Accessories Fair - June
Venue: Hong Kong Convention and Exhibition Centre
Profile: Fashion Jewellery, Fashion Jewellery Materials, Fashion Accessories, Display and Packaging
Frequency: Three times a year (March, June, September)
Market Area: International
Nature: Trade only
Statistics 2012: Exhibitors 400 came from 21 countries and regions, Buyers 6,188 came from 90 countries and regions
Organizer: UBM Asia Limited

☆48
2013.6.20-23
☎ 852-2516 1677, 2585 6179
🖷 852-3749 7319
✉ salesjgf-hk@ubm.com
www.jewellerynetasia.com

HONG KONG
JEWELLERY & GEM FAIR
香港珠寶首飾展覽會
20-23 June 2013
二〇一三年六月二十至二十三日
HONG KONG CONVENTION AND EXHIBITION CENTRE 香港會議展覽中心

六月香港珠宝首饰展览会
地点：　香港会议展览中心
内容：　贵重成品首饰、已打磨钻石及有色宝石、不同类型的珍珠、首饰表、包装陈列用品，以及首饰制造设备、工具及机器
周期：　每年一届
市场范围：　国际性
上届规模 2012：展览面积56,000m^2，展商总数1,500家（来自37国家及地区），贸易买家22,452人来自104个国家及地区
主办：　亚洲博闻有限公司

June Hong Kong Jewellery & Gem Fair
Venue: Hong Kong Convention and Exhibition Centre
Profile: Wide range of products from fine finished jewellery, polished diamonds and gemstones, to all varieties of pearls, jewellery timepieces, packaging, displays, as well as jewellery-making equipment, tools and machinery.
Frequency: Annual
Market Area: International
Statistics 2012: Exhibition Area 56,000m^2, Exhibitors 1,500 came from 37 countries and regions, Buyers 22,452 came from 104 counties and regions
Organizer: UBM Asia Limited

☆49
2013/07/08-11
☎ 852-1830 668
🖷 852-2824 0249
✉ exhibitions@hktdc.org
www.hktdc.com/hkfashionweekss

HKTDC
Hong Kong Fashion Week for Spring/Summer
香港時裝節春夏系列

香港贸发局香港时装节春夏系列
地点：　香港会议展览中心
内容：　女装、男装、婴儿服装、运动服装、内衣、新娘礼服及晚礼服、泳衣、手袋、鞋、流行饰物、眼镜、布料及纱线、钮扣、唛头、时装杂志、专业商贸服务
上届规模2012：　展出面积30,277平方米，参展商1,258家
主办：　香港贸易发展局
地址：　香港湾仔博览道1号香港会议展览中心博览商场13号展览事务部

HKTDC Hong Kong Fashion Week for Spring/Summer
Venue: Hong Kong Convention & Exhibition Centre
Profile: Ladies' wear, men's wear, babies and children's wear, sportswear, lingerie, bridal & evening wear, swimwear, handbags, shoes, costume jewellery, eyewear, fabrics & yarns, buttons, labels, fashion magazines, trade services
Statistics 2012: Gross Area 30,277m^2, Exhibitors 1,258
Organiser: Hong Kong Trade Development Council
Address: Exhibitions Department, Unit 13, Expo Galleria, Hong Kong Convention and Exhibition Centre, 1 Expo Drive, Wan Chai, Hong Kong

☆50
2013/07/17-23
☎ 852-1830 668
🖷 852-2824 0249
✉ exhibitions@hktdc.org
www.hkbookfair.com

HKTDC
Hong Kong Book Fair
香港書展

香港贸发局香港书展
地点：香港会议展览中心
内容：各类书籍及刊物、儿童及青少年图书、宗教书籍、电子学习资源：电子书、电子书阅读器、数码出版、视听教材、教育软件、音像多媒体产品、各类文具及印刷品
上届规模 2012：展出面积47,953平方米，参展商535家
主办：香港贸易发展局
地址：香港湾仔博览道1号香港会议展览中心博览商场13号展览事务部

HKTDC Hong Kong Book Fair
Venue: Hong Kong Convention & Exhibition Centre
Profile: Books and publications, children's and teen's books, religious books, e-learning resources: e-books, e-book readers, digital publishing, audio-visual learning aids, educational software, multimedia products, stationery and printing products
Statistics 2012: Gross Area 47,953m^2, Exhibitors 535
Organiser: Hong Kong Trade Development Council
Address: Exhibitions Department, Unit 13, Expo Galleria, Hong Kong Convention and Exhibition Centre, 1 Expo Drive, Wan Chai, Hong Kong

☆51
2013/08/15-17
☎ 852-1830 668
🖷 852-2824 0249
✉ exhibitions@hktdc.org
www.hktdc.com/hkteafair

HONG KONG INTERNATIONAL
teafair
香港國際茶展

香港贸发局香港国际茶展
地点：香港会议展览中心
内容：各地名茶、加工茶、茶饮料、茶食品及各种茶相关加工产品、茶叶包装、茶叶机械与检测、茶具、茶业机构、茶叶技术、茶工艺品、茶叶媒体、茗茶之友
上届规模 2012：展出面积7,819平方米，参展商298家
主办：香港贸易发展局
地址：香港湾仔博览道1号香港会议展览中心博览商场13号展览事务部

Hong Kong International Tea Fair
Venue: Hong Kong Convention & Exhibition Centre
Profile: Tea, processed tea and tea product, tea packaging, tea processing equipment and testing service, tea ware, tea bar/organisation, tea technology, tea craft, tea media, friends of tea
Statistics 2012: Gross Area 7,819m^2, Exhibitors 298
Organiser: Hong Kong Trade Development Council
Address: Exhibitions Department, Unit 13, Expo Galleria, Hong Kong Convention and Exhibition Centre, 1 Expo Drive, Wan Chai, Hong Kong

☆52
2013/08/15-17
☎ 852-1830 668
🖷 852-2824 0249
✉ exhibitions@hktdc.org
www.hktdc.com/icmcm

HKTDC
International Conference & Exhibition of the Modernization of Chinese Medicine & Health Products
國際現代化中醫藥及健康產品展覽會暨會議

国际现代化中医药及健康产品展览会暨会议
地点：香港会议展览中心
内容：中药、功能食品及产品、保健食品、健康护理及疗法、原料、设备及相关服务、科研及开发、商会
上届规模 2012：展出面积3,158平方米，参展商115家
主办：香港贸易发展局，现代化中医药国际协会
地址：香港湾仔博览道1号香港会议展览中心博览商场13号展览事务部

International Conference & Exhibition of the Modernization of Chinese Medicine & Health Products
Venue: Hong Kong Convention & Exhibition Centre
Profile: Chinese medicine, functional food & products, health supplement, health care & therapy, raw materials, equipment & related services, research & development, trade association
Statistics 2012: Gross Area 3,158m^2, Exhibitors 115
Organiser: Hong Kong Trade Development Council, Modernized Chinese Medicine International Association Ltd
Address: Exhibitions Department, Unit 13, Expo Galleria, Hong Kong Convention and Exhibition Centre, 1 Expo Drive, Wan Chai, Hong Kong

☆53
2013/08/15-19
☎ 852-1830 668
🖷 852-2824 0249
✉ exhibitions@hktdc.org
www.hktdc.com/hkfoodexpo

HKTDC
Food Expo
美食博覽

香港贸发局美食博览
地点： 香港会议展览中心
内容： 食品及饮品、食品包装、标签、物流及相关服务、食品处理产品、食品科技、机械及服务
上届规模 2012：展出面积41,428平方米，参展商1,110家
主办： 香港贸易发展局
地址： 香港湾仔博览道1号香港会议展览中心博览商场13号展览事务部

HKTDC Food Expo
Venue: Hong Kong Convention & Exhibition Centre
Profile: Food & beverage products, food packaging, labelling, safety & logistic products & services, food processing products, machinery & related services
Statistics 2012: Gross Area 41,428m^2, Exhibitors 1,110
Organiser: Hong Kong Trade Development Council
Address: Exhibitions Department, Unit 13, Expo Galleria, Hong Kong Convention and Exhibition Centre, 1 Expo Drive, Wan Chai, Hong Kong

☆54
2013/09/4-6
☎ (49) 30 3038 2178
🖷 (49) 30 3038 7060
✉ info@gp-events.com
www.asiafruitlogistica.com

asia FRUIT LOGISTICA

亚洲国际水果蔬菜展览会
地点： 亚洲国际博览馆
内容： 亚洲地区的新鲜水果蔬菜农产品产业以及和该产业相关的价值链
主办： 全球产品会展有限公司
地址： 香港湾仔博览道1号香港会议展览中心博览商场13号展览事务部

ASIA FRUIT LOGISTICA 2013
Venue: AsiaWorld-Expo
Profile: International fresh fruit and vegetable business
Organiser: Global Produce Events GmbH
Address: Exhibitions Department, Unit 13, Expo Galleria, Hong Kong Convention and Exhibition Centre, 1 Expo Drive, Wan Chai, Hong Kong

☆55
2013/09/4-6
☎ (44) 207 017 7036
🖷 (44) 207 017 7818
✉ vitafoods@informa.com
www.vitafoodsasia.com

Vitafoods™ Asia
The global nutraceutical event

亚洲营养食品展 2013
地点： 亚洲国际博览馆
内容： 营养保健品、功能食品及饮品、营养补充品和养份化妆品
主办： IIR Exhibitions
地址： 香港湾仔博览道1号香港会议展览中心博览商场13号展览事务部

Vitafoods Asia 2013
Venue: AsiaWorld-Expo
Profile: Ingredients and raw materials for the nutraceutical, functional foods and drinks and dietary supplements
Organiser: IIR Exhibitions
Address: Exhibitions Department, Unit 13, Expo Galleria, Hong Kong Convention and Exhibition Centre, 1 Expo Drive, Wan Chai, Hong Kong

☆56
2013/09/04-08
☎ 852-1830 668
🖷 852-2824 0249
✉ exhibitions@hktdc.org
www.hktdc.com/hkwatchfair

HKTDC
Hong Kong Watch & Clock Fair
香港鐘表展

香港贸发局香港钟表展
地点： 香港会议展览中心
内容： 品牌钟表、成表及钟、机械及设备、机械、包装用品、配件及零件、商贸服务
上届规模 2012：展出面积32,461平方米，参展商726家
主办： 香港贸易发展局
地址： 香港湾仔博览道1号香港会议展览中心博览商场13号展览事务部

HKTDC Hong Kong Watch & Clock Fair
Venue: Hong Kong Convention & Exhibition Centre
Profile: Brand name watches & clocks, complete watches & clocks, machinery & equipment, packaging, parts & components, trade services
Statistics 2012: Gross Area 32,461m^2, Exhibitors 726
Organisers: Hong Kong Trade Development Council
Address: Exhibitions Department, Unit 13, Expo Galleria, Hong Kong Convention and Exhibition Centre, 1 Expo Drive, Wan Chai, Hong Kong

☆57
2013.9.11-14
☎ 852-2585 6179, 2516 1677
🖷 852-3749 7542
✉ salesjgf-hk@ubm.com
www.asiafja.com

九月亚洲时尚首饰及配饰展
地点： 亚洲国际博览馆
内容： 时尚首饰: 镀金和镀银的非贵金属首饰，银器首饰和配饰，晶石、方晶锆石和莱茵石首饰，珐琅、珠石、贝壳和锡镴饰物。半宝石饰物 时尚首饰制造原料: 已打磨的有色宝石、各类珠子、天然矿物和其它首饰制造原料、首饰配件；时尚配饰: 时尚手表，发饰，手袋和皮包，皮带和皮带扣，佩章、襟针和钮扣，围巾和手套，美容用品和配饰，其它饰物和配饰
周期： 每年三届（三月、六月、九月）
市场范围： 国际性
展览性质： 仅向贸易观众开放
上届规模 2012：展商总数360家（来自15国家及地区），贸易买家6,800人
主办： 亚洲博闻有限公司

Asia's Fashion Jewellery & Accessories Fair - September
Venue: Asia World – Expo
Profile: Fashion Jewellery, Fashion Jewellery Materials, Fashion Accessories
Frequency: Three times a year (March, June, September)
Market Area: International
Nature: Trade Only
Statistics 2012: Exhibitors 360 came from 15 countries and regions, Buyers 6,800
Organizer: UBM Asia Limited

☆58
2013.9.11-15
☎ 852-2516 1677, 2585 6179
🖷 852-3749 7319
✉ salesjgf-hk@ubm.com
http://exhibitions.jewellerynetasia.com

九月香港珠宝首饰展览会
——裸钻、珍珠、有色宝石、工具设备及包装
地点： 亚洲国际博览馆
内容： 贵重成品首饰、已打磨钻石及有色宝石、不同类型的珍珠、首饰表、包装陈列用品，以及首饰制造设备、工具及机器。
周期： 每年一届
市场范围： 国际性
展览性质： 仅向贸易观众开放
主办： 亚洲博闻有限公司

September Hong Kong Jewellery & Gem Fair
– Diamonds, Pearls, Gemstones, Tools, Equipment and Packaging

Venue: AsiaWorld-Expo
Profile: Wide range of products from fine finished jewellery, polished diamonds and gemstones, to all varieties of pearls, jewellery timepieces, packaging, displays, as well as jewellery-making equipment, tools and machinery.
Frequency: Annual
Market Area: International
Nature: Trade only
Organizer: UBM Asia Limited

☆59
2013.9.13-17
☎ 852-2516 1677, 2585 6179
🖷 852-3749 7319
✉ salesjgf-hk@ubm.com
http://exhibitions.jewellerynetasia.com

九月香港珠宝首饰展览会——珠宝首饰成品

地点： 香港会议展览中心
内容： 贵重成品首饰、已打磨钻石及有色宝石、不同类型的珍珠、首饰表、包装陈列用品，以及首饰制造设备、工具及机器。
周期： 每年一届
市场范围： 国际性
展览性质： 仅向贸易观众开放
主办： 亚洲博闻有限公司

September Hong Kong Jewellery & Gem Fair

Venue: Hong Kong Convention and Exhibition Centre
Profile: Wide range of products from fine finished jewellery, polished diamonds and gemstones, to all varieties of pearls, jewellery timepieces, packaging, displays, as well as jewellery-making equipment, tools and machinery.
Frequency: Annual
Market Area: International
Nature: Trade only
Organizer: UBM Asia Limited

☆60
2013.9.25-27
☎ 852-2827 6211
020-8666 0158
🖷 852-3749 7346
020-8667 2235
✉ sales@aplf.com
info-china@ubm.com
www.fashionaccess.aplf.com

2013年时尚汇集

秋季展-手袋、行李箱包、鞋类、皮衣、裘皮服装及时尚配饰展-秋季展(FAA)

地点： 香港会议展览中心
内容： 各类鞋类、箱包、手袋、皮带、钱包、皮衣、时尚配饰、传播媒介及其他
周期： 每年两届
市场范围： 国际性
展览性质： 仅向贸易观众开放
上届规模 2012： 展览面积11,019 m^2，展商总数363家（来自23个国家及地区），贸易买家3,920家
主办： 亚太区皮革展有限公司(由亚洲博闻有限公司及SIC集团合资)

2013Fashion Access -

Handbags/ Travelware/ Footwear/ Leather Garments and Fashion Accessories - Autumn Show

Venue: Hong Kong Convention & Exhibition Centre
Profile: Variety of footwear; luggage; leather products; garment and finished decoration accessories; press and others
Frequency: Biannual
Market Area: International
Nature: Trade only
Statistics 2012: Exhibition Area 11,019m2, Exhibitors 363 came from 23 countries and regions, Buyers 3,920
Organizer: Asia Pacific Leather Fair Ltd (JV with CMP Asia Ltd. & SIC Group)

☆61
2013.9.25-27
☎ 852-2827 6211
020-8666 0158
🖷 852-3749 7346
020-8667 2235
✉ sales@aplf.com
info-china@ubm.com
www.fashionaccess.aplf.com

国际羊绒交易会——国际性的专业羊绒商贸展览盛会
地点： 香港会议展览中心
内容： 羊绒原料、羊绒纱线、羊绒面料、羊绒成衣、时尚羊绒配饰、生活品味羊绒用品、配件及配饰、加工化学原料及染料、羊绒机械设备、羊绒检测、商业服务（包括:商业协会及业内媒体）
主办： 亚太区皮革展有限公司(由亚洲博闻有限公司及SIC集团合资)

Cashmere World - The International Trade Fair for the Cashmere Industry
Venue: Hong Kong Convention & Exhibition Centre
Organizer: Asia Pacific Leather Fair Ltd (JV with CMP Asia Ltd. & SIC Group)

☆62
2013.10.12-15
☎ 852- 8199 7308
🖷 852-8199 7628
✉ visit@chinasourcingfair.com
www.chinasourcingfair.com

环球资源电子产品及零件采购交易会
地点： 亚洲国际博览馆
内容： 电脑周边产、品 电脑终端机、网络产品、个人数码电子产品、消费类电子产品及配件、电子零件、连接件、电源设备、车载电子产品、全球定位系统、通信产品、智能手机、家庭影音娱乐设备、电子产品专用包、苹果产品周边配件、平板电脑及配件
主办： 环球资源

China Sourcing Fair – Electronics & Components
Venue: AsiaWorld-Expo
Profile: Computer Peripherals , iProducts Accessories, Consumer Electronics & Accessories, Personal Digital Electronics, In-Car Electronics, Telecom products, Electronic Components, Interconnects, Home Entertainment, Power Supplies, Smartphones, GPS, Tablets & accessories, Computer Terminals, Networking Products , Bags & cases
Organizer: Global Sources

☆63
2013.10.12-15
☎ 852- 8199 7308
🖷 852-8199 7628
✉ visit@chinasourcingfair.com
www.chinasourcingfair.com

环球资源韩国电子产品及零件采购交易会
地点： 亚洲国际博览馆
内容： 消费类电子产品及配件、家庭影音娱乐设备、个人数码电子产品、通信及无线产品、移动电话及配件、车载电子产品、音响设备及配件、电脑终端机及周边产品、电子零件、安防产品、苹果产品周边配件、电子产品专用包、平板电脑及移动设备配件
主办： 环球资源

Korea Sourcing Fair – Electronics & Components
Venue: AsiaWorld-Expo
Profile: Telecom Products & Wireless, iProducts Accessories , Computer Peripherals , Consumer Electronics & Accessories, In-Car Electronics
Organizer: Global Sources

☆64
2013.10.12-15
☎ 852- 8199 7308
🖷 852-8199 7628
✉ visit@chinasourcingfair.com
www.chinasourcingfair.com

环球资源安防产品采购交易会
地点： 亚洲国际博览馆
内容： CCTV及数码监视器、门禁系统及无线射频、 防盗报警器及传感器、家居安防及系统整合、安全及防火设备产品

主办：　环球资源

China Sourcing Fair – Security Products
Venue:　AsiaWorld-Expo
Profile:　CCTV & Digital Surveillance, Access Control & RFID, Home and system integration , Alarms, Fire and Safety products
Organizer:　Global Sources

☆65
2013/10/13-16
☎ 852-1830 668
Fax 852-2824 0249
✉ exhibitions@hktdc.org
www.hktdc.com/hkelectronicsfairae

HKTDC

Hong Kong Electronics Fair (Autumn Edition)
香港秋季電子產品展

香港贸发局香港秋季电子产品展
地点：　香港会议展览中心
内容：　视听产品、电脑及周边产品、数码影像产品、电子配件、电子游戏产品、电子保健产品、家用电器、汽车电子及导航系统、流动设备及配件、办公室自动化设备、个人电子产品、保安产品、电讯产品、测验及认证服务、商贸服务
上届规模 2012：展出面积79,910平方米，参展商3,322家
主办：　香港贸易发展局
地址：　香港湾仔博览道1号香港会议展览中心博览商场13号展览事务部

HKTDC Hong Kong Electronics Fair (Autumn Edition)
Venue:　Hong Kong Convention & Exhibition Centre
Profile:　Audio visual products, computer & peripherals, digital imaging, electronic accessories, electronic gaming, healthcare electronics, home appliances, in-vehicle electronics and navigation systems, mobile devices & accessories, office automation & equipment, personal electronics, security products, telecommunication products, testing, inspection & certification, trade services
Statistics 2012:　Gross Area 79,910m^2, Exhibitors 3,322
Organiser:　Hong Kong Trade Development Council
Address:　Exhibitions Department, Unit 13, Expo Galleria, Hong Kong Convention and Exhibition Centre, 1 Expo Drive, Wan Chai, Hong Kong

☆66
2013/10/13-16
☎ 852-1830 668
Fax 852-2824 0249
✉ exhibitions@hktdc.org
www.electronicasia.com

electronicAsia
國際電子組件及生產技術展

国际电子组件及生产技术展
地点：　香港会议展览中心
内容：　电子科技、元器件、组件、显示技术、太阳能光伏电子技术
上届规模 2012：展出面积10,885平方米，参展商578家
主办：　香港贸易发展局, 慕尼黑国际博览亚洲有限公司
地址：　香港湾仔博览道1号香港会议展览中心博览商场13号展览事务部

electronicAsia
Venue:　Hong Kong Convention & Exhibition Centre, Hong Kong
Profile:　Electronic components, assemblies, electronics production, display technologies, photovoltaic technology
Statistics 2012:　Gross Area 10,885m^2, Exhibitors 578
Organiser:　Hong Kong Trade Development Council, MMI Asia Pte Ltd.
Address:　Exhibitions Department, Unit 13, Expo Galleria, Hong Kong Convention and Exhibition Centre, 1 Expo Drive, Wan Chai, Hong Kong

☆67
2013/10/19-22
☎ 852-8199 7308
Fax 852-8199 7628
✉ visit@chinasourcingfair.com
www.chinasourcingfair.com

global sources Baby & Children's Products China Sourcing Fair

环球资源婴儿及儿童产品采购交易会
地点：　亚洲国际博览馆
内容：　服装、床上用品、家具、安全产品、护理及沐浴产品、喂食产品、旅行产品、鞋类产品、流行服饰及配件、包袋、玩具、游戏及益智拼图、面具及服饰、户外游乐设施
主办：　环球资源

China Sourcing Fair – Baby & Children's Products
Venue:　AsiaWorld-Expo
Profile:　Toys, Baby & Children's Garment, Footwear, Baby Care Products, Bedding & Furniture
Organiser:　Global Sources

☆68
2013/10/19-22
☎ 852-8199 7308
🖷 852-8199 7628
✉ visit@chinasourcingfair.com
www.chinasourcingfair.com

环球资源圣诞及节日产品采购交易会
地点：　亚洲国际博览馆
内容：　圣诞装饰、圣诞饰品、万圣节装饰、节日灯饰、 派对装饰、复活节装饰、圣诞树、圣诞袜子、派对用品、情人节装饰
主办：　环球资源

China Sourcing Fair – Christmas & Seasonal Products
Venue:　AsiaWorld-Expo
Profile:　Christmas & Seasonal, Party Products
Organiser:　Global Sources

☆69
2013/10/19-22
☎ 852-8199 7308
🖷 852-8199 7628
✉ visit@chinasourcingfair.com
www.chinasourcingfair.com

环球资源礼品及赠品采购交易会
地点：　亚洲国际博览馆
内容：　运动及活动礼赠品、电子赠品、手表及时钟、文具及纸制品、礼盒、小饰品盒及珠宝盒、普通礼品、苹果产品促销配件
主办：　环球资源

China Sourcing Fair – Gifts & Premiums
Venue:　AsiaWorld-Expo
Profile:　Stationery & Paper, Electronic premiums, Watches & clocks , General gifts, Promotional Bags, Gifts, trinkets and jewelry boxes, Flags, Banners & Accessories, Souvenir Items, Promotional iProduct Accessories, Brand zone
Organiser:　Global Sources

☆70
2013/10/19-22
☎ 852-8199 7308
🖷 852-8199 7628
✉ visit@chinasourcingfair.com
www.chinasourcingfair.com

环球资源家居用品采购交易会
地点：　亚洲国际博览馆
内容：　厨具及餐桌用品、烘烤及烹饪用具、酒具及酒吧用具、玻璃及陶瓷制品、家居用品、宠物护理产品、浴室用品、家居装饰品、家用纺织品、家用电器、户外家具及装饰用品、运动及休闲用品、运动包袋及旅行产品、DIY及家居装饰产品
主办：　环球资源

China Sourcing Fair – Home Products
Venue:　AsiaWorld-Expo
Profile:　Kitchenware & Tableware, Bakeware & cookware, Sports Bags & Travel Goods, Bathroom Products & Accessories, Household products , Home Decor , Glassware & Ceramic , Home Textiles, Home appliances, Outdoor furniture and decorations, Petcare Products, Wine and bar accessories, Sports & Leisure
Organiser:　Global Sources

☆71
2013/10/19-22
☎ 852-8199 7308
🖷 852-8199 7628
✉ visit@chinasourcingfair.com
www.chinasourcingfair.com

环球资源医疗及健康用品采购交易会
地点：　亚洲国际博览馆
内容：　个人护理产品、健康及保健、家用医疗设备及供应、水疗设备及用品、美容化妆品
主办：　环球资源

China Sourcing Fair – Medical & Health Products
Venue: AsiaWorld-Expo
Profile: Medical & Health Products
Organiser: Global Sources

☆72
2013/10/19-22
☎ 852-8199 7308
🖷 852-8199 7628
✉ visit@chinasourcingfair.com
www.chinasourcingfair.com

global sources Gifts & Premiums Korea Sourcing Fair

环球资源韩国礼品及赠品采购交易会
地点： 亚洲国际博览馆
内容： 普通礼品、电子赠品、 运动礼赠品、 圣诞及节日礼品、旅行用品、 礼品包装及配饰、纪念品、工艺品、保健及美容用品、家用电子产品、玻璃制品、家用器具、婴儿用品及护理品
主办： 环球资源

Korea Sourcing Fair – Gifts & Premiums
Venue: AsiaWorld-Expo
Profile: Korean Gifts & Premiums
Organiser: Global Sources

☆73
2013/10/27-30
☎ 852- 8199 7308
🖷 852- 8199 7628
✉ visit@chinasourcingfair.com
www.chinasourcingfair.com

global sources Fashion Accessories China Sourcing Fair

环球资源流行服饰配件采购交易会
地点： 亚洲国际博览馆
内容： 休闲及时尚手袋、晚装包、皮包、发饰及配件、 头饰品、时尚珠宝首饰、围巾及披肩、时尚腰带、 时尚鞋类、手套类产品、袜类产品、 伞类产品
主办： 环球资源

China Sourcing Fair – Fashion Accessories
Venue: AsiaWorld-Expo
Profile: Headwear, Scarves & Gloves, Casual & Fashion Bags , Fashion jewelry , Socks, Fashion Belts, Evening Bags, Fashion Footwear
Organiser: Global Sources

☆74
2013/10/27-30
☎ 852- 8199 7308
🖷 852- 8199 7628
✉ visit@chinasourcingfair.com
www.chinasourcingfair.com

global sources Garments & Textiles China Sourcing Fair

环球资源服装及面料采购交易会
地点： 亚洲国际博览馆
内容： 服装成衣、运动装/休闲装、儿童服饰、毛衣及针织衫、面料、花边及服装辅料
主办： 环球资源

China Sourcing Fairs - Garments & Textiles
Venue: AsiaWorld-Expo
Profile: Casual wear, Garments, Sweater & Knitwear , Fabrics, Lace and Trimmings , Children's wear
Organiser: Global Sources

☆75
2013/10/27-30
☎ 852- 8199 7308
🖷 852- 8199 7628
✉ visit@chinasourcingfair.com
www.chinasourcingfair.com

global sources Underwear & Swimwear China Sourcing Fair

环球资源内衣及泳衣采购交易会
地点： 亚洲国际博览馆
内容： 内衣、泳衣及沙滩装、睡衣
主办： 环球资源

China Sourcing Fair – Underwear & Swimwear
Venue: AsiaWorld-Expo
Profile: Underwear & sleepwear , Swimwear & Beachwear
Organiser: Global Sources

☆76
2013/10/27-30
☎ 852- 8199 7308
🖷 852- 8199 7628
✉ visit@chinasourcingfair.com
www.chinasourcingfair.com

global sources
Garments & Accessories
India Sourcing Fair

环球资源印度服装及配饰采购交易会
地点： 亚洲国际博览馆
内容： 休闲及时尚手袋、晚装包、皮包、发饰及配件、帽类产品、太阳镜、时尚珠宝首饰、针织品、领带、围巾及披肩、时尚腰带、休闲及时尚鞋类产品、手套类产品、袜类产品、伞类产品、男女服装、服装辅料
主办： 环球资源

India Sourcing Fair - Garments & Accessories
Venue: AsiaWorld-Expo
Profile: Indian Garments & Accessories
Organiser: Global Sources

☆77
2013/10/28-30
☎ 852-1830 668
🖷 852-2824 0249
✉ exhibitions@hktdc.org
www.hktdc.com/hkbdh

HKTDC
Hong Kong International Building and Decoration Materials & Hardware Fair
香港國際建築裝飾材料及五金展

香港贸发局香港国际建筑装饰材料及五金展
地点： 亚洲国际博览馆
内容： 建筑装饰五金、建筑科技、天花及幕墙、陶瓷及石材、涂料及化学建材、门及窗、家具、环保建材、室内装饰材料、厨房及卫浴、检测及认证
上届规模 2012：展出面积5,000平方米，参展商153家
主办： 香港贸易发展局
地址： 香港湾仔博览道1号香港会议展览中心博览商场13号展览事务部

HKTDC Hong Kong International Building and Decoration Materials & Hardware Fair
Venue: AsiaWorld-Expo
Profile: Building & decorative hardware, building technology, ceiling & curtain wall, ceramics, stone & marble, coating & chemicals, door & window, furniture, green building, indoor decorative materials, kitchen & bath, testing, inspection & certification
Statistics 2012: Gross Area 5,000m^2, Exhibitors 153
Organiser: Hong Kong Trade Development Council
Address: Exhibitions Department, Unit 13, Expo Galleria, Hong Kong Convention and Exhibition Centre, 1 Expo Drive, Wan Chai, Hong Kong

☆78
2013.10.27-30
☎ 852-1830 668
🖷 852-2824 0249
✉ exhibitions@hktdc.org
www.hktdc.com/hklightingfairae

HKTDC
Hong Kong International Lighting Fair (Autumn Edition)
香港國際秋季燈飾展

香港贸发局香港国际秋季灯饰展
地点： 香港会议展览中心
内容： 商业照明、家居照明、LED及环保照明、灯饰配件及零件、灯饰管理、设计及技术、户外照明、贸易服务及刊物
上届规模 2012：展出面积69,288平方米，参展商2,279家
主办： 香港贸易发展局
地址： 香港湾仔博览道1号香港会议展览中心博览商场13号展览事务部

HKTDC Hong Kong International Lighting Fair (Autumn Edition)
Venue: Hong Kong Convention & Exhibition Centre
Profile: Commercial lighting, household lighting, LED & green lighting , lighting accessories, parts & components, lighting management, design & technology, outdoor lighting, trade service & publication
Statistics 2012: Gross Area 69,288m^2, Exhibitors 2,279
Organiser: Hong Kong Trade Development Council
Address: Exhibitions Department, Unit 13, Expo Galleria, Hong Kong Convention and Exhibition Centre, 1 Expo Drive, Wan Chai, Hong Kong

☆79
2013/10/28-31
☎ 852-1830 668
🖷 852-2824 0249
✉ exhibitions@hktdc.org
www.ecoexpoasia.com

Hong Kong Optical Fair
香港眼鏡展

国际环保博览
地点： 亚洲国际博览馆
内容： 空气质素、能源效益及能源、废物处理及循环再造、环保产品、环保工程方案及服务、水质、管理/监测及实验室技术、环保服务及研究、绿色建筑方案及服务、绿色运输、检测及认证服务
上届规模 2012：展出面积9,000平方米，参展商271家
主办： 香港贸易发展局，法兰克福展览(香港)有限公司
地址： 香港湾仔博览道1号香港会议展览中心博览商场13号展览事务部

Eco Expo Asia –
International Trade Fair on Environmental Protection
Venue: AsiaWorld-Expo
Profile: Air quality , energy efficiency & energy, waste management & recycling, eco-friendly product, environmental protection solution & service, water quality, control/ measuring and laboratory technology, environmental protection service, & research, green, building solution & service, green transportation, testing, inspection & certification
Statistics 2012: Gross Area 9,000m^2, Exhibitors 271
Organisers: Hong Kong Trade Development Council, Messe Frankfurt (HK) Ltd.
Address: Exhibitions Department, Unit 13, Expo Galleria, Hong Kong Convention and Exhibition Centre, 1 Expo Drive, Wan Chai, Hong Kong

☆80
2013/10/28-30
☎ 852-1830 668
🖷 852-2824 0249
✉ exhibitions@hktdc.org
www.sportssource-asia.com

亚洲运动用品展
地点： 亚洲国际博览馆
内容： 球类运动装备、自行车运动用品、运动服装布料／物料、健身及健美器材、高尔夫球用品、室内运动、户外运动及休闲用品、球拍运动、滚轴及滑板用品、体育防护配件、运动鞋、运动用品店装置及设备、运动服装及配件、田径运动、水上运动、冰上运动、期刊及服务、运动用品贸易组织
上届规模 2012：展出面积5,000平方米，参展商140家
主办： 香港贸易发展局，慕尼黑国际博览亚洲有限公司
地址： 香港湾仔博览道1号香港会议展览中心博览商场13号展览事务部

Sports Source Asia
Venue: AsiaWorld-Expo
Profile: Ball game equipment, cycling, fabrics & materials for sportswear, fitness & gymnastic training equipment, golf equipment & supplies, indoor sports, outdoor sports, racket sports, skating & skateboarding supplies, sports safety & protection gear, sports shoes, sports shop fittings & equipment, sportswear & accessories, track & field sports, water sports, winter sports, publications & services, sporting goods trade organisations
Statistics 2012: Gross Area 5,000m^2, Exhibitors 140
Organisers: Hong Kong Trade Development Council, MMI Asia Pte Ltd
Address: Exhibitions Department, Unit 13, Expo Galleria, Hong Kong Convention and Exhibition Centre, 1 Expo Drive, Wan Chai, Hong Kong

☆81
2013/11/06-08
☎ 852-1830 668
🖷 852-2824 0249
✉ exhibitions@hktdc.org
www.hktdc.com/hkopticalfair

香港贸发局香港眼镜展
地点： 香港会议展览中心
内容： 隐形眼镜、镜框及镜架、镜片、眼镜配件、护目镜、运动眼镜、太阳眼镜、视光仪器及机械、眼镜盒及眼镜袋、相关之机械及技术、相关之化学原料、相关之包装物料、相关之服务及专业刊物

上届规模 2012：展出面积25,099平方米，参展商629家
主办： 香港贸易发展局
地址： 香港湾仔博览道1号香港会议展览中心博览商场13号展览事务部

HKTDC Hong Kong Optical Fair
Venue: Hong Kong Convention & Exhibition Centre
Profile: Contact lenses, frames & mountings, lenses, parts & accessories, safety eyewear, sportswear, sunglasses, optometric instruments & machinery, spectacle cases & holders, related equipment & technology, related chemical & materials, related packaging materials, related services and publications
Statistics 2012: Gross Area 25,099m^2, Exhibitors 629
Organiser: Hong Kong Trade Development Council
Address: Exhibitions Department, Unit 13, Expo Galleria, Hong Kong Convention and Exhibition Centre, 1 Expo Drive, Wan Chai, Hong Kong

☆82
2013/11/07-09
☎ 852-1830 668
🖷 852-2824 0249
✉ exhibitions@hktdc.org
www.hktdc.com/hkwinefair

HKTDC
Hong Kong International Wine & Spirits Fair
香港國際美酒展

香港贸发局香港国际美酒展
地点： 香港会议展览中心
内容： 含酒精饮品、酒业服务、葡萄酒投资产品、酒类配件及器具、美酒之友
上届规模 2012：展出面积21,582平方米，参展商957家
主办： 香港贸易发展局
地址： 香港湾仔博览道1号香港会议展览中心博览商场13号展览事务部

HKTDC Hong Kong International Wine & Spirits Fair
Venue: Hong Kong Convention & Exhibition Centre
Profile: Liquor & beverage products, wine services, wine investment, wine accessories & equipment, friends of wine
Statistics 2012: Gross Area 21,582m^2, Exhibitors 957
Organiser: Hong Kong Trade Development Council
Address: Exhibitions Department, Unit 13, Expo Galleria, Hong Kong Convention and Exhibition Centre, 1 Expo Drive, Wan Chai, Hong Kong

☆83
2013/11/07
☎ 852-1830 668
🖷 852-2824 0249
✉ alc@hktdc.org
www.asianlogisticsconference.com

亚洲物流及航运会议
地点： 香港会议展览中心
内容： 会议为物流和航运服务供应商和使用者提供平台，探讨环球物流、航运及供应链管理趋势，发掘区内商机。
主办： 香港贸易发展局
地址： 香港湾仔港湾道一号会展广场办公大楼38字楼

Asian Logistics and Maritime Conference
Venue: Hong Kong Convention & Exhibition Centre
Profile: The Conference brings together services providers and users to discuss regional business opportunities and trends in logistics, supply chain management and maritime services.
Organiser: Hong Kong Trade Development Council
Address: 38/F, Office Tower, Convention Plaza, 1 Harbour Road, Wan Chai, Hong Kong

☆84
2013/11/13-15
☎ 852-2827 6211
020-8666 0158
🖷 852-3749 7345, 3749 7310
020-8626 6186, 8667 7120
✉ cosmasia-hk@ubm.com
info-china@ubm.com
www.cosmoprof-asia.com

COSMOPROF
ASIA HONG KONG
亞 太 區 美 容 展

亚太区美容展
地点： 香港会议展览中心
内容： 专业美容院及身心健康产品及设备；美发产品、仪器及发廊家具；包装、原料、机械、私人品牌及承包生产；香水、化妆品及护肤品；膳食补助品、替代及亚洲传统医疗、保健食品及饮料、原材料及私人品牌生产。
周期： 每年一届
市场范围： 国际性
展览性质： 仅向贸易观众开放
上届规模 2012：展览面积68,000m^2，展商总数1,780家（来自42国家及地区），贸易买家48,500人
主办： 亚太区美容展有限公司（由亚洲博闻有限公司与BolognaFiere合办）

Cosmoprof Asia
Venue: Hong Kong Convention and Exhibition Centre

Profile: Professional Beauty Salon and Well-being Products and Equipment; Hair Products, Equipment and Salon Furnishings; Packaging, Raw Materials, Machinery, Private Label and Contract Manufacturing; Perfumery, Cosmetics and Toiletries; Dietary supplements, Alter
Frequency: Annual
Market Area: International
Nature: Trade only
Statistics 2012: Exhibition Area 68,000m^2, Exhibitors 1,780 (came from 42 countries) , Buyers 48,500
Organizer: Cosmoprof Asia Ltd. (JV by CMP Asia and BolognaFiere)

☆85
2013/11/27-29
☎ +33(0)1 49 52 14 07
🖷 +33(0)1 49 52 14 48
✉ nev-hk@europ-expo.com
www.nev-hk.com

China
NEW ENERGY
VEHICLE
Show Hong Kong

中国新能源汽车展览会
地点: 亚洲国际博览馆
内容: 汽车
主办: EUROPEXPO

China NEW ENERGY VEHICLE Show
Venue: AsiaWorld-Expo
Profile: Electric vehicles, Hybrid vehicles, Hydrogen & Gas vehicles and Connected car & other services
Organiser: EUROPEXPO

☆86
2013/12
☎ 852-1830 668
🖷 852-2824 0249
✉ hktdc@hktdc.org
www.hktdc.com/worldsmeexpo

香港贸发局国际中小企博览
地点: 香港会议展览中心
内容: 一站式国际商贸平台，提供中小企业支持服务及环球商机：中国及海外市场商机、中国商务策略、企业顾问、市场推广、理财融资、电子商贸、法律、会计、创业营商、特许经营商机、商业资讯及支援机构
上届规模 2012: 展出面积10,500平方米，参展商317家
主办: 香港贸易发展局
地址: 香港湾仔港湾道一号会展广场办公大楼38字楼

HKTDC World SME Expo
Venue: Hong Kong Convention & Exhibition Centre
Profile: A one-stop international marketplace for SMEs, providing business solutions and market opportunities: China and overseas opportunities, China trade strategies, corporate management consultancy and marketing services, financial services, IT and e-Business, legal and accounting, new start-up and franchising, business intelligence, institutional support
Statistics 2012: Gross Area 10,500m^2, Exhibitors 317
Organiser: Hong Kong Trade Development Council
Address: 38/F, Office Tower, Convention Plaza, 1 Harbour Road, Wan Chai, Hong Kong

☆87
2013.12
☎ 852-1830 668
🖷 852-2824 0249
✉ hktdc@hktdc.org
www.hktdc.com/innodesigntechexpo

HKTDC
Inno Design Tech Expo
設計及創新科技博覽

香港贸发局设计及创新科技博览
地点: 香港会议展览中心
内容: "设计及创新科技博览"是创意及科技业界发掘生意契机，物色合适商贸伙伴的理想平台
上届规模 2012: 展出面积13,219平方米，参展商400家
主办: 香港贸易发展局
地址: 香港湾仔港湾道一号会展广场办公大楼38字楼

HKTDC Inno Design Tech Expo
Venue: Hong Kong Convention & Exhibition Centre
Profile: Inno Design Tech Expo (IDT Expo) provides a unique platform for creative and technology professionals to exchange ideas and explore business opportunities
Statistics 2012: Gross Area 13,219m^2, Exhibitors 400
Organiser: Hong Kong Trade Development Council
Address: 38/F, Office Tower, Convention Plaza, 1 Harbour Road, Wan Chai, Hong Kong

☆88
2013.12
☎ 852-1830 668
📠 852-2824 0249
✉ bipasia@hktdc.org
www.bipasiaforum.com

亚洲知识产权营商论坛

地点： 香港会议展览中心
内容： “亚洲知识产权营商论坛”是一年一度的国际盛事，为世界各地的商家和专业人士提供理想平台，聚首一堂，就知识产权贸易活动互相交流，探讨国际知识产权市场的最新发展，发掘生意契机。
上届规模 2012：参加者超过700人
主办： 香港贸易发展局
地址： 香港湾仔港湾道一号会展广场办公大楼38字楼

Business of IP Asia Forum

Venue: Hong Kong Convention & Exhibition Centre
Profile: Business of Intellectual Property Asia Forum (BIP Asia), an annual global conference on IP, brings together businessmen and professionals from around the world with an interest in IP. The forum focuses on the latest trends and opportunities in IP business, helping participants to explore new business opportunities while keeping up with the latest developments in the IP arena.
Statistics 2012: Participants over 700
Organiser: Hong Kong Trade Development Council
Address: 38/F, Office Tower, Convention Plaza, 1 Harbour Road, Wan Chai, Hong Kong

中国澳门展览会议

Exhibitions in Macao China

2013/11 -
☎ 010-8260 6899
🖷 010-8260 6883
✉ www.cnaico.com.cn, www.autochina.com.cn

013年中国（澳门）国际汽车博览会

地点：中国澳门
主办：中国汽车工业国际合作总公司
地址：北京市海淀区中关村丹棱街3号A座

China (Macao) Auto Expo

Venue: Macao, China
Organizer: China Natl Automotive Industry Intl Corp
Address: Tower A, 3 Danling Street, Haidian District, Beijing, China

中国台湾展览信息

Exhibitions in Taiwan

2013/11/15-18
☎ 852-2827 6211
🖷 852-3749 7342
✉ info-hk@ubm.com
www.jewellerynetasia.com

TAIWAN
JEWELLERY & GEM FAIR
台灣珠寶首飾展覽會
15-18 November 2013
Taipei World Trade Center, Hall 3

台湾珠宝首饰展览会

地点：台湾台北
主办：亚洲博闻有限公司
地址：香港湾仔港湾道26号华润大厦17楼

Taiwan Jewellery & Gem Fair

Venue: Taipei World Trade Center Exhibition, Taibei, Taiwan
Organizer: UBM Asia Ltd
Address: 17/F, China Resources Building, 26 Harbour Road, Wan Chai, Hong Kong

中国及海外会展概览2013-2014

Directory of China & Overseas Exhibitions and Meetings

229元/本
RMB 229/COPY

令您掌握未来一至两年中国（包括香港、澳门）及海外展览会议信息，全书按照行业分为机械、建筑、汽车、纺织服装、化工、电子、通讯、农业、食品、消费等82个类，每个展览会议信息有详细介绍，包括举办日期、地点、范围内容、参展费用、入场券价格、上界规模、主办介绍及联系方式。全书的会展信息以通过实践、地点和行业三种方式轻松查找。

中国会展中心指南2013

China Convention and Exhibition Directory Center

189元/本
RMB 189/COPY

全国展览中心、会议中心和活动场所全集。全国会展中心排名、行业专业报道及详细会展中心数据构成《中国会展中心指南2013》权威、翔实。会展中心介绍部分包括各展览会议场馆总面积、展览面积、会议面积、可搭建展位数、会议室面积、可容纳座位、地面承重、场馆高度、负责人地址、电话和场馆平面图。

联系我们：
电话　Tel: 010-6340 0061
传真　Fax: 010-8312 7130
邮箱　Email: dcoem@live.cn, dcoem@qq.com
网站　Web: www.dcoem.com

DCOEM

中国经济信息
真正价值所在
欢迎订阅
《中国经济信息》半月刊
国家重点期刊
经济日报 主办
地址 北京王府井大街277号
邮编 100006
电话 010-65141774
传真 010-65283638
E-mail zgjjxx@sohu.net
www.zgjjxx.net.cn
全年定价 240元
邮发代号 82-43

海外展览会议

Exhibitions and Fairs Overseas

阿尔及利亚
Algeria

安哥拉
Angola

阿根廷
Argentina

澳大利亚
Australia

奥地利
Austria

巴林
Bahrain

孟加拉
Bengal

巴西
Brazil

英国
Britain

柬埔寨
Cambodia

加拿大
Canada

智利
Chile

哥伦比亚
Columbia

埃及
Egypt

法国
France

德国
Germany

匈牙利
Hungary

印度
India

印度尼西亚
Indonesia

伊朗
Iran

伊拉克
Iraq

以色列
Israel

意大利
Italy

日本
Japan

哈萨克斯坦
Kazakhstan

韩国
Korea

科威特
Kuwait

马来西亚
Malaysia

墨西哥
Mexico

蒙古
Mongolia

摩洛哥
Morocco

缅甸
Myanmar

荷兰
Netherlands

尼日利亚
Nigeria

挪威
Norway

巴基斯坦
Pakistan

巴拿马
Panama

秘鲁
Peru

菲律宾
Philippines

波兰
Poland

葡萄牙
Portugal

卡塔尔
Qatar

俄罗斯
Russia

沙特阿拉伯
Saudi Arabia

新加坡
Singapore

南非
South Africa

西班牙
Spain

斯里兰卡
Sri Lanka

泰国
Thailand

突尼斯
Tunisia

土耳其
Turkey

阿联酋
UAE

乌克兰
Ukraine

美国
USA

委内瑞拉
Venezuela

越南
Vietnam

阿尔及利亚
Algeria

阿尔及利亚国际汽配展
日期：2013/03/04-07
地点：阿尔及利亚阿尔及尔
周期：每年一届
承办：北京中杰城投国际展览有限公司
联系人：李娜
☎ 010-5979 9850转858
🖷 010-5979 9850转ext 810，5885 7468
www.top-fairs.com.cn
www.build-ccpit.org

第16届阿尔及利亚国际建筑材料和建筑机械展览会
日期：2013/05/06-10
地点：阿尔及利亚阿尔及尔
内容：建筑材料及设备、建筑机械、陶瓷及石材、五金工具、建筑玻璃和幕墙、玻璃机械、地面铺装材料、室内及室外门、涂料、门窗及配件、室内装饰材料、木艺、铁艺、装饰纺织品、灯具、家具、地毯、安防产品、太阳能、电梯、园艺设备、厨房设备、卫浴洁具、冷暖通风设备等
主办：Algiers, Algeria
承办：中国贸促会建设行业分会
地址：北京市海淀区三里河路9号建设部大院北附楼503(100835)
联系人：云鹏
☎ 010-8837 0844
🖷 010-5893 3930
✉ 1492095643@qq.com
www.build-ccpit.org

国际工程及施工设备展览会
日期：2013/11 -
地点：阿尔及利亚阿尔及尔
周期：每年一届
主办：中国贸促会机械行业分会
地址：北京市西城区三里河路46号(100823)
☎ 010-6859 4811，6859 4994，6859 4910
🖷 010-6859 4995
✉ info@ccpitmsc.org
www.chinamachine.org.cn

安哥拉
Angola

国际贸易博览会
日期：2013/07/17-22
地点：安哥拉罗安达
周期：每年一届
主办：中国贸促会机械行业分会
地址：北京市西城区三里河路46号(100823)
☎ 010-6859 4811，6859 4994，6859 4910
🖷 010-68594995
✉ info@ccpitmsc.org
www.chinamachine.org.cn

阿根廷
Argentina

国际机床工具展览会
日期：2013/04/09-13
地点：阿根廷布宜诺斯艾利斯
周期：两年一届
主办：中国贸促会机械行业分会
地址：北京市西城区三里河路46号(100823)
☎ 010-6859 5495，6859 5247，6859 5406，6859 5431
🖷 010-6859 4995
✉ info@ccpitmsc.org
www.chinamachine.org.cn

国际矿业展览会
日期：2013/05/07-09
地点：阿根廷布宜诺斯艾利斯
主办：中国贸促会机械行业分会
地址：北京市西城区三里河路46号(100823)
☎ 010-6859 4939，6859 4951，6859 5176，6859 4805
🖷 010-6859 4995
✉ info@ccpitmsc.org
www.chinamachine.org.cn

2013年第12届阿根廷国际建筑材料、五金、管道配件、涂料展览会
日期：2013/09/04-07
地点：阿根廷Costa Salguero Exhibition Center, Buenos, Aires-Argentina
内容：建筑材料；五金机械、工具及设备；综合五金制品；卫浴配件；涂料、粘合剂、密封剂、化学制品；安全防护产品；锁具及装饰五金；润滑产品、园艺产品、小家电等
周期：每年一届
主办：中国贸促会建设行业分会
地址：北京市海淀区三里河路9号建设部大院机关门诊楼503(100835)
联系人：云鹏
☎ 15110286537
🖷 010-5893 3930
✉ rocyun@hotmail.com

澳大利亚
Australia

国际工程机械展览会
日期：2013/02/21-23
地点：澳大利亚墨尔本
周期：每年一届
主办：中国贸促会机械行业分会
地址：北京市西城区三里河路46号(100823)
☎ 010-6859 4939，6859 4951，6859 5176，6859 4805
🖷 010-68594995
✉ info@ccpitmsc.org
www.chinamachine.org.cn

国际汽车配件及售后服务博览会
日期：2013/04/11-13
地点：澳大利亚墨尔本
周期：两年一届
主办：中国贸促会机械行业分会
地址：北京市西城区三里河路46号(100823)
☎ 010-6859 4952，6859 4804，6859 4931，6859 5220
🖷 010-68594995
✉ info@ccpitmsc.org
www.chinamachine.org.cn

澳大利亚国际机械制造周展览会
NMW
日期：2013/05/07-10
地点：澳大 利亚墨尔本
内容：工业技术及产品，车床设备及配件，电子工业产品及配件，自动化设备，电机，流动动力技术与产品，阀门，仪器仪表，焊接及热处理；各种泵/阀/管件/紧固件等
周期：每年一届
主办：北方国际展览有限公司North International Exhibition Co Ltd
地址：北京市西城区菜园街1号中环假日酒店写字间1102室(100053)
联系人：赖彦平，陈思
☎ 010-8354 0342, 8354 0341
🖷 010-6354 7597
✉ yanping.lai@northexpo.com.cn; freya_chen@northexpo.com.cn
主办：中国贸促会机械行业分会
地址：北京市西城区三里河路46号(100823)
☎ 010-6859 5499，6859 4803，6859 4807，6859 4989，6859 5055
🖷 010-6859 4995
✉ info@ccpitmsc.org
www.chinamachine.org.cn

国际建材及设备展览会
日期：2013/05-
地点：澳大利亚墨尔本
周期：每年一届
主办：中国贸促会机械行业分会
地址：北京市西城区三里河路46号(100823)
☎ 010-6859 5499，6859 4803，6859 4807，6859 4989，6859 5055
🖷 010-68594995
✉ info@ccpitmsc.org
www.chinamachine.org.cn

国际包装机械展览会
日期：2013/05/07-10
地点：澳大利亚悉尼
周期：两年一届
主办：中国贸促会机械行业分会
地址：北京市西城区三里河路46号(100823)
☎ 010-6859 4192，6859 4826，6859 5406
🖷 010-6859 4995
✉ info@ccpitmsc.org
www.chinamachine.org.cn

国际机床及板材展览会
日期：2013/05/07-10
地点：澳大利亚悉尼
周期：每年一届
主办：中国贸促会机械行业分会
地址：北京市西城区三里河路46号(100823)
☎ 010-6859 5495，6859 5247，6859 5406，6859 5431
🖷 010-68594995
✉ info@ccpitmsc.org
www.chinamachine.org.cn

澳大利亚建材展
DESIGN BUILD EXPO
日期：2013/06-
地点：澳大利亚悉尼
内容：浴室、厨房设备；装饰、装修材料；电气、照明设备；五金制品等
主办：北方国际展览有限公司North Intl Exhibition Co Ltd
联系人：吴江，刘硕
地址：北京市西城区菜园街1号，中环假日酒店写字间1102室(100053)
☎ 010-8354 0336，8351 3705
🖷 010-6354 7597
✉ wujiang@northexpo.com.cn
liushuo@northexpo.con.cn

澳大利亚（悉尼）国际游艇展览会
日期：2013/08/02-06
地点：澳大利亚悉尼
主办：中国贸促会机械行业分会
地址：北京市西城区三里河路46号(100823)
☎ 010-6859 4985，6859 5855
🖷 010-6859 4995
✉ info@ccpitmsc.org
www.chinamachine.org.cn

亚太国际矿业展览会
日期：2013/08/20-23
地点：澳大利亚悉尼
周期：两年一届
主办：中国贸促会机械行业分会
地址：北京市西城区三里河路46号(100823)
☎ 010-6859 4811，6859 4994，6859 4910
🖷 010-6859 4995
✉ info@ccpitmsc.org
www.chinamachine.org.cn

悉尼亚太国际矿业展
AIMEX: Asia Pacific's Intl Mining Exhibition
日期：2015/09 -
地点：澳大利亚悉尼奥林匹克公园悉尼展览场
内容：面向世界采矿以及相关工程行业最大的产品及服务展会之一。产品及服务：采矿设备、供应及服务、计算机－软件及硬件、传送装置及相关操作设备、电子设备、消防设备、安全设备、地下采矿、运输、环境保护及尘埃控制、露天采矿、矿物

开采、矿物加工及选煤、粉碎、碾压及筛选设备、发电、传送、布缆、能源系统、进程控制、水泵及阀门。**周期：**四年一届
市场范围：国际性
性质：面向贸易观众
上届规模 2011：展览面积18,600m²，参展商519家，贸易观众10,947人
主办：励展澳大利亚公司
联络：励展博览集团国际销售部 张志超
地址：北京市朝阳区新源南路1-3号平安国际金融中心A座15层01-03,05
☎ 010-5933 9266
🖷 010-5933 9233
✉ ivy.zhang@reedexpo.com.cn
联系人：张志超
www.aimex.com.au
www.aimex.reedexhibitions.com.au

奥地利 Austria

奥地利国际汽车生产设备及加油站设备、化学品及环境技术展
Auto Zum:
Intl Trade Fair for the Car & Vehicle Industry
日期：2013/01/16-19
地点：奥地利奥地利萨尔斯堡贸易展览中心Salzburg Trade Fair Center
内容：AutoZum 是奥地利最大的汽车零部件及加油站设备、汽车化学产品及环保产品国际专业展览会。该展是在奥地利地区汽车行业人士汇聚的的唯一场所，同时它也无可置疑成为奥地利主要的国际贸易展览会。作为衡量下一个财政年度的标准，该展被称为是在多瑙河和阿尔卑斯山区域的市场指南针。展览会具有明确的主题，高质量的专业讲座、专业的观众，这些都为参展提供了必要的增值服务。作为专业贸易展览会，AutoZum是接触新客户、增进现有客户关系，扩大贸易的最好机会。也是为专业观众展示革新产品的最好场所。
周期：两年一届
市场范围：国际性
性质：面向贸易观众
主办：励展奥地利公司
联络：励展博览集团国际销售部
地址：北京市朝阳区新源南路1-3号平安国际金融中心A座15层01-03,05 (100738)
☎ 010-5933 9209
🖷 010-5933 9233
联系人: 杜一鸣
✉ martin.du@reedexpo.com.cn
www.autozum.at

奥地利国际木材加工、处理、装配、木匠用品展
BWS:
Intl Trade Fair for Woodworking
日期：2013/03 -
地点：奥地利萨尔茨堡展览中心
内容：木工五金配件、防护衣及工作安全用品、铰链和配件、工具、锁具及锁具技术、安全设备、金属加工、紧固及固定技术、环境技术、木具加工及成套设备、木工材料和加工材料、木工和细木供应，表面磨光、加工聚合材料机器和工具、木工和细木机械工具、锯木技术、锯木机械及工具、门窗设备、结构设备、森林伐木设备，机械，工具
周期：两年一届
市场范围：国际性
性质：面向贸易观众
主办：励展奥地利公司Messe Salzburg
联络：励展博览集团国际销售部
地址：北京市朝阳区新源南路1-3号平安国际金融中心A座15层01-03,05
☎ 010-5933 9206
🖷 010-5933 9233
✉ eric.xue@reedexpo.com.cn()
联系人：薛光
www.bwsmesse.at

欧洲国际电力、电网及能源展览会
PENN WELL
日期：2013/06/04-06
地点：奥地利维也纳
周期：每年一届
主办：中国贸促会建设行业分会会展部；北京中杰城设国际展览有限公司
联系人：王艳玲
☎ 010-8836 3688，5979 9850转813，13691545669
🖷 010-5885 7468，5979 9850转 810
✉ wangyanling@top-fairs.com.cn
20204846
www.btfi.cn
www.power-gen.org.cn
www.top-fairs.com.cn

欧洲国际电力展览会
日期：2013/06/04-06
地点：奥地利维也纳
周期：每年一届
主办：中国贸促会机械行业分会
地址：北京市西城区三里河路46号(100823)
☎ 010-6859 4802，6859 4934
🖷 010-6859 4995
✉ info@ccpitmsc.org
www.chinamachine.org.cn

巴林 Bahrain

第十八届中东石油及天然气展览会暨研讨会
MEOS 2013
日期：2013/03/10-13
地点：巴林
主办：北京邦企展览服务有限公司
地址：北京市朝阳区惠新东街11号紫光发展大厦B1座501(100029)
☎ 010-6482 3808, 6482 3670
✉ bbes@china.com

第二十二届中东国际珠宝钟表展
Jewellery Arabia 2013
日期：2013/11/19-23
地点：巴林
主办：北京邦企展览服务有限公司
地址：北京市朝阳区惠新东街11号紫光发展大厦B1座501(100029)
☎ 010-6482 3808, 6482 3670
✉ bbes@china.com

孟加拉 Bengal

孟加拉国际染料和化工展
Dye+Chem Bangladesh
日期：2013/09/05-08
地点：孟加拉达卡
主办：全国化工国际展览交流中心
☎ 010-6524 2231转ext 608
✉ fany@icif.cn

巴西 Brazil

巴西纺织机械展
ITMEX Americas:
Intl Textile Machinery Trade Fair
日期：2013 -
地点：巴西圣保罗
内容：再次展出创新型高技术非织造品，机械装备、必需件及零件、卫生用品（尿布、卫生巾、湿纸巾），非织造品转换器，转换用机械及装备，转换必需材料及零件。同时举办的展会还有 Fenatec, Feimaco, Expolav and Ponto Final。产品及服务包括非织造品、高技术纺织品、其它技术纺织品、机械和设备，生产必需品和零件、一次性卫生用品（尿布、卫生巾、湿纸巾）、非织造品转换器、转换机械及设备、转换器必需品及零件。
周期：两年一届
市场范围：国际性
性质：面向贸易观众
参展费用：光地展位260美元，标准展位340美元
主办：励展巴西公司；励展博览集团国际销售部
地址：北京市东长安街1号东方广场东一办公楼1204室(100738)
联系人：宫卫
☎ 010-8518 5787, 8515 1375
🖷 010-8515 1304
✉ david.gong@reedexpo.com.cn
www.reedexport.cn

巴西国际电子展
FIEE Elétrica
日期：2013/03 -
地点：巴西圣保罗安年比展览中心Anhembi, Sao Paulo
内容：能源生产，传送和分配装备—GTD必需元件－供电组件－电力安装材料－电力工具和自动控制－公用设施组件－电力工程，安装和维修－银行服务，实体公司，贸易发布及服务。
始办年份：1985
周期：两年一届
主办：励展巴西公司Reed Exhibitions Alcantara Machado, Brizal
联络：励展博览集团国际销售部
地址：北京市朝阳区新源南路1-3号平安国际金融中心A座15层01-03,05
☎ 010-5933 9268
🖷 010-5933 9233
✉ daisy.zang@reedexpo.com.cn
联系人：臧威
www.fiee.com.br

FIEE Elétrica
Date: 2013/03 -
Venue: Anhembi, Sao Paulo, Brazil
Profile: Intl Electrical, Energy & Automation Industry Trade Fair. Automation and instrumentation; Electrical components for machines, equipment Industrial equipment; Generation, Transmission and Distribution; Construction materials; The Environment; Energy generation, transmission and distribution utility companies; Banks, associations, publications, services and others.
Established Year: 1985
Frequency: Biennial
Organizer: Reed Exhibitions Alcantara Machado, Brizal
☎ 86-10-5933 9268
🖷 86-10-5933 9233
✉ daisy.zang@reedexpo.com.cn
www.fiee.com.br

巴西纺织机械展
ITMEX Americas:
Intl Textile Machinery Trade Fair
日期：2013/03 -
地点：巴西圣保罗
内容：创新型高技术非织造品，机械装备、必需件及零件、卫生用品（尿布、卫生巾，湿纸巾），非织造品转换器，转换用机械及装备，转换必需材料及零件。
周期：四年一届
市场范围：国际性
性质：面向贸易观众
主办：励展巴西公司
联络：励展博览集团国际销售部
地址：北京市朝阳区新源南路1-3号平安国际金融中心A座15层01-03,05
☎ 010-5933 9268
🖷 010-5933 9233
✉ daisy.zang@reedexpo.com.cn
联系人：臧威
www.itmex.com.br

巴西圣保罗工程机械与零部件展
SP Infrastructure:
Exhibition Fair of Infrastructure Works' Products & Services
日期：2013/03 -
地点：巴西圣保罗安年比展览中心
内容：为工程机械制造商、设备供应商以及零部件制造企业提供了一个绝佳的展示及贸易平台，并将成为你打开巴西市场的唯一通路。
主办：励展博览集团
联络：励展博览集团国际销售部 张志超
地址：北京市朝阳区新源南路1-3号平安国际金融中心A座15层01-03,05
☎ 010-5933 9266
🖷 010-5933 9233
✉ ivy.zhang@reedexpo.com.cn
联系人：张志超
www.spinfra.com.br

圣保罗国际建材及五金展
FEICON BATIMAT
日期：2013/03/12-16
地点：巴西圣保罗
内容：各类五金工具及DIY产品、室内建材、各类五金配件、门窗、楼梯、卫浴、供暖加热通风空调设备，管道、阀门、电气照明设备；园艺及户外用品等
主办：北方国际展览有限公司North Intl Exhibition Co Ltd
联系人：吴江，刘硕
地址：北京市西城区菜园街1号，中环假日酒店写字间1102室(100053)
☎ 010-8354 0336，8351 3705
🖷 010-6354 7597
✉ wujiang@northexpo.com.cn
liushuo@northexpo.con.cn

南美国际动力传动及物流设备展览会
日期：2013/03/19-22
地点：巴西圣保罗
周期：每年一届
主办：中国贸促会机械行业分会
地址：北京市西城区三里河路46号(100823)
☎ 010-6859 5499，6859 4803，6859 4807，6859 4989，6859 5055
🖷 010-6859 4995
✉ info@ccpitmsc.org
www.chinamachine.org.cn

国际农业机械展览会
日期：2013/04 -
地点：巴西圣保罗
主办：中国贸促会机械行业分会
地址：北京市西城区三里河路46号(100823)
☎ 010-6859 4939，6859 4951，6859 5176，6859 4805
🖷 010-6859 4995
✉ info@ccpitmsc.org
www.chinamachine.org.cn

巴西国际电力及电子元器件展
FIEE 2013
日期：2013/04/01-05
地点：巴西圣保罗
周期：两年一届
主办：中国贸促会建设行业分会会展部；北京中杰城设国际展览有限公司
联系人：王艳玲
☎ 010-8836 3688，5979 9850转813，13691545669
🖷 010-5885 7468，5979 9850转810
✉ wangyanling@top-fairs.com.cn
QQ 20204846
www.btfi.cn
www.power-gen.org.cn
www.top-fairs.com.cn

巴西国际塑料机械展览会
BrasilPlast:
Intl Plastic Industry Trade Fair
日期：2013/04/08-12
地点：巴西圣保罗Anhembi, Sao Paulo
内容：塑料产品生产商、人造树脂、原材料与电子元件塑料衬底、化工产品，机械、设备与零件，模具，仪器、控制与自动设备，服务与技术项目，交易宣传及其他服务。
始办年份：1998
周期：两年一届
主办：励展巴西公司Alcantara Machado
联络：励展博览集团国际销售部
地址：北京市朝阳区新源南路1-3号平安国际金融中心A座15层01-03,05
☎ 010-5933 9268
🖷 010-5933 9233
✉ daisy.zang@reedexpo.com.cn
联系人：臧威
www.brasilplast.com.br

BrasilPlast: Intl Plastic Industry Trade Fair
Date: 2013/04/08-12
Venue: Anhembi, Sao Paulo, Brazil
Profile: Manufacturers of Plastic Products-Synthetic Resins-Raw Materials and Base Input Industries-Chemical Products-Machines, Equipment and Accessories-Molds-Instruments, Control and Automation-Services and Technical Projects-Trade Publications and Services
Established Year: 1998
Frequency: Biennial
Organizer: Reed Exhibitions
☎ 86-10-5933 9268
🖷 86-10-5933 9233
✉ daisy.zang@reedexpo.com.cn
www.brasilplast.com.br

巴西国际汽车零配件、设备及服务贸易展览会
AUTOMEC 2013
日期：2013/04/16-19
地点：巴西圣保罗
周期：两年一届
承办：北京中杰城投国际展览有限公司
联系人：李娜
☎ 010-5979 9850转858
🖷 010-5979 9850转810，5885 7468
www.top-fairs.com.cn
www.build-ccpit.org

国际安防展览会
日期：2013/05 -
地点：巴西圣保罗
周期：每年一届
主办：中国贸促会机械行业分会
地址：北京市西城区三里河路46号(100823)
☎ 010-6859 5499，6859 4803，6859 4807，6859 4989，6859 5055
🖷 010-6859 4995
✉ www.chinamachine.org.cn
www.chinamachine.org.cn

巴西国际机床工具及成套设备展
FEIMAFE:
Intl Machine Tools & Integrated Manufacturing Systems Trade Fair
日期：2013/05/20-25
地点：巴西圣保罗安年比展览中心Anhembi, Sao Paulo, BRAZIL
内容：机床、自动化、质量控制整合生产技术、辅助设备、配件和零部件、工具、服务
周期：两年一届
主办：励展巴西公司
联络：励展博览集团国际销售部
地址：北京市朝阳区新源南路1-3号平安国际金融中心A座15层01-03,05
☎ 010-5933 9268
🖷 010-5933 9233
✉ daisy.zang@reedexpo.com.cn
联系人：臧威
www.feimafe.com.br

FEIMAFE:
Intl Machine Tools & Integrated Manufacturing Systems Trade Fair
Date: 2013/05/20-25
Venue: Anhembi, Sao Paulo, Brazil
Profile: Machine Tools, Automation, Quality Control Integrated with Production, Auxiliary Equipment, Accessories and Components, Tools, Services
Frequency: Biennial
Organizer: Reed Exhibitions
☎ 86-10-5933 9268
🖷 86-10-5933 9233
✉ daisy.zang@reedexpo.com.cn
www.feimafe.com.br

国际塑料工业贸易展览会
日期：2013/05/20-24
地点：巴西圣保罗
周期：两年一届
主办：中国贸促会机械行业分会
地址：北京市西城区三里河路46号(100823)
☎ 010-6859 4192，6859 4826，6859 5406
🖷 010-6859 4995
✉ info@ccpitmsc.org
www.chinamachine.org.cn

2013巴西机场建设及设备供应展览会
日期：2013/05/22-24
地点：巴西圣保罗泛美国际会展中心
内容：机场建设设备和技术有废水处理，飞机棚设计和建设，规划、咨询和建设，技术设备安装，咨询与建设等其他活动-油库技术，跑道设计和建设，供电和电缆，废物收集与处理升降平台、高空作业车、机场物流系统，机场电梯、通信设备、机场新能源大巴车。 地面支持设备和服务有飞机发动机起动器和PCA系统，飞机处理系统，飞机拖引，机场服务设备，行李装载，货物处理，事故、火灾和救援，装卸系统（起重机和提升台），移动货物处理系统（运输车和推移动车），乘客运输，供水和厕所用车，其他地面支持设备和服务-飞机除冰，飞机加油，飞机冲洗，行李处理。技术系统；航站楼建设与安装；航站楼内部装修；相关服务机构；信息技术；软件和服务；咨询机构
主办：SATORS；上海杜德会展服务有限公司
地址：上海白兰路137号绿洲广场A座812号
联系人：敖雨轩
☎ 021-3126 3306
🖷 021-3255 3878
✉ dude803@expodude.com
ada1106@hotmail.com
QQ 2218465956

国际食品、饮料工业加工技术和包装工业博览会
日期：2013/06-
地点：巴西圣保罗
周期：每年一届
主办：中国贸促会机械行业分会
地址：北京市西城区三里河路46号(100823)
☎ 010-6859 4192，6859 4826，6859 5406
🖷 010-6859 4995
✉ info@ccpitmsc.org
www.chinamachine.org.cn

国际机床工具与制造技术展览会
日期：2013/06/03-08
地点：巴西圣保罗
周期：两年一届
主办：中国贸促会机械行业分会
地址：北京市西城区三里河路46号(100823)
☎ 010-6859 5495，6859 5247，6859 5406，6859 5431
🖷 010-6859 4995
✉ info@ccpitmsc.org
www.chinamachine.org.cn

国际工程技术与设备展览会
日期：2013/06/05-08
地点：巴西圣保罗
周期：三年一届
主办：中国贸促会机械行业分会
地址：北京市西城区三里河路46号(100823)
☎ 010-6859 4811，6859 4994，6859 4910
🖷 010-6859 4995
✉ info@ccpitmsc.org
www.chinamachine.org.cn

巴西国际海洋石油及天然气工业设备展览会
Brazil Offshore:
Intl Offshore Oil and Gas Industry Trade Show and Conference
日期：2013/06/11-14
地点：巴西里约州马珈耶Macaé, Roberto Marinho展

览中心
内容：作为世界第三大海洋石油工业产品贸易展会，巴西国际海洋石油天然气工业设备展是众多成功业内贸易展会之一，在参展公司和观众的数量和质量上有突飞猛进的增长。
周期：两年一届
市场范围：国际性
性质：面向贸易观众
主办：励展巴西公司
联络：励展博览集团国际销售部
地址：北京市朝阳区新源南路1-3号平安国际金融中心A座15层01-03,05
☎ 010-5933 9268
🖷 010-5933 9233
✉ daisy.zang@reedexpo.com.cn
联系人：臧威
www.brasiloffshore.com

巴西国际食品博览会
SIAL Brazil
日期：2013/06/25-28
地点：巴西圣保罗
内容：各类食品原料、食品配料及调料、冷冻食品、绿色食品、水果、蔬菜、饮料、肉类、水产品、糖果、厨房器具、金属及塑料制品、保鲜膜、塑料袋等
主办：北方国际展览有限公司North International Exhibition Co Ltd
地址：北京市西城区菜园街1号中环假日酒店写字间1102室(100053)
联系人：王子威，李松林
☎ 010-8355 7740，8353 3198
🖷 010-6354 7597
✉ w.ziwei@northexpo.com.cn
reanna@northexpo.com.cn

国际混凝土设备展览会
日期：2013/08 -
地点：巴西圣保罗
周期：每年一届
主办：中国贸促会机械行业分会
地址：北京市西城区三里河路46号(100823)
☎ 010-6859 4811，6859 4994，6859 4910
🖷 010-6859 4995
✉ info@ccpitmsc.org
www.chinamachine.org.cn

国际矿业机械及工程机械展览会
日期：2013/08 -
地点：巴西贝洛
周期：两年一届
主办：中国贸促会机械行业分会
地址：北京市西城区三里河路46号(100823)
☎ 010-6859 4811，6859 4994，68594910
🖷 010-6859 4995
✉ info@ccpitmsc.org
www.chinamachine.org.cn

巴西造船、航运及海事展暨学术研讨会

NAVALSHORE
MARINTEC SOUTH AMERICA 2013
Feira e Conferência da Indústria Naval e Offshore

Navalshore
日期：2013/08/13-15
地点：巴西里约热内卢
主办：亚洲博闻有限公司
地址：香港湾仔港湾道26号华润大厦17楼
☎ 00852-2827 6211
🖷 00852-3749 7342
✉ info-hk@ubm.com
www.ubmnavalshore.com.br

Navalshore
Date: 2013/08/13-15
Venue: Centro de Conven??es SulAmérica, Brazil
Organizer: UBM Asia Ltd
Address: 17/F, China Resources Building, 26 Harbour Road, Wan Chai, Hong Kong
☎ 852-2827 6211
🖷 852-3749 7342
✉ info-hk@ubm.com
www.ubmnavalshore.com.br

巴西圣保罗国际影像展览会
Photoimage Brazil
日期：2013/08/28-30
地点：巴西圣保罗
内容：传统及数码照相机和摄像机；摄影摄像器材；摄影摄像配件及附件；摄影工作室器材；数字成像和出版；数码产品；存储产品
主办：北方国际展览有限公司North International Exhibition Co Ltd
地址：北京市西城区菜园街1号中环假日酒店写字间1102室(100053)
联系人：王子威，李松林
☎ 010-8355 7740，8353 3198
🖷 010-6354 7597
✉ w.ziwei@northexpo.com.cn
reanna@northexpo.com.cn

巴西国际制冷、空调、通风、供暖和空气处理贸易展
Febrava:
Intl Refrigeration, Air-conditioning, Ventilation, Heating and Air Treatment Trade Fair
日期：2013/09 -
地点：巴西圣保罗Imigrantes会展中心
内容：美洲第二大制冷、空调、通风、供暖和空气处理行业展会。展会吸引来自巴西和国际的业内最重要公司，是发布推动行业发展的解决方案和创新技术的理想场所。
周期：两年一届
市场范围：国际性
性质：面向贸易观众
参展费用：光地展位每平米260美元，标准展位每平米340美元
主办：励展巴西公司Alcantara Machado
联络：励展博览集团国际销售部
地址：北京市朝阳区新源南路1-3号平安国际金融中心A座15层01-03,05
☎ 010-5933 9268
🖷 010-5933 9233
✉ daisy.zang@reedexpo.com.cn
联系人：臧威
www.brasiloffshore.com
www.febrava.com.br

巴西国际涂料展
ABRAFATI
日期：2013/09/16-18
地点：巴西圣保罗
主办：全国化工国际展览交流中心
☎ 010-6524 2231转608
✉ fany@icif.cn

巴西国际无纺布贸易展
NT&TT:
Intl Nonwovens & Technical Textiles Trade Fair
日期：2013/10 -
地点：巴西圣保罗北方展览中心Expo Center Norte
内容：展示以下领域的创新项目：无纺布与产业用纺织品、机械与设备、物料与零部件、卫生耗材（尿布、卫生棉与湿纸巾）、无纺布转换器、转换机械与设备、无纺布转换物料与零部件等。
周期：两年一届
主办：励展巴西公司Alcantara Machado
联络：励展博览集团国际销售部
地址：北京市朝阳区新源南路1-3号平安国际金融中心A座15层01-03,05
☎ 010-5933 9268
🖷 010-5933 9233
✉ daisy.zang@reedexpo.com.cn
联系人：臧威
www.brasiloffshore.com
www.nt-ttshow.com.br

巴西国际造纸展
ABTCP-TAPPI
日期：2013/10 -
地点：巴西圣保罗
主办：全国化工国际展览交流中心
☎ 010-6524 2231转608
✉ fany@icif.cn

巴西国际交通展览会
Fenatran:
Intl Transport Industry Trade Show
日期：2013/10 -
地点：巴西圣保罗安年比展览中心（Anhembi）
内容：展示货物运输领域技术的发展状况，为众多观众及买家提供了巨大的商机。巴西国际交通展览会被公认为是拉丁美洲最大的技术性运输方面的展会，本展会将展示国际运输产品与设备，主要涉及公路运输方面。产品与服务有货物运输企业、交通工具组装、工具制造商、汽车部件制造商、发动机与轮胎生产商、汽油及衍生产品经销商、设备维修站、行业情报。
周期：两年一届
主办：励展巴西公司Alcantara Machado
联络：励展博览集团国际销售部
地址：北京市朝阳区新源南路1-3号平安国际金融中心A座15层01-03,05
☎ 010-5933 9268
🖷 010-5933 9233
✉ daisy.zang@reedexpo.com.cn
联系人：臧威
www.brasiloffshore.com
www.fenatran.com.br

巴西国际两轮车展览会
Intl Motorcycle, Bicycle, Parts & Equipment Show
日期：2013/10 -
地点：巴西圣保罗市安年比展览中心（ANHEMBI）
内容：自行车，摩托车，单脚滑行车，轻型摩托车，三轮车，四轮车，设备，配件，摩托车配件，自行车配件，汽油和润滑剂，综合服务，出版刊物。
周期：两年一届
主办：励展巴西公司（Alcantara Machado）
联络：励展博览集团国际销售部
地址：北京市朝阳区新源南路1-3号平安国际金融中心A座15层01-03,05
☎ 010-5933 9268
🖷 010-5933 9233
✉ daisy.zang@reedexpo.com.cn
联系人：臧威
www.feiradasamericas.com.br
www.reedexport.cn

国际管道、阀门、管件及配件展览会
日期：2013/10 -
地点：巴西圣保罗
周期：两年一届
主办：中国贸促会机械行业分会
地址：北京市西城区三里河路46号(100823)
☎ 010-6859 5296，6859 4938，6851 2883
🖷 010-6859 4995
✉ info@ccpitmsc.org
www.chinamachine.org.cn

巴西圣保罗国际紧固件展览会
FASTENER FAIR/BRASIL
日期：2013/11 -
地点：巴西圣保罗
内容：各类标准及非标准紧固件、相关加工设备、检测设备、工具等
主办：北方国际展览有限公司North International Exhibition Co Ltd
主办：北方国际展览有限公司North International Exhibition Co Ltd
地址：北京市西城区菜园街1号中环假日酒店写字间1102室(100053)
联系人：赖彦平，陈思
☎ 010-8354 0342, 8354 0341
🖷 010-6354 7597
✉ yanping.lai@northexpo.com.cn
freya_chen@northexpo.com.cn

巴西圣保罗户外家具、露营设备及园林工具展览会
日期：2013/10/10-13
地点：巴西圣保罗

内容：花园家具及家居用品、露营及休闲用品、烧烤设备、花园机械和设备、花园手工具和附件、其它设备和花园布置、植物和植物护理、水处理和室外照明
主办：北方国际展览有限公司North International Exhibition Co Ltd
地址：北京市西城区菜园街1号中环假日酒店写字间1102室(100053)
主办：北方国际展览有限公司
地址：北京市西城区菜园街1号中环假日酒店写字间1102室(100053)
联系人：王子威，李松林
☎ 010-8355 7740，8353 3198
🖷 010-6354 7597
✉ w.ziwei@northexpo.com.cn
reanna@northexpo.com.cn

英国
Britain

2013年伦敦国际绿色建筑和节能环保展览会
日期：2013/03/05-07
地点：英国伦敦 ExCel 展览中心
内容：环保建筑材料：石材、陶瓷、玻璃、门窗、型砖、钢材、有色金属、木材、瓷砖、地板与地毯、石膏、木材、油毯、粗绒、铺路材料、水泥、涂料、油漆、内饰和家具等；可再生及新能源建筑：生物能源、光伏建筑一体化、热泵、热电联供、太阳能、风能、太阳-热能、微发电，综合供热供电，光伏能、风能、热泵、绝缘保温；节能卫浴、器材：水暖器材、暖通管道、PVC管道及附件、洁具/五金配件；建筑装饰材料、保温隔热材料：玻璃纤维、羊毛、箔、聚苯乙烯；采暖、通风材料：空调、通风系统、供水和下水、供煤气、防火安全系统、采暖设施、通风网络、管道，电气设施、照明系统和仪表、工程管网、制冷系统、卫浴设施；建筑设备；建筑结构；水资源管理
周期：每年一届
主办：ExCel
承办：中国贸促会建设行业分会
地址：北京市海淀区三里河路9号建设部大院机关门诊楼503(100835)
联系人：云鹏
☎ 010-8837 0844
🖷 010-5893 3930
✉ rocyun@hotmail.com
www.build-ccpit.org

英国食品、饮料包装机械、设备展览会
Pro2Pac: Processing & Packaging Solutions for the Food & Drink Industry
日期：2013/03/17-20
地点：英国伦敦ExCeL会展中心
内容：食品&饮料加工和包装解决方案包括，主要包括：包装设备，机械，系统，技术，服务及原料。
周期：两年一届
参展费用：光地展位261英镑，标准展位313英镑
主办：励展英国公司
联络：励展博览集团国际销售部
地址：北京市朝阳区新源南路1-3号平安国际金融中心A座15层01-03,05
☎ 010-5933 9209
🖷 010-5933 9233
✉ martin.du@reedexpo.com.cn
联系人：杜一鸣
www.pro2pac.co.uk

英国国际食品与饮料展
IFE:
Intl Food and Drink Exhibition
日期：2013/03/17-20
地点：英国伦敦ExCel会展中心
内容：展会将为大家带来来自英国及世界各地的食品和饮料，其中包括：烘焙食品和糖果，奶酪和奶制品，饮料，冷冻食品，儿童食品及饮料，方便食品，风俗食品，肉类和家禽类，英国特产和地方食品，有机及天然食品，功能食品，零食与速食等。
周期：两年一届
参展费用：光地展位261英镑，标准展位313英镑
主办：英国Fresh RM
联络：励展博览集团国际销售部
地址：北京市朝阳区新源南路1-3号平安国际金融中心A座15层01-03,05
☎ 010-5933 9209
🖷 010-5933 9233
✉ martin.du@reedexpo.com.cn
联系人：杜一鸣
www.pro2pac.co.uk

国际物流与运输展览会
日期：2013/03/19-23
地点：英国伯明翰
周期：三年一届
主办：中国贸促会机械行业分会
地址：北京市西城区三里河路46号(100823)
☎ 010-6859 4811，6859 4994，6859 4910
🖷 010-6859 4995
✉ info@ccpitmsc.org
www.chinamachine.org.cn

国际工程机械作业展览会
日期：2013/05/14-16
地点：英国伯明翰
周期：两年一届
主办：中国贸促会机械行业分会
地址：北京市西城区三里河路46号(100823)
☎ 010-6859 4939，6859 4951，6859 5176，6859 4805
🖷 010-6859 4995
✉ info@ccpitmsc.org
www.chinamachine.org.cn

2013年英国电子元器件及设备展览会
日期：2013/05/18-19
地点：英国伯明翰
周期：每年一届
主办：中国贸促会建设行业分会会展部；北京中杰城设国际展览有限公司
联系人：王艳玲
☎ 010-8836 3688，5979 9850转813，13691545669
🖷 010-5885 7468，5979 9850转810
✉ wangyanling@top-fairs.com.cn
QQ 20204846
www.btfi.cn
www.power-gen.org.cn
www.top-fairs.com.cn

英国国际包装新技术展览会
Total Processing & Packaging
日期：2013/06/04-06
地点：英国伯明翰国家展览中心
内容：涵盖加工和包装行业各领域，提供完整的生产线方案、行业内情及创新信息。产品及服务有包装原料和容器、加工设备、包装机械、包装设计、其他相关产品及服务。
周期：三年一届
市场范围：国际性
性质：面向贸易观众
主办：励展英国公司
联络：励展博览集团国际销售部
地址：北京市朝阳区新源南路1-3号平安国际金融中心A座15层01-03,05
☎ 010-5933 9206
🖷 010-5933 9233
✉ eric.xue@reedexpo.com.cn
联系人：薛光
www.totalexhibition.com
www.totalexhibition.com
联络：中国贸促会机械行业分会
地址：北京市西城区三里河路46号(100823)
☎ 010-6859 4192，6859 4826，6859 5406
🖷 010-6859 4995
✉ info@ccpitmsc.org
www.chinamachine.org.cn

国际分包展览会
日期：2013/06/07-09
地点：英国伯明翰
主办：中国贸促会机械行业分会
地址：北京市西城区三里河路46号(100823)
☎ 010-6859 4927，6851 3586，6851 2883
✉ info@ccpitmsc.org
www.chinamachine.org.cn

英国伯明翰国际花五金工具及园艺展
GLEE
日期：2013/09 -
地点：英国伯明翰
内容：花园家具及家居用品、露营及休闲用品、烧烤设备、花园机械和设备、花园手工具和附件、其它设备和花园布置、植物和植物护理、水处理和室外照明
主办：北方国际展览有限公司North Intl Exhibition Co Ltd
联系人：吴江，刘硕
地址：北京市西城区菜园街1号，中环假日酒店写字间1102室(100053)
☎ 010-8354 0336，8351 3705
🖷 010-6354 7597
✉ wujiang@northexpo.com.cn
liushuo@northexpo.con.cn

英国石油工业技术展
SPE Offshore Europe:
Oil & Gas Exhibition & Conference
日期：2013/09/03-06
地点：英国阿伯丁会展中心
内容：作为东半球最重要的石油勘探及生产工业展会，英国石油工业技术展一直不断发展，全面真实地反映着世界石油工业不断发展的技术要求。产品及服务涉及石油勘探与生产各个环节的上游油田技术/服务。
周期：两年一届
市场范围：国际性
性质：面向贸易观众
主办：励展英国公司
联络：励展博览集团国际销售部
地址：北京市朝阳区新源南路1-3号平安国际金融中心A座15层01-03,05
☎ 010-5933 9268
🖷 010-5933 9233
✉ daisy.zang@reedexpo.com.cn
www.offshore-europe.co.uk

英国国际海洋勘探技术展
Oceanology Intl
日期：2014/03 -
地点：英国伦敦ExCeL会展中心
内容：海洋及船舶科学与技术
周期：两年一届
参展费用：光地展位290英镑/m²，标准展位336英镑/m²
上届规模 2010：展览面积7,338m²，参展商538家，贸易观众4,490人)
主办：励展英国公司
联络：励展博览集团国际销售部
地址：北京市朝阳区新源南路1-3号平安国际金融中心A座15层01-03,05
☎ 010-5933 9268
🖷 010-5933 9233
✉ daisy.zang@reedexpo.com.cn
www.oceanologyIntl.com

柬埔寨
Cambodia

第八届柬埔寨进出口商品与各省特色产品博览会
2013第二届中国出口商品（柬埔寨）展览会
2013东盟（柬埔寨）中国农林牧渔出口商品展
2013柬埔寨农林牧渔供应商对接中国买家采购会
The 8th Cambodia Import-Export and One Province One Product Exhibition 2013
日期：2013/12 -
地点：柬埔寨金边钻石岛国际会展中心
主办：越中会展商务有限公司
☎ 0771-261 5620
🖷 0771-263 0917

2013柬埔寨国际建筑建筑装饰博览会
Cambodia Intl Construction & Building Material and Decoration Expo
日期：2013/12/26-30
地点：柬埔寨金边
内容：建筑和房地产、建材、室内外建筑装饰产品、家居用品等
主办：越中会展商务有限公司
☎ 0771-261 5620
🖷 0771-263 0917

2013东盟(柬埔寨)中国建筑建材及家居用品博览会
China Construction-Building Materials & Interior-Exterior Decoration Exhibition in Cambodia 2013
日期：2013/12/26-30
地点：柬埔寨金边
内容：建筑和房地产、建材、室内外建筑装饰产品、家居用品等
主办：越中会展商务有限公司
☎ 0771-2615 620
🖷 0771-2630 917

加拿大
Canada

加拿大国际食品展览会
SIAL Canada
日期：2013/05/09-11
地点：加拿大蒙特利尔
内容：农产品、畜产品、水产品、肉加工品、罐头食品、副食品、保健食品、有机食品、调味品、各类面点及甜点、各类酒精饮料、不含酒精的饮料、保健饮料等 农产品、畜产品、水产品、肉加工品、罐头食品、副食品、保健食品、有机食品、调味品、各类面点及甜点、各类酒精饮料、不含酒精的饮料、保健饮料等 洋食品、清真食品、烘焙食品、食品供应、快餐、鱼、肉类食品、待许经营、蔬菜、饮料及厨房设备等
主办：北方国际展览有限公司North International Exhibition Co Ltd
地址：北京市西城区菜园街1号中环假日酒店写字间1102室(100053)
联系人：王子威，李松林
☎ 010-8355 7740，8353 3198
🖷 010-6354 7597
✉ w.ziwei@northexpo.com.cn
reanna@northexpo.com.cn

国际塑料工业展览会
日期：2013/05/14-16
地点：加拿大多伦多
周期：三年一届
主办：中国贸促会机械行业分会
地址：北京市西城区三里河路46号(100823)
☎ 010-6859 4192，6859 4826，6859 5406
🖷 010-6859 4995
✉ info@ccpitmsc.org
www.chinamachine.org.cn

加拿大制造技术展览会
日期：2013/10 -
地点：加拿大多伦多
周期：两年一届
主办：中国贸促会机械行业分会
地址：北京市西城区三里河路46号(100823)
☎ 010-6859 5495，6859 5247，6859 5406，6859 5431
🖷 010-6859 4995
✉ info@ccpitmsc.org
www.chinamachine.org.cn

智利
Chile

2013智利圣地亚哥国际建筑展览会
日期：2013/05/08-11
地点：智利智利圣地亚哥Espacio Riesco
内容：厨房浴室成套家具、设备及其配套产品；门窗及配套五金件、建筑玻璃、型材；幕墙、天蓬、屋顶、暖房、活动房等；工程机械（钻机、搅拌机、起重机、凿岩机械）、矿业装备；暖通空调、制冷设备、泵阀管，水处理设备；石材及石材加工工具；地板、地毯、壁纸等铺装材料；陶瓷制品、砖瓦、马赛克及彩色路砖；建筑装饰板材、线材、饰面板；墙体材料、石膏、隔热隔音与保温材料；住宅、公共场所等照明及配套电子元器件；建筑涂料、油漆、化学粘合剂；防盗、防火报警系统及出入口控制设备；楼梯、泳池及桑拿设备、康体休闲设施；停车库(场)管理系统；电梯、自动扶梯及校准及测量设备；建筑工程设备、机械、施工工具
周期：两年一届
主办：中国贸促会建设行业分会会展部
地址：北京市海淀区三里河路9号建设部大院机关门诊楼503(100835)
联系人：云鹏
☎ 15110286537
🖷 010-5893 3930
✉ www.build-ccpit.org
QQ 1492095643

国际矿业展览会
日期：2013/06/17-21
地点：智利安托法加斯塔
主办：中国贸促会机械行业分会
地址：北京市西城区三里河路46号(100823)
☎ 010-6859 4811，6859 4994，6859 4910
🖷 010-6859 4995
✉ info@ccpitmsc.org
www.chinamachine.org.cn

哥伦比亚
Columbia

哥伦比亚国际汽车及零部件展览会
Expo Partes 2013
日期：2013/06/05-07
地点：哥伦比亚波哥大
周期：两年一届
主办：北京中杰城投国际展览有限公司
联系人：李娜
☎ 010-5979 9850转858
🖷 010-5979 9850转810, 5885 7468
www.top-fairs.com.cn
www.build-ccpit.org

埃及
Egypt

国际汽车及零配件展览会
日期：2013/01/21-25
地点：埃及开罗
周期：每年一届
主办：中国贸促会机械行业分会
地址：北京市西城区三里河路46号(100823)
☎ 010-6859 4952，6859 4804，6859 4931，6859 5220
🖷 010-6859 4995
✉ info@ccpitmsc.org
www.chinamachine.org.cn

国际博览会
日期：2013/03 -
地点：埃及开罗
周期：每年一届
主办：中国贸促会机械行业分会
地址：北京市西城区三里河路46号(100823)
☎ 010-6859 5499，6859 4803，6859 4807，6859 4989，6859 5055
🖷 010-68594995
✉ info@ccpitmsc.org
www.chinamachine.org.cn

国际机床工具展览会
日期：2013/11 -
地点：埃及开罗
周期：每年一届
主办：中国贸促会机械行业分会
地址：北京市西城区三里河路46号(100823)
☎ 010-6859 5495，6859 5247，6859 5406，6859 5431
🖷 010-6859 4995
✉ info@ccpitmsc.org
www.chinamachine.org.cn

埃及国际电力能源及照明展览会
日期：2013/12 -
地点：埃及开罗
周期：每年一届
主办：中国贸促会建设行业分会会展部；北京中杰城设国际展览有限公司
联系人：王艳玲
☎ 010-8836 3688，5979 9850转813，13691545669
🖷 010-5885 7468，5979 9850转810
✉ wangyanling@top-fairs.com.cn
QQ 20204846
www.btfi.cn
www.power-gen.org.cn
www.top-fairs.com.cn

法国
France

法国戛纳音乐节
MIDEM: The World's Music Market
日期：2013/01 -
地点：法国戛纳影节宫Palais des Festivals
内容：与音乐产业及其关联产业相关的所有产品与服务。通过丰富的会议与联络活动帮助参会代表全面、深入了解产业与市场的最新资讯和发展趋势。
周期：每年一届
主办：励展法国公司Reed MIDEM
联络：励展博览集团国际销售部
地址：北京市朝阳区新源南路1-3号平安国际金融中心A座15层01-03,05
☎ 010-5933 9299
🖷 010-5933 9233
✉ jerry.shen@reedexpo.com.cn
联系人：申健
www.midem.com

巴黎国际服装、珠宝、银饰及配件展览会
Eclat de Mode / Bijorhca Paris:
The Fashion side of Jewellery
Bi-annual Intl Trade Show
日期：2013/01 -
地点：法国巴黎凡尔赛门展览中心Paris Expo - Porte de Versailles
内容：巴黎专为世界时尚珠宝业举办的唯一国际展会。集中展示秋／冬时装珠宝、银质珠宝、高级女士时装及时尚附件等产品。Eclat de Mode 是时尚世界的旗帜性展会，每年两届在巴黎举办（一月及九月）。展商包括来自全球30多个国家的设计师、厂商、批发商、进口商。 产品及服务：设计师珠宝及服装珠宝、银质及镀金珠宝、时尚手表、品牌及高级定制珠宝、春夏时尚配件。
周期：每年两届
市场范围：国际性
性质：面向贸易观众
主办：励展法国公司Reed Expositions France
联络：励展博览集团国际销售部
地址：北京市朝阳区新源南路1-3号平安国际金融中心A座15层01-03,05
☎ 010-5933 9299
🖷 010-5933 9233
✉ jerry.shen@reedexpo.com.cn
联系人：申健
www.bijorhca.com

法国国际地产投资交易会
MIPIM featuring MIPIM Horizons:
The World's Property Market
日期：2013/03 -
地点：法国戛纳影节宫Palais des Festivals
内容：为投资者、公司最终用户、当地及地区官员、开发商、经纪商、资产管理者以及服务供应商提供商业机会。另有内容丰富的研讨会活动以及各

种社交联络活动，令参会者深刻理解房地产业并获取国际房地产业的最新资讯动态。
周期：每年一届
主办：励展法国展览公司Reed MIDEMReed MIDEM, FRANCE
联络：励展博览集团国际销售部
地址：北京市朝阳区新源南路1-3号平安国际金融中心A座15层01-03,05
☎ 010-5933 9299
🖷 010-5933 9233
✉ jerry.shen@reedexpo.com.cn
联系人：申健
www.mipim.com

法国尼斯卫生纸业展览会
日期：2013/03/18-21
地点：法国尼斯Acropolis Palais des Expositions
周期：两年一届
上届规模 2011：展览面积4,353m^2，参展商184家，贸易观众2,250人
主办：亚洲博闻有限公司UBM Asia
地址：广州中国大酒店商业大厦1159-1164,博闻(广州)展览有限公司(510015)
联系人：020-8666 0158
http://tissueworld.com/world

巴黎国际航空航天展览会
日期：2013/06/20-23
地点：法国巴黎
周期：每年一届
主办：中国贸促会机械行业分会
地址：北京市西城区三里河路46号(100823)
☎ 010-6859 4985，6859 5855
🖷 010-6859 4995
✉ info@ccpitmsc.org
www.chinamachine.org.cn

法国国际汽车配件及工艺装备展览会
EQUIP AUTO 2013
日期：2013/10/16-19
地点：法国巴黎
周期：两年一届
主办：北京中杰城投国际展览有限公司
联系人：李娜
☎ 010-5979 9850转858
🖷 010-5979 9850转810，5885 7468
www.top-fairs.com.cn
www.build-ccpit.org
主办：中国贸促会机械行业分会
地址：北京市西城区三里河路46号(100823)
☎ 010-6859 4952，6859 4804，6859 4931，6859 5220
🖷 010-6859 4995
✉ info@ccpitmsc.org
www.chinamachine.org.cn

国际工业配件市场展览会
日期：2013/11 -
地点：法国巴黎
周期：每年一届
主办：中国贸促会机械行业分会
地址：北京市西城区三里河路46号(100823)
☎ 010-6859 4927，6851 3586，6851 2883
🖷 010-6859 4995
✉ info@ccpitmsc.org
www.chinamachine.org.cn

2013年法国国际卫浴展览会
日期：2013/11/04-08
地点：法国巴黎维勒班特国际展览中心
内容：陶瓷洁具，浴室地板，卫浴配件及装饰，卫生设备，淋浴/供水设备，卫浴照明，土耳其浴，桑拿，水疗，矿物质产品，卫浴家具，各式浴缸，电暖气，毛巾烘干机，水龙头，管道技术
周期：每年一届
主办：IDEO BAIN
承办：中国贸促会建设行业分会
地址：北京市海淀区三里河路9号建设部大院机关门诊楼503(100835)
联系人：云鹏
☎ 010-8837 0844
🖷 010-5893 3930
✉ rocyun@hotmail.com
QQ 1492095643

第28届法国巴黎国际建筑展览会
BATIMAT :
The World's Leading Construction Exhibition
日期：2013/11 -
地点：法国巴黎
内容：主体工程区包括屋架、结构构件、屋顶、防水材料、保温隔热材料、主体结构材料和构配件、水处理系统、排水系统；门窗及五金区；装饰装修区包括各种隔段材料、橱柜、墙地面装饰材料、瓷砖、大理石、花岗石、其它石材、石板、木质板材、木地板、油漆涂料、壁炉及烟道、厨房装饰、照明、装饰材料、游泳池装修及其设备、露天家具及设施、户外运动及娱乐设施；建筑施工设备区。观众构成：承包商、建筑工匠39%，建筑师、开发商 24%，零售商、分销商17%，制造商15%。
周期：两年一届
主办：励展博览集团
联络：励展博览集团国际销售部
地址：北京市朝阳区新源南路1-3号平安国际金融中心A座15层01-03,05
☎ 010-5933 9208
🖷 010-5933 9233
✉ winnie.wang@reedexpo.com.cn
联系人：王颖
www.batimat.com
www.reedexport.cn

巴黎国际殡葬展
Funéraire Paris 2013 :
The Exhibition for Funeral Suppliers & Distributors
日期：2013/11 -
地点：法国巴黎
主办：励展法国公司（Reed Expositions France）
地址：励展博览集团国际销售部 北京市朝阳区新源南路1-3号平安国际金融中心A座15层01-03,05
联系人：王颖
☎ 010-5933 9208
🖷 010-5933 9233
✉ winnie.wang@reedexpo.com.cn
www.reedexport.cn

德国
Germany

国际智能城市技术博览会
UrbanTec
日期：2013 -
地点：德国科隆国际展览中心
主办：科隆国际展览公司
联络：科隆展览中国有限公司
地址：北京市东三环北路8号亮马河大厦2座1018室(100004)
☎ 010-6590 7878/7766
🖷 010-6590 6139
✉ info@koelnmesse.cn
www.koelnmesse.cn

烹饪 · 享受 · 生活
LivingKitchen
日期：2013/01/14-20
地点：德国科隆科隆国际博览中心容：展会吸引了来自20个国家的185家参展商，展品范围涵盖了厨房家具，厨房电器及相关配件。
主办：科隆展览国际有限公司KOELNMESSE
地址：北京东三环北路8号亮马河大厦2座1018室(100004)
联系人：陈琬
☎ 010-6590 7766转751
✉ s.chen@koelnmesse.cn
www.livingkitchen-cologne.com
www.livingkitchen-cologne.cn

LivingKitchen
Date: 2013/01/14-20
Venue: Cologne Exhibition Center，Germany
Profile: Covering an area of 42,000 m^2, more than 180 well-known national and Intl suppliers will bring their latest ideas and innovations to the trade fair – from kitchen furniture and built-in appliances to sinks, fixtures, worktops, lighting and accessories.
Organizer: KOELNMESSE
Address: Unit 1018, Landmark Tower II, No. 8 Dongsanhuan North Rd,, Beijing 100004, China
Contact: Sunny Chen
☎ 010-6590 7766 ext 751
✉ s.chen@koelnmesse.cn
www.livingkitchen-cologne.com
www.livingkitchen-cologne.cn

科隆国际家具展
imm cologne
日期：2013/01/14-20
地点：德国科隆国际展览中心Cologne Exhibition Center
内容：世界最负盛名的家具展览会。每年一月份在德国科隆国际展览中心举行。展品无以伦比的广度和深度是科隆国际家具展作为全球第一品牌的独特性。在这里，全球的观众将领略到来自世界范围的包罗万象的设计一流的家具以及经典家居用品世界，其间，丰富多彩的配套活动也为科隆国际家具展增色不少
周期：每年一届
市场范围：国际性
性质：面向公众
主办：德国科隆展览国际有限公司Koelnmesse GmbH
地址：北京市朝阳区东三环北路8号亮马河大厦二座1018室(100004)
联系人：陈瑞
☎ 010-6590 7766转750
🖷 010-6590 6139
✉ r.chen@koelnmesse.cn
www.imm-cologne.cn

imm cologne
Date: 2013/01/14-20
Venue: Cologne Exhibition Center, Germany
Profile: imm cologne is the Intl leading trade fair for the furnishing sector. Each year, imm cologne is the first event to present the latest home trends for Europe and overseas.The unparalleled breadth and depth of the exhibits is the trademark and claim to top quality of imm cologne. Here, Intl trade visitors discover furniture and home style ideas from all over the world.
Frequency: Annual
Market Area: International
Nature: Open to public
Organizer: Koelnmesse GmbH
Contact: Ryan Chen
Address: Unit 1018 Landmark Tower II, No. 8 Dongsanhuan N. Road, Beijing 100004
☎ 86-10-6590 7766 ext 750
🖷 86-10-6590 6139
✉ r.chen@koelnmesse.cn
www.imm-cologne.cn

科隆国际糖果原料和机械展览会
ProSweets Cologne 2013
日期：2013/01/27-30
地点：德国德国科隆国际博览中心Cologne Exhibition Center
内容：甜食生产原材料，甜食包装材料，甜食包装机械，甜食工业机器与设备，甜食生产中冷藏与空调技术，甜食生产中的食品安全、质量管理，甜食生产中的自动化、数据处理、开环和闭环控制技术，甜食生产用加工设备和辅助装置。服务提供商、组织机构、出版社 垃圾处理、废物循环利用
始办年份：2006
周期：每年一届
市场范围：国际性
性质：面向贸易观众
主办：科隆国际展览有限公司Koelnmesse GmbH
地址：北京市东三环北路8号亮马河大厦2座1018室(100004)
联系人：潘容
☎ 010-6590 7766 转ext 715
🖷 010-6590 6139
✉ g.pan@koelnmesse.cn
www.prosweets.cn

ProSweets Cologne 2013
Date: 2013/01/27-30
Venue: Cologne Exhibition Center, Germany
Profile: Raw materials and ingredients for confectionery production Confectionery packaging Packaging machines for confectionery Machines and systems for the confectionery industry Refrigeration and air conditioning technology for confectionery production Food safety and quality management in confectionery production (incl. operating hygiene) Automation, data processing, control technology for confectionery production &61548; Operating equipment and auxiliary devices for confectionery production &61548; Service providers, organisations, publishers; Waste disposal / Recycling
Established Year: 2006
Frequency: Annual
Market Area: International
Nature: Trade Only
Organizer: Koelnmesse GmbH
Address: Unit 1018, Landmark Tower II, No.8 Dongsanhuan North Rd., Beijing 100004
Contact: Grace Pan
☎ 010-6590 7766 ext 715
🖷 010-6590 6139
✉ g.pan@koelnmesse.cn
www.prosweets.cn

科隆国际糖果及休闲食品展
ISM- Intl Sweets and Biscuits Fair
日期：2013/01/27-30
地点：德国科隆国际博览中心Cologne Exhibition Center
内容：ISM是全球市场成功的标志 在德国科隆举办的科隆国际糖果及休闲食品展（ISM）是全球最大、最重要的甜食和休闲食品的展览会。每年，来自全球贸易界的专业人士汇聚在这里，相互介绍、发掘和探讨国际最新流行趋势、最新的产品，寻找最近最好的商机。始办年份：1972
周期：每年一届
市场范围：国际性
性质：面向贸易观众
入场费：人民币600元
参展费用：标准摊位要求最小12m^2 420欧元/m^2（最小12m^2） 光地 （最小36m^2）：150欧元/m^2
主办：Koelnmesse
联络：科隆展览中国有限公司
地址：北京东三环北路8号亮马河大厦2座1018室(100004)
联系人：潘容
☎ 010-6590 7766 转715
🖷 010-6590 6139
✉ g.pan@koelnmesse.cn
www.ism-cologne.cn
www.ism-cologne.com

ISM- Intl Sweets and Biscuits Fair
Date: 2013/01/27-30
Venue: Cologne Exhibition Center, Germany
Profile: ISM is the largest and most important sweets and iscuits fair in the world. Every year the Intl sector meets to introduce,discover and discuss the latest trends, the newest products and the most up-to-dates perspectives.
Established Year: 1972
Frequency: Annual
Market Area: International
Nature: Trade Only
Organizer: Koelnmesse
Address: Unit 1018, Landmark Tower II, No. 8 Dongsanhuan North Rd, Beijing 100004, China
Contact: Grace Pan
☎ 86-10-6590 7766 ext 715
🖷 86-10-6590 6139
✉ g.pan@koelnmesse.cn
www.ism-cologne.cn
www.ism-cologne.com

春季马术用品展
spoga horse(spring)
日期：2013/02/03-05
地点：德国科隆国际展览中心
内容：马术用品和相关服务
始办年份：2008
周期：每年两届
市场范围：国际性
性质：面向贸易观众
主办：科隆展览中国有限公司Koelnmesse Co., Ltd.
地址：北京市东三环北路8号亮马河大厦2座1018室(100004)
联系人：张昱
☎ 010-6590 7766 转738
🖷 010-6590 6139
✉ j.zhang@koelnmesse.cn
www.spogahorse.cn
www.spogahorse.com

spoga horse(spring)
Date: 2013/02/03-05
Venue: Cologne Exhibition Center, Germany
Established Year: 2008
Frequency: Biannual
Market Area: International
Nature: Trade Only
Organizer: Koelnmesse Co., Ltd.
Address: Unit 1018, Landmark Tower II, No.8 Dongsanhuan North Rd., Beijing 100004
Contact: Joesy Zhang
☎ 86-10-6590 7766 ext 738
🖷 86-10-6590 6139
✉ j.zhang@koelnmesse.cn
www.spogahorse.cn
www.spogahorse.com

科隆国际电动汽车大会暨展览会
elektromobilia
日期：2013/02/13-14
地点：德国德国科隆国际博览中心Koelnmesse GmbH, Germany
主办：科隆展览中国有限公司Koelnmesse Co., Ltd.
地址：北京市朝阳区东三环北路8号亮马河大厦二座1018室(100004)
☎ 010-6590 7766
🖷 010-6590 6139
✉ info@koelnmesse.cn
www.elektromobilia.com

elektromobilia
Date: 2013/02/13-14
Venue: Koelnmesse GmbH, Germany, Germany
Organizer: Koelnmesse Co Ltd
Address: Unit 1018, Landmark Tower II, No. 8 Dongsanhuan North Rd, Beijing 100004, China
☎ 86-10-6590 7766
🖷 86-10-6590 6139
✉ info@koelnmesse.cn
www.elektromobilia.com

德国斯图加特紧固件展览会
FASTENER FAIR/STUTTGART
日期：2013/02/26-28
地点：德国斯图加特
内容：各类标准及非标准紧固件、相关加工设备、检测设备、工具等
周期：两年一届
主办：北方国际展览有限公司North International Exhibition Co Ltd
地址：北京市西城区菜园街1号中环假日酒店写字间1102室(100053)
联系人：赖彦平，陈思
☎ 010-8354 0342, 8354 0341
🖷 010-6354 7597
✉ yanping.lai@northexpo.com.cn
freya_chen@northexpo.com.cn

科隆亚太采购交易会—五金、家居、家电、园艺产品展
ASIA PACIFIC SOURCING
日期：2013/03/03-05
地点：德国科隆
内容：各种五金工具、小型机械、锁具及安防设备、建筑及DIY产品、五金配件、紧固件、卫生洁具、灯光照明设备等
周期：两年一届
主办：北方国际展览有限公司North Intl Exhibition Co Ltd
地址：北京市西城区菜园街1号，中环假日酒店写字间1102室(100053)
联系人：吴江，刘硕
☎ 010-8354 0336，8351 3705
🖷 010-6354 7597
✉ wujiang@northexpo.com.cn
liushuo@northexpo.con.cn

科隆教育与培训展览会
Didacta
日期：2013/03/06-09
地点：德国科隆国际博览中心
市场范围：国际性
主办：科隆展览国际有限公司KOELNMESSE
地址：北京市东三环北路8号亮马河大厦2座1018室(100004)
☎ 010-6590 7766
🖷 010-6590 6139
✉ info@koelnmesse.cn
www.bildungsmesse.com

Didacta
Date: 2013/03/06-09
Venue: Cologne Exhibition Center, Germany
Market Area: International
Organizer: KOELNMESSE
Address: Unit 1018, Landmark Tower II, No. 8 Dongsanhuan North Rd, Beijing 100004, China
☎ 86-10-6590 7766
🖷 86-10-6590 6139
✉ info@koelnmesse.cn
www.bildungsmesse.com

涂料—外观装饰展览会
Farbe-Ausbau&Fassade
(Paint-Finishing & Facade)
日期：2013/03/06-09
地点：德国科隆国际展览中心Cologne Exhibition Center
入场费：日票18欧元，两日票25欧元，通票39欧元
主办：科隆国际展览公司
地址：北京市东三环北路8号亮马河大厦2座1018室(100004)
☎ 010-6590 7766
🖷 010-6590 6139
✉ info@koelnmesse.cn
www.faf-cologne.com

Farbe-Ausbau&Fassade
(Paint-Finishing & Facade)
Date: 2013/03/06-09
Venue: Cologne Exhibition Center, Germany
Organizer: KOELNMESSE
Address: Unit 1018, Landmark Tower II, No. 8 Dongsanhuan North Rd, Beijing 100004, China
☎ 86-10-6590 7766
🖷 86-10-6590 6139
✉ info@koelnmesse.cn
www.faf-cologne.com

法兰克福暖通卫浴展
ISH
日期：2013/03/12-16
地点：德国法兰克福
内容：浴室、卫生间：卫生洁具、浴室及卫生间配件、厕所设施、厨房与家居设备、热水器、水处理设备；安装技术：管道技术及金属加工技术、卫生间安装部分、连接件、管件、及相关的工具，密封件等；楼宇及能源技术：供热工程、散热器、泵类等；通风和制冷。
周期：两年一届
主办：北方国际展览有限公司North Intl Exhibition Co Ltd
联系人：吴江，刘硕
地址：北京市西城区菜园街1号，中环假日酒店写字间1102室(100053)
☎ 010-8354 0336，8351 3705
🖷 010-6354 7597
✉ wujiang@northexpo.com.cn
liushuo@northexpo.con.cn

科隆国际牙科展
IDS-Intl Dental Show
日期：2013/03/12-16
地点：德国科隆国际展览中心
内容：牙科临床实践，牙科技工室，感染控制与维护，服务、信息、交流和机构
始办年份：1945
周期：两年一届
市场范围：国际性
性质：面向贸易观众
主办：科展览有中国限公司Koelnmesse Co., Ltd.
地址：北京市亮马河大厦2座1018室(100004)
联系人：齐志宇
☎ 010-6590 7766 转727
🖷 010-6590 6139
✉ k.qi@koelnmesse.cn
www.ids-cologne.cn english.ids-cologne.de

IDS-Intl Dental Show
Date: 2013/03/12-16
Venue: Cologne exhibition centre, Germany
Profile: Dental practice, Dental laboratory, Infection control and maintenance, services, information, communication and organization
Established Year: 1945
Frequency: Biennial
Market Area: International
Nature: Trade Only
Organizer: Koelnmesse Co Ltd
Address: Unit 1018, Landmark Tower 2, No.8 Dongsanhuan North Rd., Beijing
Contact: Kevin Qi
☎ 86-10-6590 7766 ext 727
🖷 86-10-6590 6139
✉ k.qi@koelnmesse.cn
www.ids-cologne.cn
english.ids-cologne.de

德国汉诺威工业博览会
HANNOVER MESSE
日期：2013/04/08-12
地点：德国汉诺威
内容：动力传动与控制展；工业零部件和分承包技术展；工业自动化展；能源展；风能及风力发电技术产品；电厂技术；环保技术展；数字化工业展；研发与技术展；线圈及绕线技术展；新能源汽车技术展；表面处理技术；空压及真空技术展。
主办：北方国际展览有限公司North Intl Exhibition Co Ltd
联系人：吴江，刘硕
地址：北京市西城区莱园街1号，中环假日酒店写字间1102室(100053)
☎ 010-8354 0336，8351 3705
🖷 010-6354 7597
✉ wujiang@northexpo.com.cn
liushuo@northexpo.con.cn

德国慕尼黑国际工程机械博览会
bauma 2013
日期：2013/04/15-21
地点：德国 新慕尼黑国际博览会中心
内容：建筑工地包括建筑工程车辆，建筑机械，起重及输送设备，建筑设备、工具及特殊系统，工地用水泥和砂浆处理及施工设备，结构件及脚手架，其他建筑工地设施；采矿、原材料开采及加工包括原材料开采与采矿机械，原材料运送，材料预加工技术（含炼焦厂设备）；建材生产包括水泥、石灰及石膏复合建材生产，混凝土制品及预制件生产机械和系统，沥青生产机械与系统，干混砂浆、石膏、抹灰及建材店产品生产机械及系统，石灰砂岩、电厂废渣（粉煤灰、炉渣等）再造建材生产机械及系统，其他附属建材生产机械及系统，建材（厂内）运送；部件及服务供应商包括传动工程、流体工程、供电组件，附件及高使用率备件，服务，测试、测量、控制及控制系统工程，通讯及导航，作业安全
周期：三年一届
上届规模 2011：展览面积555,000m^2，参展商3,150家来自190个国家及地区)，参观人数500,000人
承办：北京麦田通会国际展览有限公司（Beijing Cornfairs Intl Exhibition Co Ltd
地址：北京市丰台区南四环中路公益西桥北城南大道2座1217室
联系人：吴珊，高飞
☎ 010-5165 9302转8009
🖷 010-5165 9302转8004
✉ wanyingmissyou@163.com
✉ xiaoxiangzhishui@hotmail.com
QQ 1983315902
www.cornfairs.com
主办：中国贸促会机械行业分会
地址：北京市西城区三里河路46号(100823)
☎ 010-6859 4939，6859 4951，6859 5176，6859 4805
🖷 010-68594995
✉ info@ccpitmsc.org
www.chinamachine.org.cn

科隆国际艺术展
ART COLOGNE
日期：2013/04/18-22
地点：德国科隆国际展览中心Cologne Exhibition Center
内容：科隆艺术展是一个以传播和销售被国际认可的现代及当代艺术作品展览会。科隆艺术展是世界上最重要的艺术展览会之一。 主要展品范围： 油画作品 绘图作品 雕塑作品 行为艺术 摄影作品
始办年份：1967
周期：每年一届
市场范围：国际性
性质：面向贸易观众
主办：科隆展览中国有限公司Koelnmesse Co Ltd
地址：北京市朝阳区东三环北路8号亮马河大厦二座1018室(100004)
联系人：潘容
☎ 010-6590 7766转 715
🖷 010-6590 6139
✉ g.pan@koelnmesse.cn
www.artcologne.cn

USETEC
二手机械设备、机械系统及技术贸易国际展览会
日期：2013/04/22-24
地点：德国科隆国际展览中心Cologne Exhibition Center
内容：世界最大的二手机械设备系统展将与EISENWARENMESSE -科隆国际五金展同期举行。届时，全面蓬勃发展的二手机械设备 系统产品将会在这座落在黄金地段的开阔展览场地上等待您的光临。
周期：每年一届
入场费：日票28欧元，长期票43欧元
主办：科隆展览中国有限公司
地址：北京市东三环北路8号亮马河大厦2座1018室（100004）
☎ 010-6590 7878, 6590 7766
🖷 010-6590 6139
www.usetec.com

科隆国际家具生产、木工及室内装饰展
interzum cologne
日期：2013/05/13-16
地点：德国科隆国际展览中心Koelnmesse Trade Fair Center
内容：针对家具生产及其原辅料方面的一个全球性盛会，是目前世界上木工机械、家具生产设备及家具原材料、配件领域规模最大、影响力最大的专业展览会之一，每两年举办一届（逢单年举办），其展品范围之广位居所有同类展会之首。
始办年份：1959
周期：两年一届
市场范围：国际性
性质：面向公众
主办：德国科隆展览国际有限公司Koelnmesse GmbH
地址：北京市朝阳区东三环北路8号亮马河大厦二座1018室(100004)
联系人：贾宁
☎ 010-6590 7766转 729
🖷 010-6590 6139
✉ m.jia@koelnmesse
www.interzum.cn
主办：北方国际展览有限公司North Intl Exhibition Co Ltd
联系人：吴江，刘硕
地址：北京市 西城区莱园街1号，中环假日酒店写字间1102室(100053)
☎ 010-8354 0336，8351 3705
🖷 010-6354 7597
✉ wujiang@northexpo.com.cn
liushuo@northexpo.con.cn

interzum cologne
Date: 2013/05/13-16
Venue: Koelnmesse Trade Fair Center，Germany
Profile: interzum is the leading global event for the furniture and interior construction industries' supplying sections. This is where the trends and visions that will create future living spaces using modern materials, outstanding design, and exclusive innovations come to life.
Established Year: 1959
Frequency: Biennial
Market Area: International
Nature: Open to Public
Organizer: Koelnmesse GmbH
Address: Unit 1018 Landmark Tower II, No. 8 Dongsanhuan N. Road, Beijing 100004
Contact: Maggie Jia
☎ 86-10-6590 7766 ext 729
🖷 86-10-6590 6139
✉ m.jia@koelnmesse
www.interzum.cn

国际林业木工机械展览会
日期：2013/05/14-18
地点：德国汉诺威
周期：两年一届
主办：中国贸促会机械行业分会
地址：北京市西城区三里河路46号(100823)
☎ 010-6859 5499，6859 4803，6859 4807，6859 4989，6859 5055
🖷 010-6859 4995
✉ info@ccpitmsc.org
www.chinamachine.org.cn

创新材料学术大会
InnoMateria
日期：2013/05/14-15
地点：德国科隆国际展览中心Cologne Exhibition Center
主办：科隆展览中国有限公司
地址：北京市东三环北路8号亮马河大厦2座1018室(100004)
☎ 010-6590 7766转788/ 716
🖷 010-6590 6139
✉ info@koelnmesse.cn
www.innomateria.com

2013德国柏林国际线圈、电机、绝缘材料及电器制造展
CWIEME
日期：2013/06/04-06
地点：德国柏林国际展览中心
内容：全球最大的电磁线圈、电机、变压器制造和重绕及电气绝缘专业性展览会。该展览会为我国企业开拓欧洲市场，扩大出口提供了绝佳的平台。展品范围：各类电磁线圈、磁性材料、电机、变压器、绕线机、插片机、浸漆机、测试仪器及其它变压器制造设备、电气绝缘材料等。
始办年份：1996
周期：每年一届
市场范围：国际性
性质：面向贸易观众
参展费用：454.50欧元/m^{2}标准展位
上届规模 2012：展出面积30,000m^2，参展商730家（德国展商177家，中国展商140家被上届增长17%）
主办：广东粤召展览有限公司
地址：广州市天河区体育东路122号羊城国际商贸中心东塔1202, 1208室(510620)
联系人：周文槟
☎ 13710318991
✉ 1979wenbin@163.com
gdwenbin@hotmail.com
QQ 406372636

柏林国际会展及媒体技术展览会
SHOWTECH:
Intl. Show & Conference for Stage Technology, Eqpt. & Event Svs
日期：2013/06/18-20
地点：德国柏林展览中心
内容：国际会展技术及媒体技术展览会是针对舞台表演及展会活动行业的著名欧洲展览会，是向业内技术决策人、制造商、展会活动经理人、主办者及经销商展示灯光、音响科技领域最新创新、解决方案及行业潮流的高水平业务交流平台。由展会赞助机构德国影剧院技术协会（DTHG）于展会同期主办的专业会议将邀请顶级业内专家介绍最新的国际影剧院技术及管理经验。产品及服务 舞台技术、演播室技术、灯光及投影技术、音响及舞台专业音响（PA）技术、影像及通讯技术、展会活动技术、会议技术、影剧院设备及效果、展会活动服务、安全、初级及高级培训学院、媒体、协会机构。
周期：两年一届
性质：面向贸易观众
主办：励展德国公司
联络：励展博览集团国际销售部
地址：北京市朝阳区新源南路1-3号平安国际金融中心A座15层01-03,05
☎ 010-5933 9268
🖷 010-5933 9233
✉ daisy.zang@reedexpo.com.cn
联系人：臧威
www.showtech.de

2013科隆游戏展
gamescom
日期：2013/08/21-25
地点：德国德国科隆国际博览中心Cologne Exhibition Center, Germany
内容：欧洲最专业的综合性互动式游戏软件、信息软件和硬件设备展览，也是德国唯一一个集中了游戏软件、硬件、娱乐设备、信息软件和设备的大型国际展会。科隆国际游戏展由科隆国际展览公司与联邦互动娱乐软件协会(BIU)联合举办。
始办年份：2002
周期：每年一届
市场范围：国际性
性质：面向贸易观众
主办：科隆展览国际有限公司KOELNMESSE
地址：北京东三环北路8号亮马河大厦2座1018室科隆展览中国有限公司(100004)
联系人：陈瑞
☎ 010-6590 7766 转750
🖷 010-6590 6139
✉ r.chen@koelnmesse.cn
www.gamescom-cologne.cn

gamescom
Date: 2013/08/21-25
Venue: Cologne Exhibition Center, Germany，Germany
Established Year: 2002
Frequency: Annual
Market Area: International
Nature: Trade Only
Organizer: KOELNMESSE
Address: Unit 1018, Landmark Tower II, No. 8 Dongsanhuan North Rd, Beijing 100004, China
Contact: Ryan Chen
☎ 86-10-6590 7766 ext 750
🖷 86-10-6590 6139
✉ r.chen@koelnmesse.cn
www.gamescom-cologne.cn

国际自动贩卖机展览会
Eu'Vend
日期：2013/09/05-07
地点：德国科隆国际博览中心Cologne Exhibition Center
内容：Eu'Vend为观众提供了自动贩卖机制造商的全方位概览。无论是自动贩卖机还是软件提供商，Eu'Vend在同一时间、同一地点展示了各类创新理念和创新技术。
始办年份：2003
周期：两年一届
市场范围：国际性
主办：科隆展览国际有限公司KOELNMESSE
联络：科隆展览中国有限公司
地址：北京东三环北路8号亮马河大厦2座1018室
☎ 010-6590 7878/7766转715
🖷 010-6590 6139
✉ g.pan@koelnmesse.cn
www.euvend.cn

2013年国际体育用品、露营设备及园林生活博览会 科隆国际园艺博览会
spoga+gafa
日期：2013/09/08-10
地点：德国德国科隆国际展览中心
内容：户外生活（户外家具）；户外运动（烧烤设备，露营休闲用品，体育及比赛用品）；户内和户外休闲（植物和植物护理，花卉栽培和装饰，水处理和室外照明，花园规划和维护，其它设备和花园布置，宠物用品）；马术用品及服务
始办年份：1960
周期：每年一届
主办：科隆展览中国有限公司Koelnmesse Co Ltd
地址：北京市东三环北路8号亮马河大厦2座1018室(100004)
联系人：张昱
☎ 010-6590 7766 转 738
🖷 010-6590 6139
✉ j.zhang@koelnmesse.cn
www.spogagafa.cn

欧洲机床展览会
日期：2013/09/16-21
地点：德国汉诺威
周期：两年一届
主办：中国贸促会机械行业分会
地址：北京市西城区三里河路46号(100823)
☎ 010-6859 5495，6859 5247，6859 5406，6859 5431
🖷 010-6859 4995
✉ info@ccpitmsc.org
www.chinamachine.org.cn

数码营销博览会
dmexco
日期：2013/09/18-19
地点：德国科隆国际博览中心Cologne Exhibition Center
内容：展品涵盖数码产业所有领域的展览外，主题多样、规模巨大、娱乐性强。内容包括数码创意、数码效率和数码智能等。
市场范围：国际性
上届规模 2012：展览面积50,000m²，参展商578家，参观人数22,200人
主办：科隆展览国际有限公司KOELNMESSE
地址：北京东三环北路8号亮马河大厦2座1018室科隆展览中国有限公司(100004)
联系人：张昱
☎ 010-6590 7766 转 738
🖷 010-6590 6139
✉ j.zhang@koelnmesse.cn
www.dm-exco.cn
www.dm-exco.com

国际咖啡与茶展览会
coffeena- Intl Coffee Fair
日期：2013/09/19-21
地点：德国科隆国际博览中心
市场范围：国际性
主办：科隆展览国际有限公司KOELNMESSE
地址：北京东三环北路8号亮马河大厦2座1018室
☎ 010-6590 7878/7766
🖷 010-6590 6139
✉ info@koelnmesse.cn
www.coffeena.biz

coffeena- Intl Coffee Fair
Date: 2013/09/19-21
Venue: Cologne Exhibition Center，Germany
Market Area: International
Organizer: KOELNMESSE
Address: Unit 1018, Landmark Tower II, No. 8 Dongsanhuan North Rd, Beijing 100004, China
☎ 86-10-6590 7878/7766
🖷 86-10-6590 6139
✉ info@koelnmesse.cn
www.coffeena.biz

国际少儿用品展览会
Kind und Jugend
日期：2013/09/19-22
地点：德国科隆国际展览中心
内容：儿车及附件，安全座椅及设备，家具及附件，纺织品，婴儿、儿童、青年时装及孕妇装，玩具，育婴用品，电器，出版物，团体，其它
始办年份：1960
周期：每年一届
市场范围：国际性
性质：面向公众
主办：科展览有中国限公司Koelnmesse Co., Ltd
地址：北京市亮马河大厦2座1018室(510620)
联系人：潘容
☎ 010-6590 7766 转715
🖷 010-6590 6139
✉ g.pan@koelnmesse.cn
www.kindundjugend.cn

Kind und Jugend
Date: 2013/09/19-22
Venue: Cologne exhibition centre，Germany
Profile: Prams, car/bicycle seats, childrens` furniture, hygiene articles, electric appliances, textiles, baby cosmetics, toys and games for babies and toddlers, fashion for babies and toddlers, maternity wear, shop equipment, publications, organizations
Established Year: 1960
Frequency: Annual
Market Area: International
Nature: Open to Public
Organizer: Koelnmesse Co Ltd
Address: Unit 1018, Landmark Tower 2, No.8 Dongsanhuan North Rd., Beijing
Contact: Grace Pan
☎ 010-6590 7766 ext 715
🖷 010-6590 6139
✉ g.pan@koelnmesse.cn
www.kindundjugend.cn

国际游艇及水上运动展览会
日期：2013/09/22-30
地点：德国腓特烈港
周期：每年一届
主办：中国贸促会机械行业分会
地址：北京市西城区三里河路46号(100823)
☎ 010-6859 4985，6859 5855
🖷 010-6859 4995
✉ info@ccpitmsc.org
www.chinamachine.org.cn

世界食品博览会
Anuga
日期：2013/10/05-09
地点：德国科隆国际博览中心
内容：全世界的食品展数不胜数，但只有Anuga才是食品和饮料行业规模最大、地位最重要的展览会，也是唯一一个为您的未来精心规划的展览会。展品范围有基本食品和精细食品，冷冻食品，肉制品，冷藏食品，奶制品，面包、焙烤食品和热饮，饮料，有机食品，餐饮技术，零售技术；其他有非处方药OTC论坛、健康及功能性食品论坛、协会、组织、贸易媒体、服务提供商和信息技术
始办年份：1922
周期：两年一届
市场范围：国际性
性质：面向贸易观众
主办：科隆国际展览有限公司KOELNMESSE
地址：北京东三环北路8号亮马河大厦2座1018室科隆展览中国有限公司(100004)
联系人：张昱
☎ 010-6590 7766 转738
🖷 010-6590 6139
✉ j.zhang@koelnmesse.cn
www.anuga.cn
www.anuga.com

Anuga
Date: 2013/10/05-09
Venue: Cologne Exhibition Center，Germany
Profile: Trade Fair for the Intl Food Industry Leading fair for industry, trade and catering trade in the food and beverage sector Manufacturers, importers and wholesalers - of food and drinks - of catering technology - of retail technology/shop fittings - Suppliers of services for the catering sector and the food retail trade - Trade agencies - Suppliers of specialties - Suppliers of fresh convenience products
Established Year: 1922
Frequency: Biennial
Market Area: International
Nature: Trade Only
Organizer: KOELNMESSE
Address: Unit 1018, Landmark Tower II, No. 8 Dongsanhuan North Rd, Beijing 100004, China
Contact: Joesy Zhang
☎ 86-10-6590 7766 ext 738
🖷 86-10-6590 6139
✉ j.zhang@koelnmesse.cn
www.anuga.cn
www.anuga.com

国际塑料橡胶工业展览会
日期：2013/10/16-23
地点：德国杜塞尔多夫
周期：三年一届
主办：中国贸促会机械行业分会
地址：北京市西城区三里河路46号(100823)
☎ 010-6859 4192，6859 4826，6859 5406
🖷 010-6859 4995
✉ info@ccpitmsc.org
www.chinamachine.org.cn

2013欧洲世界原料制药包装欧洲展
日期：2013/10/22-24
地点：德国法兰克福展览中心
内容：生物碱、氨基酸、抗体、抗生素、细胞因子、酶、激素及人工合成物质、酞类、磷脂、前列腺素、血清和疫苗。定制生产：原料药的委托生产、植物提纯和分离、原料药、合同制造/精细化学品、免疫组织化学、有机合成化学。中间体：生物催化剂、中间体、组织培养媒体。精细化学品：高级中间体、规范精细化工，医药中间体。辅料：抗菌防腐剂，抗氧化剂，胶囊/封装、涂层剂、颜色和分散体，药物输送系统、乳化/溶剂、香精香料、配方开发、微胶囊、软膏基质、溶剂、硬化剂、栓剂基地、粘度增加剂、脱臭剂、片剂粘结剂、片剂崩解剂、片剂填充剂、粘合剂、片剂润滑剂。润湿/溶剂、成品制剂
主办：博闻展览公司UBM
联络：上海国卓会展有限公司
联系人：黄叶
☎ 021-6072 3398
🖷 021-5171 4607
✉ hzxshzy@163.com
www.wstzcj.com

国际桑拿及泳池设备展
Aquanale
日期：2013/10/22-25
地点：德国科隆国际博览中心
内容：游泳池、桑拿房的设计、建设及其维护；游泳池、桑拿房相关设施、设备、器材、用品；游泳休闲设备、疗养设备4私人spa；服务、专业媒体及其它；人工日光浴装置包括技术仪器；spa治疗
始办年份：1953
周期：两年一届
市场范围：国际性
性质：面向贸易观众
主办：科隆展览中国有限公司Koelnmesse Co., Ltd.
地址：北京市朝阳区东三环北路8号亮马河大厦二座1018室(100004)
联系人：贾宁
☎ 010-6590 7766 转729
🖷 010-6590 6139
✉ m.jia@koelnmesse.cn
www.aquanale.cn
www.aquanale.com

Aquanale
Date: 2013/10/22-25
Venue: Cologne Exhibition Center, Germany
Profile: Project planning, construction and equipping of pool facilities; Project planning, construction and equipping of sauna facilities and similar bath shapes; Ambience and fittings for pool and Wellness; Private SPA; Service and media; Synthetic Tanning Devices incl. technical equipment; Spa Treatment
Established Year: 1953
Frequency: Biennial
Market Area: International
Nature: Trade Only
Organizer: Koelnmesse Co Ltd
Address: Unit 1018, Landmark Tower II, No. 8 Dongsanhuan North Rd, Beijing 100004, China
Contact: Maggie Jia
☎ 86-10-6590 7766 ext 729
🖷 86-10-6590 6139
✉ m.jia@koelnmesse.cn
www.aquanale.cn
www.aquanale.com

国际休闲、体育设施及泳池设备展
FSB -
the Intl Trade Fair for Amenity Areas, Sports and Pool Facilities
日期：2013/10/22-25
地点：德国科隆国际博览中心Cologne Exhibition Center
内容：运动设施，公共泳池设施，公共桑拿设施，运动场的规划设计、建设及其配套设施，城市规划、景观建筑，服务及专业媒体
始办年份：1969
周期：两年一届
市场范围：国际性
性质：面向贸易观众
主办：科隆展览国际有限公司KOELNMESSE
地址：北京东三环北路8号亮马河大厦2座1018室科隆展览中国有限公司(100004)
联系人：张昱
☎ 010-6590 7766 转738
🖷 010-6590 6139
✉ j.zhang@koelnmesse.cn
www.fsb-cologne.cn

FSB -
the Intl Trade Fair for Amenity Areas, Sports and Pool Facilities
Date: 2013/10/22-25
Venue: Cologne Exhibition Center，Germany
Established Year: 1969
Frequency: Biennial
Market Area: International
Nature: Trade Only
Organizer: KOELNMESSE
Address: Unit 1018, Landmark Tower II, No. 8 Dongsanhuan North Rd, Beijing 100004, China
Contact: Joesy Zhang
☎ 86-10-6590 7766 ext 738
🖷 86-10-6590 6139
✉ j.zhang@koelnmesse.cn
www.fsb-cologne.cn

国际博物馆及展示技术博览会
EXPONATEC COLOGNE
日期：2013/11/20-22
地点：德国科隆国际展览中心Cologne Exhibition Center
内容：国际博物馆及展示技术展览会是全球最大的博物行业的展会。 主要展品范围：楼宇新建、重建与规划；人事服务供应商；公共关系；观众研究与定位；展览设计；建筑与展览技术；媒体；入口出口区域；博物馆商店；博物馆餐饮；安全与运输；行政后勤；修复与保存；分解；材料测试；继续教育；研究机构
始办年份：2004
周期：两年一届
市场范围：国际性
性质：面向贸易观众
主办：科隆展览国际有限公司KOELNMESSE
地址：北京东三环北路8号亮马河大厦2座1018室科隆展览中国有限公司(100004)
☎ 010-6590 7766
🖷 010-6590 6139
✉ info@koelnmesse.cn
www.exponatec.com

EXPONATEC COLOGNE
Date: 2013/11/20-22
Venue: Cologne Exhibition Center，Germany
Established Year: 2004
Frequency: Biennial
Market Area: International
Nature: Trade Only
Organizer: KOELNMESSE
Address: Unit 1018, Landmark Tower II, No. 8 Dongsanhuan North Rd, Beijing 100004, China
☎ 86-10-6590 7766
🖷 86-10-6590 6139
✉ info@koelnmesse.cn
www.exponatec.com

欧洲模具展览会
日期：2013/12 -
地点：德国法兰克福
周期：每年一届
主办：中国贸促会机械行业分会
地址：北京市西城区三里河路46号(100823)
☎ 010-6859 5495，6859 5247，6859 5406，6859 5431
🖷 010-6859 4995
✉ info@ccpitmsc.org
www.chinamachine.org.cn

科隆国际家装生活展
Living Interiors
日期：2014/01/13-19
地点：德国科隆科隆国际博览中心Cologne Exhibition Center
主办：科隆展览国际有限公司KOELNMESSE
地址：北京东三环北路8号亮马河大厦2座1018室(100004)
☎ 010-6590 7766
www.livinginteriors-cologne.de
www.livinginteriors-cologne.com

Living Interiors
Date: 2014/01/13-19
Venue: Cologne Exhibition Center, Germany
Profile: The new Intl event for interior furnishing — celebrated its premiere in January 2012 in parallel with imm cologne in hall 4.2. LivingInteriors stands for holistic interior and furnishing concepts. 120 exhibiting companies from the baths, flooring, walls and lighting segments came from Germany and abroad and showcased perfectly staged worlds of home design. All of these were a success with trade visitors and end consumers alike
Organizer: KOELNMESSE
Address: Unit 1018, Landmark Tower II, No. 8 Dongsanhuan North Rd,, Beijing 100004, China
☎ 010-6590 7766
www.livinginteriors-cologne.de,
www.livinginteriors-cologne.com

科隆国际五金博览会
INL HARDWARE FAIR COLOGNE
日期：2014/03/09-12
地点：德国科隆国际展览中心Koelnmesse Trade Fair Center
内容：国际五金行业规模最大最有影响力的盛会，代表着国际化的发展和顶级品质。全球没有任何其他展会能在一次展会上涵盖如此全面和齐备的展品范围，科隆国际五金博览会现在及将来都是全球这一行业内最具竞争力和主导博览会。科隆国际五金博览会在2010 年采用新的LOGO 和名称后，在五金领域将更加专业化。博览会包括三大展品系列一工具；锁具及安全系统；紧固件和家居改进，来自全球相关领域的零售商、供应商及采购商都聚集在此。随着中国产品的国际竞争力的增强以及参展取得的卓越的效果，中国企业参加科隆国际五金博览会的规模和数量也在最近数年内有着突飞猛进的增长。

始办年份：1952
周期：两年一届
市场范围：国际性
性质：面向公众
参展费用：标准摊位540 欧元/m^2 含光地租金、摊位装修、公共能源费、德国展览业协会 费用（AUMA费）、基本会刊登录费用、观众推广费用 359 欧元/家、垃圾清运费、摊位电费、其它杂费，及19 %增值税
主办：德国科隆展览国际有限公司Koelnmesse GmbH
地址：北京市朝阳区东三环北路8号亮马河大厦二座1018室(100004)
联系人：郑志强
☎ 010-6590 7766转7878
🖷 010-6590 6139
✉ k.zheng@koelnmesse.cn
www.ihf-cologne.cn

INTL HARDWARE FAIR COLOGNE
Date: 2014/03/09-12
Venue: Koelnmesse Trade Fair Center, Germany
Profile: The world's leading trade fair for the hardware sector regarding: Intlity of exhibitors and visitors, Comprehensive survey of the hardware industry: "One-Stop-Shopping
Established Year: 1952
Frequency: Biennial
Market Area: International
Nature: Open to Public
Organizer: Koelnmesse GmbH
Address: Unit 1018 Landmark Tower II, No. 8 Dongsanhuan N. Road, Beijing 100004
Contact: Ken Zheng
☎ 86-10-6590 7766 ext 7878
🖷 86-10-6590 6139
✉ k.zheng@koelnmesse.cn
www.ihf-cologne.cn

世界影像博览会
photokina
日期：2014/09/16-21
地点：德国科隆国际博览中心
内容：照相与成像工业领域领先的展览会，是世界上唯一的为大众消费者和专业人士提供所有成像介质、成像技术与成像市场综合性展示的展览会。因此，世界影像博览会（photokina）在成像领域具有独特的竞争优势，使其成为所有影像用户提供综合性解决方案的展示平台。 世界影像博览会（photokina）不仅为照相与成像产业部门提供新的销售动力，而且是集中展示面向未来的 各种技术和产品的趋势论坛
始办年份：1950
周期：两年一届
市场范围：国际性
性质：面向公众
入场费：8,95 EUR欧元
主办：科隆展览国际有限公司KOELNMESSE
地址：北京东三环北路8号亮马河大厦2座1018室(100004)
☎ 010-6590 7766
🖷 010-6590 6139
✉ g.pan@koelnmesse.cn
www.photokina.com

photokina
Date: 2014/09/16-21
Venue: Cologne Exhibition Center, Germany
Established Year: 1950
Frequency: Biennial
Market Area: International
Nature: Open to Public
Cost to Attend: 8,95 EUR
Organizer: KOELNMESSE
Address: Unit 1018, Landmark Tower II, No. 8 Dongsanhuan North Rd, Beijing 100004, China
☎ 86-10-6590 7766
🖷 86-10-6590 6139
✉ g.pan@koelnmesse.cn
www.photokina.com

匈牙利
Hungary

中国出口商品展览会
日期：2013/05 -
地点：匈牙利布达佩斯
周期：每年一届
主办：中国贸促会机械行业分会
地址：北京市西城区三里河路46号(100823)
☎ 010-6859 5499，6859 4803，6859 4807，6859 4989，6859 5055
🖷 010-6859 4995
✉ info@ccpitmsc.org
www.chinamachine.org.cn

印度
India

第三届印度南亚地球勘探科学展览会暨研讨会
GEO India 2013
日期：2013/01/23-25
地点：印度新德里
主办：北京邦企展览服务有限公司
地址：北京市朝阳区惠新东街11号紫光发展大厦B1座501(100029)
☎ 010-6482 3808, 6482 3670
✉ bbes@china.com

国际机床（切削技术）与工具展览会
日期：2013/01/24-30
地点：印度班加罗尔
周期：两年一届
主办：中国贸促会机械行业分会
地址：北京市西城区三里河路46号(100823)
☎ 010-6859 5495，6859 5247，6859 5406
🖷 010-6859 4995
✉ info@ccpitmsc.org
www.chinamachine.org.cn

印度国际铸造技术及设备展览会
IFEX
日期：2013/01/27-29
地点：印度班加罗尔班加罗尔国际展览中心 Bangalore Intl Exhibition Center
周期：每年一届
主办：科隆展览中国有限公司
地址：北京市东三环北路8号亮马河大厦2座1018室(100004)
☎ 010-6590 7766
🖷 010-6590 6139
✉ info@koelnmesse.cn
www.ifexindia.com

印度国际铝工业展（第三届）
ALUMINIUM INDIA
日期：2013/02 -
地点：印度孟买展览中心(Bombay Exhibition Centre)
内容：作为印度领先的铝业生态系统及其应用工业的企业间行业展会，印度国际铝工业展汇聚生产商、加工商、技术供应商和消费用户，即从原材料到半成品和成品的完整价值链。展品范围有原材料、原生金属制品；半成品、铸造、薄片、带条、平板、挤出铝制品；适于建筑建造、运输、电子及机械行业应用的铝制品；表面处理及链接技术；铝提取、处理及精炼机械、设备及配件；轻金属贸易及回收再用；服务、咨询、专业意见及信息。
周期：两年一届
上届规模 2010：展览面积5,000m^2，国外展商75家
主办：励展印度公司
联络：励展博览集团国际销售部
地址：北京市朝阳区新源南路1-3号平安国际金融中心A座15层01-03,05
联系人：王颖
☎ 010-5933 9208
🖷 010-5933 9233
✉ winnie.wang@reedexpo.com.cn
www.aluminium-india.com

国际工程机械、建材机械、矿山机械及工程车辆博览会
日期：2013/02/05-08
地点：印度孟买
周期：两年一届
主办：中国贸促会机械行业分会
地址：北京市西城区三里河路46号 100823
☎ 010-6859 4811，6859 4994，6859 4910
🖷 010-68594995
✉ info@ccpitmsc.org
www.chinamachine.org.cn
主办：中国贸促会机械行业分会
地址：北京市西城区三里河路46号(100823)
☎ 010-6859 4939，6859 4951，6859 5176，6859 4805
🖷 010-68594995
✉ info@ccpitmsc.org
www.chinamachine.org.cn

2013年印度国际汽车零部件及售后服务展览会
ACMA Automechanika New Delhi 2013
日期：2013/02/07-10
地点：印度新德里
周期：两年一届
主办：北京中杰城投国际展览有限公司
联系人：李娜
☎ 010-5979 9850转ext 858
🖷 010-5979 9850转ext 810,5885 7468
www.top-fairs.com.cn
www.build-ccpit.org
主办：中国贸促会机械行业分会
地址：北京市西城区三里河路46号(100823)
☎ 010-6859 4952，6859 4804，6859 4931，6859 5220
🖷 010-6859 4995
✉ info@ccpitmsc.org
www.chinamachine.org.cn

印度国际宝石及珠宝展览会（晨奈）
Gem and Jewellery India Intl Exhibition

Gem & Jewellery
India International Exhibition
16 - 18 March 2013
Chennai Trade Centre, Chennai, India

日期：2013/03/16-18
地点：印度晨奈
主办：亚洲博闻有限公司
地址：香港湾仔港湾道26号华润大厦17楼
☎ 00852-2827 6211
🖷 00852-3749 7342
✉ info-hk@ubm.com
www.jewelleryfair.in

Gem and Jewellery India Intl Exhibition
Date: 2013/03/16-18
Venue: Chennai, India
Organizer: UBM Asia Ltd
Address: 17/F, China Resources Building, 26 Harbour Road, Wan Chai, Hong Kong
Contact:
☎ 852-2827 6211
🖷 852-3749 7342
✉ info-hk@ubm.com
www.jewelleryfair.in

2013印度国际礼品、文具及家庭用品博览会
日期：2013/03/21-24
地点：印度孟买展览中心
内容：礼品类：各种工艺礼品、银器、珠宝盒、游戏机、玩具、布娃娃、装饰织物。 家居用品：餐桌用品、厨房用具、清洁用品、收纳用具、小家电、便携式电子设备；家庭装饰、室内家具、家用纺织品。 文具类：笔记本、信纸及各种纸制品；铅笔、钢笔及各种文具用品和学校、办公用品、办公设

备、体育用品教学器材。
主办：福建金福国际商务会展有限公司
联系人：许小姐
☎ 0591-6335 3882, 13763897042
📠 0591-8767 4271
✉ jfexpo-02@jfexpo.cn,
jinfuyuandian@163.com
jinfuyuandian@live.cn
1852705532
www.jfexpo.cn

印度化工技术设备展
ChemProTech India
日期：2013/04/10-10
地点：印度孟买展览中心
主办：科隆展览国际有限公司KOELNMESSE
地址：北京东三环北路8号亮马河大厦2座1018室(100004)
☎ 010-6590 7766
✉ info@koelnmesse.cn
www.chemprotechindia.com

ChemProTech India
Date: 2013/04/10-10
Venue: Mumbai, India
Organizer: KOELNMESSE
Address: Unit 1018, Landmark Tower II, No. 8 Dongsanhuan North Rd,, Beijing 100004, China
☎ 010-6590 7766
✉ info@koelnmesse.cn
www.chemprotechindia.com

印度精细化工展
Chemspec India
日期：2013/04/10-12
地点：印度孟买
主办：全国化工国际展览交流中心
☎ 010-6524 2231转608
✉ fany@icif.cn

印度CBME孕婴童展
CBME India
日期：2013/04/10-13
地点：印度孟买Bombay Exhibition Centre
主办：亚洲博闻有限公司亚洲博闻有限公司 UBM Asia Ltd
地址：香港湾仔港湾道26号华润大厦17楼
☎ 00852-2827 6211
📠 00852-3749 7342
✉ info-hk@ubm.com
http://cbmeindia.com/visitorregistrationform.aspx

CBME India
Date: 2013/04/10-13
Venue: Bombay Exhibition Centre, India
Organizer: UBM Asia Ltd
Address: 17/F, China Resources Building, 26 Harbour Road, Wan Chai, Hong Kong
☎ 852-2827 6211
📠 852-3749 7342
✉ info-hk@ubm.com
http://cbmeindia.com/visitorregistrationform.aspx

世界节能环保与生态建筑印度展
Ecobuild India

日期：2013/04/16-18
地点：印度孟买Bombay Exhibition Centre
主办：亚洲博闻有限公司
地址：香港湾仔港湾道26号华润大厦17楼
☎ 00852-2827 6211
📠 00852-3749 7342
✉ info-hk@ubm.com
www.ecobuild-india.com

Ecobuild India
Date: 2013/04/16-18
Venue: Bombay Exhibition Centre, India
Organizer: UBM Asia Ltd
Address: 17/F, China Resources Building, 26 Harbour Road, Wan Chai, Hong Kong
☎ 852-2827 6211
📠 852-3749 7342
✉ info-hk@ubm.com
www.ecobuild-india.com

印度孟买紧固件展览会
FASTENER FAIR/MUMBAI
日期：2013/04/17-18
地点：印度孟买
内容：各类标准及非标准紧固件、相关加工设备、检测设备、工具等
周期：两年一届
主办：北方国际展览有限公司North International Exhibition Co Ltd
地址：北京市西城区莱园街1号中环假日酒店写字间1102室(100053)
联系人：赖彦平，陈思
☎ 010-8354 0342, 8354 0341
📠 010-6354 7597
✉ yanping.lai@northexpo.com.cn;
freya_chen@northexpo.com.cn

印度及中亚电力能源展览会
PENN WELL
日期：2013/05/06-08
地点：印度孟买
周期：每年一届
主办：中国贸促会建设行业分会会展部；北京中杰城设国际展览有限公司
联系人：王艳玲
☎ 010-8836 3688，5979 9850转813，13691545669
📠 010-5885 7468，5979 9850转810
✉ wangyanling@top-fairs.com.cn
20204846
www.btfi.cn
www.power-gen.org.cn
www.top-fairs.com.cn

海德拉巴珠宝珍珠玉石展览会
Hyderabad Jewellery, Pearl & Gem Fair
日期：2013/06/07-09
地点：印度海德拉巴海德拉巴HITEX 展览中心
主办：亚洲博闻有限公司
地址：香港湾仔港湾道26号华润大厦17楼
☎ 852-2827 6211
📠 852-3749 7342
✉ info-hk@ubm.com
www.ubmasia.com

Hyderabad Jewellery, Pearl & Gem Fair
Date: 2013/06/07-09
Venue: HITEX Exhibition Centre, India
Organizer: UBM Asia Ltd
Address: 17/F, China Resources Building, 26 Harbour Road, Wan Chai, Hong Kong
☎ 852-2827 6211
📠 852-3749 7342
✉ info-hk@ubm.com
www.ubmasia.com

印度NGO展
NGO India

日期：2013/06/14-15
地点：印度孟买
主办：亚洲博闻有限公司
地址：香港湾仔港湾道26号华润大厦17楼
☎ 00852-2827 6211
📠 00852-3749 7342
✉ info-hk@ubm.com
india-ngo.org

NGO India
Date: 2013/06/14-15
Venue: Bombay Convention & Exhibition Centre, India
Organizer: UBM Asia Ltd
Address: 17/F, China Resources Building, 26 Harbour Road, Wan Chai, Hong Kong
☎ 852-2827 6211
📠 852-3749 7342
✉ info-hk@ubm.com
india-ngo.org

国际时尚服装业印度高峰论坛
Prime Source Forum - Focus on India

日期：2013/07/16-
地点：印度
主办：亚洲博闻有限公司
地址：香港湾仔港湾道26号华润大厦17楼
☎ 00852-2827 6211
📠 00852-3749 7342
✉ info-hk@ubm.com
www.primesourceforum-india.com

Prime Source Forum-Focus on India
Date: 2013/07/16 -
Venue: India
Organizer: UBM Asia Ltd
Address: 17/F, China Resources Building, 26 Harbour Road, Wan Chai, Hong Kong
☎ 852-2827 6211
📠 852-3749 7342
✉ info-hk@ubm.com
www.primesourceforum-india.com

第八届印度国际自动化展
Automation 2013
日期：2013/09 -
地点：印度孟买
主办：北京邦企展览服务有限公司
地址：北京市朝阳区惠新东街11号紫光发展大厦B1座501(100029)
☎ 010-6482 3808, 6482 3670
✉ bbes@china.com

国际食品加工及包装机械展览会
日期：2013/09/11-13
地点：印度孟买
周期：每年一届
主办：中国贸促会机械行业分会
地址：北京市西城区三里河路46号(100823)
☎ 010-6859 4192，6859 4826，6859 5406
📠 010-68594995
✉ info@ccpitmsc.org
www.chinamachine.org.cn

印度食品配料展
Food Ingredients India

日期：2013/10/03-05
地点：印度孟买印度孟买展览中心
周期：每年一届

主办：亚洲博闻有限公司
地址：香港湾仔港湾道26号华润大厦17楼
☎ 00852-2827 6211
🖷 00852-3749 7342
✉ info-hk@ubm.com
http://fiindia.ingredientsnetwork.com

Food Ingredients India

Date: 2013/10/03-05
Venue: Bombay Exhibition Centre, Mumbai, India
Frequency: Annual
Organizer: UBM Asia Ltd
Address: 17/F, China Resources Building, 26 Harbour Road, Wan Chai, Hong Kong
☎ 852-2827 6211
🖷 852-3749 7342
✉ info-hk@ubm.com
http://fiindia.ingredientsnetwork.com

新德里珠宝及宝石展览会

Delhi Jewellery & Gem Fair

日期：2013/10/06-08
地点：印度新德里Pragati Maidan
主办：亚洲博闻有限公司
地址：香港湾仔港湾道26号华润大厦17楼
☎ 00852-2827 6211
🖷 00852-3749 7342
✉ info-hk@ubm.com
www.jewelleryfair.in

Delhi Jewellery & Gem Fair

Date: 2013/10/06-08
Venue: Pragati Maidan, India
Organizer: UBM Asia Ltd
Address: 17/F, China Resources Building, 26 Harbour Road, Wan Chai, Hong Kong
☎ 852-2827 6211
🖷 852-3749 7342
✉ info-hk@ubm.com
www.jewelleryfair.in

2013印度国际建材及建筑技术展览会
日期：2013/10/17-20
地点：印度孟买
内容：厨房、卫浴洁具产品及设施：厨房用具及配件、厨房家具、烧烤用具、抽油烟机、水槽、厨房作业系统等；浴室家具、橱柜及配件、加热及通风设备、卫生洁具、淋浴桑拿及水疗设施、瓷砖、水龙头、水处理；陶瓷、石材及机械：花岗岩、大理石、板岩、瓷砖及地砖、石材机械、陶瓷机械、切割及抛光机器、研磨剂及配件、金刚石工具、玻化瓷砖及瓷化瓦、天然石材；电子电线及照明：家用照明、商用照明、路面照明、LED、筒灯射灯、纤维光学、自动化和控制系统；电子元件、电表、变压器、工业控制及自动化系统、民用控制及自动化系统、开关、发电机、电线及其配件；门窗及装饰五金；屋面　覆盖层及外墙技术；涂料及面料；管道设施及配件；玻璃技术；防火及安保技术；家具
周期：每年一届
主办：BOMBAY EXHIBITION CENTRE
承办：中国贸促会建设行业分会
地址：北京市海淀区三里河路9号建设部大院北附楼503(100835)
联系人：云鹏
☎ 010-8837 0844
🖷 010-5893 3930
✉ 1492095643@qq.com
QQ 1492095643
www.build-ccpit.org

印度国际造纸展
Paperex
日期：2013/10/24-27
地点：印度新德里
主办：全国化工国际展览交流中心
☎ 010-6524 2231转608
✉ fany@icif.cn

第十一届印度国际机械、工程技术及机床展览会
ENGIMACH
日期：2013/10/27-01
地点：印度艾哈迈达巴德市大学广场
内容：机床，锻压、铸造设备、表面处理技术、工程机械，建筑机械，石油、化工机械，电厂设备，纺织机械，矿山机械，物流设备，医疗机械，制药机械，环保机械设备，粮食及食品加工机械，农牧渔业机械，塑胶机械，电热设备，机电设备，缝制机械，造纸机械，印刷机械，包装机械，电气机械，电子，光电子，激光设备，金属加工机械，仪器仪表，工具，模具，风机，电机，锅炉与原动机，木工机械，气体压缩与分离设备，液压设备，焊接设备，各类二手机械设备生产线，其它机械。
始办年份：1997年
周期：两年一届
市场范围：国际性
性质：面向贸易观众
参展费用：24,000元人民币(3x3m)
上届规模：展览面积 35,000m²，参展公司525个，摊位超过1500个。美国、日本、意大利、德国、中国（包括香港和台湾）、西班牙、新加坡、韩国等13个国家的许多著名企业参加了展览会；观众超过275，000人，来自全球20多个国家；贸易总额达到158亿卢比
主办：中国轻工业对外经济技术合作公司K AND D COMMUNICATION LIMITED；广东粤召展览有限公司
地址：广州市天河区体育东路122号羊城国际商贸中心东塔1202, 1208室(510620)
联系人：周文槟
☎ 020-13710318991
🖷 020-3887 0797
✉ 1979wenbin@163.com
✉ gdwenbin@hotmail.com
QQ 406372636
www.gf-hk.com

国际工程机械与技术展览会
日期：2013/11 -
地点：印度班加罗尔
周期：两年一届
主办：中国贸促会机械行业分会
地址：北京市西城区三里河路46号(100823)
☎ 010-6859 4811，6859 4994，6859 4910
🖷 010-6859 4995
✉ info@ccpitmsc.org
www.chinamachine.org.cn

Index Fairs 孟买展

Index Fairs Mumbai
日期：2013/11/14-17
地点：印度孟买
主办：亚洲博闻有限公司
地址：香港湾仔港湾道26号华润大厦17楼
☎ 00852-2827 6211
🖷 00852-3749 7342
✉ info-hk@ubm.com
www.indexfairs.com

Index Fairs Mumbai

Date: 2013/11/14-17
Venue: MMRDA Exhibition Center, Bandra Kurla Complex, India
Organizer: UBM Asia Ltd
Address: 17/F, China Resources Building, 26 Harbour Road, Wan Chai, Hong Kong
☎ 852-2827 6211
🖷 852-3749 7342
✉ info-hk@ubm.com
www.indexfairs.com

国际印刷及相关机械展览会
日期：2013/11/14-17
地点：印度新德里
周期：两年一届
主办：中国贸促会机械行业分会
地址：北京市西城区三里河路46号(100823)
☎ 010-6859 4192，6859 4826，6859 5406
🖷 010-6859 4995
✉ info@ccpitmsc.org
www.chinamachine.org.cn

Intermodal India

日期：2013/11/20-22
地点：印度孟买
主办：亚洲博闻有限公司
地址：香港湾仔港湾道26号华润大厦17楼
☎ 00852-2827 6211
🖷 00852-3749 7342
✉ info-hk@ubm.com
http://intermodalindia.com

Intermodal India

Date: 2013/11/20-22
Venue: Bombay Exhibition Centre, India
Organizer: UBM Asia Ltd
Address: 17/F, China Resources Building, 26 Harbour Road, Wan Chai, Hong Kong
☎ 852-2827 6211
🖷 852-3749 7342
✉ info-hk@ubm.com
http://intermodalindia.com

第五届亚太天然气汽车协会会议暨展览会
ANGVA 2013
日期：2013/11/27-29
地点：印度新德里
主办：北京邦企展览服务有限公司
地址：北京市朝阳区惠新东街11号紫光发展大厦B1座501(100029)
☎ 010-6482 3808, 6482 3670
✉ bbes@china.com

第十一届印度国际机械、工程技术及机床展览会
ENGIMACH
日期：2013/11/27-12/01
地点：印度艾哈迈达巴德市大学广场
内容：机床，锻压、铸造设备、表面处理技术、工程机械，建筑机械，石油、化工机械，电厂设备，纺织机械，矿山机械，物流设备，医疗机械，制药机械，环保机械设备，粮食及食品加工机械，农牧渔业机械，塑胶机械，电热设备，机电设备，缝制机械，造纸机械，印刷机械，包装机械，电气机械，电子，光电子，激光设备，金属加工机械，仪器仪表，工具，模具，风机，电机，锅炉与原动机，木工机械，气体压缩与分离设备，液压设备，焊接设备，各类二手机械设备生产线，其它机械。
始办年份：1997年
周期：两年一届
市场范围：国际性
性质：面向贸易观众
参展费用：24,000元人民币(3x3m)
上届规模 2011：展览会面积超过35,000m²，参展公司525个，摊位超过1500个。美国、日本、意大利、德国、中国（包括香港和台湾）、西班牙、新加坡、韩国等13个国家的许多著名企业参加了展览会；观众超过275，000人，来自全球20多个国家；贸易总额达到158亿卢比
主办：中国轻工业对外经济技术合作公司；广东粤召展览有限公司
地址：广州市天河区体育东路122号羊城国际商贸中

心东塔1202, 1208室(510620)
联系人：周文槟
☎ 13710318991
🖷 020-3887 0797
✉ 1979wenbin@163.com
✉ gdwenbin@hotmail.com
QQ 406372636
www.gf-hk.com

国际工业装备展览会
日期：2013/12 -
地点：印度
周期：每年一届
主办：中国贸促会机械行业分会
地址：北京市西城区三里河路46号(100823)
☎ 010-6859 5499，6859 4803，6859 4807，6859 4989
🖷 010-6859 4995
✉ info@ccpitmsc.org
www.chinamachine.org.cn

印度国际五金工具展
日期：2013/12 -
地点：印度孟买
内容：各种五金工具、小型机械、锁具及安防设备、建筑材料、五金配件、卫生洁具、灯光照明设备等；紧固件产品专区
主办：北方国际展览有限公司North Intl Exhibition Co Ltd
联系人：吴江，刘硕
地址：北京市 西城区莱园街1号，中环假日酒店写字间1102室(100053)
☎ 010-8354 0336，8351 3705
🖷 010-63547597
✉ wujiang@northexpo.com.cn
✉ liushuo@northexpo.con.cn

印度国际安全与消防技术设备展览会
IFSEC India

日期：2013/12/05-07
地点：印度大诺伊达India Expo Centre
主办：亚洲博闻有限公司
地址：香港湾仔港湾道26号华润大厦17楼
☎ 00852-2827 6211
🖷 00852-3749 7342
✉ info-hk@ubm.com
www.ifsecindia.com

IFSEC India
Date: 2013/12/05-07
Venue: India Expo Centre, India
Organizer: UBM Asia Ltd
Address: 17/F, China Resources Building, 26 Harbour Road, Wan Chai, Hong Kong
☎ 852-2827 6211
🖷 852-3749 7342
✉ info-hk@ubm.com
www.ifsecindia.com

印度国际甜食和休闲食品加工展览会
Sweet & Snack India
日期：2013/12/10-12
地点：印度印度孟买展览中心
主办：科隆国际展览有限公司
联络：科隆展览中国有限公司
地址：北京市东三环北路8号亮马河大厦2座1018室(100004)
☎ 010-6590 7766
🖷 010-6590 6139
✉ info@koelnmesse.cn
www.sweetandsnacktecindia.com

Sweet & Snack India
Date: 2013/12/10-12
Venue: Bombay Exhibition Center, India
☎ 86-10-6590 7766
🖷 86-10-6590 6139
✉ info@koelnmesse.cn
www.sweetandsnacktecindia.com

印度国际奶制品加工展览会
Dairy Universe India
日期：2013/12/10-12
地点：印度印度孟买展览中心India
主办：科隆国际展览有限公司
联络：科隆展览中国有限公司
地址：北京市东三环北路8号亮马河大厦2座1018室(100004)
☎ 010-6590 7878/7766
🖷 010-6590 6139
✉ info@koelnmesse.cn
www.dairyuniverseindia.com

Dairy Universe India
Date: 2013/12/10-12
Venue: Bombay Exhibition Center, India
Organizer: Koelnmesse GmbH
☎ 86-10-6590 7878/7766
🖷 86-10-6590 6139
✉ info@koelnmesse.cn
www.dairyuniverseindia.com

印度国际食品技术与机械展览会
日期：2014/11/14-16
地点：印度孟买展览中心
主办：科隆展览国际有限公司KOELNMESSE
地址：北京东三环北路8号亮马河大厦2座1018室(100004)
☎ 010-6590 7766
🖷 010-6590 6139
✉ info@koelnmesse.cn
www.foodtecindia.com

Intl FoodTec India
Date: 2014/11/14-16
Venue: Mumbai, India
Profile: along with PackEx India 2012 received an overwhelming response from the Indian as well as global industry with the presence of Who is Who of the respective industry and over 11,385 trade visitors. The exhibition clearly emerged as the most sought after trade fair for Packaging and Food Processing sector in India and the neighbouring countries.
Frequency: Annual
Organizer: KOELNMESSE
Address: Unit 1018, Landmark Tower II, No. 8 Dongsanhuan North Rd,, Beijing 100004, China
☎ 010-6590 7766
🖷 010-6590 6139
✉ info@koelnmesse.cn
www.foodtecindia.com

国际工业泵阀展览会
日期：2013/12/14-16
地点：印度浦那
周期：每年一届
主办：中国贸促会机械行业分会
地址：北京市西城区三里河路46号(100823)
☎ 010-6859 5296，6859 4938，6851 2883
🖷 010-6859 4995
✉ info@ccpitmsc.org
www.chinamachine.org.cn

印度尼西亚
Indonesia

国际时尚服装业印尼高峰论坛
Prime Source Forum - Focus on ASEAN

日期：2013/01/30-
地点：印度尼西亚雅加达
主办：亚洲博闻有限公司
地址：香港湾仔港湾道26号华润大厦17楼
☎ 00852-2827 6211
🖷 00852-3749 7342
✉ info-hk@ubm.com
http://primesourceforum.com

Prime Source Forum - Focus on ASEAN
Date: 2013/01/30 -
Venue: Jakarta, Indonesia
Organizer: UBM Asia Ltd
Address: 17/F, China Resources Building, 26 Harbour Road, Wan Chai, Hong Kong
☎ 852-2827 6211
🖷 852-3749 7342
✉ info-hk@ubm.com
http://primesourceforum.com

世界制药原料东南亚展
P-MEC South East Asia

日期：2013/03/20-22
地点：印度尼西亚雅加达国际展览中心
主办：亚洲博闻有限公司
地址：香港湾仔港湾道26号华润大厦17楼
☎ 00852-2827 6211
🖷 00852-3749 7342
✉ info-hk@ubm.com
www.cphi-sea.com/pmec

P-MEC South East Asia
Date: 2013/03/20-22
Venue: Jakarta Intl Expo, Indonesia
Organizer: UBM Asia Ltd
Address: 17/F, China Resources Building, 26 Harbour Road, Wan Chai, Hong Kong
☎ 852-2827 6211
🖷 852-3749 7342
✉ info-hk@ubm.com
www.cphi-sea.com/pmec

医药包装材料精品东南亚展
InnoPack South East Asia

日期：2013/03/20-22
地点：印度尼西亚雅加达国际展览中心
主办：亚洲博闻有限公司
地址：香港湾仔港湾道26号华润大厦17楼
☎ 00852-2827 6211
🖷 00852-3749 7342
✉ info-hk@ubm.com
www.cphi-sea.com/innopack

InnoPack South East Asia
Date: 2013/03/20-22
Venue: Jakarta Intl Expo，Indonesia
Organizer: UBM Asia Ltd
Address: 17/F, China Resources Building, 26 Harbour Road, Wan Chai, Hong Kong
☎ 852-2827 6211
🖷 852-3749 7342
✉ info-hk@ubm.com
www.cphi-sea.com/innopack

世界制药机械、设备与材料东南亚展
CPhI South East Asia

日期：2013/03/20-22
地点：印度尼西亚雅加达国际展览中心
主办：亚洲博闻有限公司
地址：香港湾仔港湾道26号华润大厦17楼
☎ 00852-2827 6211
🖷 00852-3749 7342
✉ info-hk@ubm.com
www.cphi-sea.com

CPhI South East Asia
Date: 2013/03/20-22
Venue: Jakarta Intl Expo, Indonesia
Organizer: UBM Asia Ltd
Address: 17/F, China Resources Building, 26 Harbour Road, Wan Chai, Hong Kong
☎ 852-2827 6211
🖷 852-3749 7342
✉ info-hk@ubm.com
www.cphi-sea.com

印度尼西亚汽摩工业展
日期：2013/03/26-29
地点：印度尼西亚雅加达
周期：每年一届
主办：北京中杰城投国际展览有限公司
联系人：李娜
☎ 010-5979 9850转858
🖷 010-5979 9850转810,5885 7468
www.top-fairs.com.cn
www.build-ccpit.org

第十一届印度尼西亚国际酒店、餐饮设备、食品和饮料展览会
FHI2013
日期：2013/04/10-13
地点：印度尼西亚雅加达
主办：北京邦企展览服务有限公司
地址：北京市朝阳区惠新东街11号紫光发展大厦B1座501(100029)
☎ 010-6482 3808, 6482 3670
✉ bbes@china.com

中国机械和电子产品展览会
日期：2013/05 -
地点：印度尼西亚雅加达
周期：每年一届
主办：中国贸促会机械行业分会
地址：北京市西城区三里河路46号(100823)
☎ 010-6859 5499，6859 4803，6859 4807，6859 4989，6859 5055
🖷 010-68594995
✉ info@ccpitmsc.org
www.chinamachine.org.cn

"国际工程机械、矿山机械、建材机械及建筑材料展览会（自办展）"
日期：2013/05/29-01
地点：印度尼西亚雅加达
周期：每年一届
主办：中国贸促会机械行业分会
地址：北京市西城区三里河路46号(100823)
☎ 010-6859 4811，6859 4994 6859 4910
🖷 010-6859 4995
✉ info@ccpitmsc.org
www.chinamachine.org.cn

印尼 SATTE 展
SATTE Indonesia

日期：2013/06/12-14
地点：印度尼西亚巴里岛
主办：亚洲博闻有限公司
地址：香港湾仔港湾道26号华润大厦17楼
☎ 00852-2827 6211
🖷 00852-3749 7342
✉ info-hk@ubm.com
www.satteindonesia.com

SATTE Indonesia
Date: 2013/06/12-14
Venue: Bali Intl Convention Centre，Indonesia
Organizer: UBM Asia Ltd
Address: 17/F, China Resources Building, 26 Harbour Road, Wan Chai, Hong Kong
☎ 852-2827 6211
🖷 852-3749 7342
✉ info-hk@ubm.com
www.satteindonesia.com

第六届印尼电工电力展览会
Electric Indonesia 2013
日期：2013/09/04-07
地点：印度尼西亚雅加达
主办：北京邦企展览服务有限公司
地址：北京市朝阳区惠新东街11号紫光发展大厦B1座501(100029)
☎ 010-6482 3808, 6482 3670
✉ bbes@china.com

2013第十六届印度尼西亚国际采矿暨设备技术展览会
Mining Indonesia 2013
日期：2013/09/04-07
地点：印度尼西亚雅加达
主办：北京邦企展览服务有限公司
地址：北京市朝阳区惠新东街11号紫光发展大厦B1座501(100029)
☎ 010-6482 3808, 6482 3670
✉ bbes@china.com

第十七届印尼国际建筑设备、建筑材料及基础设施建设展览会
Building & Construction Indonesia 2013
日期：2013/09/04-07
地点：印度尼西亚雅加达
主办：北京邦企展览服务有限公司
地址：北京市朝阳区惠新东街11号紫光发展大厦B1座501(100029)
☎ 010-6482 3808, 6482 3670
✉ bbes@china.com

2013年印尼国际电力设备技术展览会
日期：2013/09/04-09
地点：印度尼西亚雅加达
周期：两年一届
主办：中国贸促会建设行业分会会展部；北京中杰城设国际展览有限公司
联系人：王艳玲
☎ 010-8836 3688，5979 9850转813，13691545669
🖷 010-5885 7468，5979 9850转810
✉ wangyanling@top-fairs.com.cn
QQ 20204846
www.btfi.cn
www.power-gen.org.cn
www.top-fairs.com.cn

印尼机电展
Indonesia M&E Expo
日期：2013/10/24-26
地点：印度尼西亚雅加达国际展览中心
周期：每年一届
市场范围：国际性
主办：亚洲博闻公司UBM Asia Limited
地址：香港湾仔港湾道26号华润大厦17楼
☎ 00852-2827 6211
🖷 00852-3749 7342
✉ info-hk@ubm.com
www.ubmasia.com

Indonesia M&E Expo
Date: 2013/10/24-26
Venue: Jakarta Intl Expo, Jakarta, Indonesia
Frequency: Annual
Market Area: International
Organizer: UBM Asia Limited
Address: 17/F, China Resources Building, 26 Harbour Road, Wan Chai, Hong Kong
☎ 852-2827 6211
🖷 852-3749 7342
✉ info-hk@ubm.com
www.ubmasia.com

东南亚国际混凝土产业展览会
Concrete Show South East Asia
日期：2013/10/24-26
地点：印度尼西亚雅加达Jakarta Intl Expo
主办：亚洲博闻有限公司
地址：香港湾仔港湾道26号华润大厦17楼
☎ 00852-2827 6211
🖷 00852-3749 7342
✉ info-hk@ubm.com
www.concreteshowseasia.com

Concrete Show South East Asia
Date: 2013/10/24-26
Venue: Jakarta Intl Expo，Indonesia
Organizer: UBM Asia Ltd
Address: 17/F, China Resources Building, 26 Harbour Road, Wan Chai, Hong Kong
☎ 852-2827 6211
🖷 852-3749 7342
✉ info-hk@ubm.com
www.concreteshowseasia.com

印尼国际染料和化工展
Dye+Chem Indonesia
日期：2013/10/24-26
地点：印度尼西亚雅加达
主办：全国化工国际展览交流中心
☎ 010-6524 2231转608
✉ fany@icif.cn

2013年印度尼西亚国际纺织面料博览会
日期：2013/10/24-26
地点：印度尼西亚雅加达国际会展中心
内容：印度尼西亚唯一的国际专业面料及纱线展会。内容包括各类棉料，合成纤维面料（梭织/针织）、天然纤维面料（梭织/针织）、纱线与纤维、花式整理、家用纺织品、箱包、被套、毯子、配件、CAD/CAM；床上亚麻布、桌布、装饰布、厨房纺织布、室内装潢布、墙面装饰；纤维、单丝及原材料；辅料：带子、扣子、针线、刺绣、人造钻石辅料、丝带、徽章、钮扣、橡胶镶边、按钮、拉链、垫肩等。
主办：CEMS展览集团，上海爱卫客会展服务有限公司
☎ 021-3132 6575, 15900594089
🖷 021-5049 7282
联系人：李爱燕
✉ ivyli18@163.com
QQ 2632726499@qq.com
www.aweek-expo.com

2013印度尼西亚国际工业机械展览会暨第十五届中国机械（印尼）展览会
日期：2013/10/30-11/02
地点：印度尼西亚雅加达国际展览中心

内容：工程建筑机械、矿产机械、冶金机械；机电设备、风机、电机、锅炉、泵类、电子仪表仪 器、发电设备、热电设备、动力设备、光电设备、港口机械；橡塑机械、包装机械、印刷机械、造纸机械；粮、油、食品生产加工设备；木工机械、医 疗制药设备；保健设备、环保设备、电子生产设备、实验室设备、化工设备；消防及保安 设备；金属加工机械、数控设备、机床、铸锻设备、冶金设备、锻压及切割设备、焊接设备、铸造设备、激光设备、表面处理设备、模具；五金、汽车零配件、仪器仪表、基础机械；纺织、缝制及印染设备；农业、林业、养殖机械；其它机械设备。
主办：中国轻工业对外经济技术合作公司；粤召（香港）国际展览有限公司；印度尼西亚PT Kristamedia Pratama；广东粤召展览有限公司
地址：广州市天河区体育东路122号羊城国际商贸中心东塔1202、1208、1209室
联系人：叶小芳
☎ 020-8396 3610
🖷 020-3887 0797
✉ AW8008@163.com
www.gf-hk.com

第九届印尼国际石油和天然气探测、生产及精炼展览会
Oil & Gas Indonesia 2013
日期：2013/11/13-15
地点：印度尼西亚雅加达
主办：北京邦企展览服务有限公司
地址：北京市朝阳区惠新东街11号紫光发展大厦B1座501(100029)
☎ 010-6482 3808, 6482 3670
✉ bbes@china.com

印尼国际海事展
Marine Indonesia 2013
日期：2013/11/13-15
地点：印度尼西亚雅加达
主办：北京邦企展览服务有限公司
地址：北京市朝阳区惠新东街11号紫光发展大厦B1座501(100029)
☎ 010-6482 3808, 6482 3670
✉ bbes@china.com

第二十五届印尼国际食品加工、饮料、包装机械展览会
ProPak Indonesia 2013
日期：2013/11/20-23
地点：印度尼西亚雅加达
主办：北京邦企展览服务有限公司
地址：北京市朝阳区惠新东街11号紫光发展大厦B1座501(100029)
☎ 010-6482 3808, 6482 3670
✉ bbes@china.com

第二十五届印尼国际塑料橡胶展览会暨研讨会
Plastics & Rubber Indonesia2013
日期：2013/11/20-23
地点：印度尼西亚雅加达
主办：北京邦企展览服务有限公司
地址：北京市朝阳区惠新东街11号紫光发展大厦B1座501(100029)
☎ 010-6482 3808, 6482 3670
✉ bbes@china.com

国际机床及金属加工技术展览会
日期：2013/12 -
地点：印度尼西亚雅加达
周期：每年一届
主办：中国贸促会机械行业分会
地址：北京市西城区三里河路46号(100823)
☎ 010-6859 5495，6859 5247，6859 5406，6859 5431
🖷 010-6859 4995
✉ info@ccpitmsc.org
www.chinamachine.org.cn

国际汽车制造机械及零配件展览会
日期：2013/12 -
地点：印度尼西亚雅加达
周期：每年一届
主办：中国贸促会机械行业分会
地址：北京市西城区三里河路46号(100823)
☎ 010-6859 4952，6859 4804，6859 4931，6859 5220
🖷 010-6859 4995
✉ info@ccpitmsc.org
www.chinamachine.org.cn

Industrial Automation & Logistics Indonesia 2013
日期：2013/12/04-07
地点：印度尼西亚雅加达
主办：北京邦企展览服务有限公司
地址：北京市朝阳区惠新东街11号紫光发展大厦B1座501(100029)
☎ 010-6482 3808, 6482 3670
✉ bbes@china.com

印尼国际五金工具展
TOOLS & HARDWARE INDONESIA 2013
FASTENER&FIXING INDONESIA
日期：2013/12/04-07
地点：印度尼西亚雅加达
主办：北京邦企展览服务有限公司
地址：北京市朝阳区惠新东街11号紫光发展大厦B1座501(100029)
☎ 010-6482 3808, 6482 3670
✉ bbes@china.com

第二十四届印尼国际制造机械，设备，材料及服务展览会
Manufacturing Indonesia Series 2013
日期：2013/12/04-07
地点：印度尼西亚雅加达
主办：北京邦企展览服务有限公司
地址：北京市朝阳区惠新东街11号紫光发展大厦B1座501(100029)
☎ 010-6482 3808, 6482 3670
✉ bbes@china.com

伊朗
Iran

国际电力电工设备及技术展览会
日期：2013/10 -
地点：伊朗德黑兰
周期：两年一届
主办：中国贸促会机械行业分会
地址：北京市西城区三里河路46号(100823)
☎ 010-6859 4802，6859 4934
🖷 010-6859 4995
✉ info@ccpitmsc.org
www.chinamachine.org.cn

国际汽车零配件展览会
日期：2013/11 -
地点：伊朗德黑兰
周期：每年一届
主办：中国贸促会机械行业分会
地址：北京市西城区三里河路46号(100823)
☎ 010-6859 4952，6859 4804，6859 4931，6859 5220
🖷 010-6859 4995
✉ info@ccpitmsc.org
www.chinamachine.org.cn

伊拉克
Iraq

2013年第三届伊拉克苏莱曼尼亚国际建筑材料和建筑机械展览会
日期：2013/04/10-13
地点：伊拉克苏莱曼尼亚国际展览中心
内容：建筑材料类：屋面材料；门窗幕墙及型材，建筑玻璃；暖通空调,通风及供水系统；地面,墙面,天花板材料；厨房卫浴；五金产品及工具；照明,电器设备及工具；各类型材,管材；石材产品,石材相关设备及工具；建筑工程类：金属建筑结构及材料；工程建筑机械及道路施工机械；混凝土机械设备； 建材生产加工设备；石材加工设备；陶瓷制品生产设备；水泥及水泥制品生产设备；玻璃生产加工设备；涂料生产设备；石膏板设备,矿棉板设备；PVC&PE管材生产线及各种管材加工设备；免烧砖机械；铝塑钢门窗加工设备,铝幕墙加工设备；成型机
周期：每年一届
主办：Elan Expo
承办：中国贸促会建设行业分会
地址：北京市海淀区三里河路9号建设部大院机关门诊楼503
联系人：云鹏
☎ 010-8837 0844
🖷 010-5893 3930
✉ rocyun@hotmail.com
QQ 1492095643
www.build-ccpit.org

2013年伊拉克医疗展
日期：2013/05/27-29
地点：伊拉克埃尔比勒国际展览中心
内容：急救设备及相关辅助设备；救护车；麻醉系统；建筑技术与服务；通讯设备；牙科设备及实验室耗材；诊断与药物治疗；消毒处理系统；电子保健；电子医疗设备；水疗美发设备；解救、救援设备；医院账单及急救医疗服务管理系统软件；医院设备；保险方案；实验室设备；激光；生命支持设备；医疗及卫生耗材产品；诊断试剂；医学专业化妆品；外科手术器械；医用耗材；医疗器械；医疗信息技术；医用家具；光学及眼科部件及设备；矫形用品；整形外科手术设备；矫形康复设备；医药产品及用品；整形外科、美容美发设备及诊所设备；防护齿轮装备及制衣；放射学、心脏学设备；复康设备；扫描仪；担架
主办：IFP
联络：上海格博会展服务有限公司
联系人：鞠龙
☎ 021-6117 3587
🖷 021-6117 3558
✉ julongdeyouxiang@163.com
www.globalexh.com

国际工程机械与建材展览会
日期：2013/09 -
地点：伊拉克埃尔比勒
周期：每年一届
主办：中国贸促会机械行业分会
地址：北京市西城区三里河路46号(100823)
☎ 010-6859 4811，6859 4994，6859 4910
🖷 010-6859 4995
✉ info@ccpitmsc.org
www.chinamachine.org.cn

以色列
Israel

以色列国际化工展
ISRACHEM
日期：2013/04/30-02
地点：以色列特拉维夫
主办：全国化工国际展览交流中心
☎ 010-6524 2231转608
✉ fany@icif.cn

意大利
Italy

意大利印刷、印刷媒体和传播工业及意大利包装印刷和纸加工展览会
日期：2013/05/07-11
地点：意大利米兰
周期：四年一届
主办：中国贸促会机械行业分会
地址：北京市西城区三里河路46号(100823)
☎ 010-6859 4192，6859 4826，6859 5406
🖷 010-68594995
✉ info@ccpitmsc.org
www.chinamachine.org.cn

意大利(热那亚)国际游艇展览会
日期：2013/10/01-09
地点：意大利热那亚
周期：每年一届
主办：中国贸促会机械行业分会
地址：北京市西城区三里河路46号(100823)
☎ 010-6859 4985，6859 5855
010-6859 4995
✉ info@ccpitmsc.org
www.chinamachine.org.cn

日本
Japan

日本电子展
INTERNEPCON Japan
日期：2013/01 -
地点：日本东京有明国际展览中心Tokyo Big Sight
内容：电子产品包装和生产，针对电子产品生产和SMT的所有设备、材料以及技术生产线，安装器、丝印机、回流焊机、焊接机、水洗机、分配器，穿孔机，带式载体，产品生产管理系统，焊接区，焊接机、回流焊机、再加工机、烙铁、金属熔化槽，焊剂涂敷器&65381;焊锡及焊用材料/助焊剂。安装专区，贴片机/隔板，厂房设备区，工厂所需的所有设施和供应品生产线，清洗设备和清洁区，配件和相关设备等，EMS/合同加工区
周期：每年一届
上届规模 2011：展览面积69,140m²，参展商1,149家，参观人数71,322人
主办：励展日本公司
联络：励展博览集团国际销售部
地址：北京市朝阳区新源南路1-3号平安国际金融中心A座15层01-03,05
联系人：张志超
☎ 010-5933 9266
010-5933 9233
✉ ivy.zhang@reedexpo.com.cn
www.nepcon.jp/english/

日本国际照明展览会
LIGHTING JAPAN:
LED/OLED Lighting Technology Expo
日期：2013/01 -
地点：日本东京
内容：范围涉及所有照明设备、元件、生产设计材料和LED/OLED照明设备。
周期：每年一届
上届规模 2011：展览面积69,140m²，参展商314家，贸易观众24,053人
主办：励展日本公司
联络：励展博览集团国际销售部
地址：北京市朝阳区新源南路1-3号平安国际金融中心A座15层01-03,05
联系人：张志超
☎ 010-5933 9266
010-5933 9233
✉ ivy.zhang@reedexpo.com.cn
www.lightingjapan.jp

东京国际珠宝展
IJT : Intl Jewellery Tokyo
日期：2013/01 -
地点：日本东京有明展览馆Big Sight
内容：钻石、天然宝石、人工宝石、黄金、铂金、银饰、手表、钟表、古珠宝、珍珠、湖泊、珊瑚、浮雕、金银成品、宝石（裸石、裸珠、珠子、链子及其他宝石），包装材料，商店展示柜、展示框及部件、生产设备及工具，安全监测设备，OEM/ODM，加工服务等。周期：每年一届
上届规模 2011：参展商1,267家，参观人数35,902人
主办：励展日本公司
联络：励展博览集团国际销售部
☎ 010-5933 9299
010-5933 9233
✉ jerry.shen@reedexpo.com.cn
www.ijt.jp

综合医疗展及会议
Integrated Medicine Exhibition & Conference
統合医療展
Integrated Medicine Exhibition & Conference
日期：2013/02/19-20
地点：日本Tokyo Big Sight Exhibition Centre
主办：亚洲博闻有限公司
地址：香港湾仔港湾道26号华润大厦17楼
☎ 00852-2827 6211
00852-3749 7342
✉ info-hk@ubm.com
www.togo-iryo.jp

Integrated Medicine Exhibition & Conference
Date: 2013/02/19-20
Venue: Tokyo Big Sight Exhibition Centre, Japan
Organizer: UBM Asia Ltd
Address: 17/F, China Resources Building, 26 Harbour Road, Wan Chai, Hong Kong
☎ 852-2827 6211
852-3749 7342
✉ info-hk@ubm.com
www.togo-iryo.jp

eCommerce Solution 东京展
网络及手机直销方案展览会
eCommerce Solution Fair in Tokyo
Net & Mobile Direct Marketing Solution Fair

ネット&モバイル
通販
ソリューションフェア in 東京
eCommerce Solution Fair
Tokyo

日期：2010/02/27-28
地点：日本东京Sunshine City Convention Centre
主办：亚洲博闻有限公司
地址：香港湾仔港湾道26号华润大厦17楼
☎ 00852-2827 6211
00852-3749 7342
✉ info-hk@ubm.com
www.tsuhan-fair.com

eCommerce Solution Fair in Tokyo
Net & Mobile Direct Marketing Solution Fair
Date: 2010/02/27-28
Venue: Sunshine City Convention Centre，Tokyo, Japan
Organizer: UBM Asia Ltd
Address: 17/F, China Resources Building, 26 Harbour Road, Wan Chai, Hong Kong
☎ 852-2827 6211
852-3749 7342
✉ info-hk@ubm.com
www.tsuhan-fair.com

医疗保健食品博览会
Medi-Care Foods Expo
日期：2013/02/19-20
地点：日本东京有明国际展览中心
主办：亚洲博闻有限公司
地址：香港湾仔港湾道26号华润大厦17楼
☎ 00852-2827 6211
00852-3749 7342
✉ info-hk@ubm.com
www.ubmchina.com

Medi-Care Foods Expo
Date: 2013/02/19-20
Venue: Tokyo Big Sight Exhibition Centre, Tokyo, Japan
Organizer: UBM Asia Ltd
Address: 17/F, China Resources Building, 26 Harbour Road, Wan Chai, Hong Kong
☎ 852-2827 6211
852-3749 7342
✉ info-hk@ubm.com
www.ubmchina.com

东京国际光伏发电展览会
PV EXPO:
Intl Photovoltaic Power Generation Expo
日期：2013/03 -
地点：日本东京有明国际展览中心Tokyo Big Sight
内容：亚洲光伏发电产业综合性最强的展会，它汇集了与光伏制造业、太阳能电池、组件和光伏系统有关的各种材料、设备和技术。
周期：每年一届
市场范围：国际性
性质：面向贸易观众
上届规模 2011：贸易观众90,011人
主办：日本励展博览有限公司
联络：励展博览集团国际销售部
地址：北京市朝阳区新源南路1-3号平安国际金融中心A座15层01-03,05
联系人：杜一鸣
☎ 010-5933 9209
010-5933 9233
✉ martin.du@reedexpo.com.cn
www.pvexpo.jp

日本国际二次电池展
Battery Japan
日期：2013/03-
地点：日本东京有明国际展览中心Tokyo Big Sight
内容：原材料、零部件，设备制造，检测、测试、评估，可充电电池，相关仪器
周期：每年一届
上届规模 2011：参观人数90,011人
主办：励展日本公司
联络：励展博览集团国际销售部
地址：北京市朝阳区新源南路1-3号平安国际金融中心A座15层01-03,05
联系人：杜一鸣
☎ 010-5933 9209
010-5933 9233
✉ martin.du@reedexpo.com.cn
www.batteryjapan.jp/en

日本国际食品及饮料展览会
FOODEX JAPAN
日期：2013/03 -
地点：日本东京
内容：农产品、畜产品、水产品、肉加工品、罐头食品、副食品、保健食品、有机食品、调味品、各类面点及甜点、各类酒精饮料、不含酒精的饮料、保健饮料等 农产品、畜产品、水产品、肉加工品、罐头食品、副食品、保健食品、有机食品、调味品、各类面点及甜点、各类酒精饮料、不含酒精的饮料、保健饮料等 洋食品、清真食品、烘焙食品、食品供应、快餐、鱼、肉类食品、待许经营、蔬菜、饮料及厨房设备
主办：北方国际展览有限公司North International Exhibition Co Ltd
地址：北京市西城区莱园街1号中环假日酒店写字间1102室(100053)
联系人：王子威，李松林
☎ 010-8355 7740，8353 3198
010-6354 7597
✉ w.ziwei@northexpo.com.cn
✉ reanna@northexpo.com.cn

东京健康博览会
Tokyo Health Industry Show
健康博覧会
TOKYO HEALTH INDUSTRY SHOW
日期：2013/03/13-15
地点：日本东京有明国际展览中心

主办：亚洲博闻有限公司
地址：香港湾仔港湾道26号华润大厦17楼
☎ 00852-2827 6211
📠 0852-374 97342
✉ info-hk@ubm.com
www.this.ne.jp

Tokyo Health Industry Show
Date: 2013/03/13-15
Venue: Tokyo Big Sight Exhibition Centre, Japan
Organizer: UBM Media Co Ltd
Address: 17/F, China Resources Building, 26 Harbour Road, Wan Chai, Hong Kong
☎ 852-2827 6211
📠 0852-374 97342
✉ info-hk@ubm.com
www.this.ne.jp

国际模具展览会
日期：2013/04 -
地点：日本东京
周期：每年一届
主办：中国贸促会机械行业分会
地址：北京市西城区三里河路46号(100823)
☎ 010-6859 5495，6859 5247，6859 5406，6859 5431
📠 010-6859 4995
✉ info@ccpitmsc.org
www.chinamachine.org.cn

日本美食佳酿暨酒店及餐饮设备展
Wine & Gourmet Japan
日期：2013/04/03-05
地点：日本东京国际展览中心Tokyo Big Sight, Japan
内容：罐头食品、乳制品、精制烘焙食品、精制特色食品、食品配料、新鲜食品、冷冻、冷藏食品、精制巧克力、鲜美食品、肉禽制品、海鲜、非酒精饮料（茶和咖啡）、休闲食品、糖果、甜食、葡萄酒、烈酒、啤酒、食品招待和餐饮服务相关设备
始办年份：2009
周期：每年一届
市场范围：国际性
性质：面向贸易观众
主办：科隆展览国际有限公司Koelnmesse
地址：北京东三环北路8号亮马河大厦2座1018室，科隆展览中国有限公司(100004)
联系人：潘容
☎ 010-6590 7766 转715
📠 010-6590 6139
✉ g.pan@koelnmesse.cn
www.wineandgourmetjapan.com

Wine & Gourmet Japan
Date: 2013/04/03-05
Venue: Tokyo Big Sight, Japan
Established Year: 2009
Frequency: Annual
Market Area: International
Nature: Trade Only
Organizer: Koelnmesse
Address: Unit 1018, Landmark Tower Ⅱ, No. 8 Dongsanhuan North Rd, Beijing 100004, China
Contact: Grace Pan
☎ 86-10-6590 7766 ext 715
📠 86-10-6590 6139
✉ g.pan@koelnmesse.cn
www.wineandgourmetjapan.com

日本制药技术展
Pharmatec Japan

日期：2013/04/24-26
地点：日本东京有明国际展览中心
主办：亚洲博闻有限公司
地址：香港湾仔港湾道26号华润大厦17楼
☎ 00852-2827 6211
📠 00852-3749 7342
✉ info-hk@ubm.com
www.cphijapan.jp/info/pharmatec.html

Pharmatec Japan
Date: 2013/04/24-26
Venue: Tokyo Big Sight Exhibition Centre, Tokyo, Japan
Organizer: UBM Asia Ltd
Address: 17/F, China Resources Building, 26 Harbour Road, Wan Chai, Hong Kong
☎ 852-2827 6211
📠 852-3749 7342
✉ info-hk@ubm.com
www.cphijapan.jp/info/pharmatec.html

世界制药机械、设备与材料日本展
P-MEC Japan

日期：2013/04/24-26
地点：日本东京有明国际展览中心
主办：亚洲博闻有限公司
地址：香港湾仔港湾道26号华润大厦17楼
☎ 00852-2827 6211
📠 00852-3749 7342
✉ info-hk@ubm.com
www.cphijapan.jp/info/p-mec.html

P-MEC Japan
Date: 2013/04/24-26
Venue: Tokyo Big Sight Exhibition Centre, Japan
Profile: Japan' s APIs and intermediates producers, including pharmaceutical manufacturers who develop these products internally, are always on the lookout for new technologies for enhancing quality control, safety assurance, and increasing production efficiency. Exhibitors include Analyzer, Synthesizer, Chromatography, Concentration System, Centrifugal Separators, Reaction Vessels, Filtration Devices, Granulators, Agitators, Dryers
Organizer: UBM Asia Ltd
Address: 17/F, China Resources Building, 26 Harbour Road, Wan Chai, Hong Kong
☎ 852-2827 6211
📠 852-3749 7342
✉ info-hk@ubm.com
www.cphijapan.jp/info/p-mec.html

日本国际医疗设备设计与技术展览会
Medtec Japan

日期：2013/04/24-25
地点：日本东京有明国际展览中心Tokyo Big Sight Exhibition Centre
周期：每年一届
市场范围：国际性
主办：亚洲博闻有限公司
地址：香港湾仔港湾道26号华润大厦17楼
☎ 00852-2827 6211
📠 00852-3749 7342
✉ info-hk@ubm.com
✉ medtecjapan@ubm.com
http://medtecjapan.com

Medtec Japan
Date: 2013/04/24-25
Venue: Tokyo Big Sight Exhibition Centre, Japan
Frequency: Annual
Market Area: International
Organizer: UBM Asia Ltd
Address: 17/F, China Resources Building, 26 Harbour Road, Wan Chai, Hong Kong
☎ 852-2827 6211
📠 852-3749 7342
✉ info-hk@ubm.com
✉ medtecjapan@ubm.com
http://medtecjapan.com

制药业生物解决方案日本展
CPhI Japan

日期：2013/04/24-26
地点：日本东京有明国际展览中心
周期：每年一届
主办：亚洲博闻有限公司
地址：香港湾仔港湾道26号华润大厦17楼
☎ 00852-2827 6211
📠 00852-3749 7342
✉ info-hk@ubm.com
www.cphijapan.com

CPhI Japan
Date: 2013/04/24-26
Venue: Tokyo Big Sight Exhibition Centre, Japan
Frequency: Annual
Organizer: UBM Asia Ltd
Address: 17/F, China Resources Building, 26 Harbour Road, Wan Chai, Hong Kong
☎ 852-2827 6211
📠 852-3749 7342
✉ info-hk@ubm.com
www.cphijapan.com

国际合同定制服务日本展
ICSE Japan

日期：2013/04/24-26
地点：日本京东有明国际展览中心
主办：亚洲博闻有限公司
地址：香港湾仔港湾道26号华润大厦17楼
☎ 00852-2827 6211
📠 00852-3749 7342
✉ info-hk@ubm.com
www.cphijapan.jp/info/icse.html

ICSE Japan
Date: 2013/04/24-26
Venue: Tokyo Big Sight Exhibition Centre, Japan
Organizer: UBM Asia Ltd
Address: 17/F, China Resources Building, 26 Harbour Road, Wan Chai, Hong Kong
☎ 852-2827 6211
📠 852-3749 7342
✉ info-hk@ubm.com
www.cphijapan.jp/info/icse.html

日本今治海事展
Bari Ship (Japan)
日期：2013/05 -
地点：日本今治
主办：亚洲日本公司UBM Japan
联络：博闻(广州)展览有限公司
地址：广州中国大酒店商业大厦1159-1164 (510015)
联系人：020-8666 0158
www.bariship.com

Bari Ship (Japan)
Date: 2013/05 -
Venue: Imabari, Japan
Organizer: UBM Japan
Contact: UBM Asia Ltd
☎ 86-20-8626 6215
www.bariship.com

Imabari 海事展
(Bari-Ship)
Imabari Maritime Fair

日期：2013/05/23-25
地点：Texport Imabari, Japan
主办：亚洲博闻有限公司
地址：香港湾仔港湾道26号华润大厦17楼
☎ 00852-2827 6211
🖷 00852-3749 7342
✉ info-hk@ubm.com
http://secure.ubmjapan.com

Bari-Ship
Imabari Maritime Fair
Date: 2013/05/23-25
Venue: Texport Imabari，Japan
Organizer: UBM Asia Ltd
Address: 17/F, China Resources Building, 26 Harbour Road, Wan Chai, Hong Kong
☎ 852-2827 6211
🖷 852-3749 7342
✉ info-hk@ubm.com
secure.ubmjapan.com/bariship/visitor

东京国际机械零部件、材料及技术展览会
M-Tech
日期：2013/06 -
地点：日本东京
内容：机械传动零部件、紧固件、工业零配件、模具、制造及检测设备，表面处理技术及设备，粉末冶金技术及加工设备等
主办：北方国际展览有限公司North International Exhibition Co Ltd
地址：北京市西城区菜园街1号中环假日酒店写字间1102室(100053)
☎ 010-8354 0336，8351 3705
🖷 010-63547597
✉ wujiang@northexpo.com.cn
liushuo@northexpo.con.cn

eCommerce Solution 大阪展 网络及手机直销方案展览会大阪展
eCommerce Solution Fair in Osaka
Net & Mobile Direct Marketing Solution Fair in Osaka

日期：2013/06/12-13
地点：日本大阪Mydome Osaka
主办：亚洲博闻有限公司
地址：香港湾仔港湾道26号华润大厦17楼
☎ 00852-2827 6211
🖷 00852-3749 7342
✉ info-hk@ubm.com
www.tsuhan-fair-osaka.com

Commerce Solution Fair in Osaka
Net & Mobile Direct Marketing Solution Fair in Osaka
Date: 2013/06/12-13
Venue: Mydome Osaka, Japan
Organizer: UBM Asia Ltd
Address: 17/F, China Resources Building, 26 Harbour Road, Wan Chai, Hong Kong
☎ 852-2827 6211
🖷 852-3749 7342
✉ info-hk@ubm.com
www.tsuhan-fair-osaka.com

客户服务中心/客户关系管理展览会及会议大阪展
Call Centre/CRM Demo & Conference Osaka

日期：2013/06/12-13
地点：日本大阪Mydome Osaka
主办：亚洲博闻有限公司
地址：香港湾仔港湾道26号华润大厦17楼
☎ 00852-2827 6211
🖷 00852-3749 7342
✉ info-hk@ubm.com
www.callcenter-japan.com

Call Centre/CRM Demo & Conference Osaka
Date: 2013/06/12-13
Venue: Mydome Osaka，Japan
Organizer: UBM Asia Ltd
Address: 17/F, China Resources Building, 26 Harbour Road, Wan Chai, Hong Kong
☎ 852-2827 6211
🖷 852-3749 7342
✉ info-hk@ubm.com
www.callcenter-japan.com

日本国际五金及DIY展
JAPAN DIY SHOW
日期：2013/08 -
地点：日本东京
内容：手动工具、电动工具、气动工具、各类配件、锁具及安防器材、建筑构件、紧固件、照明电器、园艺工具、油漆喷涂装饰设备、泵类、供暖制冷设备、管道设备等
主办：北方国际展览有限公司North Intl Exhibition Co Ltd
联系人：吴江，刘硕
地址：北京市西城区菜园街1号，中环假日酒店写字间1102室(100053)
☎ 010-8354 0336，8351 3705
🖷 010-63547597
✉ wujiang@northexpo.com.cn
liushuo@northexpo.con.cn

日本保健及美容展
Diet & Beauty Fair

日期：2013/09/09-11
地点：日本东京有明国际展览中心Tokyo Big Sight Exhibition Centre
主办：亚洲博闻有限公司
地址：香港湾仔港湾道26号华润大厦17楼
☎ 00852-2827 6211
🖷 00852-3749 7342
✉ info-hk@ubm.com
www.ubmchina.com

Diet & Beauty Fair
Date: 2013/09/09-11
Venue: Tokyo Big Sight Exhibition Centre，Japan
Organizer: UBM Asia Ltd
Address: 17/F, China Resources Building, 26 Harbour Road, Wan Chai, Hong Kong
☎ 852-2827 6211
🖷 852-3749 7342
✉ info-hk@ubm.com
www.ubmchina.com

日本水疗及健康展
Spa & Wellness Japan

日期：2013/09/09-11
地点：日本东京有明国际展览中心
周期：每年一届
市场范围：国际性
主办：亚洲博闻有限公司
地址：香港湾仔港湾道26号华润大厦17楼
☎ 00852-2827 6211
🖷 00852-3749 7342
✉ info-hk@ubm.com
www.spaandwellness.jp
www.spajapan.info

Spa & Wellness Japan
Date: 2013/09/09-11
Venue: Tokyo Big Sight Exhibition Centre, Japan
Profile: Spa products & devices, Natural products, Amenity & gifts, Wellness programs
Frequency: Annual
Market Area: International
Organizer: UBM Asia Ltd
Address: 17/F, China Resources Building, 26 Harbour Road, Wan Chai, Hong Kong
☎ 852-2827 6211
🖷 852-3749 7342
✉ info-hk@ubm.com
www.spaandwellness.jp
www.spajapan.info

日本东京国际庭院园艺及户外家具展览会
GARDEX
日期：2013/10 -
地点：日本东京
内容：花园、草坪工具及设备、花园家具及家居用品、烧烤设备、花园规划和维护、植物和植物护理、花卉栽培和装饰
主办：北方国际展览有限公司North International Exhibition Co Ltd
地址：北京市西城区菜园街1号中环假日酒店写字间1102室(100053)
☎ 010-8354 0336，8351 3705
🖷 010-63547597
✉ wujiang@northexpo.com.cn
liushuo@northexpo.con.cn

日本健康食品原料展
安全及技术展
Health Ingredients Japan
Safety and Technology Japan

日期：2013/10/09-11
地点：日本东京有明国际展览中心
主办：亚洲博闻有限公司
地址：香港湾仔港湾道26号华润大厦17楼
☎ 00852-2827 6211
🖷 00852-3749 7342
✉ info-hk@ubm.com
www.hijapan.info

Health Ingredients Japan
Safety and Technology Japan
Date: 2013/10/09-11
Venue: Tokyo Big Sight Exhibition Centre, Japan
Organizer: UBM Asia Ltd
Address: 17/F, China Resources Building, 26 Harbour Road, Wan Chai, Hong Kong
☎ 852-2827 6211
🖷 852-3749 7342
✉ info-hk@ubm.com
www.hijapan.info

日本国际化工展
INCHEM TOKYO
日期：2013/11 -
地点：日本东京
主办：全国化工国际展览交流中心
☎ 010-6524 2231转608
✉ fany@icif.cn

日本东京国际建材展
JAPAN HOME AND BUILDING SHOW
日期：2013/11 -
地点：日本东京
内容：建材、室内装饰部分、手动工具、电动工具、气动工具等
主办：北方国际展览有限公司North Intl Exhibition Co Ltd
联系人：吴江，刘硕
地址：北京市西城区菜园街1号，中环假日酒店写字间1102室(100053)
☎ 010-8354 0336，8351 3705
🖷 010-63547597
✉ wujiang@northexpo.com.cn
liushuo@northexpo.con.cn

客户服务中心/客户关系管理展览会及会议
Call Centre/CRM Demo & Conference Tokyo

日期：2013/11/14-15
地点：日本东京阳光城市展览中心
周期：每年一届
市场范围：国际性
主办：亚洲博闻有限公司
地址：香港湾仔港湾道26号华润大厦17楼
☎ 00852-2827 6211
🖷 00852-3749 7342
✉ info-hk@ubm.com
www.callcenter-japan.com

Call Centre/CRM Demo & Conference Tokyo
Date: 2013/11/14-15
Venue: Sunshine City Convention Centre, Tokyo, Japan
Frequency: Annual
Market Area: International
Organizer: UBM Asia Ltd
Address: 17/F, China Resources Building, 26 Harbour Road, Wan Chai, Hong Kong
☎ 852-2827 6211
🖷 852-3749 7342
✉ info-hk@ubm.com
www.callcenter-japan.com

哈萨克斯坦 Kazakhstan

国际工程机械及矿业展览会
日期：2013/09 -
地点：哈萨克斯坦阿拉木图
周期：每年一届
主办：中国贸促会机械行业分会
地址：北京市西城区三里河路46号(100823)
☎ 010-6859 4811，6859 4994，6859 4910
🖷 010-6859 4995
✉ info@ccpitmsc.org
www.chinamachine.org.cn

哈萨克斯坦国际电力能源展览会
日期：2013/10 -
地点：哈萨克斯坦阿拉木图
周期：每年一届
主办：中国贸促会建设行业分会会展部；北京中杰城设国际展览有限公司
联系人：王艳玲
☎ 010-8836 3688、59799850-813；13691545669
🖷 010-5885 7468，5979 9850转ext 810
✉ wangyanling@top-fairs.com.cn
20204846
www.btfi.cn
www.power-gen.org.cn
www.top-fairs.com.cn

肯尼亚 Kenya

国际贸易展览会
日期：2013/09 -
地点：肯尼亚内罗毕
周期：每年一届
主办：中国贸促会机械行业分会
地址：北京市西城区三里河路46号(100823)
☎ 010-6859 5499，6859 4803，6859 4807
🖷 010-6859 4995
✉ info@ccpitmsc.org
www.chinamachine.org.cn

韩国 Korea

韩国涂料和胶粘剂展
Adhesive & Coating System Fair
日期：2013/03/20-20
地点：韩国仁川
主办：全国化工国际展览交流中心
☎ 010-6524 2231转608
✉ fany@icif.cn

第三十届韩国首尔国际食品酒店展
Seoul Food & Hotel 2013
日期：2013/05/14-17
地点：韩国首尔
主办：北京邦企展览服务有限公司
地址：北京市朝阳区惠新东街11号紫光发展大厦B1座501(100029)
☎ 010-6482 3808, 6482 3670
✉ bbes@china.com

韩国海事展
KORMARINE
日期：2013/10 -
地点：韩国釜山会展中心BEXCO
内容：韩国海事及造船业最主要的展会活动。产品及服务有船只设计、建造和装备、起重机械、火警与安全系统、烟气探测、防火设备、电子设备、船只及港口导航/通讯系统、引擎、海上防卫系统、分级与出版物。
周期：两年一届
市场范围：国际性
性质：面向贸易观众
主办：励展日本公司
联络：励展博览集团国际销售部
地址：北京市朝阳区新源南路1-3号平安国际金融中心A座15层01-03,05
联系人：臧威
☎ 010-5933 9268
🖷 010-5933 9233
✉ daisy.zang@reedexpo.com.cn
www.kormarine.net

韩国金属制造周
日期：2013/10 -
地点：韩国高阳
内容：各类标准及非标准紧固件、相关加工设备、检测设备、工具等
主办：北方国际展览有限公司
地址：北京市西城区菜园街1号中环假日酒店写字间1102室（100053）
联系人：赖彦平，陈思
☎ 010-8354 0342, 8354 0341
🖷 010-6354 7597
✉ yanping.lai@northexpo.com.cn
freya_chen@northexpo.com.cn

科威特 Kuwait

科威特石油天然气展览会
KOGS 2013
日期：2013/10/08-10
地点：科威特
主办：北京邦企展览服务有限公司
地址：北京市朝阳区惠新东街11号紫光发展大厦B1座501(100029)
☎ 010-6482 3808, 6482 3670
✉ bbes@china.com

马来西亚 Malaysia

马来西亚国际家具展
Malaysian Intl Furniture Fair

日期：2013/03/05-09
地点：马来西亚吉隆坡
主办：亚洲博闻有限公司
地址：香港湾仔港湾道26号华润大厦17楼
☎ 00852-2827 6211
🖷 00852-3749 7342
✉ info-hk@ubm.com
www.miff.com.my/2013

Malaysian Intl Furniture Fair
Date: 2013/03/05-09
Venue: Putra World Trade Centre and Matrade Exhibition and Convention Centre，Malaysia
Organizer: UBM Asia Ltd
Address: 17/F, China Resources Building, 26 Harbour Road, Wan Chai, Hong Kong
☎ 852-2827 6211
🖷 852-3749 7342
✉ info-hk@ubm.com
www.miff.com.my/2013

法兰克福（马来西亚）国际汽车零配件、设备及服务用品展览会
Automechanika Malaysia 2013
日期：2013/03/07-09
地点：马来西亚吉隆坡
周期：两年一届
主办：北京中杰城投国际展览有限公司
联系人：李娜
☎ 010-59799850转858
🖷 010-59799850转810、58857468
www.top-fairs.com.cn
www.build-ccpit.org

第六届东盟电力、电工设备技术展览会
Asean Elenex 2013
日期：2013/03/20-23
地点：马来西亚吉隆坡
主办：北京邦企展览服务有限公司
地址：北京市朝阳区惠新东街11号紫光发展大厦B1座501(100029)
☎ 010-6482 3808, 6482 3670
✉ bbes@china.com

Asean Industrial Automation 2013
日期：2013/03/20-23
地点：马来西亚吉隆坡
主办：北京邦企展览服务有限公司
地址：北京市朝阳区惠新东街11号紫光发展大厦B1座501(100029)
☎ 010-6482 3808, 6482 3670
✉ bbes@china.com

第十四届亚洲石油天然气及石化工程技术展览会
Oil & Gas Asia 2013
日期：2013/06/05-07
地点：马来西亚吉隆坡
主办：北京邦企展览服务有限公司
地址：北京市朝阳区惠新东街11号紫光发展大厦B1座501(100029)
☎ 010-6482 3808, 6482 3670
✉ bbes@china.com

亚洲铁路展
Rail Asia

RAILASIA'13
11-13 SEPTEMBER 2013 • KL CONVENTION CENTER

日期：2013/09/11-13
地点：马来西亚吉隆坡Kuala Lumpur Convention Centre
主办：亚洲博闻有限公司
地址：香港湾仔港湾道26号华润大厦17楼
☎ 00852-2827 6211
🖷 00852-3749 7342
✉ info-hk@ubm.com
www.railasia.org

Rail Asia
Date: 2013/09/11-13
Venue: Kuala Lumpur Convention Centre，Malaysia
Organizer: UBM Asia Ltd
Address: 17/F, China Resources Building, 26 Harbour Road, Wan Chai, Hong Kong
☎ 852-2827 6211
🖷 852-3749 7342
✉ info-hk@ubm.com
www.railasia.org

东南亚国际安全与消防技术设备展览会
Cybersec Asia

CyberSec Asia
PROTECTION • INTELLIGENCE • CYBER SECURITY

日期：2013/09/11-13
地点：马来西亚吉隆坡Kuala Lumpur Convention Centre
主办：亚洲博闻有限公司
地址：香港湾仔港湾道26号华润大厦17楼
☎ 00852-2827 6211
🖷 00852-3749 7342
✉ info-hk@ubm.com
ifsecsea.com

Cybersec Asia
Date: 2013/09/11-13
Venue: Kuala Lumpur Convention Centre，Malaysia
Organizer: UBM Asia Ltd
Address: 17/F, China Resources Building, 26 Harbour Road, Wan Chai, Hong Kong
☎ 852-2827 6211
🖷 852-3749 7342
✉ info-hk@ubm.com
ifsecsea.com

东南亚国际安全与消防技术设备展览会
IFSEC Southeast Asia

IFSEC Southeast Asia
COMMERCIAL SECURITY • FIRE • SAFETY

日期：2013/09/11-13
地点：马来西亚吉隆坡Kuala Lumpur Convention Centre
主办：亚洲博闻有限公司
地址：香港湾仔港湾道26号华润大厦17楼
☎ 00852-2827 6211
🖷 00852-3749 7342
✉ info-hk@ubm.com
ifsecsea.com

IFSEC Southeast Asia
Date: 2013/09/11-13
Venue: Kuala Lumpur Convention Centre，Malaysia
Organizer: UBM Asia Ltd
Address: 17/F, China Resources Building, 26 Harbour Road, Wan Chai, Hong Kong
☎ 852-2827 6211
🖷 852-3749 7342
✉ info-hk@ubm.com
ifsecsea.com

东南亚家具与室内装饰进出口商贸展
Southeast Asia Furniture & Interiors Import-Export Exhibition
日期：2013/09/13-16
地点：马来西亚吉隆坡Putra World Trade Centre
主办：亚洲博闻有限公司
地址：香港湾仔港湾道26号华润大厦17楼
☎ 00852-2827 6211
🖷 00852-3749 7342
✉ info-hk@ubm.com
www.seafie.com

Southeast Asia Furniture & Interiors Import-Export Exhibition
Date: 2013/09/13-16
Venue: Putra World Trade Centre，Malaysia
Organizer: UBM Asia Ltd
Address: 17/F, China Resources Building, 26 Harbour Road, Wan Chai, Hong Kong
☎ 852-2827 6211
🖷 852-3749 7342
✉ info-hk@ubm.com
www.seafie.com

世界节能环保与生态建筑东南亚展
EcoBuild Southeast Asia

ecobuild
Southeast Asia

日期：2013/09/17-19
地点：马来西亚吉隆坡Putra World Trade Centre
主办：亚洲博闻有限公司
地址：香港湾仔港湾道26号华润大厦17楼
☎ 00852-2827 6211
🖷 00852-3749 7342
✉ info-hk@ubm.com
www.ecobuildsea.com

EcoBuild Southeast Asia
Date: 2013/09/17-19
Venue: Putra World Trade Centre，Malaysia
Organizer: UBM Asia Ltd
Address: 17/F, China Resources Building, 26 Harbour Road, Wan Chai, Hong Kong
☎ 852-2827 6211
🖷 852-3749 7342
✉ info-hk@ubm.com
www.ecobuildsea.com

国际绿色建筑暨建筑设计展
Greenbuild Asia

GREENBUILD ASIA 2013
INTERNATIONAL EXHIBITION & CONFERENCE ON SUSTAINABLE BUILDING, DESIGN & CONSTRUCTION
17-19 September 2013 • Putra World Trade Centre

日期：2013/09/17-19
地点：马来西亚吉隆坡Putra World Trade Centre
主办：亚洲博闻有限公司
地址：香港湾仔港湾道26号华润大厦17楼
☎ 00852-2827 6211
🖷 00852-3749 7342
✉ info-hk@ubm.com
greenbuildasia.org

Greenbuild Asia
Date: 2013/09/17-19
Venue: Putra World Trade Centre，Malaysia
Organizer: UBM Asia Ltd
Address: 17/F, China Resources Building, 26 Harbour Road, Wan Chai, Hong Kong
☎ 852-2827 6211
🖷 852-3749 7342
✉ info-hk@ubm.com
http://greenbuildasia.org

亚洲太阳能展
Solar Asia Expo
日期：2013/09/17-19
地点：马来西亚吉隆坡Putra World Trade Centre
主办：亚洲博闻有限公司
地址：香港湾仔港湾道26号华润大厦17楼
☎ 00852-2827 6211
🖷 00852-3749 7342
✉ info-hk@ubm.com
www.solarasiaexpo.com

Solar Asia Expo
Date: 2013/09/17-19
Venue: Putra World Trade Centre，Malaysia
Organizer: UBM Asia Ltd
Address: 17/F, China Resources Building, 26 Harbour Road, Wan Chai, Hong Kong
☎ 00852-2827 6211
🖷 00852-3749 7342
✉ info-hk@ubm.com
www.solarasiaexpo.com

马来西亚国际食品加工、饮料、包装机械展览会
ProPak Malaysia 2013
日期：2013/09/17-20
地点：马来西亚吉隆坡
主办：北京邦企展览服务有限公司
地址：北京市朝阳区惠新东街11号紫光发展大厦B1座501(100029)

☎ 010-6482 3808, 6482 3670
✉ bbes@china.com

第十二届马来西亚国际酒店、餐饮设备、食品和饮料展览会
FHM 2013
日期：2013/09/17-20
地点：马来西亚吉隆坡
主办：北京邦企展览服务有限公司
地址：北京市朝阳区惠新东街11号紫光发展大厦B1座501(100029)
☎ 010-6482 3808, 6482 3670
✉ bbes@china.com

亚洲国际饲料、畜牧与肉类加工展
Livestock Asia

日期：2013/09/24-26
地点：马来西亚吉隆坡Kuala Lumpur Convention Centre
主办：亚洲博闻有限公司
地址：香港湾仔港湾道26号华润大厦17楼
☎ 00852-2827 6211
⎙ 00852-3749 7342
✉ info-hk@ubm.com
www.livestockasia.com

Livestock Asia
Date: 2013/09/24-26
Venue: Kuala Lumpur Convention Centre, Malaysia
Organizer: UBM Asia Ltd
Address: 17/F, China Resources Building, 26 Harbour Road, Wan Chai, Hong Kong
☎ 852-2827 6211
⎙ 852-3749 7342
✉ info-hk@ubm.com
www.livestockasia.com

马来西亚国际化工展
CHEMAISA
日期：2013/10/08-09
地点：马来西亚吉隆坡
主办：全国化工国际展览交流中心
☎ 010-6524 2231转608
✉ fany@icif.cn

墨西哥电力及电工设备、照明及技术展览会
日期：2013/06/05-07
地点：墨西哥墨西哥城
周期：每年一届
主办：中国贸促会建设行业分会会展部；北京中杰城设国际展览有限公司
联系人：王艳玲
☎ 010-8836 3688，5979 9850转813，13691545669
⎙ 010-5885 7468，5979 9850转810
✉ wangyanling@top-fairs.com.cn
QQ 20204846
www.btfi.cn
www.power-gen.org.cn
www.top-fairs.com.cn

国际汽车零部件、原料加工及售后服务贸易展览会
日期：2013/07 -
地点：墨西哥墨西哥城
周期：每年一届
主办：中国贸促会机械行业分会
地址：北京市西城区三里河路46号(100823)
☎ 010-6859 4952，6859 4804，6859 4931，6859 5220
⎙ 010-68594995
✉ info@ccpitmsc.org
www.chinamachine.org.cn

法兰克福（中美洲）国际汽车零配件、原料加工及售后展览会
PAACE Automechanika Mexico
日期：2013/07/10-12
地点：墨西哥墨西哥城
周期：每年一届
主办：北京中杰城投国际展览有限公司
联系人：李娜
☎ 010-59799850转858
⎙ 010-59799850转810、58857468
www.top-fairs.com.cn
www.build-ccpit.org

墨西哥国际五金展
EXPO NACIONAL FERRETERA
日期：2013/09 -
地点：墨西哥瓜达拉哈拉
内容：建筑装饰五金、日用五金、电动机手动工具、建筑设备、固定装置及电子产品；户外用品
主办：北方国际展览有限公司North Intl Exhibition Co Ltd
联系人：吴江，刘硕
地址：北京市西城区菜园街1号，中环假日酒店写字间1102室(100053)
☎ 010-8354 0336，8351 3705
⎙ 010-63547597
✉ wujiang@northexpo.com.cn
✉ liushuo@northexpo.con.cn

主办：励展博览集团
联络：励展博览集团国际销售部
联系人：王颖
地址：北京市朝阳区新源南路1-3号平安国际金融中心A座15层01-03,05
☎ 010-5933 9208
⎙ 010-5933 9233
✉ winnie.wang@reedexpo.com.cn
www.batimat.com

国际工业配件展览会
日期：2013/05 -
地点：摩洛哥卡萨布兰卡
周期：每年一届
主办：中国贸促会机械行业分会
地址：北京市西城区三里河路46号(100823)
☎ 010-6859 4927，6851 3586，6851 2883
⎙ 010-6859 4995
✉ info@ccpitmsc.org
www.chinamachine.org.cn

摩洛哥国际建筑展之暖通空调及电子系统展
BATIMAT MOROCCO HVAC
Electrical systems
日期：2013/09 -
地点：摩洛哥卡萨布兰卡
周期：两年一届
主办：励展博览集团
联络：励展博览集团国际销售部
联系人：王颖
地址：北京市朝阳区新源南路1-3号平安国际金融中心A座15层01-03,05
☎ 010-5933 9208
⎙ 010-5933 9233
✉ winnie.wang@reedexpo.com.cn
www.batimat.com

摩洛哥酒店用品展
Marocotel:
Intl show of professional equipment for hotels & catering
日期：2014/03 -
地点：摩洛哥卡萨布兰卡(Casablanca)
内容：与酒店、餐饮、食品贸易、健康与娱乐专业设备有关的国际展览会。
主办：励展法国公司摩洛哥分公司
联络：励展博览集团国际销售部
地址：北京市朝阳区新源南路1-3号平安国际金融中心A座15层01-03,05
☎ 010-5933 9268
⎙ 010-5933 9233
✉ daisy.zang@reedexpo.com.cn
联系人：臧威
www.marocotel.org

墨西哥
Mexico

国际机床展览会
日期：2013/03/05-08
地点：墨西哥墨西哥城
周期：两年一届
主办：中国贸促会机械行业分会
地址：北京市西城区三里河路46号(100823)
☎ 010-6859 5495，6859 5247，6859 5406，6859 5431
⎙ 010-68594995
✉ info@ccpitmsc.org
www.chinamachine.org.cn

国际包装展览会
日期：2013/06 -
地点：墨西哥墨西哥城
周期：每年一届
主办：中国贸促会机械行业分会
地址：北京市西城区三里河路46号(100823)
☎ 010-6859 4192，6859 4826，6859 5406
⎙ 010-68594995
✉ info@ccpitmsc.org
www.chinamachine.org.cn

蒙古
Mongolia

国际工程机械、矿山机械和矿业展览会
日期：2013/09/19-21
地点：蒙古乌兰巴托
主办：中国贸促会机械行业分会
地址：北京市西城区三里河路46号(100823)
☎ 010-6859 4811，6859 4994，6859 4910
⎙ 010-68594995
✉ www.chinamachine.org.cn
www.chinamachine.org.cn

摩洛哥
Morocco

摩洛哥国际建筑展之室内外装饰展
BATIMAT MOROCCO
Interior & outdoor Architecture
日期：2013/04/03-06
地点：摩洛哥卡萨布兰卡
周期：两年一届

缅甸
Myanmar

缅甸国际家禽、畜牧工业暨肉类加工展
Livestock Myanmar

加入LOGO

日期：2013/10/24-26
地点：缅甸仰光Tatmadaw Exhibition Hall
主办：亚洲博闻有限公司
地址：香港湾仔港湾道26号华润大厦17楼
☎ 00852-2827 6211
⎙ 00852-3749 7342
✉ info-hk@ubm.com
www.livestockmyanmar.com

Livestock Myanmar
Date: 2013/10/24-26
Venue: Tatmadaw Exhibition Hall，Yangon, Myanmar
Organizer: UBM Asia Ltd
Address: 17/F, China Resources Building, 26 Harbour

Road, Wan Chai, Hong Kong
☎ 852-2827 6211
852-3749 7342
✉ info-hk@ubm.com
www.livestockmyanmar.com

缅甸国际建筑展
Building & Construction Myanmar 2013
日期：2013/10/31-02
地点：缅甸仰光
主办：北京邦企展览服务有限公司
地址：北京市朝阳区惠新东街11号紫光发展大厦B1座501(100029)
☎ 010-6482 3808, 6482 3670
✉ bbes@china.com

缅甸国际采矿展
Mining Myanmar 2013
日期：2013/10/31-02
地点：缅甸仰光
主办：北京邦企展览服务有限公司
地址：北京市朝阳区惠新东街11号紫光发展大厦B1座501(100029)
☎ 010-6482 3808, 6482 3670
✉ bbes@china.com

缅甸国际电力&可再生能源展览会
Electric & Power & Renewable Energy Myanmar 2013
日期：2013/10/31-02
地点：缅甸仰光
主办：北京邦企展览服务有限公司
地址：北京市朝阳区惠新东街11号紫光发展大厦B1座501(100029)
☎ 010-6482 3808, 6482 3670
✉ bbes@china.com

2013缅甸国际农业博览会
2013东盟（缅甸）中国农林牧渔出口商品
2013缅甸农林牧渔供应商对接中国买家采购会
日期：2013/12 -
地点：缅甸仰光
内容：中国综合农业产品、农林牧渔产品采购对接
主办：越中会展商务有限公司
☎ 0771-2615 620
0771-2630 917

荷兰 Netherlands

荷兰国际运输及物流展
Holland Transport & Logistics Show
日期：2013/09 -
地点：荷兰鹿特丹Ahoy Rotterdam
内容：运输与多式联运服务、海外物流服务、物流服务、运输与物流的辅助服务、物流基础设施、工业产权、运输/物流技术及信息系统、生态物流
周期：两年一届
主办：励展法国展览公司Reed Expositions France
联络：励展博览集团国际销售部
联系人：臧威
地址：北京市朝阳区新源南路1-3号平安国际金融中心A座15层01-03,05
☎ 010-5933 9268
010-5933 9233
✉ daisy.zang@reedexpo.com.cn
www.hollandtransport.com

荷兰国际海事展览会
日期：2013/11/08-11
地点：荷兰鹿特丹
周期：两年一届
主办：中国贸促会机械行业分会
地址：北京市西城区三里河路46号(100823)
☎ 010-6859 4985，6859 5855
010-6859 4995
✉ info@ccpitmsc.org
www.chinamachine.org.cn

新西兰 New Zealand

2013年新西兰国际建筑展览会
日期：2013/06/23-25
地点：新西兰ASB SHOWGROUND
内容：建筑和室内装饰材料：玻璃、石材、陶瓷、钢材、木材、瓷砖、地板与地毯、门窗、涂料油漆、墙纸、百叶窗、家具等；建筑机械：加工设备、施工机械、建筑器具，工地防护用品、建筑工地设施等；五金工具：水嘴、水暖器材、洁具五金配件、门窗五金配件、阀门、紧固件、标准件、钉丝网、园艺设备等；建筑设备：采暖空调、卫浴设备、热水器、太阳能设备、厨房设备、建筑照明等；建筑智能化：家用设施智能控制系统，防火安全系统等。灯具
主办：BuildNZ
联络：中国贸促会建设行业分会
地址：北京市海淀区三里河路9号建设部大院机关门诊楼503
联系人：云鹏
☎ 010-8837 0844
010-5893 3930
✉ rocyun@hotmail.com
1492095643

尼日利亚 Nigeria

国际电力、照明及新能源展览会
日期：2013/09 -
地点：尼日利亚阿布贾
周期：每年一届
主办：中国贸促会机械行业分会
地址：北京市西城区三里河路46号(100823)
☎ 010-6859 4802，6859 4934
010-6859 4995
✉ info@ccpitmsc.org
www.chinamachine.org.cn

挪威 Norway

北极地球物理科学展览会暨研讨会
3P Arctic 2013
日期：2013/10/15-18
地点：挪威
主办：北京邦企展览服务有限公司
地址：北京市朝阳区惠新东街11号紫光发展大厦B1座501(100029)
☎ 010-6482 3808, 6482 3670
✉ bbcs@china.com

巴基斯坦 Pakistan

2013第10届巴基斯坦国际纺织服装工业展
Textile Asia 2013
日期：2013/03/08-10
地点：巴基斯坦卡拉奇卡拉奇博览中心
内容：纺织机械及附件，服装机械及附件
主办：巴基斯坦纺织工业部，巴基斯坦Jamals黄页公司，Ecommerce Gateway Pakistan(pvt) Ltd（UFI会员）
承办：上海爱卫客会展服务有限公司
联系人：李爱燕
☎ 021-3132 6575, 15900594089
021-5049 7282
✉ ivyli18@163.com
2632726499
www.aweek-expo.com

2013巴基斯坦国际纺织面料展
日期：2013/03/08-10
地点：巴基斯坦巴基斯坦卡拉奇博览中心
内容：棉面料，化纤面料，各式纱线，毛巾，浴室纺织品及辅料，餐桌及厨房用布，装饰布，窗帘，纺织窗帘配件，墙纸，家具布，地毯，男装，女装，儿童装，休闲装，户外装，游泳衣，冬装，安全防护装，床上用品
主办：巴基斯坦纺织工业部
联络：上海爱卫客会展服务有限公司
联系人：李爱燕
☎ 021-3132 6575, 15900594089
021-5049 7282
✉ ivyli18@163.com
2632726499
www.aweek-expo.com

第11届巴基斯坦国际电力能源及石油展览会
日期：2013/05/16-18
地点：巴基斯坦卡拉奇
周期：每年一届
主办：中国贸促会建设行业分会会展部，北京中杰城设国际展览有限公司
联系人：王艳玲
☎ 010-8836 3688，5979 9850转813，13691545669
010-5885 7468，5979 9850转810
✉ wangyanling@top-fairs.com.cn
20204846
www.btfi.cn
www.power-gen.org.cn
www.top-fairs.com.cn

巴拿马 Panama

2013年巴拿马第三十一届国际博览会
Expocomer 2013
日期：2013/04/17-20
地点：巴拿马城阿特拉巴国际展览中心ATLAPA CONVENTION CENTER
内容：为扩大博览会的影响，博览会的开幕式由巴拿马总统主持，邀请中南美洲多国总统、政界要人到会出席，并且巴拿马政府每年邀请中南美洲各国进口商参加该博览会。展出内容包括机械、电子、仪器、化工、五矿、五金工具、食品、服装、轻工产品、照明设备、灯具、建材、消费品、纺织品、家用电器、石油化工、加工机械、农用机械、电子通讯、轻工家电、汽车配件、五矿建材、农机具、文具玩具、体育用品、汽车、摩托车、农产品、畜牧产品等。
周期：每年一届
市场范围：国际性
性质：面向贸易观众
参展费用：24000元/9m^2
主办：巴拿马农工商协会；通用国际广告展览有限公司；广东粤召展览有限公司
地址：广州市天河区体育东路122号羊城国际商贸中心东塔1202, 1208室(510620)
联系人：周文槟
☎ 13710318991
✉ 1979wenbin@163.com
gdwenbin@hotmail.com
406372636

秘鲁 Peru

国际矿业展览会
日期：2013/09 -
地点：秘鲁阿雷基帕
周期：两年一届
主办：中国贸促会机械行业分会
地址：北京市西城区三里河路46号(100823)
☎ 010-6859 4811，6859 4994，6859 4910
010-6859 4995
✉ info@ccpitmsc.org
www.chinamachine.org.cn

菲律宾
Philippines

2013菲律宾国际建材、空调卫浴和建筑机械展览会
日期： 2013/03/13-17
地点： 菲律宾马尼拉
内容： 建筑和室内装饰材料：建筑材料、建筑五金、洁具五金配件、门窗、灯具、百叶窗和窗帘、建材、地毯、纺织品、地板、家具和装修、五金水暖产品、家用电子产品和家用器皿、室内和室外家居用品、厨房设备、生活用品、照明灯具、涂料和化学品。暖通空调卫浴：空调、空气压缩机、空气过滤和净化、空气压缩机、鼓风机、冷却器、清洗设备、压缩机、冷凝器、冷却塔、风管清洗设备、排气系统、风机和鼓风机、泡沫产品、供热系统、加湿器、工业气体、绝缘子、检漏仪、通风产品、泵和阀、发动机及汽车温度控制系统、过滤系统、液压气动设备、润滑油等，卫浴设备、阀门、热水器及配套设备加工设备、水暖器材。工程建筑机械：施工机械、挖掘机、叉车、推土机、皮带输送系统、起重机、电梯
周期： 每年一届
主办： 中国贸促会建设行业分会会展部
地址： 北京市海淀区三里河路9号建设部大院机关门诊楼503
联系人： 云鹏
☎ 15110286537
🖷 010-5893 3930
✉ rocyun@hotmail.com
QQ 1492095643
www.build-ccpit.org

菲律宾国际水工程大展
Water Philippines

WATER PHILIPPINES 2013 EXPO
INTERNATIONAL WATER & WASTEWATER INDUSTRY EVENT
20 - 22 MARCH 2013 • SMX CONVENTION CENTER, PASAY CITY, MANILA

日期： 2013/03/20-22
地点： 菲律宾巴萨市SMX Convention Centre
主办： 亚洲博闻有限公司
地址： 香港湾仔港湾道26号华润大厦17楼
☎ 00852-2827 6211
🖷 00852-3749 7342
✉ info-hk@ubm.com
www.waterphilippinesexpo.com

Water Philippines
Date: 2013/03/20-22
Venue: SMX Convention Centre, Barcelona City, Philippines
Organizer: UBM Asia Ltd
Address: 17/F, China Resources Building, 26 Harbour Road, Wan Chai, Hong Kong
☎ 852-2827 6211
🖷 852-3749 7342
✉ info-hk@ubm.com
www.waterphilippinesexpo.com

菲律宾食品配料展
Food Ingredients Philippines

Fi Food ingredients Philippines

日期： 2013/06/26-28
地点： 菲律宾马尼拉马尼拉SMX 会议中心
主办： 亚洲博闻有限公司
地址： 香港湾仔港湾道26号华润大厦17楼
☎ 00852-2827 6211
🖷 00852-3749 7342
✉ info-hk@ubm.com
http://fiphilippines.ingredientsnetwork.com/home

Food Ingredients Philippines
Date: 2013/06/26-28
Venue: SMX Convention Centre, Manila, Philippines
Profile: The first Food Ingredients (Fi) trade show ever held in the Philippines will give the domestic food industry greater access to much needed ingredients and technology from around the world.
Organizer: UBM Asia Ltd
Address: 17/F, China Resources Building, 26 Harbour Road, Wan Chai, Hong Kong
☎ 852-2827 6211
🖷 852-3749 7342
✉ info-hk@ubm.com
http://fiphilippines.ingredientsnetwork.com/home

菲律宾国际家禽、畜牧工业暨肉类加工展
Livestock Philippines

LIVESTOCK 2013 PHILIPPINES EXPO
PHILIPPINES' INTERNATIONAL LIVESTOCK INDUSTRY SHOW
7 - 9 AUGUST 2013 • SMX CONVENTION CENTRE, PASAY CITY

日期： 2013/08/07-09
地点： 菲律宾马尼拉SMX会议中心
主办： 亚洲博闻有限公司
地址： 香港湾仔港湾道26号华润大厦17楼
☎ 00852-2827 6211
🖷 00852-3749 7342
✉ info-hk@ubm.com
www.livestockphilippines.com

Livestock Philippines
Date: 2013/08/07-09
Venue: SMX Convention Centre, Manila, Philippines
Organizer: UBM Asia Ltd
Address: 17/F, China Resources Building, 26 Harbour Road, Wan Chai, Hong Kong
☎ 852-2827 6211
🖷 852-3749 7342
✉ info-hk@ubm.com
www.livestockphilippines.com

菲律宾饲料博览
Feeds Expo Philippines

FEEDS EXPO PHILIPPINES 2013
PHILIPPINES' INTERNATIONAL FEED INDUSTRY SHOW
7 - 9 AUGUST 2013 • SMX CONVENTION CENTRE, PASAY CITY

日期： 2013/08/07-09
地点： 菲律宾马尼拉马尼拉SMX会议中心
主办： 亚洲博闻有限公司
地址： 香港湾仔港湾道26号华润大厦17楼
☎ 00852-2827 6211
🖷 00852-3749 7342
✉ info-hk@ubm.com
livestockphilippines.com

Feeds Expo Philippines
Date: 2013/08/07-09
Venue: SMX Convention Centre, Manila, Philippines
Organizer: UBM Asia Ltd
Address: 17/F, China Resources Building, 26 Harbour Road, Wan Chai, Hong Kong
☎ 852-2827 6211
🖷 852-3749 7342
✉ info-hk@ubm.com
livestockphilippines.com

波兰
Poland

2013年波兰国际汽车配件展览会
日期： 2013/04 -
地点： 波兰波兹南国际展览中心
内容： 轿车、卡车、汽车装配及原理、零配件、电力系统、无线通信工程原理、警报和防盗、服务修理装备及设备、轮胎、耗材、汽车保养及保养材料；车体及车内设备、风挡玻璃、帆布、底盘、减震器、制动系统、轮毂、轮胎、转向器、万向节、电机、汽车轴承、汽车传动及变速器、离合器、刹车片、汽车空调器、加热器、冷却器、汽车电路系统及设备；车辆维修设备及工具、诊断装置、清洗、起重装置、油品及油品添加剂、车辆防护材料、车辆装饰用品及车辆养护用品、清洗材料、空气清新剂、导航系统；特殊技术服务、银行、保险。
主办： 波兹兰国际展览公司
联络： 厦门市盈拓商务有限公司
地址： 厦门市湖里大道41号联泰大厦2楼
☎ 400-8855-088
🖷 0592-239 6880
✉ web3988@showguide.cn

国际电力电子和新能源展览会
日期： 2013/05 -
地点： 波兰波兹南
周期： 每年一届
主办： 中国贸促会机械行业分会
地址： 北京市西城区三里河路46号(100823)
☎ 010-6859 4802，6859 4934
🖷 010-6859 4995
✉ info@ccpitmsc.org
www.chinamachine.org.cn

2013年波兰国际电力展览会
（展前补贴）
日期： 2013/05/14-16
地点： 波兰波兹南波兹南展览中心
周期： 每年一届
主办： 中国贸促会建设行业分会会展部；北京中杰城设国际展览有限公司
联系人： 王艳玲
☎ 010-8836 3688，5979 9850转813，13691545669
🖷 010-5885 7468，5979 9850转ext 810
✉ wangyanling@top-fairs.com.cn
QQ 20204846
www.btfi.cn
www.power-gen.org.cn
www.top-fairs.com.cn

葡萄牙
Portugal

里斯本国际食品展
Alimentaria Lisboa:
Intl Food & Beverage Exhibition
日期： 2013/04/14-17
地点： 葡萄牙里斯本国际展览馆Feira Internacional de Lisboa
内容： 一次在伊比利亚半岛上举办的食品饮料领域最重要的商业展会。在葡萄牙配销公司协会（APED）以及每个葡萄牙零售渠道的支持下，展会凝聚了食品市场最大最全面的视野，展会期间还为观众和展商提供丰富多彩的活动。
周期： 两年一届（奇数年举办）
市场范围： 国际性
性质： 面向贸易观众
参展费用： 光地展位96.5~121.8欧元/m^2
主办： 励展博览集团
联络： 励展博览集团国际销售部
联系人： 杜一鸣
地址： 北京市朝阳区新源南路1-3号平安国际金融中心A座15层01-03,05
☎ 010-5933 9209

☎ 010-5933 9233
✉ martin.du@reedexpo.com.cn
www.alimentaria-lisboa.com

卡塔尔
Qatar

中东电力展
PENN WELL
日期：2013/02/04-06
地点：卡塔尔
周期：每年一届
主办：中国贸促会建设行业分会会展部；北京中杰城设国际展览有限公司
联系人：王艳玲
☎ 010-8836 3688，5979 9850转813，13691545669
☎ 010-5885 7468，5979 9850转810
✉ wangyanling@top-fairs.com.cn
20204846
www.btfi.cn
www.power-gen.org.cn
www.top-fairs.com.cn

国际建材与工程机械博览会
日期：2013/04 -
地点：卡塔尔多哈
周期：每年一届
主办：中国贸促会机械行业分会
地址：北京市西城区三里河路46号(100823)
☎ 010-6859 4939，6859 4951，6859 5176，6859 4805
☎ 010-6859 4995
✉ www.chinamachine.org.cn
www.chinamachine.org.cn

俄罗斯
Russia

国际包装展览会
日期：2013/01 -
地点：俄罗斯莫斯科
周期：每年一届
主办：中国贸促会机械行业分会
地址：北京市西城区三里河路46号(100823)
☎ 010-6859 4192，6859 4826，6859 5406
☎ 010-68594995
✉ info@ccpitmsc.org
www.chinamachine.org.cn

俄罗斯暖通、制冷、空调、卫浴及水池设备展览会
Aqua-Therm Moscow:
Intl Exhibition for HVAC Sector & Pools
日期：2013/02 -
地点：俄罗斯莫斯科Crocus Expo会展中心
内容：HVAC（热通风与空调设备）、自动化控制系统、卫浴配件、锅炉设备、能源、燃气供给环境、水质控制设备、阀门及配件、供热技术、管道管线、泵、卫生技术与设备、热力配件水、污水处理技术、空调、通风管道及空气过滤器、空气净化器、压缩机、风扇、加湿器、除湿器、制冷、冷藏设备、通风设备、水健身与水疗、化工产品、水上乐园设备、小型游泳池、桑拿设备、水疗设备、游泳池、泳池设备及配件、水净化器、按摩浴缸
周期：每年一届
上届规模 2011：展览面积25,000m^2，参展商510家，参观人数18,505人
主办：励展俄罗斯公司
联络：励展博览集团国际销售部
地址：北京市朝阳区新源南路1-3号平安国际金融中心A座15层01-03,05
联系人：薛光
☎ 010-5933 9206
☎ 010-5933 9233
✉ eric.xue@reedexpo.com.cn
www.aquatherm-moscow.com

俄罗斯聚氨酯和复合材料展
Polyurethanex & Composite
日期：2013/02/26-28
地点：俄罗斯莫斯科
主办：全国化工国际展览交流中心
☎ 010-6524 2231转608
✉ fany@icif.cn

俄罗斯国际电力能源展
PENN WELL
日期：2013/03/05-06
地点：俄罗斯莫斯科
周期：每年一届
主办：中国贸促会建设行业分会会展部；北京中杰城设国际展览有限公司
联系人：王艳玲
☎ 010-8836 3688，5979 9850转813，13691545669
☎ 010-5885 7468，5979 9850转810
✉ wangyanling@top-fairs.com.cn
20204846
www.btfi.cn
www.power-gen.org.cn
www.top-fairs.com.cn

俄罗斯国际涂料展
INTERLAKOKRASKA
日期：2013/03/11-14
地点：俄罗斯莫斯科
主办：全国化工国际展览交流中心
☎ 010-6524 2231转608
✉ fany@icif.cn

俄罗斯国际园林工具及园林用品展
Gardentool
日期：2013/03/11-14
地点：俄罗斯莫斯科
内容：花园家具及家居用品、露营及休闲用品、烧烤设备、花园机械和设备、花园手工具和附件、其它设备和花园布置、植物和植物护理、水处理和室外照明。
主办：北方国际展览有限公司North International Exhibition Co Ltd
地址：北京市西城区莱园街1号中环假日酒店写字间1102室(100053)
联系人：王子威，李松林
☎ 010-8355 7740，8353 3198
☎ 010-6354 7597
✉ w.ziwei@northexpo.com.cn
✉ reanna@northexpo.com.cn

俄罗斯线缆展
CABEX
日期：2013/03/12-14
地点：俄罗斯莫斯科
内容：线缆（高中低压电力电缆，油田，矿业，安防专用）、线材制品（民用，工业用，电力用，通信用）、电缆（线）绝缘材料、紧固件、安装及专业工具；线材制造及精加工机械、原材料及辅助加工材料；电线电缆附件、线缆接插件、电线电缆保护设备及用品；相关领域其他产品。
主办：北方国际展览有限公司North International Exhibition Co Ltd
地址：北京市西城区莱园街1号中环假日酒店写字间1102室（100053）
联系人：王子威，李松林
☎ 010-8355 7740，8353 3198
☎ 010-6354 7597
✉ w.ziwei@northexpo.com.cn
✉ reanna@northexpo.com.cn

俄罗斯圣彼得堡紧固件展览会
FASTENER FAIR/RUSSIA
日期：2013/03/12-14
地点：俄罗斯圣彼得堡
内容：各类标准及非标准紧固件、相关加工设备、检测设备、工具等
周期：两年一届
主办：北方国际展览有限公司North International Exhibition Co Ltd
地址：北京市西城区莱园街1号中环假日酒店写字间1102室(100053)
联系人：赖彦平，陈思
☎ 010-8354 0342, 8354 0341
☎ 010-6354 7597
✉ yanping.lai@northexpo.com.cn
freya_chen@northexpo.com.cn

俄罗斯国际数字影像展览会
PHOTO FORUM
日期：2013/04 -
地点：俄罗斯莫斯科
内容：传统及数码照相机和摄像机；摄影摄像器材；摄影摄像配件及附件；摄影工作室器材；数字成像和出版；数码产品；存储产品
主办：北方国际展览有限公司North International Exhibition Co Ltd
地址：北京市西城区莱园街1号中环假日酒店写字间1102室(100053)
联系人：王子威，李松林
☎ 010-8355 7740，8353 3198
☎ 010-6354 7597
✉ w.ziwei@northexpo.com.cn
reanna@northexpo.com.cn

俄罗斯国际数字影像展览会
PHOTO FORUM
日期：2013/04 -
地点：俄罗斯莫斯科
内容：传统及数码照相机和摄像机；摄影摄像器材；摄影摄像配件及附件；摄影工作室器材；数字成像和出版；数码产品；存储产品
主办：北方国际展览有限公司North International Exhibition Co Ltd
地址：北京市西城区莱园街1号中环假日酒店写字间1102室(100053)
联系人：王子威，李松林
☎ 010-8355 7740，8353 3198
☎ 010-6354 7597
✉ w.ziwei@northexpo.com.cn
reanna@northexpo.com.cn

俄罗斯建材展
日期：2013/04 -
地点：俄罗斯莫斯科
内容：各类五金工具及DIY产品、室内建材、各类五金配件、门窗、楼梯、卫浴、供暖加热通风空调设备，管道、阀门、电气照明设备；园艺及户外用品等
主办：北方国际展览有限公司North Intl Exhibition Co Ltd
联系人：吴江，刘硕
地址：北京市西城区莱园街1号，中环假日酒店写字间1102室(100053)
☎ 010-8354 0336，8351 3705
☎ 010-63547597
✉ wujiang@northexpo.com.cn
liushuo@northexpo.con.cn

俄罗斯国际橡胶和轮胎展
TIRES AND RUBBER
日期：2013/04/23-26
地点：俄罗斯莫斯科
主办：全国化工国际展览交流中心
☎ 010-6524 2231转608
✉ fany@icif.cn

莫斯科国际家具生产、木工及室内装饰展
zum moscow / Interkomplekt
日期：2013/05/13-16
地点：俄罗斯莫斯科Crokus Expo Exhibition Cente国际博览中心
内容：莫斯科国际家具生产、木工及室内装饰展（interzum Moscow/Interkomplekt）和俄罗斯春季家具展(EEM/EuroExpoFurniture) 同期举行，后者是俄罗斯最重要的春季家具展。 作为interzum 的系列展会，莫斯科国际家具生产、木工及室内装饰展在展示一系列国际领先的家具生产材料和辅助配件的同时，也让您对俄罗斯及东欧的家具市场及潮流走向拥有更深入的了解
市场范围：国际性
性质：面向公众
入场费：380元人民币
主办：德国科隆展览国际有限公司Koelnmesse GmbH

地址：北京市朝阳区东三环北路8号亮马河大厦二座1018室(100004)
联系人：贾宁
☎ 010-65907766转ext 729
🖷 010-6590 6139
✉ m.jia@koelnmesse
www.interzum-moscow.cn
www.interzum-moscow.com

国际矿业机械展览会
日期：2013/05/14-16
地点：俄罗斯莫斯科
周期：每年一届
主办：中国贸促会机械行业分会
地址：北京市西城区三里河路46号(100823)
☎ 010-6859 4939，6859 4951，6859 5176，6859 4805
🖷 010-68594995
✉ info@ccpitmsc.org
www.chinamachine.org.cn

第12届俄罗斯电线电缆展
日期：2013/05/15-18
地点：俄罗斯莫斯科
周期：每年一届
主办：中国贸促会建设行业分会会展部；北京中杰城设国际展览有限公司
联系人：王艳玲
☎ 010-8836 3688，5979 9850转813，13691545669
🖷 010-5885 7468，5979 9850转810
✉ wangyanling@top-fairs.com.cn
QQ 20204846
www.btfi.cn
www.power-gen.org.cn
www.top-fairs.com.cn

国际机床工具展览会
日期：2013/05/27-31
地点：俄罗斯莫斯科
周期：每年一届
主办：中国贸促会机械行业分会
地址：北京市西城区三里河路46号(100823)
☎ 010-6859 5495，6859 5247，6859 5406，6859 5431
🖷 010-68594995
✉ info@ccpitmsc.org
www.chinamachine.org.cn

国际包装展览会
日期：2013/06 -
地点：俄罗斯莫斯科
周期：每年一届
主办：中国贸促会机械行业分会
地址：北京市西城区三里河路46号(100823)
☎ 010-6859 4192，6859 4826，6859 5406
🖷 010-68594995
✉ info@ccpitmsc.org
www.chinamachine.org.cn

国际电力电子展览会
日期：2013/06 -
地点：俄罗斯莫斯科
周期：每年一届
主办：中国贸促会机械行业分会
地址：北京市西城区三里河路46号(100823)
☎ 010-6859 4802, 6859 4934
🖷 010-6859 4995
✉ info@ccpitmsc.org
www.chinamachine.org.cn

国际建筑及工程机械展览会
日期：2013/06 -
地点：俄罗斯莫斯科
周期：每年一届
主办：中国贸促会机械行业分会
地址：北京市西城区三里河路46号(100823)
☎ 010-6859 4811，6859 4994，6859 4910
🖷 010-68594995
✉ info@ccpitmsc.org
www.chinamachine.org.cn

国际石油、天然气展览会
日期：2013/06 -
地点：俄罗斯莫斯科
周期：两年一届
主办：中国贸促会机械行业分会
地址：北京市西城区三里河路46号(100823)
☎ 010-6859 5296，6859 4938，6851 2883
🖷 010-6859 4995
✉ info@ccpitmsc.org
www.chinamachine.org.cn

第37届俄罗斯国际电力电子展览会
日期：2013/06/17-20
地点：俄罗斯莫斯科
周期：每年一届
主办：中国贸促会建设行业分会会展部；北京中杰城设国际展览有限公司
联系人：王艳玲
☎ 010-8836 3688，5979 9850转813，13691545669
🖷 010-5885 7468，5979 9850转810
✉ wangyanling@top-fairs.com.cn
QQ 20204846
www.btfi.cn
www.power-gen.org.cn
www.top-fairs.com.cn

国际汽车零部件展览会
日期：2013/08 -
地点：俄罗斯莫斯科
周期：每年一届
主办：中国贸促会机械行业分会
地址：北京市西城区三里河路46号(100823)
☎ 010-6859 4952，6859 4804，6859 4931，6859 5220
🖷 010-68594995
✉ info@ccpitmsc.org
www.chinamachine.org.cn

法兰克福（莫斯科）国际汽车零配件及售后服务展览会
MIMS automechanika MOSCOW
日期：2013/08/26-28
地点：俄罗斯莫斯科
周期：每年一届
主办：北京中杰城投国际展览有限公司
联系人：李娜
☎ 010-59799850转858
🖷 010-59799850转810，5885 7468
www.top-fairs.com.cn
www.build-ccpit.org

俄罗斯国际汽配展览会
InterAuto 2012
日期：2013/08/28-31
地点：俄罗斯莫斯科
周期：每年一届
主办：北京中杰城投国际展览有限公司
联系人：李娜
☎ 010-5979 9850转858
🖷 010-5979 9850转810，5885 7468
www.top-fairs.com.cn
www.build-ccpit.org

国际动力传动、表面处理及工业自动化展览会
日期：2013/09 -
地点：俄罗斯莫斯科
周期：每年一届
主办：中国贸促会机械行业分会
地址：北京市西城区三里河路46号(100823)
☎ 010-6859 5499，6859 4803，6859 4807，6859 4989
🖷 010-6859 4995
✉ www.chinamachine.org.cn
www.chinamachine.org.cn

俄罗斯国际化工展
CHEMISTRY
日期：2013/10 -
地点：俄罗斯莫斯科
主办：全国化工国际展览交流中心
☎ 010-6524 2231转608
✉ fany@icif.cn

国际印刷设备及技术展览会
日期：2013/10 -
地点：俄罗斯莫斯科
周期：两年一届
主办：中国贸促会机械行业分会
地址：北京市西城区三里河路46号(100823)
☎ 010-6859 4192，6859 4826，6859 5406
🖷 010-68594995
✉ info@ccpitmsc.org
www.chinamachine.org.cn

俄罗斯莫斯科国际紧固件展览会
日期：2013/10/08-10
地点：俄罗斯莫斯科
内容：各类标准及非标准紧固件、相关加工设备、检测设备、工具
主办：北方国际展览有限公司North International Exhibition Co Ltd
地址：北京市西城区菜园街1号中环假日酒店写字间1102室(100053)
联系人：赖彦平，陈思
☎ 010-8354 0342, 8354 0341
🖷 010-6354 7597
✉ yanping.lai@northexpo.com.cn
freya_chen@northexpo.com.cn

国际泵、阀门、压缩机、传动设备展览会
日期：2013/10/22-25
地点：俄罗斯莫斯科
周期：每年一届
主办：中国贸促会机械行业分会
地址：北京市西城区三里河路46号(100823)
☎ 010-6859 5296，6859 4938，6851 2883
🖷 010-6859 4995
✉ info@ccpitmsc.org
www.chinamachine.org.cn

莫斯科国际五金工具博览会
日期：2013/11 -
地点：俄罗斯莫斯科
内容：电动、气动、木工、加工、塑料、金属加工、机器、喷漆等工具类；电线、陶瓷、管道玻璃；汽修设备、液/气压设备和配件；精密仪器、激光切割设备
主办：北方国际展览有限公司North Intl Exhibition Co Ltd
地址：北京市西城区菜园街1号，中环假日酒店写字间1102室(100053)
联系人：吴江，刘硕
☎ 010-8354 0336，8351 3705
🖷 010-63547597
✉ wujiang@northexpo.com.cn
✉ liushuo@northexpo.con.cn

沙特阿拉伯
Saudi Arabia

第十五届沙特国际电力能源展览会
日期：2013/05/26-29
地点：沙特阿拉伯利雅得
周期：每年一届
主办：中国贸促会建设行业分会会展部；北京中杰城设国际展览有限公司
联系人：王艳玲
☎ 010-8836 3688，5979 9850转813，13691545669
🖷 010-5885 7468，5979 9850转810
✉ wangyanling@top-fairs.com.cn
QQ 20204846
www.btfi.cn
www.power-gen.org.cn
www.top-fairs.com.cn

沙特建材展
日期：2013/10 -
地点：沙特利雅得
内容：浴室、厨房设备；装饰、装修材料；电气、照明设备；五金制品等
主办：北方国际展览有限公司
联系人：吴江，刘硕

地址：北京市西城区菜园街1号，中环假日酒店写字间1102室(100053)
☎ 010-8354 0336，8351 3705
🖷 010-63547597
✉ wujiang@northexpo.com.cn
liushuo@northexpo.con.cn

国际工程建筑机械与工程车辆展览会
日期：2013/11 -
地点：沙特利雅得
周期：每年一届
主办：中国贸促会机械行业分会
地址：北京市西城区三里河路46号(100823)
☎ 010-6859 4811，6859 4994，6859 4910
🖷 010-68594995
✉ info@ccpitmsc.org
www.chinamachine.org.cn

新加坡 Singapore

第十九届新加坡精密机械及金属加工展
MTA 2013
日期：2013/04/09-12
地点：新加坡
主办：北京邦企展览服务有限公司
地址：北京市朝阳区惠新东街11号紫光发展大厦B1座501(100029)
☎ 010-6482 3808, 6482 3670
✉ bbes@china.com

亚洲宠物展
Pet Asia

日期：2013/05/30-06/02
地点：新加坡Suntec Singapore
主办：亚洲博闻有限公司
地址：香港湾仔港湾道26号华润大厦17楼
☎ 00852-2827 6211
🖷 00852-3749 7342
✉ info-hk@ubm.com
http//:aquarama.com.sg

Pet Asia
Date: 2013/05/30-06/02
Venue: Suntec Singapore，Singapore
Organizer: UBM Asia Ltd
Address: 17/F, China Resources Building, 26 Harbour Road, Wan Chai, Hong Kong
☎ 852-2827 6211
🖷 852-3749 7342
✉ info-hk@ubm.com
Htttt://aquarama.com.sg

新加坡国际观赏鱼及水族器材展览会
The 13th Intl Ornamental Fish and Accessories Exhibition 2013

日期：2013/05/30-06/02
地点：新加坡新达城国际会议展览中心
周期：两年一届
上届规模 2011：展览面积8,480m²，参展商126家来自23个国家及地区，参观人数3,755人主办：亚洲博闻UMB Asia
地址：广州中国大酒店商业大厦1159-1164，博闻(广州)展览有限公司(510015)
☎ 020-8666 0158
🖷 020-8626 6215
✉ info-china@ubm.com
www.aquarama.com.sg

The 13th Intl Ornamental Fish and Accessories Exhibition 2013
Date: 2013/05/30-02
Venue: Singapore
Frequency: Bienniel
Statistics 2011: Exhibition Area 8,480m², Exhibitors 126 came from 23 countries and regions, Visitors 3,755
Organizer: UMB Asia
☎ 86-20-8666 0158
🖷 86-20-8626 6215
✉ info-china@ubm.com
www.aquarama.com.sg

第十七届新加坡亚洲广播展
BroadcastAsia2013
日期：2013/06/18-21
地点：新加坡
主办：北京邦企展览服务有限公司
地址：北京市朝阳区惠新东街11号紫光发展大厦B1座501(100029)
☎ 010-6482 3808, 6482 3670
✉ bbes@china.com

第二十三届新加坡亚洲通讯展
CommunicAsia2013
日期：2013/06/18-21
地点：新加坡
主办：北京邦企展览服务有限公司
地址：北京市朝阳区惠新东街11号紫光发展大厦B1座501(100029)
☎ 010-6482 3808, 6482 3670
✉ bbes@china.com

亚洲海上旅游及邮轮展
Cruise Shipping Asia-Pacific
日期：2013/09 -
地点：新加坡
周期：每年一届
市场范围：国际性
主办：亚洲博闻有限公司
地址：香港湾仔港湾道26号华润大厦17楼
☎ 00852-2827 6211
🖷 00852-3749 7342
✉ info-hk@ubm.com
www.cruiseshippingasia.com

Cruise Shipping Asia-Pacific
Date: 2013/09 -
Venue: 新加坡
Frequency: Annual
Market Area: International
Organizer: UBM Asia Ltd
Address: 17/F, China Resources Building, 26 Harbour Road, Wan Chai, Hong Kong
☎ 852-2827 6211
🖷 852-3749 7342
✉ info-hk@ubm.com
www.cruiseshippingasia.com

新加坡珠宝首饰展览会
Singapore Jewellery & Gem Fair

日期：2013/10/12-15
地点：新加坡Marina Bay Sands
主办：亚洲博闻有限公司
地址：香港湾仔港湾道26号华润大厦17楼
☎ 00852-2827 6211
🖷 00852-3749 7342
✉ info-hk@ubm.com
www.jewellerynetasia.com

Singapore Jewellery & Gem Fair
Date: 2013/10/12-15
Venue: Marina Bay Sands，Singapore
Organizer: UBM Asia Ltd
Address: 17/F, China Resources Building, 26 Harbour Road, Wan Chai, Hong Kong
☎ 852-2827 6211
🖷 852-3749 7342
✉ info-hk@ubm.com
www.jewellerynetasia.com

第十四届国际实验室与分析技术及仪器展览会
AnaLabAsia2013
日期：2013/11/27-29
地点：新加坡
主办：北京邦企展览服务有限公司
地址：北京市朝阳区惠新东街11号紫光发展大厦B1座501(100029)
☎ 010-6482 3808, 6482 3670
✉ bbes@china.com

新加坡国际牙科展
IDEM Singapore
日期：2014/04/04-06
地点：新加坡SUNTEC展览中心
主办：科隆展览国际有限公司KOELNMESSE
地址：北京东三环北路8号亮马河大厦2座1018室(100004)
☎ 010-6590 7766
🖷 010-6590 6139
✉ info@koelnmesse.cn
www.idem-singapore.com

IDEM Singapore
Date: 2014/04/04-06
Venue: Singapore
Organizer: KOELNMESSE
Address: Unit 1018, Landmark Tower II, No. 8 Dongsanhuan North Rd, Beijing 100004, China
☎ 86-10-6590 7766
🖷 86-10-6590 6139
✉ info@koelnmesse.cn
www.idem-singapore.com

南非 South Africa

国际包装、食品加工及印刷机械展览会
日期：2013/03/12-15
地点：南非约翰内斯堡
周期：三年一届
主办：中国贸促会机械行业分会
地址：北京市西城区三里河路46号(100823)
☎ 010-6859 4192，6859 4826，6859 5406
🖷 010-6859 4995
✉ info@ccpitmsc.org
www.chinamachine.org.cn

南非基础建设展览会
日期：2013/05 -
地点：南非约翰内斯堡
周期：每年一届
主办：中国贸促会机械行业分会
地址：北京市西城区三里河路46号(100823)
☎ 010-6859 5499，6859 4803，6859 4807，6859 4989，6859 5055
🖷 010-6859 4995
✉ info@ccpitmsc.org
www.chinamachine.org.cn

法兰克福（南非）国际汽车零配件及售后服务展览会
Automechanika South Africa
日期：2013/05 -

地点：南非约翰内斯堡
周期：两年一届
主办：北京中杰城投国际展览有限公司
联系人：李娜
☎ 010-5979 9850转ext 858
🖷 010-5979 9850转ext 810，5885 7468
www.top-fairs.com.cn
www.build-ccpit.org

国际汽车零部件及售后服务展览会
日期：2013/05/08-11
地点：南非约翰内斯堡
周期：两年一届
主办：中国贸促会机械行业分会
地址：北京市西城区三里河路46号(100823)
☎ 010-6859 4952，6859 4804，6859 4931，6859 5220
🖷 010-6859 4995
✉ info@ccpitmsc.org
www.chinamachine.org.cn

国际五金工具展览会
日期：2013/08 -
地点：南非约翰内斯堡
周期：每年一届
主办：中国贸促会机械行业分会
地址：北京市西城区三里河路46号(100823)
☎ 010-6859 4927，6851 5863
🖷 010-6859 4995
✉ info@ccpitmsc.org
www.chinamachine.org.cn

国际建筑机械、建材机械、矿山机械及工程车辆博览会
日期：2013/09/18-21
地点：南非约翰内斯堡
周期：两年一届
主办：中国贸促会机械行业分会
地址：北京市西城区三里河路46号(100823)
☎ 010-6859 4811，6859 4994，6859 4910
🖷 010-6859 4995
✉ info@ccpitmsc.org
www.chinamachine.org.cn

国际电力、照明及新能源展览会
日期：2013/10 -
地点：南非约翰内斯堡
周期：每年一届
主办：中国贸促会机械行业分会
地址：北京市西城区三里河路46号(100823)
☎ 010-6859 4802，6859 4934
🖷 010-6859 4995
✉ info@ccpitmsc.org
www.chinamachine.org.cn

南非电力能源展览会
PENN WELL
日期：2014/03/17-19
地点：南非开普敦
周期：每年一届
主办：中国贸促会建设行业分会会展部；北京中杰城设国际展览有限公司
联系人：王艳玲
☎ 010-8836 3688，5979 9850转813，13691545669
🖷 010-5885 7468，5979 9850转810
✉ wangyanling@top-fairs.com.cn
QQ 20204846
www.btfi.cn
www.power-gen.org.cn
www.top-fairs.com.cn

西班牙
Spain

西班牙毕尔巴鄂国际五金展
Ferroforma
日期：2013/03/12-15
地点：西班牙毕尔巴鄂展览中心BILBAO EXHIBITION CENTRE
内容：锁具、安防设备及配件；工具；电动工具和木工机械；建筑五金和建材；工业供应品；劳保用品；紧固件；商店、仓储设备与配件；家居用品；装潢五金；电气产品，照明；管件；家居改进和DIY产品；园艺工具和产品
始办年份：1974
周期：两年一届
市场范围：国际性
性质：面向贸易观众
入场费：17 欧元
主办：北方国际展览有限公司North Intl Exhibition Co Ltd
联系人：吴江，刘硕
地址：北京市西城区菜园街1号，中环假日酒店写字间1102室(100053)
☎ 010-8354 0336，8351 3705
🖷 010-63547597
✉ wujiang@northexpo.com.cn
✉ liushuo@northexpo.con.cn
主办：科隆展览国际有限公司KOELNMESSE
地址：北京东三环北路8号亮马河大厦2座1018室，科隆展览中国有限公司(100004)
联系人：陈瑞
☎ 010-6590 7766 转750
🖷 010-6590 6139
✉ r.chen@koelnmesse.cn
www.ferroforma.cn

伊比利亚国际汽车零部件、设备及售后服务展览会
日期：2013/03/13-16
地点：西班牙马德里
周期：两年一届
主办：中国贸促会机械行业分会
地址：北京市西城区三里河路46号(100823)
☎ 010-6859 4952，6859 4804，6859 4931，6859 5220
🖷 010-68594995
✉ info@ccpitmsc.org
www.chinamachine.org.cn

西班牙巴塞隆拿世界卫生纸业展览会
Tissue World

日期：2013/03/18-21
地点：西班牙巴塞隆拿Fira Barcelona
主办：亚洲博闻有限公司
地址：香港湾仔港湾道26号华润大厦17楼
☎ 00852-2827 6211
🖷 00852-3749 7342
✉ info-hk@ubm.com
http://tissueworld.com

Tissue World
Date: 2013/03/18-21
Venue: Fira Barcelona–Gran Via, Hall 1, Spain
Organizer: UBM Asia Ltd
Address: 17/F, China Resources Building, 26 Harbour Road, Wan Chai, Hong Kong
☎ 852-2827 6211
🖷 852-3749 7342
✉ info-hk@ubm.com
http://tissueworld.com

西班牙游泳池展
PISCINA BCN
日期：2013/10/15-18
地点：西班牙巴塞罗那
主办：全国化工国际展览交流中心
☎ 010-6524 2231转608
✉ fany@icif.cn

斯里兰卡
Sri Lanka

斯里兰卡国际染料和化工展
Dye+Chem Sirilanka
日期：2013/02/28-02
地点：斯里兰卡科伦坡
主办：全国化工国际展览交流中心
☎ 010-6524 2231转608
✉ fany@icif.cn

坦桑尼亚
Tanzania

2013年第16届东非（坦桑尼亚）国际建筑展览会
日期：2013/05/18-20
地点：坦桑尼亚坦桑尼亚
内容：建筑材料：石材、陶瓷、家居饰品、型砖、钢材、有色金属、木材、水泥、混凝土、玻璃、石膏、密封材料、地板与地毯、墙纸及墙板镶嵌、庭院设施、园林绿化摆设等；建筑五金：水嘴、水暖器材、洁具五金配件、窗及门、五金配件、阀门、紧固件、标准件、管件、钉、丝网，电动与手动工具；建材机械：加工设备、玻璃门窗机械、木工机械、石材设备等；施工机械、建筑设备：采暖、空调、卫浴设备、热水器及配套设备、建筑照明等；家庭自动化：遥控装置、音响录像装置、家庭影院与卫星产品、有线电视系统等。工程和矿山机械：建筑工程机械、专用车辆、运输设备、工地防护用品
周期：每年一届
主办：中国贸促会建设行业分会
地址：北京市海淀区三里河路9号建设部大院机关门诊楼503(100835)
联系人：云鹏
☎ 010-8837 0844
🖷 010-5893 3930
✉ rocyun@hotmail.com
QQ 1492095643

泰国
Thailand

泰国国际化工展
CHEMEXPO THAI
日期：2013/03/19-20
地点：泰国曼谷
主办：全国化工国际展览交流中心
☎ 010-6524 2231转608
✉ fany@icif.cn

第27届泰国东盟建筑及技术博览会
日期：2013/04/30-02
地点：泰国曼谷 IMPACT会展中心
内容：房屋建筑商、设计与施工服务；门和窗户，栅栏，五金产品；家庭装饰、家具、电器；建筑材料、涂料、玻璃、窗帘；壁纸、木材、地板、墙壁；照明产品；电脑、软件、闭路电视、家庭；剧院，音响设备；屋顶材料、绝缘材料、遮篷、钢材、金属制品；混凝土材料和密封剂；卫生洁具；厨房、游泳池、桑拿；瓷砖，大理石，花岗岩；花园和景观及配件；住房和居住产品，高科技产品；工具设备；设备安装；房地产、房子、公寓、银行，金融、贷款
周期：每年一届
主办：Challenger Hall
承办：中国贸促会建设行业分会
地址：北京市海淀区三里河路9号建设部大院北附楼503(100835)
联系人：云鹏
☎ 010-8837 0844

🖷 010-5893 3930
✉ 1492095643@qq.com
1492095643
www.build-ccpit.org

国际专用工具及机械展
MOLDEX
日期：2013/05/16-19
地点：泰国曼谷国际贸易展览中心
周期：每年一届
主办：亚洲博闻有限公司
☎ 00852-2827 6211
🖷 00852-3749 7342
✉ info-hk@ubm.com
www.intermachshow.com

MOLDEX
Date: 2013/05/16-19
Venue: Bangkok Intl Trade & Exhibition Centre, Thailand
Frequency: Annual
Organizer: UBM Asia Ltd
☎ 852-2827 6211
🖷 852-3749 7342
✉ info-hk@ubm.com
www.intermachshow.com

专业运输及材料装卸展
LogisPro Thailand

日期：2013/05/16-19
地点：泰国曼谷国际贸易展览中心
周期：每年一届
市场范围：国际性
主办：亚洲博闻有限公司
地址：香港湾仔港湾道26号华润大厦17楼
☎ 00852-2827 6211
🖷 00852-3749 7342
✉ info-hk@ubm.com
www.intermachshow.com

LogisPro Thailand
Date: 2013/05/16-19
Venue: Bangkok Intl Trade & Exhibition Centre, Thailand
Frequency: Annual
Market Area: International
Organizer: UBM Asia Ltd
Address: 17/F, China Resources Building, 26 Harbour Road, Wan Chai, Hong Kong
☎ 852-2827 6211
🖷 852-3749 7342
✉ info-hk@ubm.com
www.intermachshow.com

专业焊接技术及配件工艺贸易展
WeldTech

日期：2013/05/16-19
地点：泰国曼谷国际贸易展览中心
周期：每年一届
市场范围：国际性
主办：亚洲博闻有限公司
地址：香港湾仔港湾道26号华润大厦17楼
☎ 00852-2827 6211
🖷 00852-3749 7342
✉ info-hk@ubm.com
www.intermachshow.com

WeldTech
Date: 2013/05/16-19
Venue: Bangkok Intl Trade & Exhibition Centre, Thailand
Frequency: Annual
Market Area: International
Organizer: UBM Asia Ltd
Address: 17/F, China Resources Building, 26 Harbour Road, Wan Chai, Hong Kong
☎ 852-2827 6211
🖷 852-3749 7342
✉ info-hk@ubm.com
www.intermachshow.com

工业自动化展
Industrial Automation Robotics

日期：2013/05/16-19
地点：泰国曼谷国际贸易展览中心
周期：每年一届
主办：亚洲博闻有限公司
地址：香港湾仔港湾道26号华润大厦17楼
☎ 00852-2827 6211
🖷 00852-3749 7342
✉ info-hk@ubm.com
www.intermachshow.com

Industrial Automation Robotics
Date: 2013/05/16-19
Venue: Bangkok Intl Trade & Exhibition Centre, Thailand
Frequency: Annual
Organizer: UBM Asia Ltd
Address: 17/F, China Resources Building, 26 Harbour Road, Wan Chai, Hong Kong
☎ 852-2827 6211
🖷 852-3749 7342
✉ info-hk@ubm.com
www.intermachshow.com

亚洲金属板材展
Sheet Metal Asia

日期：2013/05/16-19
地点：泰国曼谷国际贸易展览中心
周期：每年一届
市场范围：国际性
主办：亚洲博闻有限公司
地址：香港湾仔港湾道26号华润大厦17楼
☎ 00852-2827 6211
🖷 00852-3749 7342
✉ info-hk@ubm.com
www.intermachshow.com

Sheet Metal Asia
Date: 2013/05/16-19
Venue: Bangkok Intl Trade & Exhibition Centre, Thailand
Frequency: Annual
Market Area: International
Organizer: UBM Asia Ltd
Address: 17/F, China Resources Building, 26 Harbour Road, Wan Chai, Hong Kong
☎ 852-2827 6211
🖷 852-3749 7342
✉ info-hk@ubm.com
www.intermachshow.com

国际机器展
Intermach

日期：2013/05/16-19
地点：泰国曼谷国际贸易展览中心
周期：每年一届
市场范围：国际性
主办：亚洲博闻有限公司
地址：香港湾仔港湾道26号华润大厦17楼
☎ 00852-2827 6211
🖷 00852-3749 7342
✉ info-hk@ubm.com
www.intermachshow.com

Intermach
Date: 2013/05/16-19
Venue: Bangkok Intl Trade & Exhibition Centre, Thailand
Frequency: Annual
Market Area: International
Organizer: UBM Asia Ltd
Address: 17/F, China Resources Building, 26 Harbour Road, Wan Chai, Hong Kong
☎ 852-2827 6211
🖷 852-3749 7342
✉ info-hk@ubm.com
www.intermachshow.com

国际汽车生产及配件展览会
Automotive Engineering Asia

日期：2013/05/16-19
地点：泰国曼谷国际贸易展览中心
周期：每年一届
市场范围：国际性
主办：亚洲博闻有限公司
地址：香港湾仔港湾道26号华润大厦17楼
☎ 00852-2827 6211
🖷 00852-3749 7342
✉ info-hk@ubm.com
www.intermachshow.com

Automotive Engineering Asia
Date: 2013/05/16-19
Venue: Bangkok Intl Trade & Exhibition Centre, Thailand
Frequency: Annual
Market Area: International
Organizer: UBM Asia Ltd
Address: 17/F, China Resources Building, 26 Harbour Road, Wan Chai, Hong Kong
☎ 852-2827 6211
🖷 852-3749 7342
✉ info-hk@ubm.com
www.intermachshow.com

亚洲世界食品博览会
Thaifex – World of Food Asia
日期：2013/05/22-26
地点：泰国泰国曼谷IMPACT展览中心
IMPACT, Bangkok, Thailand
内容：食品和饮料、食品技术、餐饮、招待、零售和连锁
始办年份：2004
周期：每年一届
市场范围：国际性

性质：面向公众
主办：科隆展览国际有限公司KOELNMESSE
联络：科隆展览中国有限公司
地址：北京东三环北路8号亮马河大厦2座1018室(100004)
联系人：潘容
☎ 010-6590 7766 转715
🖷 010-6590 6139
✉ g.pan@koelnmesse.cn
www.world-of-food.cn

Thaifex – World of Food Asia
Date: 2013/05/22-26
Venue: IMPACT, Bangkok, Thailand
Established Year: 2004
Frequency: Annual
Market Area: International
Nature: Open to Public
Organizer: KOELNMESSE
Address: Unit 1018, Landmark Tower II, No. 8 Dongsanhuan North Rd, Beijing 100004, China
Contact: Grace Pan
☎ 86-10-6590 7766 ext 715
🖷 86-10-6590 6139
✉ g.pan@koelnmesse.cn
www.world-of-food.cn

世界清真食品博览会
World of Halal
日期：2013/05/22-26
地点：泰国泰国曼谷IMPACT 展览中心
始办年份：2004
周期：每年一届
市场范围：国际性
性质：面向公众
主办：科隆展览国际有限公司KOELNMESSE
联络：科隆展览中国有限公司
地址：北京东三环北路8号亮马河大厦2座1018室(100004)
联系人：潘容
☎ 010-6590 7766 转715
🖷 010-6590 6139
✉ g.pan@koelnmesse.cn
www.world-of-food.cn

亚洲水泵及阀门展

Pumps & Valves Asia
日期：2013/06/05-08
地点：泰国曼谷国际贸易展览中心
市场范围：国际性
主办：亚洲博闻有限公司
地址：香港湾仔港湾道26号华润大厦17楼
☎ 00852-2827 6211
🖷 00852-3749 7342
✉ info-hk@ubm.com
www.pumpsandvalves-asia.com

Pumps & Valves Asia

Date: 2013/06/05-08
Venue: Bangkok Intl Trade & Exhibition Centre, Thailand
Market Area: International
Organizer: UBM Asia Ltd
Address: 17/F, China Resources Building, 26 Harbour Road, Wan Chai, Hong Kong
☎ 852-2827 6211
🖷 852-3749 7342
✉ info-hk@ubm.com
www.pumpsandvalves-asia.com

亚洲再生能源展

Renewable Energy Asia
日期：2013/06/05-08
地点：泰国曼谷国际贸易展览中心
周期：每年一届
市场范围：国际性
主办：亚洲博闻有限公司
地址：香港湾仔港湾道26号华润大厦17楼
☎ 00852-2827 6211
🖷 00852-3749 7342
✉ info-hk@ubm.com
www.renewableenergy-asia.com

Renewable Energy Asia

Date: 2013/06/05-08
Venue: Bangkok Intl Trade & Exhibition Centre, Thailand
Frequency: Annual
Market Area: International
Organizer: UBM Asia Ltd
Address: 17/F, China Resources Building, 26 Harbour Road, Wan Chai, Hong Kong
☎ 852-2827 6211
🖷 852-3749 7342
✉ info-hk@ubm.com
www.renewableenergy-asia.com

泰国国际水工程大展暨论坛

Thai Water
日期：2013/06/05-08
地点：泰国曼谷Bangkok Intl Trade & Exhibition Centre
市场范围：国际性
主办：亚洲博闻有限公司
地址：香港湾仔港湾道26号华润大厦17楼
☎ 00852-2827 6211
🖷 00852-3749 7342
✉ info-hk@ubm.com
www.thai-water.com

Thai Water

Date: 2013/06/05-08
Venue: Bangkok Intl Trade & Exhibition Centre, Thailand
Market Area: International
Organizer: UBM Asia Ltd
Address: 17/F, China Resources Building, 26 Harbour Road, Wan Chai, Hong Kong
☎ 852-2827 6211
🖷 852-3749 7342
✉ info-hk@ubm.com
www.thai-water.com

国际环保技术展

Entech Pollutec Asia
日期：2013/06/05-08
地点：泰国曼谷国际贸易展览中心
周期：每年一届
市场范围：国际性
主办：亚洲博闻有限公司
地址：香港湾仔港湾道26号华润大厦17楼
☎ 00852-2827 6211
🖷 00852-3749 7342
✉ info-hk@ubm.com
www.entechpollutec-asia.com

Entech Pollutec Asia

Date: 2013/06/05-08
Venue: Bangkok Intl Trade & Exhibition Centre, Thailand
Frequency: Annual
Market Area: International
Organizer: UBM Asia Ltd
Address: 17/F, China Resources Building, 26 Harbour Road, Wan Chai, Hong Kong
☎ 852-2827 6211
🖷 852-3749 7342
✉ info-hk@ubm.com
www.entechpollutec-asia.com

第二十一届亚洲地区国际食品饮料，加工包装技术展览会及研讨会
ProPak Asia2013
日期：2013/06/12-15
地点：泰国曼谷
主办：北京邦企展览服务有限公司
地址：北京市朝阳区惠新东街11号紫光发展大厦B1座501(100029)
☎ 010-6482 3808, 6482 3670
✉ bbes@china.com

2013年泰国电子展：国际电子产品制造贸易展及会议
NEPCON Thailand
日期：2013/06/20-23
地点：泰国曼谷国际贸易展览中心BITEC
内容：是国际电子元器件及生产设备展览会(NEPCON)系列展会之一，曾在亚洲8个国家举办。
周期：二年一届
市场范围：国际性
性质：面向贸易观众
上届规模 2009：参观人数34,206人
主办：励展泰国公司
联络：励展博览集团国际销售部
地址：北京市朝阳区新源南路1-3号平安国际金融中心A座15层01-03,05
联系人：张志超
☎ 010-5933 9266
🖷 010-5933 9233
✉ ivy.zhang@reedexpo.com.cn
www.nepconthailand.com

第二十一届泰国国际食品酒店用品展览会
FHT2013
日期：2013/09/03-06
地点：泰国曼谷
主办：北京邦企展览服务有限公司
地址：北京市朝阳区惠新东街11号紫光发展大厦B1座501(100029)
☎ 010-6482 3808, 6482 3670
✉ bbes@china.com

国际管材线材展览会
日期：2013/09 -
地点：泰国曼谷
周期：两年一届
主办：中国贸促会机械行业分会
地址：北京市西城区三里河路46号(100823)
☎ 010-6859 5296，6859 4938，6851 2883
🖷 010-6859 4995
✉ info@ccpitmsc.org
www.chinamachine.org.cn

亚洲食品配料展

Food Ingredients Asia
日期：2013/09/11-13
地点：泰国曼谷
主办：亚洲博闻有限公司
地址：香港湾仔港湾道26号华润大厦17楼
☎ 00852-2827 6211
🖷 00852-3749 7342
✉ info-hk@ubm.com
http://fiasia-thailand.ingredientsnetwork.com

Food Ingredients Asia

Date: 2013/09/11-13
Venue: Bangkok Intl Trade & Exhibition Centre, Thailand
Organizer: UBM Asia Ltd
Address: 17/F, China Resources Building, 26 Harbour Road, Wan Chai, Hong Kong
☎ 852-2827 6211
🖷 852-3749 7342
✉ info-hk@ubm.com
http://fiasia-thailand.ingredientsnetwork.com

第21届国际亚洲电力展
PENN WELL
日期：2013/10/02-04
地点：泰国
周期：每年一届
主办：中国贸促会建设行业分会会展部；北京中杰城设国际展览有限公司
联系人：王艳玲
☎ 010-8836 3688, 5979 9850转813，13691545669
🖷 010-5885 7468，5979 9850转810
✉ wangyanling@top-fairs.com.cn
🐧 20204846
www.btfi.cn
www.power-gen.org.cn
www.top-fairs.com.cn

国际机床和金属加工机械展览会
日期：2013/11 -
地点：泰国曼谷
周期：每年一届
主办：中国贸促会机械行业分会
地址：北京市西城区三里河路46号(100823)
☎ 010-6859 5495，6859 5247，6859 5406，6859 5431
🖷 010-68594995
✉ info@ccpitmsc.org
www.chinamachine.org.cn

亚洲防卫展
Defense & Security

日期：2013/11/04-07
地点：泰国曼谷IMPACT exhibition & Convention Centre
主办：亚洲博闻有限公司
地址：香港湾仔港湾道26号华润大厦17楼
☎ 00852-2827 6211
🖷 00852-3749 7342
✉ info-hk@ubm.com
www.asiandefense.com

Defense & Security
Date: 2013/11/04-07
Venue: IMPACT exhibition & Convention Centre, Bangkok, Thailand
Organizer: UBM Asia Ltd
Address: 17/F, China Resources Building, 26 Harbour Road, Wan Chai, Hong Kong
☎ 852-2827 6211
🖷 852-3749 7342
✉ info-hk@ubm.com
www.asiandefense.com

突尼斯
Tunisia

第十一届突尼斯建材展
日期：2013/06/06-09
地点：突尼斯斯法克斯
主办：上海菲思斯会展服务有限公司
地址：上海市浦东杨南路455号郭家花园商务中心A座602室
联系人：成晓菲
☎ 021-5179 6280
🖷 021-5179 6290
✉ faye0612@sina.com
🐧 2423543880

土耳其
Turkey

中东贸易和伊拉克重建国际工业展览会
日期：2013 -
地点：土耳其加济安泰普
周期：每年一届
主办：中国贸促会机械行业分会
地址：北京市西城区三里河路46号(100823)
☎ 010-6859 4927，6851 3586，6851 2883
🖷 010-6859 4995
✉ info@ccpitmsc.org
www.chinamachine.org.cn

国际工业展览会
日期：2013/03 -
地点：土耳其伊斯坦布尔
周期：每年一届
主办：中国贸促会机械行业分会
地址：北京市西城区三里河路46号(100823)
☎ 010-6859 5499，6859 4803，6859 4807，6859 4989，6859 5055
🖷 010-6859 4995
✉ info@ccpitmsc.org
www.chinamachine.org.cn

伊斯坦堡珠宝展-三月展
ISTANBUL JEWELRY SHOW - March

21 - 24 MARCH 2013
日期：2013/03/21-24
地点：土耳其伊斯坦堡CNR国际展览中心
市场范围：国际性
主办：亚洲博闻有限公司
地址：香港湾仔港湾道26号华润大厦17楼
联系人：00852-2827 6211
✉ info-hk@ubm.com
www.istanbuljewelryshow.com

ISTANBUL JEWELRY SHOW - March
Date: 2013/03/21-24
Venue: Istanbul Expo Center (CNR Expo), Turkey
Profile: ISTANBUL JEWELRY SHOW offers you an easy access to jewellery sector professionals in Middle & Near East, Russia, CIS Nations, Eastern Europe and the Northern Coast of Africa.
Market Area: International
Organizer: UBM Asia Ltd
Address: 17/F, China Resources Building, 26 Harbour Road, Wan Chai, Hong Kong
☎ 852-3749 7342
✉ info-hk@ubm.com
www.istanbuljewelryshow.com

国际汽车零部件及售后服务展览会
日期：2013/04/11-14
地点：土耳其伊斯坦布尔
周期：两年一届
主办：中国贸促会机械行业分会
地址：北京市西城区三里河路46号(100823)
☎ 010-6859 4952，6859 4804，6859 4931，6859 5220
🖷 010-6859 4995
✉ info@ccpitmsc.org
www.chinamachine.org.cn

法兰克福（土耳其）国际汽车零配件及售后服务展览会
Automechanika Istanbul
日期：2013/04/11-14
地点：土耳其伊斯坦布尔
周期：两年一届
主办：北京中杰城投国际展览有限公司
联系人：李娜
☎ 010-5979 9850转ext 858
🖷 010-5979 9850转ext 810,5885 7468
www.top-fairs.com.cn
www.build-ccpit.org

2013土耳其第30届欧亚纺织工业展
暨 纱线、无纺布展
同期举行：
第10届国际纱线展
第5届产业用布及无纺布展
日期：2013/05/29-01
地点：土耳其伊斯坦布尔TUYAP会展中心
内容：无纺布及深加工产品：土工布、建筑用布、汽车用布、农业用布、合成革基布、过滤材料、建筑材料、电绝缘材料、环保用品、造纸、毛毯、医疗卫生用品、装饰用品、服装用品、鞋材、家庭用品、其它等多功能无纺布。无纺布及深加工技术与设备、仪器：干法造纸、缝编、热粘合等非织布设备、生产线、口罩、手术衣、成型口罩等深加工设备、途层、叠层、静电施加（驻极）、静电植绒、模压、包装等机械、纤维梳理及成网、化学粘合法、针刺法、水刺法、纺粘法、熔喷法；纤维及纱线；机械及零配件；纺织用化学品上届规模：参展商683家来自33个国家及地区，参观人数22,266人
主办：土耳其纺织机械工业协会；TUYAP展览集团公司
联络：上海爱卫客会展服务有限公司
联系人：李爱燕
☎ 021-3132 6575, 15900594089
🖷 021-5049 7282
✉ ivyli18@163.com
aiyan18@126.com
🐧 2632726499

国际包装工业展览会
日期：2013/09 -
地点：土耳其伊斯坦布尔
周期：每年一届
主办：中国贸促会机械行业分会
地址：北京市西城区三里河路46号(100823)
☎ 010-6859 4192，6859 4826，6859 5406
🖷 010-6859 4995
✉ info@ccpitmsc.org
www.chinamachine.org.cn

土耳其国际涂料展
TURKCOAT
日期：2013/09/12-14
地点：土耳其伊斯坦布尔
主办：全国化工国际展览交流中心
☎ 010-6524 2231转608
✉ fany@icif.cn

伊斯坦堡珠宝展-十月展
Istanbul Jewelry Show - October

03 - 06 OCTOBER 2013
日期：2013/10/03-06
地点：土耳其伊斯坦堡会展中心
市场范围：国际性
主办：亚洲博闻有限公司
地址：香港湾仔港湾道26号华润大厦17楼
☎ 00852-2827 6211
🖷 00852-3749 7342
✉ info-hk@ubm.com
www.istanbuljewelryshow.com

Istanbul Jewelry Show-October
Date: 2013/10/03-06
Venue: Istanbul Expo Center (CNR Expo), Turkey
Profile: ISTANBUL JEWELRY SHOW offers you an

easy access to jewellery sector professionals in Middle & Near East, Russia, CIS Nations, Eastern Europe and the Northern Coast of Africa.
Market Area: International
Organizer: UBM Asia Ltd
Address: 17/F, China Resources Building, 26 Harbour Road, Wan Chai, Hong Kong
☎ 852-2827 6211
🖷 852-3749 7342
✉ info-hk@ubm.com
www.istanbuljewelryshow.com

土耳其铝工业展览会
日期：2013/10/03-06
地点：土耳其伊斯坦布尔
周期：两年一届
主办：中国贸促会机械行业分会
地址：北京市西城区三里河路46号(100823)
☎ 010-6859 5499，6859 4803，6859 4807
🖷 010-6859 4995
✉ info@ccpitmsc.org
www.chinamachine.org.cn

土耳其汽车工业展
日期：2013/11 -
地点：土耳其伊斯坦布尔
周期：每年一届
主办：北京中杰城投国际展览有限公司
联系人：李娜
☎ 010-5979 9850转858
🖷 010-5979 9850转810, 5885 7468
www.top-fairs.com.cn
www.build-ccpit.org

国际汽车工业及配件展览会
日期：2013/11 -
地点：土耳其伊斯坦布尔
周期：每年一届
主办：中国贸促会机械行业分会
地址：北京市西城区三里河路46号(100823)
☎ 010-6859 4952，6859 4804，6859 4931，6859 5220
🖷 010-6859 4995
✉ info@ccpitmsc.org
www.chinamachine.org.cn

土耳其聚氨酯展暨欧亚复合材料展
Putech Eurasia & Eurasian Composites Show
日期：2013/11/14-16
地点：土耳其伊斯坦布尔
主办：全国化工国际展览交流中心
☎ 010-6524 2231转608
✉ fany@icif.cn

阿联酋
UAE

国际机械技术展览会
日期：2013/01 -
地点：阿联酋迪拜
周期：两年一届
主办：中国贸促会机械行业分会
地址：北京市西城区三里河路46号(100823)
☎ 010-6859 5495，6859 5247，6859 5406，6859 5431
🖷 010-6859 4995
✉ info@ccpitmsc.org
www.chinamachine.org.cn

国际管材展览会
日期：2013/01 -
地点：阿联酋迪拜
周期：两年一届
主办：中国贸促会机械行业分会
地址：北京市西城区三里河路46号(100823)
☎ 010-6859 5296，6859 4938，6851 2883
🖷 010-6859 4995
✉ info@ccpitmsc.org
www.chinamachine.org.cn

阿布扎比世界未来能源峰会暨新能源与环保展览会
World Future Energy Summit (WFES)
日期：2013/01 -
地点：阿联酋阿布扎比新国家展览中心
内容：促进了再生能源及环境保护的创新和投资机会。峰会还在汇集项目业主、解决方案提供商、公共及私营部门的投资商和采购商等方面提供了一个无与伦比的商业平台。
周期：每年一届
上届规模 2011：参展商600家来自31个国家及地区，贸易观众26,391人
主办：励展中东公司
联络：励展博览集团国际销售部
联系人：杜一鸣
地址：北京市朝阳区新源南路1-3号平安国际金融中心A座15层01-03,05
☎ 010-5933 9209
🖷 010-5933 9233
✉ martin.du@reedexpo.com.cn
www.worldfutureenergysummit.com

国际电力、照明及新能源展览会
日期：2013/02/17-19
地点：阿联酋迪拜
周期：每年一届
主办：中国贸促会机械行业分会
地址：北京市西城区三里河路46号(100823)
☎ 010-6859 4802，6859 4934
🖷 010-6859 4995
✉ info@ccpitmsc.org
www.chinamachine.org.cn

第38届中东迪拜国际电力、照明及新能源展览会
日期：2013/02/17-19
地点：阿联酋迪拜
周期：每年一届
主办：中国贸促会建设行业分会会展部；北京中杰城设国际展览有限公司
联系人：王艳玲
☎ 010-8836 3688，5979 9850转813，13691545669
🖷 010-5885 7468，5979 9850转ext 810
✉ wangyanling@top-fairs.com.cn
QQ 20204846
www.btfi.cn
www.power-gen.org.cn
www.top-fairs.com.cn

2013年法兰克福中东（迪拜）玩具婴童用品展
日期：2013/03/05-07
地点：阿联酋迪拜国际会展中心
内容：婴儿，婴儿和学龄前儿童玩具及产品：高脚椅，床，婴儿手推车，汽车座椅，婴儿服饰，婴儿家具，儿童的个人美容产品和化妆品，毛绒玩具，学习产品，木制玩具；儿童生活：儿童家具，儿童服装，鞋类及手袋，儿童娱乐，儿童手表，旅游和假日用品；玩具及游戏：发牌，卡通人物及配件，棋类游戏，视频/电脑游戏，乐器，魔术套装，笑话产品，收集工具箱；自行车及运动器材：三轮车，滑板车，滑板，运动玩具，户外玩具，户外游乐设施，幼儿园及游乐场设备；娃娃：婴儿娃娃，毛绒玩具，游戏之家，娃娃服装服饰，木偶，超级英雄和行动图玩具；模型和电子：模型套件，积木，机械玩具，电子/电动玩具，儿童电子产品（收音机，音响，时钟），录制音乐（光盘，磁带），无线遥控套件和汽车摩托车，汽车及配件曲目
主办：德国法兰克福（迪拜）展览公司
联络：杭州思诺博会展服务有限公司
地址：浙江省杭州市体育场路229号浙江粮油大厦1205室(310003)
☎ 0571-8577 8500
🖷 0571-85779709
www.sinobal.com
http://exposinobal.atobo.com.cn

2013年法兰克福中东（迪拜）文具、办公用品展
日期：2013/03/05-07
地点：阿联酋迪拜国际会展中心
内容：办公用品：办公设备，演示用品，收纳用品，邮寄/粘贴/印戳设备，办公附件，书写/绘画工具，综合产品；学校用品：书写工具，绘画材料，练习簿，文件夹，书包，文具盒；文具礼品：纪念册，日记本，书写纸，信封/创意礼品信纸，长毛绒玩具，时尚礼品，授权礼品，玩具书；包装产品：礼品包装，缎带/蝴蝶结，纸板产品；贺卡/日历：卡片，授权/设计师产品，艺术/卡通/相片等图画历；纸制品：办公类：喷墨纸，激光纸，复印纸，书写纸，透明纸，信封，包装材料，书籍装帧材料；家用类：餐巾纸、装饰透明纸
周期：每年一届
主办：德国法兰克福（迪拜）展览公司
联络：杭州思诺博会展服务有限公司
地址：浙江省杭州市体育场路229号浙江粮油大厦1205室(310003)
☎ 0571-8577 8500
🖷 0571-85779709
www.sinobal.com
http://exposinobal.atobo.com.cn

国际包装印刷机械展览会
日期：2013/04/08-11
地点：阿联酋迪拜
周期：两年一届
主办：中国贸促会机械行业分会
地址：北京市西城区三里河路46号(100823)
☎ 010-6859 4192，6859 4826，6859 5406
🖷 010-6859 4995
✉ info@ccpitmsc.org
www.chinamachine.org.cn

2013年第十届中东（迪拜）国际包装、印刷机械展览会
Gulf Pack & Print 2013
日期：2013/04/08-11
地点：阿联酋迪拜世贸中心展览馆
内容：包装区：包装机械及配件：真空包装机，糊盒机，制袋机，填充、灌装、封口、封箱、贴标机械，包装机械，日化用品包装机械、塑料软包装设备，药品包装机械，塑料机械，各种模切刀具配件；瓦楞蜂窝纸板设备，纸箱机械，纸盒，纸带，纸浆；包装材料：共挤复合、拉伸吹膜、发泡片材、纸板纸筒、铝箔铝材、胶粘带、热熔胶加工机械，塑料包装材料，金属包装材料，药品包装材料，绿色环保包装材料；包装容器：金属包装容器，玻璃包装容器，绿色环保包装技术、包装防伪科技、包装设计、包装工艺、包装出版媒体；印刷区：印刷设备：胶印机，制版设备，模切机，晒版机，商标印刷机；印前设备：桌面制作系统，广告创意制作系统，软件，扫描仪；印后设备：切纸机，装订机，复膜机，折页机，贴面机，压痕机，烫金机；特种印刷设备：凸印机，凹印机，丝印机，名片印刷机；丝网印刷技术及器材；数码印刷技术及器材；印刷材料配件器材：印刷、复合胶辊，油墨，版材，感光胶片
周期：每年一届
市场范围：国际性
性质：面向贸易观众
参展费用：28000元/9m^2
上届规模 2011: 展出面积在15000 m^2,400家企业参展来自50多个国家或地区，专业观众近万名，同比上涨9%以上。
主办：TARSUS西麦克国际展览有限责任公司；广东粤召展览有限公司
地址：广州市天河区体育东路122号羊城国际商贸中心东塔1202, 1208室(510620)
联系人：周文槟
☎ 13710318991
✉ 1979wenbin@163.com
✉ 1979wenbin@163.com
QQ 406372636

2013年中东（迪拜）水处理、能源、环保产品展览会
WETEX
日期：2013/04/15-17
地点：阿联酋迪拜阿联酋迪拜国际会展中心
内容：太阳能类光伏类：光伏电池、太阳电缆、光伏原材料、太阳能灯、-光伏转换系统、太阳能家居用、光伏工程及系统、太阳能空气调节系统、光伏发电系统、太阳能检测测及控制系统、太阳能取暖系统工程；能源类：电站设备，电气开关，发电机组，风力发电设备，燃气设备，电线电缆，电热设备，配电输电设备，电子元器件，绝缘材料，电工电子材料，电声器件，电光源，电子专业设备、室

外灯具，照明设备，灯具配件,清洁可再生型能源、风力发电设备，风力发电地热能、地热能、节能新能源、电力工业、水利水电、低压电器、高压电器、变压器、稳压器、成套设备、电器开关、防爆电器、仪器仪表、工控电器、电线电缆、电机 环境保护及水处理设备：环保材料、环保电器、环保污水处理设备、环保电池、环保动力设备、环保袋、环保漆、环保清洗设备及零配件、供水系统、排水系统、水资源检测、分析、监控仪器与设备，水环境配套设备，过滤设备仪器及材料
周期：每年一届
主办：迪拜水电部
联络：杭州思诺博会展服务有限公司
地址：浙江省杭州市体育场路229号浙江粮油大厦1205室(310003)
☎ 0571-8577 8500
📠 0571-8577 9709
www.sinobal.com
http://exposinobal.atobo.com.cn

2013年阿布扎比国际建筑建材展览会
日期：2013/04/16-18
地点：阿联酋阿布扎比国家展览中心
内容：建筑材料，再生能源，建筑五金，门窗玻璃类，空调制冷通风设备，厨房卫浴产品，水资源管理，建筑结构，建筑机械，气动工具，混凝土搅拌运输车、混凝土布料杆等建筑及工程机械；特别展览：新型建材、绿色环保建材。
周期：每年一届
主办：WORLD ecoConstruct
承办：中国贸促会建设行业分会
地址：北京市海淀区三里河路9号建设部大院机关门诊楼503(100835)
联系人：云鹏
☎ 010-8837 0844
📠 010-5893 3930
✉ rocyun@hotmail.com
QQ 1492095643

迪拜国际铝工业展
Gateway to the Middle East's Aluminium Industry
日期：2013/04/23-25
地点：迪拜国际会议展览中心Dubai Intl Convention and Exhibition Centre
内容：原材料，主要金属产品，半成品，半成品制作，特殊用途铝产品，表面处理，轻金属贸易与回收，铝材生产厂房、机械、零件及设备，提取、加工与提炼，服务与咨询 信息、教育及其它
始办年份：2009
周期：两年一届
性质：面向贸易观众
主办：励展中东公司
联络：励展博览集团国际销售部
地址：北京市朝阳区新源南路1-3号平安国际金融中心A座15层01-03,05
联系人：王颖
☎ 010-5933 9208
📠 010-5933 9233
✉ winnie.wang@reedexpo.com.cn
www.aluminium-dubai.com

Gateway to the Middle East's Aluminium Industry
Date: 2013/04/23-25
Venue: Dubai Intl Convention and Exhibition Centre, UAE
Profile: Raw materials, Primary metal products, Semi-finished products; Semi-fabricates; Aluminium products for special application; Surface treatment; Light-metals trade and Recycling; Plant, machinery and accessories and equipment for aluminium extraction, processing and refining; Services, consultancy; Information, Education, Others
Established Year: 2009
Frequency: Biennial
Nature: Trade Only
Organizer: Reed Exhibitions
☎ 86-10-5933 9208
📠 86-10-5933 9233
✉ winnie.wang@reedexpo.com.cn
www.aluminium-dubai.com

迪拜国际影像展览会
Photoworld-Dubai
日期：2013/04/24-26
地点：阿联酋迪拜
内容：传统及数码照相机和摄像机；摄影摄像器材；摄影摄像配件及附件；摄影工作室器材；数字成像和出版；数码产品；存储产品
主办：北方国际展览有限公司
地址：北京市西城区菜园街1号中环假日酒店写字间1102室(100053)
联系人：王子威，李松林
☎ 010-8355 7740，8353 3198
📠 010-6354 7597
✉ w.ziwei@northexpo.com.cn
reanna@northexpo.com.cn

中东迪拜国际五金工具博览会
Hardware & Tools
日期：2013/05 -
地点：阿联酋迪拜
内容：各种五金工具、小型机械、锁具及安防设备、建筑及DIY产品、五金配件、紧固件、卫生洁具、灯光照明设备等
主办：北方国际展览有限公司North Intl Exhibition Co Ltd
联系人：吴江，刘硕
地址：北京市西城区菜园街1号，中环假日酒店写字间1102室(100053)
☎ 010-8354 0336，8351 3705
📠 010-63547597
✉ wujiang@northexpo.com.cn
liushuo@northexpo.con.cn

国际汽车零配件及售后服务展览会
日期：2013/05 -
地点：阿联酋迪拜
周期：每年一届
主办：中国贸促会机械行业分会
地址：北京市西城区三里河路46号(100823)
☎ 010-6859 4952，6859 4804，6859 4931，6859 5220
📠 010-6859 4995
✉ info@ccpitmsc.org
www.chinamachine.org.cn

中东（迪拜）国际园艺及 户外休闲用品展览会
日期：2013/05 -
地点：阿联酋迪拜
内容：花园家具及家居用品、露营及休闲用品、烧烤设备、花园机械和设备、花园手工具和附件、其它设备和花园布置、植物和植物护理、水处理和室外照明，马术用品
主办：北方国际展览有限公司North International Exhibition Co Ltd
地址：北京市西城区菜园街1号中环假日酒店写字间1102室(100053)
联系人：王子威，李松林
☎ 010-8355 7740，8353 3198
📠 010-6354 7597
✉ w.ziwei@northexpo.com.cn
reanna@northexpo.com.cn

第23届迪拜国际家具及室内装饰设计展、国际办公及商用家具展
日期：2013/05/20-23
地点：阿联酋迪拜世界贸易中心
内容：家具类：卧室用具、户外家具、餐厅家具、婴儿家具、办公家具、酒店及商用家具、零配件 灯具：装饰灯、室内&室外灯、LED、建筑照明、城市照明、照明技术、有独特设计风格灯具、纺织品和室内装潢织品：布料纺织品、布类装饰、墙布、地板铺装、纺织品制造
主办：伟加展览(香港)有限公司
联系人：黄小姐
☎ 00852-2320 8978, 15018938764
✉ sales@racingchamp.com.hk
Racing_jennifer@hotmail.com.hk
QQ 1247308534

2013年第18届中东迪拜国际美容、美发展览会
日期：2013/05/28-30
地点：阿联酋迪拜世界贸易中心
上届规模 2012：展览面积34,684m²，参展商884家，参观人数21,091人
主办：法兰克福展览公司
联络：上海拓程展览服务有限公司
联系人：王姣
☎ 021-6220 7536, 15800323804
📠 021-6768 4318
✉ tuochengzhan69@163.com
tuochengzhan69@163.com
QQ 2643547948

法兰克福（中东）国际汽车零配件及售后服务展览会
Automechanika Middle East
日期：2013/06/11-13
地点：阿联酋迪拜
周期：每年一届
主办：北京中杰城投国际展览有限公司
联系人：李娜
☎ 010-5979 9850转ext 858
📠 010-5979 9850转ext 810，5885 7468
www.top-fairs.com.cn
www.build-ccpit.org

中东渔具、狩猎及户外用品展
日期：2013/09 -
地点：阿联酋阿布扎比
内容：望远镜、枪瞄、狩猎用品、帐篷、睡袋、吊床、户外服饰、烧烤及户外炊具、鱼钩、鱼线、渔网等
主办：北方国际展览有限公司North International Exhibition Co Ltd
地址：北京市西城区菜园街1号中环假日酒店写字间1102室(100053)
联系人：王子威，李松林
☎ 010-8355 7740，8353 3198
📠 010-6354 7597
✉ w.ziwei@northexpo.com.cn
reanna@northexpo.com.cn

国际石油、天然气展览会
日期：2013/10/06-08
地点：阿联酋迪拜
周期：两年一届
主办：中国贸促会机械行业分会
地址：北京市西城区三里河路46号(100823)
☎ 010-6859 5296，6859 4938，6851 2883
📠 010-6859 4995
✉ info@ccpitmsc.org
www.chinamachine.org.cn

中东国际建筑机械、车辆和设备展
PMV
日期：2013/11 -
地点：阿联酋迪拜
内容：工程机械、工程车辆，建材机械，建筑机械，生产设备，技术与服务，测量与控制系统等
主办：北京中展海外展览有限公司#
地址：北京北三环东路6号综合楼5层（100028）
联系人：宋秋爽#
☎ 010-8460 0367, 8460 0564#
✉ gaolijuan@ciec.com.cn
overseas@ciec.com.cn#
www.ciec-expo.com
www.ciec-overseas.com

乌克兰
Ukraine

乌克兰基辅国际五金工具展
INTERTOOL KIEV
日期：2013/02/27-01
地点：乌克兰基辅
内容：五金工具，小型机械，模具制造，塑料，橡胶，质量控制材料，工程工具，机床，动力手工具，精密工具等
主办：北方国际展览有限公司North Intl Exhibition Co Ltd
联系人：吴江，刘硕
地址：北京市西城区菜园街1号，中环假日酒店写字间1102室(100053)

☎ 010-8354 0336，8351 3705
🖷 010-63547597
✉ wujiang@northexpo.com.cn
liushuo@northexpo.con.cn

第17届乌克兰国际电力电工设备展览会
日期： 2013/04/23-26
地点： 乌克兰基辅
周期： 每年一届
主办： 中国贸促会建设行业分会会展部；北京中杰城设国际展览有限公司
联系人： 王艳玲
☎ 010-8836 3688，5979 9850转813，13691545669
🖷 010-5885 7468，5979 9850转810
✉ wangyanling@top-fairs.com.cn
QQ 20204846
www.btfi.cn
www.power-gen.org.cn
www.top-fairs.com.cn

2013年乌克兰国际暖通、卫浴及泳池设备展
aqua-therm
日期： 2013/05/14-17
地点： 乌克兰基辅基辅国际展览中心
内容： 空调、制冷设备、供暖/采暖设备、通风设备、加热装置、热能循环和利用、空气加热器；各类卫生洁具、浴室家具和配件、面盆、马桶、淋浴房、浴缸、花洒、水龙头及配件、浴室照明、镜子、五金挂件；厨房家具、厨房电器、通风装置、橱柜、下水道装置；各种关键、泵类、连接件、不锈钢管件、管道装置、PVF聚氟乙烯；桑拿和游泳池设备、水处理剂废水处理技术。
周期： 每年一届
主办： 杭州思诺博会展服务有限公司
地址： 浙江省杭州市体育场路229号浙江粮油大厦1205室(310003)
☎ 0571-8577 8500
🖷 0571-8577 9709
www.sinobal.com
http:// exposinobal.atobo.com.cn

2013年乌克兰国际建材、室内装饰及石材展览会
日期： 2013/05/23-26
地点： 乌克兰Odessa Sea Commercial Port Exhibition Complex
主办： 中国贸促会建设行业分会
地址： 北京市海淀区三里河路9号建设部大院机关门诊楼503
联系人： 云鹏
☎ 15110286537
🖷 010-5893 3930
✉ rocyun@hotmail.com
QQ 1492095643

美国
USA

美国职业高尔夫球协会高尔夫用品展
PGA Merchandise Show
日期： 2013/01 -
地点： 美国佛罗里达州奥兰多橙郡会议中心Orange County Convention Center
内容： 高尔夫俱乐部，高尔夫球具，人造草坪，高尔夫球包，高尔夫球，高尔夫球服饰，俱乐部产品订制，电脑系统、软件，信用服务，食品、饮料，高尔夫艺术品、工艺品，出版物，模拟练习设备，高尔夫店设备、家俱，培训机构，电子产品和游戏
周期： 每年一届
上届规模 2011：展览面积316,100平方英尺，参展商879家，参观人数42,859人
主办： 励展美国公司
联络： 励展博览集团国际销售部
地址： 北京市朝阳区新源南路1-3号平安国际金融中心A座15层01-03,05
联系人： 申健
☎ 010-5933 9299
🖷 010-5933 9233
✉ jerry.shen@reedexpo.com.cn
www.pgashow.com

美国国际电子消费展览会暨美国国际影像协会PMA影像展
(PMA@CES)
日期： 2013/01/08-13
地点： 美国拉斯维加斯
内容： 传统及数码照相机和摄像机；摄影摄像器材；摄影摄像配件及附件；摄影工作室器材；数字成像和出版；数码产品；存储产品
主办： 北方国际展览有限公司North International Exhibition Co Ltd
地址： 北京市西城区菜园街1号中环假日酒店写字间1102室(100053)
联系人： 王子威，李松林
☎ 010-8355 7740，8353 3198
🖷 010-6354 7597
✉ w.ziwei@northexpo.com.cn
reanna@northexpo.com.cn

美国拉斯维加斯射击、狩猎、户外用品展览会
SHOT SHOW
日期： 2013/01/17-20
地点： 美国拉斯维加斯
内容： 狩猎用品、配件、彩弹球、望远镜、刀剑制品、安全技术装备、装载设备、户外运动服饰、护目镜、鞋、手套、旅行用品、运动用品、动物剥制术，农场、牧场经营，狩猎野营和野生动物管理等相关书籍、出版物,影视录像、等其他与狩猎运动有关的产品
主办： 北方国际展览有限公司North International Exhibition Co Ltd
地址： 北京市西城区菜园街1号中环假日酒店写字间1102室（100053）
联系人： 王子威，李松林
☎ 010-8355 7740，8353 3198
🖷 010-6354 7597
✉ w.ziwei@northexpo.com.cn
reanna@northexpo.com.cn

国际空调、制冷和供暖展览会
日期： 2013/01/28-30
地点： 美国达拉斯
周期： 每年一届
主办： 中国贸促会机械行业分会
地址： 北京市西城区三里河路46号(100823)
☎ 010-6859 5499，6859 4803，6859 4807，6859 4989，6859 5055
🖷 010-6859 4995
✉ info@ccpitmsc.org
www.chinamachine.org.cn

国际输变电技术会议及交流展览会
日期： 2013/01/29-31
地点： 美国圣地亚哥
周期： 每年一届
主办： 中国贸促会机械行业分会
地址： 北京市西城区三里河路46号(100823)
☎ 010-6859 4802，6859 4934
🖷 010-6859 4995
✉ info@ccpitmsc.org
www.chinamachine.org.cn

美国国际线材展览会
日期： 2013/04/23-25
地点： 美国亚特兰大
周期： 两年一届
主办： 中国贸促会机械行业分会
地址： 北京市西城区三里河路46号(100823)
☎ 010-6859 5296，6859 4938，6851 2883
🖷 010-6859 4995
✉ info@ccpitmsc.org
www.chinamachine.org.cn

国际石油、天然气展览会
日期： 2013/05 -
地点： 美国休斯顿
主办： 中国贸促会机械行业分会
地址： 北京市西城区三里河路46号(100823)
☎ 010-6859 5296，6859 4938，6851 2883
🖷 010-6859 4995
✉ info@ccpitmsc.org
www.chinamachine.org.cn

美国国际五金制品及花园用品博览会
NHS
日期： 2013/05/07-09
地点： 美国拉斯维加斯
内容： 各种五金工具、小型机械、锁具及安防设备、建筑及DIY产品、五金配件、紧固件、卫生洁具、灯光照明设备等；户外用品
主办： 北方国际展览有限公司North Intl Exhibition Co Ltd
联系人： 吴江，刘硕
地址： 北京市西城区菜园街1号，中环假日酒店写字间1102室(100053)
☎ 010-8354 0336，8351 3705
🖷 010-63547597
✉ wujiang@northexpo.com.cn
liushuo@northexpo.con.cn

美国夏季国际优质食品及糖果展览会
Summer Fancy Food Show
日期： 2013/07 -
地点： 美国华盛顿
内容： 速食产品、水果蔬菜、（非）酒类饮品、烘焙类、罐头食品、糖果类、乳品类、肉类、海鲜类、休闲食品、有机食品类、天然及健康食品类、减肥食品、厨房用具等
主办： 北方国际展览有限公司North International Exhibition Co Ltd
地址： 北京市西城区菜园街1号中环假日酒店写字间1102室（100053）
联系人： 王子威，李松林
☎ 010-8355 7740，8353 3198
🖷 010-6354 7597
✉ w.ziwei@northexpo.com.cn
reanna@northexpo.com.cn

2013年美国拉斯维加斯国际美容美发展览会
日期： 2013/07/22-24
地点： 拉斯维加斯拉斯维加斯会议中心
内容： 香水、古龙水、彩妆、植物性化妆品、沙龙用专业化妆品、恒久性化装设备及技术、各式美容仪器、保养护肤用品、婴儿用保养品、芳香治疗、沐浴用品、化妆美容工业技术
主办： 美国美容美发协会
承办： 拉斯维加斯展览中心
地址： 上海市浦东新区金港路333号禹洲金桥国际大厦一期315室(201206)
联系人： 林峰
☎ 021-6064 6986, 18321918890
✉ jiaguan_linfeng@hotmail.com
QQ 1273633881

国际印刷及纸品加工展览会
日期： 2013/09/06-11
地点： 美国芝加哥
周期： 四年一届
主办： 中国贸促会机械行业分会
地址： 北京市西城区三里河路46号(100823)
☎ 010-6859 4192，6859 4826，6859 5406
🖷 010-6859 4995
✉ info@ccpitmsc.org
www.chinamachine.org.cn

国际包装展览会
日期： 2013/09/23-25
地点： 美国拉斯维加斯
周期： 每年一届
主办： 中国贸促会机械行业分会
地址： 北京市西城区三里河路46号(100823)
☎ 010-6859 4192，6859 4826，6859 5406
🖷 010-68594995
✉ info@ccpitmsc.org
www.chinamachine.org.cn

美国路易斯维尔园林机械展览会
GIE+EXPO
日期： 2013/10 -
地点： 美国路易斯维尔
内容： 花园机械和设备、花园手工具和附件、其它设备和花园布置、植物和植物护理、水处理和室外照明、露营及休闲用品
主办： 北方国际展览有限公司North International

Exhibition Co Ltd
地址：北京市西城区菜园街1号中环假日酒店写字间1102室(100053)
联系人：王子威，李松林
☎ 010-8355 7740，8353 3198
🖷 010-6354 7597
✉ w.ziwei@northexpo.com.cn
reanna@northexpo.com.cn

美国纽约城国际影像器材展览会
PDN PHOTOPLUS
日期：2013/10 -
地点：美国纽约
内容：传统及数码照相机和摄像机；摄影摄像器材；摄影摄像配件及附件；摄影工作室器材；数字成像和出版；数码产品；存储产品
主办：北方国际展览有限公司
地址：北京市西城区菜园街1号中环假日酒店写字间1102室（100053）
联系人：王子威，李松林
☎ 010-8355 7740，8353 3198
🖷 010-6354 7597
✉ w.ziwei@northexpo.com.cn
reanna@northexpo.com.cn

美国西部紧固件展览会
NATIONAL INDUSTRIAL FASTENER SHOW/WEST
日期：2013/10 -
地点：美国拉斯维加斯
内容：各类标准及非标准紧固件、相关加工设备、检测设备、工具等
主办：北方国际展览有限公司
地址：北京市西城区菜园街1号中环假日酒店写字间1102室（100053）
联系人：王子威，李松林
☎ 010-8355 7740，8353 3198
🖷 010-6354 7597
✉ w.ziwei@northexpo.com.cn
reanna@northexpo.com.cn

美国劳德岱堡国际游艇展览会
日期：2013/10/25-29
地点：美国劳德岱堡
周期：每年一届
主办：中国贸促会机械行业分会
地址：北京市西城区三里河路46号(100823)
☎ 010-6859 4985，6859 5855
🖷 010-6859 4995
✉ info@ccpitmsc.org
www.chinamachine.org.cn

美国水处理展
AWT
日期：2013/10/30-02
地点：美国安卡斯威尔
主办：全国化工国际展览交流中心
☎ 010-6524 2231转608
✉ fany@icif.cn

美国国际汽车零部件展览会
AAPEX 2013
日期：2013/11/05-07
地点：美国拉斯维加斯
周期：每年一届
主办：北京中杰城投国际展览有限公司
联系人：李娜
☎ 010-5979 9850转858
🖷 010-5979 9850转810，5885 7468
www.top-fairs.com.cn
www.build-ccpit.org
主办：中国贸促会机械行业分会
地址：北京市西城区三里河路46号(100823)
☎ 010-6859 4952，6859 4804，6859 4931，6859 5220
🖷 010-68594995
✉ info@ccpitmsc.org
www.chinamachine.org.cn

国际金属加工和管材展览会
日期：2013/11 -
地点：美国芝加哥
周期：每年一届
主办：中国贸促会机械行业分会
地址：北京市西城区三里河路46号(100823)
☎ 010-6859 5495，6859 5247，6859 5406，68595431
🖷 010-6859 4995
✉ info@ccpitmsc.org
www.chinamachine.org.cn

美国改装车展览会
SEMA 2013
日期：2013/11/05-08
地点：美国拉斯维加斯
周期：每年一届
主办：北京中杰城投国际展览有限公司
联系人：李娜
☎ 010-5979 9850转858
🖷 010-5979 9850转810，5885 7468
www.top-fairs.com.cn
www.build-ccpit.org

国际电力博览会
日期：2013/12 -
地点：美国拉斯维加斯
周期：每年一届
主办：中国贸促会机械行业分会
地址：北京市西城区三里河路46号(100823)
☎ 010-6859 4802，6859 4934
🖷 010-6859 4995
✉ info@ccpitmsc.org
www.chinamachine.org.cn

美国电力展览会
PENN WELL
日期：2013/12/12-14
地点：美国奥兰多
周期：每年一届
主办：中国贸促会建设行业分会会展部；北京中杰城设国际展览有限公司
联系人：王艳玲
☎ 010-8836 3688，5979 9850转813，13691545669
🖷 010-5885 7468，5979 9850转ext 810
✉ wangyanling@top-fairs.com.cn
QQ 20204846
www.btfi.cn
www.power-gen.org.cn
www.top-fairs.com.cn

乌兹别克斯坦 Uzbekistan

第十三届乌兹别克斯坦国际食品、食品加工和包装展
日期：2013/04/03-05
地点：乌兹别克斯坦塔什干国家展览中心
内容：食品、饮料(酒精类&软饮料)；食品配料，添加剂，调味品；食品生产设备；过滤筛选设备；冷冻冷藏设备；包装材料及设备；饮料及酒类包装设备及配件
周期：每年一届
主办：英国国际贸易与展览有限公司(英国ITE集团)
联系人：郭先生，刘小姐
☎ 010-5610 5196
🖷 010-8157 0329

委内瑞拉 Venezuela

中国工业产品（委内瑞拉）展览会
日期：2013/06 -
地点：委内瑞拉加拉加斯
周期：每年一届
主办：中国贸促会机械行业分会
地址：北京市西城区三里河路46号(100823)
☎ 010-6859 5499，6859 4803，6859 4807，6859 4989，6859 5055
🖷 010-6859 4995
✉ www.chinamachine.org.cn
www.chinamachine.org.cn

越南 Vietnam

2013越南国际医药技术、化妆品加工、药装设备和材料展
PIA Vietnam 2013
日期：2013/03/20-20
地点：越南胡志明市
主办：北京邦企展览服务有限公司
地址：北京市朝阳区惠新东街11号紫光发展大厦B1座501(100029)
☎ 010-6482 3808, 6482 3670
✉ bbes@china.com

第七届越南国际加工、填充技术、包装机械展览会暨研讨会
ProPak Vietnam 2013
日期：2013/03/20-20
地点：越南胡志明市
主办：北京邦企展览服务有限公司
地址：北京市朝阳区惠新东街11号紫光发展大厦B1座501(100029)
☎ 010-6482 3808, 6482 3670
✉ bbes@china.com

2013年越南（河内）国际建筑、建材及家居产品展览会
VIETBUILD
日期：2013/03/28-04/01
地点：越南河内讲武国际会展中心VIETBUILD
内容：建材和装饰：建筑工程、建筑结构、建筑材料、装饰材料、室内装饰、家用纺织品等；玻璃&门窗：玻璃、玻璃制品、玻璃装饰、玻璃加工机械；门窗、幕墙、门控五金配件、门窗加工机械、加工技术与检测设备等；机械&设备：工程机械、建筑机械、施工设备、建材机械、建材生产设备等；五金&工具：建筑装饰五金、工具类、丝网铁钉、铁艺、篱笆、护栏、楼梯电梯等；厨房&卫浴：厨房用品及设备、家用电器；卫生间设备、管道管件、水龙头、阀门、其他配件等；照明&灯饰：照明设备、开关、插座等电气控制元器件、各类灯饰产品等；暖通&空调：空调、管道技术及水处理；制冷产品、设备及技术；太阳能产品及技术等；化学&建材：化学建材、油漆涂料、粘合剂、建筑胶、胶带、建筑防水防火、保暖隔热等；其他&相关：楼宇智能自动化、监控管理系统及技术、城市安防、建筑设计与规划、园艺与环境规划、室内设计、施工技术。
始办年份：1958年
周期：每年两届
市场范围：国际性
性质：面向贸易观众
参展费用：13000元/9m²
主办：中国贸促会建设行业分会；广东粤召展览有限公司
地址：广州市天河区体育东路122号羊城国际商贸中心东塔1202，1208室(510620)
联系人：周文槟
☎ 13710318991
🖷 020-3887 0797
✉ 1979wenbin@163.com
gdwenbin@hotmail.com
QQ 406372636
主办：越中会展商务有限公司#
☎ 0771-261 5620
🖷 0771-263 0917

第二十三届越南国际贸易博览会
The 23 Vietnam Intl Trade Fair
日期：2013/04/10-14
地点：越南河内VEFC
内容：综合商品展示和交易
主办：越中会展商务有限公司#
☎ 0771-261 5620
🖷 0771-263 0917

第三届中国品牌消费品(越南)展览交易会
China Brands Of Consumer Goods Fair In Vietnam
日期：2013/04/10-13

地点：越南河内VEFC
内容：家电、消费电子、家纺、服装、鞋帽箱 包、眼镜钟表、玩具及婴儿用品、文具 与办公用品、体育休闲用品、礼品、工 艺品等
主办：越中会展商务有限公司#
☎ 0771-261 5620
🖷 0771-263 0917

2013中国-东盟美容美发（越南）展览会
日期：2013/04/10-13
地点：越南河内讲武国际会展中心
上届规模：展览面积12,000m²，参展商家来自10个国家及地区，参观人数70,000人
主办：越南国家工贸部；越南计划投资部；越南建设部；越南美容美发协
承办：广西南宁鸿越展览服务有限公司
地址：广西南宁市民族大道125号展厦景湾A1-902室(530021)
联系人：周雨浓
☎ 0771-555 5004, 13647815672
🖷 0771-571 5301
✉ william5555004@126.com

越南国际轮胎和橡胶展
RUBBER+TIRE VIETNAM
日期：2013/04/11-13
地点：越南胡志明市
主办：全国化工国际展览交流中心
☎ 010-6524 2231转608
✉ fany@icif.cn

第七届越南国际食品、饮料和酒店设备展览会
Food & Hotel Vietnam 2013
日期：2013/04/24-26
地点：越南胡志明市
主办：北京邦企展览服务有限公司
地址：北京市朝阳区惠新东街11号紫光发展大厦B1座501(100029)
☎ 010-6482 3808, 6482 3670
✉ bbes@china.com

2013第三届越南中国汽车摩托车零配件及用品展暨采购对接会
China Autotech & Accessories Show in Vietnam
日期：2013/05/30-06
地点：越南胡志明市西贡展览会议中心（SECC）
内容：汽摩制造装备、零配件、汽车用 品、交通配套设施、加油站设备等
主办：越中会展商务有限公司
☎ 0771-261 5620
🖷 0771-263 0917

2013第九届越南汽车摩托车制造工业技术展览会
Saigon Intl Autotech & Accessories Show
日期：2013/05/30-06/06
地点：越南胡志明市西贡展览会议中心（SECC）
内容：汽摩制造装备、零配件、汽车用 品、交通配套设施、加油站设备等
主办：越中会展商务有限公司
☎ 0771-261 5620
🖷 0771-263 0917

越南国际造纸展
PAPER VIETNAM
日期：2013/06/06-08
地点：越南河内
主办：全国化工国际展览交流中心
☎ 010-6524 2231转608
✉ fany@icif.cn

第七届印尼泗水国际制造机械设备，材料及金属工具技术展览会
Manufacturing Surabaya 2013
日期：2013/06/12-15
地点：越南泗水
主办：北京邦企展览服务有限公司
地址：北京市朝阳区惠新东街11号紫光发展大厦B1座501(100029)
☎ 010-6482 3808, 6482 3670
✉ bbes@china.com

第四届国际机床、金属加工及相关行业展览会
Machine Tool Surabaya 2013
日期：2013/06/12-15
地点：越南泗水
主办：北京邦企展览服务有限公司
地址：北京市朝阳区惠新东街11号紫光发展大厦B1座501(100029)
☎ 010-6482 3808, 6482 3670
✉ bbes@china.com

2013越南住博会国际建筑陶瓷石材博览会
VIETBUILD 2013
日期：2013/06/13-17
地点：越南胡志明市西贡展览会议中心（SECC）
内容：建筑陶瓷、石材等
主办：越中会展商务有限公司
☎ 0771-261 5620
🖷 0771-263 0917

2013第十届越南（河内）汽车摩托车制造工业技术展览会
VietNam Intl Autotech & Accessories Show
日期：2013/06/19-20
地点：越南河内VEFC
内容：汽摩制造装备、零配件、汽车用 品、交通配套设施、加油站设备等
主办：越中会展商务有限公司
☎ 0771-261 5620
🖷 0771-263 0917

2013越南国际水产展览会
VIETFISH
日期：2013/06/25-27
地点：越南胡志明市西贡展览会议中心（SECC）
内容：渔业养殖技术、水产品加工设备、饲料及添加剂、病防治、环保养殖技术、仓储运输、捕捞技术
主办：越中会展商务有限公司
☎ 0771-261 5620
🖷 0771-263 0917

2013中国水产养殖加工技术产品（越南）展览会暨双向买家采购会
日期：2013/06/25-27
地点：越南胡志明市西贡展览会议中心（SECC）
内容：渔业养殖技术、水产品加工设备、饲料及添加剂、病防治、环保养殖技术、仓储运输、捕捞技术等
主办：越中会展商务有限公司
☎ 0771-261 5620
🖷 0771-263 0917

国际机床工具展览会
日期：2013/07 -
地点：越南胡志明市
周期：每年一届
主办：中国贸促会机械行业分会
地址：北京市西城区三里河路46号(100823)
☎ 010-6859 5495，6859 5247，6859 5406，6859 5431
🖷 010-68594995
✉ info@ccpitmsc.org
www.chinamachine.org.cn

第九届越南国际精密机械及金属加工展
MTA Vietnam 2013 (Ho Chi Minh City)
日期：2013/07/02-05
地点：越南胡志明市
主办：北京邦企展览服务有限公司
地址：北京市朝阳区惠新东街11号紫光发展大厦B1座501(100029)
☎ 010-6482 3808, 6482 3670
✉ bbes@china.com

越南国际鞋类、皮革制成品展览会
IFLE – VIETNAM 2013
Intl Footwear & Leather Products Exhibition – Vietnam

日期：2013/07/11-13
地点：越南胡志明市西贡会议展览中心
内容：所有鞋类、皮包和箱包、皮革衣服和产品、时尚皮制饰物配件、知名品牌产品
始办年份：1999
周期：每年一届
市场范围：国际性
上届规模 2012：参展商108家，贸易观众6,180人
主办：越南皮革和鞋类协会；显辉国际展览有限公司；越南显达展览服务有限公司
地址：香港干诺道中168-200号信德中心西座2802室
联系人：刘小姐
☎ 852-2851 8603
🖷 852-2851 8637
✉ topreput@top-repute.com
www.ifle-vietnam.com

IFLE – VIETNAM 2013
–Intl Footwear & Leather Products Exhibition – Vietnam
Date: 2013/07/11-13
Venue: Saigon Exhibition & Convention Center, (SECC), Ho Chi Minh City, Vietnam
Profile: All kinds of footwear, Bags & Suitcases, Leather Garments & Leather Product, Fashion Accessories, Brand Name Products
Established Year: 1999
Frequency: Annual
Market Area: International
Participated Fee: Standard Booth USD 2,700/9m²
Statistics '12: Exhibitors 108, Trade visitors 6,180
Organizer: Vietnam Leather and Footwear Association (LEFASO VIETNAM); Top Repute Co. Ltd. Vietnam Liaison Office
Address: Unit 2802, Shun Tak Centre, West Tower, Nos.168-200 Connaught Road Central, Hong Kong.
Contact: Ms. Mandy Lau
☎ 852-2851 8603
🖷 852-2851 8637
✉ topreput@top-repute.com
www.ifle-vietnam.com

越南国际鞋类、皮革及工业设备展览会
SHOES & LEATHER – VIETNAM 2013
Intl Shoes & Leather Exhibition – Vietnam

日期：2013/07/11-13
地点：越南胡志明市西贡会议展览中心
内容：鞋类机械、制革机、皮具机、皮革、原皮料、鞋材、化工、配件/辅料、成品
始办年份：1999
周期：每年一届
市场范围：国际性
参展费用：标准展位2,700美金 / 9m²
上届规模 2012：参展商108家，贸易观众6,180人
主办：越南皮革和鞋类协会；显辉国际展览有限公司；越南显达展览服务有限公司
地址：香港干诺道中168-200号信德中心西座2802室
联系人：刘小姐
☎ 852-2851 8603
🖷 852-2851 8637
✉ topreput@top-repute.com
www.shoeleather-vietnam.com

SHOES & LEATHER–VIETNAM 2013
Intl Shoes & Leather Exhibition–Vietnam
Date: 2013/07/11-13
Venue: Saigon Exhibition & Convention Center, Ho Chi Minh City, Vietnam
Profile: Tanning machinery, shoes machinery, raw materials, leather, chemicals, accessories, finished products, etc.
Established Year: 1999

Frequency: Annual
Market Area: International
Participated Fee: Standard Booth USD 2,700/9m²
Statistics '12: Exhibitors 108, Trade visitors 6,180
Organizer: Vietnam Leather and Footwear Association (LEFASO VIETNAM); Top Repute Co. Ltd. Vietnam Liaison Office
Address: Unit 2802, Shun Tak Centre, West Tower, Nos.168-200 Connaught Road Central, Hong Kong.
Contact: Ms. Mandy Lau
☎ 852-2851 8603
🖷 852-2851 8637
✉ topreput@top-repute.com
www.shoeleather-vietnam.com

越南国际制衣机械设备、面料展览会

Vietnam Intl Exhibition on Garment Manufacturing Equipment and Fabric
(GARMENT & FABRIC – VIETNAM 2013)

日期：2013/07/11-13
地点：越南胡志明市西贡会议展览中心
内容：所有服装机器和配饰、布料
始办年份：2012
周期：每年一届
市场范围：国际性
参展费用：标准展位: 2,700美金 / 9m²
上届规模 ' 12: 参展商108家，贸易观众6,180人
主办：显辉国际展览有限公司；越南显达展览服务有限公司
地址：香港干诺道中168-200号信德中心西座2802室
联系人：刘小姐
☎ 852-2851 8603
🖷 852-2851 8637
✉ topreput@top-repute.com
www.garmentfabric-vietnam.com

GARMENT & FABRIC–VIETNAM 2013 –Vietnam Intl Exhibition on Garment Manufacturing Equipment and Fabric

Date: 2013/07/11-13
Venue: Saigon Exhibition & Convention Center (SECC), Ho Chi Minh City, Vietnam
Profile: All kinds of apparel machinery, accessory and fabric
Established Year: 2012
Frequency: Annual
Market Area: International
Participated Fee: Standard Booth USD 2,700/9m²
Statistics '12: Exhibitors 108, Trade visitors 6,180
Organizer: Top Repute Co. Ltd. Vietnam Liaison Office
Address: Unit 2802, Shun Tak Centre, West Tower, Nos.168-200 Connaught Road Central, Hong Kong.
Contact: Ms. Mandy Lau
☎ 852-2851 8603
🖷 852-2851 8637
✉ topreput@top-repute.com
www.garmentfabric-vietnam.com

越南国际塑胶机械及技术展览会

Vietnam Plastic Fair

日期：2013/07/18-20
地点：越南胡志明市西贡会议展览中心
内容：塑胶机械、产品、塑胶及橡胶原材料、模具、吹模机、注塑机
始办年份：1993
周期：每年一届
市场范围：国际性
参展费用：标准展位2,700美元/9m²
上届规模 '12：参展商108家来自12个国家及地区，贸易观众6,188人
主办：显辉国际展览有限公司；越南显达展览服务有限公司
地址：香港干诺道中168-200号信德中心西座2802室
联系人：林先生, 林小姐
☎ 852-2851 8603
🖷 852-2851 8637
✉ topreput@top-repute.com
www.machinery-vietnam.com

Vietnam Plastic Fair

Date: 2013/07/18-20
Venue: Saigon Exhibition & Convention Centre (SECC), Ho Chi Minh City, Vietnam
Profile: Plastic machinery, Product, Plastic & rubber raw material, Mould, Blow molding, Injection molding, etc.
Established Year: 1993
Frequency: Annual
Market Area: International
Participated Fee: Standard Booth USD 2,700/9m²
Statistics '12: Exhibitors 108 came from 12 countries and regions, Visitors 6,188
Organizer: Top Repute Co., Ltd. Top Repute Co. Ltd. Vietnam Liaison Office
Address: Unit 2802, Shun Tak Centre, West Tower, Nos.168-200 Connaught Road Central, Hong Kong
Contact: Mr. Dennis Lam, Ms. Melody Lam
☎ 852-2851 8603
🖷 852-2851 8637
✉ topreput@top-repute.com
www.machinery-vietnam.com

越南国际金属加工设备及技术展览会

Metaltech - Vietnam

日期：2013/07/18-20
地点：越南胡志明市西贡会议展览中心
内容：金属加工设备、压缩机、工具及测试仪器、螺杆、切割机及各类金属零件等
始办年份：1993
周期：每年一届
市场范围：国际性
参展费用：标准展位2,700美元/9m²
上届规模 '12：参展商108家来自12个国家及地区，贸易观众6,188人
主办：显辉国际展览有限公司；越南显达展览服务有限公司
地址：香港干诺道中168-200号信德中心西座2802室
联系人：林先生, 林小姐
☎ 852-2851 8603
🖷 852-2851 8637
✉ topreput@top-repute.com
www.machinery-vietnam.com

Metaltech–Vietnam

Date: 2013/06/18-20
Venue: Saigon Exhibition & Convention Centre (SECC), Ho Chi Minh City, Vietnam
Profile: Metalworking machines, Compressor, Tools and testing equipments, Screws barrel, Cutting tools, and Metal parts, etc.
Established Year: 1993
Frequency: Annual
Market Area: International
Participated Fee: Standard Booth USD 2,700/9m²
Statistics '12: Exhibitors 108 came from 12 countries and regions, Visitors 6,188
Organizer: Top Repute Co. Ltd. Vietnam Liaison Office
Address: Unit 2802, Shun Tak Centre, West Tower, Nos.168-200 Connaught Road Central, Hong Kong
Contact: Mr. Dennis Lam, Ms. Melody Lam
☎ 852-2851 8603
🖷 852-2851 8637
✉ topreput@top-repute.com
www.machinery-vietnam.com

越南国际印刷、包装机械设备及技术展览会

Print & Pack – Vietnam

日期：2013/07/18-20
地点：越南胡志明市西贡会议展览中心
内容：丝刷及移印机、标签机、包装机、膜纸、封口机、制袋机等
始办年份：1993
周期：每年一届
市场范围：国际性
参展费用：标准展位2,700美元/9m²
上届规模 '12：参展商108家来自12个国家及地区，贸易观众6,188人
主办：显辉国际展览有限公司；越南显达展览服务有限公司
地址：香港干诺道中168-200号信德中心西座2802室
联系人：林先生, 林小姐
☎ 852-2851 8603
🖷 852-2851 8637
✉ topreput@top-repute.com
www.machinery-vietnam.com

Print & Pack–Vietnam

Date: 2013/07/18-20
Venue: Saigon Exhibition & Convention Centre (SECC), Ho Chi Minh City, Vietnam
Profile: Screen & pad printing, Labeling machines, Packaging machines, Film, Sealer machine, Bag making machine, etc.
Established Year: 1993
Frequency: Annual
Market Area: International
Participated Fee: Standard Booth USD 2,700/9m²
Statistics '12: Exhibitors 108 came from 12 countries and regions, Visitors 6,188
Organizer: Top Repute Co. Ltd. Vietnam Liaison Office
Address: Unit 2802, Shun Tak Centre, West Tower, Nos.168-200 Connaught Road Central, Hong Kong
Contact: Mr. Dennis Lam, Ms. Melody Lam
☎ 852-2851 8603
🖷 852-2851 8637
✉ topreput@top-repute.com
www.machinery-vietnam.com

越南国际食品包装机械及技术展览会

Foodpack - Vietnam

日期：2013/07/18-20
地点：越南胡志明市西贡会议展览中心
内容：食品包装机械、食品加工机, 标签及条码机、称量及封盖机、饮料瓶装机等
始办年份：1993
周期：每年一届
市场范围：国际性
参展费用：标准展位2,700 美元/ 9m²
上届规模 '12：参展商108家来自12个国家及地区，贸易观众6,188人
主办：显辉国际展览有限公司；越南显达展览服务有限公司
地址：香港干诺道中168-200号信德中心西座2802室
联系人：林先生, 林小姐
☎ 852-2851 8603
🖷 852-2851 8637
✉ topreput@top-repute.com
www.machinery-vietnam.com

Foodpack – Vietnam

Date: 2013/07/18-20
Venue: Saigon Exhibition & Convention Centre (SECC), Ho Chi Minh City, Vietnam

Profile: Food packaging machine, Food processing, Labeling & bar coding machine, Weighing & Capping Machine, Soft drink bottling
Established Year: 1993
Frequency: Annual
Market Area: International
Participated Fee: USD 2,700 / booth (9 m^2)
Statistics '12: Exhibitors 108 came from 12 countries and regions, Visitors 6,188
Organizer: Top Repute Co. Ltd. Vietnam Liaison Office
Address: Unit 2802, Shun Tak Centre, West Tower, Nos.168-200 Connaught Road Central, Hong Kong
Contact: Mr. Dennis Lam, Ms. Melody Lam
☎ 852-2851 8603
🖷 852-2851 8637
✉ topreput@top-repute.com
www.machinery-vietnam.com

越南国际自动化工业展览会

Automation – Vietnam

日期：2013/07/18-20
地点：越南胡志明市西贡会议展览中心
内容：各类自动化机械
始办年份：1993
周期：每年一届
市场范围：国际性
参展费：标准展位2,700美金/9m^2
上届规模 '12：参展商108家来自12个国家及地区，贸易观众6,188人
主办：显辉国际展览有限公司；越南显达展览服务有限公司
地址：香港干诺道中168-200号信德中心西座2802室
联系人：林先生, 林小姐
☎ 852-2851 8603
🖷 852-2851 8637
✉ topreput@top-repute.com
www.machinery-vietnam.com

Automation–Vietnam

Date: 2013/07/18-20
Venue: Saigon Exhibition & Convention Centre (SECC), Ho Chi Minh City, Vietnam
Profile: Industrial automatic machinery
Established Year: 1993
Frequency: Annual
Market Area: International
Participated Fee: Standard Booth USD 2,700/9m^2
Statistics '12: Exhibitors 108 came from 12 countries and regions, Visitors 6,188
Organizer: Top Repute Co. Ltd. Vietnam Liaison Office
Address: Unit 2802, Shun Tak Centre, West Tower, Nos.168-200 Connaught Road Central, Hong Kong
Contact: Mr. Dennis Lam, Ms. Melody Lam
☎ 852-2851 8603
🖷 852-2851 8637
✉ topreput@top-repute.com
www.machinery-vietnam.com

越南国际建筑展览会

VICB 2013 -
Vietnam Intl Construction & Building Exhibition 2013

日期：2013/07/18-20
地点：越南胡志明市西贡会议展览中心
内容：建筑/楼宇工程机械、设备、工具、建材及技术
市场范围：国际性
参展费用：标准展位2,430 美元/9m^2
上届规模 '12：参展商108家来自12个国家及地区，贸易观众6,188人
主办：显辉国际展览有限公司；越南显达展览服务有限公司
地址：香港干诺道中168-200号信德中心西座2802室
联系人：林先生
☎ 852-2851 8603
🖷 852-2851 8637
✉ topreput@top-repute.com
dennis@top-repute.com
www.toprepute.com.hk
www.construction-vietnam.com

VICB 2013 –Vietnam Intl Construction & Building Exhibition 2013

Date: 2013/07/18-20
Venue: Saigon Exhibition & Convention Center (SECC), Ho Chi Minh City, Vietnam
Profile: Machinery, Equipment, Material & technology for construction and building industries
Market Area: International
Participated Fee: Standard Booth USD 2,430/9m^2
Statistics '12: Exhibitors 108 came from 12 countries and regions, Visitors 6,188
Organizer: Top Repute Co. Ltd. Vietnam Liaison Office
Address: Unit 2802, Shun Tak Centre, West Tower, Nos.168-200 Connaught Road Central, Hong Kong
Contact: Mr. Dennis Lam
☎ 852-2851 8603
🖷 852-2851 8637
✉ topreput@top-repute.com
✉ dennis@top-repute.com
www.toprepute.com.hk
www.construction-vietnam.com

越南国际安防、技防、消防设备和技术展览会

SECURITY & FIRE VIETNAM 2013

日期：2013/07/18-20
地点：越南胡志明市西贡会议展览中心
内容：安防、技防、消防产品、设备和技术
市场范围：国际性
参展费用：标准展位2,430美元/9m^2
上届规模 '12：参展商108家来自12个国家及地区，贸易观众6,188人
主办：显辉国际展览有限公司；越南显达展览服务有限公司
地址：香港干诺道中168-200号信德中心西座2802室
☎ 852-2851 8603
🖷 852-2851 8637
✉ topreput@top-repute.com
✉ dennis@top-repute.com
www.toprepute.com.hk
www.construction-vietnam.com

SECURITY & FIRE VIETNAM 2013 –Vietnam Intl Security System, Fire Protection Equipment and Technology Exhibition 2013

Date: 2013/06/18-20
Venue: Saigon Exhibition & Convention Center (SECC), Ho Chi Minh City, Vietnam
Profile: System products, equipment & technology for security & fire industry
Market Area: International
Participated Fee: Standard Booth USD 2,430/9m^2
Statistics '12: Exhibitors 108 came from 12 countries and regions, Visitors 6,188
Organizer: Top Repute Co. Ltd. Vietnam Liaison Office
Address: Unit 2802, Shun Tak Centre, West Tower, Nos.168-200 Connaught Road Central, Hong Kong
Contact: Mr. Dennis Lam
☎ 852-2851 8603
🖷 852-2851 8637
✉ topreput@top-repute.com
dennis@top-repute.com
www.construction-vietnam.com

越南国际制冷、空调、供暖、通风系统展览会

RAHV 2013
Intl Exhibition on Refrigeration, Air-conditioning, Heating & Ventilation Systems

日期：2013/07/18-20
地点：越南胡志明市西贡会议展览中心
内容：制冷、空调、供暖、通风、冷冻设备及技术
市场范围：国际性
参展费用：标准展位2,430 美元/9m^2
上届规模 '12：参展商108家来自12个国家及地区，贸易观众6,188人
主办：显辉国际展览有限公司；越南显达展览服务有限公司
地址：香港干诺道中168-200号信德中心西座2802室
联系人：林先生
☎ 852-2851 8603
🖷 852-2851 8637
✉ topreput@top-repute.com,
www.construction-vietnam.com

RAHV 2013 –Intl Exhibition on Refrigeration, Air-conditioning, Heating & Ventilation Systems

Date: 2013/07/18-20
Venue: Saigon Exhibition & Convention Center (SECC), Ho Chi Minh City, Vietnam
Profile: Machinery, equipment & technology for refrigeration, air-conditioning, heating & ventilation
Market Area: International
Participated Fee: Standard Booth USD 2,430/9m^2
Statistics '12: Exhibitors 108 came from 12 countries and regions, Visitors 6,188
Organizer: Top Repute Co. Ltd. Vietnam Liaison Office
Address: Unit 2802, Shun Tak Centre, West Tower, Nos.168-200 Connaught Road Central, Hong Kong
Contact: Mr. Dennis Lam
☎ 852-2851 8603
🖷 852-2851 8637
✉ topreput@top-repute.com
www.construction-vietnam.com

越南国际照明器材及技术展览会

LIGHTING VIETNAM 2013

日期：2013/07/18-20
地点：越南胡志明市西贡会议展览中心
内容：照明应用产品、系统、技术和设计
市场范围：国际性
参展费用：标准展位2,430 美元/9m^2
主办：显辉国际展览有限公司；越南显达展览服务有限公司
地址：香港干诺道中168-200号信德中心西座2802室
联系人：林先生
☎ 852-2851 8603
🖷 852-2851 8637
✉ topreput@top-repute.com,
www.construction-vietnam.com

LIGHTING VIETNAM 2013 Vietnam Intl Lighting Equipment & Technology Exhibition

Date: 2013/07/18-20
Venue: Saigon Exhibition & Convention Center (SECC), Ho Chi Minh City, Vietnam

Profile: Lighting system, products, equipment & technology
Market Area: International
Participated Fee: Standard Booth USD 2,430/9m^2
Organizer: Top Repute Co. Ltd. Vietnam Liaison Office
Address: Unit 2802, Shun Tak Centre, West Tower, Nos.168-200 Connaught Road Central, Hong Kong
Contact: Mr. Dennis Lam
☎ 852-2851 8603
🖷 852-2851 8637
✉ topreput@top-repute.com
www.construction-vietnam.com

第十四届中国机械(越南)展览会
14TH CHINA MAC FAIR-VIENAM
日期： 2013/07/31-03
地点： 越南胡志明市西贡展览会议中心（SECC）
内容： 工程建筑机械、矿产机械、冶金机械；金属加工机械、数控设备及机床、锻压设备、切割设备、激光设备、表面处理设备、模具；机电设备、发电设备、输变电设备、焊接设备、风机、电机、锅炉、泵类、电子机械、仪器仪表、光电设备；木工机械、船舶设备、商业设备、实验室设备、阀门、五金加工设备、输送设备、电梯、铸造设备、动力设备、起重设备、冷冻设备、分离设备、成型设备，零部件，其它机械设备。农业机械、食品生产加工设备，包装机械；空调设备、环保设备、化工设备、运输设备、橡塑机械、包装机械、印刷机械、造纸机械 医疗制药设备；纺织、缝制及印染设备；农林养殖机械
周期： 每年一届
市场范围： 国际性
性质： 面向贸易观众
参展费用： 22000元/9m^2
主办： 越南国家工贸部；中国轻工业对外经济技术合作公司；广东粤召展览有限公司
地址： 广州市天河区体育东路122号羊城国际商贸中心东塔1202, 1208室(510620)
联系人： 周文槟
☎ 020-8396 3610转706，13710318991
🖷 020-3887 0797
✉ 1979wenbin@163.com
✉ gdwenbin@hotmail.com
QQ 406372636
www.gf-hk.com

2013越南国际金属加工及焊接技术展览会
Intl Exhibition on Metalworking & Welding Technology
日期： 2013/07/31–08/03
地点： 越南胡志明市西贡展览会议中心（SECC）
内容： 焊接机械设备：矽钢片焊接机、焊接机器人、氩弧焊机、埋弧焊机、弧焊机、对焊机、气体保护焊、塑料焊接机、回流焊机、MAG焊机、TIG焊机、激光焊接机、专用焊接机、点焊设备、缝焊机、超声波焊接设备、焊接生产线、其它焊接设备、数控切割机、线切割设备、激光切割机、火焰切割机、砂轮切割机、水刀切割机、等离子切割机、氩弧切割机、汽油焊割机、其它类切割机、数控切割机、线切割设备、激光切割机、火焰切割机、砂轮切割机、过滤设备、风机、排风设备、清洗、测试仪、无损检测仪器、气体检测仪器、焊缝探伤仪器、焊缝金相分析器、焊接工艺装备焊接辅助器具。金属加工设备：金属切削机床。金属成形机床；模具制造机床；
周期： 每年一届
市场范围： 国际性
性质： 面向贸易观众
参展费用： 22,000元（人民币）(3x3m)
主办： 越南国家工贸部；中国轻工业对外经济技术合作公司；广东粤召展览有限公司
地址： 广州市天河区体育东路122号羊城国际商贸中心东塔1202, 1208室(510620)
联系人： 周文槟
☎ 020-8396 3610转706，13710318991
🖷 020-3887 0797
✉ 1979wenbin@163.com
✉ gdwenbin@hotmail.com
QQ 406372636
www.gf-hk.com

2013第六届越南国际安防展览会
Secutech Vietnam 2013
第四届中国安防技术产品越南买家采购会
日期： 2013/08/08-10
地点： 越南胡志明市西贡展览会议中心（SECC）
内容： 视频监控防范系统、社区安全系统、楼宇自动化系统、消防报警器材、警用装备、智能交通系统、生物识别技术、防伪技术等
主办： 越中会展商务有限公司
☎ 0771-261 5620
🖷 0771-263 0917

2013东盟（越南胡志明）中国建筑建材及家居用品博览会
China Construction-Building Materials & Interior-Exterior Decoration Exhibition in Saigon Vietnam
日期： 2013/08/14-18
地点： 越南胡志明市西贡展览会议中心（SECC）
内容： 建筑和房地产、建材、室内外建筑装饰产品、家居用品等
主办： 越中会展商务有限公司
☎ 0771-261 5620
🖷 0771-263 0917

第十六届越南胡志明市国际建筑建材装饰博览会
VIETBUILD HO CHI MINH CITY 2013
日期： 2013/08/14-18
地点： 越南胡志明市西贡展览会议中心（SECC）
内容： 建筑和房地产、建材、室内外建筑装饰产品、家居用品等
主办： 越中会展商务有限公司
☎ 0771-261 5620
🖷 0771-263 0917

2013第十七届越南国际食品饮料工业博览会暨中国食品加工及包装技术设备越南专题展
17th Vietnam Intl Exhibition on Food & Beverage
日期： 2013/09/10-14
地点： 越南胡志明市TBECC
内容： 食品饮料加工设备、印刷包装机械、标签、食品加工原材料及添加剂、冰淇淋设备等
主办： 越中会展商务有限公司
☎ 0771-261 5620
🖷 0771-263 0917

2013年越南国际木工机械暨家具配件展
日期： 2013/09/25-28
地点： 越南胡志明市西贡国际会展中心
VIETNAMWOOD
内容： 干燥设备、锯木机械、锯木厂设备,木材车削机、木材弯曲机、黏合机、钻孔及填装 圆木榫机、人造板生产设备,粉尘收集设备；木材前处理机械及设备,木材加工机械及设备气动工具、电动工具等；木材加工机械及设备；木材及木器传送技术；油漆，喷涂及抛光技术、涂料及粘合剂等；油漆，喷涂、胶合；原木及木匠工具；家具装饰材料、家具配件与家具五金、家具生产材料、家具半成品与部件；家具构配件家具装饰五金；喷漆及干燥设备、刀具及配件等各式家具的生产设备和工具,贴面、装饰纸及表面处理材料、封边条、织物与皮革、原辅材料与配件，家居配套用品；原木、木材、人造板及板材、木皮、贴面、装饰纸及表面处理材料、木材及木器传送技术；林业成套设备,营林采伐设备。
始办年份： 2001
周期： 两年一届2010(在河内和胡志明交替举办)
市场范围： 国际性
性质： 面向贸易观众
参展费用： 16800元（人民币）/9m^2
上届规模 2011：展览面积12,500m^2，参展商250家（来自全球19个国地/地区），观众10,062人
主办： 中国贸易促进行委员会建设行业分会；广东粤召展览有限公司
地址： 广州市天河区体育东路122号羊城国际商贸中心东塔1202, 1208室(510620)
联系人： 周文槟
☎ 020-8396 3610转706，13710318991
🖷 020-3887 0797
✉ 1979wenbin@163.com
✉ gdwenbin@hotmail.com
QQ 406372636

越南机电展
M&E Vietnam
日期： 2013/10/16-18
地点： 越南胡志明市Saigon Exhibition & Convention Centre
主办： 亚洲博闻有限公司
地址： 香港湾仔港湾道26号华润大厦17楼
☎ 852-2827 6211
🖷 852-3749 7342
✉ info-hk@ubm.com
www.ubmasia.com

M&E Vietnam
Date: 2013/10/16-18
Venue: Saigon Exhibition & Convention Centre，Ho Chi Minh City, Vietnam
Organizer: UBM Asia Ltd
Address: 17/F, China Resources Building, 26 Harbour Road, Wan Chai, Hong Kong
☎ 852-2827 6211
🖷 852-3749 7342
✉ info-hk@ubm.com
www.ubmasia.com

越南国际水工程大展暨论坛
VIETWATER

VIET WATER 2013
VIETNAM'S NO.1 WATER & WASTEWATER INDUSTRY SHOW
16-18 OCTOBER 2013 • SAIGON EXHIBITION & CONVENTION CENTER(SECC), HCMC

日期： 2013/10/16-18
地点： 越南胡志明市SECC
市场范围： 国际性
主办： 亚洲博闻有限公司
地址： 香港湾仔港湾道26号华润大厦17楼
☎ 00852-2827 6211
🖷 00852-3749 7342
✉ info-hk@ubm.com
http://vietwater.com

VIETWATER
Date: 2013/10/16-18
Venue: Saigon Exhibition & Convention Centre, Vietnam
Profile: Internaltional Water Supply, Sanitation, Industrial Wastewater Treatment & Purification Event
Market Area: International
Organizer: UBM Asia Ltd
Address: 17/F, China Resources Building, 26 Harbour Road, Wan Chai, Hong Kong
☎ 852-2827 6211
🖷 852-3749 7342
✉ info-hk@ubm.com
http://vietwater.com

2013越南国际工业展览会
Vietnam Intl Industrial Fair
日期： 2013/10/17-21
地点： 越南河内VEFC
内容： 数控机床及金属加工、工业自动化、信息与通信技术应用信息感知、智能工业控制与应用、新能源与电力电工、环保技术设备等
主办： 越中会展商务有限公司
☎ 0771-261 5620
🖷 0771-263 0917

2013第十三届越南国际农业博览会
暨东盟（越南）中国农林牧渔出口商品展
2013越南农林牧渔供应商对接中国买家采购会
Agroviet
日期： 2013/11 -
地点： 越南河内
内容： 农业生产用种子、肥料、农药；农业机械 及

农产品加工、饲料及畜牧养殖技术、茶 业种植加工技术、粮油加工机械设备及技 术、食用油及食品、农业高新科技等
主办：越中会展商务有限公司
☎ 0771-261 5620
🖷 0771-263 0917

国际工程、建材机械、工程车辆及设备展览会
日期：2013/12 -
地点：越南胡志明市
周期：每年一届
主办：中国贸促会机械行业分会
地址：北京市西城区三里河路46号(100823)
☎ 010-6859 4811，6859 4994，6859 4910
🖷 010-6859 4995
✉ info@ccpitmsc.org
www.chinamachine.org.cn

国际工程、建材机械、工程车辆及设备展览会
日期：2013/12 -
地点：越南胡志明市
周期：每年一届
主办：中国贸促会机械行业分会
地址：北京市西城区三里河路46号(100823)
☎ 010-6859 4811，6859 4994，6859 4910
🖷 010-68594995
✉ info@ccpitmsc.org
www.chinamachine.org.cn

2013第十一届越南胡志明市国际贸易博览会
11th Vietnam Intl Trade Fair in Ho Chi Minh City
日期：2013/12/04-07
地点：越南胡志明市西贡展览会议中心（SECC）
内容：综合商品展示和交易
主办：越中会展商务有限公司
☎ 0771-261 5620
🖷 0771-263 0917

2013 第四届中国品牌消费品（越南）展览交易会
China Brands of Consumer Goods Fair in Vietnam
日期：2013/12/04-07
地点：越南胡志明市西贡展览会议中心（SECC）
内容：家电、消费电子、家纺、服装、鞋帽箱 包、眼镜钟表、玩具及婴儿用品、文具 与办公用品、体育休闲用品、礼品、工艺品等
主办：越中会展商务有限公司
☎ 0771-261 5620
🖷 0771-263 0917

海外展览会议行业分类

Exhibitions Overseas Listed by Industry Category

综合博览会
General Fairs

2013年巴拿马第三十一届国际博览会
Expocomer 2013
2013/04/17-20
巴拿马巴拿马城Panama- Panama City

安全
Safety and Security

越南国际安防、技防、消防设备和技术展览会
"SECURITY & FIRE VIETNAM 2013" - Vietnam International Security System, Fire Protection Equipment and Technology Exhibition 2013
2013/06/18-20
越南Vietnam

"SECURITY & FIRE VIETNAM 2013" - 越南国际安防、技防、消防设备和技术展览会
"SECURITY & FIRE VIETNAM 2013" - Vietnam International Security System, Fire Protection Equipment and Technology Exhibition 2013
2013/07/18-20
越南Vietnam

印度国际安全与消防技术设备展览会
IFSEC India
2013/12/05-07
印度大诺伊达India-Greater Noida

日本健康食品原料展 / 安全及技术展
Health Ingredients Japan / Safety and Technology Japan
2013/10/09-11
日本东京Japan-Tokyo

包装
Packaging

英国国际包装新技术展览会
Total Processing & Packaging
2013
英国Britain

2013年第十届中东（迪拜）国际包装、印刷机械展览会
Gulf Pack & Print 2013
2013/04/08-11
阿联酋迪拜UAE-Dubai

英国国际包装新技术展览会
Total Processing & Packaging
2013/05/21-23
英国Britain

越南国际印刷、包装机械设备及技术展览会
Print & Pack - Vietnam
2013/06/18-20
越南Vietnam

越南国际印刷、包装机械设备及技术展览会
Print & Pack - Vietnam
2013/07/18-20
越南Vietnam

材料
Materials

创新材料学术大会
InnoMateria
2013/05/14-15
德国科隆Germany-Koln

英国国际包装新技术展览会
Total Processing & Packaging
2013
英国Britain

英国国际包装新技术展览会
Total Processing & Packaging
2013/05/21-23
英国Britain

船艇、海事
Boats,Ship Building and Marine

日本今治海事展
Bari Ship (Japan)
2013/05
日本Japan

亚洲海上旅游及邮轮展
Cruise Shipping Asia-Pacific
2013/09
新加坡Singapore

国际游艇及水上运动展览会
2013/09/22-30
德国腓特烈港Germany-frederikshavn

意大利(热那亚)国际游艇展览会
2013/10/01-09
意大利热那亚Italy-Genoa

美国劳德岱堡国际游艇展览会
2013/10/25-29
美国劳德岱堡USA-Fort Lauderdale

韩国海事展
KORMARINE
2013/10
韩国Korea

荷兰国际海事展览会
2013/11/08-11
荷兰鹿特丹Netherlands-Rotterdam

英国国际海洋勘探技术展
Oceanology International
2014/03
英国Britain

灯光照明、灯饰
Lighting

日本国际照明展览会
LIGHTING JAPAN: LED/OLED Lighting Technology Expo
2013/01
日本Japan

"LIGHTING VIETNAM 2013" 越南国际照明器材及技术展览会2013
"LIGHTING VIETNAM 2013" Vietnam International Lighting Equipment & Technology Exhibition
2013/07/18-20
越南Vietnam

电力、电工
Electric Power,Electrical Engineering

国际输变电技术会议及交流展览会
2013/01/29-31
美国圣地亚哥USA-Santiago

国际电力、照明及新能源展览会
2013/02/17-19
阿联酋迪拜UAE- Dubai

巴西国际电子展
FIEE El é trica
2013/03
巴西Brazil

国际电力电子展览会
2013/04/01-05
巴西圣保罗Brazil-St.Paul

国际建材及设备展览会
2013/05
澳大利亚墨尔本Australia-Melbourne

国际电力电子和新能源展览会
2013/05
波兰波兹南Poland-Poznan

欧洲国际电力展览会
2013/06/04-06
奥地利维也纳Austria-Vienna

国际电力电子展览会
2013/06
俄罗斯莫斯科Russia-Moscow

国际电力、照明及新能源展览会
2013/09
尼日利亚阿布贾Nigeria-Abuja

印尼机电展
Indonesia M&E Expo
2013/10/24-26
印度尼西亚雅加达Indonesia-Jakarta

国际电力、照明及新能源展览会
2013/10
南非约翰内斯堡South Africa-Johannesburg

国际电力博览会
2013/12
美国拉斯维加斯USA-Las Vegas

电子 Electronics

日本国际照明展览会
LIGHTING JAPAN: LED/OLED Lighting Technology Expo
2013/01
日本Japan

日本电子展
INTERNEPCON Japan
2013/01
日本Japan

2013年泰国电子展：国际电子产品制造贸易展及会议
NEPCON Thailand 2013: The International Electronics Manufacturing Technology Trade Exhibition and Conference
2013/06
泰国Thailand

2011年泰国电子展：国际电子产品制造贸易展及会议
NEPCON Thailand
2013/06/20-23
泰国Thailand

房地产 Real Estate

法国国际地产投资交易会
MIPIM featuring MIPIM Horizons: The World's Property Market
2013/03
法国France

纺织、服装、服饰及相关机械 Clothing and Textile

巴西纺织机械展
ITMEX Americas : International Textile Machinery Trade Fair
2013
巴西Brazil

越南国际制衣机械设备、面料展览会
Vietnam International Exhibition on Garment Manufacturing Equipment and Fabric (GARMENT & FABRIC - VIETNAM 2013)
2013/07/11-13
越南Vietnam

越南国际制衣机械设备、面料展览会
Vietnam International Exhibition on Garment Manufacturing Equipment and Fabric (GARMENT & FABRIC - VIETNAM 2013)
2013/07/18-20
越南Vietnam

工程机械 Construction Machinery

巴西纺织机械展
ITMEX Americas : International Textile Machinery Trade Fair
2013
巴西Brazil

印度国际铸造技术及设备展览会
IFEX
2013/01/27-29
印度班加罗尔India-Bangalore

国际工程机械、建材机械、矿山机械及工程车辆博览会
2013/02/05-08
印度孟买India- Bombay

国际工程机械展览会
2013/02/21-23
澳大利亚墨尔本Australia- Melbourne

西班牙毕尔巴鄂国际五金展
2013/03/12-15
西班牙毕尔巴鄂Spain- Bilbao

法兰克福暖通卫浴展
ISH
2013/03/12-16
德国法兰克福Germany- Frankfurt

国际物流与运输展览会
2013/03/19-23
英国伯明翰Britain- Birmingham

巴西圣保罗工程机械与零部件展
SP Infrastructure: Exhibition Fair of Infrastructure Works' Products & Services
2013/03
巴西Brazil

俄罗斯建材展
2013/04
俄罗斯莫斯科Russia- Moscow

德国汉诺威工业博览会
HANNOVER MESSE
2013/04/08-12
德国汉诺威Germany- Hanover

国际建材与工程机械博览会
2013/04
卡塔尔多哈Qatar- Doha

国际农业机械展览会
2013/04
巴西圣保罗Brazil- St.Paul

德国慕尼黑国际工程机械博览会（bauma 2013）
2013/04/15-21
德国Germany

迪拜国际铝工业展
Gateway to the Middle East\'s Aluminium Industry
2013/04/23-25
阿联酋UAE

国际矿业展览会
2013/05/07-09
阿根廷布宜诺斯艾利斯Argentina-Buenos Aires

美国国际五金制品及花园用品博览会
NHS
2013/05/07-09
美国拉斯维加斯USA- Las Vegas

国际矿业机械展览会
2013/05/14-16
俄罗斯莫斯科Russia- Moscow

国际工程机械作业展览会
2013/05/14-16
英国伯明翰Britain- Birmingham

德国科隆木工机械展
INTERZUM
2013/05
德国科隆Germany- Koln

中东迪拜国际五金工具博览会
Hardware & Tools
2013/05
阿联酋迪拜UAE- Dubai

巴西国际机床工具及成套设备展
FEIMAFE: Intl Machine Tools & Integrated Manufacturing Systems Trade Fair
2013/05/20-25
巴西Brazil

"国际工程机械、矿山机械、建材机械及建筑材料展览会 (自办展)"
2013/05/29-01
印度尼西亚雅加达Indonesia- Djakarta Djakarta

澳大利亚建材展
DESIGN BUILD EXPO
2013/06
澳大利亚悉尼Australia- Sydney

国际工程技术与设备展览会
2013/06/05-08
巴西圣保罗Brazil- St.Paul

国际建筑及工程机械展览会
2013/06
俄罗斯莫斯科Russia- Moscow

国际贸易博览会
2013/07/17-22
安哥拉罗安达Angola-Luanda

国际矿业机械及工程机械展览会
2013/08
巴西贝洛Brazil- Belo

亚太国际矿业展览会
2013/08/20-23
澳大利亚悉尼Australia- Sydney

国际工程机械及矿业展览会
2013/09
哈萨克斯坦阿拉木图Kazakhstan- Alma-Ata

国际工程机械、矿山机械和矿业展览会
2013/09/19-21
蒙古乌兰巴托Mongolia- Ulan Bator

国际工程机械与建材展览会
2013/09
伊拉克埃尔比勒Iraq- Erbil

国际矿业展览会
2013/09
秘鲁阿雷基帕Peru- Arequipa

国际建筑机械、建材机械、矿山机械及工程车辆博览会
2013/09/18-21
南非约翰内斯堡South Africa- Johannesburg

巴西国际无纺布贸易展
NT&TT: International Nonwovens & Technical Textiles Trade Fair
2013/10
巴西Brazil

国际工程及施工设备展览会
2013/11
阿尔及利亚阿尔及尔Algeria- Algiers

国际工程机械与技术展览会
2013/11
印度班加罗尔India- Bangalore

国际工程建筑机械与工程车辆展览会
2013/11
沙特利雅得Saudi Arabia- Riyadh

国际工程、建材机械、工程车辆及设备展览会
2013/12
越南胡志明市Vietnam- Ho Chi Minh City

国际工程、建材机械、工程车辆及设备展览会
2013/12
越南胡志明市Vietnam- Ho Chi Minh City

广播、电影、电视、舞台设备
Broadcasting, Film, Television&Stage Equipment

柏林国际会展技术及媒体技术展览会
SHOWTECH – International Trade Show & Conference for Event Technology & Services
2013/06
德国Germany

柏林国际会展及媒体技术展览会
SHOWTECH: Intl. Show & Conference for Stage Technology, Eqpt. & Event Svs
2013/06/18-20
德国Germany

焊接
Welding

2013年汉诺威工业博览会
HANNOVER MESSE 2013
2013/04/08-12
德国汉诺威Germany- Hanover

专业焊接技术及配件工艺贸易展
WeldTech
2013/05/16-19
泰国曼谷Thailand-Bangkok

第十一届印度国际机械、工程技术及机床展览会
ENGIMACH
2013/10/27-11/01
印度艾哈迈达巴德市India- Ahmedabad

第十一届印度国际机械、工程技术及机床展览会
ENGIMACH
2013/11/27-01
印度艾哈迈达巴德市India- Ahmedabad

航空航天
Aviation, Aerospace&Airport

巴黎国际航空航天展览会
2013/06/20-23
法国巴黎France-Paris

澳大利亚（悉尼）国际游艇展览会
2013/08/02-06
澳大利亚悉尼Australia-Sydney

化工
Chemical Industry

斯里兰卡国际染料和化工展
Dye+Chem Sirilanka
2013/02/28-03/02
斯里兰卡科伦坡Sri Lanka- Colombo

涂料-外观装饰展览会
Farbe-Ausbau&Fassade (Paint-Finishing & Facade)
2013/03/06-09
德国科隆Germany-Koln

泰国国际化工展
CHEMEXPO THAI
2013/03/19-20
泰国曼谷Thailand- Bangkok

印度精细化工展
Chemspec India
2013/04/10-12
印度孟买India- Bombay

以色列国际化工展
ISRACHEM
2013/04/30-05/02
以色列特拉维夫Israel- Tel Aviv

孟加拉国际染料和化工展
Dye+Chem Bangladesh
2013/09/05-08
孟加拉达卡Bengal- Dacca

俄罗斯国际化工展
CHEMISTRY
2013/10
俄罗斯莫斯科Russia- Moscow

马来西亚国际化工展
CHEMAISA
2013/10/08-09
马来西亚吉隆坡Malaysia- Kuala Lumpur
8416
印尼国际染料和化工展
Dye+Chem Indonesia
2013/10/24-26
印度尼西亚雅加达Indonesia- Djakarta

日本国际化工展
INCHEM TOKYO
2013/11
日本东京Japan- Tokyo

环境保护
Environment Protection

阿布扎比世界未来能源峰会暨新能源与环保展览会
World Future Energy Summit (WFES)
2013/01
阿联酋UAE

亚洲再生能源展
Renewable Energy Asia
2013/06/05-08
泰国曼谷Thailand-Bangkok

国际环保技术展
Entech Pollutec Asia
2013/06/05-08
泰国曼谷Thailand-Bangkok

机械、制造、工业装备、自动化
Machinery, Machine Tools and Technology&Automation

中东贸易和伊拉克重建国际工业展览会
2013
土耳其加济安泰普Turkey-Gaziantep

国际包装展览会
2013/01
俄罗斯莫斯科Russia- Moscow

国际机械技术展览会
2013/01
阿联酋迪拜UAE- Dubai

国际机床（切削技术）与工具展览会
2013/01/24-30
印度班加罗尔India- Bangalore

国际空调、制冷和供暖展览会
2013/01/28-30
美国达拉斯USA- Dallas

国际工程机械、建材机械、矿山机械及工程车辆博览会
2013/02/05-08
印度孟买India- Bombay

德国斯图加特紧固件展览会
FASTENER FAIR/STUTTGART
2013/02/26-28
德国斯图加特Germany-Stuttgart

国际博览会
2013/03
埃及开罗Egypt- Cairo

国际工业展览会
2013/03
土耳其伊斯坦布尔Turkey- Istanbul

国际机床展览会
2013/03/05-08
墨西哥墨西哥城Mexico- Mexico City

俄罗斯圣彼得堡紧固件展览会
FASTENER FAIR/RUSSIA
2013/03/12-14
俄罗斯圣彼得堡Russia-

国际包装、食品加工及印刷机械展览会
2013/03/12-15
南非约翰内斯堡South Africa- Johannesburg

南美国际动力传动及物流设备展览会
2013/03/19-22
巴西圣保罗Brazil- St.Paul

国际模具展览会
2013/04
日本东京Japan- Tokyo

2013年汉诺威工业博览会
HANNOVER MESSE 2013_
2013/04/08-12
德国汉诺威Germany- Hanover

汉诺威工业博览会
2013/04/08-12
德国汉诺威Germany- Hanover

国际包装印刷机械展览会
2013/04/08-11
阿联酋迪拜UAE- Dubai

国际机床工具展览会
2013/04/09-13
阿根廷布宜诺斯艾利斯Argentina-Buenos Aires

印度孟买紧固件展览会
FASTENER FAIR/MUMBAI
2013/04/17-18
印度孟买India-Bombay

USETEC 二手机械设备、机械系统及技术贸易国际展览会
2013/04/22-24
德国科隆Germany-Koln

国际工业配件展览会
2013/05
摩洛哥卡萨布兰卡Morocco-Casablanca

中国机械和电子产品展览会
2013/05
印度尼西亚雅加达Indonesia- Djakarta

南非基础建设展览会
2013/05
南非约翰内斯堡South Africa- Johannesburg

国际安防展览会
2013/05
巴西圣保罗Brazil- St.Paul

国际机械制造周
2013/05
澳大利亚墨尔本Australia- Melbourne

中国出口商品展览会
2013/05
匈牙利布达佩斯Hungary- Budapest

国际机床及板材展览会
2013/05/07-10
澳大利亚悉尼Australia- Sydney

澳大利亚国际机械制造周展览会
NMW
2013/05/07-10
澳大 利亚墨尔本Australia-Melbourne

国际包装机械展览会
2013/05/07-10
澳大利亚悉尼Australia- Sydney

意大利印刷、印刷媒体和传播工业及意大利包装印刷和纸加工展览会
2013/05/07-11
意大利米兰Italy- Milan

国际塑料工业展览会
2013/05/14-16
加拿大多伦多Canada- Toronto

国际林业木工机械展览会
2013/05/14-18
德国汉诺威Germany- Hanover

国际机器展
Intermach
2013/05/16-19
泰国曼谷Thailand-Bangkok

国际专用工具及机械展
MOLDEX
2013/05/16-19
泰国曼谷Thailand-Bangkok

工业自动化展
Industrial Automation Robotics
2013/05/16-19
泰国曼谷Thailand-Bangkok

国际塑料工业贸易展览会
2013/05/20-24
巴西圣保罗Brazil- St.Paul

巴西国际机床工具及成套设备展
FEIMAFE: Intl Machine Tools & Integrated Manufacturing Systems Trade Fair
2013/05/20-25
巴西Brazil

国际机床工具展览会
2013/05/27-31
俄罗斯莫斯科Russia- Moscow

中国工业产品（委内瑞拉）展览会
2013/06
委内瑞拉加拉加斯Venezuela- Caracas

东京国际机械零部件、材料及技术展览会
M-Tech
2013/06
日本东京Japan-Tokyo

国际食品、饮料工业加工技术和包装工业博览会
2013/06
巴西圣保罗Brazil- St.Paul

国际包装展览会
2013/06
墨西哥墨西哥城Mexico- Mexico City

国际机床工具与制造技术展览会
2013/06/03-08
巴西圣保罗Brazil- St.Paul

2013德国柏林国际线圈、电机、绝缘材料及电器制造展
CWIEME
2013/06/04-06
德国柏林Germany- Berlin

国际包装工业展览会
2013/06/04-06
英国伯明翰Britain- Birmingham

国际分包展览会
2013/06/07-09
英国伯明翰Britain-Birmingham

越南国际塑胶机械及技术展览会
Vietnam Plastic Fair
2013/06/18-20
越南Vietnam

越南国际金属加工设备及技术展览会
Metaltech - Vietnam
2013/06/18-20
越南Vietnam

越南国际自动化工业展览会
Automation - Vietnam
2013/07/18-20
越南Vietnam

2013越南国际金属加工及焊接技术展览会
International Exhibition on Metalworking & Welding Technology
2013/07/31-08/03
越南胡志明市Vietnam-Ho Chi Minh City

第十四届中国机械(越南)展览会
THE 14th CHINA MAC FAIR-VIENAM
2013/07/31-08/03
越南胡志明市Vietnam-Ho Chi Minh City

国际机床工具展览会
2013/07
越南胡志明市Vietnam- Ho Chi Minh City

第十四届中国机械(越南)展览会
THE 14th CHINA MAC FAIR-VIENAM
2013/07/31-08/03
越南胡志明市Vietnam- Ho Chi Minh City

2013越南国际金属加工及焊接技术展览会
International Exhibition on Metalworking & Welding Technology
2013/07/31-08/03
越南胡志明市Vietnam- Ho Chi Minh City

第十四届中国机械(越南)展览会
THE 14th CHINA MAC FAIR-VIENAM
2013/07/31-08/03
越南胡志明市Vietnam- Ho Chi Minh City

国际包装工业展览会
2013/09
土耳其伊斯坦布尔Turkey- Istanbul

国际贸易展览会
2013/09
肯尼亚内罗毕Kenya-Nairobi

国际动力传动、表面处理及工业自动化展览会
2013/09
俄罗斯莫斯科Russia-Moscow

国际印刷及纸品加工展览会
2013/09/06-11
美国芝加哥USA- Chicago

国际食品加工及包装机械展览会
2013/09/11-13
印度孟买India- Bombay

欧洲机床展览会
2013/09/16-21
德国汉诺威Germany- Hanover

国际包装展览会
2013/09/23-25
美国拉斯维加斯USA- Las Vegas

国际印刷设备及技术展览会
2013/10
俄罗斯莫斯科Russia- Moscow

加拿大制造技术展览会
2013/10
加拿大多伦多Canada- Toronto

韩国金属制造周
2013/10
韩国高阳Korea-Gao Yang

美国西部紧固件展览会
NATIONAL INDUSTRIAL FASTENER SHOW/WEST
2013/10
美国拉斯维加斯USA-Las Vegas

巴西国际无纺布贸易展
NT&TT: International Nonwovens & Technical Textiles Trade Fair
2013/10
巴西Brazil

土耳其铝工业展览会
2013/10/03-06
土耳其伊斯坦布尔Turkey-Istanbul

俄罗斯莫斯科国际紧固件展览会
2013/10/08-10
俄罗斯莫斯科Russia-Moscow

国际塑料橡胶工业展览会
2013/10/16-23
德国杜塞尔多夫Germany- Dusseldorf

国际机床工具展览会
2013/11
埃及开罗Egypt- Cairo

国际机床和金属加工机械展览会
2013/11
泰国曼谷Thailand- Bangkok

国际金属加工和管材展览会
2013/11
美国芝加哥USA- Chicago

巴西圣保罗国际紧固件展览会
FASTENER FAIR/BRASIL
2013/11
巴西圣保罗Brazil-St.Paul

国际工业配件市场展览会
2013/11
法国巴黎France-Paris

国际印刷及相关机械展览会
2013/11/14-17
印度新德里India- New Delhi

第十一届印度国际机械、工程技术及机床展览会
ENGIMACH
2013/11/27-01
印度艾哈迈达巴德市India-Ahmedabad city

国际工业装备展览会
2013/12
印度India

国际机床及金属加工技术展览会
2013/12
印度尼西亚雅加达Indonesia- Djakarta

欧洲模具展览会
2013/12
德国法兰克福Germany- Frankfurt

家具、木工机械
Furniture&Woodwoking

科隆国际厨房展
LivingKitchen
2013/01/14-20
德国Germany

科隆国际家具展
imm cologne
2013/01/14-20
德国Germany

马来西亚国际家具展
Malaysian International Furniture Fair
2013/03/05-09
马来西亚吉隆坡Malaysia-Kuala Lumpur

奥地利国际木材加工、处理、装配、木匠用品展
BWS: International Trade Fair for Woodworking
2013/03
奥地利Austria

科隆国际家具生产、木工及室内装饰展
interzum cologne
2013/05/13-16
德国Germany

莫斯科国际家具生产、木工及室内装饰展
zum moscow / Interkomplekt
2013/05/13-16
俄罗斯Russia

2013年越南国际木工机械暨家具配件展
2013/09/25-28
越南胡志明市Vietnam- Ho Chi Minh City

建筑、建材、装饰及相关机械
Building,Construction,Decoration&Materials

国际工程机械、建材机械、矿山机械及工程车辆博览会
2013/02/05-08
印度孟买India- Bombay

国际工程机械展览会
2013/02/21-23
澳大利亚墨尔本Australia- Melbourne

法国国际地产投资交易会
MIPIM featuring MIPIM Horizons: The World's Property Market
2013/03
法国France

西班牙毕尔巴鄂国际五金展
2013/03/12-15
西班牙毕尔巴鄂Spain- Bilbao

法兰克福暖通卫浴展
ISH
2013/03/12-16
德国法兰克福Germany- Frankfurt

国际物流与运输展览会
2013/03/19-23
英国伯明翰Britain- Birmingham

2013东盟（越南河内）中国建筑建材及家居用品博览会
China Construction-Building Materials & Interior-Exterior Decoration Exhibition In Hanoi Vietnam 2013
2013/03/28-01
越南河内Vietnam-Hanoi

2013年越南（河内）国际建筑、建材及家居产品展览会
VIETBUILD
2013/03/28-01
越南河内Vietnam- Hanoi

2013年越南（河内）国际建筑、建材及家居产品展览会
VIETBUILD
2013/03/28-01
越南河内Vietnam- Hanoi

俄罗斯建材展
2013/04
俄罗斯莫斯科Russia- Moscow

国际农业机械展览会
2013/04
巴西圣保罗Brazil- St.Paul

国际建材与工程机械博览会
2013/04
卡塔尔多哈Qatar- Doha

摩洛哥国际建筑展之室内外装饰展
BATIMAT MOROCCO Interior & outdoor Architecture
2013/04/03-06
摩洛哥Morocco

德国汉诺威工业博览会
HANNOVER MESSE
2013/04/08-12
德国汉诺威Germany- hanover

中东迪拜国际五金工具博览会
Hardware & Tools
2013/05
阿联酋迪拜UAE- Dubai

德国科隆木工机械展
INTERZUM
2013/05
德国科隆Germany- Cologne

美国国际五金制品及花园用品博览会
NHS
2013/05/07-09
美国拉斯维加斯USA- Las Vegas

国际矿业机械展览会
2013/05/14-16
俄罗斯莫斯科Russia- Moscow

国际工程机械作业展览会
2013/05/14-16
英国伯明翰Britain- Birmingham

"国际工程机械、矿山机械、建材机械及建筑材料展览会(自办展)"
2013/05/29-01
印度尼西亚雅加达Indonesia- Djakarta

澳大利亚建材展
DESIGN BUILD EXPO
2013/06
澳大利亚悉尼Australia- Sydney

国际建筑及工程机械展览会
2013/06
俄罗斯莫斯科Russia- Moscow

国际工程技术与设备展览会
2013/06/05-08
巴西圣保罗Brazil- St.Paul

“VICB 2013” -越南国际建筑展览会
“VICB 2013” - Vietnam International Construction & Building Exhibition 2013
2013/06/18-20
越南Vietnam

国际贸易博览会
2013/07/17-22
安哥拉罗安达Angola- Luanda

“VICB 2013” -越南国际建筑展览会
“VICB 2013” - Vietnam International Construction & Building Exhibition 2013
2013/07/18-20
越南Vietnam

日本国际五金及DIY展
JAPAN DIY SHOW
2013/08
日本东京Japan- Tokyo

国际矿业机械及工程机械展览会
2013/08
巴西贝洛Brazil- Bello

亚太国际矿业展览会
2013/08/20-23
澳大利亚悉尼Australia- Sydney

摩洛哥国际建筑展之暖通空调及电子系统展
BATIMAT MOROCCO HVAC / Electrical systems
2013/09
摩洛哥Morocco

墨西哥国际五金展
EXPO NACIONAL FERRETERA
2013/09
墨西哥瓜达拉哈拉Mexico- Guadalajara

国际工程机械及矿业展览会
2013/09
哈萨克斯坦阿拉木图Kazakhstan- Alma-Ata

国际工程机械与建材展览会
2013/09
伊拉克埃尔比勒Iraq- Erbil

国际矿业展览会
2013/09
秘鲁阿雷基帕Peru- Arequipa

国际建筑机械、建材机械、矿山机械及工程车辆博览会
2013/09/18-21
南非约翰内斯堡South Africa- Johannesburg

国际工程机械、矿山机械和矿业展览会
2013/09/19-21
蒙古乌兰巴托Mongolia- Ulan Bator

2013年越南国际木工机械暨家具配件展
2013/09/25-28
越南胡志明市Vietnam- Ho Chi Minh City

沙特建材展
2013/10
沙特利雅得Saudi Arabia- Riyadh

第28届法国巴黎国际建筑展览会 第28届法国巴黎国际建筑展览会 第28届法国巴黎国际建筑展览会 第28届法国巴黎国际建筑展览会
BATIMAT : The World\'s Leading Construction Exhibition
2013/11
法国France

西班牙毕尔巴鄂国际五金展
2013/03/12-15
西班牙毕尔巴鄂Spain- Bilbao

国际物流与运输展览会
2013/03/19-23
英国伯明翰Britain- Birmingham

俄罗斯建材展
2013/04
俄罗斯莫斯科Russia- Moscow

国际农业机械展览会
2013/04
巴西圣保罗Brazil- St.Paul

国际建材与工程机械博览会
2013/04
卡塔尔多哈Qatar- Doha

德国汉诺威工业博览会
HANNOVER MESSE
2013/04/08-12
德国汉诺威Germany- Hanover

中东迪拜国际五金工具博览会
Hardware & Tools
2013/05
阿联酋迪拜UAE- Dubai

德国科隆木工机械展
INTERZUM
2013/05
德国科隆Germany- Koln

美国国际五金制品及花园用品博览会
NHS
2013/05/07-09
美国拉斯维加斯USA- Las Vegas

国际矿业机械展览会
2013/05/14-16
俄罗斯莫斯科Russia- Moscow

国际工程机械作业展览会
2013/05/14-16
英国伯明翰Britain- Birmingham

"国际工程机械、矿山机械、建材机械及建筑材料展览会(自办展)"
2013/05/29-01
印度尼西亚雅加达Indonesia- Djakarta

国际建筑及工程机械展览会
2013/06
俄罗斯莫斯科Russia- Moscow

国际工程技术与设备展览会
2013/06/05-08
巴西圣保罗Brazil- St.Paul

国际贸易博览会
2013/07/17-22
安哥拉罗安达Angola-Luanda

国际矿业机械及工程机械展览会
2013/08
巴西贝洛Brazil- Belo

亚太国际矿业展览会
2013/08/20-23
澳大利亚悉尼Australia- Sydney

国际矿业展览会
2013/09
秘鲁阿雷基帕Peru- Arequipa

国际工程机械及矿业展览会
2013/09
哈萨克斯坦阿拉木图Kazakhstan- Alma-Ata

国际工程机械与建材展览会
2013/09
伊拉克埃尔比勒Iraq- Erbil

国际建筑机械、建材机械、矿山机械及工程车辆博览会
2013/09/18-21
南非约翰内斯堡South Africa- Johannesburg

国际工程机械、矿山机械和矿业展览会
2013/09/19-21
蒙古乌兰巴托Mongolia- Ulan Bator

国际工程及施工设备展览会
2013/11
阿尔及利亚阿尔及尔Algeria- Algiers

国际工程机械与技术展览会
2013/11
印度班加罗尔India- Bangalore

国际工程建筑机械与工程车辆展览会
2013/11
沙特利雅得Saudi Arabia- Riyadh

国际工程、建材机械、工程车辆及设备展览会
2013/12
越南胡志明市Vietnam- Ho Chi Minh City

国际工程、建材机械、工程车辆及设备展览会
2013/12
越南胡志明市Vietnam- Ho Chi Minh City
交通、运输、物流、铁路、仓储
Transportation &Logistics &Storage

巴黎国际实时运输及物流展
SITL Real Time: International Show for Logistics Solutions
2013/03
法国France

专业运输及材料装卸展
LogisPro Thailand
2013/05/16-19
泰国曼谷Thailand-Bangkok

荷兰国际运输及物流展
Holland Transport & Logistics Show
2013/09
荷兰Netherlands

巴西国际交通展览会
Fenatran: International Transport Industry Trade Show
2013/10
巴西Brazil

金属加工、冶金、铸造锻造
Metalworking, Metallurgy&Foundry

迪拜国际铝工业展
Gateway to the Middle East\'s Aluminium Industry
2013/04/23-25
阿联酋UAE

亚洲金属板材展
Sheet Metal Asia
2013/05/16-19
泰国曼谷Thailand-Bangkok

越南国际金属加工设备及技术展览会
Metaltech - Vietnam
2013/06/18-20
越南Vietnam

越南国际金属加工机械及技术展览会
Metaltech - Vietnam
2013/07/18-20
越南Vietnam

酒店业
Hote&Restaurant

摩洛哥酒店用品展
Marocotel: Intl show of professional equipment for hotels & catering
2014/03
澳大利亚Australia

空调、制冷、供暖
Air-conditioning, Heating, Refrigeration &Ventilation

“RAHV 2013” - 越南国际制冷、空调、供暖、通风系统展览会
“RAHV 2013” - International Exhibition on Refrigeration, Air-conditioning, Heating & Ventilation Systems
2013/06/18-20
越南Vietnam

“RAHV 2013” - 越南国际制冷、空调、供暖、通风系统展览会
“RAHV 2013” - International Exhibition on Refrigeration, Air-conditioning, Heating & Ventilation Systems
2013/07/18-20
越南Vietnam

巴西国际制冷、空调、通风、供暖和空气处理贸易展
Febrava: International Refrigeration, Air-conditioning, Ventilation, Heating and Air Treatment Trade Fair
2013/09
巴西Brazil

矿业
Mining

悉尼亚太国际矿业展
AIMEX: Asia Pacific's International Mining Exhibition
2015/09
澳大利亚Australia

零售业
Retail and Marketing

客户服务中心/客户关系管理展览会及会议
Call Centre/CRM Demo & Conference Tokyo
2013/11/14-15
日本东京Japan-Tokyo

美容美发、化妆品、
Cosmetics,Hairdressing

2013年第18届中东迪拜国际美容、美发展览会
2013/05/28-30
阿联酋迪拜UAE-Dubai

日本水疗及健康展
Spa & Wellness Japan
2013/09/09-11
日本东京Japan-Tokyo

能源、节能
Energy &Energy-Saving

阿布扎比世界未来能源峰会暨新能源与环保展览会
World Future Energy Summit (WFES)
2013/01
阿联酋UAE

俄罗斯暖通、制冷、空调、卫浴及水池设备展览会
Aqua-Therm Moscow: International Exhibition for HVAC Sector & Pools
2013/02
俄罗斯Russia

日本国际二次电池展
Battery Japan
2013/03
日本Japan

东京国际光伏发电展览会
PV EXPO: International Photovoltaic Power Generation Expo
2013/03
日本Japan

2013德国柏林国际线圈、电机、绝缘材料及电器制造展
CWIEME
2013/06/04-06
德国柏林Germany- Berlin

亚洲再生能源展
Renewable Energy Asia
2013/06/05-08
泰国曼谷Thailand-Bangkok

农业、林业、畜牧业、渔业、花卉 Agriculture, Animal Husbandary, Fishery&Forestry

奥地利国际木材加工、处理、装配、木匠用品展
BWS: International Trade Fair for Woodworking
2013/03
奥地利Austria

英国伯明翰国际花五金工具及园艺展
GLEE
2013/09
英国伯明翰Britain- Birmingham

汽车、摩托车 Automobile &Motorcycles

奥地利国际汽车生产设备及加油站设备、化学品及环境技术展
Auto Zum: International Trade Fair for the Car & Vehicle Industry
2013/01/16-19
奥地利Austria

国际汽车及零配件展览会
2013/01/21-25
埃及开罗Egypt- Cairo

国际汽车零部件及售后服务展览会
2013/02/07-10
印度新德里India- New Delhi

伊比利亚国际汽车零部件、设备及售后服务展览会
2013/03/13-16
西班牙马德里Spain- Madrid

国际汽车配件及售后服务博览会
2013/04/11-13
澳大利亚墨尔本Australia- Melbourne

国际汽车零部件及售后服务展览会
2013/04/11-14
土耳其伊斯坦布尔Turkey- Istanbul

国际汽车零部件展览会
2013/04/16-20
巴西圣保罗Brazil- St.Paul

国际汽车零配件及售后服务展览会
2013/05
阿联酋迪拜UAE- Dubai

国际汽车零部件及售后服务展览会
2013/05/08-11
南非约翰内斯堡South Africa- Johannesburg

国际汽车生产及配件展览会
Automotive Engineering Asia
2013/05/16-19
泰国曼谷Thailand-Bangkok

国际汽车零部件、原料加工及售后服务贸易展览会
2013/07
墨西哥墨西哥城Mexico- Mexico City

国际汽车零部件展览会
2013/08
俄罗斯莫斯科Russia- Moscow

国际电力电工设备及技术展览会
2013/10
伊朗德黑兰Iran- Teheran

巴西国际两轮车展览会
Salão Duas Rodas: Intl Motorcycle, Bicycle, Parts & Equipment Show
2013/10
巴西Brazil

国际汽车零配件展览会
2013/10
法国巴黎France- Paris

国际汽车零部件展览会
2013/11
美国拉斯维加斯USA- Las Vegas

国际汽车工业及配件展览会
2013/11
土耳其伊斯坦布尔Turkey- Istanbul

国际汽车零配件展览会
2013/11
伊朗德黑兰Iran- Teheran

国际汽车制造机械及零配件展览会
2013/12
印度尼西亚雅加达Indonesia- Djakarta

石油、燃气 Petroleum,Petrochemicals

阿布扎比世界未来能源峰会暨新能源与环保展览会
World Future Energy Summit (WFES)
2013/01
阿联酋UAE

俄罗斯暖通、制冷、空调、卫浴及水池设备展览会
Aqua-Therm Moscow: International Exhibition for HVAC Sector & Pools
2013/02
俄罗斯Russia

日本国际二次电池展
Battery Japan
2013/03
日本Japan

国际石油、天然气展览会
2013/05
美国休斯顿USA-Houston

国际石油、天然气展览会
2013/06
俄罗斯莫斯科Russia-Moscow

巴西国际海洋石油及天然气工业设备展览会
Brazil Offshore: International Offshore Oil and Gas Industry Trade Show and Conference
2013/06/11-14
巴西Brazil

英国石油工业技术展
SPE Offshore Europe: Oil & Gas Exhibition & Conference
2013/09/03-06
英国Britain

国际石油、天然气展览会
2013/10/06-08
阿联酋迪拜UAE-Dubai

食品、咖啡、酒、饮料及相关机械 Food, Beverage, Spirit&Processing

科隆国际糖果原料和机械展览会
ProSweets Cologne 2010
2013/01/27-30
德国Germany

科隆国际糖果及休闲食品展
ISM- international Sweets and Biscuits Fair
2013/01/27-30
德国Germany

英国食品、饮料包装机械、设备展览会
Pro2Pac : Processing & Packaging Solutions Event, Exclusively for the Food & Drink Industry
2013/03
英国Britain

英国国际食品与饮料展
IFE: Intl Food and Drink Exhibition
2013/03/17-20
英国Britain

英国食品、饮料包装机械、设备展览会
Pro2Pac: Processing & Packaging Solutions for the Food & Drink Industry
2013/03/17-20
英国Britain

日本美食佳酿暨酒店及餐饮设备展
Wine & Gourmet Japan
2013/04/03-05
日本东京Japan-Tokyo

里斯本国际食品展
Alimentaria Lisboa : International Food & Beverage Exhibition
2013/04/14-17
葡萄牙Portugal

加拿大国际食品展览会
SIAL Canada
2013/05/09-11
加拿大蒙特利尔Canada-Montreal

世界清真食品博览会
World of Halal
2013/05/22-26
泰国Thailand

亚洲世界食品博览会
Thaifex - World of Food Asia
2013/05/22-26
泰国Thailand

世界清真食品博览会
World of Halal
2013/05/22-26
泰国Thailand

亚洲世界食品博览会
Thaifex - World of Food Asia
2013/05/22-26
泰国Thailand

巴西国际食品博览会
SIAL Brazil
2013/06/25-28
巴西圣保罗Brazil-St.Paul

菲律宾食品配料展
Food Ingredients Philippines
2013/06/26-28
菲律宾马尼拉Philippines-Manila

美国夏季国际优质食品及糖果展览会
Summer Fancy Food Show
2013/07
美国华盛顿USA-Washington

越南国际食品包装机械及技术展览会
Foodpack - Vietnam
2013/07/18-20
越南Vietnam

亚洲食品配料展
Food Ingredients Asia
2013/09/11-13
泰国曼谷Thailand-Bangkok

印度食品配料展
Food Ingredients India
2013/10/03-05
印度孟买India-Mumbai

世界食品博览会
Anuga
2013/10/05-19
德国科隆Germany-Koln

日本健康食品原料展 / 安全及技术展
Health Ingredients Japan / Safety and Technology Japan
2013/10/09-11
日本东京Japan-Tokyo

印度国际甜食和休闲食品加工展览会
Sweet & Snack India
2013/12/10-12
印度India

印度国际奶制品加工展览会
Dairy Universe India
2013/12/10-12
印度India
摄影、影像
Photography &Image

美国国际电子消费展览会暨美国国际影像协会PMA影像展
（PMA@CES）
2013/01/08-13
美国拉斯维加斯USA-Las Vegas

世界影像博览会
photokina
2014/09/16-21
德国科隆Germany-Koln

水
Water

泰国国际水工程大展暨论坛
Thai Water
2013/06/05-08
泰国曼谷Thailand-Bangkok

越南国际水工程大展暨论坛
VIETWATER
2013/10/16-18
越南胡志明市Vietnam-Ho Chi Minh City

塑料、橡胶
Plastics & Rubbers

巴西国际塑料机械展览会
BrasilPlast: Intl Plastic Industry Trade Fair
2013/04/08-12
巴西Brazil

越南国际轮胎和橡胶展
RUBBER+TIRE VIETNAM
2013/04/11-13
越南胡志明市Vietnam- Ho Chi Minh City

俄罗斯国际橡胶和轮胎展
TIRES AND RUBBER
2013/04/23-26
俄罗斯莫斯科Russia- Moscow

越南国际塑胶机械及技术展览会
Vietnam Plastic Fair
2013/06/18-20
越南Vietnam

越南国际塑胶机械及技术展览会
Vietnam Plastic Fair
2013/07/18-20
越南Vietnam

体育、休闲
Sports and Leisure

美国职业高尔夫球协会高尔夫用品展
PGA Merchandise Show
2013/01
美国USA

美国拉斯维加斯射击、狩猎、户外用品展览会
SHOT SHOW
2013/01/17-20
美国拉斯维加斯USA-Las Vegas

科隆亚太采购交易会—五金、家居、家电、园艺产品
Asia Pacific Sourcing
2013/03/03-05
德国Germany

中东（迪拜）国际园艺及 户外休闲用品展览会
2013/05
阿联酋迪拜UAE-Dubai

中东渔具、狩猎及户外用品展
2013/09
阿联酋阿布扎比UAE-Abu Dhabi

日本东京国际庭院园艺及户外家具展览会
GARDEX
2013/10
日本东京Japan-Tokyo

美国路易斯维尔园林机械展览会
GIE+EXPO
2013/10
美国路易斯维尔USA-Louisville

巴西国际两轮车展览会
Salão Duas Rodas: Intl Motorcycle, Bicycle, Parts & Equipment Show
2013/10
巴西Brazil

国际休闲、体育设施及泳池设备展
FSB - the International Trade Fair for Amenity Areas, Sports and Pool Facilities
2013/10/22-25
德国科隆Germany-Koln

国际桑拿及泳池设备展
Aquanale
2013/10/22-25
德国科隆Germany-Koln

文具、办公用品
Stationery and Office Products

沙特建材展
2013/10
沙特利雅得Saudi Arabia- Riyadh

五金、工具
Hardware and Tools

国际管材展览会
2013/01
阿联酋迪拜UAE-Dubai

科隆亚太采购交易会—五金、家居、家电、园艺产品
Asia Pacific Sourcing
2013/03/03-05
德国Germany

西班牙毕尔巴鄂国际五金展
2013/03/12-15
西班牙毕尔巴鄂Spain- Bilbao

法兰克福暖通卫浴展
ISH
2013/03/12-16
德国法兰克福Germany- Frankfurt

俄罗斯建材展
2013/04
俄罗斯莫斯科Russia- Moscow

德国汉诺威工业博览会
HANNOVER MESSE
2013/04/08-12
德国汉诺威Germany- Hanover

德国科隆木工机械展
INTERZUM
2013/05
德国科隆Germany- Koln

美国国际五金制品及花园用品博览会
NHS
2013/05/07-09
美国拉斯维加斯USA- Las Vegas

中东迪拜国际五金工具博览会
Hardware & Tools
2013/05
阿联酋迪拜UAE- Dubai

澳大利亚建材展
DESIGN BUILD EXPO
2013/06
澳大利亚悉尼Australia- Sydney

日本国际五金及DIY展
JAPAN DIY SHOW
2013/08
日本东京Japan- Tokyo

墨西哥国际五金展
EXPO NACIONAL FERRETERA
2013/09
墨西哥瓜达拉哈拉Mexico- Guadalajara

莫斯科国际五金工具博览会
2013/11
俄罗斯莫斯科Russia- Moscow

日本东京国际建材展
JAPAN HOME AND BUILDING SHOW
2013/11
日本东京Japan- Tokyo

印度国际五金工具展
2013/12
印度孟买India- Bombay

科隆国际五金博览会
INTERNATIONAL HARDWARE FAIR COLOGNE
2014/03/09-12
德国科隆Germany-Koln

消费品、家居
Consumer Goods, Houseware

科隆亚太采购交易会—五金、家居、家电、园艺产品
Asia Pacific Sourcing
2013/03/03-05
德国Germany

西班牙毕尔巴鄂国际五金工具展
Ferroforma
2013/03/12-15
西班牙毕尔巴鄂Spain-Bilbao

鞋、皮革
Shoes &Leather

越南国际自动化展览会
Automation – Vietnam
2013/06/18-20
越南Vietnam

越南国际食品包装机械及技术展览会
Foodpack - Vietnam
2013/06/18-20
越南Vietnam

越南国际鞋类、皮革制成品展览会
International Footwear & Leather Products Exhibition – Vietnam (IFLE – VIETNAM 2013)
2013/07/11-13
越南Vietnam

越南国际鞋类、皮革制成品展览会
International Footwear & Leather Products Exhibition – Vietnam (IFLE – VIETNAM 2012)
2013/07/18-20
越南Vietnam

越南国际鞋类、皮革及工业设备展览会
International Shoes & Leather Exhibition – Vietnam (SHOES & LEATHER – VIETNAM 2013)
2013/07/18-20
越南Vietnam

信息技术、通信技术
Information Technology & Communication Technology

科隆教育与培训展览会
Didacta
2013/03/06-09
德国科隆Germany-Koln

数码营销博览会
dmexco
2013/09/18-19
德国科隆Germany-Koln

国际博物馆及展示技术博览会
EXPONATEC COLOGNE
2013/11/20-22
德国Germany

客户服务中心/客户关系管理展览会及会议
Call Centre/CRM Demo & Conference Tokyo
2013/11/14-15
日本东京Japan-Tokyo

医药、医疗设备、保健、生物
Medical Equipment Pharmaceuticals &Health Care

综合医疗展及会议
Integrated Medicine Exhibition & Conference
2013/02/19-20
日本Japan

科隆国际牙科展
IDS-International Dental Show
2013/03/12-16
德国Germany

东京健康博览会
Tokyo Health Industry Show
2013/03/13-15
日本Japan

世界制药机械、设备与材料东南亚展
CPhI South East Asia
2013/03/20-22
印度尼西亚雅加达Indonesia-Jakarta

国际合同定制服务日本展
ICSE Japan
2013/04/24-26
日本京东Japan-Tokyo

制药业生物解决方案日本展
CPhI Japan
2013/04/24-26
日本京东Japan-Tokyo

日本国际医疗设备设计与技术展览会
Medtec Japan
2013/04/24-25
日本东京Japan-Tokyo

世界制药机械、设备与材料日本展
P-MEC Japan
2013/04/24-26
日本东京Japan-Tokyo

艺术
Arts

法国戛纳音乐节
MIDEM: The World's Music Market
2013/01
法国France

科隆国际艺术展
ART COLOGNE
2013/04/18-22
德国科隆Germany-Koln

印刷
Printing

2013年第十届中东（迪拜）国际包装、印刷机械展览会
Gulf Pack & Print 2013
2013/04/08-11
阿联酋迪拜UAE- Dubai

2013年第十届中东（迪拜）国际包装、印刷机械展览会
Gulf Pack & Print 2013
2013/04/08-11
阿联酋迪拜UAE- Dubai

越南国际印刷、包装机械设备及技术展览会
Print & Pack – Vietnam
2013/06/18-20
越南Vietnam

越南国际印刷、包装机械设备及技术展览会
Print & Pack – Vietnam
2013/07/18-20
越南Vietnam

纸业
Paper

法国尼斯卫生纸业展览会
2013/03/18-21
法国France

越南国际造纸展
PAPER VIETNAM
2013/06/06-08
越南河内Vietnam- Hanoi

巴西国际造纸展
ABTCP-TAPPI
2013/10
巴西圣保罗Brazil- St.Paul

印度国际造纸展
Paperex
2013/10/24-27
印度新德里India- New Delhi

珠宝
Jewelry

巴黎国际服装、珠宝、银饰及配件展览会
Eclat de Mode / Bijorhca Paris: The Fashion side of Jewellery. Bi-annual International Trade Show
2013/01
法国France

东京国际珠宝展
IJT : International Jewellery Tokyo
2013/01
日本Japan

伊斯坦堡珠宝展-三月展
ISTANBUL JEWELRY SHOW - March
2013/03/21-24
土耳其伊斯坦堡Turkey-Istanbul

海德拉巴珠宝珍珠玉石展览会
Hyderabad Jewellery, Pearl & Gem Fair
2013/06/07-09
印度海德拉巴India-Hyderabad

2013年美国拉斯维加斯国际美容美发展览会
2013/07/22-24
拉斯维加斯USA-Las Vegas

伊斯坦堡珠宝展-十月展
Istanbul Jewelry Show - October
2013/10/03-06
土耳其伊斯坦堡Turkey-Istanbul

自行车
Bikes

巴西国际两轮车展览会
Salão Duas Rodas: Intl Motorcycle, Bicycle, Parts & Equipment Show
2013/10
巴西Brazil

居室
Habitable room

科隆亚太采购交易会—五金、家居、家电、园艺产品
Asia Pacific Sourcing
2013/03/03-05
德国Germany

管道
Pipeline

亚洲水泵及阀门展
Pumps & Valves Asia
2013/06/05-08
泰国曼谷Thailand-Bangkok

婴幼儿用品
Products for babies

国际少儿用品展览会
Kind und Jugend
2013/09/19-22
德国科隆Germany-Koln

园林与休闲
Gardens&Recreation

其它
Others

印度NGO展
NGO India
2013/06/14-15
印度孟买India-Mumbai

巴黎国际殡葬展
Fun é raire Paris 2011 : The Exhibition for Funeral Suppliers & Distributors
2013/11
法国巴黎France-Paris

行业先锋
展览会议组织与管理

亚洲博闻

亚洲博闻有限公司隶属於伦敦股票交易所上市的博闻公司(UBM plc)。亚洲博闻总部设於香港，子公司遍布亚洲，包括在上海、杭州、广州及北京的博闻中国。集团拥有逾200项产业，涵盖商贸展会、会议、专业杂志、商业对商业或面对消费者的网站及网上虚拟会议及展会。亚洲博闻是亚洲首要的展会主办单位，也是中国和印度两大快速发展的市场之最大的商贸展会主办商。公司举办150个商贸展会、出版34本高质专业杂志，以及营运14个垂直网站，为来自全球逾1,000,000名参展商、买家、会议代表、广告商及读者提供高质素的会面商贸配对、即时市场动向、网上贸易网络、行业资讯中心及采购和市场推广平台。亚洲博闻的办事处遍布亚洲，东达日本，西至土耳其，在21个主要城市共有超过1,000名员工。

公司在中国的主要展览包括：
- 九月香港珠宝首饰展览会（香港)-全球最大型的珠宝展
- 中国国际家具展览会(上海)-世界三大家具展之一
- 中国国际海事技术学术会议和展览会(上海)
  -亚洲最大规模的海事展
- 上海国际儿童、婴儿、孕妇产品博览会(上海)
  -亚洲最大型的儿童、婴儿、孕妇产品展会
- 广东国际广告/LED展(广州)
  -全球广告行业 “奥斯卡” 年度盛会及全球最大LED产业盛会

香港总办事处：
香港湾仔港湾道26号华润大厦17楼
电话：+852 2827 6211
传真：+852 3749 7310
电邮：info-hk@ubm.com
网址：www.ubmasia.com

博闻(广州)展览有限公司
中国广州市流花路中国大酒店商业大厦1159-1164室 （邮编：510015)
电话：+ 86 20 8666 0158
传真：+ 86 20 8667 7120
电邮：info-china@ubm.com
网站：www.gz.ubmchina.com

亿百媒会展（上海）有限公司
中国上海市南京西路388号仙乐斯广场9楼（邮编:200003)
电话：+86 21 6157 7288
传真：+86 21 6157 7299
电邮：info-sh@ubm.com
网站：www.sh.ubmchina.com

杭州博贝广告有限公司
中国杭州市温州路69号南北商务港大厦2幢11楼（邮编:310015)
电话：+86 571 8839 5884
传真：+86 571 8838 8829
电邮：info-hz@ubm.com
网站：www.hz.ubmchina.com

博闻科媒信息技术咨询（北京）有限公司
北京市朝阳区建国路108号丰树大厦604室（邮编：100022)
电话：+ 86 10 879 51980
传真：+ 86 10 8795 1990
电邮：info-bj@ubm.com
网站：www.bj.ubmchina.com

上海博华国际展览有限公司
中国上海市襄阳南路218号现代大厦7-8楼（邮编：200031)
电话：+ 86 21 6437 1178
传真：+ 86 21 6437 0982
电邮：info@ubmsinoexpo.com
网站：www.ubmsinoexpo.com

广州闻信展览服务有限公司
中国广州市天河区林和东路华庭路4号富力天河商务大厦1306室（邮编：510015)
电话：+ 86 20 3810 6261
传真：+ 86 20 3810 6200
电邮：info-trust@ubm.com
网站：www.ubmtrust.com

显辉国际展览有限公司

显辉国际展览有限公司成立于1989年，是一家发展迅速、专业从事在中国及东南亚地区筹办各类形专业展览会和会议服务的公司。

自成立以来，本公司便专注于发展展览业务，致力筹办不同的工业展览会，展览题材范围主要包括 ： 鞋类、皮革及工业设备；医疗设备及技术；动漫画展；金属加工、塑料、印刷、食品包装的工业机械设备和技术；制冷、空调、供暖、通风及食品冷冻技术；建筑工程及建材设备；酒店、餐饮设备及服务；食品博览会；国际展销会和博览会等。

凭著已累积了20年的展览服务业经验，对亚洲各国和地区的市场动态充分了解、加上高效益的管理与营运，以及广阔的人脉网络，时至今天，我们每年所举办的国际大型展览会都已成为区内的触目盛事，部分的展览会更成为业内翘楚，亦是参展商及供应商推广业务的有效平台。 其中，在广州举办的“国际鞋类、皮革及工业设备展览会”已被誉为国内同类专业展中规模最大及最成功的国际展；还有在越南举办的工业机械展，包括“国际塑胶机械及技术展”；“国际金属加工设备及技术展”；“国际印刷、包装机械设备及技术展”；“国际食品包装机械设备及技术展”均在行内享有相当的美誉和地位。

为配合业务的迅速发展及日益频繁的商业活动需求，我们除了以香港作为总部外，亦早于公司成立之初在上海，广州，越南开设分公司，并在世界各国（包括中国大陆，台湾地区，日本，韩国，新加坡，巴基斯坦，澳大利亚，意大利，西班牙，德国等国家）建立代理服务网络，提供快捷和尽善尽美的服务。

显辉公司力求至臻，凭借广阔的人脉网络极富经验的管理层 ，具专业、富动力的员工团队，我们挚诚为世界各地的客户提供最全面的信息，最完善的服务。

地址：香港上环禧利街27号富辉商业中心2403室
电话：00852-2851 8603
传真：00852-2851 8637
电邮：topreput@hkabc.ne
网址：www.toprepute.com.hk

澳门贸易投资促进局
为您提供全方位的商业服务

作为澳门特别行政区促进贸易和投资的机构，我们的使命是：促进本地对外贸易及引进外资，推动澳门与世界各地之间经贸关系的发展，加强相互了解，发展友好合作。

具体来讲，我们提供以下服务：

对投资者的“一站式”服务

对于在澳门的投资计划，我们向投资者提供有专人跟进的“一站式”服务：接受咨询、评估项目、专责公证办理成立公司手续、指引投资程序及所需牌照／准照申請、寻找合作伙伴、跟进有关行政手续及其它协助以便落实投资项目。为了使此项服务更加便捷完善，本局内设“专责公证员”，并且也设立了由九个政府部门主管组成的“投资委员会”。

离岸服务

本局负责非金融离岸业务的审批、技术协助和监管工作，并通过推广活动促进非金融离岸业务在澳之发展。允许在澳门经营的离岸机构分为“离岸商业服务机构”和“离岸辅助服务机构”。政府向离岸商业活动提供多项税务优惠。离岸机构只需向本局繳付一次性的设立费，及每半年一次的运作费。

经贸推广活动

本局每年主办、协办及参与在澳门及全球各地举行的经贸会展和贸易投资合作活动，主要包括：澳门国际贸易投资展览会(MIF)、中国内地及葡语国家的大型经贸洽谈会，以及各地区的投资环境推介会等。同时，本局每年亦曾组织经贸代表团出外考察访问，并接待外地代表到访，促进澳门与海内外企业家的交流与合作。此外，本局对澳门企业参加世界各地的展览会提供多方面支持，包括资助部分的参展及宣传品印刷经费，提供全球多项展览会信息等。

澳门商务促进中心

“中心”的设立是为了让外來投资者在低成本及短时间內了解澳门的营商环境和办理有关行政手续，减低在澳经商的启动成本，并为本地的企业和商会提供一个直接与外地企业和商会交流与合作的服务平台。“中心”向企业提供：

设施设备－包括现代化办公室、洽谈室、产品展示区、电脑设备、无线宽频互联网。另设有收费多功能会议厅、影印及传真等商务设备。

商贸服务—包括“贸促局咨询服务专柜”、“内地商务咨询服务”、秘书服务，以及提供有关本地企业、驻“中心”商会、政府部门行政手续及本地统计资料。另外，尚有与商会合作举办商贸推介及交流活动等。

企业之间及企业与办事处互相交流的平台—“中心”有多间外地商会、团体、机构、组织代表处(统称：办事处)进驻，如“渝澳经济合作促进会澳门秘书处”、“世界华商组织联盟”、“葡中工商协会”、“国际葡语市场企业家商会”、“中国国际贸易促进委员会驻港澳代表处”、“澳门德国商会”、“澳洲商务署澳门办事处”、“欧洲咨询中心”、“澳门葡萄牙商务中心”、“澳门英国商会”及“日资商业服务中心(澳门)有限公司”。企业可向驻“中心”的办事处直接咨询。“中心”为企业及各驻场办事处提供了交流与合作的机会。

中小企服务中心

为加強本澳中小企业之综合竞争力，把握澳门经济发展所带来之商机，并按照澳门政府支持中小企业发展的政策，于澳门贸易投资促进局属下之“澳门商务促进中心”將推出一系列协助本地中小企业之服务，并设立“中小企服务中心”，目的是协助本地中小企开拓海外和本地市场，并结合海外及本地市场需求，促进企业交流合作，引导中小企把握澳门服务业及会展业所带來之商机。

咨询服务

为了推广澳门的经贸环境，向海内外商界提供最新的商贸讯息，本局定期出版“贸易投资快讯”和“澳门经济之窗”，也經常发行“投资者指南”及有关宣传性刊物及光碟。本局的网页是我们向公众提供资讯的。

主要途径：

除了关于澳门和本局的一般资料及主要刊物內容，还有本澳制造商和出口商的资料库以及免费的主商易站等一系列丰富及不断更新的资料，为用户提供在世界各地寻找贸易投资伙伴的机会。

资讯中心

资讯中心也是我们对外提供信息咨询服务的重要窗口之一。公众可以阅读、直接向服务人员或通过电脑查寻资料，并可借阅一些特定刊物。

资讯中心主要有以下的参考资料：

外国及本澳经贸方面的基本情况
本澳经贸政策与规例
本澳及海內外统计数据
本澳及海内外厂商名录

申请居留

在本澳作出有利于澳门特别行政区的重大投资计划或重大投资的权利人、或获本地雇主聘用的、其所具备的学历、专业资格及经验被视为特别有利于本澳的管理人员或具备特别资格的技术人员，均可透过本局的投资居留暨法律处申请本澳的临时居留许可。

地址：澳门友谊大马路918号世界贸易中心一至四楼
电话：853-28 710300
传真：853-28 590309, 710304
电邮：ipim@ipim.gov.mo
网址：www.ipim.gov.mo
24小时电话查询热线 853-28 881212

澳门贸易投资促进局
-商汇馆(Macao Ideas)

澳门「商汇馆」(Macao Ideas)，海内外采购商、代理商或有意引进澳门商品企业的一个最快捷搜罗澳门本地名优商品的采购目的地。

由澳门贸易投资促进局筹备及设置，统一向外宣传「澳门制造」、「澳门品牌」、「澳门设计」及「葡语国家代理产品」的长期商品展示中心。汇聚了近89间澳门企业的商品，包括衣饰、礼服、鞋、手袋、珠宝、食品、咖啡、茶、酒类、保健产品、药物、家具、工业用品、科技信息产品、电单车、眼镜、文化创意设计产品及手工艺制品等。

展馆更安排多位驻场工作人员，为到访之客商提供馆内展品及参展企业资料，更会向相关参展商转达有意洽谈合作企业的要求及意向，并协助邀约双方作面谈，促成贸易。

地址：澳门高美士街431号，旅游活动中心地下展厅
电话：00853 – 2870 0620，2870 2123
传真：00853 – 2870 0621
电邮：macaoideas@ipim.gov.mo
网址：macaoideas.ipim.gov.mo

香港贸易发展局

香港贸易发展局(香港贸发局)成立于1966年，是专责推广香港对外贸易的法定机构，服务对象包括以香港为基地的贸易商、制造商及服务业者。我们在世界各地设有40多个办事处，其中11个在中国内地，为有意开拓海外和内地市场的港商提供服务，同时致力推广香港作为全球企业与中国内地及亚洲经商的平台。

香港贸发局通过不同的服务，包括：贸易展览会、网上的贸易平台及产品杂志，把全世界数以百万计的买家及供货商联系起来。

香港贸发局每年在香港举办超过30个国际贸易展览会，其中10个是亚洲同类型展览中规模最大的，当中3个更是全球之冠。

香港贸发局的网站www.hktdc.com，广受全球商家欢迎，载有来自香港、中国内地及海外近100万名注册买家及12万名供货商的数据。用户可于网站搜寻超过8,000个产品类别，寻找所需的产品或服务，简单快捷。

香港贸发局出版的15本产品杂志及行业专刊，读者超过500万，遍及全球。我们每年又出版150份贸易研究报告、针对个别行业的快讯及商业通讯，提供有关香港、中国内地及海外市场的最新情报。

同时，香港贸发局为中小企业提供商贸配对服务，能为企业物色理想的合作伙伴。

香港贸发局每年举办超过160项研讨会、大型会议、工作坊及论坛，协助港商拓展新市场。此外，我们每年在世界各地举办约600项贸易推广活动，把香港的产品、服务及讯息传达给约10万名来自主要市场的商家，并在香港接待约600个访港贸易代表团。

香港贸发局与七个国家或地区，包括日本、美国、韩国、欧盟、英国、法国及台湾，成立了双边贸易协会。同时，香港贸发局亦担任「环球香港商业协会联盟」秘书处，通过遍及全球的香港商业协会，与世界各地建立连系。

有关香港贸发局的最新信息，请浏览：www.hktdc.com

上海里扬展览服务有限公司

2002年1月成立的里扬集团，下属公司分别有：（上海里扬展览服务有限公司、里扬展览（香港）有限公司、上海尼奥建筑装潢有限公司、韩国成都设计（株）。我们紧紧把握时代脉搏，凭借对现代展览、展示形式和内涵的深刻理解，逐渐发展成为具实力和影响力的综合型专业展览公司，是上海市会展行业协会、北京展览馆协会、上海展览展示工程协会、上海韩国商会的会员单位，同时也是韩国釜山国际展览馆上海办事处。公司的主要业务包括：主办、承办、合作举办大型国际展览会；组织出国展览；策划大型商务活动；展台搭建以及品牌产品专柜设计。

目前，公司每年自主举办"上海国际幼儿教育展"、中韩技术转移暨投资洽谈会、产业机器人高峰论坛，专业代理海外28个知名展览会，涉及的行业有建材、电子、教育、食品、IT、化妆品等，并参与400多场展会的特装设计和制作，与SAMSUNG、INTEL、MICROSOFT、GOODYEAR、HYUNDAI、HITACHI、SIEMENS、中国电信等众多国际知名企业建立了良好的合作关系，并吸引了一批韩国和中国优秀的展览技术人才。

上海里扬展览服务有限公司
上海市北京翟路1178号鑫达大厦408-419室
电话：021-5216 4991，5216 4992
传真：021-5218 9400

法国爱博西雅展览（北京）有限公司

爱博集团（EXPOSIUM）是世界最著名的展览公司之一，具有五十年主办展会的经验和专长，得到国际展览界的公认。

爱博集团目前举办115个展览会，其中11个展览会在法国以外的国家举办。爱博集团办展的领域包括：农牧业、工业设备、建筑、印刷、电子、电信、信息、信息技术、食品、食品加工、包装、销售、城市规划与生活环境、旅游等。

爱博集团积极推行国际发展战略，以自己的强势市场为依托，围绕农业，食品工业，公共工程以及物流运输等行业开发市场，并以有潜力的亚洲和拉美地区的新兴国家作为开拓重点。

2004年，爱博集团在北京建立了自己的展览公司（北京爱博西雅展览有限公司），在上海设有代表处。其任务是为在法国举办的展会组织各种宣传促进活动，同时和中国的行业机构或展览公司发展合作关系，积极在华开拓新的展览会业务。

SIAL法国国际食品和饮料展览会创建于1964年，每两年一届，迄今已有40多年的历史，现已成为世界第一品牌的食品专业展会。自2000年SIAL展移植中国以来，SIAL CHINA 中国国际食品和饮料展览会已成功举办了七届。SIAL CHINA展会秉承其母展-SIAL巴黎国际食品展国际性、专业性、贸易性的特点，以客户服务作为展会组织工作的中心，规模不断扩大，现已发展成为中国国际食品第一大展，是国内外食品厂商开拓中国大陆市场、亚洲市场和海外市场的不二选择，是您不容错过的贸易和合作交流平台。

法国爱博西雅展览（北京）有限公司
北京市朝外大街22号泛利大厦1605室
邮编：100020
电话：010-6588 6235, 8879
传真：010-6588 6233
电邮：info@sialchina.cn
网址：www.sialchina.cn

上海国际展览公司

上海市国际展览有限公司成立于1984年是全国首家国营企业专业从事国际来展的展览公司，现由上海世博（集团）有限公司与上海市国际贸易促进委员会共同投资；公司成立以来，已成功举办各类展览会近500个，展览面积近500万平方米；公司现为国际博览联盟（UFI）正式会员，举办的"中国国际模具技术和设备展览会"、"上海国际汽车工业展览会"和"中国国际染料工业暨有机颜料、纺织化学品展会"是国际博览联盟认证的展览会；在2005年会展行业协会首次试评的上海首批8个优质展览会中，本公司举办的5个展览会榜上有名；公司下属的一些投资和合资公司，提供从展览运输、展馆管理、展览搭建、广告业务、展品留购和会议会务等全方位的会展服务产业链。

地址：上海市延安中路841号东方海外大厦8楼
邮编：200040
电话：021-6279 2828
传真：021-6545 5124
网址：www.siec-ccpit.com
电邮：info@siec-ccpit.com

义乌中国小商品城展览有限公司

义乌中国小商品城展览有限公司创办于1998年，注册资金800万元，拥有60多人年轻化、高学历的专业团队，专门从事国内外展览组织业务，是历届中国义乌国际小商品博览会的唯一展务执行机构，也是UFI、IAEE的会员企业。

公司成立多年以来，先后承办过浙江旅交会、浙江农博会、全国百货会、全国化洗会、中国会展财富论坛等国家级、省级会展项目，并自主培育及合作开发了多个品牌展览项目，包括中国义乌文化产品交易博览会、中国国际五金电器博览会、义乌消费品出口交易会、中国国际旅游商品博览会、义乌国际针织及服装机械展、中国水晶及玻璃制品博览会、中国义乌国际森林产品博览会。其中，公司承办的义博会已跻身为广交会、华交会之后的中国第三大出口商品展，成为唯一经国务院批准的日用消费品类国际大型展会。同时，公司还积极走出去，拓展境外展会义乌，组织展商参加法兰克福、拉斯维加斯、伯明翰、马契夫、迪拜等境外知名展会，并取得部分境外知名展览会的出国组展权。

在中国经济新一轮发展的重要时期，我们将继续以“搭建会展平台，促进贸易机会”为宗旨，努力做好工业经济和商业经济的产业纽带。我们愿意在各界朋友的大力支持下，密切同行合作，提升企业服务，打造精英团队，逐步向国际一流的现代展览服务企业迈进。

地址：浙江省义乌市宾王路301号梅湖会展中心三楼
电话：0579-8541 5888
传真：0579-8541 5777
网址：www.yiwufairs.com

宁波雅卓展览服务有限公司

地址：宁波百丈东路650号贵都商务楼7楼
邮编：315040
电话：0574-2771 6625
传真：0574-8784 9306
电邮：younage@younage
网址 rwww.chinamaching.cn

晋江市展务有限公司

地址：福建省晋江市青阳外经贸大厦3楼
邮编：362200
电话：0595-8560 0609, 8530 3030
传真：0595-8567 4572
电邮：jif@cn-jif.com
网址：www.cn-jif.com

中国演艺设备技术协会

地址：北京市东城区安定门东大街28号雍和大厦东楼C座10层
邮编：100007
电话：010-8402 9994,6403 3098转ext201/203
传真：010-8401 0152
电邮：chen@palmexpo.com
网址：www.palmexpo.com

中国哈尔滨国际经济贸易洽谈会

地址：哈尔滨市南岗区美顺街35号
邮编：150090
电话：0451-8234 0100
传真：0451-8234 0226
电邮：chn@ichtf.com
网址：www.ichtf.com

中国机械工程学会及其焊接分会

地址：北京市海淀区莲花小区2-5-1607
邮编：100036
电话：010-6397 2404, 6398 2928
传真：010-6398 0554
电邮：Whj@cmes.org
网址：essen.cmes.org

中国贸促会轻工行业分会

地址：北京阜外大街乙22号
邮编：100833
电话：010-6839 6330
传真：010-6839 6422
电邮：ccpitsli@public3.bta.net.cn
网址：www.fi-c.com

行业先锋
展览设计与施工搭建

奥克坦姆集团大中华区 -奥克坦姆系统科技（苏州）有限公司

OCTANORM Vertriebs GmbH在中国投资成立了奥克坦姆系统科技（苏州）有限公司。德国产品素以其出色的品质、信誉和技术水准闻名于世。作为亚洲地区唯一一家工厂，奥克坦姆系统科技（苏州）有限公司秉承OCTANORM全球质量标准和享誉世界的德国技术以及服务理念，所有产品都依照最严格的德 国标准设计生产，以满足在全球化浪潮中日益增长的中国市场需要。

随着中国会展经济的不断高速发展，奥克坦姆在华业务日益扩大，为了进一步发挥奥克坦姆的全方位优势，将展览展示系统行业最优越的技术尽快地转化为中国用户有价值的解决方案，帮助用户更有成效地开展业务，增强竞争优势，降低交易成本，奥克坦姆先后在北京、上海等地设立了分公司及办事处。

奥克坦姆以先进的理念创造出美观环保的铝制系统产品。这些新颖的产品除了可以应用于展览行业外，在室内设计，展示，洁净室等方面也可以广泛使用。并且具有安装快捷、容易拆除，可以重复使用等显著优点，同时也非常方便运输和储存，并提供完善的技术咨询和服务。

奥克坦姆为您化繁为简，以系统实现美。

江苏省苏州工业园区星龙街428号苏春工业坊3A
电话：0512-6283 3338
电话：0512-6283 3332
传真：0512-6283 3330
邮箱：info@octanorm.cn
网址：www.octanorm.cn

上海里扬展览服务有限公司

2002年1月成立的里扬集团，下属公司分别有：（上海里扬展览服务有限公司、里扬展览（香港）有限公司、上海尼奥建筑装潢有限公司、韩国成都设计（株））。我们紧紧把握时代脉搏，凭借对现代展览、展示形式和内涵的深刻理解，逐渐发展成为具实力和影响力的综合型专业展览公司，是上海市会展行业协会、北京展览馆协会、上海展览展示工程协会、上海韩国商会的会员单位，同时也是韩国釜山国际展览馆上海办事处。公司的主要业务包括：主办、承办、合作举办大型国际展览会；组织出国展览；策划大型商务活动；展台搭建以及品牌产品专柜设计。

目前，公司每年自主举办“上海国际幼儿教育展”、中韩技术转移暨投资洽谈会、产业机器人高峰论坛，专业代理海外28个知名展览会，涉及的行业有建材、电子、教育、食品、IT、化妆品等，并参与400多场展会的特装设计和制作，与SAMSUNG、INTEL、MICROSOFT、GOODYEAR、HYUNDAI、HITACHI、SIEMENS、中国电信等众多国际知名企业建立了良好的合作关系，并吸引了一批韩国和中国优秀的展览技术人才。

上海里扬展览服务有限公司
上海市北京翟路1178号鑫达大厦408-419室
电话：021-5216 4991，5216 4992
传真：021-5218 9400

上海尼奥建筑装潢有限公司
电话：021-5216 4996，5216 4997

韩国釜山展览馆上海办事处
021-5216 4993，5216 4994

里扬展览（香港）有限公司
九龙旺角亚皆街113号2607室
电话；852-2384 2778
传真：852-2384 2778

行业先锋
展览会议中心

中国国际展览中心集团公司

中国国际展览中心集团公司（简称“中展集团”）是中国国际贸易促进委员会直属企业，中国展览馆协会理事长单位、国际展览业协会（UFI）成员和国际展览与项目协会（IAEE）成员。中展集团的业务范围涵盖场馆经营管理、国内外组展以及各种展览配套服务。

中国国际展览中心位于北京市朝阳区北三环东路6号，占地面积13.6万平方米，室内展馆面积6万多平方米。每年举办各类展会100多个，展出面积超过100万平方米。

2008年初开业运营的中国国际展览中心（新馆）位于北京顺义天竺空港城商务区，紧邻首都国际机场，第一期工程建筑面积24万平方米、室内展馆面积10万平方米。中国国际展览中心（新馆）是目前北京市规模最大、设施先进、功能完备的展览场馆。

电话：010-8460 0000
网址：www.ciec-expo.com

哈尔滨国际会展体育中心有限公司

哈尔滨国际会展体育中心是黑龙江省及哈尔滨市重点工程项目，由黑龙江省人民政府、哈尔滨市人民政府、哈尔滨工大集团股份有限公司、黑龙江省体育局共同投资建设。总占地面积63公顷，总建筑面积40万平方米，坐落在哈尔滨最具现代城市风范和魅力的经济技术开发区东北部，是全国唯一将会展、体育合二为一；会议、酒店互为一体；休闲、购物相辅相成；展览、洽谈有机结合、互补生辉的超大型综合性场馆，以其宏伟的气势、完美的设计和精良的设施成为哈尔滨市的城市标志。

经过六年多的运营，哈尔滨国际会展体育中心已经形成了强大的会展经济辐射力、体育经济冲击力、商业物流经济聚合力、休闲文化经济影响力。

依托黑龙江省对俄通路咽喉要道的独特地理位置优势，哈尔滨国际会展体育中心为促进国际对俄经济贸易发展发挥着重要平台作用，正逐步成为国际间日益频繁的经贸往来的重要舞台，并以蓬发昂扬的朝气向世界经济发展的大舞台迈进。

地址：哈尔滨市南岗区红旗大街301号
电话：0451-8227 8855
传真：0451-8227 8855
网址：www.hrbhuizhan.com

沈阳国际展览中心

沈阳国际展览中心（以下简称：中心）坐落于苏家屯区会展路9号，距市区12公里，距桃仙国际机场13公里。

项目总用地面积95.96万平方米，计划分两期建设。其中一期工程总建筑面积16.6万平方米，室内展览面积10.52万平方米，室外展览面积5万平方米，行政服务区面积2.2万平方米。展馆按照国际专业化水准进行设计和建设。每个展厅既可独立办展，又能通过内部连廊彼此连通，使展区浑然一体。

中心主体结构由8个单层、无柱、大跨度独立展厅组成，每厅面积1.32万平方米，可设625个国际标准展位。室内展馆由东西两侧各4个展厅组成，中间由双层连廊衔接，总体可容纳5000个国际标准展位，东、南、西、北面均设有观众登录厅，可举行各类礼仪活动。中心北广场可举行开幕式、庆典及大型公益活动。

中心设有1间1000人会议厅（内部可灵活分割），1间600人新闻发布厅，5间200人会议厅，6间50人会议室，3间贵宾会议室，4间洽谈室，可承接各种会议、会见、签约等活动，可为国内外客商和旅游人员提供住宿和餐饮服务。

地址：辽宁省沈阳市苏家屯区会展路9号
电话：024-8956 6755
传真：024-8956 6778
电邮：marketing@shenyang-expo.com
网址：www.shenyang-expo.com

广东现代国际展览中心

广东现代国际展览中心GDE，位于广东省东莞市厚街镇-著名的加工制造产业基地。室内展览面积为10 万平万米，室外广场面积为11万平方米；

引入ISO9000质量管理认证休系；一站式A+服务；

2003，2004年；分别获“会展综合服务最佳场馆、中国会展业最佳场馆”称号；

先后成为香港展览厅会议业协会海外成员、中国展览馆协会会员、2004年加人全球展览业协会(UFI)；

2010年会展信息：
广东（厚街）茶业博览会
第二十三届国际名家具（东莞）展览会

第十一届中国（东莞）国际纺织制衣工业技术展览会
第十一届中国（东莞）国际鞋机鞋材工业技术展览会
励华国际瓦楞展2010中国展/2010励华国际彩盒展
2010中国东莞国际鞋类、皮革制品、配件与生产技术展览会
第十九届华南(东莞)国际电子制造采购博览会
第十届东莞国际印刷造纸胶粘带及广告展览会
广东外商投资企业产品（内销）博览会
第二十四届国际名家具（东莞）展览会
第十五届国际集成电路研讨会暨展览会
2010中国东莞国际鞋类、皮革制品、配件与生产技术展览会
第十二届东莞国际模具展及金属加工展
第十二届东莞国际橡塑胶、包装、压铸和铸造展
2010第十届东莞嘉年华时尚生活用品购物节

地址：广东省东莞市厚街镇家具大道广东现代国际展览中心
邮编：523952
电话：0769-8598 1885
传真：0769-8590 9318
邮箱：Dickson@deexpo.com
网址：www.gdeexpo.com

澳门威尼斯人®酒店-会展中心

澳门威尼斯人®是您的最佳会展专业伙伴，为展览筹办者提供一站式支援服务。金光会展™提供总面积达75,000平方米的展览场地，另设有108间可灵活分割的多功能会议厅，配合首屈一指的硬件设施和专业的会展團队，助你成就每个出色活动。澳门威尼斯人拥有3,000间宽敞舒适的豪华套房、330间国际名店及30间寰宇食府，更有多项精彩的现场娱乐表演，各项设施配套，应有尽有，保证让您实现一个完美无暇的活动。此外，我们还可以助您与澳门政府联系，申请各项资助会展行业的补助计划。

详情登录：www.venetianmacao.com
电话：853-2882 8800

上海新国际博览中心

上海新国际博览中心(SNIEC)由上海陆家嘴(集团)有限公司、德国汉诺威展览公司、德国杜塞尔多夫展览公司、德国慕尼黑展览有限公司联合投资建造。

自2001年11月2日正式开业以来，上海新国际博览中心(SNIEC)已取得了快速的增长，每年举办约60余场知名展览会，并正吸引着越来越多的展会在此举行。位于上海浦东中国的商业中心，SNIEC凭借其方便的交通地理位置、单层无柱式为特点的展馆设施以及多种多样的现场服务，已博得世界的广泛关注。作为一个多功能的场馆，SNIEC也是举办各种社会、公司活动的理想场地。

目前，SNIEC拥有9个无柱展厅，面积达103,500平方米，室外展览面积100,000平方米。

SNIEC的全面扩建将于2010年完成，届时室内面积将达到200,000平方米，室外面积130,000平方米。SNIEC的扩建将进一步巩固其在中国市场的领导地位，并确保上海作为东亚地区会展中心的领导地位。

地址：上海市浦东新区龙阳路2345号
邮编：201204
电话：021-3876 0488
传真：021-6856 6089
网址：www.sniec.ne

郑州国际会展中心

郑州国际会展中心由郑州市人民政府投资建造，集会议、展览、商务、餐饮、娱乐演出和旅游观光为一体，功能齐备、设施一流的会展场馆，是郑州市的地标性建筑之一。

郑州国际会展中心由国际著名建筑设计大师黑川纪章规划设计，主体建筑由会议中心和展览中心两部分组成。2003年元月20日开工建设，2005年10月21日投入试运营。于2006年6月1日引入国际化管理，由中外合资的专业场地管理公司 — 郑州香港会展管理有限公司专责管理。

郑州国际会展中心占地面积68．6万平方米，建筑面积达22．68万平方米，其设施包括会议中心、展览中心、3.8万平方米的室外展场及4.5万平方米的室外停车场。

会议中心主体建筑共六层，建筑面积6.08万平方米。其中轩辕堂剧院式会议可容纳5000人，课桌式会议可容纳3,160人，10人台圆桌宴会可容纳1,660人；剧院式九鼎厅可容纳1,090人、大河厅、太室厅分别可容纳400人。另外，还有17个大中小型会议室、贵宾接待室和中餐厅、西餐厅、咖啡厅。轩辕堂、九鼎厅拥有8+1路同声传译系统，大河厅、太室厅拥有4+1路同声传译系统。

展览中心主体建筑两层，辅楼六层，建筑面积16.68万平方米。由两个展馆、68个会议室、餐饮间、洽谈间办公室及各类服务商店等组成。室内展览面积6.5万平方米，可设3,394个国际标准展位。一号展馆和二号展馆内均有推拉式活动隔断，可将每个展馆分隔成4个6,000平方米和2个4,500平方米的独立展厅。一号展馆层高14米，地面承重5吨/平方米；二号展馆层高17.6米，地面承重1.5吨/平方米。
地址：郑州市郑东新区商务内环路中央公园1号
网址：www.zzicec.com

亚洲国际博览馆

亚洲国际博览馆位处香港国际机场旁，坐拥完善的海陆空运输网络，交通四通八达，是香港首屈一指的展览及活动场馆，提供超过70,000平方米的可租用面积。

博览馆10个展览馆均采用单层地面无柱式的灵活设计，备有新世代的资讯及通讯科技服务，可独立或打通连接使用，切合不同类型展览活动的需要。自2005年年底开幕以来，已举行众多不同主题的大型国際展览及活动，当中包括：香港有史以来最大型的国际商贸展览暨会议—“国际电信联盟2006世界电信展”、2007年9月更首次举行由新加坡移师至香港的全球最大型民用航天及航空业务及产品展览会暨论壇—“亚洲国际航空展览会暨论坛”及每年4月及10月的“环球资源系列采购交易会”，均吸引大量海内外买家及参展商参与，足证博览馆提供一个有效的商贸平台促进中外贸易交流，让内地企业毋须远涉重洋便能有效地开拓全球市场，同时亦是外商进入中国市场的门槛，发挥双向跳板的作用。

除此之外，博览馆拥有香港规模最大的室内多用途场馆，可容纳多达 13,500 位观众，至今已举行了几十个国际级大型演唱会及会议。

地址：香港大屿山香港国际机场
电话：852-3606 8888
传真：852-3606 8889
电邮：info@asiaworld-expo.com
网址：www.asiaworld-expo.com

香港会议展览中心

位处香港心脏地带的会展中心，临近闻名中外的维多利亚港，于1988年开幕，于1997年及2009年先后完成了两次扩建工程，现时是一所占地广达306,000平方米的会议及展览设施，提供91,500平方米可租用面积，用作展览、大型会议、公司活动、文娱表演、讲座和宴会等用途，并以提供独有的便利和世界级服务而享誉国际。

会展中心曾赢得无数业内奖项，专业水准毋庸置疑。在2012年，会展中心更第九次荣获《亚太会议展览及旅游杂志》(CEI Asia Pacific Magazine) 的读者推选为「亚洲最佳会议及展览中心」。

会展中心座落于香港商业区的黄金地段，城中热点近在咫尺，不但毗邻两间国际级酒店，在短短数分钟的步行范围内亦有多间酒店供应超过6,000间客房。

每年，逾1,200项活动在会展中心举行，包括四项全球最大型的展览及七个亚洲最大型的展览和多项国际盛事，不仅为香港带来巨大的经济效益，更有助提升香港的国际形象。

会展中心于刚过去的2010-2011财政年度（即2010年7月至2011年6月）录得5,969,789访客人数，打破自1988年开始营运的记录，同时较前一年激增25%。这显着的增长受惠于活动更多元化的发展，从美食博览到艺术品及古董拍卖，医学会议到爵士音乐会等，形形色色。自过去23年营运以来，会展管理公司为共39,606 项于会展中心举行的活动提供服务，招待近7,000 万名买家、参展商、访客及嘉宾。

会展中心的业权由香港特区政府和香港贸易发展局共同拥有。而香港会议展览中心（管理）有限公司（简称「会展管理公司」）是一家专业私营的场地管理和营运公司，专责会展中心的日常营运。凭着多年举办大型展览和其他崭新活动的成功经验，会展管理公司的团队不断成功吸引新的主办机构和新的活动于会展中心举行。

地址：中国香港湾仔博览道一号
电话：852-2582 1111
电邮：info@hkcec.com
网址：www.hkcec.com

行业先锋

展览运输

全球国际货运有限公司

全球国际货运有限公司在全世界约有1500个办事处，55,000名员工。作为世界领先的综合物流服务供应商之一，全球货运能为您提供一系列物流和运输服务，包括：海运，空运和陆运，展览物品运输，移民搬迁运输，特殊项目运输以及为全球体育赛事提供物流服务。全球货运于1979年开始进军中国大陆，目前已在全中国拥有33家办事处和物流中心，4,300多名员工，可为您提供全方位的卓越的物流解决方案。

全球货运有限公司是德国铁路股份公司下属运输和物流子公司。SCHENKER中国被指定为2008年奥运会货运代理和清关服务供应商，并成功地为此世界体育盛事服务。

对于展览会相关的需求，Schenker公司专业的展览队伍会提供给您最适合的私人专属服务。凭借特别的物流平台，专业的解决方案，高等的运作效率，平等的服务态度，我们保证您可以在第一时间以自己的语言得到所需的服务，确保问题永远可以从您的利益角度进行协商解决，协助您在世界各地的展会上马到成功。

我们的优势：
•环球网络：1500个办事处，全球海陆空无缝服务
•现场服务：世界各大主要展览中心驻馆办公，德国15个展会城市均有驻馆
•自有资源：仓库，专业机械设备及特殊工具
•从业人员：经验丰富，高效，专业，灵活，多种语言服务

我们的服务：
•物流方案：私人专属，量身定做，按需出发
•呈送方式：海运，空运，陆运，火车运输，快件服务及海空联运
•货品承揽：展台材料，展览品，展会宣传材料，专业艺术品
•展品清关：与海关及商检部门无间隙沟通，保证展品在正确的时间出现在正确的位置
•展会现场：专业有素的现场督导，展前展中展后全程空箱存储相关服务，包装箱处理
•撤展相关：展览会闭幕后安排货物和设备退返原地，或续往下一个展览地点
•其他服务：展览品运输保险，展会期间安排座谈、会议及舞台所需之设备和物料

华南区－全球国际货运有限公司
香港湾仔港湾道26号华润大厦38楼
电话：852-2585 9688
传真：852-2824 0328
电邮：fairs.hk@schenker.com

华中区－全球国际货运代理（中国）有限公司
上海西藏中路268号来福士广场3802-3806室
邮编：200001
电话：021-6122 5888,2890 6226
传真：021-5292 5194,2890 6223
电邮：fairs.sha@schenker.com

华北区－全球国际货运代理（中国）有限公司北京分公司
北京顺义区天竺空港工业区天纬四街5号
邮编：101312
电话：010-8048 0099
传真：010-8048 0077
电邮：fairs.bjs@schenker.com

保昌展览搬运有限公司

在1987年成立的保昌展览搬运有限公司，「保昌展运」总部设于香港，面向中国以及全球庞大的展览物流市场，为展览业提供专业的货运服务，客户遍布世界各地。

保昌展运以精英团队和环球网络，致力为国际展览市场提供全方位的优质物流服务，以专业经验及优质服务备受业界认同。

目前「保昌展运」服务的范畴包括：在华展览会（中国和香港）、海外展览会（中国和香港以外的国家和地区）、大型汽车赛事以及贵重艺术品的物流方案。现时保昌每年为逾百个中外国际大型展览会指定的运输总代理，同时提供体育赛事以及贵重文物艺术品的物流全方案，以专业经验及优质服务备受国际市场认同。

二十多年来，保昌展运坚持提供高增值的服务，与客户并肩同行，博奕未来。

电话：852-2798 6628
传真：852-2796 5606
电邮：info.hkg@exhibition.baltrans.com
网址：www.baltrans-exhibition.com

北京分公司
电话：010-6561 4171
传真：010-6561 4170
电邮：info.bjs@exhibition.baltrans.com

上海分公司
电话：021-6228 1933
传真：021-6229 3933
电邮：info.sha@exhibition.baltrans.com

泛联展览物流香港有限公司

Agility Fairs & Events(泛联展览物流香港有限公司) 是业内公认的领先企业，可为客户在全球的交易会，博览会和贸易展会运输提供端到端的全方位管理服务。我们敬业的专业人员遍布亚太、中东、欧洲、非洲和美洲等地区各重要展会地点的办事处。我们是一间每年营业收入达60亿美元的上市公司，是业内公认的领先国际性企业，在全球100多个国家和地区内设有超过550家办事处，员工总数超过32,000人。

我们向展览会及项目组织者、推广者和参展商提供一站式的物流解决方案，确保所有展示用品及时、完好地抵达现场。我们的服务包括：

- 展品清关
- 为特殊展品获得政府许可/临时性进口
- 海运/空运/陆运服务
- 仓储和派送
- 展馆物流管理
- 现场派送及开箱
- 展品就位及拼装
- 包装、空箱存储及回运

泛联展览物流香港有限公司
香港湾仔洛克到33号中央广场福利商业中心29楼
电话：852-2866 2505
传真：852-2866 2421
电邮：fairs-china@agilitylogistics.com
网址：www.agilitylogistics.com

泛联展览物流香港有限公司
香港湾仔骆克道33号中央广场福利商业中心29楼
电话：852-2594 9233
联络人：曾浩婷小姐

泛联国际货运代理(上海)有限公司
上海市延安西路2299号上海世贸商城1606室
邮编：200336
电话：13911992219 / 021-6236 6060
联络人：张维聪先生

泛联国际货运代理(上海)有限公司 北京分公司
北京市朝阳区朝外大街22号泛利大厦 1211室
邮编 100020
电话：13911992219 / 010-6588 1961/1962/1963/1964
联络人：张维聪先生

泛联国际货运代理(上海)有限公司 广州分公司
中国广州市东风东路726号704/706室
邮编：510080
电话：020-37655886
联络人：叶岭阳先生

The Industry Leaders

Exhibition Management and Conference Planners

UBM Asia Limited

Owned by UBM plc listed on the London Stock Exchange, UBM Asia operates in 18 market sectors with headquarters in Hong Kong and subsidiary companies across Asia, including UBM China in Shanghai, Hangzhou, Guangzhou and Beijing. We have over 200 products including trade fairs, conferences, trade publications, B2B/B2C portals and virtual event services. As Asia's leading exhibition organiser and the biggest commercial organiser in the two fastest growing markets in Asia: China and India, we stage the leading events of their kind across Asia. Our 150 events, 34 publications and 14 vertical portals serve a 1,000,000 plus quality exhibitors, visitors, conference delegates, advertisers and subscribers from all over the world with high value face-to-face business-matching events, quality and instant news on market and industry trends and round-the-clock online trading networks and sourcing platforms. We have 1,000 staff in 21 major cities across Asia, stretching from Japan to Turkey.

Our leading events in China include:
September Hong Kong Jewellery & Gem Fair (Hong Kong)
–world's number one jewellery event
Furniture China (Shanghai)
–one of the biggest international furniture exhibitions in the world
Marintec China (Shanghai) – Asia's largest maritime event
Shanghai International Children-Baby-Maternity Products Expo (Shanghai)–the largest children, baby and maternity products fair in Asia
Sign/LED China (Guangzhou)
–China's definitive sign event and the world's largest LED event

Regional Head Office:
17/F China Resources Building
26 Harbour Road, Wanchai, Hong Kong
Tel: +852 2827 6211
Fax: +852 3749 7310
Email: info-hk@ubm.com
Website: www.ubmasia.com

UBM China (Guangzhou) Co Ltd
Room 1159 – 1164, China Hotel Office Tower, Liu Hua Lu
Guangzhou, 510015, P.R. China
Tel: + 86 20 8666 0158
Fax: + 86 20 8667 7120
Email: info-china@ubm.com
Website: www.gz.ubmchina.com

UBM China (Shanghai)
9/F CIROS Plaza, No. 338 West Nanjing Road
Shanghai 200003, China
Tel: +86 21 6157 7288
Fax: +86 21 6157 7299
Email: info-sh@ubm.com
Website: www.sh.ubmchina.com

UBM China (Hangzhou)
11th Floor, No.2 Building, Mansion Commerce Plaza
69 Wenzhou Road, Hangzhou 310015, China
Tel: +86 571 8839 5884
Fax: +86 571 8838 8829
Email: info-hz@ubm.com
Website: www.hz.ubmchina.com

UBM China (Beijing)
Room 604, Mapletree Tower, 108 Jianguo Road
Chaoyang District, Beijing 100022, China
Tel: + 86 10 879 51980
Fax: + 86 10 8795 1990
Email: info-bj@ubm.com
Website: www.bj.ubmchina.com

Shanghai UBM Sinoexpo International Exhibition Co Ltd
7&8/F, Xian Dai Mansion, 218 Xiang Yang Road (S)
Shanghai 200031, P.R. China
Tel: + 86 21 6437 1178
Fax: + 86 21 6437 0982
Email: info@ubmsinoexpo.com
Website: www.ubmsinoexpo.com

UBM Trust Co Ltd
Room 1306, Fu Li Tian He Business Mansion
No. 4, Hua Ting Road, Lin He Dong Road
Guangzhou 510610, China
Tel: + 86 20 3810 6261
Fax: + 86 20 3810 6200
Email: info-trust@ubm.com
Website: www.ubmtrust.com

Hong Kong Trade Development Council

Established in 1966, the Hong Kong Trade Development Council (HKTDC) is a statutory organisation with a mission to create business opportunities for Hong Kong companies. We are the international marketing arm for Hong Kong-based traders, manufacturers and service providers. With more than 40 global offices, including 11 on the Chinese mainland, the HKTDC promotes Hong Kong as a platform for doing business with China and throughout Asia. The HKTDC connects millions of international buyers and sellers through a variety of integrated services, namely its trade fairs, online marketplace and product magazines.

One of the world's major trade fair organisers, the HKTDC holds more than 30 international trade fairs annually in Hong Kong. Ten of these are the biggest of their kind in Asia, and three are the largest in the world. The HKTDC website, www.hktdc.com, features nearly one million registered buyers and 120,000 suppliers from Hong Kong, the Chinese mainland and beyond. Users can browse through nearly 8,000 clearly defined product categories to find products and services quickly and efficiently. With 15 product magazines and industry supplements and more than five million readers around the world, the HKTDC is a major publisher. The HKTDC also produces about 150 trade reports, sector-specific updates and business newsletters a year, providing timely market intelligence on Hong Kong, the Chinese mainland and international markets. Supporting these services is HKTDC Business Matching, which helps companies find the right partners. The HKTDC also produces more than 160 seminars, conferences, workshops and forums a year to help Hong Kong companies develop new markets for their products and services. As well, it organises about 600 Hong Kong promotional events around the world, reaching nearly 100,000 business people in key markets each year, and receives about 600 international business missions a year. The HKTDC's international reach is reflected in the seven bilateral committees it serves. These high-level business forums promote economic ties between Hong Kong and Japan, the United States, Korea, the European Union, the United Kingdom, France and Taiwan. The HKTDC also serves as Secretariat for the Federation of Hong Kong Business Associations Worldwide.

For more information about the HKTDC, visit www.hktdc.com.

Tel: 852-1830 668
Fax: 852-2824 0249
E-mail: hktdc@tdc.org.hk
www.hktdc.com

Top Repute Company Limited

Top Repute Company Limited, established in 1989, is a rapid growing professional exhibition and conference organizer based in Hong Kong. We expertise in organizing international exhibitions, conferences and events in Mainland China and South East Asia.

Our business scope covers Mainland China and South East Asia markets. Every year, we organize numerous of large-scale international exhibitions in Shanghai, Guangzhou, Vietnam and Cambodia such as: "Shoes & Leather", "Medical Equipment & Technology", "Metalworking & Industrial Machinery", "Rubber & Plastics", "Print & Pack","Food Packaging Machinery & Technology", "Construction, Building Industry & Materials", "Refrigeration, Air-conditioning, Heating & Ventilation System", and "International Trade Fair" etc.

With over 20 years of experience and expertise in the exhibition industry, we have maintained good contacts and have a wide consultancy network with the related industry. We have organised numerous leading events each year, such as the largest and most reputable fairs in China, "Shoes & Leather - Guangzhou" and "Medical - Shanghai" as well as the "International Industrial Machinery Exhibition (IIME)" in Vietnam. All our exhibitions have already gained international reputations in their respective fields of industry.

Whether you plan to tap into new markets, expand existing markets, or enhance your corporate communication, Top Repute Company Limited is always your reliable working partner. We and our well-trained energetic staff will, at all times, assure the best services to our worldwide clients.

Add: Room 2403, Fu Fai Commercial Centre, 27 Hillier Street, Sheung Wan, Hong Kong
Tel: 852-2851 8603
Fax: 852-2851 8637
E-mail: topreput@top-repute.com
Web: www.toprepute.com.hk

Shanghai Neon Exhibition Ltd

Neon Group was established in January, 2001, and it has subsidiaries: Shanghai Neon Exhibition Ltd, Neon Exhibition (Hong Kong) Ltd, Shanghai Neon Construction & Decorate Ltd, Korea Chengdu Design Ltd. With our understanding of trends in the industry and modern exhibition forms, we are growing to be a comprehensive and professional exhibition enterprise. We are a member of Shanghai Convention & Exhibition Industries Association,Beijing Exhibition Center. Meanwhile, we are the Shanghai office of Busan Exhibition and Convention Center. Our services include: organizing, undertaking and co-organizing large scale international exhibitions; organizing exhibitors and visitors to participate overseas exhibitions; planning business activities; booth construction and showcase design. At present, we are the organizer of Kids Education Expo Shanghai, the overseas agent of 28 well-known exhibitions, and we take part in the design and construction of special stands for about 400 exhibitions.We establish cooperating relations with many famous international enterprises, such as SAMSUNG, INTEL, MICROSOFT, GOODYEAR, Hyundai Motor, HITACHI, SIEMENS, China Telecommunication and so on. As a result, Neon appeal to many talents from China and Korea.

Tel: 021-5216 4991, 5216 4992
Fax: 021-5218 9400

Macao Trade and Investment Promotion Institute

Always at Your Service

As the trade and investment promotion institute in Macau, IPIM's mission is to promote Macau's externaltrade and attract investment, to develop and strengthen economic and trade relationship between Macao and other parts of the world.

One-Stop Service

IPIM provides a personal service "One-Stop Service" for investors, including information enquiries, project assessment, company registration assistance by our notary, guidance on administrative application procedures for licenses, looking for partnership, project follow-up, and assistance in the implementation project. In order to facilitate this service, an independent notary and an investment committee, compose of senior officials from nine different government departments have been established.

Offshore Services

IPIM is responsible for the issuing of licenses, technical assistance and supervision for nonfinancial offshore institutions, and to promote offshore development through various activities. A lot of incentives are offered to offshore businesses, while there is only a set-up fee, and an operating fee every six months.

Economic and Trade Promotional Activities

IPIM annually organized or co-organzized and participated different kinds of local and international trade exhibition and investment cooperation promotional activities, namely: Macao Trade and Investment Fair (MIF), China and Portuguese Speaking Countries Economic Forum and Business Environment Presentation of different parts of the world. Moreover, we organize annually various finding tour for local entrepreneurs and welcome overseas delegation, thus creating a co-operation exchange between Maao and Overseas enterprises.

Besides, for international trade and investment fairs, we actively give subsidies for local enterprises: participation and the printing of promotional materials, to provide international information on Exhibition and Convention Industry.

Macao Business Support Centre

The Centre serves to reduce the initial setup costs for foreign investors, enabling the enterprisesto be familiar with Macao's business environment and the relevant administrative procedures in a relatively short time and to facilitate the implementation of their investment projects, as well as providing a service platform for cooperation exchange between local and overseas enterprises and business association. The center offers the following:Facilities/equipments --- inclue modern offices, meeting rooms, Display Gallery, computers and broad-band Internet services. Apart, there are chargeable fees on multi-functional conference rooms, printing and facsimile services among others business facilities.

Business Service - include "Consultation Service Counter", "Mainland China Business Advisory Service", Secretarial Service and provide administrative procedures and statistical information of local enterprises, business associations stationed in the Centre and Government Services. Moreover, is frequently the organization of Trade and Economic Presentation and Exchange Activities in co-operation with Business Association.

Platform of mutual co-operation between Enterprises and stationed repseresentative offices - several local and overseas business associations/ organizations/ institutions/ representative offices, such as Chongqing-Macao Economic Promotion Association-Macao Office, World Federation of Chinese Entrepreneurs Organization, Portuguese - Chinese Chamber of Commerce and Industry, International Lusophone Markets Business Association, China Council for the Promotion of International Trade Hong Kong and Macau Representative Office, German Macau Business Association, Australian Trade Commission- Austrade, Euro-Info Centre, Macau, Macao-Portuguese Businesse Center, Macau British Business Association and Japan Business Service Centre are stationed at MBSC. Enterprises can either contact these offices directly or through the assistances of MBSC to arrange for various business exchanges or cooperations.

Small and Medium Enterprises Service Centre (SMEC)

In order to enhance the comprehensive competitiveness of local Small and Medium Enterprises (SMEs) and assist them to grasp the opportunities brought about by Macao's economic development and in accordance withto Macao government policies to support SMEs, the Macao Trade and Investment Promotion Institute (IPIM) will launch a series of services to assist local SMEs, which includes the setting-up of the Small and Medium Enterprises Service Centre (SMEC) in the Macao Business Support Centre (MBSC). SMEC will help local SMEs to develop overseas and local markets and provide exchanges between enterprises and cooperation in accordance with overseas and local market's demands. Thus, it will give Macao's SMEs guidance to grasp the business opportunities brought about by the service, conventions and exhibition industries.

Information Services and Information Centre

In order to promote Macau's business environment and to furnish the business community with the most up-to-date information, we publish "Newsletter", "Macao Image","Investor's Guide"and related promotional CD-Roms or printing materials.The website is our chief means to deliver quality information service. All our major publications have now an on-line version.Not only general information about Macao and our Institute can be found in the site, a business database of all manufacturers and exporterss also open to free access. Moreover, a free "Etrade" service is provided, helping users in their search for suitable trade or investment partners around the globe.

Information Centre

There is an Information Centre located on the 2nd floor of World Trade Center. The Information Centre is one of the means by which we provide information enquiry services. The public can read, search for information by computer or by direct enquiry and borrow some of the materials. Reference materials available at the Information Centre include:

General information on local and worldwide economic and trade situation

Local economic and trade policies and regulations

Local and overseas statistical data, updated information on imports and exports

Local and overseas trade directories

Application for the Right of Residence

Those who have submitted investment projects or made a significant investment; or managerial staff and specialist technicians hired by local employers, who due to their qualifications or professional experience, are considered beneficial to Macao may apply to our Residence Application and Legal Affairs Division for a temporary residency in Macao.

Add: Av. Amizade no 918, Edif. World Trade Centre,
1-4 andares, Macau
Tel: 853-2871 0300
Fax: 853-2859 0309, 2871 0304
E-mail: ipim@ipim.gov.mo
Web: www.ipim.gov.mo
24-hour enquiry hotline 853-28 881212

"Macao Ideas"
The Macao Trade and Investment Promotion Institute

"Macao Ideas", a central location for overseas buyers, distributors or enterprises who are interested in sourcing and importing Macao's branded products.

Set up by the Macao Trade and Investment Promotion Institute (IPIM), "Macao Ideas" is a brand new product display centre, jointly promoting "Made in Macao", "Macao Brand", "Macao Design" and "Sole Distributorship of Portuguese-Speaking Countries Products". "Macao Ideas" has displaying a wide array of products from about 89 local enterprises. The product categories include garments, formal attire shoes, accessories, handbags, jewellery, food, coffee, tea, wine, health products, medical products, furniture, industrial products, technical products, motorcycles, glasses, cultural and creative products and handicrafts, etc.

"Macao Ideas" has on-site professional staff to explain in detail any questions you may have on products as well as background information on companies exhibiting, assist interested visitors to contact and even arrange business matching with these exhibiting companies.

Add: Rua Luis Gonzaga Gomes, Ground floor of Tourism Activities Centre, Macau
Tel: 853 - 2870 0620, 2870 2123
Fax: 853 - 2870 0621
Email: macaoideas@ipim.gov.mo
http://macaoideas.ipim.gov.mo

Shanghai International Exhibition Co Ltd

Shanghai International Exhibition Co Ltd was found in 1984 as the first state enterprise specialized in international exhibitions, which is now jointly invested by Shanghai World Expo (Group) Co., Ltd and CCPIT Shanghai Sub Council. SIEC has held 500 international exhibitions of various themes in China since its founding. SIEC is a full member of Union des Foires International (UFI). Die & Mould China, Auto Shanghai and China Interdye are the approved events of UFI. The five of its show are among the first eight exhibitions awarded as High Quality Trade Show by the Evaluation Committee of Shanghai Convention & Exhibition Industries. The affiliated organizations of SIEC providing a comprehensive solution on exhibition services including Freight Forwarding, Venue Management, Booth Fitting, Advertisement,Trade Liaison and etc.

Add: 8/F, OOCL Plaza, 841 Yan An Zhong Rord,
Shanghai 200040, China
Tel: 021-6279 2828
Fax: 021-6545 5124
E-mail: info@siec-ccpit.com
Web: www.siec-ccpit.com

China Commodities City Exhibition Co Ltd

Yiwu China Commodities City Exhibition Co Ltd (hereinafter referred as "CCC Exhibition" below) is a holding company of Zhejiang China Commodities City Group Co Ltd with registered capital of 8 million Yuan, professional teams composed of over 60 well-educated young people, specially engaging in dometic and overseas exhibition organizing service, as a member of UFI (The Global Association of the Exhibition Industry) & IAEE (International Association of Exhibitions and Events).

As the first exhibition enterprise in Yiwu district, the company was founded in 1998, and was the only execution agency of the past China Yiwu International Commodities Fairs. Dominantly government-guided but specifically hosted by Yiwu China Commodities City Exhibition Co Ltd China Yiwu International Commodities Fair has become the third biggest export commodities exhibition following Caton Fair and East China Fair, and is the sole large international fair for daily consumer goods approved by State Council.

Since the foundation, the company has hosted many national or provincial large convention & exhibition projects, such as National General Merchandise Conference, National Cosmetics & Lavation Conference, China Convention & Exhibition Fortune Forum, Zhejiang Tourism Trade Fair, and Zhejiang Agriculture Fair, Yiwu Sourcing Fair: Consumer Goods, Yiwu International Knitting & garment Machinery Exhibition, China Crystal & Glass industry Fair, China International Woodon Products Fair, and organized the exhibitors' participation in the overseas well-known exhibitions like Frankfurt, LasVegas, Birmingham, Macef, Dubai, achieving the organizing right of part of the overseas well-known exhibitions.

In the newround important economic develepment of China, we'll continue to function as the bridge between industrial economy and commercial economy, with the aim of "build exhibition platform, and promote trade opportunities". We would like to tighten the cooperation with the company in the same industry, improve the service quality, and build an elite team, gradually close to the international first-class modem exhibition service company, under the support of friends from all walks of life.

Add: 3/F, China Commodities City Exhibition (Meihu)
Centre, Binwang road 301#, Yiwu, Zhejiang.
Tel: 0579-8541 5888
Fax: 0579-8541 5777
www.yiwufairs.com

Younage Exhibition Co Ltd

7/F, No. 650 Baizhang East Road Ningbo, China
Tel: 0574-2771 6625, 2771 6618
Fax: 0574-8784 9306, 2771 6616
E-mail: younage@younage.com
Web: www.meonline.com.cn

Jinjiang Exhibition Affairs Co Ltd, Fujian

3F Foreign Economy & Trade Building Qingyang, Jinjiang, Fujian. 362200 China
Tel: 0595-8566 4572, 8567 1572
Fax: 0595-8567 4572, 8560 0610
E-mail: jif@cn-jif.com
Web: www.cn-jif.com

Trade and Economic Cooperation International China Harbin Fair for

35, Meishun Street, Nangang District, Harbin 150090
Tel: 0451-8234 0100
Fax: 0451-8234 0226
E-mail: zhanlanchu@00615.com.cn
E-mail: qying@00615.com.cn
Web: www.00615.com.cn

China Entertainment Technology Association (Formally China Theatrical Equipment Association)

No.1 Xilou Alley,Yonghegong Str., Beijing 100007, China
Tel: 010-8402 9994, 6403 3098 ext 201/ 203
Fax: 010-8401 0152
E-mail: zhao@calmexpo.com.cn
Web: www.calmexpo.com.cn

Chinese Mechanical Engineering Scociety

2-5-1607 Lianhuaxiaoqu, Haidian District, Beijing 100036, China
Tel: 010-6397 2404, 6398 2928
Fax: 010-6398 0554
E-mail: Whj@cmes.org/ Fanx@cmes.org
Web: essen.cmes.org

CCPIT Sub-council of Light Industry

22B, Fuwai Dajie, Beijing 100833 China
Tel: 010-6839 6330
Fax: 010-6839 6422
E-mail: ccpitsli@public3.bta.net.cn
Web: www.fi-c.com

Exhibit Designers and Producers

OCTANORM® Group Great China - OCTANORM System Technology (Suzhou) Co Ltd

It was in 1968 that a great idea matured into a concept and the concept was transformed into an ingenious product - the OCTANORM® exhibition system. After 40 years development, OCTANORM® has been recognised as the world leader in the manufacture and distribution of aluminium profiles and systems for the exhibition, retail and display industries. Recommended and appreciated by designers to contractors, our range of products has represented the benchmark of quality.

With the years of experience and hard work, OCTANORM® System Technology (Suzhou) Co Ltd (www.octanorm.cn), subsidiary of OCTANORM®-Vertriebs-GmbH, was funded in SIP China in May 2003. We inherit the global standardization of produce and service from Germany. The need to implement exhibit designs more efficiently, more logically and considerably more professionally fired the imagination that eventually resulted in the world of systems.

Boasting over 2,000 product innovations, OCTANORM® is not only the original exhibition system but is also the world market leader in system construction. From the very start OCTANORM® set about identifying and consistently applying the latest developments in both technology and design. Also, from the outset, OCTANORM® pursued a marketing strategy that was based on a partnership concept.

The secret of our success has always been in our innovative ideas, experienced staff, state-of-the-art production methods and meticulous quality control. With the increasing development of exhibition in China, OCTANORM® has got great progress and we have opened the offices in Beijing and Shanghai. We are always focusing on research and development in order to create the most scientific system solutions. Every year, we bring surprising products to the public. Meanwhile, with the support of accumulated experience from thousands experiments and more than 158 OSPI members all over the world, OCTANORM® is providing the most professional exhibition service everywhere.

Add: 3A, 428 Xinglong Street, Suzhou Industrial Park,
Jiangsu, China
Tel: 0512-6283 3338
Fax: 0512-6283 3330
E-mail: info@octanorm.cn
Web: www.octanorm.cn

Shanghai Neon Exhibition Ltd

Neon Group was established in January, 2001, and it has subsidiaries: Shanghai Neon Exhibition Ltd, Neon Exhibition(Hong Kong) Ltd, Shanghai Neon Construction & Decorate Ltd, Korea Chengdu Design Ltd. With our understanding of trends in the industry and modern exhibition forms, we are growing to be a comprehensive and professional exhibition enterprise. We are a member of Shanghai Convention & Exhibition Industries Association,Beijing Exhibition Center. Meanwhile, we are the Shanghai office of Busan Exhibition and Convention Center. Our services include: organizing, undertaking and co-organizing large scale international exhibitions; organizing exhibitors and visitors to participate overseas exhibitions; planning business activities; booth construction and showcase design.At present, we are the organizer of Kids Education Expo Shanghai,the overseas agent of 28 well-known exhibitions, and we take part in the design and construction of special stands for about 400 exhibitions.We establish cooperating relations with many famous international enterprises, such as SAMSUNG, INTEL, MICROSOFT, GOODYEAR, Hyundai Motor, HITACHI, SIEMENS, China Telecommunication and so on. As a result, Neon appeal to many talents from China and Korea.

Tel: 021-5216 4991, 5216 4992
Fax: 021-5218 9400

Convention and Exhibition Centers

China International Exhibition Center Group Corporation (CIEC)

China international exhibition center group corporation (CIEC) , subordinate to China council for the promotion of international trade (CCPIT) , chairs the China association of exhibition centers (CAEC) and is a member of the global association of the exhibition industry (UFI) and the international association for exhibitors and events (IAEE). CIEC business scope covers venue operation and management, domestic and overseas show organization and various relevant exhibition services.

China international exhibition center, located at 6 east beisanhuan road, Chaoyang District, Beijing, covers an area of 136,000m^2 with over 60,000 m^2 of indoor exhibiting space. More than 100 shows and exhibitions take place in CIEC venue annually with exhibiting space totaling over 1,000,000 m^2 .

New China international exhibition center (NCIEC) , put into operation in early 2008, is located in Tianzhu Airport industrial Zone, Shunyi District, Beijing, close to Beijing capital international Airport. Being the largest exhibition venue with integrated and modern facilities in Beijing, the first phase of NCIEC covers an area of 240,000 m^2 with 100,000 m^2 of indoor exhibiting space.

Tel: 010-8460 0000
Web: www.ciec-expo.com

Harbin International Conference Exhibition and Sports Center Co., Ltd

Harbin International Conference , Exhibition and Sports Center is a key project for Heilongjiang province and Harbin city, co-invested by Hei- Longjiang Provincial Government, Harbin Municipal Government, Harbin Institute of Technology Group Inc. and Heilongjiang Provincial Sports Bureau . It is located in the northeast part of economic technical development area of Harbin, known for her modern city style and glamour, which covers a total area of 63 hectares and building area of 400,000. It is the only one super large integrated halls that have complementary advantages and make perfect combinations of exhibitions and sports, hotels and conference center, recreation and shopping as well as an organic combination of exhibitions and negotiations in the whole country. As a result, it's been Harbin's city landmark with magnificent vigor, perfect design and excellent facilities.

After six year's operation, Harbin International Conference , Exhibition and Sports Center has already developed a powerful radiation of conferences and exhibitions economy, impact of sports economy, polymerizing power of commercial logistics and force of leisure culture economy.

With the unique geographic advantages in Heilongjiang province as an access and major route of trade to Russia, Harbin International Conference, Exhibition and Sports Center plays a key role of creating the platform for promoting the growth of the international economic trade with Russia and becomes an important stage for a gradual increase of international economic and trade exchanges, as well as steps forward to the big stage of global economic development with an enterprising spirit.

Shenyang International Exhibition Center

Shenyang International Exhibition Center (SYIEC) is located in No. 9 Huizhan road, Sujiatun district. It is 12 km away from the urban district and 13 km from Taoxian International Airport.

It overall planning 959,600 square meters and it is implemented in two phases, the first one covers 166,000 square meters, including 105,200 square meters indoor and 50,000 square meters outdoor. The comprehensive executive council area occupies 22,000 square meters. It is designed as international standard. Each hall can be used for holding mini-exhibitions separately and they are also connected by corridors. It is propitious to hold large-scale fairs.

It is made up of 8 separated, single-level, column-free and spacious halls. Each hall occupies 13,200 square meters and it can hold 625 international standard booths. They are connected by corridors with 4 landing halls on east, north, west and south. We can supply 5,000 international standard booths. The north square can hold opening ceremony, celebration and public welfare activities.

One meeting room that can hold 1000 people(it can divided as you need), one conference room can hold 600 people, five meeting rooms can hold 200 people, and six meeting rooms can hold 50 people, three VIP meeting rooms and four negotiation rooms of which have advanced conference facilities and quality services. We can provide the high-quality service for the domestic and international customers.

Address: No.9 Huizhan Road, Sujiatun District, Shenyang
Tel: 024-8956 6755
Fax: 024-89566778
Email: marketing@shenyang-expo.com
Web: www.shenyang-expo.com

Shanghai New International Expo Center

Shanghai New International Expo Center (SNIEC) is China's leading expo center, boasting state-of-the-art facilities. Situated in Shanghai's Pudong district, the heart of Chinese business, SNIEC has attracted worldwide attention since its opening in November, 2001. Featuring a prime, easily accessible location, a pillar-free, single story structure and a wide array of expert on-site services, SNIEC has been experiencing rapid growth. It now hosts more than 60 world-class exhibitions each year and this number is set to grow in the future.

Currently, SNIEC has 9 exhibition halls with 103500 square meters of indoor exhibition space and 100000 square meters of outdoor exhibition space.

SNIEC plans to complete of all its facilities and reach full exhibition capacity by 2010. By then, the Center will contain 200,000 square meters of indoor floor area and 130,000 square meters of outdoor area. SNIEC's future expansions will cement its market leadership in China and secure Shanghai's position on the forefront of East Asian exhibition destinations.

SNIEC is a multi-functional venue that also caters to a diverse range of both social and corporate events.

Shanghai New International Expo Centre (SNIEC) opened on November 2, 2001, and is jointly owned by Shanghai Lujiazui Development (Group) Co Ltd, Deutsche Messe AG, Messe Duesseldorf GmbH and Messe Muenchen GmbH.

Tel: 021-3876 0488
Fax: 021-6856 6089
Web: www.sniec.net

Guangdong Modern International Exhibition Center (GDE)

Located at the middle of Canton-Hong Kong Golden corridor -HouJie Dong Guan, the acknowledged base of processing and manufacturing.

100,000 m^2 indoor space, 110,000m^2 outdoor.
ISO900 quality management system
"One-stop " services
The Best Exhibition Venue of year 2003 & 2004 in China.
A member of HKECIA, CAEC, UFI

2010 Exhibition Program:
Guangdong (Houjie) Tea Expo
The 23th International Famous Furniture Fair (Dongguan)
The 11th China (Dongguan) Int'l Textile & Clothing Industry fair
The 11th China (Dongguan) Int'l Footwear Machinery &Material Industry
The 10th Dongguan Shoes/ China Shoetes
The 19th (Dongguan) south China Eletronic Fair
The 10th Dongguan International Printing and Packaging and paper advertising, adhesive tape, protective film exhibition
Guangdong Foreign-invested Enterprises Commodities Fair
The 24th International Famous Furniture Fair (Dongguan)
The 15th International IC-China Conference & Exhibition
The 11th Dongguan Shoes/ China Shoetes
The 12th China Dongguan International Mould and Metalworking Exhibition
12th China Dongguan International Plastics Packing Rubber Diecasting & Foundry Exhibition

Hong Kong Convention and Exhibition Centre

The award-winning 306,000 square metre HKCEC, which opened in 1988, is located on a prime waterfront site in the heart of Hong Kong. Following the second expansion completed in 2009, the HKCEC now offers 91,500 square metres of rentable space for exhibitions, conferences, meetings, corporate functions, entertainment and hospitality events, along with uniquely convenient, world-class services.

Top industry awards for every major catagory of events have reaffirmed the global reputation of HKCEC for professional service excellence. In 2012, HKCEC was recognised for the 9th time as the Best Convention and Exhibition Centre in Asia by leading industry peers and readers of the CEI Asia magazine.

Hong Kong's Central Business District and the best of the city's attractions are right on the HKCEC's door step. Adjacent and linked to the HKCEC are two world-class hotels and there are over 6,000 rooms within walking distance.

Over 1,200 events are held at the HKCEC every year, including four of the world's biggest exhibitions and seven of the Asia's biggest exhibitions. These events contribute significant economic benefits to the city and help raise the international image of Hong Kong.

The HKCEC achieved a record event attendance of 5,969,789 for its fiscal year 2010-2011 (July 2010 – June 2011), a surge of 25% from the previous year. This significant jump in attendance was the result of an enlarged event portfolio. Over its 23 years of operation, the HML team has hosted 39,606 events and has collectively served around 70 million buyers, exhibitors, visitors and guests.

The HKCEC is owned by the Hong Kong SAR Government and the Hong Kong Trade Development Council. Hong Kong Convention and Exhibition Centre (Management) Limited ("HML") is a professional private management and operating company responsible for providing day to day management for the HKCEC. Its continued success in handling mega-exhibitions regularly attracts new organisers and new events to the HKCEC for debut.

Add: 1 Expo Drive, Wanchai, Hong Kong, China
Tel: 852-25852 1111
E-mail: inf@hkcec.com
Web: www.hkcec.com

AsiaWorld-Expo

AsiaWorld - Expo is Hong Kong's leading exhibition and events venue offering over 70,000 square metres of rentable space. It is fully integrated with the Hong Kong International Airport and located at the centre of an extensive and efficient air, land and marine transport network.

AsiaWorld-Expo has 10 ground-level, column-free, high specification halls. All of the halls are equipped with advanced ICT services, and can be used either separately or in conjunction with each other to provide one continuous space for events. Since its opening in 2005, AsiaWorld-Expo has already staged a lot of large-scale international events, including "ITU TELECOM WORLD 2006" the largest-ever trade exhibition cum forum in Hong Kong; "Asian Aerospace International Expo and Congress" the world's largest dedicated commercial aviation and aerospace event which has moved to AsiaWorld-Expo since September 2007 after 25 years held in Singapore; "China Sourcing Fairs" in April and October each year, which attracted lots of overseas and local exhibitors and visitors; and also act as an excellent platform for Mainland Chinese enterprises to venture into the global marketplace.

In addition, AsiaWorld-Expo includes the Hong Kong's largest indoor seated venue: AsiaWorld-Arena, which accommodates a maximum capacity of 13,500. The venue has already hosted various world-class concerts and conferences.

Tel: 852-3606 8888
Fax: 852-3606 8889
E-mail: info@asiaworld-expo.com
Web: www.asiaworld-expo.com

Zhengzhou International Convention & Exhibition Center

Zhengzhou International Convention & Exhibition Center (ZZICEC) is a fully integrated convention & exhibition facility. It is invested by Zhengzhou Municipal Government, and it integrates convention rooms, exhibition halls, business centres, restaurants, entertainments and performance and tourism facilities all into one. It is one of the signature buildings in Zhengzhou.

Zhengzhou International Convention & Exhibition Centre (ZZICEC) is designed by an internationally acclaimed architect Kisho Kurokawa. The main body of the building is consisted of convention center and exhibition center. ZZICEC has been built since January 20th,2003 and started its operation in October 21st2005 and is managed by Hong Kong - Shanghai Venue Management (Zhengzhou) Limited since June 1st 2006.

ZZICEC covers an area of 686,000 square meters, with a construction area of 226,800 square meters. It consists of a convention centre, an exhibition centre, an outdoor exhibition area of 38,000 square meters and 45,000 square meters of parking space.

The Convention Centre offers 6 levels of multi-purposed function space, with a total construction area of 60,800 square meters. The Grand Hall is an ideal venue for meetings of theatre type up to 5,000 people, meetings of classroom type up to 3,160 people and seated banquets of up to 1,660 guests, the International Theatre can accommodate 1,090 audiences and two theatres seat 400 audiences each. Also included are 17 meeting rooms of varied sizes, VIP reception rooms, a Chinese restaurant, a western restaurant, and a cafe. Simultaneous interpretation can be provided for up to 8 languages plus 1 within the Grand Hall and International Theatre, while the two theatres can provide 4 languages plus 1 simultaneous interpretation.

The Exhibition Centre offers 2 levels multi-purposed function space of the main body and 6 levels of the secondary body. It was built on a construction area of 166,800 square meters. It consists of two exhibition halls and a variety of auxiliary support facilities, including 68 meeting rooms, food concessions, offices and shops.

The inner exhibition space is 65,000 square meters which could set 3,394 international standard booths. Hall 1 and Hall 2 can be divided into 4 6,000 square meters sections and 2 4,500 square meter sections by floor-to-ceiling operable walls, for independent exhibition use. The ceiling height of Hall 1 is 14 meters and floor loading capacity is 5 tons per square meter. The ceiling height of Hall 2 is 17.6 meters and the floor loading capacity is 1.5 tons per square meter.

Exhibition Transportation

Schenker

With a network of around 55,000 people in about 1,500 offices around the world, DB Schenker is one of the world's leading providers of integrated logistics services, offering air, ocean freight and land concepts as well as logistics services for fairs, relocations, projects and global sports events. DB Schenker first entered Mainland China in 1979 and subsequently expanded its presence to nowadays more than 35 locations throughout China with over 4,300 employees working on advanced logistics solutions from one single source.

DB Schenker is part of DB Logistics, the Transportation and Logistics Division of Deutsche Bahn AG.

For all your Fairs & Exhibitions requirements, DB Schenker's dedicated team of specialists will develop the most efficient and suitable solution.

We offer a full range of exhibition services:

•Worldwide coordination of shipments–multimodal transports by air, sea and land

•Consolidated shipments of stand building materials, exhibits and promotional materials

•Expertise in documentation and customs clearance procedures

•Planning and execution of time-defined transports

•On-site handling by experienced and trained staff

•Professional storage at state-of-the-art facilities and handling of "empties"

•Return shipments of complete equipment to the point of origin or to the next fair site

•Arrangements of seminar and conference materials as well as stage equipment

•Professional transport of art material

In 2008 DB Schenker has been appointed as the Official Freight Forwarding & Customs Clearance Exclusive Supplier of the Beijing Olympic Games.

Our contacts:
South China office-Schenker Intl (H.K.) Ltd.
Add: 38/F, China Resources Building No. 26 Harbour RoadWanchai, Hong Kong
Tel: 852-2585 9688
Fax: 852-2827 5363
E-mail: fairs.hk@schenker.com

Central China office-Schenker China Ltd.
Add: Rm.3802-3806, Raffles City (Office Tower) No.268 Xi Zhang Zhong Road, Shanghai 200001, P.R. China
Tel: 021-6122 5888, 2890 6226
Fax: 021-5292 5194, 2890 6223
E-mail: fairs.sha@schenker.com

North China office-Schenker China Ltd., Beijing Branch
5 Tianwei Sijie
Tianzhu Airport Industrial Area A Beijing 101312, P.R. China
Tel: 010-8048 0099
Fax: 010-8048 0077
E-mail: fairs.bjs@schenker.com

BALtrans Exhibition & Removal Ltd.

BALtrans Exhibition & Removal Ltd. was established in 1987 and headquarter is located in Hong Kong. The major serving sectors of BALtrans Exhibition are: Fairs in China and overseas, Mega Sports Events and Artmove.

With our strong workforce and global network, BALtrans Exhibition has been committed to providing total quality logistics solutions to the world of exhibitions.

Every year, we are serving as the official freight forwarder for over 100 international industrial and art exhibitions, as well as sporting events in China and around the World.

Our expansion today, as then, continues to bear the imprint of providing the most value-added solutions to fulfilling the needs of our every individual customer around the world.

Agility

Agility Fairs & Events is the recognized leader in full-service, end-to-end management of global fairs, expositions and trade-show transportation. Our dedicated professionals are in key exhibition venue offices throughout Asia-Pacific, the Middle East, Europe, Africa and the Americas. A publicly traded company, with over US$6 billion in annual revenue, we are part of one of the largest international logistics and freight management companies in the world, with over 550 offices in 100 countries and 32,000 employees.

We provide a one-stop fairs and events logistics service for trade fair organizers, show promoters and exhibitors ensuring that displays arrive on time and in perfect condition. Our services include:

- Customs clearance
- Obtaining Government permits for special cargoes/temporary import
- Sea/air transportation and transhipment
- Storage and delivery
- Venue on-site logistics
- Site handling and unpacking
- Positioning and rigging of exhibits
- Repacking, storage of empties and re-export handling

AGILITY FAIRS & EVENTS LOGISTICS LIMITED
29/F Fook Lee Comm Centre, Town Place,
33 Lockhart Road, Wanchai, Hong Kong
Tel: 852-2594 9233
Contact: Ms Kenly Tsang

AGILITY FAIRS & EVENTS LOGISTICS (SHANGHAI) CO. LTD
Room 1606, Shanghai Mart, No. 2299, Yan'an Road (West),
Shanghai 200336, P. R. China
Tel: 021-6236 6060, 13911992219
Contact: Mr Mitch Zhang

AGILITY FAIRS & EVENTS LOGISTICS (SHANGHAI) CO. LTD
Beijing Branch
Room 1211 Prime Tower, No.22 Chaowai Street,
Chaoyang District, Beijing 100020, PR China
Tel: 010-6588 1961 / 1962 / 1963 / 1964
Mobile: 13911992219
Contact: Mr Mitch Zhang

AGILITY FAIRS & EVENTS LOGISTICS (SHANGHAI) CO. LTD
Guangzhou Branch
Rm.704/706,7F, No 726 Dong Feng Road East,
Guangzhou 510080 PR China
Tel: 020-3765 5886
Contact: Mr Eric Ye